EDUCATIONAL PSYCHOLOGY 92/93

Seventh Edition

Editor

Kathleen M. Cauley
Virginia Commonwealth University

Kathleen M. Cauley received her Ph.D. in educational studies/human development from the University of Delaware in 1985. Her research interests center on applying cognitive developmental research to school learning. Currently, she is studying children's construction of the logic of the borrowing algorithm in multidigit subtraction.

Editor

Fredric Linder
Virginia Commonwealth University

Fredric Linder received an A.B. in American civilization from the University of Miami, Florida, an M.A. in psychology from the New School for Social Research, and a Ph.D. in educational psychology from the State University of New York at Buffalo. His research and publications focus on the value, locus of control, and cognitive learning styles of students in higher education.

Editor

James H. McMillan
Virginia Commonwealth University

James H. McMillan received his bachelor's degree from Albion College in 1970, his M.A. from Michigan State University in 1972, and his Ph.D. from Northwestern University in 1976. He has reviewed and written extensively on many topics in educational psychology. Currently, he is researching critical thinking, values, and student outcomes assessment.

Cover illustration by Mike Eagle

Annual Editions
A Library of Information from the Public Press

The Dushkin Publishing Group, Inc.
Sluice Dock, Guilford, Connecticut 06437

The Annual Editions Series

Annual Editions is a series of over 55 volumes designed to provide the reader with convenient, low-cost access to a wide range of current, carefully selected articles from some of the most important magazines, newspapers, and journals published today. Annual Editions are updated on an annual basis through a continuous monitoring of over 300 periodical sources. All Annual Editions have a number of features designed to make them particularly useful, including topic guides, annotated tables of contents, unit overviews, and indexes. For the teacher using Annual Editions in the classroom, an Instructor's Resource Guide with test questions is available for each volume.

VOLUMES AVAILABLE

Africa
Aging
American Government
American History, Pre-Civil War
American History, Post-Civil War
Anthropology
Biology
Business and Management
Business Ethics
Canadian Politics
China
Commonwealth of Independent States and Central/Eastern Europe (Soviet Union)
Comparative Politics
Computers in Education
Computers in Business
Computers in Society
Criminal Justice
Drugs, Society, and Behavior
Early Childhood Education
Economics
Educating Exceptional Children
Education
Educational Psychology
Environment
Geography
Global Issues
Health
Human Development
Human Resources
Human Sexuality

International Business
Japan
Latin America
Life Management
Macroeconomics
Management
Marketing
Marriage and Family
Microeconomics
Middle East and the Islamic World
Money and Banking
Nutrition
Personal Growth and Behavior
Physical Anthropology
Psychology
Public Administration
Race and Ethnic Relations
Social Problems
Sociology
State and Local Government
Third World
Urban Society
Violence and Terrorism
Western Civilization, Pre-Reformation
Western Civilization, Post-Reformation
Western Europe
World History, Pre-Modern
World History, Modern
World Politics

Library of Congress Cataloging in Publication Data
Main entry under title: Annual Editions: Educational Psychology 1992/93.
    1. Educational psychology—Periodicals. 2. Teaching—Periodicals.
I. Cauley, Kathleen M., comp.; Linder, Fredric, comp.; McMillan, James H., comp.
II. Title: Educational psychology.
ISBN 1-56134-087-1   370.15'05   82-640517

Seventh Edition

Manufactured by The Banta Company, Harrisonburg, Virginia 22801

Editors/ Advisory Board

EDITORS

Kathleen M. Cauley
Virginia Commonwealth University

Fredric Linder
Virginia Commonwealth University

James H. McMillan
Virginia Commonwealth University

ADVISORY BOARD

Roberta Ahlquist
San Jose State University

Thomas J. Bennett
Bowling Green State University

Karen Duffy
SUNY College, Geneseo

Godfrey Franklin
University of West Florida

Al Gardner
University of Maryland
College Park

Christian Gerhard
George Washington University

William Goodwin
University of Colorado
at Denver

William M. Gray
University of Toledo

Cheryl Greenberg
University of North Carolina
Greensboro

Elaine C. Koffman
Northeastern Illinois University

Golam Mannan
Indiana University-
Purdue University

Laura Massey
Montana State University

Thomas S. Parish
Kansas State University

Donald H. Saklofske
University of Saskatchewan

Fred Schultz
University of Akron

Thomas J. Shuell
State University of New York
Buffalo

Julia Thomas
Loyola University

Lani Van Dusen
Utah State University

Members of the Advisory Board are instrumental in the final selection of articles for each edition of Annual Editions. Their review of articles for content, level, currentness, and appropriateness provides critical direction to the editor and staff. We think you'll find their careful consideration well reflected in this volume.

To the Reader

In publishing ANNUAL EDITIONS we recognize the enormous role played by the magazines, newspapers, and journals of the *public press* in providing current, first-rate educational information in a broad spectrum of interest areas. Within the articles, the best scientists, practitioners, researchers, and commentators draw issues into new perspective as accepted theories and viewpoints are called into account by new events, recent discoveries change old facts, and fresh debate breaks out over important controversies.

Many of the articles resulting from this enormous editorial effort are appropriate for students, researchers, and professionals seeking accurate, current material to help bridge the gap between principles and theories and the real world. These articles, however, become more useful for study when those of lasting value are carefully *collected, organized, indexed,* and *reproduced* in a *low-cost format*, which provides easy and permanent access when the material is needed. That is the role played by *Annual Editions*. Under the direction of each volume's *Editor*, who is an expert in the subject area, and with the guidance of an *Advisory Board*, we seek each year to provide in each *ANNUAL EDITION* a current, well-balanced, carefully selected collection of the best of the public press for your study and enjoyment. We think you'll find this volume useful, and we hope you'll take a moment to let us know what you think.

Educational psychology is an interdisciplinary subject that includes human development, learning strategies, intelligence, motivation, measurement, and classroom management. It also gives special attention to the application of this knowledge to teaching.

Annual Editions: Educational Psychology 92/93 is presented in six units. An overview precedes each unit and explains how the articles in the unit are related to the broader issues within educational psychology. The first unit presents issues central to the teaching role. The authors discuss the challenges of responding to calls for educational reform and the role of educational research in meeting those challenges.

The second unit is concerned with human development and covers the cognitive, social, and emotional development of children and adolescents. The articles in this unit discuss the developmental implications of early childhood thinking for teachers, the social forces affecting children and adolescents, and the personal and social skills they need in order to cope with developmental phases and school learning tasks.

The third unit includes articles about theories of learning and instructional strategies. The different views of learning, such as information processing, behaviorism, and humanistic learning, represent the accumulation of years of research on the way humans change in thinking or behavior due to experience. The principles generated from each approach have important implications for teaching. These implications are addressed in a subsection on instructional strategies, covering such topics as instructional methods, grouping students, using controversy, questioning, and creativity.

The topic of motivation is perhaps one of the most important aspects of school learning. Effective teachers need to motivate their students both to learn and to behave responsibly. How to manage children and what forms of discipline to use are issues that concern parents as well as teachers and administrators. The articles in the fourth unit present a variety of perspectives on motivating students, and approaches to managing student behavior are discussed.

The fifth unit, concerning exceptional children, focuses on the learning disabled, the culturally different, and the gifted. All of these children are different in some way and require an individualized approach to education. The articles in this unit discuss the characteristics of these children and suggest programs and strategies to meet their needs.

The articles in unit six review assessment approaches that can be used to diagnose learning and improve instruction. The focus is on grading practices and appropriate uses of standardized tests. Performance-based assessment is introduced as a promising new approach to classroom measurement.

This seventh edition of *Annual Editions: Educational Psychology* has been revised to present articles that are current and useful. Your response to the selection and organization of materials are appreciated. Please fill out and return the article rating form on the last page of the book.

Kathleen M. Cauley

Fredric Linder

James H. McMillan
Editors

Unit 1

Overview: Psychology Applied to Education and Teaching

Four selections discuss the importance of research and the value of scientific inquiry to the teaching process.

Unit 2

Development

Eight articles examine how social interaction in the classroom influences a child's development.

The concepts in bold italics are developed in the article. For further expansion please refer to the Topic Guide and the Index.

Unit 3

Learning

Twelve selections explore the important types of student/teacher interaction.

The concepts in bold italics are developed in the article. For further expansion please refer to the Topic Guide and the Index.

Unit
4

Motivation and Classroom Management

Eight selections discuss student control and motivation in the classroom.

The concepts in bold italics are developed in the article. For further expansion please refer to the Topic Guide and the Index.

Unit 5

Exceptional Children

Eight articles look at the problems and positive *effects*
of educational programs for exceptional children.

Unit 6

Measurement and Evaluation

Five articles discuss the implications of educational measurement for the classroom decision-making process and for the teaching profession.

The concepts in bold italics are developed in the article. For further expansion please refer to the Topic Guide and the Index.

Topic Guide

This topic guide suggests how the selections in this book relate to topics of traditional concern to educational psychology students and professionals. It is useful for locating articles that relate to each other for reading and research. The guide is arranged alphabetically according to topic. Articles may, of course, treat topics that do not appear in the topic guide. In turn, entries in the topic guide do not necessarily constitute a comprehensive listing of all the contents of each selection.

TOPIC AREA	TREATED IN:	TOPIC AREA	TREATED IN:
Action Research	3. Using Action Research to Navigate an Unfamiliar Teaching Assignment	Disabilities	27. Development of Intrinsic Motivation in Students With Learning Problems 33. Masks Students Wear 35. Facilitating Mainstreaming Through Cooperative Learning
At-Risk Students	28. Motivation for At-Risk Students		
Authentic Testing	43. Teaching to the (Authentic) Test 44. Innovation or Enervation? Performance Assessment in Perspective	Discipline	29. Good Teachers Don't Worry About Discipline 31. Order in the Classroom 32. Corporal Punishment: Used in a Discriminatory Manner?
Behaviorism	15. Practicing Positive Reinforcement 16. Implementing a Classroom Reward System 30. Accentuate the Positive . . . Eliminate the Negative 31. Order in the Classroom	Early Childhood Education	5. How Well Do We Respect the Children in Our Care? 6. Developmentally Appropriate Education for 4-year-olds 9. Encouraging Prosocial Behavior in Young Children
Character Development	18. Caring Kids	Educational Reform	1. Improving Education for the Twenty-First Century
Child/Adolescent Development	5. How Well Do We Respect the Children in Our Care? 6. Developmentally Appropriate Education for 4-Year-Olds 8. Development of Self-Concept 10. Changing Conditions for Young Adolescents 12. Affective Dimensions of Effective Middle Schools	Effective Teaching	4. Colors of Teaching 29. Good Teachers Don't Worry About Discipline
		Emotionally Disturbed	34. Working With Disturbed Adolescents
Classroom Research	3. Using Action Research to Navigate an Unfamiliar Teaching Assignment 20. Productive Teaching and Instruction	Gifted Children and Youth	36. Synthesis of Research on Gifted Youth 37. Success Strategies for Learners Who Are Learning Disabled as Well as Gifted 38. Identifying and Serving the Gifted New Immigrant
Cognitive Development	6. Developmentally Appropriate Education for 4-year-olds		
Cognitive Learning	13. Putting Learning Strategies to Work 14. Linking Metacognition to Classroom Success	Grading	41. It's a Good Score! Just a Bad Grade 42. Classroom Standard Setting and Grading Practices
Computer-Assisted Instruction	20. Productive Teaching and Instruction	Grouping Students	20. Productive Teaching and Instruction
Cooperative Learning	19. Cooperative Learning and the Cooperative School 25. Competition Doesn't Belong in Public Schools	Humanistic Education	18. Caring Kids
		Individual Differences	22. Research on Learning Styles
Creativity	24. Fostering Creativity	Information Processing	13. Putting Learning Strategies to Work 14. Linking Metacognition to Classroom Success
Criterion-Referenced Tests	42. Classroom Standard Setting and Grading Practices 43. Teaching to the (Authentic)Test		
Critical Thinking	21. Critical Thinking Through Structured Controversy	Learning Styles/ Strategies	13. Putting Learning Strategies to Work 22. Research on Learning Styles 23. Critique of the Research on Learning Styles

Overview: Psychology Applied to Education and Teaching

The teaching-learning process in schools is enormously complex. Many factors influence pupil learning—such as family background, developmental level, prior knowledge, motivation, and of course, effective teachers. Educational psychology investigates these factors to better understand and explain student learning. We begin our exploration of the teaching-learning process by considering the teaching role, particularly as it is being defined in the educational reform movement.

In the first article, Harold G. Shane looks into the future to describe the social and technological changes that will require educational reform. To meet these needs, teachers will continue to be under pressure to raise standards and improve standardized test scores. Some reports argue for more homework and longer school days.

In the second article, David J. Flinders argues that technical expertise and subject matter knowledge are insufficient to characterize the professionalism of teachers. He believes that the artistry of teaching is being overlooked in the reform movements. Flinders suggests that the artistry of teaching is evident in the complexity of interpersonal interactions as teachers are perceptive of and sensitive to students, and as they negotiate their cooperation in learning.

Another perspective in the reform of education is that teachers need to engage in more systematic inquiry—or research. As the professional development schools envisioned by the Holmes Group and others are established, teacher research will become more widespread. As the next selection illustrates, teacher researchers are an important tool in implementing educational change. Teachers who engage in action research have immediate feedback about how their new approaches are working.

The final selection offers two perspectives about teaching in American society from the perspective of a student teacher. It asks how we can improve education in these two settings.

Educational psychology is a resource for teachers that emphasizes disciplined inquiry, a systematic and objective analysis of information, and a scientific attitude toward decision-making. The field provides information for decisions that are based on quantitative and qualitative studies of learning and teaching, rather than intuition, tradition, authority, or subjective feelings. It is our hope that this aspect of educational psychology is communicated throughout these readings, and that as a student you will adopt the analytic, probing attitude that is a part of the discipline.

While educational psychologists have helped to establish a knowledge base about teaching and learning, the unpredictable, spontaneous, evolving nature of teaching suggests that the best they will ever do is provide concepts and skills that teachers can adapt for use in their classrooms. The issues raised in these articles about the impact of the reform movement on teachers help us understand the teaching role and its demands. As you read articles in other chapters, consider the demands they place on the teaching role as well.

Looking Ahead: Challenge Questions

Can teachers effectively perform all the roles expected of them?

Do you agree that educational reform is not addressing the right issues?

If educational reform succeeds, what new demands do you think it will place on teachers?

Improving Education for The Twenty-first Century

How can today's educators prepare for schooling in the next century? What will tomorrow's students be like and what will they need to know? What kinds of information can help us to prepare for that future? In this article, noted educator and futurist Harold G. Shane provides an overview of the challenges facing us today and their implications for the twenty-first century.

Harold G. Shane

HAROLD G. SHANE is University Professor Emeritus of Education at Indiana University, Bloomington, Indiana.

WHEN ONE contemplates improving education for the next century, a potent question arises: Do we actually have the foresight needed to give us reasonably accurate images of tomorrow's world? Roy Amara, a dedicated futurist and the president of the Institute for the Future, cautioned that "anything you forecast is by definition uncertain."[1] Therefore, our planning to shape better ways of life must be based on a blend of interpretations of projections as well as our aspirations.

It is encouraging to note that thoughtful scholars very often have given us a reliable picture of things to come. The work of journalist John Elfreth Watkins provides historical evidence of the reliability of many learned opinions.[2] In 1899 he interviewed a number of scholars and recorded their views regarding probable changes. Among the many accurate predictions: electric kitchen appliances, taller Americans, high-speed trains, airplanes, color photography, global telephone systems, subsidized university education, subsidized medical aid, free lunches for needy children, and dozens of other ameliorative conditions. Thus, it appears that we can study new developments and project with reasonable accuracy outcomes related to education for the twenty-first century.

The Present Challenges the Future

Current books, articles, and statements from a wide spectrum of scholars suggest many contemporary trends that imply social, economic, educational, and diverse other futures.[3] Let us examine a small sampling of these elements with implications that will possibly challenge and complicate educational planning in the next decade or two.

The new minority. Sometime in the new millennium—perhaps even before its debut—our schools will enroll a minority composed of the present white majority. As of 1989, fifty-three of America's one hundred largest cities had schools in which Hispanics,

From *Educational Horizons*, Vol. 69, No. 1, Fall 1990, pp. 11-15. Reprinted with permission from *Educational Horizons*, quarterly journal of Pi Lambda Theta, National Honor and Professional Association in Education, Bloomington, IN 47407-6626.

American Indians, Asians, and African Americans had begun to outnumber children and adolescents of white Anglo-Saxon or European ancestry.[4] Fifteen percent or more of the pupils in our schools speak English as a second language.[5] High birthrates among poor Hispanics and African Americans will further divide the U.S. along ethnic lines.

The accumulation of new ethnic educational admixtures challenges our quest for new ways to teach children with multicultural backgrounds. A recent Carnegie Council on Adolescent Development notes a related difficulty:

> By age 15, millions of American youth are at risk of reaching adulthood unable to meet adequately...the responsibilities of participation in a multicultural society and of citizenship in a democracy.[6]

Trends in population and in aging. A rapid increase in the growth of America's older residents is under way and brings with it a myriad of potential problems. By the year 2000, about 13 percent of the population will be sixty-five years old or older, and in the next thirty years, senior citizens will constitute well over 20 percent of an appreciably larger U.S. population.[7] The average life span may well approach over eighty years by the year 2020.[8]

Costs related to medical and custodial care and social security are likely to create an increasing burden for younger employed Americans. Interestingly, present trends indicate that in the next decade the greatest population growth will take place in California, Texas, and Florida.[9]

Environmental problems. So much has been written about threats to the environment that little elaboration is needed. Hazards include land erosion, deforestation in the tropics, acid rain, misuse of energy resources, oceanic pollution, the ozone depletion, and the "green house" effect.

Education that addresses these problems and issues in the 1990s may help young learners understand that our security as a nation does not necessarily depend on numerous, elabo-

rate weapons and large military forces. It also resides in policies regarding our environment and our natural resources and our ability to participate actively and intelligently in these issues.

Changes in the traditional American family. Forty or more years ago most families in the U.S. presented a rather simple profile: fathers worked and mothers reared families, despite the lack of modern conveniences such as garbage disposals, air conditioning, two bathrooms, or second cars.

Today's family is different. Part of the change may be due to a steady decline in home ownership in the past ten years and a dearth of low-cost rental property and subsidized housing for the poor, which is available to only about 25 percent of those who seek it.[10] Other sources of change in family dynamics are single-parent families, endemic homelessness, and working mothers. Approximately 70 percent of U.S. women were employed in 1990 (one-third with children five or younger) as compared with 31 percent in 1950.[11]

Melissa Ludtke succinctly summarized some of the difficulties of our clanking industrial era:

> Some call them the sandwich generation, that bulging demographic cohort of thirtysomethings and fortysomethings who face an onerous triple duty: caring for young children and elderly parents while holding down

By the year 2000, about 13 percent of the population will be sixty-five years old or older, and in the next thirty years, senior citizens will constitute well over 20 percent of an appreciably larger U.S. population.

full-time jobs. More than one-third of the U.S. work force confronts this problem, a number that is sure to rise as the population continues to age and as more women, the family's traditional care givers, enter the job market.[12]

Thus, schools may be left with responsibilities formerly assumed by the family, such as providing day care and teaching important values and behaviors.

Debt and inflation. As of 1990, the debt load was staggering—approximately seven trillion dollars owed by our government, U.S. corporations, and individuals! The annual federal deficit was listed by the government at $147 billion last year, but it actually amounted to $244 billion if social security and other trust fund surpluses were included.[13] In view of these figures plus current inflationary trends and an international currency rate reflecting a decline in the value of the U.S. dollar, our national debt may compound the problem of finding funds for schooling.

Meeting Future Challenges to Education

Rebuilding our school environments mandates teacher, parent, and community cooperation to reverse the conditions reported by a thirty-six-member commission of community leaders, doctors, and teachers sponsored by the American Medical Association and the National Association of State Boards of Education. Among the data cited were the following eight points:

1. Suicide is attempted by 18 percent of girls and 10 percent of boys during their growing-up years.

2. Teen pregnancy in the U.S. continues at the highest rate of all developed countries; one in ten teenage girls will become pregnant.

3. Alcohol consumption involves one hundred thousand elementary schoolchildren who get drunk at least once a week.

4. Gonorrhea and syphilis among teenagers has tripled since 1965, with 2.5 million adolescents each year contracting a sexually transmitted disease.

5. Drugs affect more than 3.5 million twelve- to seventeen-year-olds who have tried marijuana and one-third who are regular users; a half-million young people have tried cocaine—half of these are regular users.

6. Arrests—in 1950 youths between fourteen and seventeen years of age had a rate of four per thousand. In 1985, the arrest rate was 118 per 1,000.

7. The dropout rate in the U.S. currently stands at 30 percent.

8. The poverty rate for young people six to seventeen years old living in families with incomes below the poverty line was 13 percent in 1969 and increased to 20 percent in 1985.[14]

Additionally, technological developments are creating other challenges for education and our society. They include the possibility for information overload with the prospect of knowledge increasing fourfold in the next decade and changes in the nature of knowledge and in what we believe. We also must learn to deal with rapidly accumulating innovations such as laptop computers and sophisticated input devices. Interactive video technology will affect our ability to access information. For example, *Compton's Multi Media Encyclopedia* on compact disk adds about ten thousand animated pictures and drawings.[15]

Other technological developments with implications for the future include robots with forms of artificial intelligence, the invasion of privacy by computerized listings (the average U.S. citizen is listed on seventy private and government computer files)[16], and the effects of televised sex, violence, and advertising on children and adolescents.

Insights into challenges of the present and the probable turbulence of tomorrow are of little use unless we consider the redesign of education. Redesigning schooling for students who will live all or most of their lives in the twenty-first century is almost certainly more essential than the swarm of current reform proposals. Since 1983, when *A Nation at Risk* was released by the National Committee on Excellence in Education, we have been overwhelmed by proposals related to improving out-of-date prac-

tices rather than preparing young learners for a new millennium.

A few ventures, such as John I. Goodlad's excellent study of schooling,[17] have focused successfully on redesign, but most proposals have failed to consider basic questions such as those raised in a report commissioned by the U.S. House of Representatives. *Information Technology and Its Impact on American Education* presents four key questions that offer guidelines for planning educational policies that need to be developed to prepare learners to cope with a rapidly changing world:

1. What needs to be learned?
2. Who needs to learn it?
3. Who will provide it?
4. How will it be provided and paid for?[18]

A major question should be added to the four listed above: Where will it be provided?

To sum up, educators in the 1990s need to avoid getting stuck with a tar baby like Brer Rabbit did.[19] We must remain diligent in dealing with changes for tomorrow and not be immobilized by trying to polish the aged mosaics of past practices.

Implications for Our Schools

We undoubtedly need to bear in mind possible educational futures to be sought because of their value to learners everywhere. First, the age range of persons served by our schools should be extended to include mature and senior learners as well as children of prekindergarten age. A downward extension of the age range is vital because of the need for benign and instructive learning environments (rather than mere custodial

Insights into challenges of the present and the probable turbulence of tomorrow are of little use unless we consider the redesign of education.

centers) for the care of children of working parents. At upper age ranges, programs for mature learners are essential when innovations may require workers to prepare for ten different jobs during a lifetime that is influenced by technological changes requiring new and diverse skills.

Second, schooling should be developed with an awareness of the flow of technological and social trends that will require substantial changes in curriculum and instruction. With the prospect of living longer, more older Americans will require new "post retirement" jobs. Also to be considered are the challenges facing younger workers who must cope with an increasing information glut.

Third, future-oriented conceptualizations of a school staff should include persons familiar with microelectronic equipment, such as computers and interactive video, combined with an awareness of the diversity and needs among students of varied ages. This also includes people trained with insights into the differences in the cultures of various ethnic groups and their languages and history.

Fourth, we also need to contemplate longer school days and ten- or eleven-month school years during which parents negotiate times when their children will be away from school. This arrangement would imply a future in which there was no traditional "school year." Rather there would be an unbroken flow of learning devoid of the summer break instituted years ago when young people were needed to help on farms where a large majority of Americans lived.

Associated with a rearrangement of the school year, a departure from the traditional K-8-4, 6-6, 6-3-3 or similar elementary-secondary structures may be required. In such a structure, children could advance at their own rate on the basis of maturity and ability rather than on the basis of time spent in a given grade or group.

Since the redesign of schooling will be unique for each district, it should be noted that there are no uniform instructional practices that should be followed in all school districts. Rather we must develop in our schools poli-

We must remain diligent in dealing with changes for tomorrow and not be immobilized by trying to polish the aged mosaics of past practices.

As we rapidly approach the new millennium, it is imperative that we endeavor to develop our foresight with regard to new designs and creative innovations for education. Only thus can we move from isolation to membership in the global community.

---

cies which are in keeping with the many different futures that coming decades will demand. We must not look for uniformity but for emerging programs that will help our oncoming generations defuse the socioeducational time bombs with which we are presently challenged.

The Role of Distance Education

Schooling in the home may find a place in the U.S. similar to its role overseas. *Distance education* originated in Britain, where Prime Minister Harold Wilson suggested it as a means "to pull Britain into the twenty-first century."[20] Distance education first began in 1971 with a curriculum transmitted by the BBC at the university level. Today, these television and radio broadcasts serve over 200,000 students with support from a full-time staff of 2,800 and 700 regional personnel.

With the varied needs of American learners that will need to be met in the future, a wide variety of learning materials designed for distance education could be planned by educators in cooperation with our public broadcasting systems. The range of possibilities is virtually infinite.

Depending on the nature of the populations that might be served by distance education, the range of those participating in home learning situations could extend from preschoolers to senior citizens. Depending on learner maturity, virtually all forms of content extending far beyond the traditional classroom could be produced.

As Lord Walter Perry, first vice chancellor of the original Open University pointed out, for mature learners an important goal also would be "...to offer to many people the chance of updating their educations with refresher courses that could be taken without having to drop out of the work force."[21]

As we rapidly approach the new millennium, it is imperative that we develop our foresight with regard to new designs and creative innovations for education. Only in this way can we move from isolation to membership in the global community.

To this task we must bring sincerity and action rather than mere talk. Through education we can strive to abate growing violence, teen pregnancy, poverty, homelessness, disease, and substance abuse. As these goals are attained we will have an infinitely better chance to defend successfully our planet from problems such as pollution, resource depletion, population growth, and other global threats.

1. Roy Amara, *The Second Decade* (Menlo Park, CA: Institute for the Future, 1990), 2.
2. John Elfreth Watkins, "What May Happen in the Next Hundred Years," *The Futurist* (October 1982): 8-13. Reprinted from *The Ladies Home Journal*, December 1900.
3. For excellent abstracts of publications dealing with potential futures, see *Future Survey* published monthly by the World Future Society, 4916 St. Elmo Avenue, Bethesda, MD 20814.
4. Joe Cappo, "Future Scope: Success Strategies for the 1990's," *Future* (November 1989): 15.
5. Ibid.
6. Carnegie Council on Adolescent Development, *Turning Points: Preparing American Youth for the 21st Century: A Report of the Task Force on Education of Young Adolescents* (Washington, DC: The Carnegie Council on Adolescent Development, 1989), 21.
7. William Van Dusen Wishard, "What in the World is Going On?" *Vital Speeches of the Day* 56 (March 1990): 314.
8. Ibid.
9. Edward Cornish, ed., *The 1990s and Beyond* (Bethesda, MD: World Future Society, 1990), 156.
10. W.C. Agar, Jr. and H.J. Brown, *The State of the Nation's Housing* (Boston: Harvard University Center for Housing Studies, 1988).
11. Harold G. Shane, "Educated Foresight for the 1990's," *Educational Leadership* 47 (September 1989): 4.
12. Melissa Ludtke, "Getting Young and Old Together," *Time Magazine*, 16 April 1990, 84.
13. H.E. Figgie, Jr., "Surviving Hyperinflation: Lessons from South America," *Vital Speeches*, 1 November 1988, 47-51.
14. "AMA and NASB Report," *Bloomington Herald-Times*, 8 June 1990, p.A3.
15. *Compton's Multi Media Encyclopedia*, (Chicago: Compton's, 1990).
16. Joseph L. Galloway, "How Your Privacy is Being Stripped Away," *U.S. News and World Report*, 30 April 1984, 46-48.
17. John I. Goodlad, *A Place Called School: Prospects for the Future* (New York: McGraw-Hill, 1984).
18. Office of Technology Assessment, *Information Technology and Its Impact on American Education* (Washington, DC: U.S. Government Printing Office, 1983).
19. Joel Chandler Harris, *Uncle Remus, His Songs and His Sayings* (New York: Groffet & Dunlap,1880).
20. "Britain's University of the Air," *The Futurist*, (July-August 1989), 25.
21. Ibid., 26.

Does the "Art of Teaching" Have a Future?

We need to broaden our image of professionalism
to include the artistic dimensions teachers
consider central to their work.

DAVID J. FLINDERS

David J. Flinders is Assistant Professor, University of Oregon, Division of Teacher Education, Eugene, OR 97403-1215.

Penelope Harper quickly takes roll, steps out from behind her desk, and glances around the classroom. Her eyes meet those of her students. Standing with her back to the chalkboard, she clasps her hands close in front of her, a ballpoint pen intertwined between her fingers. She holds her arms close to her sides and shifts her weight onto the heels of her shoes. This posture signals the beginning of class.

The students quiet down. Harper shakes back her dark hair and then addresses the class: "OK, today we need to discuss chapter two. Who would like to share something from your reading notes?" Silence. Harper breathes out, assuming a more casual and relaxed attitude. She is smiling softly now, confident that her students have read the assignment and that the silent classroom alone will motivate someone to risk putting forth an idea. Someone does. Harper listens intently and nods her head. "Good," she replies. "I really hadn't thought of it that way, but it tells us something, doesn't it? What's the author getting at here?" Harper steps forward, closer to her students, as their discussion begins to unfold.

Artistry in Professional Life

Penelope Harper (the name is a pseudonym) is good at what she does. She's a professional. But in Harper's line of work, what exactly does it mean to be a professional? Does it mean simply possessing a body of expert knowledge and a repertoire of techni-

cal skills? Climbing a career ladder toward greater autonomy and increased occupational rewards? Or, for classroom teachers, does professionalism mean something more?

These questions were the focus of a qualitative study I conducted on the nature of professional life in schools (Flinders 1987). Penelope Harper was one of six high school English teachers I observed and interviewed as part of this study. My purpose was to identify what Harper and her colleagues regard as the salient concerns of their day-to-day work experience. I hoped to view professional life through the eyes of classroom teachers.

I began my research with an understanding of professional life strongly influenced by the "new reform"

Effective communication begins with the processes of learning to see and to hear: the art of perception.

(Shulman 1987). Two prominent examples of this reform are the reports by the Carnegie Task Force (1986) and the Holmes Group (1986). These reports share a common theme: the need to increase the professional status of teaching. In particular, they call for strengthening the career advancement opportunities, the subject-matter knowledge, and the technical expertise of all classroom teachers.

This focus on career development and expert knowledge reflects a widely shared and commonsense image of professionalism (Schon 1983). However, in listening to teachers talk about their work and in observing their teaching day after day, I soon realized that this image did not match their daily routines and their concerns. This image of professionalism failed to capture the artistry that these teachers often spoke of and demonstrated as central to their work.

Perhaps I can clarify this point by referring to my description of Penelope Harper. Consider, for example, her ability to signal the beginning of class through body language or her use of silence to motivate student participation. These skills reveal something of the grace, subtlety, and drama of Harper's day-to-day teaching. Granted, these deft moves cannot be evaluated solely by conventional testing procedures or through the use of systematic rating scales. Yet

David J. Flinders, "Does the 'Art of Teaching' Have a Future?" *Educational Leadership*, Vol. 46, No. 8, May 1989, pp. 16-20.

they are no less important than Harper's technical expertise or subject-matter knowledge. As my study progressed, the challenge became to understand this other side of teaching—the artistic side.

The Arts of Teaching

Elliot Eisner (1983) has examined at a theoretical level various ways in which teaching can be regarded as art and craft. He calls attention, for example, to the dynamic and emergent qualities of classroom life, as well as to the intricate skill and grace that can characterize the teacher's classroom performance. In this context, Eisner uses the term *art* in its broad sense to signify engaging, complex, and expressive human activity. It is this sense that allows us to speak of a beautiful lesson or of a well-orchestrated class discussion.

If we want to observe artistry in teaching, where might we look in order to find it? My research suggests several possible locations. The first I have already touched on in my brief description of Harper's work: the art of communication.

Communication. On a day-to-day basis, classroom teachers rely heavily on interpersonal forms of communication. Philip Jackson's (1965) early research, for example, suggests that teachers engage in as many as a thousand interpersonal interactions each day. This is an impressive number, particularly if we consider the intricate nature of even the most routine instances of face-to-face communication. Such communication, as Harper's teaching reveals, goes far beyond the spoken and written word—it also encompasses the use of space (what sociolinguists call *proxemics*), body language, and paralinguistics (voice tone and rhythm). One teacher I observed, for example, consistently demonstrated uncanny responsiveness toward her students. When a student asked a question or made a comment, that student could feel the teacher's undivided attention. In talking with students, the teacher would face them directly, lean or step in their direction, and maintain eye contact. At appropriate moments she would raise her eyebrows, nod her head, smile, and bring the index finger of her right hand up to her lips in a gesture of serious concentration. All of these

> **The teachers I observed displayed various strategies for negotiating a cooperative relationship with their students, including using humor and providing opportunities for individual recognition.**

nonverbal cues were coordinated to signal a coherent message: *I care about what you have to say.* This unspoken message was often as important to the students as the substantive meaning of her verbal responses.

Nonverbal cues serve primarily as a form of metalanguage (Tannen 1986). That is, they help teachers establish a context for communication. Consider yet another, somewhat different example. During a literature class, one teacher I observed lighted a kerosene lamp, asked his students to sit in a circle, turned on a recording of the sound effects of a storm, and read passages from Dickens' *Bleak House*, just as a Victorian father might have read the novel to his family. This teacher's well-calculated nonverbal cues provided a context for his students to gain insight into the novel that could not be "explained to them" using words alone. Creating a setting—this too is part of communication.

Perception. It would be difficult to imagine good teachers who could not communicate well with their students. Yet effective communication does not begin with formulating a message or selecting a medium, but rather with the processes of learning to see and to hear. This notion suggests another, perhaps more fundamental art relevant to classroom teaching: the art of perception.

The teachers in my study often alluded to this art in describing their work. During an interview, for example, one teacher casually mentioned that she adapts her daily lesson plans depending on "how the group comes in at the beginning of the period." Such a comment underscores her ability to read those subtle cues in student behavior that signal the changing mood and tone of a class. Another teacher, when I asked how he evaluates his work, replied: "The real test in teaching is how the kids feel about you, and it's the vibrations that you pick up from them that tell you the most." Again, this comment suggests that perceptiveness—the ability to pick up on student attitudes, motives, beliefs, and so forth—lies at the heart of this teacher's professional expertise.

The type of perceptiveness and sensitivity to which these examples refer is a largely tacit dimension of social life. It depends on the ability to make complex and fine-grained distinctions between, for example, a wink and a blink, or between a sigh of relief and a sigh of frustration. All of us learn to make such discernments, at varying levels of sophistication, through social interaction. The point, however, is that this learning reflects an intuitive receptivity that Noddings (1984) has identified as critical to sound pedagogy. At a practical level, learning to operate in a receptive mode is basic to getting to know the students, and I was not surprised to find that all of the teachers in my study mentioned this process as central to their work.

Cooperation. Knowledge of students, of "what they are like as people," as one teacher described perception, serves as the foundation for a third art that is salient in the professional lives of teachers: cooperation. For classroom teachers this means negotiating an alliance with their students. As one teacher commented, "You have to get the students on your side with honesty and a certain amount of candor, so they understand you, and you understand them." This teacher continued, "I'm here to work *with* the kids; I'm not here just to shovel out stuff and let them grab it." The other teachers were also quick to stress the practical value of student-teacher cooperation. One teacher summed it up simply: "You can't force students to do what you want them to do, but if they know you're working hard and care about 'em, from there on it's gravy."

The teachers I observed displayed various strategies for negotiating a cooperative relationship with their students. Some of these strategies include: (1) using humor and self-disclosure to promote teacher-student solidarity, (2) allowing students to choose activities, (3) occasionally bending school and classroom rules in the students' interest, (4) providing opportunities for individual recognition, and (5) creating pockets of time that allow teachers to interact one-to-one with students.

An example of this last strategy, creating pockets of time, is illustrated by a teacher who set aside every Thursday for mini-conferences. On this day, while his students worked independently, he went around the classroom to speak individually with as many students as possible. He justified this routine by insisting that "it helps break the mannequin-like image of me standing up in front of the room. It pays tremendous dividends. It allows the students to ask questions, and I find out a lot."

Appreciation. The final art of teaching is appreciation. Unlike communication, perception, and cooperation, the art of appreciation is not primarily something that teachers *do.* Instead, it is a product of their artistry and, thus, cannot always be directly observed. Nevertheless, I found it readily apparent in how teachers describe the types of satisfaction they derive from their teaching. As Harper explained: "In almost any job you do, if you do it well, you get a certain ego-satisfaction from it. It's really a good feeling—when I run a discussion—to know that I did it well." Eisner (1983) describes the same idea in another way: "The aesthetic in teaching is the experience secured from being able to put your own signature on your own work—to look at it and say it was good (p. 13)." Both the classroom teacher and the scholar are describing the intrinsic sense of worth that comes from having

done a difficult job well. This idea is central to the daily work of classroom teachers.

A Challenge to Educational Leaders

The artistic dimensions that teachers recognize as basic to their profession stand in sharp contrast to the priorities of the new reform movement. Of course, professionalism is about opportunities for career advancement, the expert knowledge teachers possess, and the types of learning that can be easily tested. Yet the day-to-day experience of teachers reminds us that teaching is also about much more. It is about subtle interpersonal skills, discernment, caring, and "ego-satisfaction." These artistic aspects reflect highly complex forms of human expression that may well influence teacher effectiveness more than career ladders and fifth-year preparation programs.

If the art of teaching is to have a future, we must enlarge our understanding of professionalism to include the artistic skills and judgment that good teaching demands. This task presents a challenge to educational leaders for at least two reasons. First, artistry cannot be mandated by the central office. Neither can it be fostered by an afternoon of inservice training once or twice a year. Therefore, we have to think more deeply about the conditions under which teachers work, their opportunities for interacting with each other, the amount of discretionary time in their daily schedules, the number of students they see each day, and the resources with which they have to work. Second, the art of teaching is simply less well understood than technical aspects of instruction. We know more, for example, about the mechanics of lesson planning, test construction, and curriculum development than we do about how Penelope Harper is able to gracefully orchestrate a class discussion.

The profession can learn much about the complexity and artistry of teaching from colleagues like Penelope

Harper. We might begin by cultivating our own abilities to engage teachers in genuine dialogue. Basic to this dialogue is our perceptiveness—learning to see and hear teachers in ways that take us beyond stereotypical images. Like teachers, we must operate in a receptive mode. We might also promote a cooperative alliance both with and between classroom teachers, for example, by occasionally bending rules for their professional well-being and by involving them in decision making. Finally, we might strive to fully appreciate the multifaceted nature of this collaborative effort as an art and craft in its own right.

References

Carnegie Task Force on Teaching as a Profession. (1986). *A Nation Prepared: Teachers for the 21st Century.* Washington, D.C.: Carnegie Forum on Education and the Economy.

Eisner, E. W. (January 1983). "The Art and Craft of Teaching." *Educational Leadership* 40: 4-13.

Flinders, D. J. (June 1987). "What Teachers Learn from Teaching: Educational Criticisms of Instructional Adaptation." Doctoral dissertation submitted to the Graduate School of Education, Stanford University.

The Holmes Group. (1986). "Tomorrow's Teachers, A Report of the Holmes Group." East Lansing, Mich.: The Holmes Group, Inc.

Jackson, P. W. (1965). "Teacher-Pupil Communication in the Elementary Classroom: An Observational Study." Paper presented at the American Educational Research Association Annual Meeting, Chicago.

Noddings, N. (1984). *Caring: A Feminine Approach to Ethics and Moral Education.* Berkeley: University of California Press.

Schon, D. A. (1983) *The Reflective Practitioner.* New York: Basic Books.

Shulman, L. S. (February 1987). "Knowledge and Teaching: Foundations of the New Reform." *Harvard Educational Review* 57, 1: 1-22.

Tannen, D. (1986). *That's Not What I Meant!* New York: Ballantine Books.

Using Action Research to Navigate an Unfamiliar Teaching Assignment

Mary Dicker

Mary Dicker is a secondary school teacher in Burns Lake, British Columbia, Canada.

It was the last week of June, just before the summer holidays, that I learned about the change in my teaching assignment for the following year. I was teaching five mathematics courses and two drama courses in a secondary school in Burns Lake, British Columbia. Proud of my achievement in both of these areas, I assumed that this situation would continue the following year. A casual check of the next year's timetable in the principal's office, however, stopped me in my tracks. My 11th-grade drama course (Acting 11), had been cut from the schedule and in its place I had been assigned an 11th-grade English course, Communications 11. I was both angry and apprehensive—angry that my hard won victory establishing drama in our school program was so short lived and apprehensive that the course I was being assigned was in an area in which I had no professional expertise or experience.

Communications 11 was a new course developed by the ministry of education to replace an 11th-grade English course called Minimum Essentials, a course intended for students with weak English skills. The new course, aimed at the same audience, was to be implemented for the first time the following year. I was given the assignment despite the fact that I had no formal training or expertise in the teaching of English.

My anxiety increased when I learned that the only materials available from the ministry prior to September were a thin curriculum guide summarizing the learning outcomes expected in reading, writing, listening, and speaking and two writing textbooks, one of which was a reference communications handbook. It was expected that teachers would rely largely on their own knowledge of and training in the subject. The difficulties of my situation were compounded by the fact that there were not enough textbooks for each student in the class. I expressed my feelings on the matter to the administration and was assured that, although I was not qualified to teach English as such, my general professional skills combined with a knowledge base in drama would enable me to teach the new course.

Many teachers have been placed in similar predicaments, being faced with new courses outside their teaching area and limited resource materials with which to teach them. How do teachers cope in such a situation? How do they utilize their own knowledge and organize their teaching so that the learning situation becomes a viable one for their students in spite of the circumstances? Assuming the role of teacher researcher, I decided to undertake an action research project to answer these questions.

Action research is a form of self-reflective inquiry that can be utilized by teachers in order to improve the rationality and justice of (a) their own practices, (b) their understanding of these practices, and (c) the situations in which these practices are carried out (Carr & Kemmis, 1983, p. 152). It seemed an appropriate choice of inquiry for my situation. Therefore, applying the four components of the action research cycle, planning, acting, monitoring, and reflecting (Kemmis & McTaggart, 1982, p. 7), I examined the knowledge I used in teaching Communications 11 and how I used this knowledge.[1]

Examining My Knowledge

The examination of my knowledge base took place over approximately 3 months from the first day of classes in September to the beginning of December. Following the recommendations of Kemmis and McTaggart (1982), the major data collection device was my own reflective journal or diary, written each evening following a class period. The journal had two purposes: to shed a focused light on the previous lesson and to clarify plans for the following lesson. It was in fact a record of my thinking, revealing my practical knowledge and the particular way it was held and used. A further reflection was written each weekend in order to extend and deepen the reflections on the week's work and to develop a sufficiently thick description for the study.

As a second source of data, students wrote journals during the last 10 minutes of each class or for homework. Not only did this deepen the students' thinking about their work but it provided me with a different perspective on the events that were happening in the class. Anticipating that students might need some assistance in writing the journal, I posed several questions for them to answer.[2] Using the daily journal as a basis, the students wrote a longer reflection for homework every 2 weeks. Again they were asked to respond to specific questions.[3]

The students' journal writing was not only educationally valid as an assignment that encouraged writing skills as they reflected on their experiences

M. Dicker, (1990), "Using Action Research to Navigate an Unfamiliar Teaching Assignment," *Theory Into Practice*, 29 (3), pp. 203-208. (Theme issue on "Teacher as Researcher.") Copyright © 1990, College of Education, The Ohio State University.

in the class and organized their thoughts, but it also provided a basis for my future planning. The knowledge gained from my reading and reflection on the student journals became an integral part of my own journal as I commented on student writings.

A third source of data for the study of my practical knowledge use was a former teacher of English who took the role of "critical friend." In this role she read my journal and asked questions that helped me reveal the thinking that was not always fully expressed in the journal. This critical friend was an important part of the study. As I developed insights during the progress of the study, the validity of these interpretations were checked by this independent critic.

A final monitoring technique was the tape recording of the first and final lessons of the period under study and occasional other discussions, brainstorming lessons, and oral work. Not only did the tapes capture the "teacher-in-action" but, like the student journals, they also provided a student perspective. The tape recordings were a valuable check on the accuracy of my interpretations as I analyzed my journal.[4]

My Teaching Styles

The journal analysis and other monitoring devices made it clear that I had used two major teaching styles while teaching the course. As teachers gain experience in the art of teaching they inevitably develop a style reflecting a basic philosophy about how a particular subject should be taught. My two different teaching styles reflect my philosophy in each of my teaching areas, mathematics and drama. I regard mathematics as a formal and logical subject that requires a formal, ordered approach. Although students can work together to achieve understanding, the test of student mastery is their ability to solve problems individually. In my view, the British Columbia mathematics curriculum is process oriented,[5] with a correct answer for each problem. The underlying question is, "Which process has to be used in order to get the correct result?" Even if one can take several routes to solve the problem, the student is still looking for the "right" answer.

In order to achieve individual mastery of mathematical processes, I use a traditional, teacher-directed approach. I follow the curriculum by adhering to the textbook and supplementing this with worksheets. The students sit in rows facing the chalkboard. I explain, the students learn, and I check their understanding with questions, quizzes, and tests. The premise in my math teaching is that I know the correct processes and the correct answers. My job is to show the student these processes so they can find the correct answers. In addition to my own evaluation of student progress, the benchmark of my success in covering the prescribed courses is the evaluation tests the ministry gives at the end of grade 10 and the provincial exam at the end of grade 12.

My view of educational drama, on the other hand, is that it should encourage students' creative thinking by inviting them to solve problems through the drama mode. Student learning is a group process rather than an individual one. In my drama classroom, I encourage students to share ideas and possible solutions, for the problems are open ended with no one "correct" answer. The "solution" is usually the consensus of the group. Even this solution is not always the final one, but is changed and modified as circumstances require.

I also encourage students to make their own improvements to the work in progress. For the initial brainstorming sessions we are usually seated in a circle to allow all ideas to be considered equally. As the work progresses I question the students to make them think a little deeper about their work. It is a probing rather than a deliberate attempt to get at a "right" answer. Presentation is not my primary goal, although the work is frequently presented to an audience. Of most concern is the development of the work and the learning inherent in this development. The personal growth of each student is not easily evaluated. Their input is necessary to judge this, in addition to my own observations.

Thus, in my two different teaching areas, I have two different teaching styles. These teaching styles reflect not only the nature of the subjects being taught but my philosophy of how each one should be taught. Both styles were used in implementing Communications 11 but I was not aware of this while I was teaching. It was not until I had reflected on and analyzed my data that I realized that I possessed two teaching styles and that they both had had a strong impact on the progress of the course. The following description of what took place in my classroom is the result of my reflection on and analysis of the data collected. It reveals the knowledge I used when teaching Communications 11 and how I used this knowledge.

Knowledge from Drama

In teaching Communications 11 I was forced to examine what strategies I had for coping with my situation. From the outset I had felt that the only way I could cope with teaching this course was by using my background knowledge in drama. If I could interpret "communication" in its broadest sense, I could teach a quasi-acting course by disguising it as Communications 11. In this way I could combat two problems. I would have an acting class and would also be on familiar ground even though the subject area itself was unfamiliar.

As the work progressed I discovered I had chosen an approach that not only could be adapted to the course but that also allowed the course to be adapted to it. As in my drama courses, I wanted the students to be actively involved in their own learning in the course. I wanted to explore communication *with* the students instead of trying to instruct them directly. Note the journal entry made in preparation for the first lesson:

> I want to find out what students think Communications 11 means. *Discussion*—round the table—different format might help the students to think differently—they're weak students—I want to encourage their ideas and let them see I *listen* to *them*.

I was able to start the course by using a previous drama lesson plan. I observed in my journal, "Today's lesson was almost identical to the first lesson in Acting 11 last year. I changed 'teen-age interests and problems' to 'communication' but method the same." The ability to adapt materials and ideas from other sources is an integral part of the art of teaching. I had embarked on my quasi-acting course with a familiar strategy that I knew would be successful.

The first idea that was contributed by the students and which could be used in developing the course was a list of the different ways people communicate. They developed the list through their own discussion. I wrote in my journal,

> I didn't make nearly enough of their lists which had good ideas—I want to make up for this by using the lists next lesson somehow . . . . Interesting to see that the students are coming up with the wider view of "communication"—more along my conception.

Using the lists was important not only for the ideas. It was a way of demonstrating my acceptance and approval of students' suggestions. What they had to offer was worthwhile, and I wanted them to know that I thought so. We expanded the lists the next day and used the dramatic technique of "tableaux" (frozen action pictures created by students) to depict the means of communication contained in the lists. Their view of communication was even broader than mine, including such areas as sign language, Braille, Morse code, and even smoke signals. I felt my concept for the course had been justified, and I believe the "meeting of minds" enhanced students' confidence and developed rapport.

By continually being aware of and recording the general reactions of the students, I think I became more sensitive to their needs. I was ready to make adjustments if I thought them necessary. By reading the "pulse" of the class I was brought closer to them and this, in a subtle way, helped in further establishing the rapport. A few lessons later I commented,

> A nice atmosphere—relaxed. I felt this lesson was an important one. I was able to talk to all the students individually or in small groups. There was an atmosphere similar to my drama class last year. I was very pleased to be able to praise their work.

The use of my knowledge from drama appeared to be working well, and as I confidently developed lessons around themes taken from the initial communications lists, I inevitably pushed the drama mode further. As time went on, however, a change occurred in my teaching style. I slipped out of the drama mode and into the formality of my mathematics style of teaching. It was at this time that

my knowledge of class control stood me in good stead.

A Loss of Focus

Twice it happened that my teaching lost focus and direction and seemed to flounder, but my control of the class did not. I was able to continue teaching and I doubt if the students were aware of the change. In both instances the loss of focus came after active periods of group work using drama techniques. There was a need for a change of pace, a need to "settle down" for a while. It seemed to me that this was probably a good time to start using the textbook. The favorable impression I had formed about the text is recorded in my journal.

> I've been looking at the text, *Writing Sense* [Potter, 1981]. I like the way it's written and presented—pictures, activities, common-sense down-to-earth style. Emphasis seems to be on writing flow rather than grammar. The first four chapters contain ideas I have emphasized with the students—honesty in writing—reading aloud to improve writing.

Philosophically it seemed the perfect book for me to use. It also appeared to be suitable for use by students weak in English as the chapters were short and easy to read. What I did not realize at the time was that each short chapter is on a different topic with no real link between chapters. This deficiency may not create difficulties for a qualified English specialist, but for someone in my position it created an unforeseen problem that I will say more about later.

I had the feeling that I ought to use the text at some point in the course so that I could say I was following the curriculum. My instincts seemed justified when I was told that I was to be evaluated for my teaching report. This knowledge prompted me to write in my journal, "I'm wondering if I have enough marks for the class at the present time—I think I'll have to make specific parts of my lessons markable. The type of work I've been doing is difficult to mark." Not only was the text the prescribed one for the course but it also had exercises in it that were markable.

I used the text two lessons in a row to encourage a feeling of continuity. The actual lessons themselves, however, were not linked as each chapter was on a different topic. My reflection for the lessons shows that the students were not enthusiastic.

> The reading was fine but they did not really apply themselves to the questions—a few of the girls did. The reporting back was not successful—students didn't listen so I eventually abandoned this and got them down to write. . . . I did not have them read aloud as I had planned because of the previous lack of concentration. Instead I had them proof-read each other's work to themselves.

The desks went back in rows as this seemed the appropriate arrangement for students who had to concentrate on individual writing assignments. I think perhaps this was one of the subtle ways in which I was influenced by the textbook. The formality of

1. PSYCHOLOGY APPLIED TO EDUCATION AND TEACHING

using the text demanded the formality that I used in math class.

Because each lesson was on a different topic, it meant I was planning one lesson at a time. I wrote, "I'm beginning to feel the need for a little longer planning—one day at a time is difficult." As I limped from lesson to lesson a feeling of desperation began to creep into my journal.

I am now beginning to get a "swamped" feeling. I am not having enough time to plan and organize because of the work in other classes. I have marking to do all the time. I also feel I am losing my efficiency which is compounding the problem. I am needing help from colleagues. I think I have passed the "going it alone" stage. What are they actually *learning* at the moment— I am beginning to wonder . . . . I am not sure what to do about the books they are reading—do I have them write a report?—or does that kill the enjoyment of the book? Could they communicate the ideas in the book another way? Should I give a deadline by which the book should be read? Better ask my colleagues these questions.

By turning to the textbook I inadvertently moved into a series of short, teacher-directed lessons more like math teaching than drama teaching. This teacher-directed style worked well in math, where I was knowledgeable; in Communications 11, it took me into an area where my knowledge of the subject was at its weakest. I lost my original focus and although my experience as a teacher enabled me to continue teaching without a loss of control or rapport, I was not pleased with the work I was doing.

Back to a Drama Teaching Mode

Toward the end of October a resource book for the course appeared in my box in the office. I found that it contained some philosophical ideas that supported my approach to the course. It emphasized the value of student based literature content and the importance of finding situations in which students want to learn and can find success. Reading the resource book prepared the ground for the development of a new focus and a return to my drama teaching style.

I noticed in the section on short stories a story about nuclear war. Initially I asked the department head for advice on reading the story. He suggested I read it aloud, with the students following in their own books. In my journal I commented, "I thought this would be too similar to them listening to the record, but the fact that they are reading along silently will be sufficiently different." The unfamiliarity of the subject was prompting me to assume I always had to be doing a new activity or slightly varying the activity. Yet I often repeated activities when teaching in my own subject areas.

The reading of the story aloud was not only a natural progression from the silent reading I was doing with the students each lesson but also encouraged me to abandon desks in rows and place them in a circle again. I began to feel the pull of my drama background again and this was evidenced in the first lesson on the new topic of nuclear war. Having read the story to them, we did an activity

used by drama teachers called "hot-seat." Several students volunteered to be characters from the story and, in role ourselves, we all asked them questions. This was quite successful and a positive end to the lesson. I was back in my drama mode with a focus that lasted nearly 3 weeks.

Unfortunately, at the end of the 3 weeks, as I again sensed the need to vary the pace, I repeated my previous mistake of using the textbook. By the third lesson I was caught in the one-lesson-at-a-time trap and had returned to the traditional teaching style of my math classes, which included arranging the desks in rows. When I tried to conduct a discussion on phobias without changing the desks, my journal records,

The discussion tended to be "patchy." Groups would take part but often the others didn't really listen—I had to do my "policeman act."

Again I felt the need to control students' behavior, using body language, direct looks, and spoken admonitions. I was aware that part of the trouble was because of the struggle to think of what to do each lesson. I talked to my husband and he suggested that I follow the example of the head of the English department and give them a project that would last 2 weeks (survival tactics!).

Even though I had done several longer units and knew this was the answer, I needed this reminder. Teaching an unfamiliar subject seems to make a person react in a similar way to being in unfamiliar situations—thinking is thrown off balance and one can miss the obvious. A project had the advantage that, once the parameters had been established, the students would work for several lessons without the teacher having to prepare new lessons. Each lesson would be spent helping the students develop their ideas in the project. I had done many a project with eighth-grade drama students.

Teachers frequently utilize the year's calendar when planning their work. Seasons and specific dates become a meaningful focus for a variety of educational activities. As it was less than 3 weeks to the Christmas holidays I decided to devise a project on the Christmas theme that applied specifically to the course. I felt some intellectual satisfaction in arriving at an idea that would tie together the work done in the term. In groups of about four, the students would make presentations on the theme of Christmas utilizing all the means of communication used in their term's work. In my journal I described how I started the project:

We then sat in the circle again and I started the discussion on Christmas—why we have it, themes associated with it etc. We then established a list of the forms of communication used so far. They made the major suggestions in both parts of the discussion with some minor prompting from me. . . . They then split up into their groups and started to discuss the project. They seemed interested and enthusiastic.

All the elements I had hoped for at the beginning of the course and had partially lost at two stages during the term combined to make this project a satisfying one for both me and the class. The students were making a positive contribution of their own ideas. They were involved in their own learning and making their own decisions in a relaxed atmosphere under my guidance, not my direction.

A few new developments also occurred during the project. The students started to search out suitable poetry to be part of their presentation— an area we had not explored as yet in the course. Kathy,[6] who had refused to speak in front of the class during the oral presentation on music because of her shyness, read aloud with Wilma during their presentation. One group read a poem as a radio play and Don learned his part by heart. Another group unified all means of communications into an effective dramatic presentation.

The written components also showed that students had thought about their work. Wilma, Sonja, and Kathy based their writing on a dictionary exercise we had done. They thought of a long list of words associated with Christmas and gave definitions for each. Ron's group researched Christmas customs in other countries. The satisfaction I had as a teacher was in seeing how much the class had progressed as a whole, and how individuals had demonstrated a personal growth.

Knowing that one has taught and the students have learned is essential for any teacher, but it is particularly important for teachers working in a subject area outside their speciality. I did not have teaching knowledge of specific English skills. However, I do believe my own knowledge of how to teach contributed to students' ability to communicate and think clearly.

Conclusions

Teaching Communications 11 was a professional development activity that contained as much learning for me as for the students. By reflecting on my teaching decisions through action research, I was able to cope with teaching a course in a subject area that was unfamiliar. Teaching a new course outside one's own area forces teachers to examine the strategies that are available to them. My reflection made me aware that I was using the two teaching styles with which I was already familiar, and that one of these styles was more appropriate for this circumstance than the other.

My 15 years experience as a teacher has given me practical knowledge that has been constructed through time by the actions taken (Connelly & Elbaz, 1982, p. 117). An important element in my practical knowledge was the ability to maintain a disciplined learning environment. While this knowledge gave me confidence in my ability in dealing with students, it was not sufficient. During the time I was using my more traditional teaching style, the monitoring techniques of action research enabled me to see that while the situation was under control, it was not the learning atmosphere I wanted to create.

As Fullan (1982) has stated, one dimension of educational change is the possible use of new teaching approaches. For teachers faced with assignments outside their areas, the need for a new approach, or at least a modification, is highly probable. In order to cope with unfamiliar assignments teachers require not only knowledge of various teaching styles but a willingness to try them out. Action research provides the opportunity of trying out a new approach while monitoring what is occurring. Through the use of journals, tape recordings, and discussions with other educators, I was able to become a learner along with my students. Action research created the possibility for perpetual, self-generated, professional development.

I learned a lot from Communications 11, but I did not want my professional development to continue through this course for another year. My goal was to reinstate Acting 11 on the timetable and work to improve it. So I tackled the principal early in spring and elicited a firm commitment on the matter. While I do not want to repeat the experience of teaching a course for which I am unprepared, the experience of coping with new subject matter materials using action research techniques has probably made me a better teacher.

Notes

1. This article is based on a longer study undertaken as part of a M.Ed. degree in curriculum studies at the University of Victoria, British Columbia, 1986-87.
2. Examples of questions posed:
- How did *you* practice communication today?
- Did you feel your communication was successful? Why or why not?
- How well did your group work together?
- What were your thoughts when you showed your work to the class?
3. Examples of questions posed:
- What do you feel you have learned so far in this course?
- Which activities have you enjoyed the most, and why?
- Which activities have you not enjoyed, and why?
- What other activities do you think we should do?
4. See Kemmis & McTaggart (1982, pp. 39-42) for a full list of techniques to use as possible monitoring devices.
5. Since the writing of the original M.Ed. study on which this article is based, a new math curriculum has been implemented in British Columbia which is less process oriented. Considerable emphasis is now placed on the development of problem-solving skills.
6. The student names used here are not their real names.

References

Carr, W., & Kemmis, S. (1983). *Becoming critical: Knowing through action research.* Geelong, Victoria, Australia: Deakin University.

Connelly, F.M., & Elbaz, F. (1982). Conceptual bases for curriculum thought: A teacher's perspective. In A.W. Foshey (Ed.), *Considered action for curriculum improvement* (pp. 95-119). Alexandria, VA: Association for Supervision and Curriculum Development.

Fullan, M. (1982). *The meaning of educational change.* Toronto: Ontario Institute for Studies in Education.

Kemmis, S., & McTaggart, R. (1982). *The action research planner* (2nd ed.). Geelong, Victoria, Australia: Deakin University.

Potter, R. (1981). *Writing sense.* Toronto: Globe/Modern Curriculum Press.

The Colors of Teaching: A Tale of Double Vision

Cochise Jackson shares his "war stories" — and raises some important questions about teaching in contemporary American society.

POINT OF VIEW

IRA JAY WINN

IRA JAY WINN, a professor of education and urban studies at California State University, Northridge, is writing a book on educational reform: The Mirage of Teaching and Education.

WHEN Cochise Jackson began to speak of his challenges and dilemmas as a teacher, a bemused silence fell over the joint seminar of university teaching assistants and student teachers. Cochise was clearly one of the class favorites, always good for a humorous yarn or a stirring tale. He had a way with words and a way with children — and, having risen successfully out of the black inner city, he knew instinctively how to take the measure of a situation, how to take command. He knew the lingo of the streets, and he was as comfortable there as in the university setting. He was one of a small group of older student teachers and teaching assistants who had entered teaching through some back door. His gangling frame gave testimony to a basketball career long since abandoned, and when he rose and ambled to the lecturn there was a murmur of respect, mixed with ripples of good humor.

"Gentlemen . . . uh, ladies, too, in these days of equality for all people . . . I have been asked to reflect with you on some recent teaching experiences — and, I suppose, to tell a few 'war stories' to get you to thinking critically. We all love

war stories because we all want to find heroes, I suppose. That must tell us something about ourselves . . . but I haven't yet figured out what. Maybe we can figure it out together. Maybe not." Jackson smiled at the assembled group of new teachers, master teachers, and professors. He waited a few moments for his opening remarks to penetrate, for the laughter to die away.

"Now all you pale faces out there, pay special attention to the first of my stories. That don't mean you darker people can go to sleep, no way. But it do mean that we might get some differing views on my two teaching stories, based on your own particular cultural background." It was clear from his language style that Cochise was playing for effect.

"Now, as some of you that knows me know, I have what is called a double assignment in student teaching. I took this not just because I love to work double, but so I can graduate this June. One might say that I is a racing fool — racing to get out the door and into the 'real world,' where a man, or a woman, gets paid real wages (if not much) for teaching. Anyway, I teach mornings at Carver Junior in the ghetto. And afternoons, I race out to the plushy Oakwood Knolls suburbs to teach at Luther Burbank Senior High. You all remember Luther Burbank as the man with the green thumb. Green! That's kind of funny, 'cause the school is lily white except for a smattering of bus-ins. So, depending on the time of day it is,

I see the world as black or white. But how do the world see me?"

Another ripple of laughter rolled through the audience as Cochise Jackson played with his glasses and threw his classmates a bemused look. After a suitable pause, he continued.

"You see, you are looking at a man with dual vision. 'Double vision,' some might say. And double vision makes the world blurry. So I'm going to ask for your help in seeing things clear after I tell you my stories. Here goes.

"One day last week, I think Wednesday, I decided to give my ninth-grade social studies class at Carver some writing experience with a real-life situation. So I got hold of a bundle of job application forms from an employment agency.

"I set the stage for the class with some personal stories about the importance of getting a good job. We bantered about different career possibilities, as well as summer and part-time jobs. Then I stressed the importance of job application forms, and I had a student write on the blackboard these words: *neatness, legibility, presentation, ability to follow directions.* For practice, I had the class respond to some simple questions on lined 3 x 5 cards, before I passed out the two-page job application forms.

"My idea was to have the students choose jobs that interested them and then fill out the forms as if they were qualified to hold those jobs. They could choose professional careers if they wanted to. I gave them a few minutes to get started; then I began to move about the classroom, giving advice and suggestions. That was when I noticed that one student was just sitting there with her arms folded.

"I went over and spoke to her. 'Lucinda, my friend, why are you not doing your work?' I thought she might be sick — or that she didn't understand the directions (although that puzzled me, because she is one of the sharper students).

" 'Mr. Jackson,' she says to me, looking up with those big eyes of hers, 'really, I'm not filling out no such form. I'm going to be a momma in a few years.'

" 'Are you kidding me, lady?' I ask quietly. But no, she is dead serious. My mind is dazzled and racing. A 'momma,' for those of you who don't know, is someone who has babies as a way of getting on welfare. Hardly a great aspiration for a bright young girl with lots of college potential. Is this the teachable moment? I decide that it is. I risk it. I talk quietly with her for a few moments to clear the way.

"Then I say, 'Hey, class, hold up what you're doing for a minute. I have an important point to discuss, and I'd like your opinions and advice. Lucinda, is it okay if we try to think this through together?' She readily assents, glad for the attention.

" 'Lucinda thinks it's a waste of time to go filling out job applications,' I announce. 'Most people don't make it out of the ghetto, I guess, and Lucinda feels that the easy way is to have kids, get on welfare, and become a momma. Now, how do the rest of you see that?'

"Well, to make the lesson for us short and clear," Cochise went on, "more than half of the class agreed with Lucinda and were able to argue persuasively in her behalf. I think I turned a lot of them around, probably because I'm older and wiser and argue better. But I have to tell you that I was demoralized and wiped out by the experience. The problems in the central city are overwhelming. And even I, who

am a product of that environment, tend to forget this.

"So much for my first story. Put it in your right eye, while I fill up your left with my very-next-day experience at Burbank Senior." Cochise paused briefly, then plunged ahead.

"On Thursday, I drove out to Oakwood Knolls armed with a neat exercise I put together on critical thinking. The class was studying the Industrial Revolution — and, after a review of background and terms, I handed out copies of the lyrics to songs from *Mary Poppins*. You may remember the one that describes the merry life of the chimney sweeps of industrial England. We read along with the tape-recorded lyrics that tell how young boys happily kept the Industrial Revolution moving ahead by cleaning the soot from the chimneys of factories and homes. Then I had my ninth-graders write down some adjectives that would best describe the job of chimney sweep, from the description given in the song. By and large, my students reported the work in a positive light.

"At this point, I handed out a short poem, 'The Chimney Sweep,' by William Blake. The poem describes in gripping detail the horrible working conditions and the terribly shortened lives of these young boys, who were taken advantage of by the new industrial system.

" 'Now, based on the accounts before you, which is probably more believable and more accurate?' I looked at the roomful of middle-class students. Several of them had their heads on their desks; others were daydreaming or looking out the window. Several girls had mirrors on their books, and two of them were combing their hair. In fairness, there were the usual five or six eager students with their hands in the air. I decided to probe among the less interested.

" 'Jeannie,' I called, 'and the rest of you Hair People — if you would comb and speak at the same time, which of these descriptions of life in industrial England seems more on target? Come

on,' I urged, 'y'all got some good heads on those shoulders.' They looked at me, half amused and a lot bored.

" 'Really, Mr. Jackson,' Jeannie finally answered, 'I'm not much interested in past history. Couldn't we discuss something more current, like the drug problem or something?' Everyone laughed.

"I got the class back on track with some comments about how we can learn from the past and how problems today often reflect problems from other times. I also made a pitch for the importance of addressing evidence — but deep down I knew that only 50% of these kids had any real interest in the lesson. 'Ah, many a truth is said in jest,' I thought. Supposing we were discussing a current problem, such as the homeless or the lack of good jobs in minority neighborhoods. I doubt that those current problems would arouse much interest in Oakwood Knolls, either.

"Let's face it," Cochise added solemnly. "The me-generation — whether rich or poor — wants mainly to be entertained. Our students, like their parents, seek a quick fix. I do what I can, the best that I can, but something is missing.

"So those are my war stories of last week. And now I ask you, my peers and teachers, which of the two groups — one from the ghetto and one from the suburbs — is most damaged by segregation? Why do we think we are protecting young people by isolating them or by teaching them lists of key names, dates, and ideas in formulaic ways that guarantee instant recognition but not understanding or compassion? Has a long history of bad education driven out demand for good? These are the questions I went home with last week — the questions that caused my blurred vision. So I want you to help me clarify things. How can we improve education in these two communities? How can I become a more effective teacher? Are we all casting stones at the sea?"

Cochise Jackson raised his eyebrows, smiled quizzically, and waited for a response.

Development

- Childhood (Articles 5–9)
- Adolescence (Articles 10–12)

The study of human development provides us with knowledge of how children and adolescents mature and learn within the family, community, and school environment. Educational psychology focuses on the description and explanation of the developmental processes that make it possible for children to become intelligent and socially competent adults. The idea that cognitive, personal, social, and emotional development proceed in stages or patterns that are predictable is presently being studied by psychologists and educators.

Jean Piaget's theory regarding the cognitive development of children and adolescents is perhaps the best known and most comprehensive. According to this theory, the perceptions and thoughts that young children have about the world are prelogical and premoral. When compared to adolescents and adults, children think about moral and social issues in a unique way. Children need to acquire cognitive, moral, and social skills in order to interact effectively with parents, teachers, and peers. If human intelligence encompasses all of the above skills, then Piaget may have been correct in saying that human development is the child's intelligent adaptation to the environment.

Today the cognitive, moral, and social development of children takes place in a rapidly changing society. A child must develop a sense of self-worth and self-reliance, as well as a strong sense of family, in order to cope with these changes and become a competent and socially responsible adult. The contribution of the classroom in fostering prosocial values and behavior is explored in the article by Susan M. Doescher and Alan I. Sugawara.

Adolescence brings with it the ability to think abstractly and hypothetically and to see the world from the perspective of others. Adolescents strive to form goals and achieve a sense of identity, but they often become frustrated and feel alienated from the adult world. The kinds of adults they want to become and the ideals they want to believe in sometimes lead to conflicts with parents and teachers. Adolescents are also sensitive about espoused adult values versus adult behavior. The articles concerning adolescence in this unit discuss the social and personal problems that confront adolescents, and they suggest ways the school can help meet the needs of adolescents.

Looking Ahead: Challenge Questions

What is an appropriate education for young children? Is childhood still recognized as a unique stage of development? Why is it important for children to have the opportunity to solve problems on their own? How can teachers provide them with these activities?

What are some of the social pressures and risks children face in growing up? How can parents and teachers help children to develop positive self-concepts and high self-esteem?

Describe the societal and personal problems adolescents face. How can the middle school provide a balance between the physical, cognitive, and affective aspects of learning and development for adolescents?

Unit 2

How Well Do We Respect the Children in Our Care?

Stacie G. Goffin

Stacie G. Goffin is Assistant Professor, Early Childhood Education, University of Missouri - Kansas City.

Children are spending increasingly larger proportions of their early years in group settings outside their homes. Statistics abound describing the quantity of mothers currently in the workforce. Interest in early childhood education, however, is more than just the result of increasing maternal employment. There are other crucial statistics.

• Twenty-five percent of all children—47% of black children, 40% of Hispanic children and 10% of white children—are born into and spend their lives in poverty (Halpern, 1987).

• One in five children who entered 1st grade this past fall is at risk of becoming a teen parent, and one in seven is at risk of dropping out of school (Children's Defense Fund, 1988).

• The decreasing number of future workers means every potential employee needs to be competent and skilled.

In combination, these changing demographics and social circumstances have focused attention on early childhood care and education as a solution to welfare reform, teenage pregnancy, female employment and future labor needs. Noticeably absent from this list of public policy concerns, however, is the well-being of children. This omission points to the low priority the general public gives to issues associated with quality. Quality issues argue the validity of children's well-being in the present and contrast with the current focus of arguments supporting early childhood education in terms of future returns.

As early educators, however, we cannot side-step the issue of quality; we need to become more reflective about the "treatment" children are receiving. We can begin by asking the question, "How well do we respect the children in our care?"

As defined by the *New Scholastic Dictionary of American English* (Kessen, 1981), the term *respect* has the following meanings: to be mindful of; to pay attention to; to show consideration and esteem for; to avoid intruding upon; and to avoid violating. Based upon this definition, respect can be both a noun and a verb. As a noun, respect can be a result or outcome of our interactions with children; it can also be a description of our behavior, as in "respectful." The major focus of this discussion, however, is on respect as a verb— as an action word. As early educators, we show our respect *for* children by what we do *with* children.

To answer the question just posed, the various meanings of respect have been amplified in relation to daily interactions with children and their families. They have been used repeatedly to describe 12 active (and knowingly overlapping) categories that frame the ways early childhood educators can display their respect, or disrespect, to children. The intent is to provoke thinking about the meaning and impact of our actions with and for children.

TWELVE ACTIVE WAYS TO RESPECT CHILDREN

Action #1: Showing respect for childhood

The idea of childhood as a separate, developmental period is a relatively recent cultural invention; in fact, it is only several hundred years old (Kessen, 1979; Postman,

1982). Yet, many recent writers have expressed concern that the idea of childhood as a separate developmental period is disappearing (see, for example, Postman, 1982). This implies we have been guilty of intruding into and violating this unique period of growth.

In early childhood settings, examples of this kind of disrespect include ignoring the ways children learn through play and expecting them to learn in ways similar to older children. In addition to being inappropriate, when the curriculum focuses on skills and knowledge children supposedly need for later schooling (e.g., lining up, coloring within the lines, learning pre-skills), children's future development is being emphasized as more important than their current well-being. As a result, childhood becomes merely a stepping-stone to future stages of growth rather than a meaningful time for development in its own right.

Disrespect for childhood is also expressed in the frustration and outbursts of anger many adults display when children "act their age," instead of conforming to adult standards. The term *childish* has acquired a negative, rather than positive, connotation.

Early childhood teachers and caregivers are frequently praised for their patience. When they display their patience because children have failed to meet inappropriate expectations, however, they reveal misunderstandings about child growth and development (Weber-Schwartz, 1987). Those who understand children accept "childish" behavior like negativism, for example ("No! Me do it!"), as developmentally appropriate behavior for 2-year-olds. Even though respectful adults will want to help 2-year-olds learn other ways of expressing their feelings, they also recognize that children behave differently from adults because of their maturational level and inexperience.

Consequently, respect for childhood requires paying attention to and showing esteem for the characteristics of childhood—such as activity, impulsiveness, curiosity, learning through exploration—and then organizing teaching and learning to reflect these understandings. To quote Weber-Schwartz (1987), "Because I accept what *is*, I put energy into effective teaching, not into struggling against the reality that children are children" (p. 53, italics in original).

Action #2: Responding with sensitivity to children's individuality

Respectful actions in this category go beyond respect for childhood. They acknowledge the unique characteristics of individual children and the ways their uniqueness is revealed in decisions, choices, preferences and styles of responding to and interacting with objects and people. To show consideration for these qualities requires we support and encourage these characteristics as worth nurturing. Too often, children's personal ways of responding are viewed as interference with an adult's prepared plans or as misbehavior, rather than as evidence of a child's individuality or personal perceptions of the situation.

Commitment to children's individuality requires accepting and supporting children's personal goals and values as worthwhile. Early childhood settings that primarily function in whole groups and emphasize adult-prescribed learning offer limited opportunities for children to personalize learning through making their own decisions, acting as initiators of their own learning or pursuing their own interests. Yet, it is these flexible opportunities that encourage and support individuality and personal growth. In contrast, heavy doses of group instruction and standardized curriculum encourage and support conformity.

Being mindful of children's in-

dividuality also occurs when adults actively listen to children even though their comments may seem trivial. It is reflected in greetings and dismissals recognizing children's arrival and departure, in interesting alternative activities for children who are not interested in the adult-chosen activity and, most important, in consideration of children's individual ways of acting their age.

Admittedly, we cannot always be flexible in response to children's individuality, but we can give more consideration to how well we are accommodating children's needs and interests. Because we adults have more authority than children, it is easy to expect children to adjust to adult preferences; it is less easy to remind ourselves that it is often more supportive and growth-enhancing if we adjust to the individuality of children.

Action #3: Developing nurturing relationships with children
Action #4: Using adult authority with wisdom to facilitate children's growth into caring adults

Adults are bigger and stronger than children. They have more experiences and greater skills. Consequently, the power relationship between children and adults is unequal and unbalanced in favor of adults. The critical issue for children is how adults choose to use their authority. Dreikurs and Solz (1964) use the term *social equality* to describe an optimum relationship between children and adults. In this type of relationship, adults recognize that even though children are dependent upon them and have less knowledge and fewer skills, they are still entitled to respect as human beings.

This respect, however, does not suggest that adults should abdicate their responsibilities toward children. Because children are dependent upon us and are less knowledgeable and skillful, we must assume responsibility for nurturing and fostering their

Table 1
Early Educator Responses to the Question:
"How Well Do We Respect the Children in Our Care?"

I show my respect when:
- I listen to what a child has to say.
- I take time for a child when I'm very busy.
- I play with children.
- I color a picture with children.
- I recognize accomplishments.
- I allow children to settle disputes between themselves.
- I listen to a special song.
- I show interest in a child's project.
- I make eye contact.
- I encourage their viewpoints.
- I allow them to make choices.
- I try to arrange a schedule to be accommodating to a parent.
- I allow for privacy.
- I try to respond with words and actions to a child's uniqueness.
- I call children by their names.
- I know how to say "no."
- I encourage independence.
- I respond to their questions.
- I allow a child to talk uninterrupted.
- I respect a child's choice of friend and play equipment.
- I allow children to make mistakes.
- I realize their individuality.
- I am flexible.
- I allow them to disagree.
- I care for their property.
- I allow transition time.
- I listen to a child's problem and realize how upsetting the situation can be to a child.
- I talk to children as people.
- I give each child a chance to communicate.
- I ask a child for his/her solution to a problem.
- I value their opinions.
- I remember that play is of great importance in each child's life.
- I prepare myself well for class so I don't have to "waste" children's time.

I am somewhat disrespectful when:
- I do not take a child's opinion seriously.
- I avoid an issue a child felt needed immediate attention.
- I use time out.
- I leave the children alone.
- I walk away from a child while he/she is crying.
- I don't stop to listen.
- I respond with "uh-huh."
- I use a "baby-talk" tone of voice with younger children.
- I use angry words under stress.
- I cut their conversations close.
- I finish a task for them to hasten time.
- I forget to follow through on something I promised.
- I answer a question for them with a strange adult present so they are more articulate or seemingly more socially acceptable.
- I spend physical time with a child but am emotionally distant from the situation.
- I behave impatiently.
- I use sarcasm.
- I shout.
- I physically force a child into a situation in which he's uncomfortable.
- My expectations are too high.
- I rush children.
- I don't take care of myself physically or emotionally.
- I call them names; e.g., dumbbell.
- I show frustration because their needs interfere with my schedule.
- I focus on children's bad behaviors.
- I belittle their feelings.
- I sneak up on a child doing wrong.
- I ignore them.
- I stop a child who is really interested in a project.
- I don't allow a child to explain why or how a friend got hurt, or how an accident occurred.

Note: Thanks to all the early educators who shared their thoughts; their own wording has been used as much as possible.

---

growth. This is where wisdom comes in! Nurturing children's development into caring adults requires not only respect for childhood and a child's individuality, but also knowledge and understanding about child growth and development.

Furthermore, despite our frequent acknowledgment of the importance of children's emotional development, since the 1960s this aspect of growth has become a stepchild to cognitive (which often means academic) development. Yet, a nurturing relationship is the basis for child development. It is a necessary foundation for children's growth into caring human beings, as well as their relationships with peers and adults.

In fact, intellectual development and socio-emotional development are inseparable. They can be separated only for purposes of theory, pedagogy and research. This understanding requires adults to be as responsive to children's social-emotional needs as to their intellectual demands.

Action #5: Considering how day-to-day practices influence children
Children learn not only from *what* they are taught, but also from *how* they are taught. They learn from how the day is arranged, how the environment is organized and how others try to teach them. As early childhood educators, we need to become more sensitive to

the cumulative impact of our daily interactions with children, including intrusions into their play and activity, usurpation of their decision-making abilities and lack of attention to their feelings. Table 1 lists a sampling of responses to the title question from early childhood practitioners. Their answers highlight the day-in, day-out interactions that reveal respect, and unintended disrespect, for children.

We need to facilitate children's involvement in personally meaningful activities and experiences. The demands of group living can be softened by allowing children to make meaningful decisions and providing more opportunities for them to pursue their individual interests. We want to minimize the times we unnecessarily or unthinkingly forget to pay attention to children's interests and preferences.

One of the most challenging aspects of early childhood education is trying to understand a child's perspective about an experience. Lack of sensitivity to children's individual ways of making sense of their experiences often leads adults to impose their own ways of organizing and interpreting experiences (see, for example, Paley, 1986; Suransky, 1982).

For example, in one early childhood setting, a group of 4-year-olds sat cross-legged on the floor in a circle, watching as their teacher lifted a pencil, a beanbag and three baby-food jars out of a bowl and then set them on a mat. The teacher announced, "Many of these things have been on the earth for a long time." She held up a baby-food jar of soil and said, "LAND has always been here as far as we know." She returned the jar to the mat and lifted up another jar filled with water, saying, "WATER has always been here as far as we know." She set the jar back on the mat and held up the last jar (which appeared empty) and said, "AIR has always been here as far as we know." She placed the jar back on the mat and asked, "Can you see anything else that has always been here?" Antoine called out excitedly, "The bowl!!"

The teacher answered, "No. MAN made the bowl. Someone INVENTED the bowl. Can anyone think of something in our room that someone made?" Antoine raised his hand and shouted, "Horses on the wall!" The teacher pointed to the teacher-prepared horses decorating the wall above the blackboard. She asked, "What about the horse on the farm? Where did it come from?" Antoine announced excitedly, "Horses!!" The teacher smiled at Antoine and asked again, "Where did they *come*

from—did man make them or did God make them?"

This teacher appeared unaware that her way of thinking about these concepts differed from Antoine's. From Antoine's point of view, the experience probably helped him to learn self-doubt and how to "play the circle-time game." It is likely he also learned that right answers are arbitrary, since his reasoned thinking was consistently corrected. It is unlikely, however, that he learned much about the distinctions between natural and man-made materials, which appears to have been the teacher's objective.

It is equally important to pay attention to children's needs in our scheduling and organizing. Too often we feel that responding to children's needs (e.g., to receive affection, to be first in line, to take more time) interferes with classroom routines or that being tough while children are young, better prepares them for a harsh world later on. In reality, it is just the opposite. By responding to children's needs, we strengthen their abilities to accept themselves and to cope with difficult circumstances.

Sensitivity to children's perspectives is seen when adults try to understand children's thinking, their needs, preferences and reactions. Failure to consider the impact of our day-in, day-out living arrangements with children underestimates the daily impact of teacher-child interactions and can undermine children's opportunities to develop their individuality.

Action #6: Recognizing discipline as a learning experience for children and viewing mistakes as potential learning opportunities
Discipline is frequently confused with punishment; its purpose is often mistakenly limited to stopping inappropriate behavior. Discipline, however, describes the guidance provided to help children understand adult expectations and develop control from within. It is

an ongoing process of guiding children's development.

When children and adults cooperate with each other, classroom life proceeds smoothly. When children do not comply with a teacher's request, the result is usually a discipline encounter. The term *encounter* highlights that the outcome desired by the teacher is not shared by the child, reminding us that children are active decision-makers (Goffin, 1987). These disagreements often result in conflict between teachers and children.

It is this aspect of discipline that has received the most discussion and unfairly earned discipline the one-sided reputation of being negative and unpleasant. Still, the important point is that discipline in general, and discipline encounters in particular, are both learning experiences for children. The ways teachers and caregivers structure these daily experiences clearly reveal their consideration and esteem for children.

A major characteristic of adult-child relationships is the discrepancy between the power and authority of children and adults. We intrude upon children when we use our authority and power to coerce them (most easily characterized by the phrase "Because I said so, that's why!") to fulfill our needs (for order or schedule, for example) without being mindful of their needs, interests and individuality. Respectful adults carefully use their power and authority to help children learn appropriate behaviors and inner controls in ways that show consideration for their feelings and developing capabilities; for example, by acknowledging feelings, providing explanations and linking behavior with rational consequences.

Action #7: Acknowledging children's competencies
Action #8: Organizing a curriculum that provides children with interesting things to think about
We often fail to be mindful of what

2. DEVELOPMENT: Childhood

children are capable of doing. There is a tendency to narrowly focus on skills and information children do not yet possess. As a result, some early childhood educators see their major responsibility as teaching children the next item in a series of learnings. This emphasis, however, fails to show esteem for children's capabilities. Learning experiences should be organized as extensions and elaborations of children's current interests and understandings—the basis for meaningful learning.

Research reveals that children are much more capable than we have credited them (Bruner & Harste, 1987; Donaldson, 1978; Gelman, 1979). It is demeaning, as well as boring, to have weekly units on fragmented skills or topics such as the color *blue*, the shape of a circle or the letter *C*. It is also frequently meaningless. A 4-year-old, working to create an octopus by gluing precut construction paper tentacles on a yellow circle of paper, turned to his teacher standing nearby and asked, "What am I making?" "Octopuses," the teacher responded. "Why?" he followed up. "Because," the teacher replied, "the letter we're learning about is *O* and octopus begins with it." "Oh," he said as he returned to his gluing.

Children are entitled to activities and experiences that are engrossing and that permit the teacher to challenge their thinking. Learning is more than memorizing labels and making associations between objects. Esteem for children demands we pay attention to their abilities and provide meaningful, relevant and interesting ways for them to expand their understandings. It also requires talking *with* children (instead of *at* them) by attending to what they are doing and asking questions related to their actions.

As the following anecdote clearly reveals, we dominate the learning process when our teaching primarily focuses on what *we*

think children ought to know, regardless of its relationship to their current interests and activities.

During a circle-time activity, the teacher flashed picture cards to the seated children. "And, what is this?" she asked. "A boat," children shouted. "Where does it go?" A child interjected, "Teacher, I rode a boat on my vacation." Another child yelled, "I did, too." "I have a boat at my house," a third child contributed. The children then began talking with each other, sharing comments like: "We went to Disney World on our vacation ...We went to Colorado." "Quiet!" the teacher shouted. "Now, I said quiet. That's enough about vacations; you can talk about that at free time. We have to get through this."

> *Research reveals that children are much more capable than we have credited them.*

Action #9: Supporting and strengthening parents in their childrearing responsibilities
Many children spend the majority of their waking hours with their teachers and caregivers. It is easy, therefore, for early childhood educators to lapse into a possessive attitude about the children in their care. This feeling is often heightened by tensions between parents and teachers/caregivers surrounding differing views on issues such as values, discipline, the importance of play and a child-centered curriculum (see Galinsky, 1988). These tensions are perhaps inescapable in any relationship where two unrelated adults care about the well-being of the same child. Still, it must be remembered that it

is parents who have made an unending commitment to their child, and it is with their parents that children are most emotionally intertwined.

Parenting is becoming respected as a challenging as well as highly personalized family enterprise. Parent programs based upon these premises are being called family support programs (Weissbourd, 1983). These programs strive to strengthen parenting by being responsive to parents' individuality and respecting the responsibilities they have assumed as parents.

We can show our support to parents in four ways: 1) by acknowledging the challenge of parenting, 2) by coming to know parents as individuals with their own personalities and family circumstances that help define their parenting, 3) by using these understandings to avoid judgmental interpretations of parents and their decisions, and 4) by acting as advocates for the parent-child relationship (Goffin & Caccamo, 1986). By strengthening and supporting parents in their parenting role, we show consideration for the importance of family in a child's life and express esteem for the challenge of parenthood.

Action #10: Acknowledging the expertise needed to be a professional in early childhood education
Action #11: Speaking out on behalf of early childhood education as a profession
The status of those who care for children is a leading indicator of how society views childhood and shows esteem for children. In general, society expresses limited interest in other people's children and therefore has little regard for those who do (Grubb & Lazerson, 1988). Society's attitude toward child care and caregivers, in particular, reveals the still dominant assumption that parents—mothers in particular—should be held totally responsible for the daily care

and education of their own children. This viewpoint encourages a custodial approach to child care outside the home.

As the number of women in the workforce and concerns for quality education increase, however, the importance of supplementing parents' responsibilities is gaining greater acceptance. We know the importance of our jobs and the contributions we make to children and their families. We know we are both underpaid and undervalued. But too many of us are also uninformed and undereducated about how to fulfill our responsibilities as early childhood educators.

For example, after beginning an afternoon kindergarten session with a 20-minute whole group handwriting exercise, a teacher announced, "Every day, after we have writing, we will have Center Time. Who knows what Center Time is?" "Well," the teacher answered, "if you went to preschool, they probably called it Play Time. And what is the difference between preschool and kindergarten? One is like babysitting and one is real school. And we are in real school here and we do real work, but sometimes we think play is learning, too."

This is a significant time in the history of early childhood education. The field is rapidly expanding. Simultaneously, early childhood educators are attempting to upgrade their status and compensation. Yet, at the same time, we are trying to convince many of the "outsiders" entering the field, as well as those already within our ranks, that early childhood education has a distinctive, professional knowledge base.

Knowledge of child development and early childhood education informs our practice and assures young children of programming specific to their needs and interests. It also provides a rationale for fending off the inappropriate expectations held by those

unfamiliar with the issues unique to early childhood education (Goffin, 1989). More clearly articulating our purposes and convincing educational decision-makers and others about the unique characteristics of early childhood education remain two of our major professional challenges.

Action #12: Speaking out on behalf of children's needs to parents, school administrators, business and community representatives, and policymakers

Recent political and economic events have sensitized us to the realization that children's issues are not above politics. Policies made by business and government structure many of the decisions early childhood educators make for children and the kinds of experiences children live.

As early educators, we experience, either directly or indirectly, the personal stories behind the statistics. Our relationships with parents create the opportunity to release parents' power on behalf of their own as well as other children (Goffin, 1988). Our relationships with the community place us in a unique position to inform others about the needs of children and families. Our knowledge and experiences enable us to help policymakers better understand the lives of their youngest constituents. Therefore, we are violating our responsibility to children when we fail to act on our beliefs and to share our knowledge with others.

Advocacy on behalf of children is a critical vehicle for actualizing our commitment to children. It is a necessary component of an expanded vision of the role of the early childhood educator.

It is important to recognize that advocacy includes, but is not limited to, political activity. Everyone can participate in personal advocacy (Goffin, 1988). When we personally reach out or speak out to others and, by our interpersonal actions, try to help children and

their families achieve needed or desired outcomes, we are performing personal advocacy. Personal advocacy takes advantage of opportunities to use our expertise on behalf of children and families.

A child care director's presentation to architects and a church committee about the importance of low windows in children's classrooms—despite her uncomfortable feelings of "exceeding her proper limits"—demonstrates personal advocacy. This director spoke out on behalf of children's needs for light and an aesthetically pleasing environment, despite her discomfort and anxiety. Her personal advocacy efforts resulted in differently designed, more appropriate classrooms for children.

Early childhood educators are among those who speak on behalf of others' children, not just their own. Our caring cannot be restricted to classrooms if we truly want to improve the lives of children.

Conclusion

This article began by emphasizing respect as an action word. It was suggested that educators show their respect *for* children by what they do *with* children. The 12 categories just described, however, reveal that showing our respect requires we go beyond our interactions with children. Esteem for childhood requires not only respectful actions with children but respectful actions on their behalf.

References

Bruner, J., & Harste, H. (1987). Introduction. In J. Bruner & H. Harste (Eds.), *Making sense: The child's construction of the world* (pp. 1-25). New York: Methuen.

Children's Defense Fund. (1988). *A children's defense budget FY89: An analysis of our nation's investment in children.* Washington, DC: Author.

Donaldson, M. (1978). *Children's minds.* New York: W. W. Norton & Company.

2. DEVELOPMENT: Childhood

Dreikurs, R., & Solz, V. (1964). *Children: The challenge*. New York: Dutton.

Galinsky, E. (1988). Parents and teacher-caregivers: Sources of tension, sources of support. *Young Children*, 43(3), 4-12.

Gelman, R. (1979). Preschool thought. *American Psychologist, 34*, 900-905.

Goffin, S. G. (1987). Introduction. In S. G. Goffin & S. Vartuli (Eds.), Classroom management in new context: Teacher as decision-maker [special issue]. *Dimensions, 15*(4).

Goffin, S. G. (1988). Putting our advocacy efforts into a new context. *Young Children*, 3(3), 52-56.

Goffin, S. G. (1989). Developing an early childhood research agenda: What can we learn from the research on teaching? *Early Childhood Research Quarterly, 4*, 187-204.

Goffin, S. G., with Caccamo, J. (1986). *In partnership with parents*. Jefferson City, MO: State Department of Elementary and Secondary Education, Division of Special Education.

Grubb, N. W., & Lazerson, M. (1988). *Broken promises: How Americans fail their children*. Chicago: University of Chicago Press.

Halpern, R. (1987). Major social and demographic trends affecting young families: Implications for early childhood care and education. *Young Children, 42*(6), 34-40.

Kessen, W. (1979). The American child and other cultural inventions. *American Psychologist, 34*, 815-820.

Kessen, W. (1981). (Ed.). *New scholastic dictionary of American English*. New York: Scholastic, Inc.

Paley, V. G. (1989). On listening to what children say. *Harvard Education Review, 56*(2), 122-131.

Postman, N. (1982). *The disappearance of childhood*. New York: Delacorte.

Suransky, V. P. (1982). *The erosion of childhood*. Chicago: The University of Chicago Press.

Weber-Schwartz, N. (1987). Food for thought: Patience or understanding? *Young Children, 42*(3), 52-54.

Weissbourd, B. (1983). The family support movement: Greater than the sum of its parts. *Zero to Three, 4*(1), 8-10.

Developmentally Appropriate Education for 4-Year-Olds

David Elkind

David Elkind is professor of child study and senior resident scholar at Tufts University.

The education of 4-year-old children in our public schools is a social experiment with consequences for the entire society. The kind of education young children receive in the early years does make a difference later (Miller & Bizzell, 1983; Schweinhart, Weikart, & Larner, 1986). In my opinion, developmentally appropriate education gives young children the wherewithal to succeed in school and become productive members of society. I believe that teaching young children in a didactic way, as if they were miniature second or third graders, can have lasting negative effects on their academic careers and their successful adaptation to the larger society. Accordingly, in this article I present the developmental approach to early childhood education, which I believe has the best chance of providing children from all walks of life the best start in schooling.

To present this approach, I elaborate on three principles that are the foundation upon which developmental early childhood teaching practices are based. The first principle is multi-age grouping, which derives from the normal variability among young children. The second is nongraded curricular materials, which can be used with profit by children at different developmental levels. The third is interactive teaching, in which the teacher serves as a matchmaker between child and materials. Effective interactive teaching means the teacher must have a solid understanding of both the intellectual demands of the materials and the cognitive abilities of the children.

The Variability of Young Children

Young children are extremely variable with respect to their levels of intellectual, emotional, and social development. A child learning to walk, for example, may not talk until walking is mastered. Another child may do exactly the reverse. Neither child is really slow in the neglected domain. Young children attend to only one skill at a time and the other will receive its due in good time.

Despite these clear differences, children's age levels are often characterized in an all-encompassing way, such as the "terrible twos." The 4-year-old age has sometimes been called the period of *Trotzalter*,[1] the age of pride. Such catch phrases fail to recognize the variability of young children

D. Elkind, "Developmentally Appropriate Education for 4-Year-Olds," *Theory Into Practice*, 28(1), Winter 1989, pp. 47-52. (Theme is on "Public Schooling At 4?") Copyright © 1989, College of Education, The Ohio State University.

and are counterproductive in planning educational programs for these children. The variability of young children requires a closer look.

In the Darwinian scheme of things, variability plays a crucial role. The variability among members of the same species makes evolution possible. As environmental conditions change, variability permits those members of the species with traits adapted to the new circumstances to survive. A phenomenon called "industrial melanism" is a nice example of how variability within a species enables it to adapt to a rather abrupt change in the environment:

> During the last hundred years many different species of moths have become virtually black in industrial towns, while remaining light and protectively colored in the countryside. In these species, the melanics, or dark forms, are much hardier than the normals, but these—the light ones— are better concealed from their enemies in the unblackened countryside. So they have a selective advantage there, while the melanics are better able to resist the smoke and contamination of the industrial areas. (Huxley, 1953, p. 39)

Variability, then, makes it possible for a species to adapt to changing environmental circumstances. In most cases, this process is a gradual one as the process of variation and natural selection takes place over many generations.

I raise the issue of variability in this way, because putting 4-year-olds in school is a fairly abrupt alteration of their environment. Putting 4-year-olds in school will favor some variations more than others. Children who are socially inclined will respond positively to the availability of same-age peers. Other children, more inclined to solitary pursuits, may find this early entrance to a school setting disruptive and uncomfortable. This situation is neither bad nor good, right nor wrong. Children who are socially inclined, for example, are the ones who are deprived when 4-year-olds are not in school.

Another significant facet of variability for the issue of 4-year-olds at school has to do with certain periods in the development of our species when the range of variability is greater than at other periods. At some point in the evolution of human species, when we were much more subject to environmental control than is true today, this variability made good adaptive sense. A period during which members of the species displayed the full range of variations maximized the options for selection.

The reason for an increased range of variation at early adolescence is easy to fit within evolutionary theory. It is the period prior to sexual activity and procreation. It is thus a critical period for the selection of traits that will be passed on to the next generations. A wide display of traits makes possible the selection of those best suited to survival in the environment at that time. Up until recent times and the increased life span, families were begun in adolescence. Juliet was 13 when she and Romeo shared their fate. The display of variability in early adolescence is less adaptive today when many couples are waiting until young adulthood and later to form families. On the other hand, other forms of variability such as motivation and intellectual prowess may not emerge until later in life and these may be the adaptive traits necessary to survival in our society.

The wide range of variation at the early childhood level, however, is harder to fit within an evolutionary perspective. Clearly mate selection does not take place at this period, so why the display of variability? It may have to do with another concept within biology, namely, redundance. We are formed with a great deal of potential redundancy. We can survive with one eye, one ear, or with part of our colon removed. Even our brains can make up for early injury according to the principle of vicarious functioning. The display of variation in early childhood may be a form of redundancy, a precursor to variational displays of adolescence, which could serve as a kind of preselection even before adolescence.

Whatever the explanation, the range of variation in early childhood is greater than it will be in later childhood or in adulthood. Children of the same age vary greatly in social, intellectual, and emotional maturity. Although it is convenient to attribute these variations to variations in child rearing practices, this may be too facile an explanation. We have been made aware by infancy research (e.g., Waters, Vaughn, & Egeland, 1980) that children can shape parental behavior as much as parents can shape child behavior. If some children are treated differently from others, they may have evoked different treatments on the part of their parents.

Multi-Age Grouping

I have gone on at considerable length about variability and stressed its biological underpinnings for a reason. As educators, many of us have trouble dealing with variability. We would like all children of a given age to be at a given place intellectually. Then we can proceed with our lesson plans and our course of instruction. Children who are ahead, behind, or somewhere on the outskirts of the group present a problem. They take extra time and effort, both of which are in short supply. While such an attitude may be understandable, given the pressures on teachers, it cannot really be justified at any level of education and is least justified at periods of wide displays of variability.

The alternative to rigid age grading of children and curricula is multi-age grouping. This means having 4-, 5-, and perhaps 6-year-old children in the same classroom. The advantages to this arrangement are many. First, the advanced 4-year-olds can be grouped with the slower 5-year-olds for certain activities. Second, older children can be used to tutor the younger children, an important and beneficial learning experience for both sides. Third, the teacher gets to really know the children and can determine when they are ready to move ahead to more complex learning materials and activities. Much information is lost when, after a year, a teacher has to pass the child to another teacher who has to start from scratch.

Multi-age grouping has drawbacks. One teacher must master the curricula for two or three developmental levels. But since much overlapping occurs at these ages, the problem is not serious. A drawback from the child's point of view is the possibility of having a teacher who is not the best for 2 or 3 years. A third drawback is the resistance of parents who do not mind when their children are the youngest in the class but become concerned when they are the oldest. They wonder whether their children are receiving sufficient intellectual stimulation.

None of these problems are insurmountable and the benefits of multi-age grouping considerably outweigh them. Teachers who have taught this way generally prefer it and are reluctant to go back to single grade teaching.

Multi-age grouping is thus the most effective way of addressing the natural variability of young children. Any program for 4-year-olds that does not take account of the wide range of normal and expectable variations in their physical, social, emotional, and intellectual maturity amounts to developmentally inappropriate practice. Indeed, such practice can result in miseducation for some children to the extent that it puts children at risk for short-term stress and long-term learning difficulties (Elkind, 1987).

Developmentally Appropriate Curricula

As the foregoing discussion indicates, the primary characteristic of developmentally appropriate curricular materials for young children is that they are ungraded and can serve children at different levels of development. Effective early education classrooms are furnished with materials that have appeal for, and can be used with profit by, children at several age levels. What and how these materials are deployed in providing an appropriate environment for young children is described below.

A classroom for young children is usually arranged in interest areas. One such area is the reading or language space. This area usually contains a book rack with a wide range of books including fairy tales, poetry, and good children's fiction. Also to be found in this area are large cushions, perhaps even a child-sized rocker, tape recorder, and record player. This area can be used by individual children, small groups, or the entire class. Such an interest area can serve children at many different levels of language proficiency.

Another area is the block corner. A substantial set of large wooden blocks is an essential curriculum material for young children. Like books, blocks are naturally ungraded materials. Two-year-old children as well as 5-year-olds can enjoy and learn a

great deal from block play. Two-year-olds, for example, gain considerable motor control from handling blocks and placing one on top of another. They also learn spatial concepts such as on top of, behind, and in front of. Later, these concepts will provide the underpinnings for learning the prepositional terms to represent these motor concepts.

Five-year-olds, in contrast, use blocks creatively to express their ordering of the world. Erikson (1951), for example, showed that boys and girls construct different types of block buildings. Boys often build towers and are curious to see how tall they can make them before they topple. In contrast, girls tend to build structures such as enclosed courtyards. For this age group, block play is a way of expressing an emerging sense of self and sexual identity. Inasmuch as 5-year-olds play with blocks in groups, it reinforces their learning of social skills such as cooperation and turn-taking.

Another area that is equally nongraded is the science and math space. Such an area might be outfitted with a water and/or sand table and a cupboard filled with science materials. These materials would include magnets, magnifying glasses, balance scales, different sized weights, and a variety of materials for counting and seriating according to size, color, and thickness. Young children can begin to learn the names of the colors and geometric shapes. Older children can begin to explore which materials float or are attracted by magnets.

Regarding science at the preschool and elementary school levels, a caveat is in order. All science begins with observation. Every science goes through a natural history stage of inquiry where the basic phenomena of the discipline are classified and organized. In some disciplines such as astronomy and paleontology it is hard to go much further. Experimentation, on the other hand, is the most advanced stage of a science and only comes into play once classification has advanced to the point of unit measurement. While experimentation is the most developed stage, it should not be equated with science itself, which includes all levels of a discipline.

This point is necessary because of the tendency in education to rush children into performing "experiments." So long as this term is used in a metaphorical way, such as a teacher putting light and heavy objects into water to determine which float and which do not, no harm is done. This is an experiment in the sense that one is asking a question of nature in a way that can be answered by observation. But this exploration is not a true experiment involving measurement and control of variables in order to test a hypothesis. Yet it is just such experiments that teachers sometimes attempt to convey to children, even at the preschool level.

Attempts to teach experimentation to young children is a good example of age-inappropriate teaching practice and miseducation. Young children do not have a true sense of quantity, so measurement is beyond them. They have difficulty keeping two dimensions in mind simultaneously, so the concept of control is meaningless to them. By presenting children with experiments at an early age, one runs the risk of confusing them and discouraging them from actively exploring materials with the aim of description and classification.

In fact, encouraging children to describe and classify is one of the most important science skills we can teach them. It provides a solid basis for their later science experiences. Moreover, because children are natural observers and classifiers, they enjoy this activity and carry this liking on to more advanced forms of scientific endeavor. In science, as in so many other curricular domains, earlier is not better. When we help children realize their skills as naturalists, we are doing more to encourage their scientific curiosity and enthusiasm for science than they would ever get from observing formal experiments.

From this perspective, the presence of plants and animals in the early childhood classroom is essential. Plants and animals provide materials for children to describe, classify, and draw. In this way they can discover the natural course of growth. Children also learn responsibility when they begin to take care of plants and animals. Having children plant seeds and watch them grow is another concrete science experience for children that is enjoyable as well as instructive. If the animals procreate, this provides still another arena for observation and discussion. Artificial experiments need not be imported into the early childhood classroom. A well outfitted classroom contains a multitude of opportunities for scientific observation, classification, and discussion.

Another nongraded curricular area is a space for dramatic play. This area can have discarded adult clothing such as hats, shirts, shoes, and scarves. Empty food cartons provide materials for playing store, while outdated phones and typewriters can be the starting point for playing office. Children of different age levels can play with and enjoy these materials, although the older children will engage in more elaborate dramas than the younger, whose dramatic play is more imitative.

Although dramatic play has many personal benefits for children as an expression of their competence to play adult roles and work effectively with other children, they learn much else as well. Such play encourages cooperation and role taking, gives children an opportunity to use and display the full range of their vocabularies, and often involves them in active use of their numerical and motor skills. Play for young children is an essential part of the curriculum that allows for personal expression as well as teaching socially adaptive dispositions.

The foregoing description in no way exhausts the range of materials appropriate for young children. Indeed, I have not even ventured to describe the outside play area, which would demand a separate discussion. What I have tried to emphasize is that the criterion for good early childhood education materials is that they be appropriate for children at different age levels. As such the materials are somewhat less structured and more open ended than curricula at later educational levels. What the materials demand, as will be seen in the next section, is a great deal of skill on the part of teachers in using them effectively.

Interactive Teaching

Although the basic trappings of good early childhood education programs have not changed much over the years, our knowledge of how to use those trappings most effectively has grown manyfold. In part this derives from the work of Piaget and Inhelder (e.g., Inhelder & Piaget, 1964) and those who have extended their work to young children (e.g., Kamii & Williams, 1986); and in part it derives from the influence of Montessori education, which has grown extensively and which puts heavy emphasis on training teachers in the use of manipulative materials (e.g., Montessori, 1917/1965).[2]

The effective use of the nongraded materials of the early childhood classroom requires both a knowledge of the intellectual demands and derivatives of the materials and an understanding of the child's cognitive level. With this knowledge the teacher can serve as a kind of matchmaker between the child and the materials. In effect the teacher introduces the child to the materials, gets a "conversation" going between them, and then discreetly moves out of the scene. It is this sort of teaching that I call *interactive*.

To make this concept more concrete, I would like to deal with teaching practices in the domain of number. Familiarity with Piaget's work on the child's conception of number (Piaget, 1952) is basic to effective interactive teaching in this domain. Piaget argued that although we may have only one word for number, there are several different levels of numerical understanding that are obscured by our imprecise language.

The child's first understanding of number is *nominal* in the sense that at this stage number is no more than a name. A number on a football or baseball player's jersey is an example of a nominal number. Next, by the age of 4, most children grasp *ordinal* number, used to designate a rank, e.g., when we say someone came in third in a race. The runner's position tells us nothing with regard to how far behind the other two runners the third runner was, only that the third runner came in behind the first two runners. The runner could have been 2 seconds, 2 minutes, or 2 hours behind the second runner but the numerical rank would remain the same.

Finally, by the age of 6 or 7, most children attain a *true* or *interval* concept of number in the sense that they now have a unit concept of number.

What sets the unit concept apart from the nominal and ordinal number is the awareness of equal intervals. Using an interval scale, a runner who came in third would also have a time designation that would indicate the length of time behind the next runner. Once children understand units as representing equal intervals, they can fully grasp the basic units and operations of arithmetic.

How then does a young child progress to this interval, or unit, concept of number? Piaget's research and that of others (e.g., Kamii, 1982) make clear that the child progresses toward a unit concept of number by engaging in a great deal of classification and seriation (ordering size, intensity, etc.). Young children can classify a few elements and progress to larger numbers of elements as they mature.

What does such classification and seriation have to do with the child's attainment of number? A good deal. A unit concept, the idea of equal intervals, is gleaned from combining the classification and seriation relationships. What children gain from classifying many different things, in addition to the disciminations involved, is the more general notion of sameness, just as they learn the concept of difference from seriating materials that vary in amount. Eventually, they put together the concepts of sameness and difference that together constitute the unit concept. A unit, a number, is both like every other number (the sameness relation) yet different from it (the difference relation). The number 3 is different from every other number in the sense that it is the only number that comes before 4 and after 2. But it is also like every other number in that it is a number.

Armed with this knowledge and a sense of where children are with respect to classification and seriation the teacher is in a position to engage in interactive instruction. The teacher will provide materials for classification and seriation matched to the child's level of ability, and then model how these materials are to be used and provide verbal labels where appropriate. Once children have mastered the classification and seriation skills, they can extend them on their own to a larger number of elements and a wide variety of materials. They can also choose the times when they wish to engage in this activity. The aim of interactive teaching is to get children started in the right way, but then for them to take over and be responsible for their own learning.

Interactive teaching is not easy. Finding materials that are neither too structured nor too open is always a struggle. Materials need enough structure to give children guidance, but also enough openness to pose a challenge to their intelligence. In the same way, the teacher is constantly searching for words and phrasing that will get children started on the activity and give them direction without unduly constraining their manipulations of the materials. Moreover, the teacher has to be aware of individual differences and what types of materials and verbalizations are most appropriate for particular children or groups of children.

Summary and Conclusion

This article has described three major principles, or goals, with respect to the education of 4-year-old children in the public schools. First, early childhood is a period of increased variability, which is a species characteristic as much or more than a product of diverse child rearing. Any group of young children will be much more variable intellectually, socially, and emotionally than it will be at, say, age 10. The most effective way to deal with this variability is multi-age grouping. Such grouping enables the teacher to move children along at their own pace rather than trying to force them into a rigidly age-graded curriculum.

The second principle is that the curriculum materials and activities for young children should be nongraded in the sense that they can be engaged in with profit by children from 2 to 5. A good set of wooden blocks can be used by 2-year-olds to acquire basic spatial concepts whereas older children can use them to express an emerging sense of identity as well as to learn a number of social skills. Reading materials including fairy tales, poetry, and children's fiction are examples of nongraded material in the sense that children of many different age levels can enjoy and profit from them.

A final principle or goal of educational programs for young children is that the teaching be interactive. In such instruction the teacher serves as a matchmaker between the child and the materials. An effective match depends on the teacher's knowledge of the demands and cognitive derivatives of the materials and the child's cognitive strengths and weaknesses. Once a match is made, the teacher must know how to move to the background and let the relationship between child and materials develop. While these principles may be considered ideal and difficult to achieve, ideals are important to guide us in our efforts to provide the best possible education for the increasing numbers of young children in our schools. A quiet reading corner in a classroom, a bit of matchmaking between a child and a book or puzzle, can mean a lot to a young learner.

In the end, of course, the principles of healthy education at the early childhood level are the principles of sound pedagogy at all grade levels. If we institute solid programs of early childhood education in our schools, perhaps we can improve the quality of schooling for all students.

Notes

1. The term *Trotzalter* is a combination of two German words, *Trotz*, used in the sense of pride, and *alter* or age. The term was used frequently by German child psychologists such as the Buhlers.
2. The Waldorf school movement, which is becoming a force on the national scene, is another early childhood

2. DEVELOPMENT: Childhood

program that emphasizes manipulatives (e.g., Edmunds, 1979).

References

Edmunds, F. (1979). *Rudolf Steiner education.* London: Rudolf Steiner Press.

Elkind, D. (1987). *Miseducation: Preschoolers at risk.* New York: Knopf.

Erikson, E. (1951). Sex differences in the play configurations of pre-adolescents. *American Journal of Orthopsychiatry, 21,* 667-692.

Huxley, J. (1953). *Evolution in action.* New York: Signet.

Inhelder, B., & Piaget, J. (1964). *The early growth of logic in the young child.* New York: Norton.

Kamii, C. (1982). *Number in preschool and kindergarten: Educational implications of Piaget's theory.* Washington, DC: National Association for the Education of Young Children.

Kamii, C., & Williams, C.K. (1986). How do children learn by handling objects? *Young Children, 42*(1), 23-26.

Miller, L.B., & Bizzell, R.P. (1983). Long term effects of four preschool programs: 6th, 7th and 8th grades. *Child Development, 54,* 725-741.

Montessori, M. (1965). *Spontaneous activity in education.* New York: Schocken. (Original work published 1917)

Piaget, J. (1952). *The child's conception of number.* London: Routledge & Kegan Paul.

Schweinhart, L.J., Weikart, D.P., & Larner, M.B. (1986). Consequences of three preschool curriculum models through age 15. *Early Childhood Research Quarterly, 1,* 15-45.

Waters, E., Vaughn, B.E., & Egeland, B. (1980). Individual differences in infant mother attachment relationships at age one: Antecedents in neonatal behavior in an urban, economically disadvantaged sample. *Child Development, 51,* 208-216.

THE CHANGING FAMILY

The Great Experiment

Today's parents are raising children in ways that little resemble their own youth. The question that haunts them: Will the kids be all right?

PHILIP ELMER-DEWITT

In Houston a stay-at-home dad kisses his pregnant wife goodbye as she heads for the office, and then turns back to the task of getting their four children fed, washed and ready for the day ahead. In Long Branch, N.J., parents work alternate shifts—she during the day at a hospital accounting office; he at night, as a security guard—so that their three kids won't be left with strangers. In Lincoln, Neb., a divorced mother of four—one of the nation's 9.3 million single parents—depends on her eldest daughter to fill in while she is at work. In cities from Providence to Portland, both parents dash to work in the morning, handing their kids off to a variety of nannies, sitters, schools, day-care centers, neighbors and relatives.

These families generally have three things in common. The parents are not raising their children the way they themselves were raised. None have any idea how it will all turn out. And all live in perpetual fear that some piece of their carefully crafted child-care structure will fall out of place and bring the fragile edifice of their lives tumbling down like a toddler's tower of blocks.

Child care in America has become a kind of vast social experiment. Not only has the archetypal nuclear family of the 1950s (working father, stay-at-home wife) given way to a myriad of customized arrangements, each as unique as a baby's toeprint, but this historic shift has been accompanied by a new awareness of the importance of attachment and family ties in the emotional development of a child. Parents today, primed by racks of bestselling child-care manuals, are haunted by questions about their changing roles. What kind of bonding takes place when a child is passed from one paid caretaker to another? What are the risks of growing up without a stable nuclear family or any real community support? How do values get passed from one generation to the next when the dominant cultural influences on children are television, pop music and Nintendo?

Not that the workadaddy-housewife family is dead. Homemaking mothers married to breadwinning fathers still make up the largest category of families with young children. The "Ozzie and Harriet" arrangement represents one-third of the na-

tion's 14.8 million families with preschool children, although dual-income households (28.8% as of 1987) are rapidly catching up. Also gaining is the single-parent family, because of divorce and the explosive rise in births to unwed mothers: up from 5% of all births in 1960 (and 22% of all black births) to 22% in 1985 (60% of blacks).

But a family of any type is subject to sudden change. Social historian Barbara Dafoe Whitehead, writing in the journal *Family Affairs,* points out that just as today's at-home mother may be tomorrow's working mom, today's career woman may soon be pregnant and thinking about remaining at home. "One day the Ozzie and Harriet couple is eating a family meal," says Whitehead. "The next day, they are working out a joint-custody arrangement."

As a result, no parent is immune to the uncertainty and guilt that make the child-rearing dilemma the No. 1 topic of conversation among young mothers today, and of more than passing interest to fathers. The job is a tangle of double binds. Should a mother stay at home, providing the values, discipline and security her children need, and let her hard-earned job skills go fallow? Or should she take a chance that her kids will be O.K. and pursue a life that brings more personal satisfaction and economic advantages? "It's very hard," says Stephanie Burchfield, a Los Angeles public-relations executive and mother of an 8-month-old. "I see her only an hour in the morning and an hour in the evening. I don't have a single friend who has worked full time who doesn't regret how little time she's spent with her children."

Nor does it help that in subtle ways—a look across the grocery aisle, a comment at the nursery school—the two kinds of moms exacerbate each other's guilt. Debbie Ippolito of Lakewood, N.J., seethes whenever a working mother makes a comment about all the "free time" she has. "People think you're eating bonbons all day," she rails. "I had a baby, not a lobotomy!" Heightening the rivalry, some of those who gave up the fast track pursue full-time parenting with a competitive drive honed in the business world. "It's not O.K. to just have an average child; you must have an *improved* child," complains psychologist Shari Thurer, of Boston University.

Much of the turmoil felt by parents in the '90s derives from the fact that so many are children of the '50s. Their image of an ideal family comes from TV shows like *Father Knows Best;* their notion of the ideal mother is the one played by Jane Wyatt: never rattled, always at home. The irony is that this "family of nostalgia," as Madeleine Stoner at the University of Southern California calls it, was largely an aberration that flourished for only a couple of decades after World War II.

In colonial America, according to Maris Vinovski, professor of history at the University of Michigan, the job of raising children was shared by the two parents. Mothers swaddled the baby and put food on the table, but fathers were responsible for the child's intellectual and moral upbringing. The majority of women have worked throughout U.S. history, first in the home, then in the shop and factory. With wave after wave of cheap immigrant labor available during the late 19th and early 20th centuries, even middle-class families had nannies. Nor is there anything new about day-care centers. In the 1820s 30% of all three-year-olds in Massachusetts were going to "infant schools," though such institutions fell out of favor within a decade.

The deeper change, according to Penelope Leach, author of the popular parenting manual *Your Baby and Child*, stems from the Industrial Revolution, which forced a split between the home and the workplace. "Home and its surrounding community used to be everybody's operating base, with work and play and family pretty much intermixed," she says. "Now work has moved into geographically separate production centers and takes the form of specialized jobs that cannot be shared, swapped or carried on with a baby strapped to your back." Home has been left an impoverished place, little more than a dormitory, a spot for a shower and a change of clothes. And as mothers have increasingly departed for the office or factory, children's isolation from the adult world has accelerated dramatically.

How will these marginalized kids turn out? Experts caution that it is difficult to generalize, but a study by the American Academy of Pediatrics describes some pitfalls. Children from single-parent homes face an array of risks, ranging from mild cognitive delays in preschoolers to withdrawal and depression in older kids. Children pressured by aggressive scheduling often show signs of chronic stress. "With the amount of anxiety and juggling," suggests San Francisco clinical psychologist Jeree Pawl, there is a risk that the next generation could grow up "thinking that they're nuisances. An unhandy bundle, a shelf for which is not always easy to find."

America's two most famous pediatricians, T. Berry Brazelton of Harvard and Benjamin Spock, worry about the disappearance of discipline, particularly when both parents work. "Parents don't want to spend what little time they have with their children reprimanding them," says Spock. "This encourages children to push limits and test parental authority." Brazelton is also concerned that working mothers are so overwhelmed by guilt that they "detach from the baby, because it's the only way they have of coping."

The feminist movement has always insisted that women's liberation must go hand in hand with changing roles for men, particularly at home. Such changes are coming about, though women still do the lion's share of the den keeping. Not only are fathers present in the birthing room (90% are there, as opposed to 10% twenty years ago) and willing to change diapers, but their entire job has been reinterpreted from passive bill payer to activist player. "It's no longer seen as unmasculine to be caring for young children," says Hanne Sonquist, a family therapist in Santa Barbara, Calif.

There is also a movement afoot to extend to American parents the kind of government support—in day care, parental leaves and tax deductions—that their European counterparts have long enjoyed. Sweden, for instance, provides parents 90% salary reimbursement for the first nine months after birth. But the battle in the U.S. for even limited family programs remains an uphill march: industry lobbied so hard against legislation that would have required most businesses to provide 12 weeks of *unpaid* parental leave that President Bush vetoed it last June [1990].

Though that veto was lamented by many parents, the debate over government policies does not necessarily touch what Barbara Whitehead calls "the emotional core of family concerns." These are centered, she says, not on the material needs of parents, but on the moral education of their children. Parents fear that, in the absence of more benevolent influences, children are adopting the values of the aggressively materialistic, consumerist culture portrayed on TV. "In their eyes," says Whitehead, "children are no longer acquiring an identity at home, as much as they are attempting to buy one in the marketplace."

What's to be done? Subsidized child care and tax credits would ease the pressure on parents to leave home before they want to. What is more difficult is finding a way to undo the damage to the family done by a century of economic and social upheaval. As Penelope Leach puts it, the most important question for parents is "not what day care to choose or when to go back to work, but how to reintegrate our children into our world." That is a challenge that is likely to be with the nation when today's children are preparing to have kids of their own.

—Reported by Deborah Edler Brown/Los Angeles and Michele Donley/Chicago, with other bureaus

The Development of Self-Concept

Janie says "I can't" a lot, often before she even tries an activity. She seems to need constant encouragement from the teacher just to try.

Timmy speaks so softly that he is rarely heard. Even the teacher sometimes does not respond to his initiatives.

Maria describes all the things she can draw as she completes her picture. She tells the teacher about waiting for her mother in the doctor's waiting room by herself and not being afraid.

Hermine H. Marshall

Hermine H. Marshall, Ph.D., is Associate Professor, Department of Elementary Education, San Francisco State University. For the past 15 years, she has been involved in research concerning self-concept and self-evaluation.

*This is one of a regular series of Research in Review columns. The column was edited by **Celia Genishi**, Ph.D., Associate Professor of Educational Theory and Practice at The Ohio State University.*

Positive self-image correlates with good mental health, good academic achievement, and good behavior.

Picture Gold

Why is it that some children try new things with enthusiasm and approach peers and adults with confidence, whereas other children seem to believe that they are incapable of succeeding in many situations? Children (and adults) behave consistently with the way they see themselves. Young children's beliefs about whether they can or cannot do things, therefore, influence how they approach new situations. In turn, their success in new situations affects the way they see themselves—in a seemingly circular process (Marsh, 1984).

Our concern with children like Janie and Timmy is justified by research that shows that low self-concept is related to poor mental health, poor academic achievement, and delinquency (e.g., Harter, 1983). But what can we learn from research that will allow us to help children approach new situations and other people with confidence?

To understand the factors that may influence the development of self-concept, we need first to be aware of the difference between such terms as *self-concept, self-image, self-esteem,* and *self-confidence.* We also need to recognize the relationships among self-concept, perceived competence, and locus of control. Based on our knowledge of factors that influence the development of positive self-concept, we can then take steps that will benefit young children.

Definitions and differentiation

We generally think of *self-concept* as the perceptions, feelings, and attitudes that a person has about himself or herself. The terms *self-concept* and *self-image* are often used interchangeably to designate a global conception of self. This global self-concept is made up of many dimensions.

One dimension is *self-esteem* (or self-

Implications and applications

Ways to explore self-concept in young children

The level of self-esteem in some children, such as those cited at the beginning of this article, is more apparent than in others. It is easy to overlook some quiet children. Nevertheless, observing a child's willingness to explore the environment and assume control of events may be a way of assessing self-esteem in preschool children. For example, watch children's responses as they approach or are presented with a new task. Do they hang back or eagerly jump in? Do they say they can't before they try?

Another way to attend to young children's self-concepts is to listen deliberately to spontaneous statements of "I can" and "I am" or "I can't." You might also try open-minded questioning techniques, such as "I would like to write about you. What can I write? . . . What else can I say about you?" Other questions that teachers of young children have found revealing are

- "What can you tell me about yourself? . . . Why is that important?"
- "What can you tell me that is best about you?"
- "What are you good at doing?"

Remember that recent but temporary events influence young children's self-concepts; therefore, judgments about self-concept or self-esteem should not be based on only one or two statements.

Ways to influence self-concept

Because most of the studies reported in this review use correlational methods that do not indicate cause and effect, we need to be cautious in making interpretations. Nevertheless, many of the findings do suggest steps likely to enhance self-concept.

Help children feel they are of value

Listen attentively to what children say. Ask for their suggestions. Soliciting and respecting children's ideas and suggestions helps children feel that they are of value.

Help children identify their own positive and prosocial behavior. When children display cooperation, helpfulness, and other prosocial behavior, give children the words to describe themselves with these terms. For example, "You are being very helpful." They may then come to see themselves in a positive manner and act accordingly. This is a positive use of the self-fulfilling prophecy.

Highlight the value of different ethnic groups. Find ways of demonstrating the value of the cultures of your group's children. Read books that include children of different cultures. Find people of various ethnic groups to share their expertise with the children. Display pictures of women, men, and children of different ethnic groups succeeding in a variety of tasks.

Help children feel they are competent

Provide experiences for children where they can succeed. For some children, we need to provide a series of tasks that can be accomplished initially with little effort but that gradually increase in difficulty. Try to relate the task to something that children already recognize they can do.

Provide new challenges and comment on positive attempts. Some children appear to need a lot of encouragement and verbal reinforcement. Encouragement and statements of confidence in the child's ability to succeed may be necessary at first. However, the effects of verbal praise and persuasion may be short-lived (Hitz & Driscoll, 1988). Children will be more likely to benefit by seeing for themselves that they can, in fact, succeed.

Teach strategies to accomplish tasks. "I can't" sometimes means "I don't know how." Rather than encouragement, children sometimes need specific instruction in particular strategies to carry out a task. Break down these strategies into smaller steps.

Allow children to carry out and complete tasks by themselves. Because self-concept reflects perceived competence, allowing children to do for themselves whatever they can is important—even when some struggle to accomplish the task is necessary. Avoid the temptation to finish a task or button coats to save time. Help them do it themselves. Doing it for them may convey to children the message that they are not competent.

Help children feel they have some control

Provide opportunities for choice, initiative, and autonomy. Provide opportunities for children to accomplish a variety of tasks at a variety of levels. Give young children simple choices: for example, which task to do first or which of two colors to use. Let children choose which song to sing or game to play next.

Avoid comparison between children. Avoid competition. The self-concept of many children suffers when comparisons between children are made. Comparison and competition point not only to winners, but also to those who have not come out on top. Support each child's accomplishments independently.

Help children learn to evaluate their own accomplishments. Children need to learn to evaluate their own performance so that they will not become dependent on adults for feelings of self-worth. Ask them what their favorite part of their picture or story is, or ask them to look at how their letters compare with those they did last month.

Help children learn interpersonal skills

Help children learn skills to enter interactions with others. Give children the words they need to express their desires and feelings. Help them learn how to enter play and how to resolve conflicts. Knowledge of how to interact appropriately with peers is likely to enhance peer acceptance and liking. This in turn, is related to children's social self-concept.

Become aware of your own expectations for children

Be open to perceiving new information about children and looking at them in new ways. Young children can surprise us. All of a sudden they seem to show new skills. Reappraise your expectations frequently. Let them know you have confidence in their ability to learn new skills.

Be aware of whether your expectations differ for girls and boys. Different expectations for girls and boys may convey cues to children about areas where it is appropriate to become competent. If we expect boys rather than girls to play with the blocks, for example, we may deprive girls of developing positive attitudes and becoming competent in skills needed for success in mathematics and certain types of problem-solving. Initiate activities in all areas that both boys and girls may explore.

worth). Self-esteem refers specifically to our self-evaluations—that is, our judgments about our own worth—whereas self-concept refers to other aspects as well—physical characteristics, psychological traits, and gender and ethnic identity. Our self-esteem may be affected by possessing culturally valued traits, such as helpfulness and honesty. It is also influenced by seeing that others perceive us as significant and worthy or possessing culturally valued traits.

Self-esteem develops in part from being able to perceive ourselves as competent. *Perceived competence* reflects our beliefs about our ability to succeed at particular tasks. According to White (1959), feelings of competence result from being able to act effectively and master one's environment. When our capacities are stretched to new heights, we feel competent.

Self-esteem and feelings of competence are related to acquiring a sense of *personal control* (Harter, 1983)—particularly in mainstream American culture. (In other cultures personal control may not be important for self-esteem.) As children perceive themselves gaining competence in a gradually widening sphere, they begin to see themselves as causal agents and are able to feel that they have greater ability to control more of their environment. This sense of personal control is often referred to as an *internal locus of control.* In contrast, external locus of control means decisions are in the hands of others or of fate.

As children develop, self-concept becomes increasingly differentiated into multiple domains. Perceptions of competence in the social skills domain become differentiated from perceptions of competence in cognitive and physical domains (Harter & Pike, 1984). Self-perceptions about interactions with peers become separated from those about interactions with parents and teachers. Cognitive or academic self-concept gradually further differentiates into math and verbal areas (Marsh, 1984).

Furthermore, the importance of each of these domains differs for individuals and families, and among cultures. A low self-evaluation in one domain, such as athletic ability, may have little effect on the individual if it is not considered important in a particular family or culture. On the other hand, in families or cultures where athletic skills are important or where skills that underpin academic ability are highly valued, low self-esteem in these culturally relevant areas may have increasingly devastating effects as children move through school (Harter, 1986).

Self-concept measurement

Unfortunately, many problems have hampered progress in understanding the development of self-concept. First, different investigators sometimes use different definitions and examine different dimensions of self-concept. This makes it difficult to compare and synthesize results from different studies (Shavelson, Hubner, & Stanton, 1976).

At the early childhood level, problems in measuring self-concept have further hindered progress. Few formal instruments are suitable for children younger than age 8, in part because of the difficulties young children have in understanding and verbalizing abstract ideas and internal processes like self-concept. In addition, the influence of momentary events on young children's self-concepts, such as a temporarily frustrating experience, often causes indicators of self-concept to vary over time and appear "unstable." Children's ability to see characteristics as stable over time develops gradually.

Furthermore, many instruments to measure self-concept have not considered developmental differences in children's levels of understanding and in how children think about themselves (Damon & Hart, 1982). Items appropriate for older elementary school children, such as "I'm not doing as well in school as I'd like to" may be meaningless for preschoolers. Other items, for example

Parents who use an "authoritative"—as opposed to an authoritarian or permissive—childrearing pattern are more likely to have children with high self-esteem.

"I'm pretty sure of myself," may be difficult for preschoolers to understand.

Rather than attempt to adapt for preschoolers instruments designed for older children, one investigation used several types of open-ended questions, asking 3- to 5-year-olds what the experimenter could "write about" each child (Keller, Ford, & Meacham, 1978). Others have used pictures of children succeeding or having difficulty with tasks (Harter & Pike, 1984).

To supplement knowledge based on research conducted with young children, we can also look at studies using older elementary children. At these age levels, self-concept is easier to measure. Although we do not know how early the relationships between self-concept and other variables such as the environment or childrearing practices begin, reviewing studies of preschool and elementary age children can give us clues about what we need to provide for young children so that they can develop a positive self-concept.

One note of caution: Much of the research on self-esteem in children has been conducted within mainstream Anglo culture. Items on self-esteem scales reflect the values of this culture. The childrearing and educational factors that have been found to be correlated with these indexes of self-esteem are, consequently, relative to this culture. Many of today's classrooms include children from diverse cultures with differing values. Therefore, we need to be sensitive to others' values and find ways of minimizing conflicts based on cultural differences.

Cognitive development and self-concept development

Preschool

The level of children's cognitive development influences self-concept development. Preschool children can often use multiple categories to describe themselves, but these categories are not yet very stable or consistent. For example, we may hear a preschooler say, "I am a boy," but "I will be a mommy when I grow up." Preschoolers' self-descriptions are also constrained by the particular events they are experiencing. A girl may say, "I'm strong. I can lift this rock." But she is not bothered if she cannot lift a chair.

In making judgments that may appear to reflect self-esteem, preschoolers' attention is often focused on the value of a specific act. A child who says, "I am a good boy" may mean "I did something good," such as share his candy. Preschoolers also appear to view themselves, as well as others, as either all good or all bad. They do not believe they can be both at the same time. The evaluation may shift to the opposite pole as the child shifts attention to

Self-esteem develops when children possess culturally valued traits and feel competent.

other actions or events (Selman, 1980).

Preschoolers see the self in both physical and action terms (Damon & Hart, 1982). When asked what an observer could "write about you," 3- to 5-year-old children most frequently described themselves in terms of physical actions, such as "I can ride a bike" or "I can help set the table" (Keller et al., 1978). Kindergartners, too, describe themselves largely in terms of activities such as play (Damon & Hart, 1982). Young children seem to see themselves as "good at doing things" or not—without making the distinction between physical and academic competence that older children do (Harter & Pike, 1984). Nevertheless,

about 5% of the responses of the youngest children in the Keller study referred to psychological aspects, such as likes and dislikes.

Primary grades

Primary grade children begin to acquire more mature thinking skills, such as the ability to organize logically and classify hierarchically, and can extend these abilities to their thinking about the self. By age 7 or 8, they are also able to make comparisons between themselves and their peers concerning their abilities (Ruble, Boggiano, Feldman, & Loebl, 1980). By third grade, children still frequently describe themselves in terms of activities, but add comparison with their peers in their self-descriptive statements, such as "I can ride a bike better than my little brother" (Damon & Hart, 1982). They are also able to think inductively and may conclude that "I'm not very smart because I'm in the low group in reading and math."

Primary grade children also acquire new perspective-taking skills that allow them to imagine what other people are thinking, especially what others think of them. Children of this age begin to be more influenced by their perceptions of what significant adults think of them. With further development, what peers think becomes increasingly important.

External factors related to the development of self-concept

Responsiveness of caregivers

Self-concept develops largely within a social context. The interpersonal envi-

Research shows that low self-concept is related to poor mental health, poor academic achievement, and delinquency. But what can we learn from research that will allow us to help children approach new situations and other people with confidence?

ronment that caregivers provide has important influences on the development of self-concept. The quality, consistency, and timing of adults' responses to infants may carry messages about trust, caring, and the value of the infant. Caregiver responsiveness may also convey information about the developing child's capacity to become competent and to control her or his environment (see Honig, 1984). When caregivers respond positively and consistently to infants' cues, infants may come to learn that they are of value and that they can influence their social environment (Harter, 1983). This may contribute to beginning feelings of self-worth, personal control, and competence.

Physical environment

A number of aspects of the physical environment may influence the development of self-concept. For example, if we make developmentally appropriate materials (those that provide both challenge and success) easily accessible to young children for exploration in an encouraging environment, these children are likely to acquire feelings of competence and confidence in approaching new materials (see Bredekamp, 1987).

Other aspects of the environment may influence the development of infants' and toddlers' conceptions of their physical self and of themselves as separate and different from others. Mirrors and similar light-reflecting surfaces, for example, provide opportunities for very young children to learn not only about their physical characteristics but also about themselves as independent agents who can make things happen. When infants can see both themselves and their image moving at the same time, they can learn about the effects of their own actions and their ability to control their world (Lewis & Brooks-Gunn, 1979).

Parental attitudes and childrearing practices

Sears (1970) found that parents who were warm and accepting when their children were young (age 5) had children with high self-esteem measured at age 12. Parents who use an "authoritative"—as opposed to an authoritarian or permissive childrearing pattern (see Honig, 1984)—are also more likely to have children with high self-esteem. These parents make rea-

sonable demands that are accepted by children, but they do not impose unreasonable restrictions and they allow their children some choice and control (Maccoby & Martin, 1983).

Training in effective parenting, where parents learn to be more accepting of their children's feelings and behavior, has led to an increase in kindergarten and second grade children's self-concepts (Summerlin & Ward, 1978). Studies such as these point to the importance of efforts to help parents understand and implement practices that enhance self-esteem.

Feeling in control also helps children develop positive self-esteem.

Expectations

Teachers' and parents' expectations may influence children's self-esteem, both (a) directly through opportunities adults provide for children to learn and become competent and (b) indirectly through more subtle cues that children eventually come to perceive. If adults believe that certain children can learn or do more than others, they may furnish additional materials for these children. In this way, they provide opportunities to become competent in more areas and thus directly influence the children's perceived competence.

In addition, teachers' and parents' expectations influence self-concept in more subtle ways as children gradually become more adept at "reading" environmental cues. Young children are not very accurate in judging adults' expectations for them. They generally hold higher expectations for themselves than their teachers hold for them (Weinstein, Marshall, Sharp, & Botkin, 1987). The discrepancy between young children's expectations and those of their teachers may be due to their relatively undeveloped ability to take the perspective of others. Young children may also have less need to focus on what their teachers expect of them because most preschool and kindergarten classrooms do not emphasize evaluation. However, even at the kindergarten level, if teach-

ers make their evaluations of children salient—such as pointing out the children's best work—children's self-evaluations can show some consistency with those of the teacher (Stipek & Daniels, 1988). Consequently kindergarten and primary teachers need to be aware of subtle ways that their expectations may be conveyed to children and thus influence their self-esteem.

Classroom environments

Classroom structure and teachers' control orientations may influence children's self-concepts as well (Marshall & Weinstein, 1984). This is exemplified in studies comparing the effects of "unidimensional" with those of "multidimensional" classrooms (Rosenholtz & Rosenholtz, 1981). In unidimensional classrooms, teachers emphasize a narrow range of students' abilities (e.g., they value reading ability to the neglect of artistic ability), group students according to ability, assign similar tasks, and publicly evaluate performance. In multidimensional classrooms, in contrast, teachers emphasize multiple dimensions of ability (e.g., artistic and problem-solving skills as well as reading skills), have students work on a variety of different tasks using different materials at the same time, and evaluate students more privately. Although preschools are more often similar to multidimensional classrooms, some kindergarten and "academic" preschools are under pressure to become more unidimensional. In classrooms that emphasized academics, with characteristics similar to unidimensional classrooms, kindergartners' perceptions of their ability were lower than those of kindergartners in more multidimensional classrooms—although the two groups were learning the same skills (Stipek & Daniels, 1988). Teachers need to be aware, therefore, that pressures to prepare children for academics and to include and evaluate more school-like tasks may have detrimental effects on children's self-concepts of ability.

Whether teachers support children's autonomy or tend to control children through external means also affects children's perceptions of competence and self-esteem. Children in classrooms that supported autonomy had higher perceptions of their own cognitive competence, self-worth, and mastery motivation than those in classrooms

Sensitive parents and teachers may be better able to assess a child's self-concept than researchers are. Differences in definitions and dimensions make it difficult to compare and synthesize studies, but a child with good self-concept radiates it.

where teachers retained control (Ryan, Connell, & Deci, 1985). Because this study was conducted with older children, we do not know at what age this effect may begin. We should be aware, nevertheless, that providing opportunities for children to strive toward independence and to develop a sense of personal control is likely to have a positive effect on children's perceptions of competence and self-esteem.

Peers

Some research suggests that peer interactions may have an influence on self-esteem and social self-concept earlier than previously believed. In an attempt to explore sources of esteem, preschoolers were asked the question "Who likes you?" More than 50% of the children mentioned peers and 49% mentioned siblings (Kirchner & Vondraek, 1975).

Older children (third through eighth graders) who have a high self-concept in the social domain have higher status with their peers—as might be predicted (Kurdek & Krile, 1982). Again, we do not know how early this finding may hold, nor do we know the direction of causality. That is, (a) social self-concept may influence peer relationships, or (b) peer relationships may influence social self-concept, or (c) knowledge of interpersonal skills may affect peer relationships and/or social self-concept. Taken together, these results suggest that helping children learn the skills needed to interact successfully with their peers may ultimately affect their social self-concept.

References

Bredekamp, S. (Ed.). (1987). *Developmentally appropriate practice in early childhood programs serving children from birth through age 8.* Washington, DC: NAEYC.

Damon, W., & Hart, D. (1982). The development of self-understanding from infancy through adolescence. *Child Development, 53,* 841–864.

Harter, S. (1983). Developmental perspectives on the self-system. In E.M. Hetherington (Ed.), *Handbook of child psychology: Vol. 4. Socialization, personality and social development* (4th ed., pp. 275–386). New York: Wiley.

Harter, S. (1986). Processes underlying the construction, maintenance, and enhancement of the self-concept in children. In J. Suls & A. Greenwald (Eds.), *Psychological perspectives of the self* (Vol. 3, pp. 137–181). Hillsdale, NJ: Erlbaum.

Harter, S., & Pike, R. (1984). The pictorial scale of perceived competence and social acceptance for young children. *Child Development, 55,* 1969–1982.

Hitz, R., & Driscoll, A. (1988). Praise or encouragement? New insights into praise: Implications for early childhood teachers. *Young Children, 43*(5), 6–13.

Honig, A. (1984). Research in review: Risk factors in infants and young children. *Young Children, 39*(4), 60–73.

Keller, A., Ford, L., & Meacham, J. (1978). Dimensions of self-concept in preschool children. *Developmental Psychology, 14,* 483–489.

Kirchner, P., & Vondraek, S. (1975). Perceived sources of esteem in early childhood. *Journal of Genetic Psychology, 132,* 169–176.

Kurdek, L., & Krile, D. (1982). A developmental analysis of the relation between peer acceptance and both interpersonal understanding and perceived social self-competence. *Child Development, 53,* 1485–1491.

Lewis, M., & Brooks-Gunn, J. (1979). *Social cognition and the acquisition of self.* New York: Plenum.

Maccoby, E., & Martin, J. (1983). Socialization in the context of the family: Parent-child interaction. In E.M. Hetherington (Ed.), *Handbook of child psychology: Vol. 4. Socialization, personality, and social development* (4th ed., pp. 1–102). New York: Wiley.

Marsh, H. (1984). Relations among dimensions of self-attributions, dimensions of self-concept and academic achievement. *Journal of Educational Psychology, 76,* 1291–1308

Marshall, H., & Weinstein, R. (1984). Classroom factors affecting students' self-evaluations. *Review of Educational Research, 54,* 301–325.

Rosenholtz, S.J., & Rosenholtz, S.H. (1981). Classroom organization and the perception of ability. *Sociology of Education, 54,* 132–140.

Ruble, D., Boggiano, A., Feldman, N., & Loebl, J. (1980). Developmental analysis of the role of social comparison in self-evaluation. *Developmental Psychology, 16,* 105–115.

Ryan, R., Connell, J., & Deci, E. (1985). A motivational analysis of self-determination and self-regulation in education. In C. Ames & R. Ames (Eds.), *Research on motivation in education: Vol. 2. The classroom milieu* (pp. 13–52). New York: Academic.

Sears, R. (1970). Relation of early socialization experiences to self-concepts and gender role in middle childhood. *Child Development, 41,* 267–289.

Selman, R. (1980). *The growth of interpersonal understanding.* New York: Academic.

Shavelson, R., Hubner, J., & Stanton, G. (1976). Self-concept: Validation of construct interpretations. *Review of Educational Research, 46,* 407–442.

Stipek, D., & Daniels, D. (1988). Declining perceptions of competence: A consequence of changes in the child or in the educational environment. *Journal of Educational Psychology, 80,* 352–356.

Summerlin, M.L., & Ward, G.R. (1978). The effect of parental participation in a parent group on a child's self-concept. *Psychological Reports, 100,* 227–232.

Weinstein, R., Marshall, H., Sharp, L., & Botkin, M. (1987). Pygmalion and the student: Age and classroom differences in children's awareness of teacher expectations. *Child Development, 58,* 1079–1093.

White, R. (1959). Motivation reconsidered: The concept of competence. *Psychological Review, 66,* 297–333.

For further reading

Young Children has had a continuing series of Ideas That Work With Young Children by Polly Greenberg emphasizing encouraging self-esteem in infants and children. If you missed them, you may want to read:

"Positive Self-Image: More Than Mirrors" (May 1988)

"Avoiding 'Me Against You' Discipline" (November 1988)

"Learning Self-Esteem and Self-Discipline Through Play" (January 1989)

"Parents as Partners in Young Children's Development and Education: A New American Fad? Why Does It Matter?" (May 1989)

Encouraging Prosocial Behavior in Young Children

Susan M. Doescher and Alan I. Sugawara

Susan M. Doescher and Alan I. Sugawara are Professors, Human Development and Family Studies, Oregon State University, Corvallis.

"That's mine!" "I want it!" "Give me that!" In a preschool classroom, two 3-year-old children are fighting over possession of a favorite truck. Moments earlier they were playing side-by-side in the block area, each one building a road. Both go to the truck shelf in search of the dump truck. One child grabs the truck, and the other tries to pull it away. The noise catches the attention of a nearby teacher who quickly approaches. Similar incidents frequently occur in the classroom setting. What can early childhood educators do to minimize such situations and maximize positive social interactions such as cooperating, sharing and helping among children? Often children's prosocial behaviors go unnoticed, while teachers attend to less desirable behaviors.

Defined as acts that aid or benefit another person (Mussen & Eisenberg-Berg, 1977), prosocial behaviors are viewed as central to the development of a child's social competence. Research has indicated that prosocial behavior develops at an early age (Bar-Tal, Raviv & Leiser, 1980; Hay, 1979; Yarrow & Waxler, 1976). Before the age of 2, children display prosocial actions with their parents such as helping and comforting (Johnson, 1982; Rheingold, 1982). In a school setting, prosocial behaviors occur among most children, although in low amounts (Yarrow & Waxler, 1976). Perhaps young children may not have the ability to accurately perceive and react to the needs of others, or adults may be reinforcing aggressive rather than prosocial actions. Children who have greater role-taking abilities and are more sensitive to the needs of others seem to be more prosocial (Eisenberg-Berg & Hand, 1979; Eisenberg-Berg & Neal, 1979).

Prosocial behaviors are observed in both girls and boys, although research results have not been conclusive. One group of studies found no significant gender differences in prosocial responses among preschoolers (Bar-Tal, Raviv & Goldberg, 1982; Hartup & Keller, 1960; Yarrow & Waxler, 1976). These studies argue that both girls and boys can and do display prosocial abilities equally. On the other hand, another group of studies report significant gender differences in preschool children's prosocial behaviors (Eisenberg, Bartlett & Haake, 1983; Harris & Siebel, 1975; Midlarsky & Bryan, 1972). In these studies girls were found to be more prosocial than boys. The differential socialization experience of girls and boys may help to explain these gender differences. Girls may experience prosocial models and may be expected to demonstrate the prosocial actions they have observed more frequently than boys (Mussen & Eisenberg-Berg, 1977).

Prosocial behavior has also been evidenced in children from various socioeconomic classes. When directly examined, mixed findings have resulted concerning the relationship between the family's socioeconomic class and prosocial actions. Some studies found no significant differences among children from different social classes (DePalma, 1974), while others indicated that lower-economic class children were more cooperative than upper-middle class children (Knight & Kagan, 1977; Madsen, 1967). Perhaps parental expectations and children's experiences can explain the differences in the development of prosocial abilities in children of various socioeconomic classes.

Recently there has been a great deal of research interest in the area of social competence. Current investigations have emphasized the importance of children's social development during the preschool years. Social experiences such as

From *Childhood Education*, Summer 1989, pp. 213-216. Reprinted by permission of the authors and the Association for Childhood Education International, 11141 Georgia Avenue, Suite 200, Wheaton, MD. Copyright © 1989 by the Association.

those preschoolers encounter in a classroom environment can enhance the prosocial skills of young children (Kim & Stevens, 1987; Floody, 1980; Moore, 1977). Early childhood educators have continually sought, therefore, to find effective methods that encourage the development of prosocial behavior in young children. If prosocial behavior occurs among preschoolers, what can teachers do to encourage these behaviors in the classroom setting? This article describes several strategies teachers may use in developing a more prosocial classroom environment for preschool children.

Strategy I: Examining Teacher Attitudes About Prosocial Behavior Among Preschool Children

Awareness of children's developmental levels and abilities. With an understanding of children's developmental levels, teachers are able to recognize that preschoolers are egocentric and have subjective perspective-taking social abilities (Selman & Bryne, 1974). Preschool children are primarily centered within themselves. They are beginning to recognize, however, that others have feelings, too. It is helpful, therefore, to provide young children with descriptions of thoughts and feelings of others different from their own. Teachers can point out how happy a child feels when included in an activity in which the child would like to participate. Imagine the following example: A child approaches a teacher with the request, "I want a trike." With the teacher's help, the child who is riding a tricycle can be asked for a turn by the child in need. "When you are done with the trike, can I use the trike next?" The teacher may add, "That would make Lisa happy for you to share the trike with her." When the trike is traded, a follow-up acknowledgment—e.g. "Lisa likes the way you shared the trike with her"—would reinforce the desired behaviors.

Verbalization of children's thoughts and feelings. Talking about one's own feelings, as well as listening to others describe their feelings, helps children consider other points of view outside themselves. Assistance can be given when children attempt to express their thoughts and feelings to others. Teachers can discuss the feelings of an excluded child to onlooking peers by asking, "How does Todd feel?" "Do you feel sad when someone won't play with you?" "What would make him feel happier?" "What can he be in your house?" Upon admittance into the play, the teacher can mention, "I see Todd is the new uncle in your house." "That must make him feel happy to be playing with you."

Belief in the capabilities of young children. Teachers who have the knowledge, understanding and conviction that all preschoolers are capable of displaying prosocial behavior in the classroom reflect these expectations in their social interactions. Despite gender, race or ethnic origin, all children have the ability to exhibit prosocial behavior. For example, teachers can expect both boys and girls to help one another secure paint smocks, which cannot be done alone. Children can ask one another for help in fastening the backs of their smocks. They can also share art materials such as construction paper, scissors and bottles of glue while working on a collage together.

Strategy II: Examining Teaching Techniques for the Classroom

Use of modeling to facilitate prosocial behaviors. Teachers are powerful models who can be influential in encouraging prosocial behavior among children. Research indicates that children learn while observing the behavior of others (Midlarsky & Suda, 1978). Children who see their teachers sharing or helping are more likely to share or help in return. For instance, when cleaning up materials at the end of activity time, a teacher can hold one end of a small table while two children hold the other end. The teacher may say, "I like the way we work together to move this table." In another situation, when playing catch with balls, a teacher may simply share a ball with a child and say, "I'll share this ball with you."

Children's responses to encouragement. Modeling and encouraging techniques are effective in eliciting prosocial behavior (Rogers-Warren & Baer, 1976). When children behave prosocially with peers or teachers, expressions of approval (a smile or touch on the arm) or a praising statement ("I like the way you are sharing with me!") will help maintain desired behaviors. Table 1 provides examples of modeling and encouraging strategies useful in facilitating children's prosocial behavior.

Use of reasoning as a guidance technique. When teachers reason rather than use power-oriented strategies to guide children's behavior, prosocial behaviors are more likely to occur. Children receive information to help them understand the consequences of their actions and sharpen their perspective-taking skills. Power-oriented techniques such as strict warnings or punishments do little to model prosocial behavior (Kim & Stevens, 1987). They involve strategies that tend to emphasize satisfying individual needs rather than helping a child empathize with others. When one child wants a truck that another child is using, a teacher can reason or explain how sharing or working together with the vehicle could solve the problem. Taking the truck from the child or providing a second truck for the child in need does not result in the learning of cooperative behavior.

Strategy III: Evaluating the Classroom Environment and Curriculum

Creation of a prosocial environment. Teachers can examine their classroom to see whether the development of prosocial skills is enhanced or hindered by the room setup. For example, is the room divided to separate rather than facilitate interactions between children? Barriers may prevent children from working together in adjacent play areas, such as the block and dramatic play areas. Furthermore, are there enough scissors, paint brushes and tricycles to go around? When materials are available for all children to use individually, a less prosocial environment is created. An environment with a limited but reasonable amount of supplies requires children to work together on projects. For instance, one set of crayons can be shared by three children who are drawing pictures at an art table. By examining the classroom environment and activity setup, teachers are able to evaluate their roles in facilitating prosocial behavior among preschool children.

Selection of appropriate curriculum activities. Children can benefit from the use of prosocial activities. A curriculum encompassing various areas of development can be used to encourage children's involvement in prosocial activities throughout the preschool day (Doescher & Sugawara, 1986). Cooperative cooking projects and dramatic airline play, in which children have limited supplies and need to work together in order to play, are good examples of prosocial experiences. Squeezing oranges for juice with the help of a hand juicer encourages children to cooperate and take turns. One child can hold the juicer while the other squeezes; later these roles may be switched. With airline play, children can take turns acting out the roles of pilot, passenger or travel agent. Turn-taking will encourage the sharing of materials (steering wheel, suitcases and travel brochures).

Summary

Aware that children are capable of displaying prosocial behavior in the preschool classroom, early childhood educators can be instrumental in creating an environment that nurtures their prosocial development. When positive social behavior is modeled and encouraged by teachers, children learn to respect others' needs and to re-

---

Table 1

Application of Teacher Modeling and Encouraging Strategies

Situation	Modeling Techniques	Encouraging Statements
1. "Row, Row, Row Your Boat" sung at group time	1. Demonstrate with one child how to sit facing one another and rock, with legs and arms interlocked.	1. "We need to work together to row our boat." "I like the way you two are cooperating to row your boat."
2. Pegboards at manipulative table	2. Demonstrate the sharing of pegs with a child next to you. Take one peg, and give one to your partner.	2. "I'll share the pegs with you." "I found a red peg." "May I share it with you?"
3. Waterplay at the watertable	3. Demonstrate helping with the child next to you by holding a funnel while he/she tries to fill the container.	3. "I like to help you." "We are working well together." "Can you help me fill this up?"
4. Teeter-totter during outside play	4. Demonstrate cooperative efforts with the child on the seesaw. Push your partner in order for his/her feet to touch the ground.	4. "We need to cooperate to get the teeter-totter to work." "I'll push you down, then you push me down."

spond accordingly. They may seek approval using such statements as, "Look, Jason and I are cooperating!" Or they may encourage each other by expressing such ideas as, "We like to help, don't we, Mary?" Strategies like those provided here can be incorporated effectively by early childhood educators in a variety of preschool settings.

Authors' Acknowledgment: Special thanks to Virginia Adduci and Joanne Sorte for comments on an earlier draft of this manuscript.

References

Bar-Tal, D., Raviv, A., & Goldberg, M. (1982). Helping behavior among preschool children: An observational study. *Child Development, 53,* 396-402.

Bar-Tal, D., Raviv, A., & Leiser, T. (1980). The development of altruistic behavior: Empirical evidence. *Developmental Psychology, 16,* 516-525.

DePalma, D. (1974). Effects of social class, moral orientation and severity of punishment on boys' moral responses to transgression and generosity. *Developmental Psychology, 10,* 890-900.

Doescher, S., & Sugawara, A. (1986). *Prosocial activity guide.* (Available from Dr. Susan M. Doescher, Department of Human Development & Family Studies, Oregon State University, Corvallis, OR 97331.)

Eisenberg-Berg, N., & Hand, M. (1979). The relationship of preschoolers' reasoning about prosocial moral conflicts in prosocial behavior. *Child Development, 50,* 356-363.

Eisenberg-Berg, N., & Neal, C. (1979). Children's moral reasoning about their own spontaneous prosocial behavior. *Developmental Psychology, 15,* 228-229.

Eisenberg, N., Bartlett, K., & Haake, R. (1983). The effects of nonverbal cues concerning possession of a toy on children's proprietary and sharing behaviors. *The Journal of Genetic Psychology, 143,* 79-85.

Floody, D. (1980). An early childhood educator's guide to prosocial development. ERIC document, #ED164 116.

Harris, M., & Siebel, C. (1975). Affect, aggression and altruism. *Developmental Psychology, 11,* 623-627.

Hartup, W., & Keller, E. (1960). Nurturance in preschool children and its relation to dependency. *Child Development, 31,* 681-689.

Hay, D. (1979). Cooperative interactions and sharing between very young children and their parents. *Developmental Psychology, 15,* 647-653.

Johnson, D. (1982). Altruistic behavior and the development of the self in infants. *Merrill-Palmer Quarterly, 28,* 379-388.

Kim, Y-O., & Stevens, J. (1987). The socialization of prosocial behavior in children. *Childhood Education, 63,* 200-206.

Knight, G., & Kagan, S. (1977). Acculturation of prosocial and competitive behaviors among second- and third-generation Mexican-American children. *Journal of Cross-Cultural Psychology, 8,* 273-283.

Madsen, M. (1967). Cooperative and competitive motivation of children in three Mexican sub-cultures. *Psychological Reports, 20,* 1307-1320.

Midlarsky, E., & Bryan, J. (1972). Affect expressions and children's imitative altruism. *Journal of Experimental Research in Personality, 6,* 195-203.

Midlarsky, E., & Suda, W. (1978). Some antecedents of altruism in children: Theoretical and empirical perspectives. *Psychological Reports, 43,* 187-208.

Moore, S. (1977). Research in review: Considerateness and helpfulness in young children. *Young Children, 32,* 73-76.

Mussen, P., & Eisenberg-Berg, N. (1977). *Roots of caring, sharing and helping.* San Francisco: W. H. Freeman.

Rheingold, H. (1982). Little children's participation in the work of adults. *Child Development, 53,* 114-125.

Rogers-Warren, A., & Baer, D. (1976). Correspondence between saying and doing: Teaching children to share and praise. *Journal of Applied Behavior Analysis, 9,* 335-354.

Selman, R., & Byrne, D. (1974). A structural-developmental analysis of levels of role-taking in middle childhood. *Child Development, 45,* 803-806.

Yarrow, M., & Waxler, C. (1976). Dimensions and correlates of prosocial behavior in young children. *Child Development, 47,* 118-125.

Changing Conditions for Young Adolescents:

Reminiscences and Realities

Today's young adolescents face many societal problems in addition to the innate personal problems of their age group. Middle schools—like it or not—must assist with these problems.

Judith A. Brough

JUDITH A. BROUGH is chair of and associate professor in the Department of Education at Gettysburg College, Gettysburg, Pennsylvania. Dr. Brough would like to acknowledge the assistance of Drs. Robert Curtis, Gettysburg College, and George White, Lehigh University, in the preparation of this article.

MY HOW THINGS have changed! Fade back to your days in junior high or middle school. Close your eyes and try to visualize your life back then. What did you look like? What did you most often think about? What activities occupied your time? What did you worry about? I remember worrying about the absence of a boyfriend; about my physical underdevelopment; about a "tough" English teacher. Those are "normal" worries for a thirteen-year-old. Contrast that to the following matters of concern reported by youngsters polled in 1987:

1. Kidnapping (76 percent very concerned; 16 percent sort of concerned).

2. The possibility of nuclear war (65 percent very concerned; 20 percent sort of concerned).

3. The fear of the spread of AIDS (65 percent very concerned; 20 percent sort of concerned).

4. Drug use by professional athletes (52 percent very concerned; 25 percent sort of concerned).

5. Air and water pollution (47 percent very concerned; 38 percent sort of concerned).

6. "Having to fight a war" (47 percent very concerned; 26 percent sort of concerned).

7. Increasing divorce (39 percent very concerned; 33 percent sort of concerned).[1]

My how things have changed. Permit me to particularize further.

Changes in the Family

My personal family situation made me rather a novelty during my middle level school days; I lived in a single-parent home. Today I would be the rule rather than the exception. The population of children involved in family changes has more than doubled over the past twenty-five years.[2] For example, more than one-third of the families in the United States are step-families. And, according to the U.S. census, 59 percent of the children born in 1983 will experience life in a single-parent home.[3]

Beaver Cleaver and his family used to represent the typical American family. Hodgkinson's data show that in 1955, 60 percent of U.S. households consisted of a working father, a housewife mother, and two or more kids (probably a station wagon and a dog, too). By 1980 that number had decreased to 11 percent, and by 1985 only 7 percent of our families could be so described.[4]

With a divorce rate of 50 percent in this country, teachers can no longer assume that a child and his/her parents share a common surname. In increasing instances, through multiple divorces and remarriages, children have come to live in families absent of biological parents.

Often the parents wait to divorce until the kids are "old enough to understand." However, during the middle level stage of development, ten- to fourteen-year-olds must unravel the mysteries of boy/girl relationships, test and study intricacies of adult and peer relationships, establish a sense of belonging as outlined by Maslow, and develop a sense of identity versus role confusion as described by Erikson. What a time to experience the break-up of the family!

The end of a marriage often involves fighting and custody battles. Children often feel guilty and somehow to blame for the break-up. Divorce can also mean

Reprinted with permission of *Educational Horizons*, Vol. 68, No. 2, Winter 1990, pp. 78-81. *Educational Horizons*, quarterly journal published by Pi Lambda Theta, national honor and professional association, Bloomington, IN 47407-6626.

a drop in family income or available money (even if child support payments are made, if a parent moves out s/he must pay additional monies for rent, for example), a move, and/or less adult supervision. Unfortunately, parents are understandably preoccupied at this point in their lives and cannot spend enough time and emotions in dealing with their youngsters. To many, school is the only stable environment and teachers the only stable adult role models. Certainly these youngsters cannot concentrate on subject matter until some of the emotional upheaval is resolved. They need adult guidance to help diminish the self-blame, to regain a sense of optimism about adult relationships, and to learn to accept the divorce and concomitant circumstances.

Other changes have also occurred in the American family. More than 50 percent of women have entered the work force, and that number is expected to increase. Before- and after-school care have become as important an issue as day care.

Kids today, therefore, do not have as much adult supervision as we did in the past. It is not uncommon to see kids in fast food restaurants buying their own suppers and eating with peers in like situations. These same kids go to local malls with credit cards in hand to buy their own clothes and do other shopping. A visit to the video arcade, today's equivalent of the pool hall of yesteryear, is inevitable.

DEALING WITH THE TOUGH TOPICS
Substance Use

When many of us were students, our major social decisions did not have to be made until we were at least sixteen or seventeen years old. In fact, some decisions could be postponed until even later. Despite the "drug culture" of the 1960s, there seemed to be little pressure for junior high or even high school students to become involved in substance abuse. Today, our fifth graders must make difficult decisions about illicit drug use. It's tough to "just say no" when you're ten years old and want to be accepted by your peers. And, unfortunately, these decisions may adversely affect the rest of our youngsters' lives. Deadly drugs like "crack" are now widely used. Children are experimenting with drugs and alcohol. As Packard reported, the extent is alarming:

1. The average age of a child taking

his/her first drink of alcohol is now twelve years.

2. Over one million of our youngster aged twelve to seventeen have a serious drinking problem.

3. Arrests of children for drug use or

T o many, school is the only stable environment and teachers the only stable adult role models.

dealing rose 4,600 percent in fifteen years.[5]

A survey of over eight thousand youngsters revealed that 12 percent of the fifth-grade students polled had used marijuana over the past year; 10 percent of the sixth graders admitted to use of the drug; 11 percent of the seventh graders; about 12 percent of the eighth graders; and 21 percent of the ninth graders.[6] Further, 40 percent of the fifth graders admitted to worrying about drugs and alcohol "quite a bit" or "very much."[7] Compare those data with your own fifth- through ninth-grade experiences.

Decisions About Sex

Certainly I didn't worry about this topic when I was in junior high school. I don't think I even knew about sex until I was well into my high school years. Nowadays, however, children are reaching puberty earlier—the average age in the U.S. is twelve. There are several theories to explain this phenomenon. Some of the most logical involve our advanced medical technology: better prenatal care, nutritional information and habits, fitness programs, etc. Further, some physicians maintain that the energy once used by the body to fight childhood diseases (e.g., measles, mumps, and whooping cough) is now put toward child growth, since many of these diseases have been eradicated.

Whatever the reason, the fact remains that children now develop reproductive capabilities much earlier. Several implications exist. One centers

on the idea that earlier maturation necessarily means more time needed to keep the reins on sexual activity. The body, the hormones, and peers all scream at the young adolescent to "do it," while adults coax, "Don't do it." We're outnumbered three to one.

Second, earlier physical maturation is not necessarily matched by earlier emotional maturation. Therefore, typical thirteen-year-old emotions interject into a decision played out by an "older" body. We expect that if a youngster looks like a seventeen-year-old, s/he will act and reason like a seventeen-year-old. But, to borrow a phrase, it just ain't necessarily so.

So what has occurred as a result of earlier maturation compounded by other societal and familial changes? Kids have sex earlier. Packard reported that one-fifth of all youngster become sexually experienced within one year of reaching puberty.[8] He stated that a series of studies found that "the proportion of sexually experienced teenage girls doubled in less than a decade."[9] A report to the U.S. House Select Committee on Children, Youth and Families included the following statement:

Although the birth rates for all adolescents have actually dropped in recent years, the rates for the youngest "teens" (those from ten to fourteen years old) have actually risen. There are currently between 20 and 29 million adolescent boys and girls in the United States, of whom one-third to one-half are sexually active: this reflects a rate that is not dropping. More and more young adolescents are becoming sexually active and subsequently pregnant at earlier ages.[10]

Such premature sexual behavior has its perils. In addition to the obvious risk of unwanted and/or imprudent teenage pregnancy, as well as its concurrent medical hazards to mother and baby, is the danger of sexually transmitted disease. It has been reported that one-fourth of sexually active youngsters will contract a sexually transmitted disease prior to high school graduation.[11]

Certainly for each of us, decisions regarding sexual activity were serious. For youngsters today, they are critical. Not only are the decisions being made earlier, it has become a matter of life and death because of the advent of the deadly AIDS virus. If youngsters become sexually active during their middle level school years, how many partners will they have before settling into a monogamous relationship? Former Surgeon General Koop stated that "adolescents and pre-adolescents are those whose behavior we wish especially to influence because of their vulnerability when they are exploring their own sexuality (heterosexual and homosexual) and perhaps experimenting with drugs."[12]

When I was thirteen, there was no such threat. How about you?

Mobility

Because of various factors, including divorce, factory shut-downs, and job transfers (now more likely as more women enter the job force), our society has become increasingly mobile. About seven million children must enroll in a new school district each year.[13]

One of the results of this mobility is the dissolution of the extended family. Grandma no longer lives around the block. Therefore, a once-used and effective family support system has been removed. Grandma and grandpa were good "sounding boards." A middle level youngster could ask grandparents questions which couldn't possibly have been addressed to mom or dad. Another result is that extended family members are no longer close by and, therefore, available to baby-sit. Since middle level kids would balk at the idea of a baby-sitter being hired to watch them, often the kids are left home alone.

The middle level school years are a particularly difficult time to adjust to a relocation. It is during this time that belongingness and peer relationships are so important. A move necessitates making new friends in both school and home environments. It is difficult to break into already established young adolescent cliques. Packard concluded that by their teens, children who had frequently moved became "supercool," developed behav-

ior patterns to attract attention, and/or became loners.[14] Being too lonely may be more dangerous than being too boisterous.

Since the world is changing for our students, so must their educational program change.

Suicide

I will never be able to accept the fact that some ten- to fourteen-year-olds feel so beset with problems that they attempt suicide. Although it is presumed that for every suicide there are one hundred unsuccessful attempts, no one can give us reliable statistics. The National Center for Health Statistics reported that in 1984 about 1,900 youngsters aged twelve to nineteen years committed suicide. Of these, 205 were between the ages of twelve and fourteen. "The suicide rate of teens aged 15-19 has more than doubled since 1960..."[15]

And how many accidents aren't really accidental? How many suicides are otherwise recorded on a death certificate?

The Middle Level Mandate

Middle level schools need to respond with programs and activities which help students cope with these changing societal structures. The purpose of any educational organization is to promote healthy physical, social,

emotional, and cognitive growth of the students it serves. Since the world is changing for our students, so must their educational program change. It must evolve continually in order to keep pace with the changing needs and characteristics of our nation's youth. Strategies, such as team planning, comprehensive guidance and counseling, advisor-advisee programs, and decision-making skills, must be components of the all-school program. It doesn't matter if we "turned out okay" without these and other current middle level strategies. How would we "turn out" if we were between ten and fourteen years old in the 1990s? Would we be able to cope with today's society, pressures, and stresses? Fade back. I'm not sure I could.

1. Roper Organization, Inc., *The American Chicle Youth Poll* (Morris Plains, N.J.: Warner-Lambert Co., The American Chicle Group, 1987), p. 19.
2. K. Appel, *Changing Families: A Guide for Educators*, Fastback #219 (Bloomington, Ind.: Phi Delta Kappa, 1985), p. 7.
3. H. Hodgkinson, *All One System: Demographics of Education -- Kindergarten through Graduate School* (Washington, D.C.: Institute for Educational Leadership, Inc., 1985), p. 3.
4. Ibid.
5. V. Packard, *Our Endangered Children: Growing Up in a Changing World* (Boston: Little, Brown and Company, 1983), p. 16.
6. P. Benson, D. Williams, and A. Johnson, *The Quicksilver Years: The Hopes and Fears of Young Adolescents* (San Francisco: Harper and Row, 1987), p. 150.
7. Ibid., p. 70.
8. V. Packard, *Our Endangered Children*, p. 15.
9. Ibid.
10. U.S. Congress, House Select Committee on Children, Youth and Families, *U.S. Children and Their Families: Current Conditions and Recent Trends, 1987* (Washington, D.C.: U.S. Government Printing Office, 1987), p. 71.
11. Carnegie Council on Adolescent Development, *Turning Points: Preparing American Youth for the 21st Century: A Report of the Task Force on Education of Young Adolescents* (Washington, D.C.: Carnegie Council on Adolescent Development, 1989), p. 25.
12. A. Lewis, "A Dangerous Silence," *Phi Delta Kappan* (January 1987): 348.
13. V. Packard, *Our Endangered Children*, p. 53.
14. Ibid., p. 57.
15. U.S. Congress, House Select Committee on Children, Youth and Families, *Infancy to Adolescence: Opportunities for Success*, National Center for Health Statistics, (Washington, D.C.: U.S. Government Printing Office, 1989), p. 53.

Meeting the Needs Of Young Adolescents:
Advisory Groups, Interdisciplinary Teaching Teams, and School Transition Programs

For each of the key practices studied, there is good evidence that strong implementation yields benefits that are educationally significant, Mr. Mac Iver reports. But the movement to implement these practices still has a long way to go.

DOUGLAS J. MAC IVER

DOUGLAS J. MAC IVER is an associate research scientist in the Center for Research on Elementary and Middle Schools and in the Center for Research on Effective Schooling for Disadvantaged Students, Johns Hopkins University, Baltimore.

ACROSS THE nation, a consensus appears to be emerging. Researchers specializing in early adolescent development, leading educators in the middle school movement, state departments of education, and foundations are all recommending similar changes in practice in the middle grades and in the organization of schools that include those grades — changes designed to lessen the current debilitating mismatch between the developmental needs of young adolescents and the characteristics of middle-grade programs.[1] The Carnegie Task Force on Education of Young Adolescents stated the problem succinctly:

> Middle grade schools — junior high, intermediate, and middle schools — are potentially society's most powerful force to recapture millions of youth adrift, and help every young person thrive during early adolescence. Yet all too often these schools exacerbate the problems of young adolescents.[2]

Prominent among the recommended practices are the use of group advisory periods, the establishment of interdisciplinary teacher teams, and the use of "articulation" activities with students, parents, and school staff members to ease students' transition from one level of schooling to the next. In this article I address questions concerning the structure, use, and effects of these practices. To what extent are middle-grade schools currently using these recommended practices? Does the use of these practices differ in schools serving different grade spans, in different locations, and serving different types of student populations? What are the effects of these practices on a school's level of success (e.g., on the overall strength of a school's program or on a school's ability to reduce its retention and dropout rates)?

In addressing these questions I use data from the recent national survey of practices and trends in middle-grade education conducted by the Johns Hopkins University Center for Research on Elementary and Middle Schools (CREMS). These data describe in detail the education of early adolescents in a large, representative sample of public schools that include grade 7.[3]

GROUP ADVISORY PERIODS

One major challenge facing educators in the middle grades is how to provide early adolescents with the social and emotional support they need to succeed as students. As young adolescents strive for autonomy, as they grapple with learning how to regulate their own behavior and make responsible choices, their need for close, caring adult supervision and guidance is paramount.

But how can schools that enroll young adolescents meet this need? The typical organization of instruction in schools that enroll young adolescents interferes with the development of close, trusting relationships between students and teachers.[4] For example, in a worthy attempt to provide students with high-quality instruction from subject-matter experts, many schools that serve middle grades establish departmentalized programs in which students receive instruction from a different teacher for each academic subject. (Even schools with semidepartmentalized programs or interdisciplinary teams often assign students to four or more different teachers.) As students change teachers every period (perhaps six or seven times a day), they may feel that no teacher or other adult in the school really knows them, cares about them, or is available to help them with problems. And their engagement in learning is likely to diminish as they begin to look outside the school for attention and rewards.

To reduce this risk, many schools are developing more responsive support systems, including homerooms, advisory groups, counseling services, and other activities designed to provide guidance and to monitor the academic, social, and emotional welfare of individual students.[5] Group advisory periods assign a small group of students to a teacher, administrator, or other staff member for a regularly scheduled (often daily) meeting to discuss topics important to students.

Sixty-six percent of the schools in the CREMS national survey have one homeroom or group advisory period, and 9% have two such periods. Although advisory or homeroom periods are common, many of the activities that occur during these periods are the mechanical tasks of keeping school (e.g., taking attendance, distributing notices, making announcements, orienting students to rules and programs) rather than social or academic support activities that use teachers' talents as advisors and that help students feel that someone is looking out for their interests and needs. Social and academic support activities include discussing problems with individual students, giving career information and guidance, developing student self-confidence and leadership, and discussing academic issues, personal or family problems, social relationships, peer groups, health issues, moral or ethical issues and values, and multicultural issues and intergroup relations.

We asked principals to tell us how frequently each of the support activities listed above occurred during group advisory periods at their schools. The principals responded using a five-point scale ranging from "never" (1) to "daily" (5). The overall mean for the nine support activities was 2.3; each activity tended to occur only a few times per year. Only 28% of the schools reported that most support activities occurred at least monthly.

Middle schools (6-8), along with K-8, K-12, and 7-8 schools, provide supportive group advisory activities to their students more frequently than do junior high schools (7-9) and middle/high combination schools (7-12).[6] But junior high schools and middle/high schools are more likely than other schools to have at least one professional guidance counselor on staff. (Every junior high school and 99% of the middle/high schools in our sample had at least one guidance counselor.) Our analyses reveal that, regardless of grade span, schools that have guidance counselors are significantly less likely to use supportive group advisory activities.

On the other hand, our analyses also reveal that grade span predicts a school's use of support activities even after statistically removing the effect of having a guidance counselor.[7] The finding that 7-9 and 7-12 schools use supportive group advisory activities less even after "removing" this effect suggests that including one or more of the high school grades in a school that begins in the middle years makes it less likely that the school will establish a strong group advisory program for its young adolescents. Carnegie unit requirements concerning course offerings (which begin in ninth grade) may limit the number of periods available for group advisory activities in the high school years. Although nothing prevents junior high schools or middle/high schools from offering frequent group advisory activities to their seventh- and eighth-graders (even if they can't offer them to their ninth-graders), these schools usually choose not to differentiate their programs in this way.

Schools serving large numbers of economically disadvantaged students are more likely than other schools to establish group advisory periods that provide social and emotional support for students. Similarly, urban schools or schools serving predominantly black student populations provide more frequent support activities.

> **O**ur findings suggest that the majority of teaching teams lack the common planning time they need.

We also analyzed the measurable benefits obtained by schools that provide frequent support activities during a group advisory period.[8] We wanted to know whether principals are more likely to report that their schools are successfully meeting students' needs for guidance, advice, and counseling when their schools use group guidance activities frequently or whether principals view these activities as pretty much a waste of time. We also wanted to know whether a strong group advisory program helps a school to "rescue" students who are en route to dropping out (e.g., by reducing students' feelings of anonymity and alienation in school). We found that, according to principals' estimates (with other geographic, demographic, and school variables taken into account), schools that have strong group advisory programs are more successful at meeting students' needs for guidance, advice, and counseling and at lowering the proportion of students who will drop out before finishing high school.

Thus the evidence suggests that there are important benefits associated with providing a strong group advisory program. However, the use of group advisory periods should not be viewed as a panacea. The impact of a group advisory program on these indicators of a school's success was significant but modest. For example, our data indicate that a school in which an average of nine supportive group advisory activities occur each month rather than never typically saves 2% of its students from dropping out before high school graduation and raises the principal's rating of the excellence of the schools' guidance services by just over one-fifth of a point on a four-point scale.

INTERDISCIPLINARY TEACHING TEAMS

The recommendations issued by the numerous task forces concerned with reforming education in the middle grades highlight interdisciplinary teams of teachers as a keystone for effective education in the middle grades.[9] Interdisciplinary teams are composed of colleagues who teach different subjects but share the same students. For example, four teachers may share 150 students. Because they share the same students, teachers on a team may be able to respond more quickly, personally, and consistently to the needs of individual students. In theory, teachers on a team know how their students are doing in all subjects, discuss the students' needs for special help with other teachers, arrange extra time for learning, and so on. Teachers on interdisciplinary teams may also meet as a team with each student's parents to review the student's progress and to plan interventions.

Interdisciplinary teams may eliminate the isolation that many teachers feel by providing a working group of colleagues to conduct activities and to discuss and solve mutual problems. In theory, instruction will be more effective in schools that use interdisciplinary teaming because the teachers on a team can plan thematic units that enable students to make connections between ideas in different disciplines. For example, an interdisciplinary unit called "The Day the World Changed" might explore how important rebellions, revolutions, and paradigm shifts in history, science, mathematics, and literature can be seen to fit together.

Students in schools using interdisciplinary teaming become members of a small unit with which they can identify; a stable clustering of peers and teachers allows them to develop close associations. Assignment to interdisciplinary teams theoretically helps students build "team spirit," enhances their motivation to learn, and improves their attitudes toward school because of the closer, more coherent supervision and caring that teams can provide.

About 42% of early adolescents (in 37% of the schools surveyed) receive instruction from interdisciplinary teams of teachers at some time between grades 5 and 9. Teams of teachers range from two to seven or more. More students (34%) have teams of four teachers than teams of other sizes. (However, more schools use two-teacher teams; smaller schools, especially K-8 and K-12 schools, tend to use two-teacher or three-teacher teams.) Although there is great variety in team composition, the most typical four-teacher team consists of one math, one English, one social studies, and one science teacher.

More 6-8 middle schools (just over 40%) use interdisciplinary teaming than do other types of schools included in our survey. However, most schools do not use interdisciplinary teams, including about 60% of the middle schools and about 75% of the schools with other grade organizations. In any case, interdisciplinary teaching teams offer a variety of possibilities and present a variety of challenges.

Common planning time and its use. If teachers on an interdisciplinary team are not given sufficient planning time in common, they cannot do the collaborative work that makes teams successful. Yet about 30% of the schools that use interdisciplinary teaming have a master schedule that contains no officially scheduled common planning time for team teachers, and only 36% of the schools that use interdisciplinary teaming give team members two or more hours of common planning time each week. Without officially scheduled common planning time, interdisciplinary team members must meet before or after school or during lunch period. This makes it much more difficult to coordinate the efforts of the team, to design interdisciplinary units, to meet with parents, and to discuss students needs. Our findings suggest that the majority of teams do not have the common planning time they need to become truly effective.

Even if team members are assigned common planning time, teachers do not always use a meaningful portion of this time for team activities. According to principals' estimates, teachers devote nearly half of their common planning periods to working on their own lessons, tests, and grades rather than to team planning and coordination. Of course, this may be necessary if teachers are provided only one planning or preparation period each day; even teachers who are on teams need time for individual preparation.

The principals in our survey estimated that team members did devote some (rather than little or none) of their common planning time to the following team activities: deciding on common themes and related topics for instruction, discussing the problems of specific students and arranging help, meeting as a team with parents to solve problems and provide assistance for individual students, and arranging assemblies, trips, or other team activities. On the other hand, teams rarely used team planning time for regrouping students (in order to better match lessons to abilities) or for revising schedules (to allow for activities that need more time). In theory, interdisciplinary teaming facilitates flexible grouping and scheduling practices; in reality, regrouping and flexible scheduling seldom occur, even in schools using interdisciplinary teaming.

Finally, the data indicate that increases in the amount of common planning time are strongly associated with increases in the amount of time the team spends coordinating content, diagnosing individual student needs, planning special events, conducting parent conferences, regrouping, and rescheduling. Thus the provision of adequate planning time does make a real difference in how a team functions.

Benefits and problems of teaching teams. Principals were asked to estimate how frequently 10 benefits or problems resulted from the use of interdisciplinary teams of teachers. The most commonly agreed-on benefits were that teachers received social support and understanding from other team members, that instruction was more effective because of increased integration and coordination across subjects and courses, that students' problems were recognized quickly and solved effectively, and that students identified with the team, developed team spirit, and improved both their work and their attitudes.

The most commonly agreed-on problems were that the teams did not have enough planning time, that the teachers were insufficiently trained in the team approach, and that the school schedule prevented flexibility in regrouping students or in varying time for different subjects. Principals did not think that teachers' personality clashes or preferences for identifying with subject-area departments posed problems for the success of interdisciplinary teams. Overall, those principals who were not using interdisciplinary teams in their schools thought that the problems of teaming would be more severe and that the benefits would be smaller than did the principals whose schools were using interdisciplinary teams.

As anticipated, in order to obtain the greatest benefit from interdisciplinary teaming, a school must provide teachers with adequate common planning time. Schools that provide more than two hours per week of common planning time that is regularly used for team coordination report obtaining substantially greater benefits from teaming than do schools that provide little or no common planning time.

Commitment to interdisciplinary teaming. Although 32% of all public schools use interdisciplinary teaming in the seventh or eighth grades, only 10% of schools show a strong commitment to teaming by providing adequate common planning time and by having the team use a significant portion of that time for team planning and activities.[10] Middle schools (6-8) and 7-8 schools have a significantly stronger commitment to interdisciplinary teaming than do K-8, K-12, and junior high (7-9) schools. Schools that serve especially advantaged or disadvantaged populations are also more likely than the average school to make a deep commitment to interdisciplinary teaming. Schools that serve many children whose parents are professionals or managers are the most likely of all to establish well-organized interdisciplinary teaming programs. But schools serving students whose achievement is considerably below national norms and who are at great risk of dropping out before finishing high school are also more likely than the average school to make a strong commitment to interdisciplinary teaming.

Although leaders of the middle school movement have sometimes implied that a departmental organization is incompatible with the use of interdisciplinary teams, the data show that schools that organize their teachers into departments (with department heads or common planning periods for departments) or that use single-subject teaching teams are not significantly less likely than others to make a deep commitment to interdisciplinary teaming. A departmental emphasis and an interdisciplinary emphasis coexist in many of the schools that use interdisciplinary teaming.

Our data support the claim that a well-organized interdisciplinary team approach can strengthen a school's overall program for students in the middle grades. With other geographic, demographic, and school variables taken into account, principals in schools with a deeper commitment to teaming are more likely than other principals to perceive that the present practices at their schools are meeting students' needs effectively and that the schools' overall middle-grade programs are "solid" or "exemplary."[11] Similarly, schools that have a strong commitment to interdisciplinary teaming report obtaining more frequent benefits from their interdisciplinary teams than do schools with less well-organized teaming programs.

Assignment of teachers. In 76% of the schools that use interdisciplinary teams in the seventh and eighth grades, administrators make the team assignments rather than allow teachers to choose the members of their teams. In about 40% of these schools, teams can be adjusted if teachers dislike their team assignment. In junior high schools or middle/high combination schools, where teams are least frequently used overall, it is more often up to teachers to organize their own teams.[12]

Recently, there has been a call to give middle-grade teachers a more significant voice in the decisions that affect them.[13] Does it matter how teachers are assigned to teams? Are teams more effective when teachers choose the other teachers on their teams?

The evidence suggests that the advantages associated with giving teachers a primary role in making team assignments are significant but modest. Teachers on "self-chosen" teams spend more of their common planning time in team planning and coordination. In addition, according to the principals surveyed, self-chosen teams are more likely than administrator-appointed teams to achieve more effective instruction through "integration and coordination across subjects and courses." On the other hand, administrator-appointed teams are as effective as self-chosen teams in building team spirit among students, in recognizing and solving the problems of individual students, and in using other team members as sources of social support.

Establishing team leaders. One might assume that having a team leader — someone who is directly responsible for coordinating and organizing team activities — would help a team to be more successful. However, among schools that use interdisciplinary teams in the seventh or eighth grades, about 40% have no team leaders. In about 28% of the schools, team leaders are appointed by the principal. In still other schools, team leadership is determined by the members of the team: the leader is elected by the other members of the teaching team in 16% of the schools, and the teachers

establish a system in which team leadership rotates among members in 5% of the schools. Finally, in 9% of the schools, principals report that a team leader emerges informally as the team works together.

Our data clearly show that having a formal team leader (whether elected, appointed, or rotating) is better than having no leader at all. Teams with a for-

> **G**iving teachers a primary role in making team assignments has significant but modest advantages.

mal leader spend significantly more of their common planning time on team activities. Similarly, principals report more frequent benefits from interdisciplinary teams in schools where there are formally designated leaders. Our data also suggest that the method by which leaders are selected has a slight impact on a team's effectiveness: teams with elected or rotating leadership devote more of their common planning time to team activities than do teams with appointed leaders.

SCHOOL TRANSITION PROGRAMS

Social scientists have expressed considerable concern about the potential negative effects of school transitions on young adolescents.[14] Our data indicate that more than 88% of the public school students in the U.S. enter a new school when they begin the middle grades, and this transition brings many changes in the school and classroom environments.[15] Furthermore, as students enter the middle grades, they are simultaneously undergoing the social and biological changes associated with early adolescence. Although a transition to a school that has a more appropriate environment may have a positive effect on students,[16] there is clearly a risk that these simultaneous adaptational challenges will overwhelm

the coping skills of some students and have pathogenic effects on their psychological adjustment, self-esteem, and motivation to learn.

We asked principals to report on their use of 10 articulation activities designed to help students make a smooth transition to the middle grades. These included several activities designed to orient incoming students and their parents to the programs and procedures at the middle-grade school and to prepare them for the new responsibilities and the new curricular and social demands they would face (e.g., having elementary students visit the middle-grade school for an assembly, having parents visit the middle-grade school while their children are still in elementary school, or having middle-grade students present information to elementary school students); activities to provide incoming students with sources of social support as they adjust to the new school (e.g., establishing buddy or big brother/big sister programs to pair new students with older ones); and activities that bring elementary and middle-grade educators together so that they can inform one another about the programs, courses, and requirements of their schools.

In our survey the average number of articulation activities used to help students make a smooth transition to the middle grades was 4.5. Even schools that enroll younger students along with early adolescents (e.g., K-8 and K-12 schools) usually conduct at least one or two activities to help students adjust to the middle grades. This indicates that principals recognize that a significant "school transition" occurs between the elementary and middle grades even if the students don't change buildings.

The three most common activities for easing the transition from the elementary to the middle grades (reported by more than 40% of the principals) were: having elementary school students visit the middle-grade school, having the administrators of middle-grade and elementary schools meet to discuss programs and articulation, and having middle-grade counselors meet with elementary counselors or staff members.

Some potentially promising activities were infrequently used, perhaps because they are more difficult to implement. Only 20% or fewer of the principals reported the following practices to ease the transition to a middle-grade school: having elementary school students attend regular classes at the middle-grade school, having summer meetings at the middle-grade school for incoming students, and having a buddy program that pairs new students with older ones.[17]

Which types of middle-grade schools have the most extensive articulation and transition activities in preparing students for entry? Middle schools, junior high schools, and 7-8 schools have similarly extensive articulation programs. Articulation activities are less extensive in 7-12 schools than in schools that enroll only middle-graders. Schools containing a large percentage of students living in poverty have less extensive articulation programs, while schools in populous metropolitan areas, schools serving a large percentage of professional or managerial families, and schools serving a large percentage of high-ability students have more extensive programs.

Principals were asked to rate the quality of their articulation activities. On a four-point scale ranging from "weak — need to design new practices and major changes" (1) to "excellent — practices fit students' needs exactly" (4), the average rating reported was 2.8. This indicates that many principals perceived their articulation programs to be good ones and believed that only minor changes were needed. As might be expected, schools using numerous and diverse articulation activities were more likely than others to earn high ratings from their principals. A more important finding is that fuller and more diversified articulation programs actually do help students succeed in their first year at a middle-grade school. That is, fewer students are retained in the transition grade in schools that have extensive articulation programs, even after taking account of other variables that influence retention rate.[18]

Easing the transition to high school. Not only must middle-grade schools insure that students make a smooth transition to the middle grades, but they must also prepare students for the transition to high school. For schools in our survey, the average number of articulation activities used to help students make a smooth transition to the high school grades was 3.9, significantly less than the average of 4.5 activities used to help students enter the middle grades. Middle schools and 7-8 schools offer the most extensive programs for smoothing the transition to high school; junior high schools offer less help with this transition than do middle and 7-8 schools but offer considerably more help than do K-8 schools. Schools in which the transition to high school does not involve a change of buildings (7-12 and K-12 schools) offer even fewer articulation activities at this transition point. Most K-12 schools provide no special articulation activities to assist stu-

dents with their entry into the high school grades.

Overall, schools with more extensive "elementary to middle grade" articulation programs also have more extensive "middle grade to high school" articulation programs. The most common articulation activities found in school transition programs are similar for both transitions: students visit the school they are about to enter, and administrators or counselors from the sending schools discuss articulation and programs with their counterparts from the receiving schools.

> # More data are needed on how key practices affect students' motivation to learn, attitudes, and achievement.

Teachers in the middle grades are significantly less likely than counselors and administrators to be given the opportunity to interact with their counterparts in elementary and high schools. Although teachers are expected to prepare their students for the coursework at the next level of schooling, they are typically not given the opportunity to discuss articulation with colleagues at other levels of schooling.

Parent involvement in transition programs. Articulation activities that involve parents at both points of transition are used by many schools, including most middle, 7-8, and junior high schools. Helping parents understand their children's new schools should help the students entering these schools and should also help the schools to maintain parent involvement.

Our data indicate that schools that involve parents in their articulation practices are, indeed, much more likely to maintain a strong partnership with parents (independent of other variables that influence the level of parent involvement found in a school). For example, 45% of the middle-grade schools that involve parents in at least two "elementary to

middle grade" articulation activities also formally recruit and train parents to work as school volunteers (as opposed to only 23% of schools that do not involve parents in the transition activities). Seventy-six percent of the middle-grade schools that involve parents in at least two "elementary to middle grade" articulation practices also have parent/teacher organizations with elected officers and active committees; only 62% of the schools that don't involve parents in articulation activities have similarly active parent/teacher groups. Finally, when parents are taken seriously in a school's articulation activities, the teachers at the school are more likely to continue to involve parents in the education of their children by frequently sending information and ideas to parents on how to help their children with homework and study skills.

SUMMARY AND CONCLUSIONS

The advocates of the middle-grade reform movement (educators, associations, foundations, state boards of education, and researchers) have often recommended the use of interdisciplinary teams, advisory groups, and transition activities as key components of a responsive and responsible educational program for young adolescents. Our analyses of national data from a large representative sample of public schools enrolling seventh-graders explored the use of these components in the "real world" in 1988 and tested the effects of these components on a school's level of success.

Our research essentially answered two key questions: Are the leaders of the reform movement barking up the right trees? (Are these practices effective? Do schools that adopt these practices reap important benefits?) And is anyone paying attention to the barking? (To what extent have middle-grade schools across the nation adopted credible versions of these practices? To what extent have they ignored the suggested reforms or implemented them poorly?) Our data permit at least three clear conclusions.

1. *There are important benefits associated with establishing extensive and well-organized implementations of these practices.* For each of the key practices studied, we found good evidence that strong implementation yields benefits that are educationally significant. For example, by helping a school better meet young adolescents' social and emotional needs, a group advisory program can play an important role in dropout prevention. Based on principals' estimates, a school that provides students with extensive social support and frequent oppor-

tunities to discuss topics that are important to them by means of a regularly scheduled group advisory period is more successful than other schools in increasing the proportion of its students who stay in school until high school graduation.

Likewise, interdisciplinary teams of teachers — if they have an appropriate leader, sufficient common planning time, and the willingness to use this planning time for team activities — were reported to produce a wide variety of benefits. These teams were seen to increase the effectiveness of instruction, to provide teachers with a much-needed support system, to help insure that students' problems will be recognized and solved, to improve students' work and attitudes, and to have a positive impact on the school's overall program for the middle grades.

Finally, school transition programs that use numerous and diverse articulation activities were seen to help students succeed in their first year following a school transition.

2. *If a major goal is to see most schools adopt effective implementations of these practices, the movement to restructure education in the middle grades still has a long way to go.* Although more than two-thirds of the schools that include grade 7 have a group advisory period, these periods are usually short and are focused on taking attendance, distributing notices, making announcements, and so on. Only 28% of the schools have a group advisory program that provides frequent social and academic support activities. Similarly, most middle-grade schools (63%) do not use interdisciplinary teaming at any grade level, and those that do use teaming often provide insufficient common planning time or have groups with no leader to coordinate and organize the team activities. Finally, although most schools do something to try to ease student transitions to and from the middle grades, some of the most

promising articulation activities (e.g., having a buddy program that pairs new students with older ones upon entry to the school) are rarely used.

3. *Additional data are needed to help us understand and improve education in the middle grades.* Although the information I have reported in this article should be useful to middle-grade educators who are making decisions about their schools, more data are needed to study how students' motivation to learn, attitudes, and achievement are directly influenced by these and other key practices. Only by collecting a great deal more information on the diversity of educational approaches and practices in schools for the middle grades and on young adolescents' academic achievement and attachment to school will we be able fully to document and understand the effects of different practices on the progress of students.

1. Jacquelynne Eccles and Carol Midgley, "Stage-Environment Fit: Developmentally Appropriate Classrooms for Young Adolescents," in Carole Ames and Russell Ames, eds., *Research on Motivation in Education*, vol. 3 (New York: Academic Press, 1989), pp. 139-86; Joan Lipsitz, *Growing Up Forgotten* (New Brunswick, N.J.: Transaction Books, 1980); Anne Petersen, "Adolescent Development," *Annual Review of Psychology*, vol. 39, 1988, pp. 583-607; Roberta Simmons and Dale Blyth, *Moving into Adolescence: The Impact of Pubertal Change and School Context* (Hawthorne, N.Y.: Aldine de Gruyter, 1987); William Alexander and Paul George, *The Exemplary Middle School* (New York: Holt, Rinehart & Winston, 1981); John Lounsbury, *Perspectives: Middle School Education, 1964-1984* (Columbus, Ohio: National Middle School Association, 1984); *Caught in the Middle: Educational Reform for Young Adolescents in California Public Schools* (Sacramento: California State Department of Education, 1987); Maryland Task Force on the Middle Learning Years, *What Matters in the Middle Grades?* (Baltimore: Maryland State Department of Education, 1989); and *Making the Middle Grades Work* (Washington, D.C.: Children's Defense Fund, 1988).
2. Carnegie Task Force on Education of Young Adolescents, *Turning Points: Preparing American Youth for the 21st Century* (New York: Carnegie

Council on Adolescent Development of the Carnegie Corporation, 1989), p. 8.
3. Joyce L. Epstein and James M. McPartland, *Education in the Middle Grades: A National Survey of Practices and Trends* (Baltimore: Johns Hopkins University Center for Research on Elementary and Middle Schools, 1988). For more details on the sample, participation rates, and survey topics, see Joyce L. Epstein and Douglas J. Mac Iver, *Education in the Middle Grades: Overview of a National Survey of Practices and Trends* (Baltimore: Johns Hopkins University Center for Research on Elementary and Middle Schools, 1989), pp. 2-3.
4. Eccles and Midgley, pp. 165-66.
5. Epstein and Mac Iver, pp. 16-20.
6. Douglas J. Mac Iver and Joyce L. Epstein, *Responsive Education in the Middle Grades: Teacher Teams, Advisory Groups, Remedial Instruction, School Transition Programs, and Report Card Entries* (Baltimore: Johns Hopkins University Center for Research on Elementary and Middle Schools, 1989), pp. 6-8.
7. Ibid., p. 7.
8. Ibid., pp. 8-9.
9. See also Epstein and Mac Iver, pp. 21-28.
10. Mac Iver and Epstein, pp. 10-13.
11. Ibid., pp. 14-16.
12. Epstein and Mac Iver, p. 24.
13. See, for example, Carnegie Task Force . . . , p. 55.
14. See, for example, Dale Blyth, Roberta Simmons, and Steven Carlton-Ford, "The Adjustment of Early Adolescents to School Transitions," *Journal of Early Adolescence*, vol. 3, 1983, pp. 105-20; Eccles and Midgley, op. cit.; Maurice Elias, Michael Gara, and Michael Ubriaco, "Sources of Stress and Support in Children's Transition to Middle School: An Empirical Analysis," *Journal of Clinical Child Psychology*, vol. 14, 1985, pp. 112-18; Simmons and Blyth, op. cit.; and Lisa Crockett et al., "School Transitions and Adjustment During Early Adolescence," *Journal of Early Adolescence*, vol. 9, 1989, pp. 181-210.
15. Jacquelynne Eccles, Carol Midgley, and Terry Adler, "Grade-Related Changes in the School Environment: Effects on Achievement Motivation," in J. G. Nicholls, ed., *The Development of Achievement Motivation* (Greenwich, Conn.: JAI Press, 1984), pp. 283-331.
16. Eccles and Midgley, op. cit.; and L. Mickey Fenzel, "Role Strains and the Transition to Middle School: Longitudinal Trends and Sex Differences," *Journal of Early Adolescence*, vol. 9, 1989, pp. 211-26.
17. Epstein and Mac Iver, pp. 37-38.
18. Mac Iver and Epstein, p. 20.

Affective Dimensions of Effective Middle Schools

Effective middle schools are sensitive to the affective development of young adolescents. While advisory programs play an important part in fostering personal growth, the whole school environment should relate the cognitive and affective domains. Seven areas where middle school educators need to give attention to affective development are discussed.

James A. Beane

JAMES A. BEANE is a faculty member in the Department of Interdisciplinary Studies at the National College of Education. This article is based on a paper presented at the 9th Annual Seminar on Teaching the Transescent, University of Wisconsin, Platteville.

IN THE THIRTY-YEAR evolution of what we now call the middle school movement, a hallmark characteristic has been the sensitivity given to the development of early adolescence. In fact, we now recognize that, beyond the debate over what grade levels to include and what organizational features to use, this is the more crucial point; an effective middle school is one that is developmentally appropriate to early adolescence. As a result of this understanding, many middle schools have been able to break away from the over-emphasis on academics that characterized the junior version of the high school and subsequently provide a more bal-anced response to the physical, cognitive, and affective aspects of learning and development.

Of these three, perhaps the most serious and sustained attention has been given to the area of affective development. This article examines the reasons behind this attention and explores possibilities for extending these affective dimensions. While substantial gains have been made in this area, there is still much work left to do if the affective dimensions of the middle school are to be appropriate, complete, and coherent.

Why Affect in the Middle?

Most middle level educators are by now able to recite the litany of characteristics that generally describe the developmental stage of early adolescence. Prominent among these are the emergence of issues centering around self-identity, a compelling desire to earn a place in the peer group, and the ex-

From *Educational Horizons*, Vol. 68, No. 2, Winter 1990, pp. 109-112. Reprinted with permission from *Educational Horizons*, quarterly journal of Pi Lambda Theta, National Honor and Professional Association in Education, Bloomington, IN 47407-6626.

ploration of moral/value themes. Furthermore, most educators are aware, in theory at least, that these personal/social issues are the most powerful factors in the lives of young adolescents—much more so, for example, than the academics and skills that fill most of the school agenda. Indeed, even the physical developments that figure so prominently in this stage are eventually embedded in the personal/social context: the appearance of acne and secondary sexual characteristics, for instance, has virtually no meaning except in the context of the "omniscient" peer group. Thus, in becoming *effective*, middle schools must place affect at the very center of the school program or risk missing the essential point of what it means to be appropriately sensitive to the developmental needs of young adolescents.

*M*iddle level educators need to think about how the spirit and affective concerns of advisory programs might be extended across the whole school and brought to life throughout.

In their work so far, many middle schools have demonstrated particular concern for the issues of self-concept and self-esteem or what one might call personal development. This is not surprising for several reasons. First, many believe, as did their junior high school predecessors, that early adolescence should mark the end of adult-dependent childhood and the beginning of self-sufficiency. Second, positive self-esteem is generally thought to be a crucial and necessary quality for coping with the myriad pressures of current society and fending off the self-

destructive behaviors endemic to the young adolescent population. Third, positive self-esteem as *learner* has been shown to correlate with such concerns as participation, self-direction, school completion, pro-social behavior, and achievement. In fact, the correlation to academic achievement most powerfully drives the present interest in self-esteem.

However, in thinking about affect in the middle school, we must remember two important points. First, the purpose of enhancing self-esteem ought to be based largely upon a concern for personal efficacy as an essential part of healthy living. Beyond academics and coping skills, we should want to help young adolescents to be fully functioning human beings. Second, affective development involves more than self-esteem; it includes social as well as personal development, and, thus, efforts to extend affective dimensions of a middle school must also address values, morals, ethics, and other aspects of our relations with others.

Progress to Date

The function of guidance that has historically been attached to middle level schools, though not always sufficiently practiced, coupled with the concern for self-esteem, has led to the emergence of teacher-based guidance programs, known variously as *adviser-advisee*, *advisory*, *teacher-advisory*, and *home-based guidance programs*. Though common in purpose, from school to school these programs vary widely in grouping arrangements, schedule allotments, and the use of local versus commercially packaged programs.[1] It is here that middle schools have placed the programmatic response to the need for self-esteem enhancement.

As we look at progress in reforming middle level education, particularly in the sense of attention to affect, we cannot overestimate the significance of advisory programs. Their widespread and increasing appearance is certainly partial evidence of such progress and the kind of commitment it requires. Aside from offering direct learning experiences related to personal/social development, advisory programs also have contributed greatly to creating "smaller, more knowable" groups within large schools where anonymity threatens to alienate many young adolescents and put them at risk of falling through the cracks in the system.[2]

However, advisory programs have also posed something of a problem in

terms of constructing a complete and coherent framework for affective development in the school. Specifically, in compartmentalizing the responsibility for affective development within the advisory program, other parts of the school may come to see themselves exempted from attention to personal/social development. This view has been compounded in situations where middle schools have purchased commercially prepared "affective education" packages whose developers claim that participation in their program during a daily set-aside time slot will enhance self-esteem and interpersonal relations and thereby greatly reduce self-destructive and anti-social behaviors.

We have known since the late 1920s that such claims are not warranted by the evidence on personal/social development. At that time, Hugh Hartshorne and Mark May studied the relation between what young people were taught in popular "character education" programs and their real-life behavior.[3] The major finding was that themes of the lessons did not transfer into actual situations unless the environment in which young people lived consistently promoted and demonstrated those themes. Thus, it is not surprising to learn that more recent evidence on packaged and/or set-aside "affective" programs indicates that even when such programs are sponsored by the schools and structured within their programs, young people who participate in them do not show significant improvements in their overall self-esteem in school.[4] Put another way, whatever gains might be made in enhancing self-esteem in set-aside time slots during the school day are most likely washed away if the rest of school is inconsistent in promoting those efforts, that is, if it is unsympathetic or uncaring toward the affective concerns and needs of young people.

Moreover, such programs sustain the historical mistake that affective and cognitive learning and development are unrelated. While we may conveniently separate out these domains for theoretical discussion and analysis, in the flow of real-life they are inextricably intertwined.[5] Affective beliefs and behaviors are not empty categories. We believe and act upon *something*. And what we believe and act upon, except in cases involving the most base visceral responses, is some concept or idea that has been shaped by our previous experiences and reflected upon through some kind of thinking that may be relatively rational, but certainly not irrational.

Three lessons may be learned from this analysis. First, self-esteem and other affective variables are not affected in lasting ways by simple programs slotted in set-aside time segments. Second, self-esteem and other affective attitudes and behaviors are not simply *figured out* by individual young people; they are greatly influenced by the environment in which young people live and the consistent opportunity to try out and reflect upon possibilities for affective ideas. Third, set-aside programs may be useful, but they must be part of a larger effort that influences the environment in which young people live—an effort and concern that enters into every nook and cranny of the school, including every part of the middle school's institutional features and curriculum plans.

Extending Affect in the Middle School

Given the larger meaning of affect and its place in the lives of young adolescents, middle schools need to expand and extend the place of affect in the school if they are to be effective. At the very least, middle schools must seek the following affective outcomes:

1. the development of clear self-concept and positive self-esteem;

2. the desire and skills to get along with others and to prize human and cultural diversity;

3. the development of values and morals that point the way toward ethical responsibility;

4. an appreciation for and experience with the democratic way of life; and

5. the development and use of critical and creative thinking in considering the many social issues that face our society and our world.

Certainly it is not reasonable or even appropriate to expect that all affective development can be adequately approached in an advisory program, particularly one that consists mainly of a collection of personal development activities. However, this does not mean that advisory programs are useless. They *do* create small, knowable groups that provide a setting for personal security and persistent guidance. Also, they offer an opportunity to deal directly with topics like self-esteem, the power of the peer group, value and moral alternatives on various issues, etc. This is the kind of direct path that is necessary in a coherent approach to affect in the curriculum. But, beyond this, middle level educators need to think about how the spirit and affective concerns of advisory programs might be extended across the whole school and brought to life throughout.

In interviews conducted with young adolescents, they often attach positive self-esteem in school to the presence of "nice" teachers, opportunities to work with friends, and experiences that culminate in making, doing, and creating things—where they own a piece of the curriculum.[6] If we put any stock in what kids think (and we ought to), then we ought to consider broader use of cooperative learning as one area where we can give attention to affective development. This should be under the guidance of caring, supportive teachers who emphasize the use of a hands-on approach to learning. For example, in engaging young people in constructing an Egyptian tomb, Robert Stromberg and Joan Smith demonstrated that such teaching variables can bring even something as "dead" as a unit on ancient Egypt to life.[7]

A second area of attention should be given to moral and value exploration, since early adolescence is a stage where serious questions about life emerge. Here, middle level educators need to place a greater premium on critical examination of issues, such as racism, environmental destruction, poverty, homelessness, and nuclear destruction, as both problems and issues of morality.[8] The curriculum in an effective middle school cannot be sterile, simply sticking to the facts and cleaning the controversy out of real life. For example, many middle school learners get a chance to study commercial advertising, but few are encouraged to think about the morality of commercialism as it feeds on problems of self-esteem and status within their peer group. Moreover, our diverse culture cannot be relegated to a Black History Month nor our heritage to the historical customs of the upper middle class, that is, to a selective view of what is important. Those who think that young adolescents are too young to hear about such things as homelessness and racism or that they ought to be left with their "innocence" need to open their eyes and see that kids are living with these issues everyday; they know about them first-hand.

Work in this area will require that reforming middle school curriculum be more than simply correlating traditional subject areas within an interdisciplinary team. Instead, middle school educators will have to rethink what they mean by the "core" of the curriculum and imagine the possibility of thematic units developed around compelling personal and social issues without regard for subject area lines—themes that engage young adolescents in direct and critical study and action.

The curriculum in an effective middle school cannot be sterile, simply sticking to the facts and cleaning the controversy out of real life.

Third, as we reconvene efforts to empower local educators, particularly teachers, middle level educators need to think about how to extend that empowerment to young people. We cannot pretend that young adolescents can learn the ways of democracy and develop a legitimate sense of self-esteem if they are disenfranchised in decision making in their schools. Instead, new ways must be created (and old ways rediscovered) to involve young people in the curriculum and in school governance decisions so that they can truly experience what it means to have a say in what goes on and learn responsibility through "ownership." Here, greater emphasis must be placed upon involving young adolescents as members of various school improvement committees, curriculum development groups, and as participants in "town meetings" that take on school-wide issues.

A fourth area of attention is that middle schools need to expand community service projects so that young adolescents might experience first-hand the issues that face others and learn the ways of compassion. Many middle schools already make some efforts in this area, but too often they are limited to school-wide charity drives that lack the commitment that comes from personally working with elders, tutoring younger children, conducting community surveys, confronting environmental problems, and so on. Moreover, community service projects must be extended beyond mere "acts of mercy" to "acts of justice" through moral reflection about how some people come to face the problems that they do.[9]

Fifth, middle schools must continue to carefully rethink and reconstruct the deep and traditional institutional features that create negative affect in the everyday school lives of young adolescents. For instance, the issue of heterogeneous versus homogeneous grouping ought not to be argued merely within the bounds of academic achievement. More importantly is the fact that homogeneous grouping reflects the race and class divisions in the larger society that detract from human dignity and are undemocratic.[10] Surely the middle schools do not mean to replicate or contribute to such social injustice. Surely this level of concern is part of the deeper commitment the middle school movement means to make.

Sixth, more thought must be given to the implications of continuing to narrowly define human possibilities by minimum competency programs and expected scores on standardized achievement tests. Even though many middle level educators are sensitive to young adolescents, their schools still fall prey to the trap of labeling young people and placing them in stereotyped groups. This problem arises partially from the fact that middle school reform ideas are not related to larger educational trends and pressures.

Finally, middle level educators must begin to remember what it means to speak out and be active on behalf of young adolescents outside the school. No matter how sensitive adults are within the school or how salutary their efforts, affective effects are constantly under threat of being washed away by the problems of growing up in a society that is largely ambiguous, unjust, and indifferent. One of the original purposes behind the middle school movement was to create a national constituency of advocates for young adolescents, the age group that is probably more misunderstood and disliked than any other.[11] The larger mission of the middle school movement is to find the lever long enough to move our society toward more justice, more happiness, and a better quality of living for early adolescence.[12] It is only by looking outside the school that such a mission might be carried out.

While these suggestions are only a partial set, they do, in the end, represent how we ought to think about affective development in an effective middle school. They raise more than the question of how to get an advisory program, although that may be important. Oddly enough, they recall many of the concerns originally framed in work on values clarification that is so widely misinterpreted today and from which many commercial "affective education" packages have separated out their simple collections of personal development activities.[13] Then, as now, issues like the trend toward imposition of values and the undercurrents of racism in society are difficult and complex. They compel us to think about affect in larger ways—helping young people think about themselves and their world in critical ways and creating environments that promote personal and social efficacy. Clearly this is not the "soft" side of the curriculum that so many people accuse it of being or the isolated concern for personal development they pretend it is.

1. M. James, *Adviser-Advisee Programs: Why, What, and How* (Columbus, Oh.: National Middle School Association, 1986).
2. Carnegie Council on Adolescent Development, *Turning Points: Preparing American Youth for the 21st Century: A Report of the Task Force on Education of Young Adolescents,* (Washington, D.C.: Carnegie Council on Adolescent Development, 1989).
3. H. Hartshorne and M.A. May, *Studies in the Nature of Character,* Vol.I, *Studies in Deceit,* Vol. II, and *Studies in Service and Self-Control,* Vol. III (With F.K. Shuttleworth) of *Studies in the Organization of Character,* (New York: Macmillan, 1928, 1929, 1930 respectively).
4. See, for example, A.L. Lockwood, "The Effects of Values Clarification and Moral Development Curricula on School-Age Subjects: A Critical Review of Research," *Review of Educational Research* 48 (1978): 325-64; and Pat Eva Crisci, "The Quest National Center: A Focus on Prevention of Alienation," *Phi Delta Kappan* 67 (1986): 440-442.
5. J.A. Beane, *Affect in the Curriculum: Toward Democracy, Dignity, and Diversity* (New York: Teachers College Press, 1990).
6. J.A. Beane and R.P. Lipka, *Self-Concept, Self-Esteem, and the Curriculum* (New York: Teachers College Press, 1986) and *When the Kids Come First: Enhancing Self-Esteem* (Columbus, Oh.: National Middle School Association, 1987).
7. R.B. Stromberg and J.M. Smith, "The Simulation Technique Applied in an Ancient Egypt I.D.U.," *Middle School Journal* 18 (1987): 9-11.
8. J.A. Beane, *Affect in the Curriculum.*
9. R.J. Starrat, *Sewing Seeds of Faith and Justice* (Washington, D.C.: Jesuit Secondary Education Association, undated).
10. See, for example, J. Oakes, *Track: How Schools Structure Inequality* (New Haven, Conn.: Yale University Press, 1985).
11. J. Lipsitz, *Successful Schools for Young Adolescents* (New Brunswick, N.J.: Transaction, 1984).
12. J.A. Beane, "A Middle School Manifesto," *Transition* 1 (1982): 9-11.
13. L.E. Raths, M. Harmin, and S.B. Simon, *Values and Teaching,* (Columbus, Oh.: Charles E. Merrill, 1966).

Learning

- Information Processing/Cognitive Learning (Articles 13–14)
- Behavioristic Learning (Articles 15–16)
- Humanistic/Social Psychological Learning (Articles 17–19)
- Instructional Strategies (Articles 20–24)

Learning can be broadly defined as a relatively permanent change in behavior due to experience. Learning is not a result of change due to maturation or drugs. Changes in behavior result from a complex interaction between individual characteristics of students and environmental factors. One of the continuing challenges in education is understanding these interactions so that learning results can be predicted. This section focuses on approaches within educational psychology that represent unique ways of viewing the learning process. Each approach emphasizes a different set of personal and environmental factors that influence certain behaviors. While

no one approach can fully explain learning, each is a valuable contribution to our body of knowledge about the process.

The discussion of each learning approach includes suggestions for specific techniques and methods of teaching to guide teachers in understanding student behavior and in making decisions about how to teach. The articles in this section reflect a recent emphasis on applied research conducted in schools rather than in laboratories. The relatively large number of articles on information processing/cognitive learning and instruction, as opposed to behaviorism, also reflects a change in

emphasis. Behaviorism, however, remains very important in our understanding of learning and instruction.

Researchers have recently made significant advances in understanding the way our minds work. Information processing refers to the way that the mind receives sensory information, stores it as memory, and recalls it for later use. This procedure is basic to all learning, no matter what teaching approach is taken, and we know that the method used in processing information determines to some extent how much and what we remember. The articles in this subsection present some of the fundamental principles of information processing, and examine concepts of thinking.

In cognitive learning, new knowledge is obtained as existing knowledge is reorganized and altered. This process is often stimulated when we are presented with information that disagrees or is incompatible with knowledge we already possess. Cognitive learning is practiced continually by children as they learn about their world; they make discoveries by perceiving things that pique their curiosity or raise questions in their minds.

Behaviorism is probably the best-known approach to learning. Most prospective teachers are familiar with concepts such as classical conditioning, reinforcement, and punishment, and there is no question that behaviorism has made significant contributions to understanding learning. But behaviorism has also been subject to much misinterpretation because it seems so simple. In fact, the effective use of behavioristic principles is complex and demanding, as the articles in this subsection point out.

Humanistic/social psychological learning emphasizes the affective, social, and personal development of students. Humanistic learning involves an acceptance of the uniqueness of each individual, and stresses character, human feelings, values, and self-worth. To the humanist, learning is the personal discovery of the meaning of information, not simply a change in behavior or thinking. A central theme in humanistic learning is the development of self-concept and self-esteem through self-perception.

Social psychology is the study of the nature of interpersonal relationships in social situations. In education, this approach looks at teacher-pupil relationships and group processes to derive principles of interaction that affect learning. One of this area's most significant contributions

to learning is the understanding of how teacher expectations affect student behavior. The first article in this subsection reviews how expectations are expressed, and maintains that teachers need to monitor their interactions carefully to communicate the appropriate expectations. The third article summarizes research about a specific method of instruction—cooperative learning—that is based on social psychological principles.

Instructional strategies are the methods of conveying information and teacher behaviors that affect student learning. Teaching methods or techniques can vary greatly, depending on objectives, group size, types of students, and personality of the teacher. For example, discussion classes are generally more effective for enhancing thinking skills than are individualized sessions or lectures. For this subsection, we have selected some major instructional strategies to illustrate the variety of approaches. Most effective teaching strategies are based on learning principles. The first article summarizes research on effective teaching to indicate instructional strategies that promote student learning. How controversy can be used to enhance critical thinking and other important outcomes is addressed in the second article. The third article suggests methods of instruction that match learning styles of students, while the next article challenges the research on learning styles. The last article discusses methods to encourage student creativity.

Looking Ahead: Challenge Questions

Compare and contrast the different approaches to learning. What approach do you think is best? What factors are important to your answer (e.g., objectives, types of students, setting, personality of the teacher)?

What are some teaching strategies that you could use to promote greater student retention of material? What is the best way to attract and keep students' attention? Is it necessary for a teacher to be an entertainer?

How can a teacher promote positive self-concepts, values, and attitudes? Is this more important than cognitive achievement?

How do teacher expectations affect student learning? How much emphasis should be put on cultivating positive student interactions? Do you think cooperative learning is feasible? Why or why not?

Putting Learning Strategies to Work

By increasing students' repertoires of tactics for learning, we can prepare them to develop their own strategies for problem solving in the classroom and beyond.

SHARON J. DERRY

Sharon J. Derry is Associate Professor and Chair, Cognitive and Behavioral Sciences, Department of Psychology, Florida State University, Tallahassee, FL 32306-1051.

Recent research in cognitive and educational psychology has led to substantial improvements in our knowledge about learning. Researchers have identified certain mental processing techniques—learning strategies—that can be taught by teachers and used by students to improve the quality of school learning. Let me illustrate.

As a professor of educational and cognitive psychology, I often begin the semester with a simulation exercise designed to illustrate major principles about the role of learning strategies in classroom instruction. For example, recently I presented my students with the following scenario:

You are a high school student who has arrived at school 20 minutes early. You discover that your first-period teacher is planning to give a test covering Chapter 5. Unfortunately, you have prepared the wrong chapter, and there is no one around to help you out. Skipping class is not the solution, since this results in an automatic "F," and you would never dream of cheating. So you open your book and use the next 15 minutes as wisely as you can.

I gave my students 15 minutes to study. They then took a quiz with eight main idea questions and two application questions. At the end of the quiz, I asked them to write in detail exactly what they did when they studied. Quizzes (without names) were collected and then distributed randomly to the class for scoring and for analyz-

Learning is a form of problem solving that involves analyzing a learning task and devising a strategy appropriate for that particular situation.

ing the study strategies reported in them.

Few people performed well on this test. A student who did wrote the following:

There wasn't enough time for details. So I looked at the chapter summary first. Then I skimmed through the chapter and tried to understand the topic paragraphs and the summary paragraphs for each section. I also noticed what the headings said, to get the organization, and I noticed certain names that went with each heading, figuring they did something related to each topic, a study or something. I started to do some memory work on the headings, but time was up before I finished.

By comparison, most students answered only two or three of the main idea questions, reporting a study strategy something like the following.

Panic. There was not enough time! I started going over the chapter and got as far as I could, but it was hopeless. I assume you do not plan to grade this quiz, because that would be unfair!

As illustrated in these two examples, the differences between successful and unsuccessful learning

strategies often are clear and striking. Whereas the successful learners assessed the learning situation and calmly developed a workable plan for dealing with it, the less successful learners were occupied with fruitless worries and vague strategies but little planning effort.

Such an exercise serves to introduce the following important principles about self-directed learning:

1. The plan that one uses for accomplishing a learning goal is a person's learning strategy. Learning strategies may be simple or complex, specific or vague, intelligent or unwise. Obviously, some learning strategies work better than others.

2. Learning strategies require knowledge of specific learning skills, or "tactics" (e.g., Derry and Murphy 1986), such as skimming, attending to chapter structure, and memorization techniques. The ability to devise appropriate learning strategies also requires knowledge about when and when not to use particular types of learning tactics.

3. Learning is a form of problem solving that involves analyzing a learning task and devising a strategy appropriate for that particular situation. Different learning situations may call for different strategies.

Further, I asked my students to determine whether any reported learning strategy had produced useful knowledge. Alas, no participant had applied the knowledge acquired in the 15-minute study session to the two application questions on the quiz. Even when learning strategies are apparently successful according to one form of measurement, the resultant learning is not necessarily usable later

Sharon J. Derry, "Putting Learning Strategies to Work," *Educational Leadership*, December 1988/January 1989, pp. 4-10.

Category	Examples	Some Conditions of Use	Strengths or Weaknesses
Attentional Focusing			
Simple focusing	Highlighting. Underlining.	Structured, easy materials. Good readers.	No emphasis on importance or conceptual relations of ideas.
Structured focusing	Looking for headings, topic sentences. Teacher-directed signaling.	Poor readers. Difficult but considerate materials.	Efficient, but may not promote active elaboration, deep thinking.
Schema Building	Use of story grammars, theory schemas. Networking.	Poor text structure. Goal is to encourage active comprehension.	Inefficient, but develops higher-order thinking skills.
Idea Elaboration	Some types of self-questioning. Imagery.	Goal is to comprehend and remember specific ideas.	Powerful, easy to combine. Difficult for some students unassisted. Will not ensure focus on what is important.

Fig. 1. Tactics for Learning Verbal Information

in problem solving. Thus, we added a fourth principle to our list:

4. In most school learning situations, strategies should be devised with the aim of creating usable, rather than inert, knowledge. Clearly, not all learning strategies will lead to the formation of usable knowledge structures.

Next I will elaborate these principles in greater detail, suggesting how they can influence classroom practice.

Strategies as Learning Plans

There is much confusion about the term *learning strategy*. The term is used to refer to (1) specific learning tactics such as rehearsal, imaging, and outlining (e.g., Cook and Mayer 1983, Levin 1986); (2) more general types of self-management activites such as planning and comprehension monitoring (e.g., Pressley et al. in press a); and (3) complex plans that combine several specific techniques (e.g., Derry and Murphy 1986, Snowman and McCown 1984).

To clarify the uses of the term, I distinguish between the specific tactics and the learning strategies that combine them. Thus, a learning strategy is a complete plan one formulates for accomplishing a learning goal; and a learning tactic is any individual processing technique one uses in service of the plan (Derry and Murphy 1986, Snowman and McCown 1984). That is,

a learning strategy is the application of one or more specific learning tactics to a learning problem. Within this definition, the plethora of learning techniques (popularly called "strategies") being promoted by various researchers and practitioners can be viewed as potentially useful learning tactics that can be applied in various combinations to accomplish different learning jobs.

This definition points to the need for two distinct types of strategies instruction: specific tactics training and training in methods for selecting and combining tactics into workable learning plans. Teachers can incorporate both types of training into regular classroom instruction by thoughtfully combining different study tactics—outlining plus positive self-talk, for example—and assigning them along with regular homework.

Learning Strategies Employ Specific Learning Tactics

In this section I discuss tactics in three major categories: (1) tactics for acquiring verbal knowledge, that is, ideas and facts fundamental to disciplines such as science, literature, and history; (2) tactics for acquiring procedural skills such as reading, using language, and solving problems that underlie various curriculum disciplines; and (3) support tactics for self-motivation,

which are applicable to all types of learning situations. (For a more thorough treatment of these topics, see the reviews by Derry and Murphy 1986, Weinstein and Mayer 1985, Levin 1986, and Pressley et al. in press b.)

Verbal learning tactics

Strategies aimed at improving comprehension and retention of verbal information should build upon tactics that enhance these mental processes: (1) focusing attention on important ideas, (2) schema building, and (3) idea elaboration (see fig. 1).

Attentional focusing. Two types of attention-focusing tactics are simple focusing and structured focusing. In the simple focusing category, highlighting and underlining are common examples. Unfortunately, the use of simple focusing procedures does not necessarily ensure identification of important information. I have often confirmed this point by requesting to see the textbooks of students who are having academic problems. Frequently I find almost every word in their texts highlighted.

Students, weaker ones in particular, should be taught to combine simple focusing with structured focusing, whereby the learner directs primary attention to headings, topic sentences, or other signals provided by the instructional presentation. The teaching

3. LEARNING: Information Processing/Cognitive

Category	Examples	Some Conditions of Use	Strengths or Weaknesses
Pattern Learning			
Hypothesizing	Student reasons and guesses why particular pattern is or isn't example of concept.	Goal is to learn attributes of concepts and patterns.	Inefficient unless feedback given. Encourages independent thinking.
Seeking reasons for actions	Student seeks explanations why particular actions are or are not appropriate.	Goal is to determine which procedures are required in which situations.	Develops meta-cognitive knowledge. Inefficient if not guided. If too guided, might not promote thinking skills.
Reflective Self-Instruction	Student compares reification of own performance to expert model.	Goal is to tune, improve complex skill.	Develops understanding of quality performance. May increase self-consciousness, reduce automaticity.
Practice			
Part practice	Student drills on one specific aspect of performance.	A few specific aspects of a performance need attention.	Develops subskill automaticity. Doesn't encourage subskill integration.
Whole practice	Student practices full performance without attention to subskills.	Goal is to maintain or improve skill already acquired or to integrate subskills.	May consolidate poorly executed subskills. Helps develop smooth whole performance.

Fig. 2. Tactics for Learning Procedural Knowledge

of structured focusing is a well-established practice in English classes, and it can profitably be reinforced in other courses to help students identify information they need to learn. However, the success of structured focusing depends heavily on well-structured, considerate instructional presentations (as well as on considerate teachers who test for the main ideas). And the use of these tactics does not ensure that the ideas identified will actually be remembered.

Schema building. A more powerful type of verbal-learning tactic is schema building, which encourages active analysis of an instructional presentation and formation of a synthesizing framework. One well-known form of schema building is networking (Dansereau 1985, Dansereau et al. 1979), whereby a student draws a node-link map representing the important ideas in a text and the interrelationships among them. This technique is powerful, but it is difficult to teach and time-consuming to apply (McKeachie 1984). Simpler forms of schema building include the use of teacher-suggested schemas, such as the well-known tactic of requiring students to

analyze stories in English literature by identifying the theme, setting, plot, resolution, and so on. Similar assignments can facilitate verbal learning in other courses of study. For example, Dansereau (1985) improved students'

> **A learning strategy is a complete plan one formulates for accomplishing a learning goal; and a learning tactic is any individual processing technique one uses in service of the plan.**

performance on science tests by teaching them to use a theory schema as a study aid for scientific text.

Schema building encourages in-depth analysis and is particularly useful if instruction is inconsiderate or unclear. Schema-building strategies are generally employed as comprehension aids; however, they also aid memory through the organization and elaboration of ideas.

Idea elaboration. Idea elaboration is a memory-enhancing process whereby students link each important new idea with prior knowledge so as to connect them. These linkages can be based on an image, a logical inference, or on anything else that serves to connect new ideas to prior knowledge (Gagne 1985).

Many elaboration tactics capitalize on imagery, a powerful memory-enhancing technique. For example, the key-word method for acquiring foreign vocabulary involves creating a mental image (prior knowledge) representing the sound of a foreign word (new information), and relating that image to another image (prior knowledge) representing the meaning of the word's English equivalent. Many types of elaboration tactics facilitate memorization (e.g., Bransford and Stein 1984), and these can be employed to great advantage in many courses.

Category	Examples	Some Conditions of Use	Strengths or Weaknesses
Behavioral Self-Management	Student breaks task into sub-goals, creates goal-attainment plan, rewards.	Complex, lengthy task; low motivated students.	Promotes extrinsic, rather than intrinsic, motivation. Very powerful.
Mood Management			
Positive self-talk	Student analyzes, avoids negative self-statements, creates positive self-statements.	Preparation for competitive or difficult performance; presence of negative ideas.	Good intrinsic motivator; requires conscious attention during performance.
Relaxation techniques	Student uses deep breathing, counting, other clinical relaxation methods.	Text anxiety; highly anxious students.	Techniques controversial in some districts.
Self-Monitoring	Student stops self during performance to consciously check mood, progress, etc.	Goal is to increase conscious awareness and control of thinking process.	May interrupt concentration.

Fig. 3. Tactics for Developing Motivation

Procedural learning tactics

Most learning strategies research has examined tactics for acquiring verbal information. However, some strategy researchers are developing techniques for acquiring procedural skills. Procedural learning has three aspects (Anderson 1983, Gagne 1985): (1) learning how to carry out basic actions such as performing long division or executing a tennis lob; (2) learning to recognize the conceptual patterns that indicate when it is appropriate to perform particular actions (such as recognizing that a word problem is a division situation or that a tennis lob is required); and (3) learning to combine many pattern-action pairs into a smooth overall system of response. Consider, for example, the complex combining of subskills that underlies the actual playing of a tennis match.

Based on this view, Figure 2 presents three categories of mental tactics for procedural learning: (1) tactics for learning conceptual patterns that cue applicability of associated actions; (2) tactics for acquiring the component actions (performance subskills) themselves; and (3) tactics for perfecting and tuning complex overall performance.

Pattern-recognition tactics. Pattern recognition plays an important role in the development of procedural performance; however, students are probably not aware of this. Thus, developing students' procedural learning abilities includes both conveying the important function of pattern recognition and helping students develop tactics for acquiring performance-related patterns.

Examples of tactics in the patterns-acquisition category include hypothesizing and seeking reasons for actions. In applying these tactics, the learner attempts to discover the identifying features of a pattern or concept through guesswork, reasoning, and investigation. For example, while watching a tennis pro at work, the student might hypothesize about the features of play that cause the pro to execute a lob or a groundstroke. Hypotheses are confirmed or altered through continued observation, until the pattern features are known. Alternatively, the student might seek reasons by consulting the tennis pro directly. Seeking information overcomes the major weakness of the hypothesizing tactic, inefficiency. However, the virtue of hypothesizing is that it can be used in situations where expert advice is not available.

Practice tactics. Other aspects of procedural learning include the acquisition of basic component actions (subskills) and, ultimately, the development of smooth complex performances that combine those subskills. There are learning tactics that can help students derive maximum benefit from their practice sessions. One example is part practice, whereby the student attempts to improve a complex performance by perfecting and automating an important subcomponent of that performance. For example, a student might greatly improve performance on mathematics tests by memorizing and practicing square-root tables. Or performance in tennis might be improved by concentrating practice on service and smashes. Part practice should be alternated with whole practice (Schneider 1985), whereby the student practices the full complex performance with little attention to individual subskills.

Reflective self-instruction. Another class of procedural learning tactics is reflective self-instruction, whereby the student attempts to improve personal performance by studying an expert model. For example, a student might videotape her tennis swing and compare that to a tape of an expert's swing. Or the student might critically compare her homework solution for a geometry proof to the teacher's expert solution presented on the board. Reflective self-instruction can concentrate either on specific component subskills or on whole complex performances. One key to successful self-instruction is the availability of adequate performance models. By providing models of expert performance and guiding students in how to benefit from those models while learning, teachers can provide training in the valuable technique of reflective self-instruction.

Mental support tactics

Acquiring useful knowledge in school is a lengthy and difficult process demanding a great investment of time and effort on the part of the student. Thus, tactics are needed for helping learners maintain a positive attitude and a high state of motivation during learning and practice. Researchers (e.g., Dansereau et al. 1979, 1985; Meichenbaum 1980; McCombs 1981-82) recommend several types of support tactics: (1) behavioral self-management, (2) mood management, and (3) self-monitoring (see fig. 3).

The behavioral self-management category includes such tactics as breaking a complex learning chore into subgoals, developing a schedule for meeting subgoals, devising a reporting procedure for charting progress, and devising a self-reward system for completing major subgoals. Mood management tactics include concentration and relaxation techniques (useful for combating test anxiety); and positive self-talk, used to establish and maintain a positive frame of mind before and during learning and performance (e.g., Meichenbaum 1980). Finally, an example of self-monitoring is the technique of stopping periodically during learning and practice to

Verbal information is likely to be called into service only if it is understood when learned and only if it is stored in memory within well-structured, well-elaborated networks of meaningfully related ideas.

check and, if necessary, readjust strategy, concentration, and mood.

Frequently used by professional athletes, mental support tactics can also be used by students to increase academic performance and motivation

and to decrease tension associated with evaluation. They are applicable to all types of learning situations and can be combined with both verbal and procedural learning tactics in study assignments. For example, to study for a history test, a student might devise a learning strategy that orchestrates several specific tactics, such as positive self-talk with self-checking (to maintain motivation), networking (to help organize facts in a meaningful way), and use of imagery or mnemonics (to help with memorization).

Strategy-Building as Problem Solving

The ultimate aim of tactics training is to provide students with tools that will enable them, as autonomous learners, to devise their own strategies. Unfortunately, a persistent problem in strategy training has been students' failure to apply tactics in situations outside the class in which they were learned originally.

However, several training techniques can alleviate these problems. A large number of researchers (e.g., Baron 1981, Bransford and Stein 1984) suggest teaching students to respond to all learning tasks using a general problem-solving model. For example, Derry, Jacobs, and Murphy (1987) taught soldiers to use the "4C's" to develop plans for study reading. The 4C's stood for: clarify learning situation, construct a learning strategy, carry out the strategy, and check results.

One presumed advantage of such plans is that they remind students to stop and think reflectively about each learning situation prior to proceeding with the task (Baron 1981). Also, such plans may serve as mnemonic devices that help students recall previously learned tactics associated with each step. There is some empirical support for the idea that problem-solving models enhance tactics transfer (Belmont et al. 1982).

Another procedure for inducing tactics transfer is informed training (Campione et al. 1982, Pressley et al. 1984). This procedure enhances direct tactics instruction with explicit information regarding the effectiveness of various tactics, including how and when they should be used. As Levin (1986) points out, there are different learning tools for different learning jobs. With informed training,

students learn that tactics selection is always influenced by the nature of the instructional material as well as the nature of the learning goal. For example, if a text is not highly struc-

Two distinct types of strategies instruction are needed: specific tactics training and training in methods for selecting and combining tactics into workable learning plans.

tured and the primary aim of study is to comprehend and remember important ideas, a strategy that combines networking with idea elaboration would be appropriate. However, if the aim is primarily comprehension rather than retention, a schema-building technique alone would suffice. Informed training is superior to "blind training" in producing transfer and sustained use of specific learning tactics (Pressley et al. 1984, Campione et al. 1982).

Previously I suggested that teachers can help develop students' learning skills by devising, assigning, and explaining learning strategies and by providing feedback on strategy use. Such established classroom practices are excellent vehicles for informed training.

Learning Strategies Should Produce Useful Knowledge

Cognitive psychology has taught us much about the nature and structure of usable knowledge. Verbal information is likely to be called into service only if it is understood when learned and only if it is stored in memory **within well-structured, well-elaborated networks of meaningfully related ideas. Procedural skills, on the other hand, are likely to be accessed and accurately executed only if they have been devel-**

oped through extensive practice and only if the environmental patterns that indicate their applicability are well learned. If the primary aim of schooling is the creation of useful knowledge, then strategy application should result in the deliberate creation of a well-structured knowledge base, whether verbal, procedural, or both.

It is unlikely that reliance on any single learning tactic alone will ensure the creation of well-constructed knowledge. Rather, multiple tactics are usually required. For example, if an elaboration technique is applied for the purpose of enhancing individual ideas, another schema-building tactic may be needed to tie related ideas together. Or if practice is used to perfect a specific aspect of procedural performance, a pattern-learning tactic may still be needed to ensure that the skill is executed only when appropriate. Thus, useful knowledge is most likely to evolve through a dynamic process requiring, first, an informed analysis of each learning problem, then selection and combining of all the learning tactics needed to produce a well-formed mental structure.

Not every learning strategy produces useful knowledge. Some strategies lead to isolated, unstructured bits of learning that will remain forever inert. For this reason, both teachers and students should be aware of the nature and form of useful knowledge and of learning strategies that are likely to facilitate its creation.

Strategy Training for Lifelong Learning

Students who receive good strategy training during their years in school can acquire a form of knowledge especially useful in coping with the wide variety of learning situations they will encounter throughout their lives. Given the amount of time that people spend in school, in job-related training, and in acquiring knowledge associated with their interests and hobbies, the ability to find good solutions to learning problems may be the most important thinking skill of all.

References

Anderson, J.R. (1983). *The Architecture of Cognition*. Cambridge, Mass.: Harvard University Press.
Baron, J. (1981). "Reflective Thinking as a Goal of Education." *Intelligence* 5: 291-309.
Belmont, J.M., E.C. Butterfield, and R.P. Ferretti. (1982). "To Secure Transfer of Training Instruct Self-Management Skills." In *How and How Much Can Intelligence Be Increased*, edited by D.K. Detterman and R.J. Sternberg, pp. 147-154. Norwood, N.J.: ABLEX.
Bransford, J.D., and B.S. Stein. (1984). *The Ideal Problem Solver: A Guide For Improving Thinking, Learning, and Creativity*. New York: Freeman.
Campione, J.C., A.L. Brown, and R.A. Ferrara. (1982). "Mental Retardation and Intelligence." In *Cognitive Strategy Research: Educational Applications*, edited by R.J. Sternberg, pp. 87-126. New York: Springer-Verlag.
Cook, L.K., and R.E. Mayer. (1983). "Reading Strategies Training for Meaningful Learning from Prose." In *Cognitive Strategy Research: Educational Applications*, edited by M. Pressley and J.R. Levin, pp. 87-126. New York: Springer-Verlag.
Dansereau, D.F. (1985). "Learning Strategy Research." In *Thinking and Learning Skills*, edited by J. W. Segal, S.F. Chipman, and R. Glaser, vol. 1, pp. 209-240. Hillsdale, N.J.: Erlbaum.
Dansereau, D.F., K.W. Collins, B.A. McDonald, C.D. Holley, J.C. Garland, G.M. Diekhoff, and S.H Evans. (1979). "Development and Evaluation of an Effective Learning Strategy Program." *Journal of Educational Psychology* 79: 64-73.
Derry, S.J., J. Jacobs, and D.A. Murphy. (1987). "The JSEP Learning Skills Training System." *Journal of Educational Technology Systems* 15, 4: 273-284.
Derry, S.J., and D.A. Murphy. (1986). "Designing Systems That Train Learning Ability: From Theory to Practice." *Review of Educational Research* 56, 1: 1-39.
Gagne, E.D. (1985). *The Cognitive Psychology of School Learning*. Boston: Little, Brown and Company.
Levin, J.R. (1986). "Four Cognitive Principles of Learning-Strategy Instruction." *Educational Psychologist* 21, 1 and 2: 3-17.
McCombs, B.L. (1981-82). "Transitioning Learning Strategies Research in Practice: Focus on the Student in Technical Training." *Journal of Instructional Development* 5: 10-17.
McKeachie, W.J. (1984). "Spatial Strategies: Critique and Educational Implications." In *Spatial Learning Strategies: Techniques, Applications, and Related Issues*, edited by C.D. Holley and D.F. Dansereau, pp. 301-312. Orlando, Fla.: Academic Press.
Meichenbaum, D.H. (1980). "A Cognitive-Behavioral Perspective on Intelligence." *Intelligence* 4: 271-283.
Pressley, M., J.G. Borkowski, and J.T. O'Sullivan. (1984). "Memory Strategy Instruction Is Made of This: Metamemory and Durable Strategy Use." *Educational Psychologist* 19: 94-107.
Pressley, M., J.G. Borkowski, and W. Schneider. (In press a). "Cognitive Strategies: Good Strategy Users Coordinate Metacognition and Knowledge." In *Annals of Child Development*, edited by R. Vasta and G. Whitehurst, vol. 4. Greenwich, Conn.: JAI Press.
Pressley, M., F. Goodchild, J. Fleet, R. Zajchowski, and E.D. Evans. (In press b). "The Challenges of Classroom Strategy Instruction." In *The Elementary School Journal*.
Schneider, W. (1985). "Training High-Performance Skills: Fallacies and Guidelines." *Human Factors* 27: 285-300.
Snowman, J., and R. McCown. (April 1984). "Cognitive Processes In Learning: A Model for Investigating Strategies and Tactics." Paper presented at the annual meeting of the American Educational Research Association, New Orleans.
Weinstein, C.E., and R.E. Mayer. (1985). "The Teaching of Learning Strategies." In *Handbook of Research on Teaching*, 3rd ed., edited by M.C. Wittrock. New York: Macmillan.

Linking Metacognition to Classroom Success

Martin N. Ganz
Incarnate Word College

Barbara C. Ganz
Pima Community College

Traditionally, the task of teaching students the fundamentals of study strategies has been in the domain of elementary educators. For the most part, their efforts have been satisfactory for students at this stage of intellectual growth. However, problems begin to arise as elementary students enter secondary education and begin their transition to the next developmental stage. The study strategies they developed in the elementary school are often incomplete for the secondary school setting with its more formalized learning environment.

In response to this, and to the ever-increasing problem of retaining students in school by preventing failure, secondary teachers are showing interest in helping their students master skills necessary to study and learn. Teachers and administrators who recognize the importance of learning skills also understand the importance of going beyond the classroom framework to develop the whole person. To these professionals, helping students develop useful study habits and positive attitudes and ultimately graduate is as important as the subject matter that may be their expertise.

Secondary teachers must realize that students were not likely taught how to adapt their study habits to a variety of learning situations during the elementary years. In fact, any attempt to do so would probably have met with little success, given the nature of children at that stage of intellectual development. It is therefore critical for secondary teachers to help students mature the learning skills they need for success. While the goal of improving study habits and further developing the skills the students already have is important, current methods used to reach desired outcomes must be modified and enhanced if success is to be achieved. Success should not be defined solely from the standpoint of student mastery of subject matter, but rather from the perspective of helping students develop a major self-control process, metacognitive skills processing.

Metacognitive skills are related to thinking about thinking, and more precisely, thinking about one's own learning. Teaching about this process should not be random or capricious. It can be accomplished in any classroom with a teacher who understands the learning process and wants to help students achieve. Students who develop metacognitive skills are far more likely to be able to make the changes needed in their own study habits and learning strategies when faced with unfamiliar tasks or challenges than students who do not.

What Is Metacognition?

Metacognition, or the act of thinking about one's own thinking, is necessary to ensure efficient learning. Dirkes (1985) points out that students who direct their own thinking commonly do three things: connect new information to former knowledge; select thinking abilities directly; and relate time and degrees to certainty of purpose. Dirkes refers to these activities as executive strategies and defines awareness of them as metacognition. Costa (1984) defines metacognition as the ability to know what one doesn't know. He further states, "Some people are unaware of their own thinking process. They are unable to describe the steps or strategies they use during the act of problem-solving. They cannot transform into words the visual images held in their minds. They seldom evaluate the quality of their own thinking skills" (p. 198).

The importance of spending effort on the development of thinking-about-thinking skills in all young people becomes especially clear when it is realized that students who are able learners develop these skills intuitively. The simplest example of a metacognitive skill is when students realized that after doing poorly on a test, they are not learning through the use of one study technique and will therefore need to try a different one. Brown and DeLoache (1977) believe that determining a desired goal and planning the steps required to achieve that goal are desirable metacognitive skills.

Many students have a goal of improving a grade at some point in their education. Fulfilling that goal can become a source of serious frustration. There are several causes for the lack of academic success many students experience, including immature metacognitive knowledge and strategies as well as the lack of motivation, attention, and effort to employ strategic activity (Ryan, 1982). Failing to determine a goal for learning or failing to think about the steps required to achieve that goal may also be included here. Students often realize that they do not understand what was read or heard, but then fail to act on this understanding. This practice can reinforce an existing negative view of their ability or lead them to believe that they are poor learners. A more precise explanation would be that they are too passive in their learning attempts. They do not practice the self-control and self-correction necessary to become better learners. It is interesting to note that at a time when these skills should be developing, the drop-out problem drops in.

Developing Metacognition

Self-interrogation is an important metacognitive technique. By asking questions of themselves, students can monitor themselves, predict and hypothesize, assess feelings of understanding or lack of understanding in order to choose and employ a self-correction strategy, and integrate new information with existing information. Examples of questions that monitor learning or comprehension include the following: Should I slow down here? Can I skip the additional clarifying explanation? Can I picture this situation or information in my mind? To predict and hypothesize, students might ask themselves such questions as, What do I think will happen next? Do I think this is fiction or nonfiction? Was that piece of information related to what I read on the last page or paragraph?

Assessing one's feelings of understanding is also important for comprehension and learning. Students could ask, Did this make sense? Can I say this in my own words? Can I make a judgment now? To assess their lack of understanding, students might ask, Is this part harder than previous information? Do I get what the author is saying here? What does this word mean? Will this make sense later? This type of introspection is critical because the selection and employment of correction strategies is based upon it. Students need to know if they should reread, continue, slow their speed, find assistance, or choose a different strategy.

After learning new information, the self-interrogation should not stop. Students should continue to reflect on their information by asking themselves such questions as, Can I make some generalizations, and are they fitting? Can I draw some conclusions, and are they plausible? Is this similar to anything that I already know?

The development of metacognitive skills is not inherited; nor is it achieved through passive attendance at school each day. It is a process that must be presented to adolescents with a cohesive, carefully planned strategy. Those who have experienced the intrinsic satisfaction that comes from being in control of their own educational success know the motivational factor that is directly connected with that control.

Using Metacognitive Skills

To examine metacognitive abilities, it is important to look at the difference between what efficient, mature learners do and what less proficient, immature learners do during their study process. Most basic is the notion that mature learners treat studying as a purposeful, attention-directing, self-questioning act, while less mature learners possess naive theories about what it takes to learn new information and to meet certain task and text demands (Brown et al., 1982). Mature learners engage in purposeful strategic learning activities tailored specifically to the demands of each task. If necessary, they develop new strategies. Less mature learners, on the other hand, do not necessarily introduce appropriate learning strategies. If they do, they may be inflexible in adapting these strategies to different text or task situations. Furthermore, they are often impeded by inferior, inefficient strategies which result in only partial success but are consistently applied in a variety of situations. Such inflexibility of approach may stem from the fact that students feel most comfortable using one kind of strategy, do not know any other strategies, or fail to realize it may be their strategic action, rather than their lack of ability, impeding their learning.

As learners mature, they become increasingly able to predict the essential elements of the text (Brown and Smiley, 1977). Evidence of this was seen during research with young through college-age learners. Some of the students spontaneously began to underline or take notes. Not only was this study strategy used spontaneously, the ideas highlighted were also considered the important elements of the text. Students induced to adopt a note-taking strategy, however, were not as sensitive to the main elements; their notations were more random. The very immature learners underlined almost all of the text when told to underline. Their skill did improve with instruction but never reached the level of the spontaneous user.

Students who are able to extract main ideas will benefit from study time. They know what to attend to first so that more detailed information may be built upon basic ideas. Mature learners use this building process to flesh out meaning. Developing learners also use it but take more trials to come upon the strategy themselves (Baker, 1980). Unless basic ideas are extracted, study time becomes an exercise in passive rereading or in rote memorization without understanding.

Self-testing, or rehearsal, is another appropriate study technique for all learners because it helps them realize what has not been learned and acts as a rehearsal procedure for learning. Rehearsal allows a transfer of information from short-term to long-term memory (Bransford, 1979). The more rehearsal attempts, the greater the probability of retention of information. The success of information retrieval for an exam or a problem-solving task depends on how specifically the information was encoded during the time of acquisition and on the quality of the retrieval schemes in the mind of the learner. Questioning gives practice in retrieving information and thus reduces the amount of forgetting. Therefore, self-interrogation is an effective study technique for recall of information and is more efficient than other techniques such as passive, desperate rereading. It is important for students to engage in self-interrogation because they often don't realize that they have inadequate preparation for a test or other similar task until it is too late.

Deciding what information needs further attention before a detailed understanding is achieved can also be accomplished through attempts to summarize materials. Baker and Brown (1980) suggest five operation for effective summarizing: delete redundance; delete trivia; provide superordinate terms or labels for items that can be grouped; select topic sentences; and invent topic sentences where missing. Summarizing can be taught and is an important check that a student both understands and remembers the material. Some students find that studying from a summary is easier than returning to the complete text.

Learning information does not always mean that the learner will be able to transfer it to different contexts, problems, or roles. Effective learners hypothesize different contexts in which information may be used. Experiences in multiple contexts increase the probability of effective transfer (Brown et al., 1982). Another element that plays a role in effective transfer is acknowledging that certain information, formulas, or concepts are meant to be applicable to various situations. Students need to see how things can be applied generally so that they too learn to put their learning in different contexts. Students also need to see how a new situation is related to one previously encountered. An understanding of situational relationships can aid information transfer.

Research Findings

Subject-matter teachers are aware of the importance of fostering good reading and study habits among students if their own efforts in the classroom are to be fruitful. Accordingly, much of the early research in the teaching of metacognitive skills has come from reading. Andre and Anderson (1979) determined that the metacognitive technique of self-generated questions during study led to improved performance on tests requiring comprehension. A recent study by Stevens (1988) demonstrated that training remedial reading students in metacognitive strategies improved their ability to identify the main idea of expository paragraphs.

Research in a variety of disciplines supports the need for metacognitive training for general classroom success. As an example, Bean et al. (1986) reported on the effect of metacognitive instruction on a tenth-grade world history class. Their study showed that the use of graphic organizer construction (a technique that expands study strategies beyond outlining) was enhanced by metacognitive training. The authors further noted that "secondary students are eager to expand their metacognitive strategies" (p. 167). Some students reported using the strategies in their biology class, especially on difficult sections of the text.

Research also suggests that metacognitive strategies training can help students be successful as young adults. Mikulecky and Ehlinger (1986) studied the higher level literacy demands placed on young people competing in today's workplace by investigating the effects of metacognitive instruction on electronic technicians. Electronic technicians, according to the study, spend nearly 2.5 hours daily in job-related reading and writing. Results indicate that "metacognitive aspects of literacy did consistently and significantly correlate to job performance" (p. 41). Also significant for students directed toward a profession requiring higher education is a study by Lundeberg (1987). This study centered on the reading strategies used by lawyers and law professors, since "legal educators profess to build minds rather than fill them" (p. 409). Lundeberg's findings indicated that metacognitive strategies significantly improved comprehension, especially of beginning law students.

As these studies suggest, waiting for students to mature into skilled learners is not an educationally viable position. There are many strategies to be learned, and while some students may discover them intuitively, others will require induced learning.

Conclusion

The key to better education for the complex world of the future is producing more efficient, independent learners who can complete their educational goals. It is only through a combination of three kinds of knowledge — strategic learning-to-learn skills, metacognitive abilities, and factual information from content courses — that students will develop self-direction and self-regulation abilities for learning. All teachers, at all levels, need to show students that successful learning is a continually active process requiring internal monitoring and control over a learning situation. Students can be shown strategies for improvements; moreover, they can be encouraged to develop them for themselves.

Individuals play the central role in their own learning. Students who do not take responsibility for their thinking and learning may exhibit symptoms of learned helplessness. If they see no relation between effort and the attainment of their goals, they may become lethargic (Thomas, 1979). Their efforts could be curtailed and their self-esteem might suffer. Sometimes after acquiring this helpless attitude, students fail to perform tasks that they could do at a previous time. Therefore, aside from the academic advantages of the learning-to-learn skills, there may be social and emotional advantages in affording students the opportunity to reduce passive, helpless attitudes that result in only a minimal effort to avoid a failing grade or even dropping out.

Considering that forgetting occurs rather quickly after exposure to material, content-area teachers who just fill students with factual knowledge soon find that students are left with very little of anything important. Thoughtful teaching professionals must move away from antiquated approaches toward a credible pedagogical alternative of teaching students to control their own learning. However, as was pointed out by Porter and Brophy (1988), "...helping students is not sufficient by itself to insure mastery of those strategies" (p. 79). Teachers need to incorporate these strategies into their lesson structure and encourage their use for class so that the strategies can be mastered. Teachers can determine if their efforts to teach and improve metacognitive skills have been successful by asking specific questions about what is going on in their students' minds as they think through various problems. Students who are developing metacognitive skills will be able to describe their thinking process, mental organization, and future strategies when coping with a problem.

As Wiens (1983) points out, "As students enter adolescence, their ability to engage in abstract thinking increases and their 'self-consciousness' takes on new meanings with real implications for being able to control their own thinking and behavior. An understanding of metacognitive skills can greatly enhance an adolescent student's ability to use appropriate strategies in learning" (p. 144).

References

Andre, M.E., and Anderson, T.H. (1970). "The Development and Evaluation of a Self-Questioning Study Technique." *Reading Research Quarterly, 14,* 605-623.

Baker, L., and Brown, A. (1980). "Metacognitive Skills and Reading." *Tech. Report 188* (November). Center for the Study of Reading, University of Illinois, Urbana-Champaign.

Bean, T.W., Singer, H., Sorter, J., and Frazee, C. (1986). "The Effect of Metacognitive Instruction in Outlining and Graphic Organizer Construction on Student's Comprehension in a Tenth-Grade World History Class."

Journal of Reading Behavior, 28(2), 153-169.

Bransford, J. (1979). "Human Cognition: Learning, Understanding, and Remembering." Belmont, Calif.: Wadsworth Publishing.

Brown, A., Bransford, J., Ferrara, R., and Campione, J. (1982). "Learning, Remembering and Understanding." *Tech. Report 244* (June). Center for the Study of Reading, University of Illinois, Urbana-Champaign.

Brown, A., and DeLoache, J. (1977). "Skills, Plans, and Self-Regulation." *Tech. Report 48* (July). Center for the Study of Reading, University of Illinois, Urbana-Champaign.

Brown, A., and Smiley, S. (1977). "Development of Strategies for Studying Prose Passages." *Tech. Report 48* (October). Center for the Study of Reading, University of Illinois, Urbana-Champaign.

Costa, A. (1984). "Thinking: How Do We Know Students Are Getting Better at It?" *Roeper Review, 6*(4), 197-199.

Dirkes, M. (1985). "Metacognition: Students in Charge of Their Thinking." *Roeper Review, 8*(2), 96-100.

Lundeberg, M.A. (1987). "Metacognitive Aspects of Reading Comprehension: Studying Understanding in Legal Case Analysis." *Reading Research Quarterly, 22*(4), 407-432.

Mikulecky, L., and Ehlinger, J. (1986). "The Influence of Metacognitive Aspects of Literacy on Job Performance of Electronic Technicians." *Journal of Reading Behavior, 18*(1), 41-62.

Porter, A.C., and Brophy, J. (1988). "Synthesis of Research on Good Teaching: Insights From the Work of the Institute for Research on Teaching." *Educational Leadership, 45*(8), 74-85.

Ryan, E.B. (1982). "Two Causes of Underachievement." *Forum, 3*(2), Winter. The English Composition Board, University of Michigan.

Stevens, R.J. (1988). "Effects of Strategy Training on the Identification of the Main Idea of Expository Passages." *Journal of Educational Psychology, 80*(1), 21-26.

Thomas, A. (1979). "Learned Helplessness and Expectancy Factors: Implications for Research in Learning Disabilities." *Review of Educational Research, 49*(2), 208-221.

Wiens, J.W. (1983). "Metacognition and the Adolescent Passive Learner." *Journal of Learning Disabilities, 16*(3), 144-149.

Practicing Positive Reinforcement

Ten Behavior Management Techniques

THOMAS R. McDANIEL

Dr. McDaniel is a professor of education and director of graduate education studies at Converse College in Spartanburg, South Carolina.

Almost all teachers know something about behavior modification. Somewhere in their training they have learned the importance of positive reinforcement. That "praise is better than punishment" in managing behavior has become almost trite. And yet, negativism abounds in public school classrooms today. For most practicing teachers it is a long step between knowing the principles of positive reinforcement and using them consistently, frequently, and successfully.

One reason that day-to-day practices of teachers do not demonstrate familiarity with behavioral psychology is that the practices often run counter to their growing-up experiences. Like their parents, teachers tend to *assume* good behavior, to accept it as commonplace, and to ignore it on the grounds that this communicates the normal expectation for good behavior. "Let sleeping dogs lie" is a common principle of child rearing. A second reason for the infrequent use of behavioral principles in classrooms is that teachers learn to intervene quickly to squelch misbehavior. Since students will test the teacher's alertness, the vigilant teacher often learns from students to apply "desist statements," which often start with negative terms: "Stop," "Don't," "No." A third reason that teachers do not frequently use positive reinforcement is that their teacher education courses seldom teach them how to apply such principles to improve discipline and classroom management. We teacher-educators often tell prospective teachers that they *should* be positive, but neglect to give them specific training to show them *how to* apply the principles in specific situations.

I list ten practical and specific techniques that are derived from behavioral psychology. Each of the ten rests on solid research of Neo-Skinnerian educators and psychologists. Each principle contains a suggestion for how to put positive reinforcement to work for more effective classroom discipline.

Teach Specific Directions

Few teachers realize how many of their discipline problems are a consequence of poor, vague, or unspecific directions. We make the mistake, especially in elementary school, of assuming that students know how to perform all kinds of instructional and behavioral assignments. It is not enough to tell students to begin work on their math assignment, to line up for lunch, and to get ready for dismissal. To maximize good behavior, teachers should teach students exactly what is required. This takes some forethought and at least a little effort, but it is well worth the time it takes.

Example: "Class, it is now time to begin work on your math assignment. When I give you the signal, I want you to (1) put all your supplies away, (2) take out your math books and two pencils, and (3) quietly open your books to page 12 and do the first five problems on that page. . . . I see that everyone is ready. Mary Lou, what are the three things you are going to do when I give you the signal? Very good. All right, begin." At this point the teacher should watch to see that every student is following the three simple steps to beginning the math work. The wise teacher will maximize good behavior by making expectations for behavior so clear, direct, and unambiguous that every student will know precisely what is expected. Such expectations increase the likelihood that students will behave the way you want them to.

Look for Good Behavior

This is the "catch 'em being good" principle so central to positive reinforcement. If the first principle asks you to communicate specific expectations, the second requires you to follow through by looking for those who are complying with the expectation. Here is a good opportunity to use "positive repetitions." You repeat each of your specific directions as you see students following them. If one seems *not* to be following the directions, use a positive repetition on the student closest to him or her if you can. This technique is called "proximity praise."

Example: You have just given directions for the assignment and then you say, "Freddy has put all his materials away; Claudette has her math book and two pencils; Clarence is starting quietly to work on the first five problems on page 12." The effect that such positive repetitions can have is sometimes amazing. It is important that you remember to find the examples of good behavior rather than criticizing those who are not following the expectations. Many students get special attention and special service by *mis*behaving so that teachers will provide them extra attention in the classroom. The message you want to give students is that your attention is always focused on those who are doing what you expect them to do.

Praise Effectively

Much research has been done on effective praise. Verbal praise can be a powerful tool if teachers understand the requirements of effective praise. One of these requirements is that the teacher give descriptive details, as in the second example. The teacher should describe the specific thing he or she likes about the student's behavior. Too often we are too general in our praise. So, a teacher should not merely say, "You are doing a good job on your drawing," but should provide specific details to give meaning to the general term "good job." Another important element of effective praise is to concentrate on the behavior rather than on the person. The phrase, "I like the way . . . " is one specific teacher assertion that can help the teacher focus on what students do rather than on who they are.

Example: "Class, you are doing a good job on your drawing. I like the way that so many of you are using the entire page for your work. I also like the way you are using contrasting colors to make your picture more interesting. I see that some of you are working hard to put details on your pictures of people. I like the way these details make the people look so real."

Praise can be overdone, of course, and it should be sincere. I suspect that teachers could use more praise,

especially to compliment students on how they came into the room quietly and promptly, how they started to work efficiently, how they took turns at the pencil sharpener, how they raised their hands to ask for permission to contribute in class, and how they kept the classroom free of trash. Some teachers even use what is called "anticipatory praise" to encourage students to behave in the way that the teacher would like. "We are about to go to lunch, class. I really appreciate your picking up the scrap paper around your desk before we leave for the lunch room." This praising *before* the fact can be much more effective than the normal practice of complaining about the messiness of the room.

Model Good Behavior

Most teachers realize that a student's behavior is learned more from example than from admonitions. Because students "do as we do" rather than "do as we say," it is important that we provide appropriate models. The teacher should demonstrate how things ought to be done. Explicit modeling is found frequently in art rooms, gymnasiums, and automotive shops. Appropriate modeling should be found more frequently in all academic classrooms. Teachers might, for example, model their thinking processes as they explain a math problem or a literary question. In the area of classroom management, a teacher can demonstrate how to move from center to center, how to enter and exit the room, how to do such simple things as sit in chairs and raise hands for permission to move. A quick review of the three previous principles might suggest that what good behavior modifiers do is set up situations that allow the teacher to use students as models.

Example: Consider your own behavior. Are you prompt and well organized when you come to class? Do you keep your voice level low and calm? When students are working quietly at their seats, do you tiptoe around and whisper softly to individuals to show that you respect their need for quiet? You should be the best example of the behavior you expect from your students. Also, consider your use of student models. Do you train demonstration groups that can be used to show how a small group discussion should be conducted? Do you select competent students to role-play good manners in a classroom? Do you take opportunities to role-play conflict resolutions so that students can demonstrate effective ways to solve interpersonal problems? If not, consider ways by which you might more effectively use the modeling principle.

Use Nonverbal Reinforcement

You can go beyond modeling to use a variety of practices that show approval for the kind of behavior you want in a classroom. Facial expressions are especially meaningful for nonverbal reinforcement. Most teachers eventually learn to use smiles, nods, and touch to show approval. Truly effective behavior modifiers use a great deal of nonverbal reinforcement. As they teach, they look at students and smile as if to say, "I see you are paying attention."

Example: "Class, I have this empty jar. Whenever I see you behaving well, I will drop a marble in the jar. At first I may tell you exactly why I am doing that, or on certain days I may tell you that I will only drop a marble in when I see examples of a particular behavior, such as concentration on your work, efficiency in completing assignments, or following the hand-raising rule." This allows you to teach students to respond to your nonverbal reinforcement system. This requires that you pair verbal and nonverbal reinforcement initially, but over time you gradually phase out the verbal part of the process.

Establish Token Economies

Students can quickly learn that each marble in the jar is a token that may represent, for example, free time. Each token might be worth fifteen seconds of free time to be cashed in at the end of the day. Or the teacher might indicate that each marble counts toward a record-playing session (music of the students' choice) to be cashed in when the students have earned 100 marbles. If your classes are small, token economies can be highly

---

. . . If you have been following the principles outlined so far, a total system of positive reinforcement is already operating in your classroom.

---

individualized. Special education teachers frequently are able to establish complex and sophisticated token economies, rewarding each student on his or her individual reinforcement card. That is more difficult to do in regular classrooms, but sometimes can be arranged with those few students who need extra structure and extra incentive. The underlying behavior principle here is contingency management. Rewards or reinforcers are contingent upon the students' demonstrating a specific behavior. This is sometimes called "Grandma's rule": if you eat your spinach, then you can have peach cobbler. Token economies are ways by which students can see their progress toward some longer range goal that is contingent upon the accumulation of successive approximations toward the goal. Tokens mark the small steps —and reward them.

Example: "Students, if you get every answer correct on this quiz, you will not have any homework tonight" (Grandma's rule). "Class, I am keeping a record of who has handed in every homework assignment during the week. Those of you who have a perfect record at the end of the week will get a special certificate. Students who get four certificates will get a special field trip" (token economy).

Premack

Premacking (a technique named after David Premack, who first described this idea in detail) asks the teacher to let students determine the reinforcers for appropriate behavior. Premacking reminds us that a reinforcer is in the eye of the beholder. The teacher must give students the opportunity to identify what they want for rewards and to exercise choice in setting up a token economy.

Example: You might observe what students prefer to do during free time when given the opportunity to exercise choice. Keep a record of which students use their free time to (a) converse with other students, (b) do their homework, (c) sleep or rest, (d) play games, (e) read comic books. If you can identify several reinforcers that motivate your students, use them to set up a reward system that the whole class will embrace.

Teach Kids to Reinforce One Another

While an effective teacher knows how to reinforce students and knows how to identify the rewards (verbal, nonverbal, token) that can be used for reinforcing expected behavior, effective teachers also teach students to praise one another. Actually, if you have been following the principles outlined so far, a total system of positive reinforcement is already operating in your classroom. If you are an effective reinforcer, you are also a good model of how people might interact with one another in positive ways. You should give students an opportunity to practice what you have been modeling in the classroom. Some teachers, following the "One-Minute Manager" prescription, ask students to take one minute to tell another student what they like about his or her behavior. Students can be not only negative toward their classmates but downright cruel. Providing opportunities for students to describe *good* things they see in their classmates can be a valuable practice. What you can do with one-minute praisings is to train students to be positive and to use the principles of positive reinforcement in their relationships with other students.

Example: "Students, we have a few minutes now at the end of the day to think about our behavior. I would like you to work in pairs to tell one of your classmates what he or she has done today that is praiseworthy. Do not discuss character or personality—only those things that your partner has done during the day that you think deserve a compliment. This should take no more than one minute. When you finish, reverse the process and let your partner compliment you on specific things you have done today that might be complimented." This can be awkward and unnatural; however, handled skillfully, these could be some of the most important minutes in the class day. This teaches students to look for good behavior in their classmates.

3. LEARNING: Behavioristic

Teach Kids to Reinforce Themselves

Students can benefit from observing their own behavior and complimenting themselves on their performance. The practice forces them to look for their strengths and can improve self-concept. This should be a serious, but not somber, enterprise. Just as we parents and teachers often do, students tend to ignore good behavior. Setting up explicit opportunities to identify one's own good behavior can counteract that tendency.

Example: "Students, we are at the end of another successful day. I would like each of you to write down on a piece of paper as many responses as you can to this phrase: 'Today I learned. . . .' When you get home be sure to share your list with a parent. Next, write down as many responses as you can to this phrase: 'My behavior was successful today because. . . .' Here, students, you should list as many kind things that you have done for yourself or others as you can. Now, get started."

Vary Positive Reinforcement

There are many practices that you can use to keep your reinforcement practices changing and improving. New techniques, new reinforcers, and new ideas can help keep your classroom sparkling.

Example: Vary any typical practices you may have by having some surprise reinforcers. If you are using the marble jar, for example, announce that the class has won some bonus marbles because of especially good behavior at the assembly program. Or, as a surprise reinforcement, cancel a homework assignment because the students have done so well on the in-class drill. Use positive notes either to parents or to students themselves. A simple personal hand-written note to a student that says, "Johnny, I certainly do appreciate how hard you have been trying to remember to bring your books to class" may do more than all of your reprimands combined. Establish a "rewards committee" to come up with some suggestions for reinforcers that would appeal to the class. Being on the rewards committee itself could be an important reward. Ask students to stop their work and to imagine themselves successfully performing a given task. Athletes frequently go through the mental process of reinforcing their imagined success on the tennis court or basketball court or track. Why not give your students an opportunity to do the same?

Example: "Students, we are getting ready to go out to the buses for the field trip. I want you to imagine yourself walking quietly down the hall in single file, getting on the bus in an orderly fashion, and conversing quietly as we move. When we get back, we will compare your mental image with your actual performance. Now, is everybody ready to go?"

These ten principles of positive reinforcement can help you practice what has been so often preached to you. If you successfully apply the principles of positive reinforcement in your day-to-day work with students, you will find that you not only develop your own skills of reinforcement but that you can help students develop theirs as well. Positive reinforcement in practice can build a positive self-concept, develop an attitude of success, and enhance instructional motivation for students. Practicing positive reinforcement principles takes work, but it is work that pays dividends for the teacher who wants to make the classroom a better place in which to live.

Guidelines for Implementing a Classroom Reward System

Ellen H. Bacon

Ellen H. Bacon, PhD, is currently an assistant professor at Western Carolina University in Cullowhee, NC. Address: Ellen H. Bacon, 215 Killian, Western Carolina University, Cullowhee, NC 28723.

Several issues must be considered before implementing a reward system in the classroom.

When special education teachers consult with regular classroom teachers, they frequently are asked about how to set up a reward system for a classroom. This article presents a practical sequence for setting up a group reward system and some guidelines for making key decisions about implementation and termination of the program.

Reward systems that can be used with all members of a class take careful planning and thought. One first-year teacher, despairing of her lack of control, brought in a bag of lemon drops and announced to the class that all children who were good would receive a lemon drop at the end of the day. While the announcement got the students' attention, it generated a number of control problems. The teacher quickly learned that she had no method for monitoring "good" behavior or any criteria by which to decide who should not receive the lemon drops. Some students began in earnest to determine what "being good" meant and if "being good" the last hour of the day would suffice. A second group, whose members did not like lemon drops, reacted as though they had had a treat taken away from them, since they would not get a desired reward for their good behavior. These problems illustrate some of the difficulties of beginning a class reward system. However, even in this reward system, there were positive results as well as negative.

The plan, though poorly conceived and implemented, succeeded in a minimal way because it clearly communicated to the students that the teacher wanted to give them rewards for good behavior and not just punishment for inappropriate behavior. Their overall reaction was that despite its faults, this game was preferable to just staying out of trouble.

Providing group or class rewards for good behavior is a fairly complex and time-consuming activity that should be considered only with clear objectives in mind. When those objectives are reached, it is time to discard the reward system and allow natural reinforcers to maintain the behavior. Using the time, energy, and resources to maintain a class reward system is defensible only when there are clear reasons to do so and when there are objectives to be met.

One of the primary reasons for using a class reward system is to train the class to follow class rules. A class reward system is a good method for teaching appropriate behaviors to children and youth who are immature. Children in the early years are learning basic school behaviors and habits as well as basic skills. A group reward system helps the teacher address those behaviors directly and provide feedback and consequences in training those behaviors. It is sometimes assumed that basic school skills, such as not talking in the hall, writing down assignments, carrying home the right books, and completing assignments, are skills that students have mastered but deliberately and defiantly refuse to do. Frequently, the child does not have the skills to ascertain when and where certain behaviors are expected and to know how to consistently carry out the expected behaviors.

A second reason for using a group reward system is to enhance academic mastery of topics and assignments. Giving prizes to those with the best grades and to those who are intellectually gifted is not likely to improve the group's motivation. Instead, students should be rewarded for completing work and for making progress. Recognition for improvement and hard work gives students the message that their work is noticed and appreciated whether they are top stu-

3. LEARNING: Behavioristic

dents or not. Although teachers can do this without a reward system, the reward system makes the teachers more aware of all students and emphasizes their need to notice progress and give feedback to each student.

A third major reason for implementing such a system is to help regain control of an unruly class. Some years, control of a class may seem to move out of the teacher's control and into the influence of a group of students. When these students behave, the class goes smoothly, and when they misbehave, the teacher has difficulty sustaining control and implementing consequences. Many young teachers become enmeshed in these group leadership dynamics, placating the power group and giving preferential treatment to its members. Use of a group reward system with clear rules and consequences can redefine power and influence within the class and return control to a teacher, even in the middle of the year.

When to Implement Class Reward Systems

The decision to use class rewards should be made on the basis of what the teacher wants to achieve. If the goal is to teach students appropriate student behaviors, the best time to implement the system is at the beginning of the year. If the reward system is to be used to encourage completion and accuracy of academic work, it may be desirable to wait until the class is involved in difficult or tedious work such as learning to regroup in subtraction, write a research paper, or use the symbols for chemical elements. Or, if class rewards are used to regain control of a class, the best time to implement the program is when control starts to slip, not after full-scale anarchy.

Whenever a system is started, it is important for the teacher to begin to plan its demise. Few reward systems need to be sustained over an entire year. Students tire of the rewards and the game, and teachers tire of the time and energy required. They may become inconsistent in rewarding and monitoring behavior. A time limit should be set to determine when the program is going to end, though it may be extended if necessary.

In summary, class reward systems should be used to accomplish specific objectives. Some of these objectives follow:

1. To teach the class to follow rules and expectations of the class
2. To motivate students to complete difficult academic assignments and tasks
3. To regain control of a class that has powerful peer influences

Based on the reasons for implementing the system, the teacher needs to decide on when to start and finish the program and what behaviors to focus on.

Class reward systems can be used effectively with all age groups. Kindergarten children can understand and respond to simple reward systems. Also, high school students will respond if behaviors and rewards are age appropriate. Starting a class reward system involves decisions about the behaviors expected, the method of monitoring, and the reinforcers to be used.

Choosing Behaviors

Several ideas are important in choosing which behaviors will be reinforced. First, the behavior must be in the child's repertoire of possible behaviors. If a boy does not know how to work independently, setting up a reward system for him will not help, but will only add to his frustration. Therefore, there must be evidence that everyone in the class is capable of meeting the requirements for the reward.

Second, the behaviors expected must be observable and countable. If teachers cannot clearly define the behaviors, they cannot expect students to be able to know what they must do. Even when behaviors are stated clearly, a brief daily review of the expected behaviors can increase the effectiveness of a token economy. Rosenberg (1986) studied token economies and compared teachers who reviewed the rules to a group who did not. He found that the number of disruptive talk-outs was reduced 12% to 50% by giving a brief rule review each day.

Third, the behaviors must be important in the students' natural environment. The behaviors must have their own natural reinforcers that maintain the behaviors when the reward system is finished (Van Houten, 1979). A good example is a reward system for doing multiplication facts. Students may work extra hard on mastering their multiplication facts if their teacher has provided a system in which they can earn a special trip by completing their multiplication tables in a certain amount of time. Knowledge and speed with multiplication facts are important in their other schoolwork, and their grades will be improved with mastery of these facts. This behavior will continue to be rewarded. On the other hand, rewarding members of a class for writing the date at the top of the page or for not writing on the back of the paper is not likely to be continued since these behaviors are not considered important in many classes. Consequently, the behavior will not be maintained when the reward system is over.

Finally, when choosing behaviors, it is important to limit the behaviors to be reinforced. Young children will respond the best to working on one or two behaviors at a time. Upper elementary and secondary students can handle five or six behaviors at once.

Keeping Track

A second major decision to be made before implementing a system is how to keep track of what the child has earned or lost. For young children, teachers frequently use some type of manipulable object or token, such as plastic poker chips, pop beads, plastic strips, or play money. Play money can be bought or made by copying and laminating pictures of play money. Teachers who use play money successfully find that it helps students learn to add and subtract money and thus serves an educational purpose.

A second method of keeping track is the use of a paper-and-pencil system, usually a sheet for adding or subtracting points. The sheet lists the behaviors expected to earn points and then has spaces for giving the student checks for meeting expectations. Some teachers have found that using a checkbook system works well for keeping track of accounts for older students. Students accrue points that are deposited in their checking account. When students want to purchase a reward, they write a check for the amount needed. In this system, misbehavior may result in fines the student would have to pay. In addition to learning appropriate behaviors, students learn to use checks and balance a checkbook (Carter, 1988).

Another important decision is determining where the tokens or point sheets will be kept. Tokens may become a problem in themselves if students take each others' tokens, or if angry students throw all their tokens in the trash. To avoid these problems, some teachers keep all the tokens at their desks or on a separate bulletin board with containers for each child's tokens. To minimize competition, it is better not to display how many tokens each child has earned.

Similarly, point sheets kept at students' desk[s] can be a source of temptation for students to add their own points or to rip up the sheets when they are frustrated. If students are given daily point sheets, the teacher can keep accumulated point sheets in a space at the front of the room where students have limited access to them.

Reinforcers

Selection of appropriate reinforcers is critical to the success of the reward system. If students are not motivated to earn the reward, they may ignore the system or sabotage the whole effort. One of the best ways to determine appropriate reinforcers is to offer the students a list of rewards, asking them which ones are their favorites and for other suggestions (Raschke, 1981). Another system is brainstorming for other ideas. Having a list or menu of possible rewards is more effective than just having one reward available. Also, it is essential to change the rewards from time to time when students seem to tire of the menu.

Devising rewards that do not cost money should be a prime objective. Natural privileges in the classroom are good choices (Marholin, McInnis, & Heads, 1974; McLaughlin & Malaby, 1972). Often other school personnel will cooperate by letting students earn the right to be a library aide, officer worker, or counselor assistant. Having a number of choices allows students to select what is reinforcing to them. One student's favorite reward was helping the janitor pick up the trash in other classrooms.

Determining the value of each reward is one of the most challenging aspects of a system. If too many points are needed to earn simple rewards, teachers may find themselves burdened with giving out large numbers of points all day. If too few points are needed to earn the reward, students may earn the reward in spite of inappropriate behavior. Some guidelines to help in determining how many points to give are listed below:

1. Decide how often to reward the students. Young children may need their rewards daily, whereas secondary students may work for several weeks before they are rewarded.

2. Decide what percentage of available points will be needed to earn the rewards. Requiring 100% of points available will not be realistic. One common method is to price different rewards so students who only have a few points can still choose a simple reward. Looking at a magazine might be possible for students who earn 60% of the possible points, whereas using the computer to play games might require 90%. Once a reasonable percentage is selected, the number of tokens required or the price for each activity is posted where students can see them.

3. Decide how often and how many points you want to give through the day. This will depend upon how frequently you need to remind the students about the expected behaviors and upon how much time you or an aide have to award points. It is useful to award more than 1 point at the end of each class so that you have more flexibility in making judgments about behavior. A child who has been in his or her seat the entire period with the exception of 5 minutes might get 4 out of 5 points. If you have only 1 point to give for that period, you are limited to an all-or-nothing decision.

4. Decide when students will be able to receive their rewards. Setting aside time at the end of the day or the week is usually necessary. Systems do not work well when teachers are inconsistent in giving rewards and promise to make it up to the students the next day or week.

Numerous reward systems have been devised and implemented. Some of the most innovative are used to teach the money system or aspects of the economy. Although there are many variations, the most common system is for students to work for classroom privileges, free time or Friday afternoon refreshments. In spite of the advantages of reward systems, teachers have not always found reward systems to work well or to be worth the trouble of implementation. There are a number of potential problems and pitfalls teachers should consider before implementing a program.

3. LEARNING: Behavioristic

Problems and Pitfalls

Basically a reward system is an attempt to increase motivation in students using positive consequences instead of negative. If the implementation of the reward system becomes negative, the system needs to be dropped. One of the most common problems with reward systems is that the teachers become erratic and disinterested in using the system. Teachers need to have a high degree of involvement and enthusiasm for the system and be willing to spend time and energy to make the program work. Enthusiastic and consistent use of a poor reward system will work better than lackadaisical use of an excellent system.

Classroom reward systems should not be used to overtly reward some children or students above others. Further, rewards should not be used to foster a competitive environment, and failure to reach objectives should not be held up to students as punishment. Rewards should be set up so that each child has a good chance to earn the reward, and failure to meet expectations should be met with disappointment on the teacher's part and encouragement to try next time. Teachers who lapse into, "I told you so," or, "Do you remember what you did?," negate the central purpose of a reward system—to set up a positive rather than a punitive environment.

Another potential problem is inflation. As students become tired of current reinforcers, teachers feel they need to add more and more attractive (and sometimes more expensive) alternatives. A better response is to introduce a new game aspect to the system. One teacher devised a large board game at the front of the class on which students had to use class points to earn a turn. The winner of the game received a prize, but the primary motivation was to have a chance to play.

Edible reinforcers are often used for very low functioning students who are not responsive to other types of rewards. Teachers in early primary grades also frequently rely on small edible reinforcers. There are some problems with use of candy, nuts, raisins, or crackers (Balsom & Bondy, 1983), though. Teachers must be aware of the problems that edible treats may cause for children who are overweight or who have allergies (Alberto & Troutman, 1986). Many parents object to their children being fed sweet food between meals. Some raise objections to use of food with sugar, food coloring, or preservatives. In addition, having food in classes where you and other children touch the food increases chances of spreading germs through the class. Bowls of candy where students reach in to get their pieces also provide considerable opportunity for spreading disease. Sweet foods, even raisins and crackers, increase the child's chance of having tooth decay.

For some children, the only effective reinforcer is food. These children are usually developmentally very young or they have severe emotional and behavioral problems. In these cases, it is best to have parental support and permission to use food consistently as a reinforcer.

Terminating the System

Behavioral theorists frequently recommend that teachers gradually fade out a reward system so that students receive fewer and fewer rewards for the same behaviors (Rusch, Rose, & Greenwood, 1988). In practice, this theoretical concept is difficult to implement. In classrooms, teachers frequently choose to terminate one system completely, perhaps replacing it with a simpler program. This seems to cause less confusion and frustration than changing the rules. For example, a class was able to earn rewards for following five basic classroom rules; after 8 weeks, the teachers decided the class knew and could follow all rules effectively.

"Teachers who lapse into, 'I told you so,' or, 'Do you remember what you did?' negate the central purpose of a reward system—to set up a positive rather than a punitive environment."

They chose to announce to the class that they were very proud of the progress they had made and their ability to meet expectations of students in the fifth grade. They had a small party with free time and games to celebrate and terminated the system. They found this easier than changing the system so that students had to earn more and more points for the rewards.

Terminating a system should be seen as an achievement by the students in meeting the objectives set for them. An alternative to terminating completely is to move to another system where the students work for new objectives and new rewards. For a classroom in which several students have behavior problems, the teacher may need to terminate the whole class program but retain the system for four or five students who still have difficulty meeting expectations.

Conclusion

Class reward systems are a powerful tool whose effectiveness is determined by the objectives of the teacher and by the amount of time and energy they put into it. Careful planning must go into selection of behaviors to be rewarded, ways of keeping track, and rewards to be used. Reward systems can be used as part of other educational games and activities. Teachers who incorporate their own ideas and creative activities into their reward systems enjoy them most and find them most useful.

References

Alberto, P. A., & Troutman, A. C. (1986). *Applied behavior analysis for teachers.* Columbus, OH: Merrill.

Balsam, P. D., & Bondy, A. S. (1983) The negative effects of reward. *Journal of Applied Behavior Analysis, 16,* 283–296.

Carter, S. J. (1988). *Hands-on education: A manual for implementation.* Unpublished manuscript.

Marholin, D., McInnis, E. T., & Heads, T. B. (1974). Effect of two free-time reinforcement procedures in a class of behavior problem children. *Journal of Educational Psychology, 66,* 872–879.

McLaughlin, T. F., & Malaby, J. (1972). Intrinsic reinforcers in a classroom token economy. *Journal of Applied Behavior Analysis,* 5, 263–270.

Raschke, D. (1981). Designing reinforcement surveys—Let the student choose the reward. *Teaching Exceptional Children, 14,* 92–96.

Rosenberg, M. S. (1986). Maximizing the effectiveness of structured classroom management programs: Implementing rule-review procedures with disruptive and distractible students. *Behavioral Disorders, 11,* 230–248.

Rusch, F. R., Rose, T., & Greenwood, C. R. (1988). *Introduction to behavior analysis in special education.* Englewood Cliffs, NJ: Prentice-Hall.

Van Houten, R. (1979). Social validation: The evolution of standards of competency for target behaviors. *Journal of Applied Behavior Analysis, 12,* 581–591.

Two Decades of Research on Teacher Expectations: Findings and Future Directions

Thomas L. Good

Good is Professor, Educational Psychology, University of Missouri-Columbia.

Good discusses the types of teacher expectation effects evidenced in the classroom. Particular attention is focused on the research that addresses teachers' expectations for and interactions with individuals believed to be of high or low potential. Good presents a model for use in understanding the dynamics of expectation communication in the classroom and highlights numerous studies relating teacher expectations with student behavior. The differential treatment of students by teachers is described by the author, with special attention given to how teachers express low expectations. The article concludes with a description of future research directions.

For about two decades, educational researchers have been concerned with the possibility that teachers communicate different performance expectations for students they believe to have low versus high achievement potential. In planning for and interacting with entire classes, small groups, and individuals, teachers are guided by their beliefs about what students need and by their expectations about how students will respond if treated in particular ways. Teacher expectations are defined here as inferences that teachers make about the future behavior or academic achievement of their students, based on what they know about these students now. Teacher expectation effects are student outcomes that occur because of the actions that teachers take in response to their own expectations.

Researchers have examined two types of teacher expectation effects (Cooper and Good, 1983): the *self-fulfilling prophecy effect* in which an originally erroneous expectation leads to behavior that causes the expectation to become true, and the *sustaining expectation effect*. In the latter effect, teachers expect students to sustain previously developed behavior patterns, to the point that teachers take these behavior patterns for granted and fail to see and capitalize on changes in student potential.

Self-fulfilling prophecy effects are more powerful than sustaining expectation effects because they introduce significant change in student behavior instead of merely minimizing such change by sustaining established patterns. Self-fulfilling prophecy effects can be powerful and dramatic when they occur, but the more subtle sustaining expectation effects probably occur much more often (Good and Brophy, 1987).

Teacher Expectations as Self-Fulfilling Prophecies

About two decades ago, Robert Rosenthal and Lenore

Research Editor: Kenneth R. Howey

Jacobson's *Pygmalion in the Classroom* (1968) created wide interest and controversy about self-fulfilling prophecies. Their book described research in which they manipulated teacher expectations for student achievement to see if these expectations would be fulfilled. Their research indicated that in the early grades teachers' artificially high expectations (teachers were given bogus test data) for student performance were associated with enhanced student performance.

At first, conclusions from this study were accepted enthusiastically. However, secondary sources sometimes made exaggerated claims that went far beyond those made by Rosenthal and Jacobson, and critics began to attack the study (Snow, 1969; Taylor, 1970). A replication attempt failed to produce the same results (Claiborn, 1969), leading to debates over the merits of the Oak School experiment. Meanwhile, other investigators conducted related studies using a variety of approaches, and attention shifted from debates over the original study to attempts to make sense of a growing literature on teacher expectation effects and related topics (Braun, 1976; Brophy and Good, 1974; West and Anderson, 1976). Research has continued in the nearly 20 years since the Oak School experiment and leads to a consensus that teachers' expectations can and sometimes do affect teacher-student interaction and student outcomes, along with the recognition that the processes involved are much more complex than originally believed (Brophy, 1983; Cooper and Good, 1983; Dusek, 1985; Marshall and Weinstein, 1984). For example, research also indicates that students influence teacher behavior.

Studies show that teachers' expectations are often an accurate assessment of student ability. Hence, teachers' expectations for student behavior are not necessarily inappropriate. The problem of low teacher expectations may not be one of simple identification or labeling of students (i.e., recognition that one student is relatively less able than another) but rather of *inappropriate knowledge* of how to respond to students who have difficulty learning.

Teachers' Expectations for Individual Students

This paper focuses on teachers' expectations for and interactions with individual students believed to be of high or low achievement potential because most research has concentrated on this area. However, it is important to recognize that teacher expectations may concern either the entire class, groups of students, or specific individuals. General expectations include teachers' beliefs about the changeability versus the rigidity of students' abilities, students' potential to benefit from instruction, the appropriate difficulty level of material for students, whether the class should be taught as a group or individually, and whether students should memorize material or interpret and apply key concepts that are presented.

There are countless ways in which teacher beliefs other than expectations for individual student performance may affect student performance. For example, some teachers believe that it is important for students to be active in the classroom, discovering knowledge on their own and assuming a great deal of independence. Other teachers believe that students should learn information that teachers present. Teachers' beliefs about subject matter may also have important effects. Depending on whether teachers believe that reading instruction basically involves teaching students phonics and

comprehension skills (being able to determine someone else's meaning of a written passage) or challenging students to develop their own meaning and to read to achieve self-determined goals, the way in which the curriculum is presented and the opportunities that students have will be quite different.

The point is that teachers' beliefs interact in complex ways and are at least responsive to, if not partially determined by, students' beliefs and behavior. A low-achieving student may receive quite different treatment in a class where a teacher believes in emphasizing meaning and understanding than in a classroom where a premium is placed on speed and accuracy. Students believed to possess less potential are more likely to receive an unending stream of drill assignments in the latter than in the former classroom.

Research shows that teachers' performance expectations vary in terms of student characteristics other than achievement potential per se. Brophy and Good (1974) found in one set of classrooms that low-achievement girls tended to have especially impoverished academic environments in the classroom, whereas high-achieving boys tended to be afforded productive and intellectually responsive environments, despite the fact that when general measures of classroom interaction were used, teachers were more critical of boys than of girls. Thus, depending on the questions researchers ask, different relationships can be obtained. Clearly, a teacher may treat girls and boys in the same classroom somewhat differently but still maintain sharply divergent interaction patterns with particular subgroups of students (high-achieving boys versus low-achieving girls).

The relationship between beliefs and behavior is complex in part because teachers hold multiple beliefs and because students possess numerous characteristics. Although the influence of beliefs on behavior is undeniable, the long history of the study of expectations (see Zuroff and Rotter, 1985) shows that conducting research in this area presents a difficult analytical challenge. Despite the difficulty of relating expectations to behavior, a considerable number of good classroom studies have been conducted. Discussion of this research is organized around the Brophy-Good model of expectation communication.

Brophy-Good Model

Much of the early classroom observational work was organized around a model used by Brophy and Good in one of the first naturalistic studies of teacher interaction with high- and low-achieving students following the publication of Rosenthal and Jacobson's (1968) *Pygmalion in the Classroom*. Brophy and Good (1970) suggested the following model for how the expectation communication process might work in the classroom:

1. Early in the year, teachers form differential expectations for student behavior and achievement.

2. Consistent with these differential expectations, teachers behave differently toward various students.

3. This treatment tells students something about how they are expected to behave in the classroom and perform on academic tasks.

4. If the teacher treatment is consistent over time and if students do not actively resist or change it, it will likely affect their self-concepts, achievement motivation, levels of

aspiration, classroom conduct, and interactions with the teacher.

5. These effects generally will complement and reinforce the teacher's expectations, so that students will come to conform to these expectations more than they might have otherwise.

6. Ultimately, this will affect student achievement and other outcomes. High-expectation students will be led to achieve at or near their potential, but low-expectation students will not gain as much as they could have gained if taught differently.

Self-fulfilling prophecy effects of teacher expectations can occur only when all the elements in the model are present. Often, however, one or more elements is missing. A teacher may not have clear-cut expectations about every student, or those expectations may change continually. Even when expectations are consistent, the teacher may not necessarily communicate them to the student through consistent behavior. In this case, the expectations would not be self-fulfilling even if they turned out to be correct. Finally, students might prevent expectations from becoming self-fulfilling by counteracting their effects or resisting them in a way that makes the teacher change them. For sustaining expectations to occur, it is only necessary that teachers engage in behaviors that maintain students' and teachers' previously formed low expectations (e.g., low students receive only drill work, easy questions, etc.).

How Teachers Form Expectations

The model begins with the statement that teachers form differential achievement expectations for individual students at the beginning of the school year. Investigators have studied the nature of the information that teachers use to form these expectations and the degree to which the expectations are accurate.

In one type of experimental study of expectation formation, subjects (not necessarily teachers) are given only carefully controlled information about, and little or no opportunity to interact with, the "students" (usually fictional) about whom they are asked to make predictions. In such a study, all of the subjects might be given cumulative record forms containing identical test scores, grades, and comments presumably written by previous teachers, but half of the forms would be accompanied by a picture of a white child and the other half by a picture of a black child (to see if knowledge about the fictional students' race would affect predictions about their achievement). Such experiments have shown that expectations can be affected significantly by information about test performance, performance on assignments, track or group placement, classroom conduct, physical appearance, race, socioeconomic status, ethnicity, sex, speech characteristics, and various diagnostic or special education labels (see reviews by Baron, Tom, and Cooper, 1985; Braun, 1976; Brophy and Good, 1974; Dusek and Joseph, 1985; Persell, 1977; Peterson and Barger, 1985; Rolison and Medway, 1985).

Most of the information in school records is accurate and likely to induce correct expectations in teachers who read it. Thus, teachers' predictions about student achievement are usually quite correct, sometimes even more accurate than predictions based on test data (Egan and Archer, 1985; Hoge and Butcher, 1984; Mitman, 1985; Monk, 1983; Pedulla, Airasian, and Madaus, 1980).

In summary, inservice teachers usually develop accurate

expectations about their students, and they tend to change these expectations as more or better information becomes available. This limits the possibility for self-fulfilling prophecy effects (which are based on false or unjustified expectations) to occur, *although it still allows sustaining expectation effects.* Self-fulfilling prophecy effects are especially likely to occur when students are new to their teachers because it is early in the school year (especially in kindergarten and first grade and in the first year of middle school, junior high, or high school) or because they have transferred from another school.

How Teachers Communicate Expectations

Considering that teachers have formed differential expectations for various students, the next step of the Brophy-Good model postulates that teachers communicate these expectations through their behavior toward students. Researchers have documented the ways that teachers interact with students who differ in current or expected achievement. Indeed, most research on the communication of teacher expectations concerns Step 2 of the Brophy-Good model.

Good and Brophy (1987) suggest that the following behaviors sometimes indicate differential teacher treatment of high and low achievers:

1. Waiting less time for "lows" to answer (Allington, 1980; Bozsik, 1982; Rowe, 1974a, b; Taylor, 1979).

2. Giving low achievers answers or calling on someone else rather than trying to improve their responses by giving clues or repeating or rephrasing questions (Brophy and Good, 1970; Jeter and Davis, 1973).

3. Rewarding inappropriate behavior or incorrect answers by low achievers (Amato, 1975; Fernandez, Espinosa, and Dornbusch, 1975; Graham, 1984; Kleinfeld, 1975; Meyer, Bachmann, Biermann, Hemplemann, Ploger, and Spiller, 1979; Natriello and Dornbusch, 1984; Rowe, 1974a; Taylor, 1977; Weinstein, 1976).

4. Criticizing low achievers more often for failure (Brophy and Good, 1970; Cooper and Baron, 1977; Good, Cooper, and Blakey, 1980; Good, Sikes, and Brophy, 1973; Jones, 1971; Medinnus and Unruh, 1971; Rowe, 1974a; Smith and Luginbuhl, 1976).

5. Praising low achievers less frequently than highs for success (Babad, Inbar, and Rosenthal, 1982; Brophy and Good, 1970; Cooper and Baron, 1977; Firestone and Brody, 1975; Good, Cooper, and Blakey, 1980; Good, et al., 1973; Martinek and Johnson, 1979; Medinnus and Unruh, 1971; Rejeski, Darracott, and Hutslar, 1979; Spector, 1973).

6. Failing to give feedback to the public responses of low achievers (Brophy and Good, 1970; Good, et al., 1973; Jeter and Davis, 1973; Willis, 1970).

7. Paying less attention to low achievers or interacting with them less frequently (Adams and Cohen, 1974; Blakey, 1970; Given, 1974; Kester and Letchworth, 1972; Page, 1971; Rist, 1970; Rubovits and Maehr, 1971).

8. Calling on low achievers less often to respond to questions (Davis and Levine, 1970; Mendoza, Good, and Brophy, 1972; Rubovits and Maehr, 1971), or asking them only easier, nonanalytic questions (Martinek and Johnson, 1979).

9. Seating low achievers farther away from the teacher (Rist, 1970).

10. Demanding less from low achievers. This differential treatment is evidenced by a variety of behaviors. Beez (1968)

found that tutors with high expectations not only taught more words, but also taught them more rapidly and with less extended explanation and repetition of definitions and examples. The studies of inappropriate reinforcement mentioned above indicate that teachers may accept low-quality or even incorrect responses from low achievers. Graham (1984) suggests that excessive teacher sympathy or offers of gratuitous, unsolicited help may communicate low expectations, especially if these behaviors occur instead of behaviors designed to help low achievers meet success criteria.

11. Interacting with low achievers more privately than publicly, and monitoring and structuring their activities more closely. Brophy and Good (1974) discuss these differences in detail.

12. Grading tests or assignments in a differential manner, in which high achievers but not low achievers are given the benefit of the doubt in borderline cases (Cahen, 1966; Finn, 1972; Heapy and Siess, 1970).

13. Having less friendly interaction with low achievers, including less smiling and fewer other nonverbal indicators of support (Babad, et al., 1982; Chaikin, Sigler, and Derlega, 1974; Kester and Letchworth, 1972; Meichenbaum, Bowers, and Ross, 1969; Page, 1971; Smith and Luginbuhl, 1976) and less warm or more anxious voice tones (Blanck and Rosenthal, 1984).

14. Providing briefer and less informative feedback to the questions of low achievers (Cooper, 1979; Cornbleth, Davis, and Button, 1972).

15. Providing less eye contact and other nonverbal communication of attention and responsiveness (e.g., forward lean, positive head nodding) in interaction with low achievers (Chaikin, Sigler, and Derlega, 1974).

16. Evidencing less use of effective but time consuming instructional methods with low achievers when time is limited (Swann and Snyder, 1980).

17. Evidencing less acceptance and use of low achievers' ideas (Martinek and Johnson, 1979; Martinek and Karper, 1982).

As indicated by the numerous studies conducted, this has been a very active research area; however, it is clear that some of the 17 points have more support than others. Also, it is critical to stress that the teacher behaviors listed above do not necessarily characterize ineffective teaching; rather, they should be used as guidelines by supervisors and teachers as they analyze their behavior and study effects of teacher behavior on particular students. Some students may need more structure and easier work than others, and there is no reason to assume that teachers should treat all students alike; however, some teachers overreact to relatively small differences among students by teaching them in sharply divergent ways that are inappropriate. The key issue is the appropriateness of students' differential treatment (e.g., work assigned, frequency of public questions).

Classrooms differ, and different students in the same classroom vary in important ways. Still, it is possible to explore research findings in order to understand some of the ways in which beliefs about achievement potential may inhibit effective classroom communication. The concepts and findings associated with expectation research provide guidelines or frames of reference that allow teachers to think about and attempt to alter classroom environments. These classroom concepts can help teachers to increase the number of dimensions they use in thinking about classroom performance and

the number (and range) of hypotheses or alternative strategies available. Concepts also encourage teachers to consider the possible consequences of selective actions on various students (Good and Power, 1976).

Some investigators have organized the behavioral research findings (e.g., 17 points raised above) into models. Rosenthal (1974) reviewed the research on mediators of teacher expectation effects and identified four general factors. Focusing on positive self-fulfilling prophecy effects, he suggests that teachers will maximize student achievement if they:

1. Create warm social-emotional relationships with the students (climate).

2. Give them more feedback about their performance (feedback).

3. Teach them more (and more difficult) material (input).

4. Give them more opportunities to respond and to ask questions (output).

Good and Weinstein (1986a) describe the effects of specific teaching behaviors in a more general way (see Table 1). We now turn to a discussion of research related to the remaining steps of the Brophy-Good model.

Student Perceptions of Differential Teacher Treatment

In addition to expectation effects that occur directly through differences in exposure to content, etc., indirect effects may occur through teacher behavior that affects students' self-concepts, motivation, performance expectations, or attributions (inferences about why they succeed or fail). This brings us to Step 3 of the Brophy and Good model, which postulates that students perceive differential treatment and its implications about what is expected of them.

Research by Weinstein (1983, 1985) and her colleagues indicates that students are aware of differences in teachers' patterns of interaction with different students in the class. Interviews with elementary school students show that they see their teachers as projecting higher achievement expectations and offering more opportunity and choice to higher achievers, while structuring the activities of low achievers more closely and providing them both with more help and with more negative feedback about academic work and classroom conduct (Weinstein, Marshall, Brattesani, and Middlestadt, 1982). Furthermore, students see these differences as applying to their own personal treatment from their teachers, not just to the treatment of other students (Brattesani, Weinstein, and Marshall, 1984).

Weinstein's research clearly indicates that students' perceptions and interpretations of teacher feedback could provide a missing link in understanding the transmission of expectations. In a study of the processes and outcomes associated with reading groups in three first-grade classrooms, Weinstein (1976) found that the relationship between teacher behavior and student achievement was difficult to reconcile. For example, the teacher "favored" low reading group members with more praise and less criticism than high-group members. Despite this "favorable" treatment, over the course of the school year the gap in achievement, peer status, and anxiety about school performance widened significantly between high and low reading group members. However, classroom observers noted that the praise to low achievers was *qualitatively* different from the praise to high achievers. Weinstein hypothesized that the more frequent critical comments concerning performance directed toward high achievers might

Table 1

General Dimensions of Teachers' Communication of Differential Expectations and Selected Examples

	Students believed to be MORE capable have:	Students believed to be LESS capable have:
TASK ENVIRONMENT Curriculum, procedures, task definition, pacing, quality of environment	More opportunity to perform publicly on meaningful tasks.	Less opportunity to perform publicly, especially on meaningful tasks (supplying alternate endings to a story vs. learning to pronounce a word correctly).
	More opportunity to think.	Less opportunity to think, analyze (since much work is aimed at practice).
GROUPING PRACTICES	More assignments that deal with comprehension, understanding (in higher-ability groups).	Less choice on curriculum assignments — more opportunity to work on drill-like assignments.
LOCUS OF RESPONSIBILITY FOR LEARNING	More autonomy (more choice in assignments, fewer interruptions).	Less autonomy (frequent teacher monitoring of work, frequent interruptions).
FEEDBACK AND EVALUATION PRACTICES	More opportunity for self-evaluation.	Less opportunity for self-evaluation.
MOTIVATIONAL STRATEGIES	More honest/contingent feedback.	Less honest/more gratuitous/less contingent feedback.
QUALITY OF TEACHER RELATIONSHIPS	More respect for the learner as an individual with unique interests and needs.	Less respect for the learner as an individual with unique interests and needs.

This table is reprinted from Good, T., & Weinstein, R. (1986a). Teacher expectations: A framework for exploring classrooms. In K. Zumwalt (Ed.), *Improving teaching*. (The 1986 ASCD Yearbook). Alexandria, VA: Association for Supervision and Curriculum Development.

suggest high expectations to those students and that the high rates of praise for low achievers (for less than perfect answers) conveyed an indiscriminant acceptance to those from whom less was expected.

Zahorik (1970) obtained similar results that suggested that various students interpret teacher statements differently. For example, if students are to feel "good" about answers and to know that their answer is correct, the teacher's verbal feedback must contain such words as "all right" or "good." Although the descriptors that would be necessary to convince students that their work was adequate would probably change dramatically from grade level to grade level or from teacher to teacher even at the same grade level, Zahorik's finding suggests that students interpret information from teachers. Along these same lines, Morine-Dershimer (1982) investigated students' perceptions of the function of teacher praise and found that students could distinguish between praise as being deserved and praise as having instructional or motivational purposes. Students' awareness of these differences generally matched teachers' intended use of praise. Students' reactions to teacher praise are a good illustration of the fact that student thinking and interpretation mediate the effect of overt teaching behavior. Brophy (1981) notes that praise may erode or enhance motivation, and Mitman (1985) reports that in some instances students may interpret teacher criticism as suggesting that the teacher cares (i.e., expects good work). It therefore is clear that in some areas of classroom life students interpret teacher behavior.

As Weinstein (1983) notes, several studies provide evidence that students make sophisticated interpretations of teacher behavior. Her own work, in particular, demonstrates that students perceive differential teacher treatment toward high-

and low-achieving students in some areas but not in others. Weinstein and Middlestadt (1979a, b) asked younger and older elementary school children to rate 60 teacher behaviors as descriptive of the treatment of a hypothetical male student, either a high or low achiever. Treatment profiles of the two types of students showed that students perceived differential treatment in one-quarter of the teacher behaviors studied. In particular, student-perceived teacher treatment of male high achievers reflected high expectations, academic demand, and special privileges. Male low achievers were viewed as receiving fewer chances but greater teacher concern and vigilance. Weinstein concludes that students are clearly aware of the greater teacher help and structure accorded low achievers in contrast to the more autonomous learning context accorded high achievers.

Students' perceptions of differential treatment at the classroom level also appear to moderate the relationship between teacher expectations and student achievement. In classrooms with perceived low differential treatment, where it was hypothesized that the teacher communicated little information about differential student ability, student achievement was best predicted by a previous measure of achievement, which accounted for 64 to 77 percent of the variance in achievement (Brattesani, et al., 1984). In other words, students continued to perform at about the same levels, relative to their classmates, as they had performed before. Other patterns were observed in classrooms with perceived high differential treatment. Because students in these classrooms reported more differential treatment of high- and low-achieving students, it was hypothesized that teachers provided more information about various students' abilities. The researchers found that in these classrooms, student achievement was less effectively predicted by prior achievement, which accounted for only 47 to 62 percent of the variance. In these high-differentiation classrooms (as perceived by students), teachers' expectations explained an additional 9 to 18 percent of the variance in student achievement, whereas teacher expectations explained only an additional one to four percent of achievement variance in low-differentiation classrooms.

Cooper and Good (1983) report similar findings. Compared to low-expectation peers, elementary students for whom their teachers held high expectations reported themselves as engaging more often in teacher-initiated public interactions but less often in teacher-initiated private interactions, supplying correct answers more frequently, and receiving more praise and less criticism from their teachers. Actual observed differences were in the same direction but less extreme, suggesting that students not only perceive differential treatment but exaggerate the degree of differentiation that exists.

To the extent that such differentiation exists in a classroom, expectation effects on student achievement are likely to occur both directly through opportunity to learn (differences in the amount and nature of exposure to content and opportunities to engage in various academic activities) and indirectly through differential treatment likely to affect students' self-concepts, attributional inferences, or motivation.

Individual differences among students also affect the size of teacher expectation effects. Some students may be more sensitive than others to voice tones or other subtle communication cues, so that they decode teachers' communications of expectations more often and accurately (Conn, Edwards, Rosenthal, and Crowne, 1968; Zuckerman, DeFrank, Hall, and Rosenthal, 1978). Younger and more teacher-dependent students may also be more susceptible to teacher expectation effects (Persell, 1977; West and Anderson, 1976). However, as Weinstein (1985) notes, we still know too little about what makes some students more sensitive to expectation effects to make accurate predictions.

Other Models for Indirect Mediation of Expectation Effects

Considering that teachers form differential expectations for various students, that teachers act on these expectations by treating students differently, and that the students perceive this differential treatment and infer implications about what is expected of them, the stage is set for teacher expectation effects on student achievement that are mediated through effects on self-concept, motivation, expectations, and attributions. The remaining steps in the Brophy-Good model suggest that such effects occur, but do not say much about how the process might work. However, others have developed models that offer such explanations.

Cooper's Model. Cooper (1979, 1985) suggests that teachers' needs to retain predictability and control over classroom interaction cause them to treat low achievers in ways that may erode achievement motivation. He notes that predictability and control are especially important issues to teachers in public interaction situations, where a student's unexpected words or actions may disrupt lesson continuity and produce classroom management problems. Because low achievers are the students most likely to cause such problems, teachers who fear loss of control may minimize these students' potential for disrupting public interaction settings by squelching their initiations and calling on them only for very brief and tightly controlled contributions. In order to exert such control, these

teachers may treat low-achieving students less warmly. In particular, they may tend not to praise strong efforts by low achievers because such praise might encourage these students to initiate interactions more often, and they may criticize low achievers' weak efforts more often because such criticism increases their control over the lows' behavior. Meanwhile, high achievers would be treated more warmly, because the teacher has less to fear from encouraging them to initiate public interactions and has less need to criticize them in order to retain control over their behavior.

Such a difference in teacher warmth alone would likely affect student motivation. In addition, however, this differential treatment might affect student motivation by decreasing low achievers' belief in a direct relationship between academic effort and achievement. Whereas high achievers would be praised or criticized in direct response to their effort (praised when efforts are strong and criticized when they do not try hard enough), low achievers sometimes would be praised or criticized more because of the teacher's desire to control their public interactions than for reasons having to do with their levels of effort. For them, good effort would often go unrecognized, and poor efforts would often be allowed because the teacher was more concerned about discouraging them from disrupting lessons than about reinforcing their learning efforts. Over time, high achievers would develop a clear sense that their learning efforts paid off, but low achievers would see less clear relationships between effort and outcome. In theory, this should lead directly to a reduction in low achievers' achievement motivation, and indirectly to a reduction in achievement itself.

Attribution Theory Models. Others (Dweck and Elliott, 1983; Eccles and Wigfield, 1985; Graham, 1984) have suggested that expectation effects are mediated by teachers' influences on students' attributional thinking about the reasons for their successes and failures. Ideally, students will believe that they have the ability to succeed at academic tasks if they apply reasonable effort ("I can succeed if I try."). However, some students, especially low achievers, fall into a failure syndrome/learned helplessness pattern ("I can't do the work — I'm dumb."). Such students are prone to discount their successes ("I was lucky.") and to attribute their failures to lack of ability rather than to insufficient effort or reliance on an ineffective strategy. Eventually, they come to believe that nothing they can do will enable them to succeed consistently, so they give up. Various authors have suggested that teacher communication of low expectations encourages low achievers to develop this pattern of attributional thinking. Teachers usually do not directly suggest that students do not have the ability to succeed (Blumenfeld, Hamilton, Bossert, Wessels, and Meece, 1983), but they may suggest this indirectly by minimizing demands on them, overreacting to minor successes, treating failures as if they were successes, or responding to failures with pity or excessive sympathy instead of problem identification and remedial instruction.

Eccles and Wigfield (1985) note that the attributional/motivational variables that are the key to the expectation communication process are similar for both students and teachers. They suggest that the issue can be summarized in three questions: Can I succeed at this task? Do I want to succeed at this task? What do I need to do to succeed at this task? From the standpoint of the student, these questions are: Can I learn this material? Do I want to complete the assignment? What do I need to do in order to complete the assignment? From the teacher's standpoint, these questions are: Can I teach this child the material? Do I want to teach this child the material? What do I have to do to teach this child the material successfully?

Although relatively little research has occurred in classrooms with regard to Steps 4, 5, and 6 of the Brophy-Good model, there is growing evidence that students are sensitive to verbal and nonverbal cues from teachers; that students perceive differences in the function of teacher behavior; and that students perceive differences in teacher behavior toward high- and low-achieving students, especially in some classrooms (Weinstein, 1985).

Weinstein's (1985) work shows that students' interview responses often indicate that students make fine distinctions in a given behavior. For example, with regard to "call-on," students said that the teacher "calls on the smart kids for the right answer . . . she expects you to know more and won't tell answers." With regard to the low achievers, students preceived that the teacher calls on them sometimes "to give them a chance" or "because they goofed off," or "often she doesn't call on them because she knows they don't know the answer."

Data from classroom observational studies suggest that not all teachers treat high- and low-expectation students differently (Good, 1980). The variability between classrooms and the occurrence of differential treatment have most often been explained in terms of individual differences in teacher type or personality (Brophy and Good, 1974; Cooper, 1979). However, as Weinstein (1985) notes, a growing body of research suggests that the activity structure adopted for classroom instruction can either facilitate or constrain the opportunities for certain kinds of teacher-student interaction (Bossert, 1979; Doyle, 1980). More research on students may help us to understand better how students perceive, internalize, and act on classroom events.

Group, Class, and School Effects

Expectation effects can operate at the level of groups, classes, or entire schools. Although the Brophy-Good model focused on teachers' communication to individual students, it is clear that teachers communicate expectations to entire classes and to groups of students and that these expectation effects are at least as important as effects on individuals.

Group Effects

Weinstein (1976) showed that reading group membership information added 25 percent to the variance in mid-year reading achievement that could be predicted beyond what was predictable from readiness scores taken at the beginning of the year. Placement into high groups accelerated achievement rates, but placement into low groups slowed them down (relative to the differences that would have been expected anyway due to variation in readiness).

Research comparing instruction in different reading groups (reviewed by Hiebert, 1983) suggests some possible reasons for this. Teachers tend to give longer reading assignments (Pflaum, Pascarella, Boswick, and Aver, 1980), to provide more time for discussion of the story (Bozsik, 1982), and to be generally more demanding (Haskett, 1968) with high groups than with low groups. They are quicker to interrupt low-group students when they make reading mistakes (Allington, 1983) and more likely to just give them the word or prompt them with graphemic (phonetic) cues during oral reading rather than to offer semantic and syntactic cues that might help them intuit the word from its context (Allington, 1980; Pflaum, et al., 1980). Teachers are also less likely to ask low groups higher-level, comprehension questions (Bozsik, 1982).

The nature and extent of such differential treatment vary from teacher to teacher, and at least some of it can be seen as appropriate differential instruction (Alpert, 1974; Brophy, 1983; Haskins, Walden, and Ramey, 1983). However, as was the case with differential treatment of individual students, consistent patterns of such differential treatment of groups are cause for concern. Too often, low groups continually get less exciting instruction, less emphasis on meaning and conceptualization, and more rote drill and practice activities (Good and Marshall, 1984).

Eder's (1981) study of reading groups in one first-grade class indicates how the process might work, at least in some instances. She found that students who were likely to have difficulty in learning to read generally were assigned to groups whose social context was not conducive to learning. Most of the students in Eder's study had similar academic abilities and socioeconomic backgrounds (middle-class). None of the students could read prior to entering first grade; however, there are probably some important differences with respect to various reading readiness skills. Still, their progress in reading could plausibly be related to the reading instruction they received in first grade. Despite the relative homogeneity of these pupils, the first-grade teacher still grouped them for reading instruction.

Because the most immature, inattentive students were assigned to low groups, it was almost certain that these groups would cause more managerial problems than others, especially early in the year. Indeed, because the teacher was often distracted from a student reader in the low group who was responding (because of the need to manage other students in the group), students often provided the correct word for the reader. Readers were not allowed time to ascertain words on their own, even though less than a third of the students interviewed reported that they liked to be helped, and most thought that this help interfered with their learning. Eder's work indicates that low students had less time than high students to correct their mistakes before other students or the teacher intervened. Eder suggests that because of management problems, frequent interruptions, and less serious teaching, low students may inadvertently have been encouraged to respond to social and procedural aspects of the reading group rather than to academic tasks.

Grant and Rothenberg (1986) concluded from an intensive study of eight classrooms that first- and second-grade reading groups create and perpetuate status distinctions among students. Students placed in top groups had more educational advantages than students placed in the lower groups. For example, students in the higher groups had (a) more opportunities to demonstrate competence, (b) work and task environments that were conducive to learning more academic skills, and (c) greater opportunity to practice autonomous, self-directed modes of learning. Grant and Rothenberg see their data as another illustration of the need to rethink the extensive use of ability grouping.

Allington (1983) notes that although there are some good reasons for oral reading (e.g., it gives the teacher a chance to identify a child's difficulties), low-achieving students do too much oral reading and too little silent reading. Allington contends that the focus on oral reading or silent reading exerts subtle pressure on the teacher to behave in a particular way. Because reading in low groups tends to be primarily oral, many teachers emphasize correct pronunciation, proper word sequence, etc. In contrast, teachers' questions of high readers following silent reading are more likely to focus on text meaning and student understanding. Hence, the *structure* of the reading group may exert subtle influences on both teachers and students.

Alloway (1984) reports that teachers may express low expectations to groups of students and that favorable expectations expressed towards individual students may be undermined by communication to students as group members. Some of the communication expressed in the classroom follows. It illustrates some of the expectations that teachers communicated to low groups: "You children are slower so please get on with your work now" (low-expectancy group); "I'll be over to help you slow ones in a moment. This group can go on by itself."; "You need this extra time, so pay attention to me please."; "The blue group will find this hard." Alloway also pointed out low expectations in the form of labels teachers give to individual students: "Hurry up, Robyn. Even you can get this right"; "Michelle, you're slow as it is. You haven't got time to look around the classroom."

The Commission on Reading (1984) summarizes the problem for low-ability students in the following way.

> There are qualitative differences in the experience of children in high and low reading groups that would be expected to place children in low groups at a disadvantage. Children in low groups do relatively more reading aloud and relatively less silent reading. They more often read words without a meaningful context on lists or flashcards, and less often read words in stories. Teachers correct a higher proportion of oral reading mistakes of children in low groups than children in high groups. When the mistake is corrected, teachers are more often likely to furnish a clue about pronunciation and less likely to furnish a clue about meaning for children in low groups. Teachers ask relatively more simple, factual questions of children in low groups and relatively fewer questions that require reasoning. (pp. 89-90)

Students in low groups often receive less interesting and less demanding reading instruction. Because of differences in vocabulary, rates of processing information, etc., there may be reasons to group students along ability lines for *some* of their instruction in reading. However, some instruction needs to occur in mixed-ability groups — such as when the meanings of stories are discussed. Too often, grouping for differential instruction is a "solution" that in a subtle fashion becomes part of the problem. Students who need a bit more structure and drill receive a curriculum that places too much emphasis on word analysis and drill.

Class Effects

Like others who have examined the literature on ability grouping and tracking, Oakes (1985) notes that there are often major differences between high- and low-track classrooms including (a) quality of knowledge, (b) amount of time assigned to learning, (c) amount of high-quality teaching, and (d) intellectual stimulation from peers. She also suggests that teachers' decisions about classroom learning opportunities are influenced by students' reactions. However,

in contrast to the view of many educators that the presence of high- and low-ability students in the same class diminishes academic demands on students, she suggests that both types of students can learn in the same class.

In an empirical examination of learning time and curriculum quality, Oakes found that 35 percent of the heterogeneous classes were more like high-track than average or low-track classes. Thirty-six percent of heterogeneous classes were like average-track classes. Thus, having high and low students in the same class does not necessarily lower standards. These results are similar to those obtained by Beckerman and Good (1981), who found that low achievers can learn in heterogeneous-ability classrooms, especially when a core of high-achieving students establishes a climate that encourages learning.

Oakes also found that teacher-student relationships (e.g., extent to which teachers were positive, supportive, etc.) in heterogeneous classes were comparable to those in 46 percent of the high-track classes, 37 percent of the average classes, and only 17 percent of the lower-track classes. Thus, in 83 percent of comparisons, slower students in heterogeneous classes had more positive interactions with teachers than they enjoyed in low-track classes.

Brophy and Evertson (1976) found that a "can-do" attitude was associated with teachers' relative levels of success in eliciting achievement from their students. The more successful teachers believed that their students could master curriculum objectives and that they (the teachers) were capable of meeting the students' instructional needs. These expectations were associated with behaviors such as augmenting or even replacing the curriculum materials or evaluation instruments if these did not appear to be suited to the needs of the students.

Ashton (1985) reported similar findings for teachers who differed in *sense of efficacy*. Sense of efficacy was measured by the teachers' responses (on a five-point scale from "strongly agree" through "strongly disagree") to the following two statements:

1. When it comes right down to it, a teacher really can't do much because most of a student's motivation and performance depends on his or her own environment.
2. If I really try hard, I can get through to even the most difficult or unmotivated students.

Teachers who rejected the first of these statements but agreed with the second were classified as high in sense of efficacy: They believed that they were capable of motivating and instructing their students successfully.

Compared to teachers with a low sense of efficacy, teachers with a high sense of efficacy were more confident and at ease in their classrooms, more positive (e.g., praising, smiling) and less negative (e.g., criticizing, punishing) in interactions with their students, more successful in managing their classrooms as efficient learning environments, less defensive, more accepting of student disagreement and challenges, and more effective in producing student achievement gains. Low-efficacy teachers revealed low expectations and a tendency to concentrate on rule enforcement and behavior management, whereas high-efficacy teachers concentrated on instructing their students in the curriculum and interacting with students about academic content. These data are correlational, but the fact that they come from parallel sections of the same courses taught to similar students in the same school suggests that they were caused by differences in the teachers rather than in the students.

As a formal research area, the relationship between teacher expectations for the class as a whole and behavior toward the class has largely been ignored. However, it seems reasonable to suggest that teachers can hold low expectations for a class as well as for individuals or groups of students. As a case in point, when R. Weinstein and I visited a school to observe differential teacher behavior toward students believed to be high and low ability, our most striking observation was the teacher's communication of low expectations to *all students* (Good and Weinstein, 1986a).

We observed one combined fifth/sixth-grade language arts class where even the physical environment of the class helped to communicate low performance expectations. We were struck by the barren nature of the room. The wall clock was broken, there were few books around, virtually nothing was on the walls, and little student work was visible.

The lesson we observed also emphasized rules and procedures. The teacher dominated, quizzing the students about the meaning of topic sentences and main ideas and about the instructions for the class assignment. The task was narrowly defined. It seems inappropriate that students who had studied paragraphing and had been reviewing related material for several days were not required to write a paragraph, or at least to read several selections and identify which groups of sentences were paragraphs. Even the latter activity would have allowed active involvement and discussion among students with regard to why some groups of sentences were not paragraphs. To us, this close monitoring of student behavior and attention to minor details (i.e., demanding procedural exactness — the precise words of the text in the precise order), and the lack of any discussion of the value or meaningfulness of the topic being studied, communicated low performance expectations for these students.

Furthermore, the pace was so painfully slow that the students (and observers) either became restless or sleepy. Although the teacher was aware of these symptoms, she attributed them to the students' lack of interest and ability. Only once did the teacher express an awareness that perhaps she was not making herself clear.

Further compounding the problem of an inappropriate task was the fact that the teacher expected students at both grade levels to cover the same material. From an inspection of the curriculum, we learned that both fifth- and sixth-graders completed the same task with similar instructions (although procedures were much clearer in the fifth-grade text) in their textbooks. The teacher also pointed out that if the fifth-grade students did not learn it now, they would have a second opportunity in sixth grade. This redundancy in curriculum, accompanied by a teacher-directed, highly passive mode of delivery, virtually assured that students would not be interested in the lesson, and they were not. Students' boredom was obvious and it caused their failure to give the teacher the answers she wanted (at least from our perspective). Sadly, the teacher probably explained the students' inadequate performance by assuming they lacked ability.

School Effects

Studies of school effectiveness and school improvement programs (reviewed by Good and Brophy, 1986) indicate that high expectations and commitment to bringing about student achievement are part of a pattern of attitudes, beliefs, and behaviors that characterizes schools that are successful in maximizing students' learning gains. Brookover, Beady, Flood, Schweitzer, and Wisenbaker (1979), for example, found that teachers in effective schools not only held higher expectations but acted on them by setting goals expressed as minimally acceptable levels of achievement rather than using prior achievement data to establish ceiling levels beyond which students would not be expected to progress. Such teachers responded to failure as a challenge, requiring students to redo failed work (with individualized help as needed) rather than writing them off or referring them to remedial classes. They responded to mistakes and response failures during class with appropriate feedback and reinstruction rather than with lowering of standards or inappropriate praise. Similar findings have been reported by Edmonds (1979) and by Rutter, Maughan, Mortimore, Ouston, and Smith (1979).

In response to such findings, school improvement programs (Proctor, 1984) and professional development programs for inservice teachers (Farley, 1982; Kerman, 1979) have begun to incorporate elements designed to reduce negative expectation effects on student achievement. Furthermore, Good and Weinstein (1986b) note that high expectations for the teachability of all students are hindered by beliefs in a single intelligence that falls in a normal distribution and have challenged educators to develop school programs for students that express high expectations but allow students to fulfill those expectations in diverse ways.

Individual Differences Among Teachers

Students appear to be differentially sensitive to the communication of expectations, and some teachers are more likely than others to differ in their behavior toward high- and low-achieving students. Teachers also express low expectations in different ways.

Different Types of Teachers

Brophy and Good (1974) suggested that teachers can be thought of as being on a continuum from proactive through reactive to overreactive. *Proactive* teachers are guided by their own beliefs about what is reasonable and appropriate in setting goals for the class as a whole and for individual students. If they set realistic goals and have the needed skills, they are likely to move their students systematically toward fulfilling the expectations associated with these goals.

At the other extreme are *overreactive* teachers who develop rigid, stereotyped perceptions of their students based on prior records or on first impressions of student behavior. Overreactive teachers tend to treat their students as stereotypes rather than as individuals, and they are the most likely to have negative expectation effects on their students.

Most teachers fall in between these extremes and are classified as *reactive* teachers who hold their expectations lightly and adjust them to take note of new feedback and emerging trends. Reactive teachers have minimal expectation effects on their students, tending merely to maintain existing differences between high and low achievers (although these differences will increase slightly because of varied student behavior that teachers do not compensate for).

Subsequent research supports these distinctions, but with an important qualification. Unfortunately, it appears that most sizable teacher expectation effects on student achievement are negative ones, in which low expectations lead to lower achievement than might have been attained otherwise (Brophy, 1983). There is little evidence that even proactive teachers significantly augment the achievement of individual students by projecting positive expectations, but much evidence that overreactive teachers minimize student progress by projecting low expectations. Work by other investigators has shown that these overreactive teachers differ from other teachers in being more rigid, authoritarian, and prone to bias and prejudice (e.g., Babad, 1985).

Differential Patterns of Teacher Communication

It is important to state again that *not all* teachers show a consistent pattern of sharply differentiated behavior toward high- and low-potential students. Also, the type of problem behavior varies from class to class; hence, no simple presumptions are possible. One estimate based on several studies that were conducted over a number of years suggests that about one-third of the teachers observed acted in a way that appears to exaggerate the initial deficiencies of low achievers (Good and Brophy, 1980). Moreover, it is clear that there are different ways in which teachers can communicate low expectations to students.

As noted earlier, studies show that some teachers criticize low achievers more frequently than high achievers per incorrect response and praise low achievers less per correct answer than high achievers. In contrast, other teachers praise marginal or incorrect responses given by low achievers. These findings reflect two different types of teachers. Teachers who criticize low achievers for incorrect responses seem to be less tolerant of these pupils. In contrast, teachers who reward marginal or even wrong answers are excessively sympathetic and unnecessarily protective of low achievers. Both types of teacher behavior illustrate to students that effort and classroom performance are not related. As illustrated in Figure 1, both the "rejecting" and excessively sympathetic teacher styles appear to stimulate less student thinking.

Over time, such differences in the way teachers treat low achievers (for example, in the third grade a student is praised or finds teacher acceptance for virtually any verbalization, but in the fourth grade the student is seldom praised and is criticized more) may reduce low students' efforts and contribute to a passive learning style. Other teacher behaviors may also contribute to this problem. Low students who are called on frequently one year (the teacher believes that they need to be active if they are to learn), but who find that they are called on infrequently the following year (the teacher doesn't want to embarrass them) may find it confusing to adjust to such different role definitions. Ironically, those students who have the least adaptive capacity may be asked to make the most adjustment as they move from classroom to classroom. The greater variation in how different teachers interact with low students (in contrast to the more similar patterns of behavior that high students receive from different teachers) may exist because teachers agree less about how to respond to students who do *not* learn readily.

Explanations for Differential Teacher Behavior

Although there is good evidence that teachers' assessments of the general achievement levels of students are accurate (e.g., Brophy and Good, 1974; Egan and Archer, 1985), classroom evidence suggests that teachers' reactions (i.e., assignments) to students with less potential indicate a limited

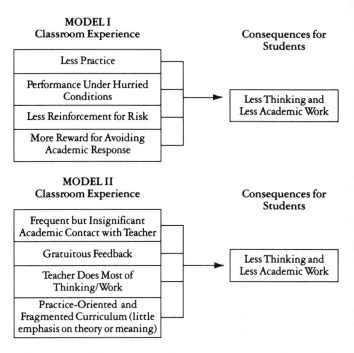

Figure 1
Passivity Model of Low Achievers

and unsuccessful repertoire of teaching strategies (i.e., drill). Thus, factors other than inaccurate assessment of students' potential account for much of the inappropriate differential behavior that occurs in the classroom. Some of these factors are briefly discussed here.

One basic cause of differential behavior is that classrooms are busy and complex environments, and it is difficult for teachers to assess accurately the frequency and quality of their interactions with individual students. Some teachers who are bright and well-prepared may behave inappropriately toward low achievers because of the complexity of the classroom.

A second explanation involves the fact that much classroom behavior must be interpreted before it has meaning. Research suggests that once a teacher develops an expectation about a student (e.g., the student is not capable of learning), the teacher interprets subsequent ambiguous classroom events in a way consistent with the original expectation (e.g., Anderson-Levitt, 1984). Good (1980) maintains that most classroom behavior is ambiguous and subject to multiple interpretations.

A third reason why some teachers differentiate their behavior toward high- and low-achieving students is related to the issue of causality. Some teachers believe that they can and will influence student learning (for example, see Brophy and Evertson, 1976). Such teachers usually interpret student failure as the need for more instruction, more clarification, and eventually increased opportunity to learn. Other teachers, because they assign blame rather than assume partial responsibility for student failure, often interpret failure as the need to provide less challenge and fewer opportunities to learn. Teachers who do not have a strong sense that they can influence student learning are therefore more likely to overreact to student error and failure (perhaps by subsequently assigning work that is too easy) than are teachers who believe that they can influence student learning and that they are a partial cause of student failure when it does take place. Along these lines, Marshall and Weinstein (1984) argue that some teachers see intelligence as fixed; others see it as changeable. Differences in views of stability of intelligence can have important effects on teacher behavior.

Another explanation for differential teacher behavior is *student self-presentation*. Students present themselves in varied ways to teachers, and these self-presentation styles may influence teachers' responses. Spencer-Hall (1981) notes that some students are able to time their misbehavior in such a way as to escape teacher attention, whereas other students who misbehave just as often are reprimanded considerably more frequently because the timing of their misbehavior is inappropriate. Carrasco (1979) suggests that some students demonstrate competence in a style that escapes teacher attention. According to Green and Smith (1983), the language some students use makes it likely that teachers will underestimate their potential.

Classroom Application

This review of the literature may stimulate teachers' thinking about the role of expectations in the classroom and the fact that classroom techniques based on research findings must be adjusted to the context of a particular classroom. As Good and Weinstein (1986a) note, teachers express expectations in so many ways (e.g., choice of curriculum topic, rationale given to students for curriculum topic, performance feedback) that it is not possible to suggest a single combination of behaviors that can lead to the communication of appropriate expectations. It is also difficult to provide advice to teachers, because the varied implications of teacher behavior (e.g., call-on, criticism, praise) depend not only on the *behavior* but also on the *context* in which it occurs (what is challenging to a sixth grader may be threatening to a first grader). The *quality* or style of the behavior, as well as students' interpretations of teacher behavior, are also important factors that determine the effects of particular behaviors on students. For example, Brophy (1981) notes that praise may erode or enhance motivation, and Mitman (1985) reports that under some conditions, students may interpret teacher criticism favorably (teacher cares — expects good work).

Teachers must be decision makers and apply concepts and research findings to their own classrooms. For example, there is ample evidence noted earlier that some teachers call on low-achieving students less often than students they believe to be more capable. It makes little sense, however, to encourage *all* teachers to call on low-achieving students more frequently simply because *some* teachers call on low-achieving students infrequently.

Similarly, it does little good to call on low-achieving students more frequently if these students are generally asked only to answer simple factual questions or asked questions they cannot answer. Likewise, it is unproductive to increase the amount of time that a teacher waits for low-achieving students to respond, independent of a consideration of the particular context. If the teacher asks a factual question, simply waiting and providing clues may be an unproductive use of classroom time (the student either knows the answer or doesn't). However, in a situation involving judgment or analysis, more time to think and more teacher clues may facilitate student response.

Still, it seems that the empirical findings and the different models that describe both teacher and student expectations

provide a rich way for thinking about and stimulating student performance. The book, *Looking in Classrooms* (Good and Brophy, 1987), outlines a series of practical considerations and guidelines for teachers based on expectation research. Good and Weinstein (1986a) offer the following suggestions for improving classrooms that feature low expectations and boring, unchallenging routines.

1. Broaden the goals of lessons and activities. Students need to practice and master basic content and skills, but they also need application opportunities. Something is wrong if students are usually working on phonics skills exercises but rarely reading, usually practicing penmanship or copying spelling words but rarely writing, or usually working on arithmetic computation exercises but rarely attempting to formulate and solve problems.

2. Pay more attention to students' ideas and interests and encourage students to play a larger role in assessing their own performance. Students are often much more passive and teacher-dependent in their learning efforts than they need to be.

3. Increase opportunities for students to participate actively in lessons and use materials in meaningful ways. Teacher-led lessons should require more than just quiet listening, and follow-up assignments should require more than just working through highly structured and routinized seatwork assignments.

4. Besides asking routine factual questions, ask students questions that require them to think, analyze, synthesize, or evaluate ideas. Include questions that have no single correct answer or that can be answered at a variety of levels and from a variety of points of view in order to encourage a greater range of students to participate and experience success.

5. Focus on the positive aspects of learning. Be encouraging and reinforcing by noting group progress toward learning goals. Minimize public comparisons of students with one another, discouraging criticism of the class as a whole or suggestions that the material to be learned is overly difficult or unrewarding.

Future Research Directions

There are many research questions that merit consideration; however, I will limit my discussion to two critical issues. First, the conceptualization of teacher expectation needs to become much more differentiated than it has been. Teachers' views of students include achievement, social, and developmental cues. To continue to study teachers' general expectations for high- and low-potential students seems needlessly limiting.

An interesting case study by King (1980) shows that a teacher's expectations for students and behavior toward students were more complex than simple beliefs about whether students were successful or not. In addition to judging whether students were high or low ability, the teacher appeared to judge whether the students' performance was due to ability or effort. King studied one sixth-grade teacher and two successful and two unsuccessful students in that class. The teacher often used the student whose success was believed to be due to ability as a role model (e.g., when she wanted to change the pace or direction of the lesson). In contrast, she developed a different relationship with the student whose success she perceived to be due largely to effort. For example, when this student requested help, the teacher expected the problem to be minor and gave the student minimum but direct feedback. However, this student was less likely to be called on as a way to change the direction of the lesson.

The teacher often provided additional academic support to the student whose lack of success was perceived as due to a lack of ability. The teacher would help the student to work through a problem, etc. Also, the teacher frequently interacted with this student. The teacher seldom interacted with the student whose lack of success the teacher perceived as due to lack of effort, and when interactions did occur, the teacher mainly checked the student's progress and determined whether or not the student was minimally involved in the activity.

This finding is similar to the conclusion that Prawat, Byers, and Anderson (1983) reached after studying 58 elementary school teachers. Specifically, the researchers found that teachers became angry when students made little effort. Thus, judgments teachers make about students are apt to involve complex and multiple criteria.

Second, it is important to recognize that other teacher beliefs and skills may increase or decrease the effects of teachers' expressed expectations. For example, teachers' general instructional style may affect student learning. Hines, Cruickshank, and Kennedy (1985) demonstrated that, at least under certain circumstances, teacher clarity is related positively to both student achievement and student satisfaction. Thus, it is not only the content of instruction or expectations that affects students, but the general way in which students are presented information in assignments. Students' sensitivity to expectation cues is also important; however, teachers' clarity (for better or worse) may make it more likely that students will be influenced by teachers' expectations.

Clearly, more research needs to examine students' awareness of teacher expectations as well as students' vulnerability to expectation communication. Rosenthal (1985) argues that much of the research on interpersonal expectancies suggests that mediation of these expectancies depends to some degree on various processes of nonverbal communication. There apparently are major differences among experimenters, teachers, and other people in the clarity of communication through different nonverbal channels. He suggests that if those teachers who best communicate their expectations for children's intellectual performance in the auditory channel were assigned to children whose best channels of reception were also auditory, expectation effects would be much more likely to occur than if those teachers were assigned to children who were less sensitive to auditory nonverbal communications. Although awareness or perception of expectations is a key issue, another vital issue is the susceptibleness of pupils to such communication. Weinstein notes that the effects of teacher expectations that Braun (1976) suggests have not been tested. It could be that students with high and low self-concepts react differently to information from teachers. Also, minority status may also play a role in students' vulnerability to teacher expectations. Differences in cultural values may insulate some children from the effects of teachers' views of their performance or alternately heighten their susceptibility to the dominant viewpoint. Parents' beliefs may also mediate expectation effects.

Several researchers point out that product measures (student performance on IQ and achievement tests) are too narrow and too restrictive to reveal much about the relationship between expectations and classroom performance (Good and Weinstein, 1986a; Hall and Merkel, 1985; Meyer, 1985). According to Meyer (1985), the long-term effects of early education programs produced by Lazar and Darling (1982) provide important evidence showing that the early Head-Start evaluations that looked only at gains in intelligence were perhaps misplaced. The Lazar and Darling (1982) report examined data from 12 well-known preschool programs; each group was matched with an appropriate control group. Outcome measures included percent of students placed in special education classes, frequency of grade retention, and various achievement and social adjustment measures. In general, the findings suggested that those students who were receiving early education programs were higher in social competence, less likely to be placed in special education programs, and felt better about themselves (treatment children were more likely to link their positive self-evaluations to school or job achievement than the controls). Lazar and Darling concluded that pupils with early education experience were better able to adapt to the social, intellectual, and behavioral demands of their school. Meyer suggests that an additional conclusion from their work is that a narrow set of aptitude/achievement outcomes or dependent variables is likely to underestimate the beneficial effects of early school experiences as well as the negative or positive effects of something like teacher-expectation phenomena.

Meyer (1985) argues that whether or not teachers use negative approaches (that have been defined in the literature) appears to be less a function of teacher expectancy for individual students but more related to how powerful an effect teachers believe they can have on the learning of children; the more powerful they perceive their influence on learning to be, the less likely they will be to use negative behaviors.

Meyer (1985) concludes that it is reasonable to assert that if teachers believe that a student with modest or lower skills is teachable, they will work hard to present information to the student, and in so doing, they will maintain the child's willingness to work. Thus, he suggests, the need exists to train teachers to believe that they can teach students, regardless of the students' current performance.

Acknowledgement

The author acknowledges the support provided by the Center for Research in Social Behavior and wishes to thank Diane Chappell for typing the manuscript and Gail Hinkel for editorial assistance.

References

Adams, G., & Cohen, A. (1974). Children's physical and interpersonal characteristics that affect student-teacher interactions. *Journal of Experimental Education, 43,* 1-5.

Allington, R. (1980). Teacher interruption behaviors during primary grade oral reading. *Journal of Educational Psychology, 72,* 371-377.

Allington, R. (1983). The reading instruction provided readers of differing reading ability. *Elementary School Journal, 83,* 548-559.

Alloway, N. (1984). *Teacher expectations.* Paper presented at the annual conference of the Australian Association for Research in Education, Perth, Australia.

Alpert, J. (1974). Teacher behavior across ability groups: A consideration of the mediation of Pygmalion effects. *Journal of Educational Psychology, 66,* 348-353.

Amato, J. (1975). *Effect of pupils' social class upon teachers' expectations and behavior.* Paper presented at the annual meeting of the American Psychological Association, Chicago.

Anderson-Levitt, K. (1984). Teacher interpretation of student behavior: Cognitive and social processes. *Elementary School Journal, 84* (3), 315-337.

Ashton, P. (1985). Motivation and the teacher's sense of efficacy. In C. Ames & R. Ames (Eds.), *Research on motivation in education. Vol. II: The classroom milieu.* Orlando, FL: Academic Press.

Babad, E. (1985). Some correlates of teachers' expectancy bias. *American Educational Research Journal, 22,* 175-183.

Babad, E., Inbar, J., & Rosenthal, R. (1982). Pygmalion, Galatea, and the Golem: Investigations of biased and unbiased teachers. *Journal of Educational Psychology, 74,* 459-474.

Baron, R., Tom, D., & Cooper, H. (1985). Social class, race and teacher expectations. In J. Dusek (Ed.), *Teacher expectancies.* Hillsdale, NJ: Erlbaum.

Beckerman, T., & Good, T. (1981). The classroom ratio of high- and low-aptitude students and its effect on achievement. *American Educational Research Journal, 18,* 317-327.

Beez, W. (1968). Influence of biased psychological reports on teacher behavior and pupil performance. *Proceedings of the 76th Annual Convention of the American Psychological Association, 3,* 605-606.

Blakey, M. (1970). The relationship between teacher expectancy and teacher verbal behavior and their effect upon adult student achievement. *Dissertation Abstracts International, 31,* 4615A.

Blanck, P., & Rosenthal, R. (1984). Mediation of interpersonal expectancy effects: Counselor's tone of voice. *Journal of Educational Psychology, 76,* 418-426.

Blumenfeld, P., Hamilton, V., Bossert, S., Wessels, K., & Meece, J. (1983). Teacher talk and student thought: Socialization into the student role. In J. Levine & M. Wang (Eds.), *Teacher and student perceptions: Implications for learning.* Hillsdale, NJ: Erlbaum.

Bossert, S. (1979). *Task and social relationships in classrooms: A study of classroom organization and its consequences.* New York: Cambridge University Press.

Bozsik, B. (1982, April). *A study of teacher questioning and student response interaction during pre-story and post-story portions of reading comprehension lessons.* Paper presented at the annual meeting of the American Educational Research Association, New York.

Brattesani, K., Weinstein, R., & Marshall, H. (1984). Student perceptions of differential teacher treatment as moderators of teacher expectation effects. *Journal of Educational Psychology, 76,* 236-247.

Braun, C. (1976). Teacher expectation: Sociopsychological dynamics. *Review of Educational Research, 46,* 185-213.

Brookover, W., Beady, C., Flood, P., Schweitzer, J., & Wisenbaker, J. (1979). *School social systems and student achievement: Schools can make a difference.* New York: Praeger.

Brophy, J. (1981). Teacher praise: A functional analysis. *Review of Educational Research, 51,* 5-32.

Brophy, J. (1983). Research on the self-fulfilling prophecy and teacher expectations. *Journal of educational psychology, 75,* 631-661.

Brophy, J., & Evertson, C. (1976). *Learning from teaching: A developmental perspective.* Boston: Allyn and Bacon.

Brophy, J., & Good, T. (1970). Teachers' communication of differential expectations for children's classroom performance: Some behavioral data. *Journal of Educational Psychology, 61,* 365-374.

Brophy, J., & Good, T. (1974). *Teacher-student relationships: Causes and consequences.* New York: Holt, Rinehart and Winston.

Cahen, L. (1966). *An experimental manipulation of the halo effect.* Unpublished doctoral dissertation, Stanford University, Palo Alto, CA.

Carrasco, R. (1979). *Expanded awareness of student performance: A case study in applied ethnographic monitoring in a bilingual classroom* (Social Linguistic Work Paper No. 60). Austin, TX: Southwest Educational Development Laboratory.

Chaikin, A., Sigler, E., & Derlega, V. (1974). Nonverbal mediators of teacher expectation effects. *Journal of Personality and Social Psychology, 30,* 144-149.

Claiborn, W. (1969). Expectancy effects in the classroom: A failure to replicate. *Journal of Educational Psychology, 60,* 377-383.

Commission on Reading. (1984). *Becoming a nation of readers.* Sponsored by the National Academy of Education, Washington, DC: National Institute of Education.

Conn, L., Edwards, C., Rosenthal, R., & Crowne, D. (1968). Perceptions of emotion and response to teachers' expectancy by elementary school children. *Psychology Reports, 22,* 27-34.

Cooper, H. (1979). Pygmalion grows up: A model for teacher expectation communication and performance influence. *Review of Educational Research, 49,* 389-410.

Cooper, H. (1985). Models of teacher expectation communication. In J. Dusek (Ed.), *Teacher expectancies.* Hillsdale, NJ: Erlbaum.

Cooper, H., & Baron, R. (1977). Academic expectations and attributed responsibility as predictors of professional teachers' reinforcement behavior. *Journal of Educational Psychology, 69,* 409-418.

Cooper, H., & Good, T. (1983). *Pygmalion grows up: Studies in the expectation communication process.* New York: Longman.

Cornbleth, C., Davis, O., & Button, C. (1972, April). *Teacher-pupil interaction and teacher expectations for pupil achievement in secondary social studies classes.* Paper presented at the annual meeting of the American Educational Research Association, Chicago.

Davis, D., & Levine, G. (1970). *The behavioral manifestations of teachers' expectations.* Unpublished manuscript, Hebrew University of Jerusalem.

Doyle, W. (1980). *Student mediating responses in teaching effectiveness.* NIE Final Report. Denton: North Texas State University.

Dusek, J. (Ed.). (1985). *Teacher expectancies.* Hillsdale, NJ: Erlbaum.

Dusek, J., & Joseph, G. (1985). The bases of teacher expectancies. In. J. Dusek (Ed.), *Teacher expectancies.* Hillsdale, NJ: Erlbaum.

Dweck, C., & Elliott, E. (1983). Achievement motivation. In P. Mussen & E. Hetherington (Eds.), *Handbook of child psychology, IV: Socialization, personality, and social development.* New York: Wiley.

Eccles, J., & Wigfield, A. (1985). Teacher expectations and student motivation. In J. Dusek (Ed.), *Teacher expectancies.* Hillsdale, NJ: Erlbaum.

Eder, D. (1981). Ability grouping as a self-fulfilling prophecy: A micro-analysis of teacher-student interaction. *Sociology of Education, 54,* 151-162.

Edmonds, R. (1979). Effective schools for the urban poor. *Educational Leadership, 37,* 15-18.

Egan, O., & Archer, P. (1985). The accuracy of teachers' ratings of ability: A regression model. *American Educational Research Journal, 22,* 25-34.

Farley, J. (1982). Raising student achievement through the affective domain. *Educational Leadership, 39,* 502-503.

Fernandez, C., Espinosa, R., & Dornbusch, S. (1975). *Factors perpetuating the low academic status of Chicano high school students.* (Memorandum No. 13). Palo Alto, CA: Stanford University, Center for Research and Development in Teaching.

Finn, J. (1972). Expectations and the educational environment. *Review of Educational Research, 42,* 387-410.

Firestone, G., & Brody, N. (1975). Longitudinal investigation of teacher-student interactions and their relationship to academic performance. *Journal of Educational Psychology, 67,* 544-550.

Given, B. (1974). Teacher expectancy and pupil performance: The relationship to verbal and non-verbal communication by teachers of learning disabled children. *Dissertation Abstracts International, 35,* 1529A.

Good, T. (1980). Classroom expectations: Teacher-pupil interactions. In J. McMillan (Ed.), *The social psychology of learning.* New York: Academic Press.

Good, T., & Brophy, J. (1980). *Educational psychology: A realistic approach* (2nd ed.). New York: Holt, Rinehart & Winston.

Good, T., & Brophy, J. (1986). School effects. In. M. Wittrock (Ed.), *Handbook of research on teaching* (3rd ed.) (pp. 570-602). New York: Macmillan.

Good, T., & Brophy, J. (1987). *Looking in classrooms* (4th ed.). New York: Harper & Row.

Good, T., Cooper, H., & Blakey, S. (1980). Classroom interaction as a function of teacher expectations, student sex, and time of year. *Journal of Educational Psychology, 72,* 378-385.

Good, T., & Marshall, S. (1984). Do students learn more in heterogeneous or homogeneous groups? In P. Peterson, L. Wilkinson, & M. Hallinan (Eds.), *The social context of instruction: Group organization and group processes.* New York: Academic Press.

Good, T., & Power, C. (1976). Designing successful classroom environments for different types of students. *Journal of Curriculum Studies, 8,* 1-16.

Good, T., Sikes, J., & Brophy, J. (1973). Effects of teacher sex and student sex on classroom interaction. *Journal of Educational Psychology, 65,* 74-87.

Good, T., & Weinstein, R. (1986a). Teacher expectations: A framework for exploring classrooms. In K. Zumwalt (Ed.), *Improving teaching. The 1986 ASCD Yearbook* (pp. 63-85). Alexandria, VA: Association for Supervision and Curriculum Development.

Good, T., & Weinstein, R. (1986b). Schools make a difference: Evidence, criticisms, and new directions. *American Psychologist, 41,* 1090-1097.

Graham, S. (1984). Teacher feelings and student thoughts: An attributional approach to affect in the classroom. *Elementary School Journal, 85,* 91-104.

Grant, L., & Rothenberg, J. (1986). The social enhancement of ability differences: Teacher-student interactions in first- and second-grade reading groups. *Elementary School Journal, 87,* 29-49.

Green, J., & Smith, D. (1983). Teaching and learning: A linguistic perspective. *Elementary School Journal, 53,* 353-391.

Hall, V., & Merkel, S. (1985). Teacher expectancy effects and educational psychology. In J. Dusek (Ed.), *Teacher expectancies.* Hillsdale, NJ: Erlbaum.

Haskett, M. (1968). An investigation of the relationship between expectancy and pupil achievement in the special education class. *Dissertation Abstracts, 29,* 4348A-4349A.

Haskins, R., Walden, T., & Ramey, C. (1983). Teacher and student behavior in high- and low-ability groups. *Journal of Educational Psychology, 75,* 865-876.

Heapy, N., & Siess, T. (1970). *Behavioral consequences of impression formation: Effects of teachers' impressions upon essay evaluations.* Paper presented at the annual meeting of the Eastern Psychological Association, Atlantic City.

Hiebert, E. (1983). An examination of ability grouping for reading instruction. *Reading Research Quarterly, 18,* 231-255.

Hines, C., Cruickshank, D., & Kennedy, J. (1985). Teacher clarity and its relationship to student achievement and satisfaction. *American Educational Research Journal, 22,* 87-99.

Hoge, R., & Butcher, R. (1984). Analysis of teacher judgments of pupil achievement level. *Journal of Educational Psychology, 76,* 777-781.

Jeter, J., & Davis, O. (1973, April). *Elementary school teachers' differential classroom interaction with children as a function of differential expectations of pupil achievements.* Paper presented at the annual meeting of the American Educational Research Association.

Jones, V. (1971). *The influence of teacher-student introversion, achievement, and similarity on teacher-student dyadic classroom interactions.* Unpublished doctoral dissertation, University of Texas, Austin.

Kerman, S. (1979). Teachers' expectations and student achievement. *Phi Delta Kappan, 16,* 716-718.

Kester, S., & Letchworth, J. (1972). Communication of teacher expectations and their effects on achievement and attitude of secondary school students. *Journal of Educational Research, 66,* 51-55.

King, L. (1980). Student thought processes and the expectancy effect. (Research Report 80-1-8). Perth, Australia: Churchlands College of Advanced Education.

Kleinfeld, J. (1975). Effective teachers of Eskimo and Indian students. *School Review, 83,* 301-344.

Lazar, I., & Darling, R. (1982). Lasting effects of early education. *Monographs of the Society for Research in Child Development, 47* (2-3, Serial No. 195).

Marshall, H., & Weinstein, R. (1984, April). *Classrooms where students perceive high and low amounts of differential teacher treatment.* Paper presented at the annual meeting of the American Educational Research Association, New Orleans.

Martinek, T., & Johnson, S. (1979). Teacher expectations. Effects on dyadic interaction and self-concept in elementary-age children. *Research Quarterly, 50,* 60-70.

Martinek, T., & Karper, W. (1982). Canonical relationships

among motor ability, expression of effort, teacher expectations, and dyadic interactions in elementary age children. *Journal of Teaching and Physical Education, 1,* 26-39.

Medinnus, G., & Unruh, R. (1971). *Teacher expectations and verbal communication.* Paper presented at the annual meeting of the Western Psychological Association.

Meichenbaum, D., Bowers, K., & Ross, R. (1969). A behavioral analysis of teacher expectancy effect. *Journal of Personality and Social Psychology, 13,* 306-316.

Mendoza, S., Good, T., & Brophy, J. (1972). *Who talks in junior high classrooms?* (Report No. 68). Austin: University of Texas, Research and Development Center for Teacher Education.

Meyer, W. (1985). Summary, integration, and perspective. In J. Dusek (Ed.), *Teacher expectancies.* Hillsdale, NJ: Erlbaum.

Meyer, W., Bachmann, M., Biermann, U., Hemplemann, M., Ploger, F., & Spiller, H. (1979). The information value of evaluative behavior: Influences of praise and blame on perceptions of ability. *Journal of Educational Psychology, 71,* 259-268.

Mitman, A. (1985). Teachers' differential behavior toward higher and lower achieving students and its relation to selected teacher characteristics. *Journal of Educational Psychology, 77,* 149-161.

Monk, M. (1983). Teacher expectations? Pupil responses to teacher mediated classroom climate. *British Educational Research Journal, 9,* 153-166.

Morine-Dershimer, G. (1982). Pupil perceptions of teacher praise. *Elementary School Journal, 82,* 421-434.

Natriello, G., & Dornbusch, S. (1984). *Teacher evaluative standards and student effort.* New York: Longman.

Oakes, J. (1985). *Keeping track: How schools structure inequality.* New Haven, CT: Yale University Press.

Page, S. (1971). Social interaction and experimenter effects in the verbal conditioning experiment. *Canadian Journal of Psychology, 25,* 463-475.

Pedulla, J., Airasian, P., & Madaus, G. (1980). Do teacher ratings and standardized test results of students yield the same information? *American Educational Research Journal, 17,* 303-307.

Persell, C. (1977). *Education and inequality: The roots and results of stratification in American schools.* New York: The Free Press.

Peterson, P., & Barger, S. (1985). Attribution theory and teacher expectancy. In J. Dusek (Ed.), *Teacher expectancies.* Hillsdale, NJ: Erlbaum.

Pflaum, S., Pascarella, E., Boswick, M., & Auer, C. (1980). The influence of pupil behaviors and pupil status factors on teacher behaviors during oral reading lessons. *Journal of Educational Research, 74,* 99-105.

Prawat, R., Byers, J., & Anderson, A. (1983). An attributional analysis of teachers' affective reactions to students' success and failure. *American Educational Research Journal, 20,* 137-152.

Proctor, C. (1984). Teacher expectations: A model for school improvement. *Elementary School Journal, 84,* 469-481.

Rejeski, W., Dararcott, C., & Hutslar, S. (1979). Pygmalion in youth sport: A field study. *Journal of Sports Psychology, 1,* 311-319.

Rist, R. (1970). Student social class and teacher expectations: The self-fulfilling prophecy in ghetto education. *Harvard Educational Review, 40,* 411-451.

Rolison, M., & Medway, F. (1985). Teachers' expectations and attributions for student achievement: Effects of label, performance patterns, and special education intervention. *American Educational Research Journal, 22,* 561-573.

Rosenthal, R. (1974). *On the social psychology of the self-fulfilling prophecy: Further evidence of Pygmalion effects and their mediating mechanisms.* New York: MSS Modular Publications.

Rosenthal, R. (1985). For unconscious experimenter bias to teacher expectancy effects. In J. Dusek (Ed.), *Teacher expectancies.* Hillsdale, NJ: Erlbaum.

Rosenthal, R., & Jacobson, L. (1968). *Pygmalion in the classroom: Teacher expectation and pupils' intellectual development.* New York: Holt, Rinehart and Winston.

Rowe, M. (1974a). Pausing phenomena: Influence on quality of instruction. *Journal of Psycholinguistic Research, 3,* 203-224.

Rowe, M. (1974b). Wait-time and rewards as instructional variables, their influence on language, logic, and fate control: Part 1: Wait-time. *Journal of Research in Science Teaching, 11,* 81-94.

Rubovits, P., & Maehr, M. (1971). Pygmalion analyzed: Toward an explanation of the Rosenthal-Jacobson findings. *Journal of Personality and Social Psychology, 19,* 197-203.

Rutter, M., Maughan, B., Mortimore, P., Ouston, J., & Smith, A. (1979). *Fifteen thousand hours: Secondary schools and their effects on children.* Cambridge, MA: Harvard University Press.

Smith, F., & Luginbuhl, J. (1976). Inspecting expectancy: Some laboratory results of relevance for teacher training. *Journal of Educational Psychology, 68,* 265-272.

Snow, R. (1969). Unfinished Pygmalion. *Contemporary Psychology, 14,* 197-199.

Spector, P. (1973). *The communication of expectancies: The interaction of reinforcement and expectancy instructions.* Unpublished manuscript. St. Louis: Washington University.

Spencer-Hall, D. (1981). Looking behind the teacher's back. *Elementary School Journal, 81,* 281-289.

Swann, W., & Snyder, M. (1980). On translating beliefs into action: Theories of ability and their application in an instructional setting. *Journal of Personality and Social Psychology, 38,* 879-888.

Taylor, C. (1970). The expectations of Pygmalion's creators. *Educational Leadership, 28,* 161-164.

Taylor, D. (1977). *Second grade reading instruction: The teacher-child dyadic interactions of boys and girls of varying abilities.* Unpublished masters thesis, Rutgers University, New Brunswick, NJ.

Taylor, M. (1979). Race, sex, and the expression of self-fulfilling prophecies in a laboratory teaching situation. *Journal of Personality and Social Psychology, 37,* 897-912.

Weinstein, R. (1976). Reading group membership in first grade: Teacher behaviors and pupil experience over time. *Journal of Educational Psychology, 68,* 103-116.

Weinstein, R. (1983). Student perceptions of schooling. *Elementary School Journal, 83,* 287-312.

Weinstein, R. (1985). Student mediation of classroom expectancy effects. In J. Dusek (Ed.), *Teacher expectancies.* Hillsdale, NJ: Erlbaum.

Weinstein, R. Marshall, H., Brattesani, K., & Middlestadt, S. (1982). Student perceptions of differential teacher treatment in open and traditional classrooms. *Journal of Educational Psychology, 74,* 678-692.

Weinstein, R., & Middlestadt, S. (1979a, April). *Learning about the achievement hierarchy of the classroom: Through children's eyes.* Paper presented at the annual meeting of the American Educational Research Association, San Francisco.

Weinstein, R., & Middlestadt, S. (1979b). Student perceptions of teacher interactions with male high and low achievers. *Journal of Educational Psychology, 71,* 421-431.

West, C., & Anderson, T. (1976). The question of preponderant causation in teacher expectancy research. *Review of Educational Research, 46,* 613-630.

Willis, B. (1970). The influence of teacher expectation on teachers' classroom interaction with selected children. *Dissertation Abstracts, 30,* 5072A.

Zahorik, J. (1970). Pupils' perception of teachers' verbal feedback. *Elementary School Journal, 71,* 105-114.

Zuckerman, M., DeFrank, R., Hall, J., & Rosenthal, R. (1978). Accuracy of nonverbal communication as determinant of interpersonal expectancy effects. *Environmental Psychology and Nonverbal Behavior, 2,* 206-214.

Zuroff, D., & Rotter, J. (1985). A history of the expectancy construct in psychology. In J. Dusek (Ed.), *Teacher expectancies.* Hillsdale, NJ: Erlbaum.

Caring Kids

The Role of the Schools

Psychological research, common sense, and the experience of an important pilot project in California offer specific guidance for helping children to grow into caring adults. Mr. Kohn provides the details.

Alfie Kohn

Alfie Kohn is an independent scholar living in Cambridge, Mass., who writes and lectures widely on human behavior and education. His books include The Brighter Side of Human Nature: Altruism and Empathy in Everyday Life *(Basic Books, 1990) and* No Contest: The Case Against Competition *(Houghton Mifflin, 1986). © 1991, Alfie Kohn.*

"Education worthy of the name is essentially education of character," the philosopher Martin Buber told a gathering of teachers in 1939.[1] In saying this, he presented a challenge more radical and unsettling than his audience may have realized. He did not mean that schools should develop a unit on values or moral reasoning and glue it onto the existing curriculum. He did not mean that problem children should be taught how to behave. He meant that the very profession of teaching calls on us to try to produce not merely good learners but good people.

Given that even the more modest task of producing good learners seems impossibly ambitious—perhaps because of a misplaced emphasis on producing good test-takers—the prospect of taking Buber seriously may seem positively utopian. But in the half-century since his speech, the need for schools to play an active role in shaping character has only grown more pressing. That need is reflected not only in the much-cited prevalence of teenage pregnancy and drug use but also in the evidence of rampant selfishness and competitiveness among young peo-

ple.* At a tender age, children learn not to be tender. A dozen years of schooling often do nothing to promote generosity or a commitment to the welfare of others. To the contrary, students are graduated who think that being smart means looking out for number one.

I want to argue, first, that something *can* be done to rectify this situation because nothing about "human nature" makes selfishness inevitable; second, that educators in particular *should* do something about the problem; and third, that psychological research, common sense, and the experience of an important pilot project in California offer specific guidance for helping children to grow into caring adults.

MUCH OF what takes place in a classroom, including that which we have come to take for granted, emerges from a set of assumptions about the nature of human nature. Not only how children are disciplined, but the very fact that influencing their actions is viewed as "discipline" in the first place; not merely how we grade students, but the fact that we grade them at all; not simply how teachers and students interact, but the fact that

---

*Our society's current infatuation with the word *competitiveness*, which has leached into discussions about education, only exacerbates the problem by encouraging a confusion between two very different ideas: excellence and the desperate quest to triumph over other people.

interaction *between students* is rarely seen as integral to the process of learning — all of these facts ultimately rest on an implicit theory of what human beings are like.

Consider the fact that most conversations about changing the way children act in a classroom tend to focus on curbing negative behaviors rather than on promoting positive ones. In part, this emphasis simply reflects the urgency of preventing troublesome or even violent conduct. But this way of framing the issue may also tell us something about our view of what comes naturally to children, what they are capable of, and, by extension, what lies at the core of our species. Likewise, it is no coincidence, I think, that the phrase "it's just human nature to be . . ." is invariably followed by such adjectives as selfish, competitive, lazy, aggressive, and so on. Very rarely do we hear someone protest, "Well, of course he was helpful. After all, it's just human nature to be generous."

The belief persists in this culture that our darker side is more pervasive, more persistent, and somehow more real than our capacity for what psychologists call "prosocial behavior." We seem to assume that people are naturally and primarily selfish and will act otherwise only if they are coerced into doing so and carefully monitored. The logical conclusion of this world view is the assumption that generous and responsible behavior must be forced down the throats of children who would otherwise be inclined to care only about themselves.

From *Phi Delta Kappan*, March 1991, pp. 496-506. Copyright © 1991 by Alfie Kohn. Reprinted by permission.

The belief persists in this culture that our darker side is more pervasive . . .

A review of several hundred studies has convinced me that this cynicism is not realism. Human beings are not only selfish and self-centered, but also decent, able to feel — and prepared to try to relieve — the pain of others. I believe that it is as "natural" to help as it is to hurt, that concern for the well-being of others often cannot be reduced to self-interest, that social structures predicated on human selfishness have no claim to inevitability — or even prudence. This is not the place for rehearsing the arguments and data that support these conclusions — in part because I have recently done so at book length.[2] But I would like to mention a few recent findings from developmental psychology that speak to the question of whether educators can aim higher than producing a quiet classroom or a nondisruptive child.

To start at the beginning, newborns are more likely to cry — and to cry longer — when they are exposed to the sound of another infant's crying than when they hear other noises that are equally loud and sudden. In three sets of studies with infants ranging in age from 18 to 72 hours, such crying seemed to be a spontaneous reaction rather than a mere vocal imitation.[3] In the view of Abraham Sagi and Martin Hoffman, who conducted one of the studies, this finding suggests the existence of "a rudimentary empathic distress reaction at birth."[4] Our species may be primed, in other words, to be discomfited by someone else's discomfort.

As an infant grows, this discomfort continues and takes more sophisticated forms. Marian Radke-Yarrow, Carolyn Zahn-Waxler, and their associates at the National Institute of Mental Health have been studying toddlers for nearly 20 years, having in effect deputized mothers as research assistants to collect data in the home instead of relying on brief (and possibly unrepresentative) observations in the laboratory. A 10- to 14-month-old child, they have found, can be expected to show signs of agitation and unhappiness in the presence of another person's distress, perhaps by crying or burying her

head in her mother's lap. As a child develops the capacity to undertake more deliberate behavior, in the period between 18 and 24 months, his response to distress will become more active: patting the head, fetching a toy, offering verbal expressions of sympathy, finding an adult to help, and so forth.[5]

I should add that, like all parents, researchers have also observed hostile and selfish actions on the part of children. To say that sympathy or helping behavior is pervasive and precocious is not to claim that every child is an angel or to deny that toddlers — particularly in a society preoccupied with possessiveness — will sometimes snatch back a toy ("Mine!") or throw it across the room. But it is to argue that the *antisocial* is no more basic or natural than the *prosocial*.

By the time children are of preschool age, comforting, sharing, and helping are regular occurrences. One study of preschoolers during free play discovered that 67 of the 77 children shared with, helped, or comforted another child at least once during only 40 minutes of observation.[6] After counting such behaviors in similar experiments of her own, Arizona State University psychologist Nancy Eisenberg became curious about why children were acting this way. To find out, she came up with a technique that few research psychologists had thought to use: she *asked* the children.

Eisenberg and a colleague simply followed 4- and 5-year-olds around a preschool and watched for unprompted prosocial behavior. Each time such an act was observed, the child was asked why he or she did it. ("How come you gave that to John?") None of the children intended to conform to adult expectations or expressed any fear of punishment. Very few said that they expected to benefit in some way by helping—such as by impressing their peers. Among the most frequent explanations heard was the simple observation that the other child had needed help.[7] This, when you come right down to it, is the heart of altruism.[8] And it is enough to suggest that parents and educators hoping to raise a child who

is responsive to the needs of others already have "an ally within the child," in Martin Hoffman's lovely phrase.

IF WE HAD to pick a logical setting in which to guide children toward caring about, empathizing with, and helping other people, it would be a place where they would regularly come into contact with their peers and where some sort of learning is already taking place. The school is such an obvious choice that one wonders how it could be that the active encouragement of prosocial values and behavior — apart from occasional exhortations to be polite — plays no part in the vast majority of American classrooms. This would seem to stem either from a lack of interest in the idea or from some objection to using the schools in particular for this purpose. Both factors probably play a role, but I will concentrate here on the latter and consider three specific reservations that parents, teachers, policy makers, and others may have — or at least may hear and thus need to answer — about classroom-based programs to help children develop a prosocial orientation.

The first objection is that an agenda concerned with social and moral issues amounts to teaching values — a dangerous business for a public institution. In response, we must concede that a prosocial agenda is indeed value-laden, but we should immediately add that the very same is true of the status quo. The teacher's presence and behavior, her choice of text, the order in which she presents ideas, and her tone of voice are as much part of the lesson as the curriculum itself. So, too, is a teacher's method of discipline or classroom management saturated in values, regardless of whether those values are transparent to the teacher. In short, to arrange our schools so that caring, sharing, helping, and empathizing are actively encouraged is not to introduce values into a neutral environment; it is to examine the values already in place and to consider trading them in for a new set.

It is sometimes said that moral con-

There is nothing about caring for others that implies not caring for oneself.

cerns and social skills ought to be taught at home. I know of no one in the field of education or child development who disagrees. The problem is that such instruction — along with nurturance and warmth, someone to model altruism, opportunities to practice caring for others, and so forth — is not to be found in all homes. The school may need to provide what some children will not otherwise get. In any case, there is no conceivable danger in providing these values in both environments. Encouragement from more than one source to develop empathic relationships is a highly desirable form of redundancy.

The second concern one hears — and this one dovetails with the broader absence of interest in the prosocial realm — is the fear that children taught to care about others will be unable to look out for themselves when they are released into a heartless society. The idea that someone exposed to such a program will grow up gullible and spineless, destined to be victimized by mean-spirited individuals, can be traced back to the prejudice that selfishness and competitiveness are efficacious social strategies — a sterling example of what sociologist C. Wright Mills used to call "crackpot realism." In fact, those whose mantra is "look out for number one" are actually at a greater disadvantage in any sort of society than those who are skilled at working with others and inclined to do so. Competition and the single-minded pursuit of narrowly conceived self-interest typically turn out to be counterproductive.

By contrast, a well-designed program of prosocial instruction will include training in cooperative conflict resolution and in methods of achieving one's goals that do not require the use of force or manipulation. But even without such a component, there is nothing about caring for others that implies not caring for or looking after oneself. A raft of research has established that assertiveness, healthy self-esteem, and popularity are all com-

patible with — and often even correlates of — a prosocial orientation.[9]

The final objection to teaching children to be caring individuals is that the time required to do so comes at the expense of attention to academics — a shift in priorities apt to be particularly unpopular at a time when we entertain ourselves by describing how much students don't know. In fact, though, there is absolutely no evidence to suggest that prosocial children — or the sort of learning experiences that help to create them — are mutually exclusive with academic achievement. To the contrary, the development of perspective-taking — the capacity to imagine how someone else thinks, feels, or sees the world — tends to promote cognitive problem solving generally. In one study, the extent to which girls had these skills at age 8 or 9 was a powerful predictor of performance on reading and spelling tests taken two years later — an even better predictor, in fact, than their original test scores.[10]

Not only are the ingredients of a prosocial orientation conducive to academic excellence, but the educational process itself does not require us to choose between teaching children to think and teaching them to care. It is possible to integrate prosocial lessons into the regular curriculum; as long as children are learning to read and spell and think critically, they may as well learn with texts that encourage perspective-taking. Indeed, to study literature or history by grappling with social and moral dilemmas is to invite a deeper engagement with those subjects. Meanwhile, literally hundreds of studies have shown that cooperative learning, which has an important place in a prosocial classroom, enhances achievement regardless of subject matter or age level.[11] So consistent and remarkable have these results been that schools and individual teachers often adopt models of cooperative learning primarily to strengthen academic per-

formance. The development of prosocial values is realized as an unintended bonus.

EDUCATION of character in Buber's sense asks of teachers something more than the mere elimination of behavior problems in the classroom. The absence of such problems is often seen as an invitation to move past behavioral and social issues and get on with the business at hand, which is academic learning. I am arguing, by contrast, that behavioral and social issues, values and character, are very much part of the business at hand. But whether we are talking about addressing misconduct or about taking the initiative to help students become more responsive to one another, a teacher can take any of several basic orientations. Here are four approaches to changing behaviors and attitudes, presented in ascending order of desirability.

1. Punishing. A reliance on the threat of punishment is a reasonably good indication that something is wrong in a classroom, since children have to be bullied into acting the way the teacher demands. Apart from the disagreeable nature of this style of interaction — which cannot be disguised, incidentally, by referring to punishment as "consequences" — it is an approach distinguished mostly by its ineffectiveness. Decades of research have established that children subjected to punitive discipline at home are *more* likely than their peers to break rules when they are away from home.

Isolating a child from his peers, humiliating her, giving him an F, loading her with extra homework, or even threatening to do any of these things can produce compliance in the short run. Over the long haul, however, this strategy is unproductive.

Why? First, at best, punishment teaches nothing about what one is supposed to do — only about what one is not supposed to do. There is an enormous difference between not beating up one's peers, on the one hand, and being helpful, on the other.

Second, the child's attention is not really focused on the intended lesson at all ("pushing people is bad"), much less on the rationale for this principle, but primarily on the punishment itself. Figuring out how to get away with the misbehavior, how to avoid detection by an authority, is a perfectly logical response. (Notice that the one who punishes be-

> ## Like sticks, carrots are artificial attempts to manipulate behavior.

comes transformed in the child's eyes into a rule-enforcer who is best avoided.) Social learning theory tells us that this attention to the punishment is also likely to *teach* the child to be punitive and thus exacerbate the behavior problems; a teacher's actions do indeed speak louder than words.

Finally, punishment breeds resistance and resentment. "The more you use power to try to control people, the less real influence you'll have on their lives," Thomas Gordon has written.[12] Since such influence is associated with helping children to develop good values, the use of power would seem ill-advised.

2. Bribing. There is no question that rewards are better than punishment. On the other hand, what these two methods share is probably more important than the respects in which they differ, and herein lies a tale that will be highly disconcerting to educators enamored of positive reinforcement. Psychological—and particularly developmental—theory and research have come a long way since the simplistic behaviorism of the last generation, but many well-meaning teachers continue to assume that what works for training the family pet must be appropriate for shaping children's actions and values as well.

Gold stars, smiley faces, trophies, certificates, high grades, extra recess time, candy, money, and even praise all share the feature of being "extrinsic" to whatever behavior is being rewarded. Like sticks, carrots are artificial attempts to manipulate behavior that offer children *no reason to continue acting in the desired way when there is no longer any goody to be gained.* Do rewards motivate students? Absolutely. They motivate students to get rewarded. What they fail to do is help children develop a commitment to being generous or respectful.

In fact, the news is even worse than this. Not only is bribing someone to act in a particular way ultimately ineffective, but, like the use of threats, it can actual-

ly make things worse. Consider the effects of rewards on achievement. Yale psychologist Robert Sternberg recently summed up what a growing number of motivation researchers now concede: "Nothing tends to undermine creativity quite like extrinsic motivators do. They also undermine intrinsic motivation: when you give extrinsic rewards for certain kinds of behavior, you tend to reduce children's interest in performing those behaviors for their own sake."[13] Once we see ourselves as doing something in order to get a reward, we are less likely to want to continue doing it in the absence of a reward — even if we used to find it enjoyable.

Readers of the *Kappan* were first exposed to research demonstrating this phenomenon more than 15 years ago,[14] and the data have continued to accumulate since then, with some studies concentrating on how extrinsic motivators reduce intrinsic interest and others showing how they undermine performance, particularly on creative tasks.[15] A number of explanations have been proposed to account for these remarkably consistent findings. First, people who think of themselves as working for a reward feel controlled, and this lack of self-determination interferes with creativity. Second, rewards encourage "ego involvement" to the exclusion of "task involvement," and the latter is more predictive of achievement. Third, the promise of a reward is "tantamount to declaring that the activity is not worth doing for its own sake," as A. S. Neill put it;[16] indeed, anything construed as a prerequisite to some other goal will probably be devalued as a result.

What is true for academic learning also applies to behavior. A little-known series of studies has pointed up the folly of trying to encourage prosocial behavior through the use of extrinsic incentives. Children who received rewards for donating to another child—and, in another experiment, adults who were paid for helping a researcher—turned out to be

less likely to describe themselves in words suggesting intrinsic motivation to help than were people who received nothing in return.[17] In another study, women offered money for answering a questionnaire were less likely to agree to a similar request two or three days later, when no money was involved, than were women who had not been paid for helping with the first survey.[18]

The implication is that, when someone is rewarded for prosocial behavior, that person will tend to assume that the reward accounts for his or her actions and thus will be less likely to help once no one is around to hand out privileges or praise. Indeed, elementary school students whose mothers believed in using rewards to motivate them were less cooperative and generous than other children in a recent study.[19] Such findings are of more than theoretical interest given the popularity of Skinnerian techniques for promoting generosity in schools. A recent *New York Times* article described elementary schools where helpful children have their pictures posted in hallways, get to eat at a special table in the cafeteria, or even receive money.[20] Such contrivances may actually have the effect of undermining the very prosocial orientation that their designers hope to promote.

3. Encouraging commitment to values. To describe the limitations of the use of punishments and rewards is already to suggest a better way: the teacher's goal should not be simply to produce a given behavior — for example, to get a child to share a cookie or stop yelling — but to help that child see himself or herself as the kind of person who is responsible and caring. From this shift in self-concept will come lasting behaviors and values that are not contingent on the presence of someone to dispense threats or bribes. The child has made these behaviors and values his or her own.

A student manipulated by currently fashionable behavioral techniques, however, is unlikely to internalize the values underlying the desired behaviors. At the heart of "assertive discipline," for example, is control: "I want teachers to learn that they have to take charge," Lee Canter explained recently.[21] I don't. I want *children* to become responsible for what they do and for what kind of people they are. The teacher has a critical role to play in making sure that this happens; in criticizing manipulative approaches I am not suggesting that children be left alone

From preschool to high school, children should learn why helping others is good.

to teach themselves responsibility. But the teacher ought to be guided less by the need to maintain control over the classroom than by the long-term objective of helping students to act responsibly because they understand that it is right to do so.

I will have more to say below about strategies for facilitating this internalization, but first I want to mention a version of this process that I believe is even more desirable — the ideal approach to helping children become good people.

4. Encouraging the group's commitment to values. What the first two approaches have in common is that they provide nothing more than extrinsic motivation. What the first two share with the third is that they address only the individual child. I propose that helpfulness and responsibility ought not to be taught in a vacuum but in the context of a community of people who learn and play and make decisions together. More precisely, the idea is not just to internalize good values *in* a community but to internalize, among other things, the value *of* community.

Perhaps the best way to crystallize what distinguishes each of these four approaches is to imagine the question that a child is encouraged to ask by each. An education based on punishment prompts the query, "What am I supposed to do, and what will happen to me if I don't do it?" An education based on rewards leads the child to ask, "What am I supposed to do, and what will I get for doing it?" When values have been internalized by the child, the question becomes "What kind of person do I want to be?" And, in the last instance, the child wonders: "How do we want our classroom (or school) to be?"

EDUCATORS eager to have children think about how they want their classrooms to be — which is to say, educators who do not feel threatened at the prospect of inviting children to share some of the responsibility for creating norms and determining goals — need to think in terms of five

broad categories: what they believe, what they say, what they do, how they relate to students, and how they encourage students to relate to one another. Let us consider each in turn.

What educators believe. The famous Pygmalion effect refers to the fact that a teacher's assumptions about a child's intellectual potential can affect that child's performance. Such self-fulfilling prophecies, however, are by no means limited to academics; they also operate powerfully on a child's actions and values. Write off a student as destructive or disruptive, and he or she is likely to "live down to" these expectations. Conversely — and here is the decisive point for anyone concerned with promoting generosity — attributing to a child the best possible motive that is consistent with the facts may set in motion an "auspicious" (rather than a vicious) circle. We help students develop good values by assuming whenever possible that they are already motivated by these values — rather than by explaining an ambiguous action in terms of a sinister desire to make trouble.

However, what we assume about a given student is also colored by our assumptions regarding human nature itself. While I am not aware of any research on this question, it seems reasonable to suppose that an educator who thinks that self-interest motivates everything we do will be suspicious of individual instances of generosity. Someone who takes for granted that a Hobbesian state of nature would exist in a classroom in the absence of a controlling adult to keep children in line, who believes that children need to be leaned on or "taught a lesson" or bribed to act responsibly, is likely to transfer these expectations to the individual child and to produce an environment that fulfills them. The belief that children are actually quite anxious to please adults, that they may simply lack the skills to get what they need, that they will generally respond to a caring environment can create a very different reality. What you believe matters.

What educators say. An immense body

of research has shown that children are more likely to follow a rule if its rationale has been explained to them and that, in general, discipline based on reason is more effective than the totalitarian approach captured by the T-shirt slogan "Because I'm the mommy, that's why." This finding applies not only to discouraging aggression but to promoting altruism. From preschool to high school, children should learn why — not merely be told that — helping others is good. Pointing out how their actions affect others sensitizes students to the needs and feelings of others and tacitly communicates a message of trust and responsibility. It implies that, once children understand how their behavior makes other people feel, they can and will choose to do something about it.

How such explanations are framed also counts. First, the level of the discourse should be fitted to the child's ability to understand. Second, the concept of using reason does not preclude passion. A prohibition on hurting people, for example, should not be offered dispassionately but with an emotional charge to show that it matters. Third, prosocial activity should not be promoted on the basis of self-interest. "Zachary, if you don't share your dump truck with Linda, she won't let you play with her dinosaur" has an undeniable appeal for a parent, but it is a strategy more likely to inculcate self-regarding shrewdness than genuine concern for others. The same goes for classroom exhortations and instruction.

A series of studies by Joan Grusec of the University of Toronto and her colleagues is also relevant. Her research provides a concrete alternative to the use of rewards or praise to elicit generosity. "Children who view their prosocial conduct as compliance with external authority will act prosocially only when they believe external pressures are present," she has written. Far preferable is for children to "come to believe that their prosocial behavior reflects values or dispositions in themselves."[22]

This result is best achieved by verbally attributing such values or dispositions to the child. In one experiment, in which children gave away some of their game winnings after watching a model do so, those who were told that they had made the donation "because you're the kind of person who likes to help other people" were subsequently more generous than those who were told that they had donated because they were expected to do so.[23] In another study, the likelihood of children's donating increased both when they were praised and when they were led to think of themselves as helpful people. But in a follow-up experiment, it was the latter group who turned out to be more generous than those who had received verbal reinforcement. In other words, praise increased generosity in a given setting but ceased to be effective outside of that setting, whereas children with an intrinsic impulse to be generous continued to act on that motivation in other circumstances.[24]

A study of adults drives home the point. Subjects who were told that a personality test showed that they were kind and thoughtful people were more likely to help a confederate who "accidentally" dropped a pile of cards than were those who were told that they were unusually intelligent or those given no feedback at all. This finding is important because it implies that being led to think of oneself as generous does not affect behavior merely because it is a kind of reinforcement or a mood-enhancer; this label apparently encourages prosocial action because it helps to build a view of the self as altruistic.[25]

This is not to suggest that a teacher's every utterance must be — or can be — geared toward internalization. Simply making sure that a classroom is a safe environment conducive to learning can require the sort of behavioral interventions on a day-to-day basis that don't do much to strengthen a child's prosocial self-concept. But the more teachers attend to the latter, the fewer problems they are likely to have over the long run.

What educators do. Children of all ages, from before the time they can read until after the time they start seeking distance from adults, learn from what they see. Studies show that children who watched, even briefly, as someone donated to charity were themselves likely to donate more than other children — even if months had elapsed since the exposure to the model.[26] The extent to which a teacher expresses concern about people in distress and takes the initiative to help

— which applies both to how the teacher treats the students themselves and how he or she refers to people outside the classroom — can set a powerful example and be even more effective than didactic instruction in promoting a sense of caring in students.

There is no shortage of suggestions about how to devise lessons that address social and ethical issues, ranging from explicit training in perspective-taking or moral reasoning to discussions about values that can, in turn, include either "clarification" of the beliefs that students already hold or old-fashioned lectures on character or morality. Most of the debate on the subject occurs between proponents of just such programs, each accusing the other of being relativistic or of seeking to indoctrinate. Far less consideration is given to the possibility of integrating such issues into the regular curriculum.

A distinction, though not a sharp one, can be made between teaching morality (or about morality) as such and helping children to be positively connected to others. The latter is my focus here, and some writers have argued that, particularly for younger children, it ought to be the primary focus in the schools, too. "Unless the young child has acquired a positive propensity towards other persons," says one educator, "subsequent moral education will become virtually impotent."[27]

As an alternative to special units devoted to one of these approaches, children can use texts in conventional subject areas that encourage perspective-taking. This option should allay the concern that moral instruction will distract us from academics.

How educators relate to students. Preceding and underlying specific techniques for encouraging particular behaviors is the practice of nesting all kinds of discipline and instruction in the context of a warm, nurturant, and empathic relationship with students. Children whose parents are interested in and supportive of them usually distinguish themselves as socially competent and psychologically healthy on a range of measures, and there is no reason to think that the teacher/student relationship is any different.

Warm, caring, empathic adults do several things at once. They provide the child with a benevolent, safe place in which to act. (If a child's experience with others leaves him or her feeling threatened rather than safe, this is likely to fos-

ter psychological damage control at the expense of any inclination to help others.) I hope that few educators take seriously the absurd dictum that teachers should display no warmth until well into the school year — after firm control of the classroom has been won. Instead, teachers should establish themselves from the beginning as the students' allies, adults with whom they can work to solve the problems that emerge during the normal course of development. In meeting a child's emotional needs we give him or her the emotional freedom to meet the needs of others.

How educators encourage students to relate to one another. Anyone interested in children as social beings must recognize the need to attend to the interactions among them in the classroom. In most American schools, children are forced to work either against one another (by competing) or apart from one another (by learning individually). The chance to work *with* one another, to learn social skills and caring, is left to happen by itself during recess, at lunch, or after school. This single fact goes a long way toward explaining why people in our society tend to regard others as potential obstacles to their own success. David Johnson and Roger Johnson of the University of Minnesota have emphasized that the relationship between student and student is at least as important as that between student and teacher or between student and curriculum. Their reference to student/student relationships is offered in the context of creating good learners, and it is all the more true in terms of creating good human beings.

How, specifically, should teachers encourage student interaction? First, students can be put in pairs or small groups so as to help one another learn. This concept, known as cooperative learning, embraces many disparate models for implementation: some depend on grades and other extrinsic incentives to insure that students work together, some involve cooperation among as well as within groups, some provide for a strict division of labor in completing assignments. A substantial number of studies have found that cooperative learning of various types has the potential to help students feel good about themselves, feel good about each other, feel good about what they are learning, and learn more effectively.

Cooperation, by virtue of being an interaction in which two or more people

Do quiet children learn more effectively or merely make fewer demands on teachers?

work together for mutual benefit, is not itself an example of prosocial behavior as the term is usually used. Neither does its successful use presuppose the existence of prosocial motives in all children. Rather, by creating interdependence and a built-in incentive to help, cooperative learning *promotes* prosocial behavior. Having children learn from one another creates powerful bonds between them and sends a message very different from that sent by a classroom in which each child is on his or her own — or, worse still, one in which the success of each is inversely related to the success of the others.[28]

In one study, fifth-graders who studied grammar in cooperative learning groups were more likely to give away prize tokens to a stranger than were those who studied on their own; in another, kindergartners who participated in cooperative activities acted more prosocially than their peers in a traditional classroom.[29] But the consequences are not limited to generosity per se. Carefully structured cooperative learning also promotes a subjective sense of group identity, a greater acceptance of people who are different from oneself (in terms of ethnicity or ability level), and a more sophisticated ability to imagine other people's points of view.[30] Cooperation is an essentially humanizing experience that predisposes participants to take a benevolent view of others. It allows them to transcend egocentric and objectifying postures and encourages trust, sensitivity, open communication, and prosocial activity.

Second, teachers can move the idea of discipline not only away from punishments and rewards but also away from the premise of these strategies — namely, that teachers should simply be figuring out by themselves how to elicit compliance with a set of rules or goals that they alone devise. The realistic alternative is not for the teacher to abdicate responsibility for what happens in the classroom but rather to bring in (and guide) children so that they can play a role in making decisions about how their classroom is to be run and why. (Must hands always be raised or only during certain kinds of discussions? What is the best way for the class as a community to balance principles of fairness and the spontaneity that encourages participation?)

Discipline would thus be reconfigured as collaborative planning and mutual problem solving. Such an approach will be preferred by anyone who favors the idea of autonomy and democratic decision making — but it can also be argued that purely practical considerations recommend it, since children are more likely to follow rules that they have helped to create than rules dictated to them. This, of course, assumes that following rules is in itself a desirable goal. More broadly, educators need to ask themselves and each other about the ultimate objective of discipline. Even if one of the conventional programs of behavior control succeeded in keeping children quiet, do quiet children learn more effectively or merely make fewer demands on the teacher? (The Johnsons like to say that a principal walking through the school corridors should be concerned if he or she hears no sound coming from a classroom; this means that real learning probably is not taking place.) And which approach is most likely to help children come to care about one another?

To invite children to participate in making decisions not only about classroom procedures but also about pedagogical matters (what is to be learned, how, and why) and housekeeping matters (how to celebrate birthdays or decorate the walls) is to bring them into a process of discussion, an opportunity to cooperate and build consensus. To this extent, it is a chance for them to practice perspective-taking skills, to share and listen and help. In short, involving children in planning and decision making is a way of providing a framework for prosocial interactions that supports other such opportunities; it turns a routine issue into another chance to learn about and practice caring—and, not so incidentally, thinking as well.[31]

Finally, educators can provide students with opportunities to be responsible for one another so that they will learn (prosocial values and skills) by doing. Ideally, this can include interaction with those of different ages. For an older child to guide someone younger is to experience firsthand what it is to be a helper and to be responsible for someone who is dependent on him or her. For the younger child, this cross-age interaction presents an opportunity to see a prosocial model who is not an adult.

ONE OF THE most exciting and innovative educational programs now in operation, the Child Development Project (CDP), is devoted specifically to helping children become more caring and responsible.[32] The experience of the CDP offers lessons in the systematic application of many of the ideas discussed here; indeed, I owe my formulation of some of these ideas to the work done by Eric Schaps, Marilyn Watson, and others involved with the project.

The CDP is the first long-term, comprehensive, school-based project in prosocial education. After being invited a decade ago to work in the San Ramon Valley (California) Unified School District, about 30 miles east of San Francisco, the staff carefully matched two sets of three elementary schools in the district for size and socioeconomic status. A coin flip then determined which of these sets would receive the program and which would serve as the comparison group. The first teachers were trained before the start of the 1982–83 school year. Staff researchers focused on a group of children in the experimental schools (then in kindergarten and now in junior high school) to assess whether their attitudes, behavior, and achievement differed significantly from those of their counterparts in the comparison schools. In the fall of 1988, the program was introduced into two elementary schools in nearby Hayward, a district more ethnically diverse than the white, affluent suburbs in San Ramon Valley,

Prosocial values come from a synthesis of adult inculcation and peer interaction.

and Schaps is now seeking funding to take the program to eight more sites around the country.

"How do we want our classroom to be?" is exactly the question that the CDP would have children ask. Rejecting punishment and rewards in favor of strategies geared toward internalization of prosocial norms and values, the CDP invites teachers and students to work together to turn their classrooms into caring communities. The primary components of the program intended to bring this about are these:

• a version of cooperative learning that does not rely on grades or other extrinsic motivators;

• the use of a literature-based reading program that stimulates discussion about values and offers examples of empathy and caring even as it develops verbal skills;

• an approach to classroom management in which the emphasis is on developing intrinsic motives to participate productively and prosocially, in which teachers are encouraged to develop warm relationships with the children, and in which periodic class meetings are held so that children can play an active role in planning, assessing progress, and solving problems; and

• a variety of other features, including pairing children of different ages to work together, setting up community service projects to develop responsibility, giving periodic homework assignments specifically designed to be done (and to foster communication) with parents, and holding schoolwide activities that may involve whole families.

In their writings, members of the CDP staff have distinguished their way of teaching values from the approaches of better-known models. Unlike certain kinds of character education, the CDP approach emphasizes helping students understand the reason for a given value rather than simply insisting that they accept it or behave in a certain way because they have been told to do so. Unlike purely child-centered approaches, however, the CDP is committed to the importance of adult socialization: the teacher's job is to teach, to guide, to enforce, to facilitate cooperation, to model behaviors — in short, to be much more than a passive bystander. Prosocial values come from a synthesis of adult inculcation and peer interaction, and these values — in contrast to the programs developed by some theorists in the area of moral reasoning — emphasize caring for others as well as applying principles of fairness.

Prior to the implementation of the CDP, students randomly selected from the three experimental and the three comparison schools proved to be similar not only demographically but also on a range of social attitudes, values, and skills. Once the program was implemented, however, structured interviews and observations turned up significant differences between students participating in the program and those in the comparison schools on some, though not all, measures.

Children taking part in the CDP engaged in a greater number of spontaneous prosocial behaviors in class, seemed better able to understand hypothetical conflict situations, and were more likely to take everyone's needs into account in dealing with such situations. They were more likely to believe that one has an obligation to speak up in a discussion even if one's position seems unlikely to prevail (which should answer those concerned about the assertiveness of caring children). While the CDP's emphasis has not required any sacrifice of conventional achievement (as measured by standardized test scores), neither has it given participants a consistent academic advantage over students in comparison schools. (In part, this finding may be due to a ceiling effect: students in the district already score in the top 10% of California school-

children, so there is not much room for improvement.) By the time the CDP group reached sixth grade, though, they were outscoring their counterparts in the comparison schools on a measure of higher-order reading comprehension (essays written about stories and poems).

It remains to be seen whether and in what ways the values and behaviors of children from schools using the CDP will continue to distinguish them from those who attended comparison schools now that they are all in junior high school. But this pilot project provides real evidence for the larger point I am making here: it is both realistic and valuable to attend to what students learn in the classroom about getting along with their peers. Children can indeed be raised to work with, care for, and help one another. And schools must begin to play an integral role in that process.

1. Martin Buber, *Between Man and Man*, trans. Ronald Gregor Smith (New York: Macmillan, 1965), p. 104.

2. Alfie Kohn, *The Brighter Side of Human Nature: Altruism and Empathy in Everyday Life* (New York: Basic Books, 1990).

3. Marvin L. Simner, "Newborn's Response to the Cry of Another Infant," *Developmental Psychology*, vol. 5, 1971, pp. 136-50; Abraham Sagi and Martin L. Hoffman, "Empathic Distress in the Newborn," *Developmental Psychology*, vol. 12, 1976, pp. 175-76; and Grace B. Martin and Russell D. Clark III, "Distress Crying in Neonates: Species and Peer Specificity," *Developmental Psychology*, vol. 18, 1982, pp. 3-9.

4. Sagi and Hoffman, p. 176.

5. See, for example, Carolyn Zahn-Waxler and Marian Radke-Yarrow, "The Development of Altruism: Alternative Research Strategies," in Nancy Eisenberg-Berg, ed., *The Development of Prosocial Behavior* (New York: Academic Press, 1982).

6. Marian Radke-Yarrow and Carolyn Zahn-Waxler, "Dimensions and Correlates of Prosocial Behavior in Young Children," *Child Development*, vol. 47, 1976, pp. 118-25.

7. Nancy Eisenberg-Berg and Cynthia Neal, "Children's Moral Reasoning About Their Own Spontaneous Prosocial Behavior," *Developmental Psychology*, vol. 15, 1979, pp. 228-29. Eisenberg and another colleague have observed that appeals to authority or punishment (which were completely absent here) are what one would expect if the chil-

dren were at Lawrence Kohlberg's first stage of moral reasoning and that the apparently altruistic needs-oriented explanations have often − and presumably unfairly − been coded as stage 2, that is, as an immature, "preconventional" way of thinking about moral problems (see Nancy Eisenberg-Berg and Michael Hand, "The Relationship of Preschoolers' Reasoning About Prosocial Moral Conflicts to Prosocial Behavior," *Child Development*, vol. 50, 1979, pp. 356-63).

8. The tendency to define *altruism* so narrowly that only Mother Teresa would qualify for the label both reflects and perpetuates a cynical view of human nature. It would never occur to us to define *aggression* so as to exclude everything short of mass murder.

9. Kohn, Ch. 3.

10. Norma Deitch Feshbach and Seymour Feshbach, "Affective Processes and Academic Achievement," *Child Development*, vol. 58, 1987, pp. 1335-47. For more research on cognitive skills and perspective-taking, see David W. Johnson and Frank P. Johnson, *Joining Together: Group Theory and Group Skills*, 3rd ed. (Englewood Cliffs, N.J.: Prentice-Hall, 1987), p. 244.

11. For example, see David Johnson et al., "Effects of Cooperative, Competitive, and Individualistic Goal Structures on Achievement: A Meta-Analysis," *Psychological Bulletin*, vol. 89, 1981, pp. 47-62; David W. Johnson and Roger T. Johnson, *Cooperation and Competition* (Edina, Minn.: Interaction Book Co., 1989), especially Ch. 3; and Robert E. Slavin, *Cooperative Learning: Theory, Research, and Practice* (Englewood Cliffs, N.J.: Prentice-Hall, 1990), especially Ch. 2.

12. Thomas Gordon, *Teaching Children Self-Discipline* (New York: Times Books, 1989), p. 7.

13. Robert J. Sternberg, "Prototypes of Competence and Incompetence," in Robert J. Sternberg and John Kolligian, Jr., eds., *Competence Considered* (New Haven: Yale University Press, 1990), p. 144.

14. Mark R. Lepper and David Greene, "When Two Rewards Are Worse Than One: Effects of Extrinsic Rewards on Intrinsic Motivation," *Phi Delta Kappan*, April 1975, pp. 565-66.

15. See, for example, Edward Deci and Richard Ryan, *Intrinsic Motivation and Self-Determination in Human Behavior* (New York: Plenum Press, 1985); Mark R. Lepper and David Greene, eds., *The Hidden Costs of Reward* (Hillsdale, N.J.: Erlbaum, 1978); and the work of John Nicholls, Teresa Amabile, Judith M. Harackiewicz, Mark Morgan, and Ruth Butler. I have reviewed some of this research in "Group Grade Grubbing Versus Cooperative *Learning*," *Educational Leadership*, February 1991, pp. 83-87.

16. Quoted in Mark Morgan, "Reward-Induced Decrements and Increments in Intrinsic Motivation," *Review of Educational Research*, vol. 54, 1984, p. 5.

17. Cathleen L. Smith et al., "Children's Causal Attributions Regarding Help Giving," *Child Development*, vol. 50, 1979, pp. 203-10; and C. Daniel Batson et al., "Buying Kindness: Effect of an Extrinsic Incentive for Helping on Perceived Altruism," *Personality and Social Psychology Bulletin*, vol. 4, 1978, pp. 86-91.

18. Miron Zuckerman, Michelle M. Lazzaro, and Diane Waldgeir, "Undermining Effects of the Foot-in-the-Door Technique with Extrinsic Rewards," *Journal of Applied Social Psychology*, vol. 9, 1979, pp. 292-96.

19. Richard A. Fabes et al., "Effects of Rewards on Children's Prosocial Motivation," *Developmental Psychology*, vol. 25, 1989, pp. 509-15.

20. Suzanne Daley, "Pendulum Is Swinging Back to the Teaching of Values in U.S. Schools," *New York Times*, 12 December 1990, p. B-14.

21. Quoted in David Hill, "Order in the Classroom," *Teacher Magazine*, April 1990, p. 77.

22. Joan E. Grusec and Theodore Dix, "The Socialization of Prosocial Behavior: Theory and Reality," in Carolyn Zahn-Waxler, E. Mark Cummings, and Ronald Iannotti, eds., *Altruism and Aggression: Biological and Social Origins* (Cambridge: Cambridge University Press, 1986), p. 220.

23. Joan E. Grusec et al., "Modeling, Direct Instruction, and Attributions: Effects on Altruism," *Developmental Psychology*, vol. 14, 1978, pp. 51-57.

24. Joan E. Grusec and Erica Redler, "Attribution, Reinforcement, and Altruism: A Developmental Analysis," *Developmental Psychology*, vol. 16, 1980, pp. 525-34.

25. Angelo Strenta and William DeJong, "The Effect of a Prosocial Label on Helping Behavior," *Social Psychology Quarterly*, vol. 44, 1981, pp. 142-47.

26. See James H. Bryan and Nancy H. Walbek, "Preaching and Practicing Generosity," *Child Development*, vol. 41, 1970, pp. 329-53; James H. Bryan and Perry London, "Altruistic Behavior by Children," *Psychological Bulletin*, vol. 72, 1970, pp. 200-211; Martin L. Hoffman, "Altruistic Behavior and the Parent-Child Relationship," *Journal of Personality and Social Psychology*, vol. 31, 1975, pp. 937-43; and Marian Radke-Yarrow, Phyllis M. Scott, and Carolyn Zahn-Waxler, "Learning Concern for Others," *Developmental Psychology*, vol. 8, 1973, pp. 240-60.

27. Ben Spiecker, "Psychopathy: The Incapacity to Have Moral Emotions," *Journal of Moral Education*, vol. 17, 1988, p. 103.

28. For an analysis of the harms of competition in the classroom and elsewhere, see Alfie Kohn, *No Contest: The Case Against Competition* (Boston: Houghton Mifflin, 1986).

29. David W. Johnson et al., "Effects of Cooperative Versus Individualized Instruction on Student Prosocial Behavior, Attitudes Toward Learning, and Achievement," *Journal of Educational Psychology*, vol. 68, 1976, pp. 446-52; and Bette Chambers, "Cooperative Learning in Kindergarten: Can It Enhance Students' Perspective-Taking Ability and Prosocial Behaviour?," unpublished manuscript, Concordia University, Montreal, 1990.

30. See, for example, the research cited in David W. Johnson and Roger T. Johnson, "The Socialization and Achievement Crisis: Are Cooperative Learning Experiences the Solution?," in Leonard Bickman, ed., *Applied Social Psychology Annual 4* (Beverly Hills, Calif.: Sage, 1983), p. 137; and Elliot Aronson and Diane Bridgeman, "Jigsaw Groups and the Desegregated Classroom: In Pursuit of Common Goals," *Personality and Social Psychology Bulletin*, vol. 5, 1979, p. 443.

31. Another classroom management issue is raised by Carolyn Zahn-Waxler. She warns that a teacher who routinely and efficiently takes care of a child in distress in order to preserve order in the classroom may unwittingly be teaching two lessons: 1) that "people do not react emotionally to upset in others" and 2) that, "if someone is hurt, someone else who is in charge will handle it" ("Conclusions: Lessons from the Past and a Look to the Future," in Zahn-Waxler, Cummings, and Iannotti, p. 310).

32. For more about the Child Development Project, see Alfie Kohn, "The ABC's of Caring," *Teacher Magazine*, January 1990, pp. 52-58; and idem, *The Brighter Side of Human Nature*, Ch. 6. For accounts written by members of the staff, see Victor Battistich et al., "The Child Development Project: A Comprehensive Program for the Development of Prosocial Character," in William M. Kurtines and Jacob L. Gewirtz, eds., *Moral Behavior and Development: Advances in Theory, Research, and Applications* (Hillsdale, N.J.: Erlbaum, 1989); and Daniel Solomon et al., "Cooperative Learning as Part of a Comprehensive Classroom Program Designed to Promote Prosocial Development," in Shlomo Sharan, ed., *Cooperative Learning: Theory and Research* (New York: Praeger, 1990).

Cooperative Learning and the Cooperative School

The availability of models that can be used in math, reading, and writing at every grade level has made it possible to plan an elementary school around the concept of everyone's working together to improve all aspects of the school.

ROBERT E. SLAVIN

Robert E. Slavin is Director of the Elementary School Program at the Center for Research on Elementary and Middle Schools, Johns Hopkins University, 3505 N. Charles St., Baltimore, MD 21218.

Photograph by Barbara Bennett

The Age of Cooperation is approaching. From Alaska to California to Florida to New York, from Australia to Britain to Norway to Israel, teachers and administrators are discovering an untapped resource for accelerating students' achievement: the students themselves. There is now substantial evidence that students working together in small cooperative groups can master material presented by the teacher better than can students working on their own.

The idea that people working together toward a common goal can accomplish more than people working by themselves is a well-established principle of social psychology. What is new is that practical cooperative learning strategies for classroom use have been developed, researched, and found to be instructionally effective in elementary and secondary schools. Once thought of primarily as social methods directed at social goals, certain forms of cooperative learning are considerably more effective than traditional methods in increasing basic achievement outcomes, including performance on standardized tests of mathematics, reading, and language (Slavin 1983a, b; Slavin in press a).

"There is now substantial evidence that students working together in small cooperative groups can master material . . . better than can students working on their own."

Recently, a small but growing number of elementary and secondary schools have begun to apply cooperative principles at the school as well as the classroom level, involving teachers in cooperative planning, peer coaching, and team teaching, with these activities directed toward effective implementation of cooperative learning in the classroom. Many of these schools are working toward institutionalization of cooperative principles as the focus of school renewal.

This article reviews the research on cooperative learning methods and presents a vision of the next step in the progression of cooperative learning: the cooperative school.

What Is Cooperative Learning and Why Does It Work?

Cooperative learning refers to a set of instructional methods in which students work in small, mixed-ability learning groups. (See p. 110 for a vignette about one day in the life of a hypothetical cooperative school.) The groups usually have four members—one high achiever, two average achievers, and one low achiever. The students in each group are responsible not only for learning the material being taught in class, but also for helping their groupmates learn. Often, there is some sort of group goal. For example, in the Student Team Learning methods developed at Johns Hopkins University (Slavin 1986), students can earn attractive certificates if group averages exceed a pre-established criterion of excellence.

For example, the simplest form of Student Team Learning, called Student Teams-Achievement Division (STAD),

consists of a regular cycle of activities. First, the teacher presents a lesson to the class. Then students, in their four-member mixed-ability teams, work to master the material. Students usually have worksheets or other materials; study strategies within the teams depend on the subject matter. In math, students might work problems and then compare answers, discussing and resolving any discrepancies. In spelling, students might drill one another on spelling lists. In social studies, students might work together to find information in the text relating to key concepts. Regardless of the subject matter, students are encouraged not just to give answers but to explain ideas or skills to one another.

At the end of the team study period, students take brief individual quizzes, on which they cannot help one another. Teachers sum the results of the quizzes to form team scores, using a system that assigns points based on how much individual students have improved over their own past records.

The changes in classroom organization required by STAD are not revolutionary. To review the process, the teacher presents the initial lesson as in traditional instruction. Students then work on worksheets or other practice activities; they happen to work in teams, but otherwise the idea of practice following instruction is hardly new. Finally, students take a brief, individual quiz.

Yet, even though changes in classroom organization are moderate, the effects of cooperative learning on students can be profound. Because one student's success in the traditional classroom makes it more difficult for others to succeed (by raising the curve or raising the teacher's expectations), working hard on academic tasks can cause a student to be labeled as a "nerd" or a "teacher's pet." For this reason, students often express norms to one another that discourage academic work. In contrast, when students are working together toward a common goal, academic work becomes an activity valued by peers. Just as hard work in sports is valued by peers because a team member's success brings credit to the team and the school, so academic work is valued by peers in cooperative learning classes because it helps the team to succeed.

In addition to motivating students to

do their best, cooperative learning also motivates students to help one another learn. This is important for several reasons. First, students are often able to translate the teacher's language into "kid language" for one another. Students who fail to grasp fully a concept the teacher has presented can often profit from discussing the concept with peers who are wrestling with the same questions.

Second, students who explain to one another learn by doing so. Every teacher knows that we learn by teaching. When students have to organize their thoughts to explain ideas to teammates, they must engage in cognitive elaboration that greatly enhances their own understanding (see Dansereau 1985).

Third, students can provide individual attention and assistance to one another. Because they work one-on-one, students can do an excellent job of finding out whether their peers have the idea or need additional explanation. In a traditional classroom, students who don't understand what is going on can scrunch down in their seats and hope the teacher won't call on them. In a cooperative team, there is nowhere to hide; there *is* a helpful, nonthreatening environment in which to try out ideas and ask for assistance. A student who gives an answer in a whole-class lesson risks being laughed at if the answer is wrong; in a cooperative team, the fact that the team has a "we're all in this together" attitude means that, when they don't understand, students are likely to receive help rather than derision.

Under What Conditions Is Cooperative Learning Effective?

Cooperative learning is always fun; it almost always produces gains in social outcomes such as race relations; and it

"Students are often able to translate the teacher's language into 'kid language' for one another."

has never been found to reduce student achievement in comparison to traditional methods. However, a substantial body of research has established that two conditions must be fulfilled if cooperative learning is to enhance student achievement substantially. First, students must be working toward a group goal, such as earning certificates or some other recognition. Second, success at achieving this goal must depend on the individual learning of all group members (see Slavin 1983a, b; in press a).

Simply putting students into mixed-ability groups and encouraging them to work together are not enough to produce learning gains: students must have a reason to take one another's achievement seriously, to provide one another with the elaborated explanations that are critical to the achievement effects of cooperative learning (see Webb 1985). If students care about the success of the team, it becomes legitimate for them to ask one another for help and to provide help to each other. Without this team goal, students may feel ashamed to ask peers for help.

Yet team goals are not enough in themselves to enhance student achievement. For example, classroom studies in which students complete a common worksheet or project have not found achievement benefits for such methods.. When the group task is to complete a single product, it may be most efficient to let the smartest or highest achieving students do most of the work. Suggestions or questions from lower-achieving students may be ignored or pushed aside, as they may interfere with efficient completion of the group task. We can all recall being in lab groups in science class or in project groups in social studies in which one or two group members did all the work. To enhance the achievement of all students, then, group success must be based not on a single group product, but on the sum of individual learning performances of all group members.

The group's task in instructionally effective forms of cooperative learning is almost always to prepare group members to succeed on individual assessments. This focuses the group activity on explaining ideas, practicing skills, and assessing all group mem-

"In a cooperative team, there is nowhere to hide; there *is* a helpful, nonthreatening environment in which to try out ideas and ask for assistance."

bers to ensure that all will be successful on learning assessments.

When cooperative learning methods provide group goals based on the learning of all members, the effects on student achievement are remarkably consistent. Of 38 studies of at least four weeks' duration comparing cooperative methods of this type to traditional control methods, 33 found significantly greater achievement for the cooperatively taught classes, and 5 found no significant differences (Slavin in press a). In contrast, only 4 of 20 studies that evaluated forms of cooperative learning lacking group goals based on group members' learning found positive achievement effects, and 3 of these are studies by Shlomo Sharan and his colleagues in Israel that incorporated group goals and individual accountability in a different way (see Sharan et al. 1980, Sharan et al. 1984).

Successful studies of cooperative learning have taken place in urban, rural, and suburban schools in the U.S., Canada, Israel, West Germany, and Nigeria, at grade levels from 2 to 12, and in subjects as diverse as mathematics, language arts, writing, reading, social studies, and science. Positive effects have been found on such higher-order objectives as creative writing, reading comprehension, and math problem solving, as well as on such basic skills objectives as language mechanics, math computations, and spelling. In general, achievement effects have been equivalent for high, average, and low achievers, for boys and girls, and for students of various ethnic backgrounds. As noted earlier, positive effects of cooperative learning have also been found on such out-

comes as race relations, acceptance of mainstreamed academically handicapped classmates, and student self-esteem and liking of class (see Slavin 1983a).

Comprehensive Cooperative Learning Methods
The cooperative learning methods developed in the 1970s—Student Teams-Achievement Divisions and Teams-Games-Tournaments (Slavin 1986); Jigsaw Teaching (Aronson et al. 1978); the Johnsons' methods (Johnson and Johnson 1986); and Group Investigation (Sharan et al., 1984)—all are generic forms of cooperative learning. They can be used at many grade levels and in many subjects. The broad applicability of these methods partly accounts for their popularity. A one- or two-day workshop given to a mixed group of elementary and secondary teachers of many subjects can get teachers off to a good start in most of the methods, which makes this an ideal focus of staff development.

However, because the early cooperative learning methods are generally applicable across grade levels and subjects, they tend not to be uniquely adapted to any particular subject or grade level. Also, the methods developed earlier are mostly curriculum-free; they rarely replace traditional texts or teaching approaches. As a result, these methods are most often applied as supplements to traditional instruction and rarely bring about fundamental change in classroom practice.

Since 1980, research and development on cooperative learning conducted at Johns Hopkins University has begun to focus on comprehensive cooperative learning methods designed to replace traditional instruction *entirely* in particular subjects and at particular grade levels. Two major programs of this type have been developed and successfully researched: Team Accelerated Instruction (TAI) in mathematics for grades 3–6, and Cooperative Integrated Reading and Composition (CIRC) in reading, writing, and language arts for grades 3–5. The main elements of these programs are described below.

Team Accelerated Instruction (TAI). Team Accelerated Instruction shares with STAD and the other Student Team Learning methods the use of four-member mixed-ability learning teams and certificates for high-performing teams. But where STAD uses a single pace of instruction for the class, TAI combines cooperative learning with individualized instruction. TAI is designed to teach mathematics to students in grades 3–6 (or older students not ready for a full algebra course).

In TAI, students enter an individualized sequence according to a placement test and then proceed at their own rates. In general, team members work on different units. Teammates check each other's work against answer sheets and help one another with any problems. Final unit tests are taken without teammate help and are scored by student monitors. Each week, teachers total the number of units completed by all team members and give certificates or other rewards to teams that exceed a criterion score based on the number of final tests passed, with extra points for perfect papers and completed homework.

Because students are responsible for checking each other's work and managing the flow of materials, the teacher can spend most class time presenting lessons to small groups of students drawn from the various teams who are working at the same point in the mathematics sequence. For example, the teacher might call up a decimals group, present a lesson, and then send the students back to their teams to work on decimal problems. Then the teacher might call the fractions group, and so on.

In TAI, students encourage and help one another to succeed because they want their teams to succeed. Individual accountability is assured because the only score that counts is the final test score, and students take final tests without teammate help. Students have equal opportunities for success because all have been placed according to their level of prior knowledge; it is as easy (or difficult) for a lower achiever to complete three subtraction units in a week as it is for a higher-achieving classmate to complete three long division units.

However, the individualization that is part of TAI makes it quite different from STAD. In mathematics, most concepts build on earlier ones. If the earlier concepts were not mastered, the later ones will be difficult or impossible to learn—a student who cannot subtract or multiply will fail to master

A Visit to a Cooperative School

It is Friday morning at "Cooper Elementary School." In Ms. Thompson's third-grade, the students are getting ready for reading. They are sitting in teams at small tables, four or five at each table. As the period begins, Ms. Thompson calls up the "Rockets." Pairs of students from several of the small groups move to a reading group area, while the remaining students continue working at their desks. In Ms. Thompson's class the students at their desks are working together on activities quite different from the usual workbooks. They are taking turns reading aloud to each other; working together to identify the characters, settings, problems, and problem solutions in stories; practicing vocabulary and spelling; and summarizing stories to one another. When Ms. Thompson finishes with the Rockets, they return to their groups and begin working together on the same types of activities. Ms. Thompson listens in on some of the students who are reading to each other and praises teams that are working well. Then she calls up the "Astros," who leave their teams to go to the reading group.

Meanwhile, in Mr. Fisher's fifth-grade, it is math period. Again, students are working in small teams, but in math, each team member is working on different materials depending on his or her performance level. In the teams students are checking one another's work against answer sheets, explaining problems to one another, and answering each other's questions. Mr. Fisher calls up the "Decimals" group for a lesson. Students working on decimals leave their teams and move to the group area for their lesson. When the lesson is over, the students return to their teams and continue working on decimals.

In Mr. Fisher's class there are five learning disabled students, who are distributed among the various teams. The special education resource teacher, Ms. Walters, is teaming with Mr. Fisher. While he is giving lessons, she is moving through the class helping students. At other times, Ms. Walters gives math lessons to groups of students who are having difficulties in math, including her five LD students, while Mr. Fisher works with students in their team areas.

In Mr. Green's fourth-grade class it is writing time. Mr. Green starts the period with a brief lesson on "and disease," the tendency to write long sentences connected by too many "ands." Then the students work on compositions in teams. They cooperatively plan what they will write and then do a draft. The students read their drafts to their teammates and receive feedback on what their teammates heard, what they liked, and what they wanted to hear more about. After revising their drafts, students hold editing conferences with teammates focusing on the mechanics of the composition.

While the students are writing, Mr. Green is moving from team to team, listening in on what they are saying to each other and conferencing with individual students to help them. Also in the class is Ms. Hill, another fourth-grade teacher. She and Mr. Green began using writing process methods at the same time and are coaching each other as they use them in their classes. At the end of the day the two teachers will meet to discuss what happened, and to plan the next steps jointly. On other days, a substitute will cover Mr. Green's class while he visits Ms. Hill's writing class.

All over Cooper Elementary School, students are working in cooperative teams, and teachers are working together cooperatively to help students learn. In the first grades, students are working in pairs taking turns reading to each other. In the sixth grades students are doing team science projects in which each team member is responsible for a part of the team's task. Second-graders are working in teams to master capitalization and punctuation rules.

At the end of the day, teachers award certificates to teams that did outstanding work that week. Those teams that met the highest standards of excellence receive "Superteam" certificates. Throughout the school the sounds of applause can be heard.

After the students have gone home, the school steering committee meets. Chaired by the principal, the committee includes representatives of teachers at several grade levels, plus two parent representatives. The committee discusses the progress they are making toward their goal of becoming a cooperative school. Among other things, the committee decides to hold a school fair to show what the school is doing, to display the students' terrific cooperative work in writing, science, and math; and to encourage parents to volunteer at the school and to support their children's success at home.

—Robert E. Slavin

long division, a student who does not understand fractional concepts will fail to understand what a decimal is, and so on. In TAI, students work at their own levels, so if they lack prerequisite skills they can build a strong foundation before going on. Also, if students can learn more rapidly, they need not wait for the rest of the class.

Individualized mathematics instruction has generally failed to increase student mathematics achievement in the past (see Horak 1981), probably because the teacher's time in earlier models was entirely taken up with checking work and managing materials, leaving little time for actually teaching students. In TAI, students handle the routine checking and management, so the teacher can spend most class time teaching. This difference, plus the motivation and help provided by students within their cooperative teams, probably accounts for the strong positive effects of TAI on student achievement.

Five of six studies found substantially greater learning of mathematics computations in TAI than in control classes, while one study found no differences (Slaven, Leavey, and Madden 1984; Slavin, Madden, and Leavey 1984; Slavin and Karweit 1985). Across all six studies, the TAI classes gained an average of twice as many grade equivalents on standardized measures of computation as traditionally taught control classes (Slavin in press b). For example, in one 18-week study in Wilmington, Delaware, the control group gained .6 grade equivalents in mathematics computations, while the TAI classes gained 1.7 grade equivalents (Slavin and Karweit 1985). These experimental-control differences were still substantial (though smaller) a year after the students were in TAI.

Cooperative Integrated Reading and Composition (CIRC). The newest of the Student Team Learning methods is a comprehensive program for teaching reading and writing in the upper elementary grades. In CIRC, teachers use basal readers and reading groups, much as in traditional reading programs. However, students are assigned to teams composed of pairs from two different reading groups. While the teacher is working with one reading group, students in the other groups are working in their pairs on a series of cognitively engaging activities, includ-

ing reading to one another; making predictions about how narrative stories will come out; summarizing stories to one another; writing responses to stories; and practicing spelling, decoding, and vocabulary. Students also work in teams to master main idea and other comprehension skills. During language arts periods, a structured program based on a writing process model is used. Students plan and write drafts, revise and edit one another's work, and prepare for publication of team books. Lessons on writing skills such as description, organization, use of vivid modifiers, and on language mechanics skills are fully integrated into students' creative writing.

In most CIRC activities, students follow a sequence of teacher instruction, team practice, team pre-assessments, and a quiz. That is, students do not take the quiz until their teammates have determined they are ready. Certificates are given to teams based on the average performance of all team members on all reading and writing activities. Two studies of CIRC (Stevens et al. in press) found substantial positive effects from this method on standardized tests of reading comprehension, reading vocabulary, language expression, language mechanics, and spelling, in comparison to control groups. The CIRC classes gained 30 to 70 percent of a grade equivalent more than control classes on these measures in both studies. Significantly greater achievement on writing samples favoring the CIRC students was also found in both studies.

A New Possibility

The development and successful evaluation of the comprehensive TAI and CIRC models has created an exciting new possibility. With cooperative learning programs capable of being used all year in the 3 Rs, it is now possible to design an elementary school program based upon a radical principle: students, teachers, and administrators can work *cooperatively* to make the school a better place for working and learning.

There are many visions of what a cooperative elementary school might look like, but there is one model that my colleagues and I have begun to work toward in partnership with some

innovative practitioners. Its major components are as follows.

1. *Cooperative learning in the classroom.* Clearly, a cooperative elementary school would have cooperative learning methods in use in most classrooms and in more than one subject. Students and teachers should feel that the idea that students can help one another learn is not just applied on occasion, but is a fundamental principle of classroom organization. Students should see one another as resources for learning, and there should be a schoolwide norm that every student's learning is everyone's responsibility, that every student's success is everyone's success.

2. *Integration of special education and remedial services with the regular program.* In the cooperative elementary school, mainstreaming should be an essential element of school and classroom organization. Special education teachers may team-teach with regular teachers, integrating their students in teams with nonhandicapped students and contributing their expertise in adapting instruction to individual needs to the class as a whole. Similarly, Chapter I or other remedial services should be provided in the regular classroom. If we take seriously the idea that all students are responsibile for one another, this goes as much for students with learning problems as for anyone else. Research on use of TAI and CIRC to facilitate mainstreaming and meet the needs of remedial readers has found positive effects on the achievement and social acceptance of these students (see Slavin 1984, Slavin et al. in press).

3. *Peer coaching.* In the cooperative elementary school, teachers should be responsible for helping one another to use cooperative learning methods successfully and to implement other improvements in instructional practice. Peer coaching (Joyce et al. 1983) is perfectly adapted to the philsophy of the cooperative school; teachers learn new methods together and are given release time to visit one another's classes to give assistance and exchange ideas as they begin using the new programs.

4. *Cooperative planning.* Cooperative activities among teachers should not be restricted to peer coaching. In addition, teachers should be given time to plan goals and strategies together, to prepare common libraries of instructional materials, and to make decisions

about cooperative activities involving more than one class.

5. *Building-level steering committee.* In the cooperative elementary school, teachers and administrators should work together to determine the direction the school takes. A steering committee composed of the principal, classroom teacher representatives, representatives of other staff (e.g., special education, Chapter I, aides), and one or more parent representatives meets to discuss the progress the school is making toward its instructional goals and to recommend changes in school policies and practices to achieve these goals.

6. *Cooperation with parents and community members.* The cooperative school should invite the participation of parents and community members. Development of a community sense that children's success in school is everyone's responsibility is an important goal of the cooperative school.

The Cooperative School Today

To my knowledge, there is not yet a school that is implementing all of the program elements listed here, but a few enterprising and committed schools are moving in this direction. In Bay Shore (New York) School District, teachers in two intermediate schools are using CIRC in reading, writing, and language arts, and STAD in math. In Alexandria, Virginia, Mt. Vernon Community School is working with the National Education Association's Mastery in Learning project to build a cooperative school plan. At Mt. Vernon, a building steering committee is planning and helping to implement a gradual phasing in of the TAI math program and CIRC reading, writing, and language arts programs. Several schools throughout the U.S. that have successfully implemented TAI math are now planning to add CIRC for reading and writing instruction, and are looking toward full-scale imple-

mentation of a cooperative school plan. Most schools that have focused school renewal efforts on widespread use of cooperative learning are at the elementary level; but several middle, junior high, and high schools have begun to work in this direction as well.

In a time of limited resources for education, we must learn to make the best use of what we have. Cooperative learning and the cooperative school provide one means of helping students, teachers, and administrators work together to make meaningful improvements in the learning of all students.

References

Aronson, E., N. Blaney, C. Stephan, J. Sikes, and M. Snapp. *The Jigsaw Classroom.* Beverly Hills, Calif.: Sage, 1978.

Dansereau, D. F. "Learning Strategy Research." In *Thinking and Learning Skills: Relating Instruction to Basic Research, Vol. 1,* edited by J. Segal, S. Chipman, and R. Glaser. Hillsdale, N.J.: Erlbaum, 1985.

Horak, V. M. "A Meta-analysis of Research Findings on Individualized Instruction in Mathematics." *Journal of Educational Research* 74 (1981): 249–253.

Johnson, D. W., and R. T. Johnson. *Learning Together and Alone.* 2d ed. Englewood Cliffs, N.J.: Prentice-Hall, 1986.

Joyce, B. R., R. H. Hersh, and M. McKibbin. *The Structure of School Improvement.* New York: Longman, 1983.

Sharan, S., R. Hertz-Lazarowitz, and Z. Ackerman. "Academic Achievement of Elementary School Children in Small-Group vs. Whole Class Instruction." *Journal of Experimental Education* 48 (1980): 125–129.

Sharan, S., P. Kussell, R. Hertz-Lazarowitz, Y. Bejarano, S. Raviv, and Y. Sharan. *Cooperative Learning in the Classroom: Research in Desegregated Schools.* Hillsdale, N.J.: Erlbaum, 1984.

Slavin, R. E. *Cooperative Learning.* New York: Longman, 1983a.

Slavin, R. E. "When Does Cooperative Learning Increase Student Achievement?" *Psychological Bulletin* 94 (1983b): 429–445.

Slavin, R. E. "Team Assisted Individualization: Cooperative Learning and Individualized Instruction in the Mainstreamed Classroom." *Remedial and Special Education* 5, 6 (1984): 33–42.

Slavin, R. E. *Using Student Team Learning.* 3d ed. Baltimore, Md.: Center for Research on Elementary and Middle Schools, Johns Hopkins University, 1986.

Slavin, R. E. "Cooperative Learning: A Best-Evidence Synthesis." In *School and Classroom Organization,* edited by R. E. Slavin. Hillsdale, N.J.: Erlbaum. In press a.

Slavin, R. E. "Combining Cooperative Learning and Individualized Instruction." *Arithmetic Teacher.* In press b.

Slavin, R. E., and N. L. Karweit. "Effects of Whole-Class, Ability Grouped, and Individualized Instruction on Mathematics Achievement." *American Educational Research Journal* 22 (1985): 351–367.

Slavin, R. E., M. Leavey, and N. A. Madden. "Combining Cooperative Learning and Individualized Instruction: Effects on Student Mathematics Achievement, Attitudes, and Behaviors." *Elementary School Journal* 84 (1984): 409–422.

Slavin, R. E., N. A. Madden, and M. Leavey. "Effects of Team Assisted Individualization on the Mathematics Achievement of Academically Handicapped and Nonhandicapped Students." *Journal of Educational Psychology* 76 (1984): 813–819.

Slavin, R. E., R. J. Stevens, and N. A. Madden. "Accommodating Student Diversity in Reading and Writing Instruction: A Cooperative Learning Approach." *Remedial and Special Education.* In press.

Stevens, R. J., N. A. Madden, R. E. Slavin, and A. M. Farnish. "Cooperative Integrated Reading and Composition: Two Field Experiments." *Reading Research Quarterly.* In press.

Webb, N. "Student Interaction and Learning in Small Groups: A Research Summary." In *Learning to Cooperate, Cooperating to Learn,* edited by R. E. Slavin, S. Sharan, S. Kagan, R. Hertz-Lazarowitz, C. Webb, and R. Schmuck. New York: Plenum, 1985.

Author's note: This article was written under funding from the Office of Educational Research and Improvement, U.S. Department of Education (Grant No. OERI-G-86–006). However, the opinions expressed are mine and do not necessarily reflect OERI positions or policy.

Productive Teaching and Instruction: Assessing The Knowledge Base

HERBERT J. WALBERG

HERBERT J. WALBERG (University of Chicago/DePaul University Chapter) is an educational psychologist and a research professor of education at the University of Illinois, Chicago. ©1990, Herbert J. Walberg.

Mr. Walberg surveys the vast literature on the effects of various instructional methods, enabling readers to consider the advantages and disadvantages of different techniques — including some effective ones that are no longer popular.

SOME TEACHING techniques have remarkable effects on learning, while others confer only trivial advantages or even hinder the learning process. Over the past decade, there has been an explosion of research activity centering on the question of what constitutes effective teaching. Ten years ago, several psychologists observed signs of a "quiet revolution" in educational research. Five years later, nearly 3,000 studies of effective teaching techniques existed. By 1987 an Australian/U.S. team was able to assess 134 reviews of 7,827 field studies and several large-scale U.S. and international surveys of learning.[1]

In this article I will give an overview of the findings to date on elementary and secondary school students and will evaluate the more recent and definitive reviews of research on teaching and instruction. Surveying the vast literature on the effects of various instructional methods allows us to consider the advantages and disadvantages of different techniques — including some effective ones that are no longer popular.

I will begin by considering the effects of the psychological elements of teaching, and I will discuss methods and patterns of teaching that a single teacher can accomplish without unusual arrangements or equipment. Then I will turn to systems of instruction that require special plan-

From *Phi Delta Kappan*, February 1990, pp. 470-478. Reprinted by permission of the author and *Phi Delta Kappan*.

ning, student grouping, and materials. Next I will describe effects that are unique to particular methods of teaching reading, writing, science, and mathematics. Finally, I will discuss special students and techniques for dealing with them and the effects of particular types of training on teachers. It is important to bear in mind that, when we try to apply in our own classrooms the methods we have read about, we may attain results that are half — or twice — as good as the average estimates reported below. Our success will depend not only on careful implementation but also on our purposes. The best saw swung as a hammer does little good.

PSYCHOLOGICAL ELEMENTS

A little history will help us to understand the evolution of psychological research on teaching. Even though educators require balance, psychologists have often emphasized thought, feeling, or behavior at the expense of the other two components of the psyche. Today, thinking or cognition is sovereign in psychology, but half a century ago behaviorists insisted on specific operational definitions (and they continue to do so). In particular, Yale psychologists John Dollard and Neal Miller, stimulated by E. L. Thorndike and B. F. Skinner, wrote about cues, responses, and positive reinforcement, especially in psychotherapy. Later Miller and Dollard isolated three components of teaching — cues, engagement, and reinforcement — that are similar to the elements of input, process, and output in physiology.[2] Their influential work led researchers to consider what teachers *do* instead of focusing on their age, experience, certification, college degrees, or other factors not directly connected to what their students learn.[3]

The behavioral model emphasized 1) the quality of the instructional cues impinging on the learner, 2) the learner's active engagement, and 3) the reinforcements or rewards that encourage continuing effort over time. Benjamin Bloom recognized, however, that in cycles of cues and effort learners may fail the first time or even repeatedly. Thus they may practice incorrect behavior, and so they cannot be reinforced. Therefore, he emphasized feedback to correct errors and frequent testing to check progress. Inspired by John Carroll's model of school learning, Bloom also emphasized engaged learning time and stressed that some learners require much more time than others.[4]

The effects of cues, engagement, re-

inforcement, and corrective feedback on student learning are enormous.[5] The research demonstrating these effects has been unusually rigorous and well-controlled. Even though the research was conducted in school classes, the investigators helped to insure precise timing and deployment of the elements and relied on short-term studies, which usually lasted less than a month. Similar effects are difficult to sustain for long time periods.

Cues. As operationalized, cues show students what is to be learned and explain how to learn it. Their quality depends on the clarity, salience, and meaningfulness of explanations and directions provided by the teacher, the instructional materials, or both. Ideally, as the learners gain confidence, the salience and number of cues can be reduced.

Engagement. The extent to which students actively and persistently participate in learning until appropriate responses are firmly entrenched in their repertoires is known as engagement. Such participation can be indexed by the extent to which the teacher engages students in overt or covert activity. A high degree of engagement is indicated by an absence of irrelevant behavior and by concentration on tasks, enthusiastic contributions to group discussion, and lengthy study.

Corrective feedback. Corrective feedback remedies errors in oral or written responses. Ideally, students should waste little time on incorrect responses, and teachers should detect difficulties rapidly and then remedy them by reteaching or using alternative methods. When necessary, teachers should also provide students with additional time for practice.

Reinforcement. The immense effort elicited by athletics, games, and other cooperative and competitive activities illustrates the power of immediate and direct reinforcement and shows that some endeavors are intrinsically rewarding. By comparison, classroom reinforcement may seem crass or jejune. The usual classroom reinforcers are acknowledgment of correctness and social approval, typically expressed by praise or a smile. More unusual reinforcers include providing contingent activity — for example, initiating a music lesson or other enjoyable activity as a reward for 90% correctness on a math test. Other reinforcers are tokens or check marks that are accumulated for discrete accomplishments and that can be exchanged for tangible reinforcers such as cookies, trinkets, or toys.

In special education programs, students have been reinforced not only for academic achievement but also for minutes spent on reading, for attempts to learn,

and for the accuracy with which they perform tasks. Margo Mastropieri and Thomas Scruggs have shown that results can be impressive when the environment can be rigorously controlled and when teachers can accurately gear reinforcement to performance, as in programs for unruly or emotionally disturbed students. Improved behavior and achievement, however, may fail to extend past the period of reinforcement or beyond the special environment.[6]

Educators ordinarily confine reinforcement to marks, grades, and awards because they must assume that students work for such intangible, long-term goals as pleasing parents, furthering their education, achieving success in later life, and the intrinsic satisfaction of learning itself. Even so, when corrective feedback and reinforcement are clear, rapid, and appropriate, they can powerfully affect learning by efficiently signaling students what to do next. In ordinary classrooms, then, the chief value of reinforcement is informational rather than motivational.

METHODS OF TEACHING

The psychological elements just discussed undergird many teaching methods and the design of most instructional media. Techniques to improve the affective or informational content of cues, engagement, correctives, and reinforcement have shown a wide range of effects.

Cues. *Advance organizers* are brief overviews that relate new concepts or terms to previous learning. They are effective if they connect new learning and old. Those delivered by the teacher or graphically illustrated in texts work best.

Adjunct questions alert students to key questions that should be answered — particularly in texts. They work best when questions are repeated on posttests, and they work moderately well when posttest questions are similar or related to the adjuncts. As we might expect, however, adjunct questions divert attention from incidental material that might otherwise be learned.

Goal setting suggests specific objectives, guidelines, methods, or standards for learning that can be spelled out explicitly. Like the use of adjunct questions, goal setting sacrifices incidental for intended learning.

Learning hierarchies assume that instruction can be made more efficient if the facts, skills, or ideas that logically or psychologically precede others are presented first. Teaching and instructional media sequenced in this way appear to be slightly more effective. However, learners may adapt themselves to apparently ill-sequenced material, and it may even be advantageous to learn to do so, since human life, as Franz Kafka showed, may depart from logic.

Pretests are benchmarks for determining how much students learn under various methods of teaching. Psychologists have found, however, that pretests can have positive cuing effects if they show students what will be emphasized in instruction and on posttests.

Several principles follow from surveying the effects of these methods. To concentrate learning on essential points and to save time (as would be appropriate in training), remove elaborations and extraneous oral and written prose. To focus learners on selected questions or to teach them to find answers in elaborated prose, use adjunct questions and goal setting. To encourage the acquisition of as much undifferentiated material as possible, as in college lecture courses, assign big blocks of text and test students on randomly selected points.

Although the means of producing certain results may seem clear, reaching a consensus on educational purposes may be difficult. Clarity at the start saves time and helps learners to see things the teacher's way, but it limits individual autonomy and deep personal insights. Zen masters ask novices about the sound of one hand clapping and wait a decade or two for an answer. Hiroshi Azuma and Robert Hess find that Japanese mothers use more indirection and vagueness in teaching their young children than do assertive American mothers, and I have observed Japanese science teachers asking questions and leaving them long unresolved. Do the Japanese cultivate initiative and perseverance by these methods?

Engagement. *High expectations* transmit teachers' standards of learning and performance. They may function both as cues and as incentives for students to put extended effort and perseverance into learning.

Frequent tests increase learning by stimulating greater effort and providing intermittent feedback. However, the effects of tests on performance are larger for quizzes than for final examinations.

Questioning also appears to work by promoting engagement and may encourage deeper thinking — as in Plato's accounts of Socrates. Questioning has bigger effects in science than in other subjects. Mary Budd Rowe and Kenneth Tobin have shown that *wait time* — allowing students several seconds to reflect rather than the usual .9 of a second — leads to longer and better answers.

> **P**raise may pale in comparison with the disincentives to achievement afforded by the youth culture.

Correctives and reinforcement. *Corrective feedback* remedies errors by reteaching, either with the same or with a different method. This practice has moderate effects that are somewhat higher in science — perhaps because learning science often involves more conceptualizing while learning other subjects may allow more memorizing.

Homework by itself constructively extends engaged learning time. Correctives and reinforcement in the form of grades and comments on homework raise its effects dramatically.

Praise has a small positive effect. For young or disturbed children, praise may lack the power of the tangible reinforcers used in psychological experiments. For students who are able to see ahead, grades and personal standards may be more powerful reinforcers than momentary encouragement. Moreover, praise may be under- or oversupplied; it may appear demeaning or sardonic; and it may pale in comparison with the disincentives to academic achievement afforded by youth culture in the form of cars, clothing, dating, and athletics.

None of this is to say that encouragement, incentives, and good classroom morale should be abandoned; honey may indeed be better than vinegar. Yet, as cognitive psychologists point out, the main classroom value of reinforcement may lie in its capacity to inform the student about progress rather than in its power to reward.

PATTERNS OF TEACHING

As explained above, methods of teaching enact or combine more fundamental psychological elements. By further extension, *patterns* of teaching integrate elements and methods of teaching. The process of determining these more inclusive formulations was another step in the evolution of psychological research on education. Behavioral research evolved in the 1950s from psychological laboratories to short-term, controlled classroom experiments on one element at a time. In the 1970s educational researchers tried to find patterns of effective practices from observations of ordinary teaching.

Thus behaviorists traded educational realism for theoretical parsimony and scientific rigor; later psychologists preferred realism until their insights could be experimentally confirmed. Fortunately, the results of both approaches appear to converge. Moreover, it seems possible to incorporate the work of cognitive psychologists of the 1980s into an enlarged understanding of teaching.

Explicit teaching. Explicit teaching can be viewed as traditional or conventional whole-group teaching done well. Since most teaching has changed little in the last three-quarters of a century and may not change substantially in the near future,[7] it is worth knowing how to make the usual practice most productive. Since it has evolved from ordinary practice, explicit teaching seems natural to carry out and does not disrupt conventional institutions and expectations. Furthermore, it can incorporate many previously discussed elements and methods.

Systematic research was initiated in the early 1960s by N. L. Gage, Donald Medley, and others who employed "process-product" investigations of the association between what teachers do and how much their students learn. Jere Brophy, Carolyn Evertson, Thomas Good, and Jane Stallings later contributed substantially to this effort. Walter Doyle, Penelope Peterson, and Lee Shulman put the results into a psychological context. Barak Rosenshine has periodically reviewed the research, and Gage and Margaret Needels recently measured the results and pointed out their implications.

The various contributors to the knowledge base do not completely agree about the essential components of explicit teaching, and they refer to it by different names, such as process-product, direct, active, and effective teaching. The researchers weigh their own results heavily, but Rosenshine, a long-standing and comprehensive reviewer, has taken an eagle's-eye view of the results.[8]

In his early reviews of the correlational studies, Rosenshine discussed the traits of effective teachers, including clarity, task orientation, enthusiasm, and flexibility, as well as their tendency to structure their presentations and occasionally to use student ideas. From later observational and control-group research, Rosenshine identified six phased functions of explicit teaching: 1) daily review, checking of homework, and reteaching if necessary; 2) rapid presentation of new content and skills in small steps; 3) guided student practice with close monitoring by teachers; 4) corrective feedback and instructional reinforcement; 5) independent practice in seatwork and homework, with a success rate of more than 90%; and 6) weekly and monthly review.

Comprehension teaching. The heirs of Aristotle and of the Anglo-American tradition of Bacon, Locke, Thorndike, and Skinner objected to philosophical "armchair" opinions; mid-century behaviorists, particularly John Watson, constructively insisted on hard empirical data about learning. But they also saw the child's mind as a blank tablet and seemed to encourage active teaching and passive acquisition of isolated facts. Reacting to such atomism and to William James' "bucket" metaphor, cognitive psychologists in the early 1980s revived research on student-centered learning and "higher mental processes," in the tradition of Plato, Socrates, Kant, Rousseau, Dewey, Freud, and Piaget. In American hands, however, this European tradition has sometimes led to vacuity and permissiveness, as in the extremes of the "progressive education" movement of the 1930s.

Oddly, the Russian psychologist Lev Vygotsky hit on an influential compromise: emphasizing the two-way nature of teaching, he identified a "zone of proximal development," which extends from what learners can do independently to the maximum that they can do with the teacher's help.[9] Accordingly, teachers should set up "scaffolding" for building knowledge and then remove it when it becomes unnecessary. In mathematics, for example, the teacher can give prompts and examples, foster independent use, and then withdraw support. This approach is similar to the "prompting" and "fading" of the behavioral cues, and it seems commonsensical. It has revived interest in granting some autonomy to students.

During the 1980s cognitive research on teaching sought ways to encourage self-monitoring, self-teaching, or "metacognition" to foster independence. Skills were seen as important, but the learner's monitoring and management of them had

priority, as though the explicit teaching functions of planning, allocating time, and reviewing were partly transferred to the learner.

For example, David Pearson outlined three phases: 1) modeling, in which the teacher exhibits the desired behavior; 2) guided practice, in which students perform with help from the teacher; and 3) application, in which students perform independently of the teacher — steps that correspond to explicit teaching functions. Anne Marie Pallincsar and Anne Brown described a program of "reciprocal teaching" that fosters comprehension by having students take turns in leading dialogues on pertinent features of a text. By assuming the kind of planning and executive control ordinarily exercised by teachers, students learn planning, structuring, and self-management. Perhaps that is why tutors learn from teaching and why we say that to learn something well, one should teach it.

Comprehension teaching encourages students to measure their progress toward explicit goals. If necessary, they can reallocate their time to different activities. In this way, self-awareness, personal control, and positive self-evaluation can be increased.[10]

LEARNER AUTONOMY IN SCIENCE

The National Science Foundation sponsored many studies of student inquiry and autonomy that showed that giving students opportunities to manipulate science materials, to contract with teachers about what to learn, to inquire on their own, and to engage in activity-based curricula all had substantial positive effects. Group- and self-direction, however, had smaller positive effects, and pass/fail and self-grading had small negative effects. Methods of providing greater learner autonomy may also work well in subjects other than science, as in the more radical approach that I discuss next.

OPEN EDUCATION

In the late 1960s, open educators expanded autonomy in the primary grades by enabling students to join teachers in planning educational purposes, means, and evaluation. In contrast to teacher- and textbook-centered education, open education gave students a voice in deciding what to learn — even to the point of writing their own texts to share with one another. Open educators tried to foster cooperation, critical thinking, constructive attitudes, and self-directed lifelong

learning. They revived the spirit of the New England town meeting, Thoreau's self-reliance, Emerson's transcendentalism, and Dewey's progressivism. Their ideas also resonate with the "client-centered" psychotherapy of Carl Rogers, which emphasizes the "unconditional worth" of the person.

Rose Giaconia and Larry Hedges' synthesis of 153 studies showed that open education had worthwhile effects on creativity, independence, cooperation, attitudes toward teachers and schools, mental ability, psychological adjustment, and curiosity. Students in open programs had less motivation for grade grubbing, but they differed little from other students in actual achievement, self-concept, and anxiety.

However, Giaconia and Hedges also found that the open programs that were more effective in producing the positive outcomes with regard to attitudes, creativity, and self-concept sacrificed some academic achievement on standardized tests. These programs emphasized the role of the child in learning and the use of individualized instruction, manipulative materials, and diagnostic rather than norm-referenced evaluation. However, they did not include three other components thought by some to be essential to open programs: multi-age grouping, open space, and team teaching.

Giaconia and Hedges speculated that children in the most extreme open programs may do somewhat less well on conventional achievement tests because they have little experience with them. At any rate, it appears that open classrooms enhance several nonstandard outcomes without detracting from academic achievement unless they are radically extreme.[11]

INSTRUCTIONAL SYSTEMS

All the techniques discussed thus far can be planned and executed by a single teacher. They may entail some extra effort, encouragement, or training, but they do not call for unusual preparation or materials. In contrast, instructional systems require special arrangements and planning, and they often combine several components of instruction. Moreover, they tend to emphasize the adaptation of instruction to individual students rather than the adaptation of students to a fixed pattern of teaching. A little history will aid our understanding of current instructional systems.

Programmed instruction. Developed in the 1950s, programmed instruction presents a series of "frames," each one of which conveys an item of information and requires a student response. *Linear programs* present a graduated series of frames that require such small increments in knowledge that learning steps may be nearly errorless and may be continuously reinforced by progression to the next frame. Able students proceed quickly under these conditions. *Branched programs* direct students back for reteaching when necessary, to the side for correctives, and ahead when they already know parts of the material. The ideas of continuous progress and branching influenced later developers, who tried to optimize learning by individualization, mastery learning, and adaptive instruction.

Individualization adapts instruction to individual needs by applying variations in speed or branching and by using booklets, worksheets, coaching, and the like. Perhaps because they have been vaguely defined and poorly operationalized, individualized programs have had small effects. Other systems (discussed below) appear more effective for adapting instruction to the needs of individual learners.

Mastery learning. Combining the psychological elements of instruction with suitable amounts of time, mastery learning employs formative tests to allocate time and to guide reinforcement and corrective feedback. In the most definitive synthesis of research on mastery learning, James Kulik and Chen-Lin Kulik reported substantial positive effects. Mastery programs that yielded larger effects established a criterion of 95% to 100% mastery and required repeated testing to mastery before allowing students to proceed to additional units (which yielded gigantic effects of one standard deviation). Mastery learning yielded larger effects with less-able students and reduced the difference between their performance and that of abler groups.

The success of mastery learning is attributable to several factors. The Kuliks, for example, found that when control groups were provided feedback from quizzes, the mastery groups' advantage was smaller. As Bloom pointed out, mastery learning takes additional time; the Kuliks found that mastery learning required a median of 16% (and up to 97%) more time than conventional instruction. The seven studies that provided equal time for mastery and control groups showed only a small advantage for mastery learning on standardized tests. However, the advantage was moderate on experimenter-made, criterion-referenced tests for nine equal-time studies. These results illustrate the separate contribu-

tions to mastery learning of cuing, feedback, and time.

Mastery learning yielded larger effects in studies of less than a month's duration than in those lasting more than four months. Retention probably declines sharply no matter what the educational method, but the decline can be more confidently noted with regard to mastery learning since it has been more extensively studied than other methods.

Bloom and his students have reported larger effects than has Robert Slavin, who reviewed their work. Thomas Guskey and S. L. Gates, for example, reported an average effect size of .78 estimated from 38 studies of elementary and secondary students. In response to Slavin, Lorin Anderson and Robert Burns pointed out two reasons for larger effects in some studies, especially those under Bloom's supervision. Bloom has been more interested in what is possible than in what is likely; he has sought to find the limits of learning. His students, moreover, have conducted tightly controlled experiments over time periods of less than a semester or less than a year.[12]

Adaptive instruction. Developed by Margaret Wang and others, adaptive instruction combines elements of mastery learning, cooperative learning, open education, tutoring, computer-assisted instruction, and comprehension teaching into a complex system whose aim is to tailor instruction to the needs of individuals and small groups. Managerial functions — including such activities as planning, allocating time, delegating tasks to aides and students, and quality control — are carried out by a master teacher. Adaptive instruction is a comprehensive program for the whole school day rather than a single method that requires simple integration into one subject or into a single teacher's repertoire. Its effects on achievement are substantial, but its broader effects are probably underestimated, since adaptive instruction aims at diverse ends — including student autonomy, intrinsic motivation, and teacher and student choice — which are poorly reflected by the usual outcome measures.

COMPUTER-ASSISTED INSTRUCTION

Ours is an electronic age, and computers have already had a substantial impact on learning. With the costs of hardware declining and with software becoming increasingly sophisticated, we may hope for still greater effects as computers are better integrated into school programs.

Computers show the greatest advan-

tage for handicapped students — probably because they are more adaptive to their special needs than teachers might be. Computers may also be more patient, discreet, nonjudgmental, or even encouraging about progress. Perhaps for the same reasons, computers generally have bigger effects in elementary schools than in high schools or colleges.

Another explanation for the disparate results is also plausible. Elementary schools provide less tracking and fewer differentiated courses for homogeneous groups. Computers may be better adapted to larger within-class differences among elementary students because they allow them to proceed at their own pace without engaging in invidious comparisons.

Simulations and games, with or without computer implementation, require active, specific responses from learners and may strike a balance between vicarious book learning and the dynamic, complicated, and competitive "real world." The interactiveness, speed, intensity, movement, color, and sound of computers add interest and information to academic learning. Unless geared to educational purposes, however, computer games can also waste time.

STUDENT GROUPING

Teaching students what they already know and teaching them what they are yet incapable of learning are equally wasteful practices and may even be harmful to motivation. For this reason, traditional whole-class teaching of heterogeneous groups can present serious difficulties — a problem that is often unacknowledged in our egalitarian age. Outside of universities, however, most educators recognize that it is difficult to teach arithmetic and trigonometry at the same time. (Even some English professors might balk at teaching phonics and deconstructionism simultaneously.) If we want to teach students as much as possible rather than to make them all alike, we need to consider how they are grouped and try to help the full range of students.

Acceleration. Accelerated programs identify talented youth (often in mathematics and science) and group them together or with older students. Such programs provide counseling, encouragement, contact with accomplished adults, grade skipping, summer school, and the compression of the standard curriculum into fewer years. The effects are huge in elementary schools, substantial in junior high schools, and moderate in senior high schools. The smaller effects at more ad-

For Japanese students, long-term adult rewards reinforce educational effort.

specific subject-matter needs rather than according to I.Q., demeanor, or other irrelevant characteristics.

Well-defined subject matter and student grouping may be among the chief reasons why Japanese students lead the world in academic achievement: the curriculum is explicit, rigorous, and nationally uniform. In primary schools, weaker students, with maternal help, study harder and longer to keep up with these explicit requirements. Subject-matter tests are administered to screen students for "lower" and "upper" secondary schools and for universities of various gradations of rigor and prestige. Each such screening determines occupational, marital, and other adult prospects; long-term adult rewards thus reinforce educational effort.[13]

There are some successful precedents for the use of media-based instruction.

vanced levels may be attributable to the smaller advantage of acceleration over the tracking and differentiated course selection already practiced in high schools.

The effects of acceleration on educational attitudes, vocational plans, participation in school activities, popularity, psychological adjustment, and character ratings have been mixed and often insignificant. These outcomes may not be systematically affected in either direction.

Ability grouping. Students are placed in ability groups according to achievement, intelligence test scores, personal insights, and subjective opinions. In high school, ability grouping leaves deficient and average students unaffected, but it has beneficial effects on talented students and on attitudes toward the subject matter. In elementary school, the grouping of students with similar reading achievement but from different grades yields substantial effects. Within-class grouping in mathematics yields worthwhile effects, but generalized ability grouping does not.

Tutoring. Because it gears instruction to individual or small-group needs, tutoring is highly beneficial to both tutors and tutees. It yields particularly large effects in mathematics — perhaps because of the subject's well-defined scope and organization.

* * *

In whole-group instruction, teachers may ordinarily focus on average or deficient students to insure that they master the lessons. When talented students are freed from repetition and slow progression, they can proceed quickly. Grouping may work best when students are accurately grouped according to their

SOCIAL ENVIRONMENT

Cooperative learning programs delegate some control of the pacing and methods of learning to groups of between two and six students, who work together and sometimes compete with other groups within classes. Such programs are successful for several reasons. They provide relief from the excessive teacher/student interaction of whole-group teaching, they free time for the interactive engagement of students, and they present opportunities for targeted cues, engagement, correctives, and reinforcement. As in comprehension teaching, the acts of tutoring and teaching may encourage students to think for themselves about the organization of subject matter and the productive allocation of time.

Many correlational studies suggest that *classroom morale* is associated with achievement gains, with greater interest in subject matter, and with the worthy outcome of voluntary participation in nonrequired subject-related activities. Morale is assessed by asking students to agree or disagree with such statements as "Most of the students know one another well" and "The class members know the purpose of the lessons."

Students who perceive the atmosphere as friendly, satisfying, focused on goals, and challenging and who feel that the classroom has the required materials tend to learn more. Those who perceive the atmosphere as fostering student cliques, disorganization, apathy, favoritism, and friction learn less. The research on morale, though plausible, lacks the specificity and causal confidence of the controlled experiments on directly alterable methods.

READING EFFECTS

Comprehension teaching, because it may extend to several subjects in elementary school, has already been discussed as a pattern of teaching. Several other methods have substantial effects on reading achievement.

Adaptive speed training involves principles that are similar to those of comprehension training. Students learn to vary their pace and the depth of their reflection according to the difficulty of the material and their reading purposes.

Reading methods vary widely, but their largest effects seem to occur when teachers are systematically trained, almost irrespective of particularities of method. Phonics or "word-attack" approaches, however, have a moderate advantage over guessing and "whole-word" approaches in the teaching of beginning reading — perhaps because early misconceptions are avoided. Phonics may also reduce the need for excessive reteaching and correctives.

Pictures in the text can be very helpful, although they add to the cost of a book and occupy space that could otherwise be used for prose. In order of their effectiveness, several types of pictures can be distinguished. Transformative pictures recode information into concrete and memorable form, relate information in a well-organized context, and provide links for systematic retrieval. Interpretive pictures, like advance organizers, make the text comprehensible by relating abstract terms to concrete ones and by connecting the unfamiliar and difficult to previously acquired knowledge. Organizational pictures, including maps and diagrams, show the coherence of objects or events in space and time. Representational pictures are photos or other concrete representations of what is discussed in the text. Decorative pictures present (possibly irrelevant or conflicting) information that is incidental to intended learning (although decoration may add interest if not information).

Pictures can provide vivid imagery and metaphors that facilitate memory, show what is important to learn, and intensify the effects of prose. Pictures may sometimes allow students to bypass the text, but memorable, well-written prose may obviate pictures.[14]

WRITING EFFECTS

Sixty well-designed studies of methods of teaching writing compared 72 experimental groups with control groups. The methods below are presented in the order of their effectiveness.

The inquiry method requires students to find and state specific details that convey personal experience vividly, to examine sets of data to develop and support explanatory generalizations, or to analyze situations that present ethical problems and arguments.

Scales are criteria or specific questions that students can apply to their own and others' writing to improve it.

Sentence combining shows students how to build complex sentences from simpler ones.

Models are presentations of good pieces of writing to serve as exemplars for students.

Free writing allows students to write about whatever occurs to them.

Grammar and mechanics include sentence parsing and the analysis of parts of speech.

SCIENCE EFFECTS

Introduced in response to the launch of Sputnik I, the "new" science curricula, sponsored by the National Science Foundation, yielded substantial effects on learning. They efficiently added value by producing superior learning on tests of their intended outcomes and on tests of general subject-matter goals. The new curricula also yielded effects ranging from small to substantial on such often-unmeasured outcomes as creativity, problem solving, scientific attitudes and skills, logical thinking, and achievement in non-science subject matter.

Perhaps these advantages are attributable to the combined efforts of teachers, psychologists, and scientists, who collaborated to insure that the curricula would be based on modern content and would foster effective teaching practices. The scientists may have been able to generate enthusiasm for teaching scientific methods, for laboratory work, and for other reforms.

The new science curricula worked well in improving achievement and other outcomes. Ironically, they are often forgotten today, despite the fact that, by international standards, U.S. students score poorly in mathematics and science.

Inquiry teaching. Often practiced in Japan, this method requires students to formulate hypotheses, reason about their credibility, and design experiments to test their validity. Inquiry teaching yields substantial effects, particularly on the understanding of scientific processes.

Audio-tutorials. These are tape-recorded instructions for using laboratory equipment, manipulatives, and readings for topical lessons or whole courses. This simple approach yields somewhat better results than conventional instruction, allows independent learning, and has the further advantage of individual pacing — allowing students to pursue special topics or to take courses on their own.

Original source papers. This method derives from the Great Books approach of the late Robert Maynard Hutchins, former president of the University of Chicago, and his colleague Mortimer Adler. They saw more value in reading Plato or Newton than in resorting to predigested textbook accounts. The use of original sources in science teaching trades breadth for depth in the belief that it is better to know a few ideas of transcending importance than to learn many unconnected bits of soon-forgotten information. Advocates of this approach have shown that such knowledge can be acquired by studying and discussing original scientific papers of historical or scientific significance.

Other methods of teaching science have effects that are near zero — that is, close to the effects of traditional methods of teaching. They include team teaching, departmentalized elementary programs, and media-based instruction. The equal results for media methods, however, suggest that choices can be based on cost and convenience. Since television programs and films can be broadcast, they can provide equally effective education in different and widespread locations (even in different parts of the world by satellite). Moreover, students today can interact "on-line" with teachers and fellow students who are far away.

There are some successful precedents for the use of media-based instruction. For a decade, the Chicago community colleges provided dozens of mainly one-way television courses to hundreds of thousands of students, who did most of their studying at home but participated in discussion and testing sessions at several sites in the metropolitan area. The best lecturers, media specialists, and test constructors could be employed, and tapes of the courses could be rebroadcast repeatedly.

In several Third World countries that are gaining in achievement and school enrollments, ministries of education make efficient and successful use of such low-cost, effective "distance education" for remote elementary and secondary schools.

The Oklahoma and Minnesota state departments of education apparently lead the nation in providing small high schools in rural areas with specialized television teachers and interactive courses in advanced science, mathematics, foreign language, and other subjects.

MATHEMATICS EFFECTS

In the heyday of its Education Directorate, the National Science Foundation sponsored considerable research not only on science but also on mathematics. Some worthwhile effects were found.

Manipulative materials. The use of Cuisenaire rods, balance beams, counting sticks, and measuring scales allows students to engage directly in learning instead of passively following abstract presentations by the teacher. Students can handle the materials, see the relation of abstract ideas and concrete embodiments, and check hypothesized answers by quick empirical testing without having to wait for quiz results or feedback from the teacher. This method apparently results in enormous effects.

Problem solving. In mathematics teaching, a focus on problem solving yields worthwhile effects. Such an approach requires comprehension of terms and their application to varied examples. It may motivate students by showing them the application of mathematical ideas to "real-world" questions.

New math. The so-called new math produced beneficial results, although it was not as successful as the new science curricula. Both reforms probably gained their learning advantages partly by testing what they taught.

SPECIAL POPULATIONS
AND TECHNIQUES

We can also gain insights from programs that lie outside the usual scope of elementary and secondary classrooms.

Early intervention. Programs of early intervention include educational, psychological, and therapeutic components for handicapped, at-risk, and disadvantaged children from the ages of one month to 5½ years. Studies of these programs found that the large, immediate effects of these programs declined rapidly and disappeared after three years.

Preschool programs. Preschool programs also showed initial learning effects that were not sustained. It appears that young children can learn more than is normally assumed, but, like other learners, they can also forget. The key to sustained gains may be sustained programs and effective families — not one-shot approaches.

Programs for the handicapped. Students classified as mentally retarded, emotionally disturbed, or learning disabled have been subjects in research that has several important implications. When they serve as tutors of one another and of younger students, handicapped students can learn well — a finding similar to those in comprehension-monitoring and tutoring studies of nonhandicapped children. Moreover, handicapped students are often spuriously classified, and we may underestimate their capacities.

Mainstreaming. Studies show that mildly to moderately handicapped students can prosper in regular classes and thereby avoid the invidious "labeling" that is often based on misclassification.

Psycholinguistic training. Providing psycholinguistic training to special-needs students yields positive effects. This approach consists of testing and remedying specific deficits in language skills.

Patient education. Educating patients about diseases and treatments can affect mortality, morbidity, and lengths of illness and hospitalization. In studies of the acquisition of knowledge regarding drug usage for hypertension, diabetes, and other chronic conditions, one-to-one and group counseling (with or without instructional material) produced greater effects than providing instruction through labels on bottles or package inserts for patients.

Labels, special containers, memory aids, and behavior modification were successful in minimizing later errors in drug usage. The most efficacious educational principles were: specification of intentions; relevance to the needs of the learner; provision of personal answers to questions; reinforcement and feedback on progress; facilitation of correct dosage, e.g., the use of unit-dose containers; and

instructional and treatment regimens suited to personal convenience, e.g., prescribing drugs for administration at mealtimes.

Inservice training of physicians. Such training shows large effects on doctors' knowledge and on their classroom or laboratory performance but only moderate effects on the outcomes of treating actual patients. Knowledge and performance, even in practical training, may help, but they hardly guarantee successful application in practice. Can an accomplished mathematician handle the intricacies of federal income tax?

Panaceas and shortcuts. At the request of the U.S. Army, the National Academy of Sciences evaluated exotic techniques for enhancing learning and performance that are described in popular psychology (and presumably are being exploited in California and the USSR).[15] However, little or no evidence was found for the efficacy of learning during sleep; for mental practice of motor skills; for "integration" of left and right hemispheres of the brain; for parapsychological techniques; for biofeedback; for extrasensory perception, mental telepathy, and "mind over matter" exercises; or for "neurolinguistic programming," in which instructors identify the students' modes of learning and mimic the students' behaviors as they teach.

The Greeks found no royal road to geometry; even kings, if they desired mastery, had to sweat over Euclid's elements. Perhaps brain research will eventually yield a magic elixir or a panacea, but for proof of its existence educators should insist on hard data in refereed scientific journals.

EFFECTS ON TEACHERS

Programs to help teachers in their work have had substantial effects — notwithstanding complaints about typical inservice training sessions. Do physicians complain about the medical care they get?

Microteaching. Developed at Stanford University in the 1960s, microteaching is a behavioral approach for preservice and inservice training that has substantial effects. It employs the explanation and modeling of selected teaching techniques; televised practice with small groups of students; discussion, correctives, and reinforcement while watching playback; and recycling through subsequent practice and playback sessions with new groups of students.

Inservice education. Inservice training for teachers also proves to have substantial effects. Somewhat like the case

> **K**nowledge
> from the field of
> psychology alone is
> not sufficient to
> prescribe practices.

of inservice training of physicians, the biggest effects are on the teacher's knowledge, but effects on classroom behavior and student achievement are also notable.

For inservice training, authoritative planning and execution seem to work best; informal coaching by itself seems ineffective. Allowing the instructor to be responsible for the design and teaching of the sessions works better than relying on presentations by teachers and group discussions. The best techniques are observation of classroom practices, video/audio feedback, and practice. The most effective training combines lectures, modeling, practice, and coaching. The size of the training group, ranging from one to more than 60, makes no detectable difference.

Some apparent effects may be attributable to the selectivity of the program rather than to its superior efficacy. For example, federal-, state-, and university-sponsored programs appear more effective than locally initiated programs. Competitive selection of participants and the granting of college credit apparently work better as incentives than extra pay, renewal of certification, or no incentives. Independent study seems to have larger effects than workshops, courses, minicourses, and institutes.

PSYCHOLOGICAL research provides first-order estimates of the effects of instructional means on educational ends under various conditions. But some instructional practices may be costly — not in terms of dollars but in terms of new or complicated arrangements that may be difficult for some teachers and districts to adopt. Thus estimates of effects are only one basis for decision making. We need to consider the productivity or value of effects in relation to total costs, including the time and energies of educators and students.

Knowledge from the field of psychology alone is not sufficient to prescribe practices, since different means bring about different ends. Educators must decide whether the learning effort is to be directed by teachers, by students, or by the curriculum. They must choose among a range of facts and concepts, breadth and depth, short- and long-term ends, academic knowledge and knowledge that has direct application in the real world, equal opportunity and equal results. They must decide which aspect of Plato's triumvirate of thinking, feeling, and acting will take precedence. Once these choices are made, educators can turn to the researchers' estimates of effects as one basis for determining the most productive practices.

1. Herbert J. Walberg, Diane Schiller, and Geneva D. Haertel, "The Quiet Revolution in Educational Research," *Phi Delta Kappan*, November 1979, pp. 179-83; Herbert J. Walberg, "Improving the Productivity of America's Schools," *Educational Leadership*, vol. 41, 1984, pp. 19-27; and Barry J. Fraser, Herbert J. Walberg, Wayne W. Welch, and John A. Hattie, "Syntheses of Educational Productivity Research," *International Journal of Educational Research*, vol. 11, 1987, pp. 73-145.
2. Neal Miller and John Dollard, *Social Learning and Imitation* (New Haven, Conn.: Yale University Press, 1941); and John Dollard and Neal Miller, *Personality and Psychotherapy* (New York: McGraw-Hill, 1950).
3. Eric A. Hanushek, "Throwing Money at Schools," *Journal of Policy Analysis and Management*, vol. 1, 1981, pp. 19-41; and Herbert J. Walberg and William F. Fowler, "Expenditure and Size Efficiencies of Public School Districts," *Educational Researcher*, vol. 16, 1987, pp. 515-26.
4. Benjamin S. Bloom, *Human Characteristics and School Learning* (New York: McGraw-Hill, 1976); and John B. Carroll, "A Model of School Learning," *Teachers College Record*, vol. 64, 1963, pp. 723-33.
5. The effects are expressed as differences between experimental and control groups in units of standard deviations. For further details and references, see my chapter in Merlin C. Wittrock, ed., *Handbook of Research on Teaching* (New York: Macmillan, 1986), and the research monograph by Fraser, myself, and others cited above. For a time I will send a table of effects and number of studies, as well as a graphic display, to readers who send a self-addressed, stamped envelope (two first-class stamps) to me at the University of Illinois, College of Education, P.O. Box 4348, Chicago, IL 60680.
6. Margo A. Mastropieri and Thomas E. Scruggs, *Effective Instruction for Special Education* (Boston: Little, Brown, 1987).
7. John Hoetker and William P. Ahlbrand, "The Persistence of the Recitation," *American Educational Research Journal*, vol. 6, 1969, pp. 145-67.
8. For a full account of most views, see Penelope L. Peterson and Herbert J. Walberg, eds., *Research on Teaching* (Berkeley, Calif.: McCutchan, 1979); and Wittrock, op. cit.
9. Lev Vygotsky, *Mind in Society* (Cambridge, Mass.: Harvard University Press, 1978).
10. Anne Marie Pallincsar and Anne Brown, "Reciprocal Teaching of Comprehension-Fostering and Comprehension-Monitoring Activities," *Cognition and Instruction*, vol. 1, 1984, pp. 117-76; David Pearson, "Reading Comprehension Instruction: Six Necessary Steps," *Reading Teacher*, vol. 38, 1985, pp. 724-38; and Paul R. Pintrich et al., "Instructional Psychology," *Annual Review of Psychology*, vol. 37, 1986, pp. 611-51.
11. Rose M. Giaconia and Larry V. Hedges, "Identifying Features of Effective Open Education," *Review of Educational Research*, vol. 52, 1982, pp. 579-602.
12. James A. Kulik and Chen-Lin Kulik, "Mastery Testing and Student Learning," *Journal of Educational Technology Systems*, vol. 15, 1986, pp. 325-45; Lorin W. Anderson and Robert B. Burns, "Values, Evidence, and Mastery Learning," *Review of Educational Research*, vol. 57, 1988, pp. 215-23; Thomas R. Guskey and S. L. Gates, "Synthesis of Research on the Effects of Mastery Learning in Elementary and Secondary Classrooms," *Educational Leadership*, May 1986, pp. 73-80; and Robert E. Slavin, "Mastery Learning Reconsidered," *Review of Educational Research*, vol. 57, 1988, pp. 175-213.
13. Herbert J. Walberg, "What Can We Learn from Japanese Education?," *The World and I*, March 1988, pp. 661-65.
14. Joel R. Levin, Gary J. Anglin, and Russell N. Carney, "On Empirically Validating Functions of Pictures in Prose," in D. M. Willows and H. A. Houghton, eds., *Illustrations, Graphs, and Diagrams* (New York: Springer-Verlag, forthcoming).
15. Daniel Druckman and John A. Swets, eds., *Enhancing Human Performance* (Washington, D.C.: National Academy Press, 1988).

Critical Thinking Through Structured Controversy

Through controlled argumentation, students can broaden their perspectives, learn material more thoroughly, and make better decisions.

DAVID W. JOHNSON
AND ROGER T. JOHNSON

David W. Johnson is Professor of Educational Psychology, and **Roger T. Johnson** is Professor of Curriculum and Instruction, both at the University of Minnesota, Cooperative Learning Center, 202 Pattee Hall, 150 Pillsbury Dr., S.E., Minneapolis, MN 55455.

Have you learned lessons only of those who admired you, and were tender with you, and stood aside for you?

Have you not learned great lessons from those who braced themselves against you and disputed the passage with you?

—Walt Whitman, 1860

Using academic conflicts for instructional purposes is one of the most dynamic and involving, yet *least-used* teaching strategies. Although creating a conflict is an accepted writer's tool for capturing an audience, teachers often suppress students' academic disagreements and consequently miss out on valuable opportunities to capture their own audiences and enhance learning.

Teachers generally avoid and subdue students' academic conflicts for several reasons. For instance, they may view conflicts as divisive, alienating students from each other, with the least capable feeling defeated and humiliated (Collins 1970, DeCecco and Richards 1974). Another reason is that teachers do not have an instructional model for structuring and controlling academic controversies to stimulate learning.

Over the past 10 years, we have developed and tested a theory about how controversy promotes positive

> **"Controversies must be defined as interesting problems to be solved rather than as win-lose situations."**

outcomes (D. Johnson 1979, 1980; Johnson and Johnson 1979, 1985). Based on our findings, we have developed a series of curriculum units on energy and environmental issues structured for academic controversies. We have also worked with schools and colleges throughout the United States and Canada to field-test and implement the units in the classroom.

We will review these efforts by discussing the process of controversy, how teachers can organize and use it, and the advantages of using it to enhance both cognitive and affective learning.

A Model for the Process of Controversy

Controversy is a type of academic conflict that exists when one student's ideas, information, conclusions, theories, and opinions are incompatible with those of another and the two seek to reach an agreement. Structured academic controversies are most commonly contrasted with concurrence-seeking, debate, and individualistic learning (fig. 1). For instance, students can inhibit discussion to avoid any disagreement and compromise quickly to reach a consensus while they discuss the issue (concurrence-seeking). Or students can appoint a judge and then debate the different positions with the expectation that the judge will determine who presented the better position (debate). Finally, students can work independently with their own set of materials at their own pace (individualistic learning).

When teachers structure controversy, students must rehearse orally the information they are learning; advocate a position; teach their knowledge to peers; analyze, critically evaluate, and rebut information; reason deductively and inductively; and synthesize and integrate information into factual and judgmental conclusions that are summarized into a joint position to which all sides can agree.

Consider the following illustration. A teacher assigns students to groups of four composed of two-person advocacy teams and asks them to prepare a report entitled "The Role of Regulations in the Management of Hazardous Waste." One team is given the position that more regulations are needed, and the other team, that fewer regulations are needed. During the first hour, both teams receive materials supporting their assigned positions. The teacher instructs them to plan how best to support their assigned positions so that they *and* the opposing team learn the information and the perspective within the materials so well that the opposing team is convinced.

During the second hour, the two teams present their positions to each other and then engage in general discussion in which they advocate their positions, rebut the opposing side, and seek to reach the best decision possible about the need to regulate hazardous waste management. This discussion continues during the third hour, and each team spends 30 minutes arguing for the opposing position.

During the fourth hour, the four group members reach consensus about the issue, synthesize the best information and reasoning from both sides, write a report on the role of regulations in hazardous waste management, and individually take a test on the factual information contained in the reading materials.

"Heterogeneity among group members leads to spirited and constructive argumentation . . . "

This illustration represents the structured use of academic controversy, a six-step process through which students advance from factual learning to reasoned judgment (fig. 2). During such a sequence, students realize that their conclusions are being contested by others who hold different views. They then become uncertain about the correctness of their own ideas, and an internal state of conceptual conflict is aroused. To resolve their uncertainty, students search for more information, new experiences, improved reasoning, and a more nearly adequate cognitive perspective. They try to understand their opponents' conclusion and rationale. The cognitive rehearsal of their own position and their attempts to understand their opponents' position result in a reconceptualization of their position. This new level of comprehension is characterized by understanding the opposing perspective, incorporating the opponents' information and reasoning, changing their own attitude and position if warranted, and using higher-level reasoning strategies. This process is repeated until the differences in conclusions among students have been resolved, a synthesis is achieved, an agreement is reached, and the controversy has ended.

Structured academic controversies require students to invest physical and

"Students must value and respect one another."

psychological energy in their educational experiences. This investment takes many forms: absorption in academic work, epistemic curiosity, effort expended toward academic achievement, and the like. Student time and energy, of course, are finite resources, and educational success can be evaluated in terms of increasing the time and energy students willingly commit to their education.

Use of Controversy in the Classroom
For the past several years, we have been training teachers to use structured academic controversies, which they are now using in a wide variety of grade levels and subject areas. At the University of Minnesota, we are using controversies in several engineering courses and with undergraduate and graduate education and psychology students. The basic format teachers use for organizing structured academic controversies consists of four steps.

1. *Choosing the discussion topic.* The choice of topic depends on the interests of the instructor and the purposes of the course. That two well-documented positions can be prepared and that students are able to manage the content are criteria for selection. Most environmental, energy, public policy, social studies, literary, and scientific issues are appropriate.

2. *Preparing instructional materials.* The following materials are needed for each position:
- a clear description of the group's task;
- a description of the phases of the controversy procedure and the collaborative skills to be used during each;
- a definition of the position to be advocated with a summary of the key arguments supporting the position;
- resource materials (including a bibliography) to provide evidence for and elaboration of the arguments supporting the position to be advocated.

3. *Structuring the controversy.* The principal requirements for a successful structured controversy are a cooperative context, skillful group members, and heterogeneity of group membership. Teachers establish a cooperative context by assigning students randomly to groups and by requiring each group to reach consen-

Controversy	Debate	Concurrence-Seeking	Individualistic
Deriving conclusions by categorizing and organizing information and experiences	Deriving conclusions by categorizing and organizing information and experiences	Deriving conclusions by categorizing and organizing information and experiences	Deriving conclusions by categorizing and organizing information and experiences
Being challenged by opposing views	Being challenged by opposing views	Quick compromise to one view	Presence of only one view
Uncertainty about the correctness of own view, cognitive conflict	Uncertainty about the correctness of own view, cognitive conflict	High certainty	High certainty
High epistemic curiosity	Moderate epistemic curiosity	Absence of epistemic curiosity	No epistemic curiosity
Active representation and elaboration of position and rationale	Active representation and elaboration of position and rationale	Active restatement of original position	No oral statement of position
High reconceptualization	Moderate reconceptualization	No reconceptualization	No reconceptualization
High productivity	Moderate productivity	Low productivity	Low productivity
High positive cathexis	Moderate positive cathexis	Low positive cathexis	Low positive cathexis

Fig. 1. Four Learning Processes

> **"Students must feel safe enough to challenge each other's ideas and reasoning."**

sus on an issue and submit a report on which all members will be evaluated. Heterogenenity among group members leads to spirited and constructive argumentation and increases appreciation of different views. (In the next section we discuss five strategies for promoting constructive controversy.)

4. *Conducting the controversy.* To guide a controversy, the teacher gives students specific instructions in five phases.

● *Learning positions.* Plan with your partner how to advocate your position effectively. Read the materials supporting your position, and plan a persuasive presentation. Make sure you and your partner master the information supporting your assigned position and present it in a way to ensure that the opposing pair will comprehend and learn the information.

● *Presenting positions.* As a pair, present your position forcefully and persuasively. Listen carefully and learn the opposing position. Take notes, and clarify anything you do not understand.

● *Discussing the issue.* Argue forcefully and persuasively for the posi-

tion, presenting as many facts as you can to support your point of view. Listen critically to the opposing pair's position, asking them for the facts that support their viewpoint, and then present counter-arguments. Remember this is a complex issue, and you need to know both sides to write a good report.

● *Reversing perspectives.* Working as a pair, present the opposing pair's position as if you were they. Be as sincere and forceful as you can. Add any new facts you know. Elaborate their position by relating it to other information you have previously learned.

● *Reaching a decision.* Summarize and synthesize the best arguments for *both* points of view. Reach consensus on a position that is supported by the facts. Change your mind only when the facts and the rationale clearly indicate that you should do so. Write your report with the supporting evidence and rationale for your synthesis that your group has agreed on.

Instruct the students to follow specific discussion rules during the controversy (see fig. 3). After the controversy, spend some time processing how well the group functioned and how its performance may be enhanced during the next controversy. It is a good idea to highlight and discuss the specific conflict management skills students need to master.

Prerequisites to Promoting Constructive Controversy
Positive outcomes do not automatically appear every time students disagree intellectually. To produce them, teachers need to know how to initiate, nurture, and manage controversies

constructively. This involves five strategies.

1. *Structuring learning activities cooperatively.* For controversies to be constructive—neither competitive nor destructive—the following conditions must be met.

● Controversies must be defined as interesting problems to be solved rather than as win-lose situations.

● Controversies must be valued as opportunities and challenges.

● Similarities as well as differences between positions must be recognized.

● Information must be accurately communicated.

● Feelings as well as information have to be communicated and responded to.

● Students must value and respect one another.

● Students must feel safe enough to challenge each other's ideas and reasoning.

2. *Ensuring that groups are heterogeneous.* Differences among students—in personality, sex, attitude, background, social class, reasoning strategies, cognitive perspective, information, ability level, and skills—

> **"A balanced presentation should be given for each side of the controversy."**

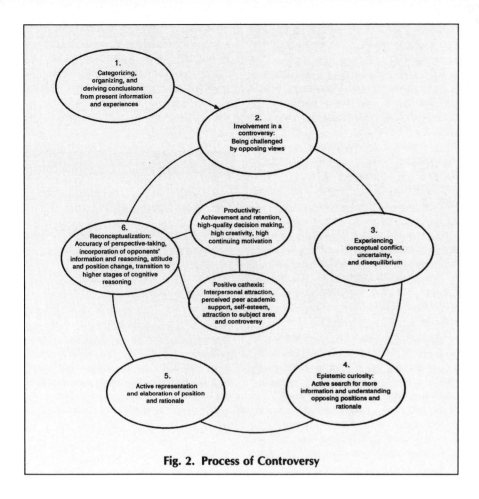

Fig. 2. Process of Controversy

1. Categorizing, organizing, and deriving conclusions from present information and experiences

2. Involvement in a controversy: Being challenged by opposing views

3. Experiencing conceptual conflict, uncertainty, and disequilibrium

4. Epistemic curiosity: Active search for more information and understanding opposing positions and rationale

5. Active representation and elaboration of position and rationale

6. Reconceptualization: Accuracy of perspective-taking, incorporation of opponents' information and reasoning, attitude and position change, transition to higher stages of cognitive reasoning

Productivity: Achievement and retention, high-quality decision making, high creativity, high continuing motivation

Positive cathexis: Interpersonal attraction, perceived peer academic support, self-esteem, attraction to subject area and controversy

"Engaging in structured academic controversies increases students' perspective-taking abilities."

dents engage in perspective-taking behaviors (e.g., paraphrasing).

A third set of skills involves the cycle of differentiation of positions and their resultant integration. Students need to perform several cycles of *differentiation* (seeking out and clarifying differences among ideas, information, conclusions, theories, and opinions) and *integration* (combining information, reasoning, theories, and conclusions of others into one new, creative solution).

5. *Teaching the procedures of rational argument.* During a controversy, students must follow the canons of rational argument. They should generate ideas, collect and organize relevant information, reason logically, empathetically enter into the perspective of their opponents, and make tentative conclusions based on current understanding. After presenting their perspectives and the rationales for their positions, as well as their conclusions, students should ask their opponents for proof that their analyses and conclusions are accurate. Students should keep an open mind, changing their conclusions if their opponents present persuasive rationales, proofs, and logical reasoning.

How Students Benefit

When students interact, conflicts among their ideas, conclusions, theories, information, perspectives, opinions, and preferences are inevitable. Teachers who capitalize on these differences find that academic conflicts can yield highly constructive dividends. Over the past 10 years, we have conducted systematic research to discover the consequences of structured controversy (Johnson and Johnson 1979, 1985). One of the most interest-

lead to differing styles of processing information, which in turn actually begin the cycle of controversy. Such differences promote learning and increase the amount of time spent in argumentation.

3. *Distributing information relevant to both sides.* A balanced presentation should be given for each side of the controversy. The more information students have about an issue, the

greater their learning tends to be. Having relevant information available, however, does not mean that students will use it. They need the interpersonal and group skills necessary to ensure that all participants contribute pertinent information and synthesize data effectively.

4. *Teaching conflict management skills.* To manage controversy constructively, students need collaborative and conflict management skills (D. Johnson 1981, Johnson and Johnson 1982). One of the most important is the ability to challenge another's ideas while at the same time confirming that individual's personal competence. Students can learn to value disagreements as interesting opportunities to learn something new, not as personal attacks.

Perspective taking is another important ability for exchanging information and opinions within a conflict (D. Johnson 1971). Additional information, both personal and impersonal, can be disclosed and is more often accurately comprehended when stu-

"To produce [positive outcomes], teachers need to know how to initiate, nurture, and manage controversies constructively."

██████████████

"Students should keep an open mind, changing their conclusions if their opponents present persuasive rationales, proofs, and logical reasoning."

1. I am critical of ideas, not people.
2. I focus on making the best decision possible, not on "winning."
3. I encourage everyone to participate and master all the relevant information.
4. I listen to everyone's ideas, even if I do not agree.
5. I restate (paraphrase) what someone has said if it is not clear.
6. I first bring out all the ideas and facts supporting both sides and then try to put them together in a way that makes sense.
7. I try to understand both sides of the issue.
8. I change my mind when the evidence clearly indicates that I should do so.

Fig. 3. Discussion Rules for Participating in an Academic Controversy

ing findings is that engaging in structured academic controversies increases students' perspective-taking abilities. Within structured academic controversies, students practice adopting a perspective, advocating it, then enlarging their view to include the opposing position as well.

Other interesting findings relate to student achievement and attitudes. For instance, compared with concurrence-seeking, debate, and individualistic learning efforts, structured controversy results in:

- greater student mastery and retention of the subject and greater ability to generalize the principles learned to a wider variety of situations;
- higher-quality decisions and solutions to problems;
- the promotion of creative insights by influencing students to view a problem from different perspectives and reformulate it in ways that allow the emergence of new orientations to the problem;
- an increase in the number and quality of students' ideas, feelings of

stimulation and enjoyment, and originality of expression in problem solving, resulting in greater emotional commitment to solving the problem, greater enjoyment of the process, and more imaginative solutions.

Within controversies are elements of disagreement, argumentation, and rebuttal that could result in divisiveness among peers and the promotion of negative attitudes. The research, however, indicates that compared with the other three learning processes, structured controversy promotes a greater liking among participants, greater perceived peer academic support, higher academic self-esteem, and more positive attitudes toward both the subject and the process of controversy.

A Generic Problem-Solving Strategy

If students are to become citizens capable of making reasoned judgments about the complex problems facing society, they must learn to use the higher-level reasoning and critical thinking processes involved in effective problem solving, especially problems for which different viewpoints can plausibly be developed. With structured controversy, students of all ages are learning how to find high-quality solutions to complex problems.

References

Collins, B. *Social Psychology*. Reading, Mass.: Addison-Wesley, 1970.
DeCecco, J., and A. Richards. *Growing Pains: Uses of School Conflict*. New York: Aberdeen Press, 1974.
Johnson, D. W. "Students Against the School Establishment: Crisis Intervention in School Conflicts and Organization Change." *Journal of School Psychology* 9 (Winter 1971): 84–92.
Johnson, D. W. *Educational Psychology*. Englewood Cliffs, N.J.: Prentice-Hall, 1979.
Johnson, D. W. "Group Processes: Influences of Student-Student Interaction on School Outcomes." In *The Social Psychology of School Learning*, edited by J. McMillan. New York: Academic Press, 1980.
Johnson, D. W. *Reaching Out: Interpersonal Effectiveness and Self-Actualization*. 2d ed. Englewood Cliffs, N.J.: Prentice-Hall, 1981.
Johnson, D. W., and F. Johnson. *Joining Together: Group Theory and Group Skills*. 2d ed. Englewood Cliffs, N.J.: Prentice-Hall, 1982.
Johnson, D. W., and R. Johnson. "Conflict in the Classroom: Controversy and Learning." *Review of Educational Research* 49 (Winter 1979): 51–61.
Johnson, D. W., and R. Johnson. "Classroom Conflict: Controversy vs. Debate in Learning Groups." *American Educational Research Journal* 22 (Summer 1985): 237–256.
Whitman, W. *Leaves of Grass*. New York: Viking Press, 1860.

Survey of Research on Learning Styles

A number of studies conducted during the last decade have found that students' achievement increases when teaching methods match their learning styles—biological and developmental characteristics that affect how they learn.

RITA DUNN, JEFFREY S. BEAUDRY, AND ANGELA KLAVAS

Rita Dunn is Professor, Division of Administrative and Instructional Leadership, and Director, Center for the Study of Learning and Teaching Styles; **Jeffrey S. Beaudry** is Assistant Professor, Division of Administrative and Instructional Leadership; and **Angela Klavas** is Assistant Director, Center for the Study of Learning and Teaching Styles, and a doctoral student in the Instructional Leadership Program—all at St. John's University, Grand Central and Utopia Parkways, Jamaica, NY 11439.

Research on learning styles has been conducted at more than 60 universities over the past decade. These investigations have yielded useful findings about the effects of environmental, emotional, sociological, physiological, and cognitive preferences on the achievement of students. Learning style is a biologically and developmentally imposed set of personal characteristics that make the same teaching method effective for some and ineffective for others.

Every person has a learning style—it's as individual as a signature. Knowing students' learning styles, we can organize classrooms to respond to their individual needs for quiet or sound, bright or soft illumination, warm or cool room temperatures, seating arrangements, mobility, or grouping preferences. We can recognize the patterns in which people tend to concentrate best—alone, with others, with certain types of teachers, or in a combination thereof. We become aware of the senses through which people remember difficult information most easily—by hearing, speaking, seeing, manipulating, writing or notetaking, experiencing, or, again, a combination of these.

Learning style also encompasses motivation, on-task persistence versus the need for multiple assignments simultaneously, the kind and amount of structure required, and conformity versus nonconformity. When a National Association of Secondary School Principals (NASSP) Task Force (1983) examined all the characteristics that influence student achievement, intake preferences (individual needs for eating and/or drinking while concentrating) achieved the highest reliability. Chronobiology is also part of style: some people are "morning people"; some are "night owls."

There are only three comprehensive models of learning style (Hill et al. 1971, Keefe et al. 1986, Dunn et al. 1975, 1979, 1981, 1985); others address only one to four elements, usually on a bipolar continuum. Although various scholars define the concept differently, only a few learning style identification instruments are reliable and valid (Curry 1987).

Correlational Studies

To investigate connections between individual preferences and other influences on learning, researchers have conducted correlational studies to establish the relationships between learning style and birth order, cognitive development, maturation, hemisphericity, field dependence/independence, global/analytic processing, temperament, and self-concept. Their comparisons examined learners at all levels from primary school through adulthood. They differentiated among gifted, musically and artistically talented, average, underachieving, at-risk, nontraditional, reading-disabled, special education, dropout, and adolescent psychiatric populations. Researchers further tested consistency of style over subject matter and time. In addition, the researchers determined the responsiveness of basal readers to style differences, and they also examined the extent to which teacher training programs complemented their student candidates.

Correlational studies also explored the similarities and differences between and among diverse groups. Thus, researchers developed profiles of the styles of a wide range of learners, including students at various levels of achievement in diverse age groups; gifted, learning disabled, and mentally retarded students; supervisors and their supervisees; teachers and their students; Southeast Asian and American Caucasian college registrants; and numerous other groups. In addition, comparisons were made of the learning styles of Bahamians and Jamaicans; Afro-Americans and Caucasians; and Afro-, Chinese, Greek, and Mexican Americans (*Annotated Bibliography* 1988; *Learning Styles Network Newsletter* 1980-1988).

3. LEARNING: Instructional Strategies

Correlations Between Learning Style and Hemisphericity

As new findings about left/right brain functions appeared, researchers investigated the connections between learning style and hemisphericity. The terms *left/right, analytic/global,* and *inductive/deductive* have been used interchangeably in the literature; descriptions of these pairs of variables parallel each other. Lefts/analytics/inductives appear to learn successively, in small steps leading to understanding; rights/globals/deductives more easily learn by obtaining meaning from a broad concept and then focusing on details.

Studies that examined the similarities and differences between hemispheric style and other elements of learning style revealed that, when concentrating on difficult academic material:

1. High school students who were less motivated than their classmates and who preferred working with *distracters* (music, low illumination, informal or casual seating, peers rather than alone or with the teacher, tactile rather than auditory or visual instructional resources) scored right-hemisphere significantly[1] more often than left-hemisphere. Also, students who scored high on persistence invariably scored high as left processors (Dunn et al. 1982). (The latter data may have implications for time-on-task research.)

2. Left-hemisphere youngsters in grades 5-12 preferred a conventional formal classroom seating design, more structure, less intake, and visual rather than tactile or kinesthetic resources during learning significantly more often than their right-preferred classmates (Cody 1983).

3. Right-hemisphere 5th through 12th graders disliked structure and were not adult motivated but *were* strongly peer motivated. Gifted and highly gifted students were significantly more often right or integrated than left processors (Cody 1983).

4. Right-hemisphere community college adult math underachievers preferred learning with sound and intake.

They wanted tactile and kinesthetic instructional resources and mobility significantly more often than their left-hemisphere counterparts, who preferred bright light and a formal design. [When the predominantly right-hemisphere students were taught alternately with both global and analytic lessons, they achieved statistically higher test scores through the global, rather than through the analytic, resources (Bruno 1988).]

Thus, correlational studies revealed sets of traits among students within the same age or grade and among those with similar talents, achievement, and interests. Even when culturally diverse groups were examined, there were as many within-group as between-group differences. Within each family, the parents, their offspring, and the siblings tend to be more different from than similar to each other.

Experimental Research

These correlational findings prompted

Researcher/Date	Sample	Subject Examined	Element Examined	Significant Effects Achievement	Attitudes
DeGregoris 1986	6th, 7th, 8th graders	Reading comprehension	Kinds of sound needed by sound preferences	+ With moderate talking	Not tested
DellaValle 1984	7th graders	Word recognition memory	Mobility/passivity needs	+	Not tested
Hodges 1985	7th, 8th graders	Mathematics	Formal/informal design preferences	+	+
Krimsky 1982	4th graders	Reading speed and accuracy	Bright/low lighting preferences	+	Not tested
MacMurren 1985	6th graders	Reading speed and accuracy	Need for intake while learning	+	+
Miller 1985	2nd graders	Reading	Mobility/passivity needs	+	Not tested
Murrain 1983	7th graders	Word recognition/ memory	Temperature preference	0	Not tested
Pizzo	6th graders	Reading	Acoustical preference	+	+
Shea 1983	9th graders	Reading	Formal/informal design preferences	+	Not tested
Stiles 1985	5th graders	Mathematics testing	Formal/informal design preferences	0	Not tested

Note: Price (1980) reported that the older students became, the less they appeared able to adapt to a conventional setting. Thus, design may be far more crucial to secondary students' ability to concentrate than to 4th graders, who may be better able to adjust to this element. Dunn and Griggs (1988) described the importance of design to high schoolers throughout the United States.
(+) = significant positive findings at p<.01 or greater; (0) = no differences or slight trend.

Fig. 1. Experimental Research Concerned with Learning Styles and Instructional Environments

researchers to conduct experimental studies to determine the effects of individual learning style on achievement, attitudes, and/or behavior.

On Instructional Environments

The extent to which classrooms appear either to stimulate or to inhibit learning for students with selected learning style characteristics has been documented in terms of individuals' needs for quiet versus sound, bright or soft lighting, warm or cool temperatures, and formal versus informal seating designs (Dunn 1987, Dunn et al. 1985; see fig. 1). These four elements affect from 10 to 40 percent of students, dependent upon age, gender, hemisphericity, and achievement. For example, the need for sound remains fairly consistent during the elementary school years but increases as adolescence begins and, as that stage passes, appears to return to its previously normal level. The younger children are, the less light they need; but about every five years most children require significantly more light than previously. Boys tend to require more mobility than girls and, thus, find sitting for any length of time difficult (Price 1980). However, teachers often view negatively the children who squirm in their seats, tap their pencils,

The need for sound remains fairly consistent during the elementary school years but increases as adolescence begins and, as that stage passes, appears to return to its previously normal level.

complain about the temperature, or become hyperactive (in some cases because of too much illumination).

On Perceptual Preferences

In addition to the instructional environment, sensory preferences influence the ways in which students learn. Eight studies within the past decade reveal that when youngsters were taught with instructional resources that both matched and mismatched their preferred modal-

ities, they achieved statistically higher test scores in modality-matched, rather than mismatched, treatments (Dunn 1988; see fig. 2). In addition, when children were taught with multisensory resources, but *initially through their most preferred modality* and then were reinforced through their secondary or tertiary modality, their scores increased even more.

Perceptual preferences affect more than 70 percent of school-age youngsters. High school teachers who have translated their curriculum into electroboards, Flip chutes, multipart task cards, and Pick-A-Holes reported increased achievement and interest when such manipulatives were available for highly tactual students (Dunn and Griggs 1988).

Data from studies conducted before the late '70s concerned with perceptual strengths often were conflicting because of inappropriate statistical designs, poor analyses, misinterpretations of the findings, and/or faulty conclusions. Those investigators examined *group* mean gain scores—which are inappropriate for determining whether individuals achieve better, the same, or less well in comparison with their own baseline data when they are taught through their preferences. In addition, the words *tactile* and *kinesthetic* often

Researcher/Date	Sample	Subject Examined	Perceptual Preference Examined	Significant Effects	
				Achievement	Attitude
Carbo 1980	Kindergartners	Vocabulary	Auditory, visual, "other" (tactile)	+	Not tested
Jarsonbeck 1984	4th grade underachievers	Mathematics	Auditory, visual, tactile	+	Not tested
Kroon 1985	9th, 10th graders	Industrial Arts	Auditory, visual, tactile, sequenced	+	Not tested
Martini 1986	7th graders	Science	Auditory, visual, tactile	+	+
Urbschat 1977	1st graders	CVC Trigram Recall	Auditory, visual	+	Not tested
Weinberg 1983	3rd graders	Mathematics	Auditory, visual, tactile	+	Not tested
Wheeler 1980	Learning disabled 2nd graders	Reading	Auditory, visual, tactile, sequenced	+	Not tested
Wheeler 1983	Learning disabled 2nd graders	Reading	Auditory, visual, tactile	+	Not tested
(+) = significant positive findings.					

Fig. 2. Experimental Research Concerned with Perceptual Learning Styles

were used interchangeably. *Tactile* suggests learning with hands through manipulation of resources, but writing is not tactile enough for children below 4th grade. *Kinesthetic* implies whole-body involvement, such as taking a trip, dramatizing, interviewing, or pantomiming. However, even when older studies identified tactile strengths, their treatments did not *introduce* the new material that way. Finally, studies that employed many diverse instruments, populations, methods, and statistical designs and that confused the terminology could not yield solid data.

On Sociological Preferences

The influence of students' social preferences also affects their achievement in school. Figure 3 shows that, in four of five studies, when students' sociological preferences were identified and the youngsters then were taught in multiple treatments both responsive and unresponsive to their diagnosed learning styles, they achieved significantly higher test scores in matched conditions and significantly lower test scores when mismatched.

How do sociological preferences interface with cooperative learning? The higher the grade level, the less teacher-motivated students become (Price 1980). Thus, there are more peer-oriented youngsters able to work in well-organized small groups than there are students willing to learn directly from their teachers. Nevertheless, in every class we have ever tested, there are students who prefer to learn by themselves with appropriate resources, others who prefer to learn with peers, and some who wish to work directly with their teachers (Price 1980).

From practical experience, educators generally consider the junior high school years a period of strong peer influence. By the beginning of grade 9, however, educators should expect movement away from that preference; Price (1980) found that students in grades 9-12 experience a greater need to learn and study alone than during any other interval. The gifted also prefer to learn alone unless the material to be mastered is difficult for them; when that happens, they prefer to learn with other gifted children (see fig. 3). Thus, except among the gifted, many students in grades 3-8 will learn better in small, well-organized groups

than either alone or with the teacher. After grade 8, however, more will learn better alone.

In a small group structure, children who are frequently chastised for not sitting quietly can move about and relieve the discomfort they experience because of mobility needs or hard chairs. This structure also permits youngsters to read together, discuss items, reason out answers, and use multisensory interactions. The various contributors may enjoy different processing styles; thus, they can help each other, especially when the teacher's dominant hemispheric style is incongruent with theirs. Despite the advan-

---

Learning Styles and Student Diversity

Sue Loper

As a young teacher, I inherited a junior high classroom from a teacher who left in midyear. The students were totally out of control. I made it through the year, but I was not pleased with my performance.

I unloaded my feelings of frustration on Margaret Payne, who taught next door. She had a reputation for being able to teach even the worst students. In fact, she often accepted problem students during the year when other teachers could no longer tolerate them. Students liked learning in her class; she made them feel special and successful. Each time they succeeded, they wanted to try again.

Ms. Payne listened to my complaints, made sympathetic sounds, and proceeded to offer practical advice: that I teach my students the way they learned best; in other words, that I determine my students' preferred learning styles and provide activities to match them. She suggested that I use several methods of presenting material and include a variety of activities—individual and group projects—ranging from the replicative to the highly creative. Ms. Payne understood that different students learn in different ways, while teachers often teach as they have been taught (Dunn and Dunn 1978).

This was certainly true in my own case. Because I learn well auditorily, I tended to teach in a lecture format. Unfortunately, this tendency shortchanged the visual, kinesthetic, and tactile learners in my classroom. Because I am a self-directed learner, I assigned mostly individual projects to be completed by a certain date. These assignments were difficult for students who learned best in a group or with the help of an adult, or who needed encouragement, assistance, or prodding to finish a project. Furthermore, I didn't like gum chewing, foot tapping, or other extraneous movements or noise, yet I had students who *needed* those activities in order to learn (Dunn and Dunn 1978).

If a teacher teaches and evaluates in only one cognitive mode, he or she is adequately serving only those students who prefer to learn in that mode. To give every learner the opportunity to succeed, teachers can expand their repertoires to include a variety of cognitive modes. Teachers should also become aware of their own learning style preferences and of how those preferences affect their teaching methods. Yet another goal is to help students move from one preferred learning mode to a base of mixed preferences, so they can benefit from various instructional modes.

If we make these changes, we will improve our chances of success at educating a diverse student population.

Reference

Dunn, R., and K. Dunn. (1978). *Teaching Students Through Their Individual Learning Styles: A Practical Approach.* Reston, Va.: Reston Publishing.

Sue Loper is Media Center Specialist, Moore County High School, Lynchburg, TN 37352.

Except among the gifted, many students in grades 3-8 will learn better in small, well-organized groups than either alone or with the teacher. After grade 8, however, more will learn better alone.

tages to group work, students who feel constrained by the slower group pacing or who enjoy the challenge of solving problems by themselves do not learn most easily through small-group instructional strategies, nor do they enjoy the experience.

Research on Time-of-Day Preferences

It is common knowledge that morning people and night owls function better at their respective times of day. The research supports our easy acceptance of these preferences. For example,

two junior high school principals revealed that the math underachievers in both their schools preferred learning in the afternoon but had been scheduled into morning math classes. When those youngsters were rescheduled into afternoon classes, they evidenced higher motivation, better discipline, and an increase in achievement. Three years later, a New York high school reported that time preference was a crucial factor in the reversal of initial and chronic truancy patterns among secondary students (Dunn et al. 1987). Similar data were reported by the di-

rector of five alternative high schools in Washington (Dunn and Griggs 1988).

In 1983, the matching of elementary students' time preferences with their instructional schedules resulted in significant achievement gains in both reading and math over a two-year period. One year later, *teachers'* time preferences were identified, and staff development was conducted during their preferred and nonpreferred times (early morning and immediately after school). Interestingly, those teachers implemented innovative in-

Researcher/Date	Sample	Subject Examined
Cholakis 1986	106 underachieving, inner-city, parochial school 7th and 8th graders	Vocabulary development was provided through three strategies—by the teacher, alone by themselves, and in a peer group treatment.
Findings: Those who preferred learning alone, scored significantly higher (.01) than those who preferred learning either with peers or the teacher. However, all students attained significantly higher achievement (.001) and attitude (.01) scores when learning with an authority figure.		
DeBello 1985	236 suburban 8th graders	Students wrote social studies compositions and then experienced revision strategies that were congruent *and* incongruent with their sociological preferences.
Findings: Peer learners scored significantly higher when matched with the peer-conferencing technique (.01). Authority-oriented learners, when revising through the teacher-conference, achieved statistically higher (.01) than when revising either through peer conferencing or self-review. And those who preferred to learn alone scored significantly higher (.01) when matched, rather than mismatched, with self-review. No learning style group achieved better than any other, but a significant interaction occurred between individual sociological style and the matched method of revision (.001). In addition, the attitudes of students who preferred to learn alone or with an adult were significantly more positive (.01) when they were assigned to approaches that matched their styles.		
Giannitti 1988	104 suburban, parochial and public school 6th, 7th, and 8th graders	Social studies taught through both a mini-Contract Activity Package (CAP) and a small-group strategy, Team Learning
Findings: Peer-oriented students achieved significantly higher test and attitudes scores when learning through Team Learning than through the mini-Cap (.01). Learning-alone preferents attained significantly higher test and attitude scores (.01) through the mini-Cap than with their peers. Non-preferred students achieved better through the mini-Cap than through the Team Learning and liked working alone better than in groups. A significant interaction occurred between learning alone and peer-preferenced learning and the method of learning (mini-Cap and Team Learning).		
Miles 1987	40 inner-city 5th and 6th graders	Twenty-two who preferred to learn alone and 18 who preferred to learn with peers were assigned randomly to two instructional groups that taught career awareness and career decision-making concepts in conditions both congruent and incongruent with their preferences.
Findings: The matching of sociological preference with complementary grouping patterns increased achievement significantly on career awareness (.01) and career decision making (.01). In addition, students' attitude scores were statistically higher when they were taught career awareness (.01) and career decision-making concepts (.05) in patterns accommodating their sociological preferences. With the exception of career awareness achievement, neither sociologically preferred group achieved better than the other but learning-alone preferents scored higher (.05) than peer-preferenced individuals.		
Perrin 1984	104 gifted and nongifted, suburban 1st and 2nd graders	Problem solving and word recognition through both individual- and peer-group strategies. Learning with the teacher was eliminated as a strategy when not a single gifted child preferred to learn that way.
Findings: Analysis of the mean gain scores revealed that achievement was significantly higher (.05) whenever students were taught through approaches that matched their diagnosed sociological preferences. Although the gifted tended to prefer to learn alone in their heterogeneously grouped classes, a small group of seven gifted, who previously had known each other from participation in a special, part-time program for the gifted, actually performed best when learning in isolation with other gifted children.		

Fig. 3. Experimental Research Concerned with Sociological Preferences

structural techniques significantly more often (as reported by their supervisors' evaluations) when *they* were taught during their most preferred hours. Then an elementary school principal in Kansas administered the *Iowa Basic Skills Tests* in reading and math to groups whose time preferences matched their test schedules—either early morning or afternoon. She reported significantly higher test gains in both subjects as compared with each youngster's previous two years' growth (Dunn et al. 1987.)

Studies of dropouts, underachievers, at-risk (Griggs and Dunn 1988), and vocational education (Tappenden 1983) students indicate that, as a group, they are *not* morning people; neither were the truants in the New York experiment. For each of these groups, learning in late morning, afternoon, or evening significantly increased achievement.

Among the more interesting findings of research with time preferences is that *most* students are *not* morning-alert. At the elementary school level, approximately 28 percent appear to be "early birds"; many do not begin to be capable of concentrating on difficult material until after 10:00 a.m., and many are at their best in the early afternoon. Only about one-third of more than a million students we have tested prefer learning in the early morning, and the majority prefer late morning or afternoon. At the high school level, almost 40 percent are early morning learners, but a majority remain most alert in the late morning and afternoon; and, for the first time identifiable after early childhood, almost 13 percent are "night owls," able to concentrate on difficult material in the evening (Price 1980). However, most teachers are early morning, high-energy people but often experience lows after 1:00 p.m. Another large group of educators merely get by much of the day and become mentally alert toward evening.

Mobility Needs

One element of learning style is the need for physical activity, and a review of this research reveals how this need can be confused with other, more alarming diagnoses. For example, Fadley and Hosler (1979) noted that children often were referred to psychologists because of their consistent

| | Means | |
	Passive b_1	Active b_2
Passive a_1	8.70	5.45
Active a_2	7.15	9.10

Note: a = preference; b = environment. N = 20.

Fig. 4. Analysis of Preference X Environment Interaction

hyperactivity; their teachers complained that such youngsters were unable to sit quietly and pay attention during lessons. Those psychologists reported that most students sent to them were not at all clinically hyperactive; instead, they were normal children in need of movement. In addition, the less interested they were in the lesson, the more mobility the children required.

During the same period, Restak (1979) substantiated that "over 95 percent of hyperactives are males" (p. 230) and that the very same characteristic, when observed in girls, correlated with academic *achievement*. He deplored that boys were required to be passive in school and were rejected for aggressive behaviors there, but were encouraged societally to engage in typical male aggressions in the world at large; this paradox could lead to role conflict. Restak added that conventional classroom environments did not provide male students with sufficient outlets for their normal needs. He warned that schools actually *caused* conflict with societal expectations that boys not be timid, passive, or conforming.

Other researchers corroborated Restak's admonitions and chastised educators for believing that physical activities prevented, rather than enhanced, learning. Indeed, when previously restless youngsters were reassigned to classes that did not require passivity, their behaviors were rarely noticed. Eventually, teachers began to report that although certain students thrived in activity-oriented environments that permitted mobility, others remained almost exclusively in the same area despite frequent attempts to coax them to move (Dunn et al. 1986). That led to Fitt's (1975) conclusions that no amount of persuasion increased certain

children's interest in movement, whereas others found it impossible to remain seated passively for extended periods. "These are cases of a child's style . . . governing his interaction with and within the environment" (p. 94).

DellaValle's (1984) research documented that almost half the 7th graders in a large urban racially mixed but predominantly black junior high school could not sit still for any length of time. Twenty-five percent could but only when interested in the lesson, and the remaining 25 percent *preferred* passivity. When preference and environment were matched, students' performance yielded significantly higher test scores than when they were mismatched. Figure 4 reports the post hoc analysis used to determine exactly where the interaction occurred. This analysis was conducted after the initial repeated measures design indicated a significant interaction at the .001 level.

Everyone Has One

Every person has a learning style—all have at least some preferences—the result of many influences. Certain learning style characteristics are biological, whereas others are developed through experience (Restak 1979, Thies 1979). Individual responses to sound, light, temperature, design, perception, intake, chronobiological highs and lows, mobility needs, and persistence appear to be biological; whereas sociological preferences, motivation, responsibility (conformity), and need for structure are thought to be developmental. The significant differences among diverse cultures tend to support this theory (*Learning Styles Network Newsletter* 1980-1988). Despite cultural influences, however, within each culture, socioeconomic strata, and classroom *there are as many within-group differences as between-group differences*. Indeed, each *family* includes parents and offspring with styles that differ.

Those who suggest that children should learn to adapt to their teachers' styles disregard the biological nature of style. They also disregard Cafferty's (1980) findings that the closer the match between each student's and the teachers' styles, the higher the grade point average; and the reverse. In addition, Kagan (1966) reported that his "success" with training impulsive students to become more reflective was

Those who suggest that children should learn to adapt to their teachers' styles disregard the biological nature of style.

evidenced only when adults were present. In addition, although Kagan's subjects learned to respond more reflectively, *their accuracy on tasks was decreased.* Thus, educators can see that learning styles are not lightly held; they demonstrate remarkable resistance to change.

Identifying learning styles as a basis for providing responsive instruction has never been more important than now, as educators meet the needs of a diverse student population. To identify their students' learning styles (Beaty 1986, Dunn et al. 1977, Marcus 1977), teachers must use a reliable and valid learning style preference instrument (Curry 1987). When permitted to learn difficult academic information or skills through their identified preferences, children tend to achieve statistically higher test and attitude scores than when instruction is dissonant with their preferences.

No learning style is either better or worse than another. Since each style has similar intelligence ranges, a student *cannot* be labeled or stigmatized by having any type of style. Most children can master the same content; *how* they master it is determined by their individual styles.

1. When we use the terms *significant* and *significantly,* we mean in a statistical sense.

Authors' note: Space limitations required the reduction from 163 primary references to the following list.

References

Annotated Bibliography. (1988). New York: Center for the Study of Learning and Teaching Styles, St. John's University.

Beaty, S.A. (1986). "The Effect of Inservice Training on the Ability of Teachers to Observe Learning Styles of Students." Doctoral diss., Oregon State University. *Dissertation Abstracts International* 47: 1998A.

Bruno, J. (1988). "An Experimental Investigation of the Relationships Between and Among Hemispheric Processing, Learning Style Preferences, Instructional Strategies, Academic Achievement, and Attitudes of Developmental Mathematics Students in an Urban Technical College." Doctoral diss., St. John's University.

Cafferty, E. (1980). "An Analysis of Student Performance Based Upon the Degree of Match Between the Educational Cognitive Style of the Teachers and the Educational Cognitive Style of the Students." Doctoral diss., University of Nebraska.

Carbo, M. (1980). "An Analysis of the Relationship Between the Modality Preferences of Kindergartners and Selected Reading Treatments as They Affect the Learning of a Basic Sight-Word Vocabulary." Doctoral diss., St. John's University, New York. *Dissertation Abstracts International* 41: 1389A.

Cholakis, M. M. (1986). "An Experimental Investigation of the Relationships Between and Among Sociological Preferences, Vocabulary Instruction and Achievement, and the Attitudes of New York, Urban Seventh and Eighth Grade Underachievers." Doctoral diss., St. John's University, New York. *Dissertation Abstracts International* 47: 4046A.

Cody, C. (1983). "Learning Styles, Including Hemispheric Dominance: A Comparative Study of Average, Gifted, and Highly Gifted Students in Grades Five Through Twelve. Doctoral diss., Temple University. *Dissertation Abstracts International* 44: 1631-6A.

Curry, L. (1987). *Integrating Concepts of Cognitive Learning Style: A Review with Attention to Psychometric Standards.* Ontario, Canada: Canadian College of Health Service Executives.

DeBello, T. (1985). "A Critical Analysis of the Achievement and Attitude Effects of Administrative Assignments to Social Studies Writing Instruction Based on Identified Eighth Grade Students' Learning Style Preferences for Learning Alone, with Peers, or with Teachers." Doctoral diss., St. John's University, New York. *Dissertation Abstracts International* 47: 68A.

DeGregoris, C. N. (1986). "Reading Comprehension and the Interaction of Individual Sound Preferences and Varied Auditory Distractions." Doctoral diss., Hofstra University, *Dissertation Abstracts International* 47: 3380A.

DellaValle, J. (1984). "An Experimental Investigation of the Word Recognition Scores of Seventh Grade Students to Provide Supervisory and Administrative Guidelines for the Organization of Effective Instructional Environments." Doctoral diss., St. John's University. *Dissertation Abstracts International* 45: 359-02A.

Dunn, R. (1987). "Research on Instructional Environments: Implications for Student Achievement and Attitudes." *Professional School Psychology* 11, 2: 43-52.

Dunn, R. (1988). "Commentary: Teaching Students Through Their Perceptual Strengths or Preferences." *Journal of Reading* 31, 4: 304-309.

Dunn, R., D. Cavanaugh, B. Eberle, and R. Zenhausern. (1982). "Hemispheric Preference: The Newest Element of Learning Style." *The American Biology Teacher* 44, 5: 291-294.

Dunn, R., J. DellaValle, K. Dunn, G. Geisert, R. Sinatra, and R. Zenhausern. (1986). "The Effects of Matching and Mismatching Students' Mobility Preferences on Recognition and Memory Tasks." *Journal of Educational Research* 79, 5: 267-272.

Dunn, R., K. Dunn, and G. E. Price. (1975, 1979, 1981, 1985). *Learning Style Inventory.* Price Systems, Box 1818, Lawrence, KS 66044-0067.

Dunn, R., K. Dunn, and G.E. Price. (1977). "Diagnosing Learning Styles: A Prescription for Avoiding Malpractice Suits Against School Systems." *Phi Delta Kappan* 58, 5: 418-420.

Dunn, R., K. Dunn, L. Primavera, R. Sinatra, and J. Virostko. (1987). "A Timely Solution: A Review of Research on the Effects of Chronobiology on Children's Achievement and Behavior." *The Clearing House* 61, 1: 5-8 (Heldreff Publications, Washington, D.C.).

Dunn, R., and S.A. Griggs. (1988). *Learning Style: Quiet Revolution in American Secondary Schools.* Reston, Va.: National Association of Secondary School Principals.

Dunn, R., J. Krimsky, J. Murray, and P. Quinn. (1985). "Light Up Their Lives: A Review of Research on the Effects of Lighting on Children's Achievement." *The Reading Teacher* 38, 9: 863-869 (The International Reading Association, Newark, Delaware).

Fadley, J.L., and V.N. Hosler. (1979). *Understanding the Alpha Child at Home and at School.* Springfield, Ill.: Charles C Thomas.

Fitt, S. (1975). "The Individual and His Environment." In *Learning Environments,* edited by T.G. David and B.D. Wright. Chigago: University of Chicago Press.

Giannitti, M. C. (1988). "An Experimental Investigation of the Relationships Among the Learning Style Sociological Preferences of Middle-School Students (Grades 6, 7, 8), Their Attitudes and Achievement in Social Studies, and Se-

3. LEARNING: Instructional Strategies

lected Instructional Strategies." Doctoral diss., St. John's University, New York.

Griggs, S.A., and R. Dunn. (September/October 1988). "High School Dropouts: Do They Learn Differently from Those Who Remain in School?" *The Principal* 35, 1: 1-8 (Board of Jewish Education of Greater New York).

Hill, J., et al. (1971). *Personalized Education Programs Utilizing Cognitive Style Mapping*. Bloomfield Hills, Mich.: Oakland Community College.

Hodges, H. (1985). "An Analysis of the Relationships Among Preferences for a Formal/Informal Design, One Element of Learning Style, Academic Achievement, and Attitudes of Seventh and Eighth Grade Students in Remedial Mathematics Classes in a New York City Junior High School." Doctoral diss., St. John's University, New York. *Dissertation Abstracts International* 45: 2791A.

Jarsonbeck, S. (1984). "The Effects of a Right-Brain and Mathematics Curriculum on Low Achieving Fourth Grade Students." Doctoral diss., University of South Florida. *Dissertation Abstracts International* 45: 2791A.

Kagan, J. (1966). "Reflection-Impulsivity: The Generality and Dynamics of Conceptual Tempo." *Journal of Abnormal Psychology* 71: 17-24.

Keefe, J., M. Languis, C. Letteri, and R. Dunn. (1986). *Learning Style Profile*. Reston, Va.: National Association of Secondary School Principals.

Krimsky, J. (1982). "A Comparative Analysis of the Effects of Matching and Mismatching Fourth Grade Students with Their Learning Style Preference for the Environmental Element of Light and Their Subsequent Reading Speed and Accuracy Scores." Doctoral diss., St. John's University, New York. *Dissertation Abstracts International* 43: 66A.

Kroon, D. (1985). "An Experimental Investigation of the Effects on Academic Achievement and the Resultant Administrative Implications of Instruction Congruent and Incongruent with Secondary Industrial Arts Students' Learning Style Perceptual Preference." Doctoral diss., St. John's University, New York. *Dissertation Abstracts International* 46: 3247A.

Learning Styles Network Newsletter. (Winter 1980-Autumn 1988). New York: National Association of Secondary School Principals and St. John's University.

MacMurren, H. (1985). "A Comparative Study of the Effects of Matching and Mismatching Sixth-Grade Students with Their Learning Style Preferences for the Physical Element of Intake and Their Subsequent Reading Speed and Accuracy Scores and Attitudes." Doctoral

diss., St. John's University, New York. *Dissertation Abstracts International* 46: 3247A.

Marcus, L. (1977). "How Teachers View Learning Styles." *NASSP Bulletin* 61, 408: 112-114.

Martini, M. (1986). "An Analysis of the Relationships Between and Among Computer-Assisted Instruction, Learning Style Perceptual Preferences, Attitudes, and the Science Achievement of Seventh Grade Students in a Suburban New York School District." Doctoral diss., St. John's University, New York. *Dissertation Abstracts International* 47: 877A.

Miles, B. (1987). "An Investigation of the Relationships Among the Learning Style Sociological Preferences of Fifth and Sixth Grade Students, Selected Interactive Classroom Patterns, and Achievement in Career Awareness and Career Decision-Making Concepts." Doctoral diss., St. John's University, New York. *Dissertation Abstracts International* 48: 2527A.

Miller, L. M. (1985). "Mobility as an Element of Learning Style: The Effect Its Inclusion or Exclusion Has on Student Performance in the Standardized Testing Environment." Master's thesis, University of North Florida.

Murrain, P. G. (1983). "Administrative Determinations Concerning Facilities Utilization and Instructional Grouping: An Analysis of the Relationships Between Selected Thermal Environments and Preferences for Temperature, an Element of Learning Style, as They Affect Word Recognition Scores of Secondary Students." Doctoral diss., St. John's University, New York. *Dissertation Abstracts International* 44: 1749A.

NASSP National Task Force. (Summer 1983). "National Task Force Defines Learning Style Operationally and Conceptually." *Learning Styles Network Newsletter* 4, 2: 1 (National Association of Secondary School Principals and St. John's University).

Perrin, J. (1984). "An Experimental Investigation of the Relationships Among the Learning Style Sociological Preferences of Gifted and Non-Gifted Primary Children, Selected Instructional Strategies, Attitudes, and Achievement in Problem Solving and Rote Memorization." Doctoral diss., St. John's University, New York. *Dissertation Abstracts International* 46: 342A.

Pizzo, J. (1981). "An Investigation of the Relationships Between Selected Acoustic Environments and Sound, an Element of Learning Style, as They Affect Sixth Grade Students' Reading Achievement and Attitudes." Doctoral diss., St. John's

University, New York. *Dissertation Abstracts International* 42: 2475A.

Price, G.E. (1980). "Which Learning Style Elements are Stable and Which Tend to Change Over Time?" *Learning Styles Network Newsletter* 1, 3: 1.

Restak, R. (1979). *The Brain: The Last Frontier*. New York: Doubleday.

Shea, T. C. (1983). "An Investigation of the Relationship Among Preferences for the Learning Style Element of Design, Selected Instructional Environments, and Reading Achievement with Ninth Grade Students to Improve Administrative Determinations Concerning Effective Educational Facilities." Doctoral diss., St. John's University, New York. *Dissertation Abstracts International* 44: 2004A.

Stiles, R. (1985). "Learning Style Preferences for Design and Their Relationship to Standardized Test Results." Doctoral diss., University of Tennessee. *Dissertation Abstracts International* 46: 2551A.

Tappenden, V. J. (1983). "Analysis of the Learning Styles of Vocational Education and Nonvocational Education Students in Eleventh and Twelfth Grades from Rural, Urban, and Suburban Locations in Ohio." Doctoral diss., Kent State University. *Dissertation Abstracts International* 44: 1326a.

Thies, A.P. (1979). "A Brain-Behavior Analysis of Learning Style." In *Student Learning Styles: Diagnosing and Prescribing Programs*. Reston, Va.: National Association of Secondary School Principals, pp. 55-61.

Urbschat, K. S. (1977). "A Study of Preferred Learning Models and Their Relationship to the Amount of Recall of CVC Trigrams." Doctoral diss., St. John's University, New York. *Dissertation Abstracts International* 38: 2536-5A.

Weinberg, F. (1983). "An Experimental Investigation of the Interaction Between Sensory Modality Preference and Mode of Presentation in the Instruction of Arithmetic Concepts to Third Grade Underachievers." Doctoral diss., St. John's University, New York. *Dissertation Abstracts International* 44: 1740A.

Wheeler, R. (1980). "An Alternative to Failure: Teaching Reading According to Students' Perceptual Strengths." *Kappa Delta Pi Record* 17, 2: 59-63.

Wheeler, R. (1983). "An Investigation of the Degree of Academic Achievement Evidenced When Second Grade Learning Disabled Students' Perceptual Preferences Are Matched and Mismatched with Complementary Sensory Approaches to Beginning Reading Instruction." Doctoral diss., St. John's University, New York. *Dissertation Abstracts International* 44: 2039A.

A Critique of the Research on Learning Styles

Like the blind men in the fable about the elephant, learning styles researchers tend to investigate only a part of the whole and thus have yet to provide a definitive picture of the matter before them.

LYNN CURRY

Lynn Curry is a Principal with Curry Adams and Associates, 130 Albert St., Ottawa, Ontario, Canada, K1P 5G4.

The primary objective for the study and application of learning styles has been to improve the immediate and long-term results of general teaching-learning episodes (for example, Biggs 1988, Papalia 1978, Smith and Renzulli 1983). Specifically, the field claims to influence four aspects of teaching and learning in schools: (1) curriculum design (Popkewitz et al. 1982, Wang 1980); (2) instructional methods (Corno and Snow 1986); (3) assessment methods; and (4) student guidance (Snow 1986). These claims for affecting the primary processes of schooling are indeed big. How good are they? Is this a new elephant we are blindly examining, or has the old beast just rearranged itself?

General Problems

The operationalization of learning style theory encompasses three pervasive general problems: (1) confusion in definitions, (2) weakness in reliability and validity of measurements, and (3) identification of relevant characteristics in learners and instructional settings.

The first issue is the bewildering array of definitions surrounding learning style conceptualizations. There is wide variation in the scale and the scope of learning, in school achievement, and in other behavior predicted by the various learning style concepts.

Some definitions claim to predict only an individual's free choice between a lecture-style instructional method versus small-group instructional method (Friedman and Stritter 1976); others endeavor to predict habitual response across all learning acts (Yando and Kagan 1970). Definitions of operation also vary widely, with loose distinctions made between *style*, *strategy*, and *tactic*. There may be some convergence emerging in the literature toward using *style* to refer to information processing routines that function in a trait-like manner at the personality level (Entwistle 1981); *strategy* to refer to cross-situational consistency in how students approach school learning (Entwistle 1988, Ramsden 1988); and

The tendency among the learning styles researchers has been to rush prematurely into print and marketing with very early and preliminary indications of factor loadings based on one dataset.

tactic to describe the specific, observable activity of learners in a specific learning situation (Snowman 1989).

Weakness in the accumulated evidence for the reliability and validity of measurements is the second continuing problem. Users of educational and psychological tests should routinely expect any conceptualization and measurement scheme to indicate that the test meets minimum standards for use and interpretation. The developers have collected varying degrees and types of evidence to support their various conceptualizations and measurement systems. The tendency among the learning styles researchers, however, has been not to pursue the necessary iterative pattern of hypothesis-investigation-modification but rather to rush prematurely into print and marketing with very early and preliminary indications of factor loadings based on one dataset. This haste weakens any claim of valid interpretation from the test scores. Nor have writers and researchers in learning style theory and measurement consistently pursued methods to carefully distinguish among like concepts in order to collect construct-related evidence. Thus, the test user has little or no indication of the degree of overlap across the various learning style conceptualizations nor much convincing evidence that the interpretations are valid for the test results observed.

An additional important standard for interpreting educational and psychological tests concerns the reliability of the measurements. Any test score is subject to many unwanted influences or sources of error or variance in the observed score for a particular individual on a particular test. But the user needs to know that the test indicates a true measure without the various sources of error. Thus, test developers have an obligation to provide information about the size and expected sources of variance in their measurement systems. Test developers in learning style have provided some information about the relevant reliabilities, but it's rare to find, for example, standard errors of measurement reported for test scores near the cutoff scores for the various learning style classification decisions. Further, most of the manuals accompanying the learning style tests report a considerable range in the simple reliabilities reported, some notably unreliable and most reported on the basis of only three or four test items.

The third pervasive problem is how to identify accurately which of the possible micro- and macro-adaptations within educational settings will be effective in interaction with which range of learning styles. To make progress here, researchers would have to require creative development of alternative structures in curriculum and instructional methods, careful matching of selected learning style concepts to these variations, and evaluation designs sensitive enough to distinguish real effects. Some learning style theorists have conducted repeated small studies that tend to validate the hypotheses derived from their own conceptualizations. However, in general, these studies have not been designed to disconfirm hypotheses, are open to expectation and participation effects, and do not involve wide enough samples to constitute valid tests in educational settings. Even with these built-in biases, no single learner preference pattern unambiguously indicates a specific instructional design (Doyle and Rutherford 1984, Good and Stipek 1983).

One approach used to evaluate the various contentions surrounding style and educational treatments is the aptitude-treatment interaction methodology. In their detailed review of this approach, Cronbach and Snow (1977) found no evidence of reliable or useful interactions between student pref-

erences and instructional treatments. Further, they noted extensive covariance of general intelligence with many measures of aptitude; the predictive effect of general intelligence on school achievement is well established.

Researchers have not resolved whether optimal results are achieved when the learning styles of individual learners are systematically matched, or systematically mismatched, to curriculum and/or instructional methods. Witkin (and colleagues 1977) suggested that matching students with teachers or instructional materials according to their cognitive styles might facilitate the students' initial acquisition of skills and provide important continued motivation. But an alternative point of view has been articulated by Shipman and Shipman (1985): "In a complex

---

Users of educational and psychological tests should routinely expect any conceptualization and measurement scheme to indicate that the test meets minimum standards for use and interpretation.

---

changing society with diverse environmental demands, students need the opportunity to become sensitive to and proficient in multiple alternative strategies." Toward such an end, Snow and Lohman (1984) suggest matching student style to instructional format for the initial stages of learning, then moving to systematic mismatches as the student becomes more proficient with the material.

Kirby (1988) and Pask (1988) argue that the best learning style for understanding instruction is the *absence* of any identified style or even any style-like consistency in approach. Both advocate that learners take a very flexible approach to instruction, one that can be easily modified as more cues be-

come available about the learning conditions. Kirby refers to this flexibility as a "synthetic style"; Pask calls it a "versatile style."

Logically, developing the flexibility to deal optimally with all sorts of instructional situations would be a laudable goal for each student. The question remains: do learning style considerations help students develop this flexibility in any way?

Problems with the Evidence

A considerable literature shows at least statistically important effects on short-term achievement when learning style scores were used to group students for intervention. (See, for example, Douglas 1979, Tanenbaum 1982, Steele 1986, DeBello 1985, Hodges 1985, Kroon 1985, and Lynch 1981.) Effects on improved test scores with testing conditions matched to student style have been published by Murrain (1983) and Shea (1983). But there are also studies showing no discernible effect attributable to learning style variation (for example, Cholakis 1986, DeGregoris 1986, Stiles 1985, and Tappenden 1983). Given the predilection in the scholarly press toward considering positive results more interesting than negative or null results, the availability of negative results regarding learning style intervention likely underestimates the true proportion of negative results found across learning style investigations.

The quality of the published evidence offered by studies in this field is also diminished by the following problems. These external threats to validity are ignored in the research designs presently used in learning style research.

1. Many studies in the learning styles literature have been conducted by graduate students preparing their Ph.D theses under the direction of faculty members with a vested interest in substantiating a particular learning style conceptualization.

2. A recurrent design problem, when comparison groups are selected on the basis of extreme scores, is the potential for statistical regression toward the mean, which subsequently biases interpretation of results.

3. Few of these studies estimate the reactive effects of pretesting for learning style, which may sensitize students to experimental instructional conditions.

What We Know about Learning Styles from Research in Special Education

Vicki E. Snider

The notion that individual differences can and must be accommodated by modifying instructional methods is a central tenet of special education. When I was a special education teacher, I advocated an eclectic approach, meaning that each student needed to be taught in a different way depending on his or her individual characteristics. Over the course of 10 years, however, I realized that, regardless of student characteristics, some approaches worked, and some didn't. I now have a better understanding of the problems that troubled me as a teacher. With the use of learning styles gaining popularity in general education, I fear that the mistakes made in special education will be repeated and learners, especially low-performing students, will suffer.

Learning styles is a type of aptitude-treatment interaction. Aptitude-treatment interactions suggest that a person's distinctive characteristics or aptitudes (in this case, learning style) can be matched to a specific treatment (instructional method) resulting in a statistical interaction (a more effective outcome than could otherwise have been achieved). But numerous reviews of the literature have failed to find support for aptitude-treatment interactions. They have not been supported by research in educational psychology (Berlinger and Cahen 1973, Cronbach and Snow 1977, Miller 1981) or in special education (Kampwirth and Bates 1980, Kavale and Forness 1987, Tarver and Dawson 1978, Ysseldyke 1973).

Learning styles are often used to determine methods of initial reading instruction. Frequently, holistic instruction is recominmended for young, inexperienced readers, whereas phonics is proposed for better readers (Carbo 1987, Carbo et al. 1986,

Carbo and Hodges 1988). This makes little sense. It seems redundant to provide phonics instruction to students who have already mastered the code. Learning styles advocates also recommend holistic instruction for low-performing students, suggesting that the cause of their reading disabilities is a mismatch between their learning styles and the instructional methods (Carbo 1987, Carbo and Hodges 1988). However, reading disabled students have difficulty with the phonological aspects of language (Bradley and Bryant 1983; Liberman and Shankweiler 1979, 1985; Stanovich 1982, 1986) and do not unravel the decoding mystery by themselves. Holistic approaches do not give them a clue. Thus, students' chances for success in school may be jeopardized by teachers who use learning styles as a basis for determining methods of initial reading instruction.

People are different, and it is good practice to recognize and accommodate individual differences. It is also good practice to present information in a variety of ways through more than one modality, but it is *not* wise to categorize learners and prescribe methods solely on the basis of tests with questionable technical qualities. For example, the Carbo, Dunn, and Dunn (1986) model of learning styles, which currently seems to be gaining the most momentum in general education, promotes two assessment instruments: the *Learning Style Inventory* (Dunn et al. 1985) and the *Reading Style Inventory* (Carbo 1983). Both struments suffer from inadequate reliability and validity (Stahl 1988). The idea of learning styles is appealing, but a critical examination of this approach should cause educators to be skeptical.

References

Berlinger, D.C. and L.S. Cahen. (1973). "Trait-Treatment Interaction and Learning." In *Review of Research in Education (Vol. 1)*. Istasca, Ill.: F.E. Peacock.

Bradley, L., and P.E. Bryant. (1983). "Categorizing Sounds and Learning to Read." *Nature* 301: 419–421.

Carbo, M. (1983). *The Reading Style Inventory*. Roslyn Heights, N.Y.: Learning Research Associates.

Carbo, M. (1987). "Matching Reading Styles: Correcting Ineffective Instruction." *Educational Leadership* 45: 55–62.

Carbo, M., and H. Hodges. (1988). "Learning Styles Strategies Can Help Students at Risk." *Teaching Exceptional Children* 20, 4: 55–58.

Carbo, M., R. Dunn, and K. Dunn. (1986). *Teaching Students to Read through their Individual Learning Styles*. Englewood Cliffs, N.J.: Prentice-Hall.

Cronbach, L.J., and R.E. Snow. (1977). *Aptitudes and Instructional Methods: A Handbook for Research on Interaction*. New York: Irvington.

Dunn, R., K. Dunn, and G.E. Price. (1985). *Learning Style Inventory*. Lawrence, Kans.: Price Systems, Inc.

Kampwirth, T.J., and M. Bates. (1980). "Modality Preference and Teaching Method: A Review of Research." *Academic Therapy* 15: 597–605.

Kavale, K.A., and S.R. Forness. (1987). "Substance Over Style: Assessing the Efficacy of Modality Testing and Teaching." *Exceptional Children* 54: 228–239.

Liberman, I.Y., and D. Shankweiler. (1979). "Speech, the Alphabet, and Teaching to Read." In *Theory and Practice of Early Reading (Vol. 2)*, pp. 109–132, edited by L. Resnick and P. Weaver. Hillsdale, N.J.: Erlbaum Associates.

Liberman, I.Y., and D. Shankweiler. (1985). "Phonology and the Problems of Learning to Read and Write." *Remedial and Special Education* 6: 8–17.

Miller, A. (1981). "Conceptual Matching Models and Interactional Research in Education." *Review of Educational Research* 51: 33–84.

Stahl, S.A. (1988). "Is There Evidence to Support Matching Reading Styles and Initial Reading Methods?" *Phi Delta Kappan* 69, 4: 317–322.

Stanovich, K.E. (1982). "Individual Differences in the Cognitive Processes of Reading: 1. Word Decoding." *Journal of Learning Disabilities* 15: 449–512.

Stanovich, K.E. (1986). "Matthew Effects in Reading: Some Consequences of Individual Differences in the Acquisition of Literacy." *Reading Research Quarterly* 31: 360–406.

Tarver, S.G., and M.M. Dawson. (1978). "Modality Preference and the Teaching of Reading: A Review." *Journal of Learning Disabilities* 11: 17–29.

Ysseldyke, J.E. (1973). "Diagnostic-Prescriptive Teaching: The Search for Aptitude-Treatment Interactions." In *First Review of Special Education (Vol. 1)*, pp. 5–31, edited by L. Mann and D.A. Sabatino. Philadelphia: JSE Press.

Vicki E. Snider is an Associate Professor, Department of Special Education, University of Wisconsin—Eau Claire, 293 Water St., Eau Claire, WI 54702–4004.

4. Students may also be reacting to the experimental arrangement instead of to the experimental variable (Hawthorne effect).

Alternate Explanations

The results observed in present studies of learning style could be, and have been, achieved through more direct mechanisms: general intelligence effects, principles of adaptive education, and instructional alignment. First, to the extent that learning styles correlate with general intelligence (Witkin's field-independence, for example), then school achievement will be highly predictable. Most learning style theorists have not distinguished their constructs sufficiently from measures of intelligence.

Second, the concept of "adaptive education" has enjoyed a long history (Snow 1980, Corno and Snow 1986) and has undoubtedly been practiced by insightful teachers throughout the ages, although tailoring instruction for individual learners has frequently received little support. During the '60s and '70s, for example, "teacher-proof" curriculum packages ignored the individual effects of teacher perceptions and knowledge about their students. Any modification by teachers was considered, at least potentially, substandard education.

Now we expect that when a student either does not master the necessary content background or supporting knowledge/skill set or has not developed skill in the information processing approach required by a curriculum, the teacher can concentrate on direct training of the missing content knowledge/skill set or information processing (McCombs 1981, 1982a and b, 1984; Palincsar and Brown 1984; Dansereau 1988). Alternatively, the teacher can choose to proceed in a manner that avoids the missing content knowledge and the inexperienced information processing, in order to preserve student motivation and self-esteem while missing links are learned. Either choice requires information about the student and about the new learning task; and both require teachers comfortable with modifying curriculum guidelines to suit individual students. These teacher-initiated adaptations are very much like the various instructional variations suggested by the learning styles literature.

Third, "instructional alignment"

Effects on improved test scores with testing conditions matched to student style have been published, but there are also studies showing no discernible effect attributable to learning style variation.

might also account for learning styles-like results. This concept grew from earlier ideas of curricular alignment (Levine 1982) to focus on the idea of specifying desired outcomes sufficiently well to allow both teachers and students to efficiently arrange learning conditions to achieve those outcomes. In 1989 Cohen and colleagues reviewed results from the leading published learning style theorists as compared to studies deemed to have the critical instructional elements (task clarity, feedback, opportunity for practice) sufficiently aligned. This critique found essentially no effects due to learning style alone, but substantial effects when instruction and testing met the following criteria for alignment: (1) the stimulus condition critical features were precisely defined; (2) instruction was designed to present those critical features and reinforce behaviors that attend to those features; (3) the same critical features occur both in the instruction and in the assessment. The argument is that those learning style studies showing effects achieve the effects by aligning instruction, not by matching instruction and style.

Old Elephants or New?

The conceptualizers, instrument developers, and researchers in the learning styles field promise to deliver the power for students, teachers, and parents to take control of learning environments and interactions. But, in general,

the learning style conceptualizations, and the claims made on their behalf, remain to be systematically and comparatively evaluated in practice. Until the fundamental concepts of validity and reliability are established and until each competing concept is carefully investigated, researchers and users alike will continue groping like the five blind men in the fable about the elephant, each with a part of the whole but none with full understanding.

References

Biggs, J. B. (1988). *Student Approaches to Learning and Studying.* Hawthorn, Victoria: Australian Council for Educational Research.

Cholakis, M. M. (1986). "An Experimental Investigation of the Relationship between and among Sociological Preferences, Vocabulary Instruction and Achievement, and the Attitudes of New York Urban Seventh and Eighth Grade Underachievers." *Dissertation Abstracts International* 47, 11: 4046A.

Cohen, S. A., J. S. Hyman, L. Ashcroft, and D. Loveless. (1989). "Mastery Learning versus Learning Styles versus Metacognition: What Do We Tell the Practitioners?" Paper presented at the annual meeting of the American Educational Research Association, San Francisco.

Corno, L., and R. E. Snow. (1986). "Adapting Teaching to Individual Differences among Learners." In *Handbook of Research on Teaching*, 3rd ed., pp. 605–629), edited by M.C. Wittrock. Washington, D.C.: American Educational Research Association.

Cronbach, L. J., and R. E. Snow. (1977). *Aptitude and Instructional Methods: A Handbook for Research on Interactions.* New York: Irvington Publishers.

Dansereau, D. F. (1988). "Cooperative Learning Strategies." In *Learning and Study Strategies: Issues in Assessment, Instruction and Evaluation*, pp. 103–120, edited by C. W. Weinstein, E. T. Goetz, and P. A. Alexander. New York: Academic Press.

DeBello, T. (1985). "A Critical Analysis of the Achievement and Attitudes Effects of Administrative Assignments to Social Studies Writing Instruction Based on Identified Eighth Grade Students' Learning Style Preferences for Learning Alone, with Peers, or with Teachers." *Dissertation Abstracts International* 47, 01: 68A.

DeGregoris, C. N. (1986). "Reading Comprehension and the Interaction of Individual Sound Preferences and Varied Auditory Distractions." *Dissertation Abstracts International* 47, 09: 3380A.

Douglas, C. B. (1979). "Making Biology Easier to Understand." *The American*

Biology Teacher 41, 5: 277–281, 298–299.

Doyle, W., and B. Rutherford. (1984). "Classroom Research on Matching Learning and Teaching Styles." *Theory Into Practice* 23: 20–25.

Entwistle, N. (1981). *Styles of Learning and Teaching*. Chichester: Wiley.

Entwistle, N. (1988). "Motivational Factors in Students' Approaches to Learning." In *Learning Strategies and Learning Styles*, pp. 21–52, edited by R.R. Schmeck. New York: Plenum Press.

Friedman, C. P., and F. T. Stritter. (November 1976). "An Empirical Inventory Comparing Instructional Preferences of Medical and Other Professional Students." *Research in Medical Education Proceedings*, pp. 85–90. 15th Annual Conference, San Francisco.

Good, T. L., and D. J. Stipek. (1983). "Individual Differences in the Classroom: A Psychological Perspective." In *Individual Differences and the Common Curriculum*, 82nd Yearbook of the National Society for the Study of Education, Part 1, edited by G.D. Fenstermacher. Chicago: University of Chicago Press.

Hodges, H. (1985). "An Analysis of the Relationships among Preferences for a Formal/Informal Design, One Element of Learning Style, Academic Achievement, and Attitude of Seventh and Eighth Grade Students in Remedial Mathematics Classes in a New York City Junior High School." *Dissertation Abstracts International* 45, 12: 2791A.

Kirby, J. R. (1988). "Style, Strategy, and Skill in Reading." In *Learning Strategies and Learning Styles*, pp. 229–274, edited by R. R. Schmeck. New York: Plenum Press.

Kroon, D. (1985). "An Experimental Investigation of the Effects on Academic Achievement and the Resultant Administrative Implications of Instruction Congruent and Incongruent with Secondary Industrial Arts Students' Learning Style Perceptual Preference." *Dissertation Abstracts International* 46, 11: 3247A.

Levine, D. (1982). "Successful Approaches for Improving Academic Achievements in Inner City Schools." *Phi Delta Kappan* 63: 523–526.

Lynch, P. K. (1981). "An Analysis of the Relationships among Academic Achievement, Attendance, and the Learning Style Time Preferences of Eleventh and Twelfth Grade Students Identified as Initial or Chronic Truants in a Suburban New York School District." *Dissertation Abstracts International* 42: 1880A.

McCombs, B. L. (1981). "Transitioning Learning Strategies Research into Practice: Focus on the Student in Technical Training." Paper presented at the Annual Meeting of the American Educational Research Association, Los Angeles.

McCombs, B. L. (1982a). "Transitioning Learning Strategies Research into Practice: Focus on the Student and Technical Training." *Journal of Instructional Development* 5, 2: 10–17.

McCombs, B. L. (1982b). "Learner Satisfaction and Motivation: Capitalizing on Strategies for Positive Self-Control." *Performance and Instruction* 21, 4: 3–6.

McCombs, B. L. (1984). "Processes and Skills Underlining Continuing Motivation: Toward a Definition of Motivational Skills Training Interventions." *Educational Psychologist* 19: 199–218.

Murrain, P. G. (1983). "Administrative Determinations Concerning Facilities Utilization and Instructional Groupings: An Analysis of the Relationships between Selected Thermal Environments and Preferences for Temperature, an Element of Learning Style, as They Affect Work Recognition Scores of Secondary Students." *Dissertation Abstracts International* 44, 06: 1749A.

Palincsar, A. S., and A. L. Brown. (1984). "Reciprocal Teaching of Comprehension Fostering and Monitoring Activities." *Cognition and Instruction* 1: 117–175.

Papalia, A. (May 1978). "Assessing Students' Learning Styles and Teaching for Individual Differences." *Hispania* 61: 318–322.

Pask, G. (1988). "Learning Strategies, Teaching Strategies, and Conceptual or Learning Style." In *Learning Strategies and Learning Styles*, pp. 83–100, edited by R. R. Schmeck. New York: Plenum Press.

Popkewitz, T. L., B. R. Tabachnick, and G. Wehlage. (1982). *The Myth of Educational Reform*. Madison, Wis.: University of Wisconsin Press.

Ramsden, P. (1988). "Context and Strategy: Situational Influences on Learning." In *Learning Strategies and Learning Styles*, pp. 159–184, edited by R. R. Schmeck. New York: Plenum Press.

Shea, T. C. (1983). "An Investigation of the Relationship among Selected Instructional Environments, Preferences for the Learning Style Element of Design, and Reading Achievements Testing in Ninth Grade Students to Improve Administrative Determinations Concerning Effective Facilities." *Dissertation Abstracts International* 44, 7: 2004A.

Shipman, S., and V. C. Shipman. (1985). "Cognitive Styles: Some Conceptual, Methodological, and Applied Issues." In *Review of Research in Education*, edited by E.W. Gordon. Washington, D.C.: American Educational Research Association.

Smith, L., and J. S. Renzulli. (1983). "The Assessment and Application of Learning Style Preferences: A Practical Approach to Classroom Teachers." Paper pre-sented at the Annual Meeting of the American Research Association, Montreal, Canada.

Snow, R. E. (1980). "Aptitude, Learner Control and Adaptive Instruction." *Educational Psychologist* 15: 151–158.

Snow, R. E. (October 1986). "Individual Differences and the Design of Educational Programs." *American Psychologist* 41, 10: 1029–1039.

Snow, R. E., and D. F. Lohman. (1984). "Towards a Theory of Cognitive Aptitude for Learning from Instruction." *Journal of Educational Psychology* 76: 347–376.

Snowman, J. (1989). "Learning Tactics and Strategies." In *Cognitive Instructional Psychology: Components of Classroom Learning*, edited by G.D. Phy and T. Andre. New York: Academic Press.

Steele, G. E. (1986). "An Investigation of the Relationships between Students' Interests and the Curricular Practices of an Alternative High School through the Perspective of Jung's Theory of Psychological Types." *Dissertation Abstracts International* 47: 3616-A.

Stiles, R. H. (1985). "Learning Style Preferences for Design and Their Relationship to Standardized Test Results." *Dissertation Abstracts International* 43, 01: 68A.

Tanenbaum, R. (1982). "An Investigation of the Relationships between Selected Instructional Techniques and Identified Field Dependent and Field Independent Cognitive Styles as Evidenced among High School Students Enrolled in Studies of Nutrition." *Dissertation Abstracts International* 43, 01: 68A.

Tappenden, V. J. (1983). "Analysis of the Learning Styles of Vocational Education and Nonvocational Education Students in Eleventh and Twelfth Grades from Rural, Urban, and Suburban Locations in Ohio." *Dissertation Abstracts International* 44, 05: 1326-A.

Wang, M. C. (1980). "Adaptive Instruction: Building on Diversity." *Theory Into Practice* 19, 2: 122–128.

Witkin, H. A., C. A. Moore, D. R. Goodenough, and P. W. Cox. (1977). "Field Dependent and Field Independent Cognitive Styles and Their Educational Implications." *Review of Educational Research* 47: 1–64.

Yando, R. M., and J. Kagan. (1970). "The Effect of Task Complexity on Reflection, Impulsivity." *Cognitive Psychological Journal* 1: 192–200.

Author's note: My synthesis of research, *Learning Styles in Secondary Schools: A Review of Instruments and Implications for Their Use*, is available from the National Center on Effective Secondary Schools at the University of Wisconsin—Madison. To order a copy, send a check or purchase order for $9, payable to Center Document Service, to Center Document Service, Rm. 242, 1025 W. Johnson St., Madison, WI 53706.

Fostering Creativity: The Innovative Classroom Environment

The standard classroom environment contains major barriers to the development of creativity in students, the author contends. He suggests methods for removing the barriers and for fostering creativity.

Randall P. Pruitt

RANDALL P. PRUITT is an instructor in the Department of Interpersonal and Public Communication at Bowling Green State University, Bowling Green, Ohio.

> Sometimes, nothing short of "a whack on the side of the head" can dislodge the assumptions that keep us thinking "more of the same."
>
> —Roger Von Oech[1]

FROM INITIAL WORK by Wallas, who classified the creative process into the four steps of preparation, incubation, illumination, and verification, to later work by Osborn, Maslow, and Arieti, the creative process has been examined from a wide variety of perspectives.[2]

In the classroom, environmental factors greatly influence the creative process. While the environment could be considered a small piece of the creative puzzle, it is, nonetheless, of vital importance with respect to how it affects innovative and creative instructor-student interaction in the classroom setting. For the purpose of this article, the instructor will be considered part of the classroom environment. The term environment itself will be defined as the aggregate of surrounding things or conditions.

Considering the teacher as part of the creative environment, J.P. Guilford, former president of the American Psychological Association, drew a direct link between the classroom instructor and the students' creativity development when he suggested that poor teaching inhibits development of creativity and that the normal conditions of mass education generally impede the development of creative individuals.[3] Arieti, Gowan and Olson, and Walker support the notion that creativity is encouraged by certain features in the environment.[4] Arieti also suggests that certain cultures have encouraged creative climates more than others. Before considering some of the advantages of a creative classroom environment, however, let us examine how to overcome some of the barriers to developing such an environment.

Overcoming Barriers to an Innovative Classroom Environment

The four major factors which impede the development of a creative classroom environment are classroom

Reprinted with permission of *Educational Horizons*, Vol. 68, No. 1, Fall 1989, pp. 51-54. *Educational Horizons*, quarterly journal published by Pi Lambda Theta, national honor and professional association, Bloomington, IN 47407-6626.

*T*orrence states that a major shortcoming in the educational system today is that too much emphasis is placed on conformity to behavioral norms and too little time is spent on encouraging original work.

control, habitual behavior, dealing with time as it relates to the creative process, and student assessment. Each is important in establishing a healthy environment for the creative process.

The Control Factor

Instructors fear that they will not be able to control the classroom in a creative learning situation. Control, in this case, does not refer to discipline, but to the process of learning within the context of the classroom. Among educators, there is often a desire to tie learning experiences into tidy little packages, but as Torrence explains, learning does not always conform to the expectations of instructors. Torrence states that a major shortcoming in the educational system today is that too much emphasis is placed on conformity to behavioral norms and too little time is spent on encouraging original work. He warns against the temptation to become confined to set patterns in learning situations and suggests that an atmosphere of "released control" be present in the classroom. "Released control" means that some control is present, but that students feel more freedom to experiment with creative alternatives because the principle of deferred judgment is practiced by the instructor.[5]

Iverson also supports the concept of a creative classroom environment, suggesting that flexibility can stimulate creative thinking in students.[6] Parnes conducted four years of research at the University of Buffalo studying the deliberate development of creative problem solving.[7] His research suggests that a "free wheeling" classroom atmosphere which includes the principle of deferred judgment can provide students with invaluable practice in viewing problems from varying vantage points. In seeking this type of environment, Parnes encouraged the creative process by giving students the freedom to apply imagination, enthusiasm, and individual creative ability in the environment where judgment of ideas was not immediate, but deferred. For some instructors, the relinquishment of immediate feedback may seem strange, but the advantage of such an atmosphere is that students can offer a great number of suggestions without the fear of immediate scrutiny by peers and superiors.

VAUGHAN discusses creativity as adventure and contends that for the creative process to develop its own direction and end, some kind of surrender of central control must be made.[8] For classroom instructors, this surrender might involve a decision to release control over expectations regarding how students should think, respond, and form ideas. To glean the advantages of a freewheeling environment, instructors may need to rethink attitudes toward students who respond and think in nonconforming ways. As Torrence suggests, students may feel more freedom to respond in creative ways if they perceive an attempt by the instructor to be open to a variety of individual learning/response styles.

In summary, the creative process can be encouraged and nurtured if instructors are willing to: (1) avoid an emphasis on conformity; (2) utilize the principle of released control; and (3) develop and practice the concept of deferred judgment.

The Habit Factor

A second barrier to a creative classroom environment is what could best be termed the habit factor. It is simply the tendency for instructors to rely on the techniques, styles, and patterns with which they are more familiar, and with which certain responses and outcomes are more predictable. Though some instructors find comfort in familiarity, the advantages of breaking the habit factor can be seen clearly in creativity research.

The Vermont Alliance for Arts in Education addressed the issue of fostering creativity in schools and communities in Vermont.[9] One of the findings of the study was that creativity needs a variety of settings. The key, according to the report, is that instructors and educators need to have a flexible attitude toward the environment. If creativity is to flourish, the environment could not, according to the alliance, be thought of as inert and immutable. Raudsepp and Hough contend that part of the reason individuals view change with considerable anxiety is because of the pressure that sometimes accompanies the change process. He contends that the only way individuals can face change is by becoming more "creatively flexible and imaginative."[10] Stanish supports the idea that for creative thinking to be encouraged, randomness and risk taking in teaching experiences and personal examples must be present in the classroom.[11]

Though instructors may use different models to foster a creative environment in the classroom, research indicates that flexibility, randomness, change, and risk taking may be important parts of breaking the habit barrier.

The Time Factor

Nicholas Murray Butler, former president of Columbia University, once said, "Time was invented by Almighty God in order to give ideas a chance." One of the biggest enemies of any instructor is time. Some instructors may find it difficult to make the time commitment that innovation and creativity demands.

*T*hough instructors may use different models to foster a creative environment in the classroom, research indicates that flexibility, randomness, change, and risk taking may be important parts of breaking the habit barrier.

Historically, many of the major models of the creative process include at least one stage involving the careful use of time. Wallas called this stage the incubation stage.[12] Rossman called it the birth of a new idea, or the invention stage.[13] Osborn referred to it as ideation.[14] And Von Oech labeled it the germination phase.[15] The emphasis is not time as it relates to preparation by the educational professional, but as it relates to the creative process itself. For students to receive the benefits of an innovative environment, it is necessary for instructors to prevent the barrier of time from rushing the birth of new ideas and approaches.

The Assessment Factor

A fourth barrier to a creative environment is the assessment factor. An assessment barrier is formed whenever judgment or assessment become a controlling factor in classroom interaction. This factor is usually present in any situation where there is the fear or actual presence of ridicule or rebuke. The object of the fear may be peers or superiors, but the result is usually an inhibition of individual willingness to risk, to question, and to fail.

Maslow asserted that the presence of a psychologically safe environment would greatly enhance creativity.[16] The Vermont Alliance for the Arts supports the need for delaying judgment in the classroom in order to encourage student creativity. One example of a delayed judgment technique is the act of brainstorming. Ideas are offered without immediate judgment or evaluation. The participants have the freedom to be creative without the fear of ridicule, failure, or rejection. The result is usually the generation of a wide variety of innovative ideas stemming from the flow of the creative process. Lobuts and Pennewell suggest the use of a classroom environment known as the open system: "The system allows students to feel comfortable trying new concepts and asking naive questions. This system facilitates learning by encouraging students to be inquisitive without feeling intimidated."[17]

The Benefits of an Innovative Environment

The Freedom to Fail

There is a great motivation to try new things and think new thoughts when the pressure of failure is removed from classroom settings. When instructors practice the principle of deferred judgment in the classroom, they encourage students to go beyond failure to innovation. It has been said that prior to Thomas Edison's patenting of the first commercially practical incandescent lamp (the light bulb), he failed over one hundred times in his attempts to find a filament that would provide a high enough degree of resistance within a vacuum. In much the same way, in-

structors need to overcome the *control and assessment factors* by allowing enough room for themselves and their students to fail in the creative process.

Mark McCormack, one of the most successful entrepreneurs in American business and author of the best-selling book, *What They Don't Teach You at Harvard Business School*, emphasizes the value of being able to face personal mistakes and failures. He considers it important for individuals to be able to admit mistakes and move on. He states that the ability to say "I was wrong" is vital to success.[18]

STUDENTS AND instructors need to be taught that rejection and failure are an important part of the creative process. And since students and instructors are likely to face setbacks and criticism when attempting to experiment, high doses of encouragement are necessary within the classroom setting to keep the creative process alive.

In *The Craft of Teaching*, Eble describes the role of the instructor as an encourager. He says that when conversing with students, "no utterances are wrong, though they may be false, off the mark, vague, wandering, irritating or whatever...all answers are good answers."[19] Instructors desiring to nurture a creative environment should be aware of the fears and setbacks associated with trying new ideas and approaches in the classroom. When students feel the freedom to experiment without the fear of failure, the creative process can become a positive experience for both students and instructors.

The Freedom to Change

By fostering creativity in the classroom through the freedom to change, instructors and students will avoid many of the pitfalls associated with stagnation. By altering the *habit factor* through cultivation of randomness, change, and risk taking, instructors and their students can move toward increased freedom in the learning environment.

CHANGE IN THE learning environment can take any number of forms. The use of guest speakers; the encouragement of student participation in course goals and planning; the use of films, videos, or music; the possibility of team teaching a course; a physical change in the

classroom environment; or the use of new subject matter and discussion techniques are all possible avenues for breaking new creative ground. Without a concerted effort to break through the habit barrier, however, educational professionals and their students may find the classroom environment mundane and the creative process limited.

The Freedom to Enjoy and Create

One of the benefits of a creative environment is the freedom to enjoy the creative process itself. The teaching techniques of Jearl Walker, an award-winning teacher of physics at Cleveland State University, have been described as a combination of Evel Knievel, Mr. Wizard, and Saturday Night Live.[20] Walker's antics have included lying on a bed of nails, breaking bricks with his bare hands, and plunging his hand into hot lead to demonstrate varying principles of physics. The point is not that instructors need to go to the extremes practiced by Walker, but that the freedom to enjoy the creative process enhances the learning experience for both instructors and their students.

The freedom to enjoy and create can also be encouraged through increasing individuals' abilities to dream and imagine in new and creative ways. Weaver and Cotrell refer to the process as imaging.[21] It is the practice of creating specific, material pictures as a source for new thoughts and feelings. Parnes calls a similar process visioneering.[22]

The Freedom to Wait

To be creative requires time; not only preparation time for instructors, but time for the creative process to germinate. Roger von Oech, who is a creative thinking consultant for Apple Computers, Colgate-Palmolive, DuPont, International Business Machines, and a host of other major industries, divides the creative process into two main phases. One of those phases, the germinal phase, involves taking the time to sprout and grow new ideas based on looking at common situations in new ways. He describes this phase as "soft thinking" and says that it involves taking the time to look at things by using ambiguity, humor, fantasy, generalization, and approximation. The environment is not pressured for time, requiring logical, precise, immediate decisions; rather, time is given to wait, to ponder, and to germinate ideas.

For instructors, this may mean taking an extra five minutes to consider a class problem in a new light or taking time to incorporate ideas that encourage students to be creative. Above all, it involves careful planning and consideration for germination of the creative process when planning course objectives, in-class discussions, and classroom activities. One example of an activity could be as simple as dividing the class into groups for the purpose of listing as many unconventional uses for a paper clip as they can think of in a two-minute period. Though the exercise may have little to do with an instructor's lesson plan for the day, the exercise can help students to begin thinking in creative ways. To overcome the *time factor*, instructors need to become sensitive to the flow of the creative process and allow enough time for its development.

The freedom to wait can also be helpful when it is applied to the *assessment factor*. In some cases, instructors might consider giving feedback but no grades on assignments in the early part of a course as a way for students to experiment with ideas and gain experience without the fear of poor grades.

The benefits associated with an innovative environment are both prac-tical and realistic. They come as a result of overcoming the barriers of control, habit, time, and assessment and by embracing the freedom to fail, the freedom to change, the freedom to enjoy and create, and the freedom to wait. In doing so, instructors and students may realize their full creative potential and take advantage of a tremendous opportunity to revitalize the classroom environment.

1. R. Von Oech, *A Whack on the Side of the Head* (New York: Warner Books, 1983).
2. G. Wallas, *The Art of Thought* (New York: Harcourt Brace, 1926); A.F. Osborn, *Applied Imagination* (New York: Charles Scribner's Sons, 1953); A.H. Maslow, "A Holistic Approach to Creativity," in *Climate for Creativity*, ed. C.W. Taylor (New York: Pergamon Press, 1972), pp. 287-293; S. Arieti, *Creativity the Magic Synthesis* (New York: Basic Books, Inc., 1976).
3. J.P. Guilford as cited in S.J. Parnes and H.F. Harding, *A Source Book for Creative Thinking* (New York: Charles Scribner's Sons, 1962).
4. Arieti, "Creativity" pp. 293-294; J.C. Gowan and M. Olson, "The Society Which Maximizes Creativity," *Journal of Creative Behavior* (3rd Qtr. 1979): 194-210; W.J. Walker, "Creativity: Fostering Golden Environments," *The Clearing House* (January 1986): 220-222.
5. E.P. Torrence, "Developing Creative Thinking Through School Experiences," in *A Source Book*, ed. S.J. Parnes and H.F. Harding (New York: Charles Scribner's Sons, 1962), pp. 31-47.
6. B.K. Iverson, "Haha, aha, ah: A Model for Play-ful Curricular Inquiry and Evaluation" (Paper presented at the Annual Meeting of the American Educational Research Association, Los Angeles, Cal., September 1981).
7. Parnes and Harding, *A Source Book*.
8. T. Vaughan, "On Not Predicting the Outcome: Creativity as Adventure," *The Journal of Creative Behavior* (4th Qtr. 1987): 300-310.
9. "First Steps: Fostering Creativity in Vermont's Schools and Communities" (Montpelier, Vt.: Vermont Alliance for Arts in Education, 1982).
10. E. Raudsepp and G.P. Hough, Jr., *Creative Growth Games* (New York: Harcourt Brace Jovanovich, 1977), p. 7.
11. B. Stanish, "The Underlying Structures and Thought About Randomness and Creativity," *The Journal of Creative Behavior* (2nd Qtr. 1986): 110-114.
12. Wallas, *The Art of Thought*.
13. J. Rossman, *The Psychology of the Inventor* (Washington, D.C.: Inventors Publishing, 1931).
14. Osborn, *Applied Imagination*.
15. Von Oech, *A Whack*.
16. Maslow, "A Holistic Approach."
17. J.F. Lobuts and C.L. Pennewell, "Do We Dare Restructure the Classroom Environment?" *The Journal of Creative Behavior* (4th Qtr. 1984): 244-246.
18. M.H. McCormack, *What They Don't Teach You at Harvard Business School* (New York: Bantam Books, 1984), p. 71.
19. K.E. Eble, *The Craft of Teaching* (San Francisco, Jossey-Bass, 1976), p. 60.
20. R. Wolkomir, "Old Jearl Will Do Anything to Stir an Interest in Physics," *Smithsonian* (October 1986): 112-120.
21. R.L. Weaver, II and H.W. Cotrell, "Imaging Can Increase Self Concept and Lecturing Effectiveness," *Education* (Spring 1985): 264-270.
22. S.J. Parnes, "Visioneering—State of the Art," *The Journal of Creative Behavior* (4th Qtr. 1987): 283-299.
23. Von Oech, *A Whack*. **EH**

Motivation and Classroom Management

- Approaches to Motivation (Articles 25–28)
- Classroom Management and Discipline (Articles 29–32)

The term motivation is used by educators to describe the processes of initiating, directing, and sustaining goal-oriented behavior. Motivation is a complex phenomenon, involving many factors that affect an individual's choice of action and perseverance in completing tasks. Furthermore, the reasons why people engage in particular behaviors can only be inferred; motivation cannot be directly measured.

Several theories of motivation, each highlighting different reasons for sustained goal-oriented behavior, have been proposed. We will discuss three of them: behavioral, humanistic, and cognitive. The behavioral theory of motivation suggests that an important reason for engaging in behavior is that reinforcement follows the action. If the reinforcement is controlled by someone else and is arbitrarily related to the behavior (such as money, a token, or a smile), then the motivation is extrinsic. In contrast, behavior may also be initiated and sustained for intrinsic reasons such as curiosity or mastery.

Humanistic approaches to motivation are concerned with the social and psychological needs of individuals. Humans are motivated to engage in behavior to meet these needs. Abraham Maslow proposes that there is a hierarchy of needs that directs behavior, beginning with physiological and safety needs and progressing to self-actualization. Some other important needs that influence motivation are affiliation and belonging with others, love, self-esteem, influence with others, recognition, status, competence, achievement, and autonomy.

The dominant view of motivation in the educational psychology literature is the cognitive approach. This set of theories proposes that our beliefs about our success and failure affect our expectations concerning future performance. Students who believe that their success is due to their ability and effort are motivated toward mastery of skills. Students who blame their failures on their inadequate abilities have low self-efficacy and tend to be discouraged and at risk for dropping out. The first selection suggests that competition in schools can make students feel like failures and consequently destroy their motivation to do well. In the second article, Margaret M. Clifford argues that many other well-established practices of schools directly contradict the principles of cognitive theories of motivation. It is these practices, she suggests, that lead students to drop out of school.

The third and fourth selections offer models for improving the motivation of children who are at risk for school failure. Geoffrey F. Schultz and Harvey N. Switzky discuss mediated learning experiences as a way to increase the intrinsic motivation of students. M. Kay Alderman presents an alternative model that focuses on helping students acquire responsibility for their own learning. She argues that students should learn to set goals and determine the learning strategies to help them reach those goals. As students reach their learning goals their success is attributed to their ability and effort.

No matter how effectively students are motivated, teachers always need to exercise management of behavior in the classroom. Classroom management is an approach to controlling behavior in order to establish a favorable learning environment. As T. R. Ellis observes, "effective teachers have the fewest discipline problems." They prevent misbehavior by setting reasonable rules and adjusting to different learning styles.

Effective teachers also have a plan for responding to students who do misbehave. Behavioral techniques such as those of assertive discipline, developed by Lee Canter, or the applied behavior analysis techniques proposed by Jo Webber and Brenda Scheuermann, are often recommended. David Hill, on the other hand, argues that some critics consider behavioral techniques such as assertive discipline to be "dehumanizing," and "humiliating." These two articles present the pros and cons of using behavioral techniques to discipline children. The final selection cautions against using corporal punishment to discipline children.

Looking Ahead: Challenge Questions

What is the most effective way to motivate learners? Are at-risk students motivated by the same techniques as typical students? When is competition and failure motivating? How are motivation and classroom management related?

How are classroom management and discipline different? Do you agree with T. R. Ellis that programs such as assertive discipline are a crutch for ineffective teachers? What are the advantages and disadvantages of the behavioral view of motivation and discipline?

145

Competition Doesn't Belong in Public Schools

Shouldn't schools be teaching children to work together instead of against each other?

Parker Damon

Parker Damon is principal of the McCarthy-Towne School in Acton, Massachusetts.

Why does competition play such a major role in our schools? Field days, science fairs, readathons, athletic contests, awards assemblies, grading practices, and ability grouping are all structured around competition. Rationalizations range from those who argue that children are naturally competitive to others who stress the need to prepare students for the competitive world they will face.

However, recent events have demonstrated the need for international cooperation in dealing with global economic and environmental problems, and for cooperation by diverse taxpayer groups at the local level to surmount fiscal constraints. Shouldn't our students be prepared to work together to meet these challenges?

Fortunately, alternatives to competition exist at the elementary school level. Cooperative learning, peer tutoring, heterogeneous cross-age grouping, performance portfolios, and parent-teacher conferences (instead of report cards) are just a few of these alternatives.

It's easy to say that competition does not belong in public schools. But saying so doesn't mean it will go away, even if educators agree that it should. There are numerous examples of conflict between concepts and practices. For example, though we may measure and record the different types of intelligences and learning styles that affect student performance, this knowledge is not reflected in our testing programs, grading systems, and report cards.

Competition in school can be harmful to students' confidence and performance. Wouldn't it be better if schools could help children to work against an objective standard or their own personal record? How do we teach students that cooperative problem solving is more important than achieving at someone else's expense?

Eliminating Competitive Practices

Schools need to pay more attention to potentially harmful competitive practices related to kindergarten enrollment, student placement, test scores, fundraising, athletic events, and achievement awards. It's time for principals to provide leadership in establishing new traditions based on collaborative expectations. But to do so, we first have to question some of our attitudes and behavior.

For example, how often do we:

• Make public comparisons of children's performance?

• Group children homogeneously to perform a task?

• Value only one correct response or solution?

• Permit only one way to perform an activity?

• Rank or rate children (or adults) arbitrarily?

• Promote contests that cause hard feelings?

• Avoid or ignore people with disabilities?

We can combat the underlying competitive nature of situations like these by acknowledging them, ceasing to participate in them or to lend them support, and by promoting activities and practices that reward cultural, racial, religious, ethnic, and linguistic diversity.

One way to begin reducing the competitive environment in our schools is by instituting cooperative learning programs that promote the development of imagination and self-confidence. Educators and parents must work together to emphasize cooperation in every arena and level of interaction with one another.

Promoting Cooperation

How can teachers and parents promote cooperation? The strategies and activities listed below require time, energy, and commitment, but they have proven that they can help promote a positive social climate, support self-esteem, and enable children to work better with others.

• Create buddy systems and partnerships that permit students to work together at the same or different grade levels.

• Provide frequent opportunities for students to know and appreciate their own and others' different learning and performance styles.

• Use instructional activities that focus on cooperative learning techniques and procedures.

• Have teachers model and describe to students techniques for cooperative teaching, planning, and problem solving.

• Implement intraschool and school-community activities that permit students to work and play with others of the same and different ages.

• Promote schoolwide efforts to support community projects.

• Schedule activities and games that are not competitive.

The Four Myths of Competition

In *No Contest: The Case Against Competition*, Alfie Kohn argues that our society teaches us to be competitive by readily accepting four myths:

1. "Competition is an unavoidable fact of life, part of 'human nature.'"
2. "Competition motivates us to do our best.... We would cease being productive if we did not compete."
3. "Contests provide the best, if not the only, way to have a good time."
4. "Competition builds character...it is good for self-confidence."

• Have parents, students, and faculty join in cooperative projects and activities.

• Schedule schoolwide events or assemblies to highlight cooperative achievements.

• Analyze cooperative and non-cooperative experiences with students so they understand their impact on themselves and others.

Strategies and activities such as these not only promote a positive school climate but provide children with the skills, attitudes, and strengths they need to withstand competitive adversity and to make effective use of cooperation.

REFERENCES

Kohn, Alfie. *No Contest: The Case Against Competition*. Boston: Houghton Mifflin Company, 1986.

Gilmore, John, and Gilmore, Eunice. *A More Productive Child: Guidelines for Parents*. Boston: The Gilmore Institute, 1978.

Students Need Challenge, Not Easy Success

Only by teaching students to tolerate failure for the sake of true success can educators control the national epidemic of "educational suicide."

MARGARET M. CLIFFORD

Margaret M. Clifford is Professor of Educational Psychology, University of Iowa, College of Education, Iowa City, IA 52242.

Hundreds of thousands of apathetic students abandon their schools each year to begin lives of unemployment, poverty, crime, and psychological distress. According to Hahn (1987), "Dropout rates ranging from 40 to 60 percent in Boston, Chicago, Los Angeles, Detroit, and other major cities point to a situation of crisis proportions." The term *dropout* may not be adequate to convey the disastrous consequences of the abandonment of school by children and adolescents; *educational suicide* may be a far more appropriate label.

School abandonment is not confined to a small percentage of minority students, or low ability children, or mentally lazy kids. It is a systemic failure affecting the most gifted and knowledgeable as well as the disadvantaged, and it is threatening the social, economic, intellectual, industrial, cultural, moral, and psychological well-being of our country. Equally disturbing are students who sever themselves from the flow of knowledge while they occupy desks, like mummies.

Student apathy, indifference, and underachievement are typical precursors of school abandonment. But what causes these symptoms? Is there a remedy? What will it take to stop the waste of our intellectual and creative resources?

We must encourage students to reach beyond their intellectual grasp and allow them the privilege of learning from mistakes.

To address these questions, we must acknowledge that educational suicide is primarily a motivational problem—not a physical, intellectual, financial, technological, cultural, or staffing problem. Thus, we must turn to motivational theories and research as a foundation for examining this problem and for identifying solutions.

Curiously enough, modern theoretical principles of motivation do not support certain widespread practices in education. I will discuss four such discrepancies and offer suggestions for resolving them.

Moderate Success Probability Is Essential to Motivation

The maxim, "Nothing succeeds like success," has driven educational practice for several decades. Absolute success for students has become the means *and* the end of education: It has

been given higher priority than learning, and it has obstructed learning.

A major principle of current motivation theory is that tasks associated with a moderate probability of success (50 percent) provide maximum satisfaction (Atkinson 1964). Moderate probability of success is also an essential ingredient of intrinsic motivation (Lepper and Greene 1978, Csikszentmihalyi 1975, 1978). We attribute the success we experience on easy tasks to task ease; we attribute the success we experience on extremely difficult tasks to luck. Neither type of success does much to enhance self-image. It is only success at moderately difficult or truly challenging tasks that we explain in terms of personal effort, well-chosen strategies, and ability; and these explanations give rise to feelings of pride, competence, determination, satisfaction, persistence, and personal control. Even very young children show a preference for tasks that are just a bit beyond their ability (Danner and Lonky 1981).

Consistent with these motivational findings, learning theorists have repeatedly demonstrated that moderately difficult tasks are a prerequisite for maximizing intellectual development (Fischer 1980). But despite the fact that moderate challenge (implying considerable error-making) is essential for maximizing learning and optimizing motivation, many educators attempt to create error-proof learning environments. They set minimum cri-

Margaret M. Clifford, "Students Need Challenge, Not Easy Success," *Educational Leadership*, Vol. 48, No. 1, September 1990, pp. 22-26. Reprinted with permission of the Association for Supervision and Curriculum Development. Copyright © 1990 by ASCD. All rights reserved.

teria and standards in hopes of ensuring success for all students. They often reduce task difficulty, overlook errors, de-emphasize failed attempts, ignore faulty performances, display "perfect papers," minimize testing, and reward error-free performance.

It is time for educators to replace easy success with challenge. We must encourage students to reach beyond their intellectual grasp and allow them the privilege of learning from mistakes. There must be a tolerance for error-making in every classroom, and gradual success rather than continual success must become the yardstick by which learning is judged. Such transformations in educational practices will not guarantee the elimination of educational suicide, but they are sure to be one giant step in that direction.

External Constraints Erode Motivation and Performance

Intrinsic motivation and performance deteriorate when external constraints such as surveillance, evaluation by others, deadlines, threats, bribes, and rewards are accentuated. Yes, even rewards are a form of constraint! The reward giver is the General who dictates rules and issues orders; rewards are used to keep the troops in line.

Means-end contingencies, as exemplified in the statement, "If you complete your homework, you may watch TV" (with homework being the means and TV the end), are another form of external constraint. Such contingencies decrease interest in the first task (homework, the means) and increase interest in the second task (TV, the end) (Boggiano and Main 1986).

Externally imposed constraints, including material rewards, decrease task interest, reduce creativity, hinder performance, and encourage passivity on the part of students—even preschoolers(Lepper and Hodell 1989)! Imposed constraints also prompt individuals to use the "minimax strategy"—to exert the minimum amount of effort needed to obtain the maximum amount of reward (Kruglanski et al. 1977). Supportive of these findings are studies showing that autonomous behavior—that which is self-determined, freely chosen, and personally controlled—elicits high task interest, creativity, cognitive flexibility, positive emotion, and persistence (Deci and Ryan 1987).

Unfortunately, constraint and lack of student autonomy are trademarks of most schools. Federal and local governments, as well as teachers, legislate academic requirements; impose guidelines; create rewards systems; mandate behavioral contracts; serve warnings of expulsion; and use rules, threats, and punishments as routine problem-solving strategies. We can legislate school attendance and the conditions for obtaining a diploma, but we cannot legislate the development of intelligence, talent, creativity, and intrinsic motivation—resources this country desperately needs.

It is time for educators to replace coercive, constraint-laden techniques with autonomy-supportive techniques. We must redesign instructional and evaluation materials and procedures so that every assignment, quiz, test, project, and discussion activity not only allows for, but routinely *requires*, carefully calculated decision making on the part of students. Instead of minimum criteria, we must define multiple criteria (levels of minimum, marginal, average, good, superior, and excellent achievement), and we must free students to choose criteria that provide optimum challenge. Constraint gives a person the desire to escape; freedom gives a person the desire to explore, expand, and create.

Prompt, Specific Feedback Enhances Learning

A third psychological principle is that specific and prompt feedback enhances learning, performance, and motivation (Ilgen et al. 1979, Larson 1984). Informational feedback (that which reveals correct responses) increases learning (Ilgen and Moore 1987) and also promotes a feeling of increased competency (Sansone 1986). Feedback that can be used to improve future performance has powerful motivational value.

Sadly, however, the proportion of student assignments or activities that are promptly returned with informational feedback tends to be low. Students typically complete an assignment and then wait one, two, or three days (sometimes weeks) for its return. The feedback they do get often consists of a number or letter grade accompanied by ambiguous comments such as "Is this your best?" or "Keep up the good work." Precisely what is

good or what needs improving is seldom communicated.

But, even if we could convince teachers of the value of giving students immediate, specific, informational feedback, our feedback problem would still be far from solved. How can one teacher provide 25 or more students immediate feedback on their tasks? Some educators argue that the solution to the feedback problem lies in having a tutor or teacher aide for every couple of students. Others argue that adequate student feedback will require an increased use of computer technology. However, there are less expensive alternatives. First, answer keys for students should be more plentiful. Resource books containing review and study activities should be available in every subject area, and each should be accompanied by a key that is available to students.

Second, quizzes and other instructional activities, especially those that supplement basic textbooks, should be prepared with "latent image" processing. With latent image paper and pens, a student who marks a response to an item can watch a hidden symbol emerge. The symbol signals either a correct or incorrect response, and in some instances a clue or explanation for the response is revealed. Trivia and puzzle books equipped with this latent image, immediate feedback process are currently being marketed at the price of comic books.

Of course, immediate informational feedback is more difficult to provide for composition work, long-term projects, and field assignments. But this does not justify the absence of immediate feedback on the learning activities and practice exercises that are aimed at teaching concepts, relationships, and basic skills. The mere availability of answer keys and latent image materials would probably elicit an amazing amount of self-regulated learning on the part of many students.

Moderate Risk Taking Is a Tonic for Achievement

A fourth motivational research finding is that moderate risk taking increases performance, persistence, perceived competence, self-knowledge, pride, and satisfaction (Deci and Porac 1978, Harter 1978, Trope 1979). Moderate risk taking implies a well-considered choice of an optimally challenging task, willingness to accept a moderate probability of success, and the anticipation of an outcome. It is this combination of events (which includes moderate success, self-regulated learning, and feedback) that captivates the attention, interest, and energy of card players, athletes, financial investors, lottery players, and even juvenile video arcade addicts.

Risk takers continually and freely face the probability of failing to attain the pleasure of succeeding under specified odds. From every risk-taking endeavor—whether it ends in failure or success—risk takers learn something about their skill and choice of strategy, and what they learn usually prompts them to seek another risk-taking opportunity. Risk taking—especially moderate risk taking—is a mind-engaging activity that simultaneously consumes and generates energy. It is a habit that feeds itself and thus requires an unlimited supply of risk-taking opportunities.

Moderate risk taking is likely to occur under the following conditions.

● The success probability for each alternative is clear and unambiguous.

● Imposed external constraints are minimized.

● Variable payoff (the value of success increases as risk increases) in contrast to fixed payoff is available.

● The benefits of risk taking can be anticipated.

My own recent research on academic risk taking with grade school, high school, and college students generally supports these conclusions. Students do, in fact, freely choose more difficult problems (a) when the number of points offered increases with the difficulty level of problems, (b) when the risk-taking task is presented within a game or practice situation (i.e., imposed constraint or threat is minimized), and (c) when additional opportunities for risk taking are anticipated (relatively high risk taking will occur on a practice exercise when students know they will be able to apply the information learned to an upcoming test). In the absence of these conditions we have seen students choose tasks that are as much as one-and-a-half years below their achievement level (Clifford 1988). Finally, students who take moderately high risks express high task interest even though they experience considerable error making.

In summary, risk-taking opportunities for students should be (a) plentiful, (b) readily available, (c) accompanied by explicit information about success probabilities, (d) accompanied by immediate feedback that communicates competency and error information, (e) associated with payoffs that vary with task difficulty, (f) relatively free from externally imposed evaluation, and (g) presented in relaxing and nonthreatening environments.

In today's educational world, however, there are few opportunities for students to engage in academic risk taking and no incentives to do so. Choices are seldom provided within tests or assignments, and rarely are variable payoffs made available. Once again, motivational theory, which identifies risk taking as a powerful source of knowledge, motivation, and skill development, conflicts with educational practice, which seeks to minimize academic risk at all costs.

We must restructure materials and procedures to encourage moderate academic risk taking on the part of students. I predict that if we fill our classrooms with optional academic risk-taking materials and opportunities so that all students have access to moderate risks, we will not only lower our educational suicide rate, but we will raise our level of academic achievement. If we give students the license to take risks and make errors, they will likely experience genuine success and the satisfaction that accompanies it.

Using Risk Can Ensure Success

Both theory and research evidence lead to the prediction that academic risk-taking activities are a powerful means of increasing the success of our educational efforts. But how do we get students to take risks on school-related activities? Students will choose risk over certainty when the consequences of the former are more satisfying and informative. Three basic conditions are needed to ensure such outcomes.

● First, students must be allowed to freely select from materials and activities that vary in difficulty and probability of success.

● Second, as task difficulty increases, so too must the payoffs for success.

● Third, an environment tolerant of error making and supportive of error correction must be guaranteed.

The first two conditions can be met rather easily. For example, on a 10-point quiz, composed of six 1-point items and four 2-point items, students might be asked to select and work only 6 items. The highest possible score for such quizzes is 10 and can be obtained only by correctly answering the four 2-point items and any two 1-point items. Choice and variable payoff are easily built into quizzes and many instructional and evaluation activities.

The third condition, creating an environment tolerant of error making and supportive of error correction, is more difficult to ensure. But here are six specific suggestions.

First, teachers must make a clear distinction between formative evaluation activities (tasks that guide instruction during the learning process) and summative evaluation activities (tasks used to judge one's level of achievement and to determine one's grade at the completion of the learning activity). Practice exercises, quizzes, and skill-building activities aimed at acquiring and strengthening knowledge and skills exemplify formative evaluation. These activities promote learning and skill development. They should be scored in a manner that excludes ability judgments, emphasizes error detection and correction, and encourages a search for better learning strategies. Formative evaluation activities should generally provide immediate feedback and be scored by students. It is on these activities that moderate risk taking is to be encouraged and is likely to prove beneficial.

Major examinations (unit exams and comprehensive final exams) exemplify summative evaluation; these activities are used to determine course grades. Relatively low risk taking is to be expected on such tasks, and immediate feedback may or may not be desirable.

Second, formative evaluation activities should be far more plentiful than summative. If, in fact, learning rather than grading is the primary objective of the school, the percentage of time spent on summative evaluation should be small in comparison to that spent on formative evaluation (perhaps about 1:4). There should be enough formative evaluation activities presented as risk-taking opportunities to satisfy the most enthusiastic and adventuresome learner. The more plentiful these activities are, the less anxiety-producing and aversive summative activities are likely to be.

Third, formative evaluation activities should be presented as optional; students should be enticed, not mandated, to complete these activities. Enticement might be achieved by (a) ensuring that these activities are course-relevant and varied (e.g., scrambled outlines, incomplete matrices and graphs, exercises that require error detection and correction, quizzes); (b) giving students the option of working together; (c) presenting risk-taking activities in the context of games to be played individually, with competitors, or with partners; (d) providing immediate, informational, nonthreatening feedback; and (e) defining success primarily in terms of improvement over previous performance or the amount of learning that occurs during the risk-taking activity.

Fourth, for every instructional and evaluation activity there should be at least a modest percentage of content (10 percent to 20 percent) that poses a challenge to even the best students completing the activity. Maximum development of a country's talent requires that *all* individuals (a) find challenge in tasks they attempt, (b) develop tolerance for error making, and (c) learn to adjust strategies when faced with failure. To deprive the most talented students of these opportunities is perhaps the greatest resource-development crime a country can commit.

Fifth, summative evaluation procedures should include "retake exams." Second chances will not only encourage risk taking but will provide good reasons for students to study their incorrect responses made on previous risk-taking tasks. Every error made on an initial exam and subsequently corrected on a second chance represents real learning.

Sixth, we must reinforce moderate academic risk taking instead of error-free performance or excessively high or low risk taking. Improvement scores, voluntary correction of errors, completion of optional risk-taking activities—these are behaviors that teachers should recognize and encourage.

Toward a New Definition of Success

We face the grim reality that our extraordinary efforts to produce "schools without failure" have not yielded the well-adjusted, enthusiastic, self-confident scholars we anticipated. Our efforts to mass-produce success for every individual in every educational situation have left us with cheap reproductions of success that do not even faintly represent the real thing. This overdose of synthetic success is a primary cause of the student apathy and school abandonment plaguing our country.

To turn the trend around, we must emphasize error tolerance, not error-free learning; reward error correction, not error avoidance; ensure challenge, not easy success. Eventual success on challenging tasks, tolerance for error making, and constructive responses to failure are motivational fare that school systems should be serving up to all students. I suggest that we engage the skills of researchers, textbook authors, publishers, and educators across the country to ensure the development and marketing of attractive and effective academic risk-taking materials and procedures. If we convince these experts of the need to employ their creative efforts toward this end, we will not only stem the tide of educational suicide, but we will enhance the quality of educational success. We will witness self-regulated student success and satisfaction that will ensure the intellectual, creative, and motivational well-being of our country.

References

Atkinson, J.W. (1964). *An Introduction to Motivation*. Princeton, N.J.: Van Nostrand.

Boggiano, A.K., and D.S. Main. (1986). "Enhancing Children's Interest in Activities Used as Rewards: The Bonus Effect." *Journal of Personality and Social Psychology* 51: 1116-1126.

Clifford, M.M. (1988). "Failure Tolerance and Academic Risk Taking in Ten- to Twelve-Year-Old Students." *British Journal of Educational Psychology* 58: 15–27.

Csikszentmihalyi, M. (1975). *Beyond Boredom and Anxiety*. San Francisco: Jossey-Bass.

Csikszentimihalyi, M. (1978). "Intrinsic Rewards and Emergent Motivation." In *The Hidden Costs of Reward*, edited by M.R. Lepper and D. Greene. N.J.: Lawrence Erlbaum Associates.

Danner, F.W., and D. Lonky. (1981). "A Cognitive-Developmental Approach to the Effects of Rewards on Intrinsic Motivation." *Child Development* 52: 1043-1052.

Deci, E.L., and J. Porac. (1978). "Cognitive Evaluation Theory and the Study of Human Motivation." In *The Hidden Costs of Reward*, edited by M.R. Lepper and D. Greene. Hillsdale, N.J.: Lawrence Erlbaum Associates.

Deci, E.L., and R.M. Ryan. (1987). "The Support of Autonomy and the Control of Behavior." *Journal of Personality and Social Psychology* 53: 1024-1037.

Fischer, K.W. (1980). "Learning as the Development of Organized Behavior." *Journal of Structural Learning* 3: 253–267.

Hahn, A. (1987). "Reaching Out to America's Dropouts: What to Do?" *Phi Delta Kappan* 69: 256–263.

Harter, S. (1978). "Effectance Motivation Reconsidered: Toward a Developmental Model." *Human Development* 1: 34–64.

Ilgen, D.R., and C.F. Moore. (1987). "Types and Choices of Performance Feedback." *Journal of Applied Psychology* 72: 401–406.

Ilgen, D.R., C.D. Fischer, and M.S. Taylor. (1979). "Consequences of Individual Feedback on Behavior in Organizations." *Journal of Applied Psychology* 64: 349–371.

Kruglanski, A., C. Stein, and A. Riter. (1977). "Contingencies of Exogenous Reward and Task Performance: On the 'Minimax' Strategy in Instrumental Behavior." *Journal of Applied Social Psychology* 2: 141–148.

Larson, J.R., Jr. (1984). "The Performance Feedback Process: A Preliminary Model." *Organizational Behavior and Human Performance* 33: 42–76.

Lepper, M.R., and D. Greene. (1978). *The Hidden Costs of Reward*. Hillsdale, N.J.: Lawrence Erlbaum Associates.

Lepper, M.R., and M. Hodell. (1989). "Intrinsic Motivation in the Classroom." In *Motivation in Education, Vol. 3*, edited by C. Ames and R. Ames. N.Y.: Academic Press.

Sansone, C. (1986). "A Question of Competence: The Effects of Competence and Task Feedback on Intrinsic Motivation." *Journal of Personality and Social Psychology* 51: 918–931.

Trope, Y. (1979). "Uncertainty Reducing Properties of Achievement Tasks." *Journal of Personality and Social Psychology* 37: 1505-1518.

The Development of Intrinsic Motivation in Students With Learning Problems

Suggestions for More Effective Instructional Practice

GEOFFREY F. SCHULTZ and HARVEY N. SWITZKY

Geoffrey F. Schultz is an associate professor of educational psychology and special education at Indiana University in Gary. Harvey N. Switzky is a professor of educational psychology at Northern Illinois University in Dekalb.

Contemporary theories of motivation document the significant effect of "intrinsic motivation" on academic performance of children with learning problems (i.e., learning disabilities and mild mental handicaps). When these children learn out of curiosity and the desire for challenge, competence, and self-determination, they display higher classroom performance levels than those predicted by assessed levels of intelligence (Harter, 1983; Haywood & Switzky, 1986b; Switzky & Haywood, 1985a, 1985b; Zigler & Balla, 1981). Moreover, these theoretical models imply that if special educators are to insure optimal educational outcomes, internal personality and motivational characteristics of learners need to be considered in the development of any instructional program for students with learning problems (Deci & Chandler, 1986; Switzky & Schultz, 1988).

In support of this consideration, there are legitimate concerns regarding traditional operant classroom approaches currently used in educating children placed in special education settings, for example, token economies (Bry & Witte, 1982; Morgan, 1981; Greene, Sternberg, & Lepper, 1976; Lepper, Greene, & Nisbett, 1973; Malouf, 1983). Special education programs that rely heavily on external rewards and incentives in modifying behavior in students with learning problems may be contrary to the instructional considerations and approaches endorsed by current theories of intrinsic motivation. The dependency on such incentives as grades, tokens and points, praise from the teacher, and other related procedures that involve rewarding behavior that the teacher wants need to be carefully examined. Even though these procedures are effective in producing the behavior sought by the teacher, behavior controlled primarily by external incentives is not likely to become internalized by the student or become an intrinsically motivated activity (Switzky, 1985; Switzky & Haywood, 1985a).

In suggesting we scrutinize current practices that rely heavily on strict reinforcement schedules, we are not pro-

From *Preventing School Failure,* Winter 1990, pp. 14-20. Reprinted with permission of the Helen Dwight Reid Educational Foundation. Published by Heldref Publications, 1319 Eighteenth St., NW, Washington, DC 20036-1802. Copyright © 1990.

posing that teachers of students with learning problems completely discard operant methodology in their classrooms. There is much that can be initially accomplished by using these techniques, and they are indeed effective for teaching basic academic skills. The problem with these kinds of instructional approaches, however, is that by themselves they are insufficient over the long term for sustaining significant and generalizable academic growth (U.S. Department of Education, 1986; Torgesen, 1986). To have a wider and more long-term effect, instructional approaches need to be tied to a broader teaching strategy or model that ultimately focuses on the internalization and the development of an intrinsic orientation toward learning. If teachers of children with learning problems are going to sustain this level and generalize the effect of their instruction, this long-term goal must be the ultimate objective of each child's Individual Educational Program.

The purpose of this paper is to offer some instructional guidelines that promote intrinsic motivation in the classroom. The major point is that teachers need to pay a great deal more attention to the mediational dynamics (i.e., the power of shared responsibility and communication between teacher and student in the learning process) if they hope to promote intrinsic motivation and significant academic growth in their instructional interactions with students.

The type of teacher/student interaction we are suggesting is most commonly described as *mediational learning experiences* (MLE) and is thought to facilitate increased intrinsic motivation in students with learning problems (Feuerstein & Rand, 1974; Feuerstein, Rand, Hoffman, & Miller, 1980). Mediational learning experiences are, in current terms, both *cognitive* and *motivational* in their effect. Through a carefully orchestrated teacher/learner interaction, the child constructs a new strategic approach to the task or a new understanding of the steps necessary to accomplish the task. This is a cognitive outcome. On the other hand, by virtue of being drawn into a goal-oriented in-

teraction under the teacher's direction, the student is acquiring a greater appreciation of why one would proceed in such a manner and of the payoff involved. This results in heightened motivation to learn and perform. Moreover, the active participation of the child and the sense of responsibility for the joint outcome engendered by the interaction leads to a greater sense of intrinsic motivation (Bandura, 1981). This instructional approach style differs from most operantly based methodologies in its reduced reliance on strict reinforcement schedules and its greater emphasis on the student as an active learner.

In presenting a case for consideration of mediational teacher approaches, we would like to do the following: (1) present the important theoretical perspectives and research that support the concept of intrinsic motivation; (2) identify how students' motivational characteristics have been reliably assessed in the classroom; (3) identify instructional guidelines and curriculum models that create MLE; and (4) discuss the implications of MLE as they relate to individual educational programming. This discussion will provide classroom teachers with guidelines that will expand the overall effectiveness of the instructional strategies they currently use with students with learning problems.

Intrinsic Motivation and Learning Performance: Important Theoretical Perspectives

The research of Carl Haywood and Harvey Switzky has examined the relationship between intrinsic motivation and academic performance and is some of the earliest work done in this area with persons who have learning problems. In a series of studies conducted over the past twenty years, these researchers have worked with the explicit assumption that intrinsic motivation is a key concept in explaining academic performance differences and deficits in children with learning problems (See Haywood & Switzky, 1986a, 1986b, for comprehensive reviews of their efforts to apply motivational concepts to mildly mentally handicapped student populations).

For Haywood and Switzky (1975, 1985), intrinsic motivation is the primary concept in a cognitive theory of motivational orientation in which the central idea is behavior for its own sake and as its own reward. Moreover, motivational orientation is defined as a learned personality trait that characterizes individual children in terms of the incentives that are effective in motivating their behavior, whether they are task intrinsic or task extrinsic. Children who characteristically seek their principal satisfactions by concentrating on task-intrinsic factors (e.g., responsibility, challenge, creativity, opportunities to learn, and task achievement) are referred to as intrinsically motivated (IM). Those who tend instead to avoid dissatisfaction by concentrating on the ease, comfort, safety, security, and practicality aspects of the environment (i.e., task-extrinsic factors) are referred to as extrinsically motivated (EM). Although all persons respond to each kind of incentive, it is the relative balance between the two sources of motivation (i.e., the relative number of situations in which one is likely to be motivated by task-intrinsic versus task-extrinsic factors) that constitutes a stable and measurable personality trait.

In two early studies involving both handicapped and nonhandicapped subjects, Haywood (1968a, 1968b) found that the IM learners worked harder and longer on a task than the EM learners did. The IM learners were characterized as "overachievers" and the EM learners as "underachievers" on tests of school achievement. It was also reported that high-achieving 10-year-olds were more IM than were low-achieving children matched on age, sex, and IQ; further, this difference in motivational orientation between high achievers and low achievers became larger as IQ became lower. Of crucial importance was the finding that these motivational influences intensity as the intellectual ability levels of the students decrease and that a disproportionate number of low-ability children were reported to be extrinsically motivated (Haywood, 1968a).

In a follow-up study (Haywood, 1968b), school achievement scores of IM and EM 10-year-olds (matched on age, sex, and IQ) in reading, spelling, and arithmetic were compared over a 3-year period. Although the achievement scores of IM and EM students in the superior intelligence groups did not differ as a function of motivational orientation in any of the achievement areas, in both the average and low normal groups the IM students were achieving in school at about one full grade level ahead of the EM students in the same IQ group. The differences were largest for students with low normal intelligence: IM students in this low-IQ ability group achieved scores that were not different from achievement levels of EM children of average IQ. Though these students were not given the test of intrinsic motivation until they were 10 years old, retrospect examination of their school achievement scores showed that the achievement differences were already present in the first grade (Haywood, 1968b). Although it does not necessarily follow that the students who were described as being internally motivated at 10 years of age were also similarly motivated in first grade, the author suggests that the significant academic differences in matched-ability students are possibly the result of a stable motivational trait already present in the children at the time they entered school.

The above studies suggest that low-ability IM students may compensate for their lower intelligence levels by increasing their effort and intrinsic involvement in academic activities (Haywood, 1968a, 1968b). This conclusion has been further validated in more recent studies (Switzky & Haywood, 1984, 1985a, 1985b, 1985c) that have investigated individual differences in nonhandicapped children and children with learning problems, in task-intrinsic and task-extrinsic motivation, and how these differences affect learning and performance in specified conditions. Again, it was found that having an intrinsically motivational (IM) orientation to learning is helpful. That is, performance levels tend to be at or above those predicted by mental age levels. Moreover, this motivational effect was reported to be most significant in children experiencing learning problems.

Susan Harter (1978, 1983) also has presented a general theory of effectance or mastery motivation that has implications for both defining and understanding the development of extrinsic and intrinsic motivational orientations in children with learning problems. Her theory is organized around the idea that effectance motivation, using one's own cognitive resources to the fullest, is intrinsically gratifying and motivating. The development of an intrinsic motivational orientation is believed to result from positive reinforcement or approval by adults for

Having an intrinsically motivational orientation to learning is helpful.

independent mastery attempts early in development; dependency on adults is not reinforced. This leads the children to develop feelings of competence and of being in control of their success and failure and increases their effectance motivation and intrinsic motivation. This increased sense of intrinsic pleasure enhances the children's motivation to engage in subsequent mastery behavior. As a result, the children internalize two critical systems—(a) a self-reward system and (b) a system of standard or mastery goals that diminishes the children's dependency on external social reinforcement.

In Harter's view, extrinsically motivated children do not develop these critical systems because adults in their lives do not encourage or may actively disapprove of independent mastery attempts. Moreover, these children become conditioned to be dependent on adults for motivational incentives (e.g., tangible rewards and punishment that validate and motivate their behavior). Consequently, as dependency behavior is reinforced, children in these circumstances increasingly manifest an ongoing and strong need for external approval and dependence on extrinsic motivational incentives controlled by significant others in their lives such as parents and teachers. Like Haywood

and Switzky, Harter reports that this developmental pattern appears to be especially characteristic of children with learning problems and further results in the intensification of their learning deficits in the classroom (Harter, Silon, & Pike, 1981; Silon & Harter, 1985).

Identification of Intrinsic Motivation in the Classroom

Relatively few instruments have been published to isolate those elements of behavior that identify students' motivational orientation in the classroom. We will discuss in detail the instruments developed by Harter and her students (Harter, 1981, 1982) and by Haywood and Switzky (Haywood & Switzky, 1986b; Switzky & Haywood, 1984).

Harter has developed a self-report instrument to measure components of her model of effectance motivation, *The Scale of Intrinsic Versus Extrinsic Orientation in the Classroom*. This instrument has been used to measure motivational orientation in the classroom in nonhandicapped children in Grades 2 through 9 (Harter, 1981) and in mildly handicapped children 9 to 12 years old (Silon & Harter, 1985) with good test-retest reliability (greater than .9). The instrument focuses on the extent to which the children's motivation for classroom learning is determined by their intrinsic interest in learning and mastery, curiosity, preference for challenge, and the degree to which their motivation is determined by a more extrinsic orientation (in which teacher approval and grades are the functional incentives). The instrument measures two factors: (a) a motivational factor labeled curiosity/interest and (b) a cognitive-informational factor labeled independent judgment versus reliance on teacher's judgment. Although there are subtle differences in what is being measured by this scale with groups of mildly handicapped and nonhandicapped children, the handicapped children appear considerably more extrinsically oriented than do nonhandicapped children (Harter, Silon, & Pike, 1981).

Kunca and Haywood (1969) developed the *Picture Choice Motivation Scale* specifically for children with learning problems, although it can be used as well with all children. This instrument is used to measure the degree to which a child is intrinsically or extrinsically motivated in terms of the learned personality trait of motivational orientation. In this scale, each item is a pair of pictures of people engaged in different activities, vocations, or endeavors determined to be qualitatively either extrinsic or intrinsic. For each of the 20 pictures illustrating an intrinsically (e.g., opportunity to learn, challenge, intense psychological satisfaction, responsibility) or extrinsically (e.g., opportunity for safety, ease, comfort, security) motivated activity, the student is asked which he would like to do. The final score used to classify the students is the number of intrinsically motivated choices out of the 20 pairs.

The Picture Choice Motivation Scale is useful with students from a mental age of 3 years up to adolescence and has yielded reliability coefficients in the eighties (e.g., Haywood, 1971; Kunca & Haywood, 1969; Miller, Haywood, & Gamon, 1975). Several studies have shown that the picture scale yields a roughly normal distribution of scores down to about the mental age of 3 years and that this distribution tends to become skewed (i.e., higher frequencies of intrinsic responses) with increasing chronological and mental age up to middle adolescence (Call, 1968; Haywood, 1966, 1968a, 1968b, 1971; Haywood & Switzky, 1986b; Switzky, 1985; Tahia, 1977). As a group, children with learning problems are more extrinsically motivated when compared with nonhandicapped children of similar age. However, it is important to note that some children with learning problems are found to be intrinsically motivated. (See Switzky & Heal, in press, for discussion of the construct validity of *The Picture Choice Motivation Scale*.)

The Development of Intrinsic Motivation Through the Creation of Mediational Learning Experiences

Children acquire knowledge and understanding in two ways (Feuerstein & Rand, 1974; Haywood, Brooks, & Burns, 1986). First, children teach themselves, that is, they learn through natural exposure to environmental stimuli where, because of their inborn intrinsic motivation to learn, they independently acquire very complex skills and abilities. Examples are ambulation and language. Second, children learn from significant others in their lives, that is, they acquire from parents and teachers knowledge and understanding of skills that are not learned independently and naturally (at least not easily). Examples are reading and writing.

Depending on how they communicate and interact with children when they are passing on skills, teachers and parents can play an important role in maintaining and further shaping the natural ability in children to learn intrinsically. As stated earlier, the promotion of intrinsic motivation to learn in children who are being taught skills by significant others is, in our opinion, best accomplished when adults create mediational learning experiences (MLE). Likewise, adult-child instructional interactions that lack this mediational quality tend to undermine the inborn intrinsic motivation that most children initially bring to the learning experiences they have with adults (Harter, 1978, 1983).

In order to qualify as mediated learning experiences (MLE), interaction between students and "mediating teachers" must meet the following criteria (Haywood, Brooks, & Burns, 1986):

1. *Intentionality.* The mediating teacher must intend to use the interaction to produce cognitive change in the student.

2. *Transcendence.* The intended change must be a generalizable one (i.e., a cognitive structural change that transcends the immediate situation and will permit the student to apply new processes of thought in new situations).

3. *Communication of meaning and purpose.* The teacher communicates to the student the long-range, structural, or developmental meaning and purpose of a shared activity or interaction (i.e., explain why one is doing a particular activity in cognitive terms).

4. *Mediation of a feeling of competence.* The teacher gives "feedback" on the child's performance by praising what is done correctly (i.e., by using correct and/or incorrect aspects of the child's performance and thus attributing the child's achievement to his own efforts and learning strategies).

5. *Promote self-regulation of student's behavior.* Student behavior is brought under control when he or she is able to focus attention on the problem or task at hand. Initially, operant controls may be needed to regulate the student's behavior; however, these controls need to be removed systematically (and gradually) so that behaviors are maintained with less direct extrinsic reinforcement.

6. *Sharing.* The student and the teacher share the quest for solutions to immediate problems and, more important, for the developmental change in the child's cognitive structures. The quest is shared because each has a defined role and function, and the interaction is characterized by mutual trust and confidence.

Of course, the more cognitive ability, intrinsic motivation, and environmental opportunity a child has, the more easily a child learns and the greater the proportion he learns naturally and independently, that is, the less the need for repeated and intense mediated learning experiences. Therefore, the need to utilize instructional guidelines that create mediated learning experiences is obviously multiplied in students with problems that impede child development, such as chaotic impoverished environments, mental retardation, learning disabilities, and emotional disturbance. Moreover, mediational learning experiences (MLE) have been successfully used with these students in a remedial fashion in both regular education and special education classrooms (Feuerstein, Rand, Hoffman, & Miller, 1980; Haywood, Brooks, & Burns, 1986; Paour, 1978; Schweinhart & Weikart, 1981).

The Use of Mediational Learning Experiences: A Research Example

Important and relevant research that exemplifies the utilization of a mediational-type approach to instructing students with learning problems in the classroom has been conducted by Annemarie

Palincsar and Ann Brown (Brown & Palincsar, 1982, 1987; Palincsar & Brown, 1984). The importance and relevance of this research, we believe, is that it is one of the few investigations on the effects of an instructional approach model that is able to report significant maintenance and generalization of academic achievement in students with learning problems.

These studies have focused on improving reading comprehension in students who are good decoders but poor comprehenders. The basic approach described involves engaging the student in a *reciprocal* teaching situation where the teacher treats the student as a coparticipant in the teaching/learning process and where the teacher and student take turns leading each other through a series of prescribed activities centered on a paragraph of text. These activities include asking a main-idea question, summarizing, and making predictions about what might occur next. The teacher assists the child in mastering these activities through a combination of modeling, prompting, clarifying, and suggesting alternatives. As the student gradually takes over more responsibility for the comprehension of strategies, the structuring provided by the teacher is withdrawn. By virtue of being drawn into a reciprocal teaching/learning interaction (mediated by the teacher), the child is acquiring a greater appreciation of why one would proceed in such a manner and of the intrinsic reward involved. This results in heightened intrinsic motivation in the student.

The results of these studies are very significant in light of our concern over long-term and generalizable effects of teacher instruction on students with learning problems. Students receiving this mediational-type teaching approach far outperformed students receiving any of several control interventions. Their eventual performance equalled that of untrained average comprehenders (Brown & Palincsar, 1982, 1987; Palincsar & Brown, 1984). The improvements were maintained over an 8-week period following training, and they generalized to compre-

hension activities embedded in ongoing classroom activities.

It should be noted that although Palincsar and Brown's subjects had not been officially identified as handicapped, the description provided suggests these children may be similar to learning-disabled and mildly mentally handicapped students with similar reading problems. Of greater importance to our discussion here are the author's comments about what they see as effective components of instructional procedures for children with learning problems of this kind. The authors note that "the teacher did not merely instruct the students and then leave them to work unaided; she entered into an interaction where the students and the teacher were mutually responsible for getting the task done" (Palincsar & Brown, 1984, p. 169). They further describe their instructional procedure as an "on-line diagnosis," designed to provide a level of teacher participation finely tuned to the student's changing cognitive status. These comments describe essential components of mediational learning experiences.

The research of Palincsar and Brown begins to provide encouraging evidence that maintenance and generalization of new learning and understanding acquired via mediational teaching approaches are possible. Moreover, these findings provide some justification for a greater focus on the use of mediational teaching approaches as a way of further promoting intrinsic motivation toward the learning process in children with learning problems.

Implications for the Individual Educational Programming of Students With Learning Problems

As stated earlier, we believe that classroom instructional practices that manipulate the learning process through extrinsic behavioral contingencies may be insufficient in the long term for maintaining significant and generalizable academic growth in students with learning problems. Moreover, it appears that some provision by teachers to promote an intrinsic orientation toward the learning process through mediational-type teaching ap-

proaches is important to sustaining academic growth across varied educational settings (Brown & Palincsar, 1982, 1987; Palincsar & Brown, 1984).

It is to be expected that the typical student with learning problems will at first require a more externally controlling instructional approach in order to be appropriately engaged in the classroom curriculum. This would seem to be especially the case with students who fail to benefit fully from instruction because of severe attention disorders or other deficiencies in behavior such as hyperactivity. It makes little sense to rigidly promote self-regulatory and intrinsic motivation in a student grossly lacking in this quality, just as it does not seem wise to regulate dogmatically the student's behavior with operant contingencies if the child is already intrinsically motivated.

In any case, it should not be construed that the external teacher control of classroom learning and behavior is the ultimate long-range objective of the Individualized Educational Program. Teachers of students with learning problems must programmatically attempt to move beyond relying on punishment-and-reward formats that can often become the primary incentives for students' involvement in the learning process and move toward more mediational approaches that permit the development of an intrinsic motivation. It is important to note that in a major review of the token-economy literature, Kazdin (1982) views token economies as only one component of school programs and states that token economies need to be removed (gradually) so that behaviors are maintained with less direct extrinsic reinforcement. The ultimate thrust of token-economy programs is the development of self-reinforcement strategies in the learner across a variety of classroom situations (Kazdin, 1982).

In attempting to move beyond an operantly controlled curriculum, researchers have developed several cognitive and motivational training programs that provide mediational learning experiences for children with learning problems. These approaches differ from the more operant styles in their reduced reliance on extrinsic reinforcement schedules and their greater emphasis on the student as an active learner. Examples of these efforts include the Instrumental Enrichment Program (Feuerstein, Rand, Hoffman, & Miller, 1980), the High/Scope Program (see, e.g., Schweinhart & Weikart, 1981), the L'Apprentissage Operatoire Model (Paour, 1978), and the Cognitive Curriculum for Young Children Program (Haywood, Brooks, & Burns, 1986).

The above noted educational approaches all provide extensive modeling and support by the teacher of task-intrinsic behavior and motivation in the student. In addition, these curriculum approaches all attempt to facilitate an intrinsic learning style through mediational-type approaches. One example is fostering a shared insight and understanding of why it is important to know how to accomplish a task or solve a problem, such as "What is the meaning and purpose of what we are doing?" Most important, these mediational classroom models include instructional components explicitly targeted at generalization and long-term retention.

Final Suggestions and Concluding Remarks

Children with learning problems are reportedly less intrinsically motivated than their nonhandicapped peers (Harter et al., 1981; Haywood, 1968a; Haywood & Switzky, 1986a; Thomas, 1979; Thomas & Pashley, 1982). And indeed, the external motivational orientation of these children does often initially require and encourage continued use of operant instructional approaches in special education classrooms and programs. On the other hand, if the developmental pathways leading to an intrinsic orientation toward learning consist of experiences that encourage intrinsically motivated, self-regulatory behavior (Feuerstein & Rand, 1974; Harter, 1983; Haywood, Brooks, & Burns, 1986; Silon & Harter, 1985), then teachers of children with learning problems must, at some point, modify and further supplement classroom practices with an instructional methodology that tends to promote and encourage intrinsic motivation.

It is reasonable to argue that an operantly controlling teacher approach, interacting with an extrinsically regulated student, does not facilitate the development of an intrinsic orientation toward learning. It is because of this limitation that we believe that operant instructional approaches are responsible, in part, for student failure to sustain and generalize academic growth. Because this kind of teaching practice tends to focus student attention away from the intrinsic dimensions of the learning process, students fail to sustain the academic gains realized or fail to exhibit them in situations such as regular education classrooms, where rewards may not be as immediate or salient to the learning process (Madden & Slavin, 1983). In essence, the reward becomes an end in itself, and it is logical to assume that when the reward is extinguished or becomes less obvious, the achievement associated with it follows suit.

Therefore, we believe that the nature of operant instructional approaches and techniques may be responsible, in part, for student failure to become intrinsically motivated and to sustain significant academic growth in the classroom. It is because of these instructional limitations that we endorse the additional use of MLE in classrooms for students with learning problems. The classroom teaching strategies developed by Palincsar and Brown do provide some evidence for the instructional power of MLE in which reciprocal interaction between teacher and student results in maintenance and generalization of newly learned information. This curriculum work and the instructional models developed by Feuerstein, Schweinhart, Paour, and Haywood are all very encouraging in this respect and need to be recognized as part of the necessary classroom methodology that will further help teachers effectively instruct students who have learning problems.

REFERENCES

Bandura, A. (1981). Self-referent thought: A developmental analysis of self-efficacy. In J. H. Flavel & L. Ross (Eds.), *Social cognitive development: Frontiers and possible futures* (pp. 200–239). Cambridge, England: Cambridge University Press.

Brown, A. L., & Palincsar, A. S. (1982). Inducing strategy learning from texts by means of informed, self-control training. *Topics in Learning & Learning Disabilities*, 2(1), 1–17.

Brown, A. L., & Palincsar, A. S. (1987). Reciprocal teaching of comprehension strategies: A natural history of one program for enhancing learning. In J. D. Day & J. G. Borkowski (Eds.), *Intelligence and exceptionality* (pp. 81–132). Norwood, NJ: Ablex.

Bry, B. H., & Witte, G. (1982). *Effect of a token economy on perceived competence and locus of causality and their relationship to outcomes*. Unpublished manuscript, Rutgers University, New Brunswick, New Jersey.

Call, R. J. (1968). *Motivation-hygiene orientation as a function of socioeconomic status, grade, race and sex*. Unpublished master's thesis, Tennessee State University, Nashville.

Deci, E. L., & Chandler, C. L. (1986). The importance of motivation for the future of the LD field. *Journal of Learning Disabilities*, 19, 587–594.

Feuerstein, R., & Rand, Y. (1974). Mediated learning experiences: An outline of the proximal etiology for differential development of cognitive functions. *International Understanding*, 10, 7–37.

Feuerstein, R., Rand, Y., Hoffman, M. B., & Miller, R. (1980). *Instrumental enrichment*. Baltimore: University Park Press.

Greene, D., Sternberg, B., & Lepper, M. R. (1976). Overjustification in a token economy. *Journal of Personality and Social Psychology*, 34, 1219–1234.

Harter, S. (1978). Effectance motivation reconsidered: Toward a developmental model. *Human Development*, 45, 661–669.

Harter, S. (1981). A new self-report scale of intrinsic versus extrinsic orientation in the classroom: Motivation and informational components. *Developmental Psychology*, 17, 300–312(b).

Harter, S. (1982). The perceived competence scale for children. *Child Development*, 53, 81–97.

Harter, S. (1983). Developmental perspectives on the self-system. In E. M. Hetherington (Ed.), *Handbook of child psychology: Socialization, personality, and social development* (Vol. 4, pp. 278–386). New York: Wiley.

Harter, S., Silon, E., & Pike, R. G. (1981). *Perceived competence, intrinsic versus extrinsic orientation, and anxiety in the educable mentally retarded: A comparison of mainstreaming and self-contained classrooms*. Unpublished manuscript, University of Denver.

Haywood, H. C. (1966). *Report of the fourth OAMR visiting professor in mental retardation*. Toronto: Ontario Association for the Mentally Retarded.

Haywood, H. C. (1968a). Motivational orientation of over achieving and under achieving elementary school children. *American Journal of Mental Deficiency*, 72, 662–667.

Haywood, H. C. (1968b). Psychometric motivation and the efficiency of learning and performance in the mentally retarded. In B. W. Richards (Ed.), *Proceedings of the First Congress of the International Association for the Scientific Study of Mental Deficiency* (pp. 276–283). Reigate Survey, England: Michael Jackson.

Haywood, H. C. (1971). Individual differences in motivational orientation: A trait approach. In H. I. Day, D. E. Berlyne, & D. E. Hunt

(Eds.), *Intrinsic motivation: A new direction in education.* Toronto: Holt, Rinehart and Winston.

Haywood, H. C., Brooks, P. E., & Burns, S. (1986). Stimulating cognitive development at developmental level: A tested, non-remedial preschool curriculum for preschoolers and older retarded children. In M. Schwebel & C. Maher (Eds.), *Facilitating cognitive development: Principles, practices, and programs* (pp. 127–147). New York: Haworth Press.

Haywood, H. C., & Switzky, H. N. (1975). Use of contingent social reinforcement to change the verbal expression of motivation by children of differing motional orientation. *Perceptual and Motor Skills, 40,* 547–561.

Haywood, H. C., & Switzky, H. N. (1985). Work response of mildly retarded adults to self versus external regulation as a function of motivational orientation. *American Journal of Mental Deficiency, 90,* 151–159.

Haywood, H. C., & Switzky, H. N. (1986a). The malleability of intelligence: Cognitive processes as a function of polygenic and experiential interaction. *School Psychology Review, 15*(2), 245–255.

Haywood, H. C., & Switzky, H. N. (1986b). Intrinsic motivation and behavior effectiveness in retarded persons. In N. R. Ellis (Ed.), *International Review of Research in Mental Retardation* (Vol. 14, pp. 1–46). New York: Academic Press.

Kazdin, A. E. (1982). The token economy: A decade later. *Journal of Applied Behavioral Analysis, 15,* 431–445.

Kunca, D. F., & Haywood, H. C. (1969). The measurement of motivational orientation in low mental age subjects. *Peabody Papers in Human Development, 7* (Whole No. 2).

Lepper, M. R., Greene, D., & Nisbett, R. E. (1973). Understanding children's intrinsic interest with extrinsic rewards: A test of the "overjustification" hypothesis. *Journal Of Personality and Social Psychology, 28,* 129–137.

Madden, M., & Slavin, G. (1983). Mainstreaming students with mild handicaps: Academic and social outcomes. *Review of Educational Research, 53,* 519–569.

Malouf, J. C. (1983). Do rewards reduce student motivation? *School Psychology Review, 12,* 1–11.

Miller, M. B., Haywood, H. C., & Gamon, A. T. (1975). Motivational orientation of Puerto Rican children in Puerto Rico and the U.S. mainland. In G. Marin (Ed.), *Proceedings of the 15th Interamerican Congress of Psychology.* Bogota: Sociedad Interamericana de Psicologia.

Morgan, M. (1981). The overjustification effect: A developmental test of self-perception interpretations. *Journal of Personality and Social Psychology, 65,* 202–210.

Palincsar, A. S., & Brown, A. L. (1984). Reciprocal teaching of comprehension fostering and monitoring activities. *Cognition and Instruction, 1,* 117–175.

Paour, J. L. (1978). Une experience d'induction des structures logiques chez des enfants deficients mentaux. *Cahier Psychologique, 21,* 79–98.

Schweinhart, L. J., & Weikart, D. P. (1981). Perry preschool effects nine years later: What do they mean? In M. J. Begab, H. C. Haywood, & H. L. Garber (Eds.), *Psychosocial influences in retarded performances: Vol. 2. Strategies for improving performances* (pp. 113–126). Baltimore: University Park Press.

Silon, E. F., & Harter, S. (1985). Assessment of perceived competence, motivational orientation, and anxiety in segregated and mainstreamed educable mentally retarded children. *Journal of Educational Psychology, 77,* 217–230.

Switzky, H. N. (1985). Self reinforcement schedules in young children: a preliminary investigation of the effects of motivational orientation in instructional demands. *Reflections of Learning Research, 1,* 3–18.

Switzky, H. N., & Haywood, H. C. (1984). A biosocial ecological perspective on mental retardation. In N. S. Endler & J. McV. Hunt (Eds.), *Personality and behavior disorder* (2nd ed., Vol. 2). New York: Wiley.

Switzky, H. N., & Haywood, H. C. (1985a). *Self-reinforcement schedules in the mildly mentally retarded: Effects of motivational orientation and instructional demands.* Paper presented at Eighteenth Annual Gatlinburg Conference on Research and Theory in Mental

Retardation and Developmental Disabilities, Gatlinburg, TN.

Switzky, H. N., & Haywood, H. C. (1985b). *Work response of mildly retarded adults to self vs. external regulation as a function of motivational orientation.* Paper presented at Eighteenth Annual Gatlinburg Conference on Research and Theory in Mental Retardation and Developmental Disabilities, Gatlinburg, TN.

Switzky, H. N., & Haywood, H. C. (1985c). *Symposium on intrinsic motivation and mental retardation.* Paper presented at 109th Annual Meeting of the American Association on Mental Deficiency, Philadelphia, PA.

Switzky, H. N., & Heal, L. (in press). Research methods in special education. In R. Gaylord-Ross (Ed.), *Issues and research in special education.* New York: Teachers College Press.

Switzky, H. N., & Schultz, G. F. (1988). Intrinsic motivation and learning performance: Implications for individual educational programming for learners with mild handicaps. *Remedial and Special Education, 9*(4), 7–14.

Tahia, R. (1977). *Modifiability of Bedouin children.* Unpublished manuscript, Bar Ilan University, School of Education, Ramat-Gan, Israel.

Thomas, A. (1979). Learned helplessness and expectancy factors: Implications for research in learning disabilities. *Review of Educational Research, 49*(2), 208–221.

Thomas, A., & Pashley, B. (1982). Effects of classroom training on LD students' task persistence and attributions. *Learning Disability Quarterly, 5,* 133–144.

Torgesen, J. K. (1986). Learning disability theory: Its current state and future prospects. *Journal of Learning Disability, 19,* 399–407.

U.S. Department of Education. (1986). *What works: Research about teaching and learning.* Washington, DC: U.S. Department of Education.

Zigler, E., & Balla, D. (1981). Issues in personality and motivation in mentally retarded persons. In M. J. Begab, H. C. Haywood, & H. L. Garber (Eds.), *Psychosocial influences in retarded performance: Vol. 1. Issues and theories in development* (pp. 197–218). Baltimore: University Park Press.

Motivation for At-Risk Students

"Helpless" students need to learn to link their
successes and failures to their own efforts.

M. Kay Alderman

M. Kay Alderman is Professor, Department of Educational Foundations, University of Akron, Akron, OH 44325.

Student motivation for learning is a major concern of most teachers, but especially for teachers of low-achieving or "at risk" students, whose numbers are on the rise (Hodgkinson 1985). In today's classrooms, motivational inequality prevails: some students persist and work on their own for their own intrinsic interest, while others work because they are required to and do not believe their actions are related to success and failure (Nicholls 1979). The encouraging news, however, is that motivation research (e.g., Alderman and Cohen 1985, Ames and Ames 1989) and cognitive learning research (e.g., Weinstein and Mayer 1986) offer teachers an abundant repertoire of strategies to foster student success and self-worth.

Understanding Motivation Levels

The motivation theory of attribution has helped us to understand students who have a pattern of failure. The reasons one assigns for achieving success or failure are called *attributions* (Weiner 1979). Students' attributions affect their future expectations and actions. The following four attributions are used most frequently:

> **Some students persist and work on their own for their own intrinsic interest, while others work because they are required to and do not believe their actions are related to success and failure.**

1. Not having the ability ("I'm just not a writer");
2. Not expending enough effort ("I could do it if I really tried");
3. Task difficulty ("the test was too hard");
4. Luck ("I guessed right").

These attributions have been further categorized into two dimensions, stable-unstable and internal-external. Stable-unstable refers to the consistency of a student's pattern of failure. Internal-external refers to the student's beliefs that the cause for failure lies either within or outside the student. For example, Teresa fails an exam on

reading comprehension—she has done this many times. Her attributions for her failure are that she can never answer those kinds of questions and that she is just not a good reader. These attributions have internal/stable characteristics: the student blames herself rather than an outside force for her failure, and she characterizes herself as someone who can never succeed.

Students with such internal/stable attributions for failure consider themselves "helpless"—they believe they can do nothing to prevent failure or assure success (Dweck and Goetz 1978). The "helpless" student actually expends less effort after failure, while a "mastery" student increases effort and looks for better strategies. Failure attributed to internal/stable ability is one of the most difficult motivational problems to remedy. And for the helpless student, simply experiencing success is not enough to ensure motivation.

For example, a student may not attribute his success to anything that he did—he attributes it to luck—so he does not expect success again. Or another student attributes her failure to "stupidity," so failure becomes a self-fulfilling prophecy. The task for teachers is to help these students break this failure/low expectation/helpless cycle.

Efficacy and Expectations

Teachers who are successful in reaching low-achieving students combine a high sense of their own efficacy with high, realistic expectations for student achievement. *Teacher efficacy* refers to teachers' confidence in their ability to influence student learning and motivation. This sense of efficacy, in turn, affects teachers' expectations concerning students' abilities. Teachers with a high sense of efficacy are more likely to view low-achieving students as reachable, teachable, and worthy of their attention and effort (Ashton and Webb 1986).

The effects of teacher expectations on student achievement are well documented (Good and Brophy 1987): the key attitudes for teachers are confidence and determination. This does not mean that they are idealistic in their expectations. Instead, it means that, although teachers are realistic—aware that students have learning problems—they look for ways to overcome the learning problems (Brophy and Evertson 1976). They let students know they want them to succeed and that they will be expected to achieve the objectives. Then they assure them that they will be taught the skills or learning strategies necessary for achieving them.

"Links" to Success

It is not enough that the student achieve success; in order to acquire a high degree of motivation, the student must know how he or she personally contributed to this success. In other words, there must be a link between what the student did and the outcome. Drawing from research on motivation and learning strategies, I have developed the "Links" for helping the "helpless" student become successful and, in turn, develop an increased sense of self-worth. These links are shown in Figure 1.

Link One: proximal goals. The first link to success is the setting of goals for performance. Goals play an important role in the cultivation of self-motivation by establishing a target or personal standards by which we can evaluate or monitor our performances (Bandura 1986). Goal setting provides the mechanism for self-assessment. Morgan (1987) concluded that there is a reciprocal relationship between goal setting and self-monitoring: either process will lead to the other. For example, Harris and Graham's (1985) instruction and training program for teaching composition skills to learning disabled students requires students to set a criterion for performance and then keep graphs to show their progress toward their goals.

But all goals are not equally effective in providing standards for self-evaluation. To be effective, the goal should be specific rather than general; harder rather than easier (but attainable); and proximal (close at hand) rather than long term (Locke 1968). It is especially important for students with a history of failure to have proximal goals so they won't be overwhelmed. Bandura and Schunk (1981) found that children who had proximal goals performed better than those with distal or long-term goals.

How do we establish a starting point to forge this proximal goal link? First, we have to find out where students are so that we can establish a baseline. The baseline can be determined by pre-tests (formal or informal) and analyses of student errors. Teachers and students can then jointly decide on the proximal goals.

Goal setting seems to benefit everyone: it has been found to have a positive effect on elementary and secondary students (Gaa 1973, 1979), as well as learning disabled students (Tollefson et al. 1984) and college students (Morgan 1987). Figure 2 shows a form that can be used and adapted to teach students to set effective goals.

I have used adaptions of these steps for students of various ages and ability and have found that most students need considerable practice in learning to make goals specific.

Link Two: learning strategies. Low-achieving students usually can be described as "inefficient learners" (Pressley and Levin 1987); that is, an inefficient learner fails to apply a learning strategy that would be bene-

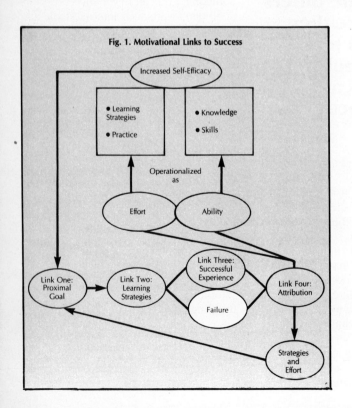

Fig. 1. Motivational Links to Success

Increased Self-Efficacy

- Learning Strategies
- Practice

- Knowledge
- Skills

Operationalized as

Effort   Ability

Link One: Proximal Goal   Link Two: Learning Strategies   Link Three: Successful Experience   Link Four: Attribution

Failure

Strategies and Effort

Fig. 2. Proximal Goals and Progress

Make your goal as specific as possible:

Planning

1. My specific learning goals for this week (today) are:

2. I will know I have accomplished my goals by:

3. Actions or steps I will take to accomplish these goals:

4. Possible blocks, both personal and outside, that may interfere with my goals:

5. If I need help, I can go to:

6. My confidence in reaching my goal is:

    no confidence   very confident
    0   25

Evaluating

7. My satisfaction with my goal attainment is:

    very unsatisfied   very satisfied
    0   25

8. Reasons for attaining or not attaining my goal:

ficial. In Link Two, the students identify the learning strategies that will help them accomplish their goals. Examples of learning strategies are: basic and complex rehearsal strategies; comprehension-monitoring strategies (Weinstein and Mayer 1986); task-limited and across-domains strategies, with metacognitive knowledge about when to use them (Pressley et al. 1989); and various reading comprehension strategies, including summarization, question asking, clarification, and prediction. In the latter example, Palincsar and Brown (1984) reported improved reading comprehension scores after students were taught the four comprehension skills.

Link Three: successful experience. A learning goal rather than a performance goal is the key to success in Link Three (Dweck 1986). The focus in a learning goal is on "how much progress I made," not on "how smart I am," a performance goal. The student measures his or her success using the proximal goal as the criterion. As teachers, we may think that success is the final link. However, consider the student who is successful but still has low expectations for future performance. It is the *attribution* the student makes for the successful experience that affects expectation: the student must link his or her personal effort or strategy to the successful outcome.

Link Four: attribution for success. In Link Four, students are encouraged to attribute success to their personal effort or abilities. The teacher's role is to help the student make the appropriate attribution. The attributions most easily changed are the internal and unstable. Thus, since students control their own effort, this is the likely starting place to influence their attributions for success. Teachers can ask, "What did you do when you tried?" Examples of student effort might be: completing all homework, correcting errors, extra practice, redoing an assignment, going to a "help" or review lesson, or using appropriate learning strategies.

Schunk (1984) concluded that for difficult tasks, attributional feedback should begin with effort, then shift to ability as skills develop. Researchers have found that effort attributions were often less valued by students than attributions for ability (Covington and Omlich 1979, Nicholls 1976). Students, especially adolescents, may not

When we help students take responsibility for their learning, we have taken a giant step in promoting motivational equality in the classroom.

view themselves as "smart" if they "tried hard." However, it is important that the student see "ability" as skills that can be learned (e.g., writing composition skills).

The teacher's role in Link Four is to model and give feedback about why the student succeeded or failed at the task. Attributional feedback is information (oral or written) about effort, strategies, or ability. Examples of feedback are: "Jenny, look at your test score, that extra practice really paid off" (effort); "Martin, the latest revision of your story shows you have really learned to use action words" (ability); "Tom, your reading scores improved because you have learned to summarize and find main ideas" (strategies).

This model then goes "full circle." Students who have succeeded and attributed the success to their own effort or ability (and not to task ease or luck) have concrete performance feedback that in turn will lead to increased self-efficacy. Self-efficacy is most enhanced by prior successful performance (Bandura 1977). This increased self-efficacy then leads to increased confidence about goal accomplishment.

In this "Links" model, we have focused on a successful experience. However, failure will occur; and when it does, students' attributions for it are important determinants of their future expectations for success. Students who attribute failure to not using the proper strategy, for example, are more likely to try again than students who attribute failure to lack of intelligence. This latter attribution for failure results in a dead end for the student. Teachers should be cautious in assigning lack of effort as the cause of failure; they should only

use this attribution when they are sure the task was within the student's capability. Often students don't know why they failed (Alderman et al. 1989). When students indicate they don't know why they failed, the teacher can provide them with a new strategy for accomplishing the task.

Classroom Structure to Support Success

To foster optimum motivation, classroom structure must support student goals, effort, and use of effective strategies. A "mastery orientation" structure fosters optimum student motivation (Ames and Archer 1988). A mastery classroom emphasizes learning and progress (Link Three) over performance and ability. Thus, errors are viewed as a natural and important part of the learning process, not as an indication that one lacks ability. Teachers in mastery classrooms give students opportunities to relearn concepts and correct errors. Low-achieving students in particular need to know exactly what they are expected to do and the criterion for measuring their success (Covington and Beery 1976). This criterion takes the focus off ability in comparison to other students as the reason for failure.

Progress, Not Miracles

The Links-To-Success model is not an algorithm but rather a guide for fostering students' motivation for success and self-worth. It is flexible: any link of the chain can be the starting point. For example, when a student fails, the cycle can begin with attributing the failure to lack of effort or use of ineffective strategies and returning to Link One: proximal goals.

This model also serves to enhance the teacher's motivation as well, through the same dynamics used with the students. When teachers see progress in their at-risk students, their teaching efficacy increases.

Finally, I make no claim that these links will work miracles with at-risk students. They only provide teachers and students with a framework for beginning the cycle of progress that fosters self-responsibility for learning. When we help students take responsibility for their learning, we have taken a giant step in promoting motivational equality in the classroom. This type of motivational intervention takes time and patience; our focus is progress, not miracles.

References

Alderman, M.K., and M.W. Cohen. (1985). *Motivation Theory and Practice for Preservice Teachers* (Teacher Education Monograph No. 4). Washington, D.C.: ERIC Clearinghouse on Teacher Education.

Alderman, M., R. Klein, M. Sanders, and S. Keck. (1989). "Metacognitive Self-Portraits: Preservice Teachers as Learners in Formation," Paper presented at the annual meeting of the American Educational Research Association, San Francisco.

Ames, C., and R. Ames. (1989). *Research on Motivation in Education: Goals and Cognition* (Vol. 3). San Diego, Calif.: Academic Press.

Ames, C., and J. Archer. (1988). "Achievement Goals in the Classroom: Students' Learning Strategies and Motivation Processes." *Journal of Educational Psychology* 80: 260–267.

Ashton, P.T., and R.B. Webb. (1986). *Making a Difference: Teachers' Sense of Efficacy and Student Achievement*. N.Y.: Longman.

Bandura, A. (1977). "Self-Efficacy: Toward a Unifying Theory of Behavioral Change," *Psychological Review* 84: 191–215.

Bandura, A., and D. Schunk. (1981). "Cultivating Competence, Self-Efficacy, and Intrinsic Interest Through Proximal Self-Motivation." *Journal of Personality and Social Psychology* 41: 586–598.

Bandura, A. (1986). *Social Foundations of Thought and Action*. Englewood Cliffs, N.J.: Prentice Hall.

Brophy, J., and C. Evertson. (1976). *Learning From Teaching: A Developmental Perspective*. Boston: Allyn & Bacon.

Covington, M. V., and R. M. Beery. (1976). *Self-Worth and School Learning*. N.Y. Holt, Rinehart, and Winston.

Covington, M.V., and C. Omlich. (1979). "Effort: The Double-Edged Sword in School Achievement." *Journal of Educational Psychology* 71: 169–182.

Dweck, C.S., and T. Goetz. (1978). "Attributions and Learned Helplessness." In *New Directions in Attribution Research*, Vol. II. Hillsdale, N.J.: Erlbaum.

Dweck, C.S. (1986). "Motivational Processes Affecting Learning." *American Psychologist* 41: 1040–1048.

Gaa, J.P. (1973). "Effects of Individual Goal-Setting Conferences on Achievement, Attitude, and Goal-Setting Behavior." *Journal of Experimental Education* 42: 22–28.

Gaa, J.P. (1979). "The Effects of Individual Goal-Setting Conferences on Achievement, Attitudes, and Modification of Locus of Control." *Psychology in the Schools* 16: 591–597.

Good, T.L., and J.E. Brophy. (1987). *Looking in Classrooms* (4th ed.). N.Y.: Harper & Row.

Harris, K.R., and S. Graham. (1985). "Improving Learning Disabled Students' Composition Skills: Self-Control Strategy Training." *Learning Disability Quarterly* 8: 27–36.

Hodgkinson, H.L. (June 1985). *All One System: Demographics of Education—Kindergarten Through Graduate School*. Washington, D.C.: Institute for Educational Leadership.

Locke, E.A. (1968). "Toward a Theory of Task Motivation and Incentives." *Organizational Behavior and Human Performance* 3: 157–189.

Morgan, M. (1987). "Self-Monitoring and Goal Setting in Private Study." *Contemporary Educational Psychology* 12: 1–6.

Nicholls, J.G. (1976). "Effort is Virtuous, But It's Better to Have Ability: Evaluative Responses to Perceptions of Effort and Ability." *Journal of Research in Personality* 10: 306–315.

Nicholls, J. (1979). "Quality and Inequality in Intellectual Development: The Role of Motivation in Education." *American Psychologist* 34: 1071–1084.

Palincsar, A.M., and A.L. Brown. (1984). "Reciprocal Teaching of Comprehension Fostering and Monitoring Activities." *Cognition and Instruction* 1: 117–125.

Pressley, M., F. Goodchild, J. Fleet, R. Zajchowski, and E. Evans. (1989). "Classroom Strategy Instruction." *The Elementary School Journal* 89: 301–342.

Pressley, M., and J. Levin. (1987). "Elaborative Learning Strategies for the Inefficient Learner." In *Handbook of Cognitive, Social, and Neuropsychological Aspects of Learning Disabilities*, edited by S.J. Ceci. Hillsdale, N.J.: Erlbaum.

Schunk, D. (1984). "Sequential Attributional Feedback and Children's Achievement Behavior." *Journal of Educational Psychology* 76: 1159–1169.

Tollefson, N., D.B. Tracy, E.P. Johnson, A. W. Farmer, and B. Buenning. (1984). "Goal Setting and Personal Responsibility Training for LD Adolescents." *Psychology in the Schools* 21: 224–232.

Weiner, B. (1979). "A Theory of Motivation for Some Classroom Experiences." *Journal of Educational Psychology* 71: 3–25.

Weinstein, C.E., and R.E. Mayer (1986). "The Teaching of Learning Strategies." In *Handbook of Research on Teaching* (3rd ed.), edited by M. Wittrock. New York: Macmillan.

GOOD TEACHERS DON'T WORRY ABOUT

DISCIPLINE

Behavior is rarely a problem when effective teaching is taking place.

T. R. Ellis

T. R. Ellis is curriculum coordinator of the Lawrenceburg Community Schools in Lawrenceburg, Indiana. This article is adapted from a presentation delivered at the Indiana Department of Education's Prime Time Fair in New Albany, Indiana, August 1988.

Discipline in the classroom has become big business. Many companies are marketing workshops, audiocassettes, videocassettes, filmstrips, workbooks, and texts, each designed to instruct teachers how to control student behavior so that effective teaching can occur.

They just may have that backwards!

Eleven years as an elementary school principal taught me many things, but no lesson clearer than this: the most effective teachers have the fewest discipline problems.

Control of student behavior *is* important. No one can teach well when students have their own agenda, and you will find no argument here in favor of disbanding whatever discipline programs you or your school have adapted. Structured discipline programs do accomplish an important educational goal: they make ineffective teachers less ineffective. But they do little to help teachers who are already effective, because those teachers need very little help.

Of all the sad stories circulating about the state of public school education today, the saddest may be the ascendancy of student discipline gurus. Their very popularity serves as a severe

indictment of our profession. When Lee Canter claims that 500,000 educators use his assertive discipline methods, we must ask why so many of our peers need such a crutch to gain control over students.

A much more positive emphasis is found in the work being done in the area of effective teaching and mastery learning by John B. Carroll, Benjamin Bloom, Madeline Hunter, Marie Carbo, and many others. In their efforts to describe effective teaching, they make little mention of student discipline. There is an inherent understanding that when the learning is meaningful, the motivation provided, and the teaching appropriate, discipline problems seldom occur.

Controlling student behavior through effective teaching requires skills that are developed through a two-step process: knowledge followed by practice. Unfortunately, most educators perform those steps backwards; they learn by trial and error—mostly the latter. How much better for their students if they followed the correct procedure: first learn what effective teaching is, then practice until they become skillful.

As a supervising principal in two dif-

ferent school systems, I have observed and evaluated scores of teachers over the years. Three of them were so inept they were fired. Several others received strongly worded directives to shape up or ship out. Most of the others, however, were very effective teachers and I learned something from each of them.

Getting Started

Getting the lesson off to a good start is as important in teaching as being on the first horse out of the gate at the Kentucky Derby. Yet, legions of teachers start every lesson with a fizzle like this: "All right, class. Open your books to page 39. Who will read first?" The most highly motivated student in the class cannot get very excited about page 39 after an introduction like that.

Madeline Hunter suggests the use of an anticipatory set for motivation and a written objective for the lesson that provides a reason for learning. One teacher who uses this technique starts every lesson with a challenge like, "Think of an important thing we learned in yesterday's lesson, then whisper it to your neighbor." While this thinking and telling is going on, the

The Dos and Don'ts of Teaching

Effective Practices	Ineffective Practices
Start every lesson with an anticipatory set (motivation to learn) and a written list of objectives (reason to learn).	"Ok, class, it's time for health. Open your books to page 39. Who remembers where we left off?"
Target individual students for performance. ("Johnny, you think about that question and try to remember. I want you to answer that before we finish.")	"Johnny, what's the answer?" (Pause two seconds.) "Sara, can you tell us?" (Pause one second.) "Hasn't anyone been paying attention in here?"
Ask How, Why, and If questions.	Ask only Who, What, When, and Where questions.
Check frequently for learning. Examples: Have each student write the answer to a question and pass it to a neighbor for checking. Or, call five or six students at random to write their answers on the board simultaneously.	Just keep plodding along in order to cover the material. Assign seatwork, paperwork, workbook pages, and unreadable ditto papers that keep the students quiet and out of your hair.
Be confident and welcome observation, particularly if constructive feedback follows.	Keep the door closed and direct very hard stare at anyone brave enough to enter, including the principal. Never ask for advice or help.
Be positive. Have high expectations for all students. ("Everyone will learn in this class, including me.")	Be negative. ("No one could teach those bozos. When's our next holiday?")
Give appropriate, personalized praise. ("Mary, you raised an interesting point. I like the connection you made.")	Give either the same praise ("Good," "OK," "Great"), undeserved praise, or no praise at all.
Provide constructive criticism and direction. Be polite while being assertive.	Use sarcasm and insults. Make punishment humiliating. Yell and scream your expectations of polite behavior.
Catch students being good and give them public recognition.	Catch students being bad and publicly embarrass them.
Expect all students to perform every day. Provide opportunities for success.	Expect only your best students to perform. Don't call on the slow learners.
Energize the class. Move around the room. Be ready to provide immediate feedback on written work.	Sit at your desk. Supervise by yelling out names. Make seatwork an individual activity with no teacher assistance.
Show personal regard for all students.	Make a big deal about Mary's vacation in Hawaii. Ignore Sam's camping trip.

teacher writes on the board one or two clear objectives for that day's lesson. Then, signaling quiet with one word—"Ready?"—she reads what she has written: "Today we will learn, starting on page 39, why . . ."

Students in that class expect a connection between thinking, recalling, anticipating, and learning. They know that learning is an overt activity and that it takes more effort than simply opening their books to the current page. They also know that the teacher expects *everyone* to recall an important part of yesterday's lesson, not just the class apple shiners with their hands raised.

Raising Expectations

For educators, the expression, "What you see is what you get," needs to be rephrased to read: "What you *expect* is what you get." We typically have low levels of expectation for many of our students. We get what we expect.

And yet, Benjamin S. Bloom says, ". . . it is difficult to conceive of any single learning task which is beyond the capabilities of most human beings who wish to learn it and who have been properly prepared for it" (Bloom 1982).

Japanese parents *expect* their chil-

dren to achieve. When they don't, their parents blame lack of *effort*.

American parents *hope* their children will achieve. When they don't, their parents blame lack of *aptitude*.

I have observed a teacher who expects all students in his class to master each learning task and who conducts the process of instruction to guarantee that outcome. It's amazing the amount of learning mastered by the "slow" students in that class. The teacher is not a magician; he is a master teacher, as these observation notes attest:

Billy seems confused and cannot respond. The teacher keeps him after the others have gone to recess. He gives individual tutoring, then lets Billy practice the skill at the board. Then, while the others are still away, he teaches Billy the next lesson and lets him know that he will be the first student called upon to respond the next day and that Billy will be his "star" pupil, since the others have not learned the lesson yet. Billy's performance the next day recovers his peer image as a worthy learner and motivates him for further success.

Meeting Student Needs

The most useless piece of furniture in an effective classroom is the teacher's chair. Teaching from the seat of one's pants is not teaching at all, but uttering.

I have seen a teacher who never pulls her chair away from the desk unless she has to open the top drawer. Once the lesson is delivered and independent practice assigned, she flitters around the room, assisting here, checking there, questioning this one, and encouraging that one. Her students see effort being modeled and they are secure in their belief that the teacher will help.

B. F. Skinner calls such behavior "immediate feedback." Bloom calls the same behavior "feedback and corrective instruction," a critical part of the quality of instruction portion of his learning model. As far as the teacher is concerned, she is simply meeting her students' needs.

Motivating and Reinforcing

Teaching in a classroom where little effort is applied to motivation and reinforcement is like pulling teeth, without the blood.

Students are curious creatures who love to learn. The trick is getting them to learn what the teacher is teaching. To succeed in that task requires motivation and reinforcement.

Motivation is complex. What motivates one student bores another. The same is true of reinforcement. Although the standard tricks of the trade include individual praise and recognition, too many teachers limit themselves to such expressions as "Good," "OK," "Great," "Nice job."

Praise and recognition must be personal to be effective: "Mary, that was a unique interpretation. Thank you for that insight." Even more effective is praise that specifically reminds the class of the lesson: "Bob just explained in his own words that a country is a political division of land, while a continent is a geographical division of land."

Madeline Hunter carries this point of reinforcement even further with her idea of "dignifying errors." Thus, even wrong answers can be accepted—and add to the learning—by correcting with dignity: "The answer you gave, Helen, correctly answers the question of why Columbus sailed west to go to the East Indies. But how did he discover America? Will you try again?"

Another common practice by teachers to reinforce student effort is their habit of displaying student papers on the walls. Unfortunately, this practice stops being reinforcing with overuse. Recognition should be special. Call everyone's attention to Susie's perfect paper. Make a big deal out of Rob's rock collection.

One teacher, after reading *Tom Sawyer* to the class, found that his students were intrigued by the idea of Tom earning "white tickets" for memorizing bible verses. That was a perfect introduction to a motivation and reinforcement program that kept his students energized all year.

Students earned white tickets for perfect papers, extra projects, special effort, and unexpected good deeds. The tickets could be "cashed in" for various prizes or entitlements. For instance, for a white ticket a child could move his desk to another location, or have one practice assignment canceled, or line up first for lunch, or leave two minutes early for recess, or get a piece of hard candy.

Five white tickets could be traded for one yellow ticket, five yellows for a green, five greens for a red, and five reds for a blue. The tickets became extremely coveted tokens. Monetarily, a white ticket was worth one cent, a yellow worth a nickel, and so on up to the $6.25 value blue ticket. Only three students managed to earn blue tickets over

the course of the year, and two of those three elected *not* to cash them in on the last day of school. They wanted them as keepsakes of a happy, successful school year.

Madeline Hunter refers to such extrinsic rewards as the lowest form of positive reinforcement, and many teachers think of them as a form of bribery. Both points of view have merit, within reason. Students should be taught the pleasure of intrinsic rewards, for example, knowledge, good grades, praise, recognition, and pride. At the same time, however, an appropriate extrinsic reward can go a long way toward motivating student effort.

Using Learning Styles

Students are not all alike. We cannot make them alike, nor should we try. Students have suffered many injustices over the years from teachers unwilling to tolerate differences. Because they are different, and not because they are handicapped in any way, hundreds of students are labeled under one or another special education category each year.

Teachers often impose ridiculous rules that reduce many students to nervous wrecks. Marie Carbo presents a typical example: "Although many of us tell children to sit up and pay attention, there is no direct relationship between how one sits and the amount of concentration devoted to what is being studied" (Carbo, Dunn, and Dunn 1986). So why hassle the kid?

Tactile learners probably suffer the most humiliation in our schools. They need to touch. They count on their fingers. Teachers hate kids who count on their fingers. They believe it represents ignorance. All it represents is a learning style.

I had a teacher who repeatedly berated a boy for counting on his fingers. "Put your hands flat on your desk," she would say. The child started bouncing his fingers. "Hold those fingers still," she yelled. The child started tapping his feet. "Hold your feet still," she shrieked.

The child's mother eventually brought him to me for after-school tutoring. He could not, said his mother, learn his math facts. As I flashed the facts cards to this nervous boy I was fascinated and saddened to watch his facial contortions. He looked to be in pain.

Do you know what he was doing? He was counting his teeth with his tongue! He could figure 8 times 9 in a few seconds by tapping his thumb against the fingers of his right hand. Can you do that? I can't! Yet we had turned this handsome youngster into a facial contortionist because we could not tolerate his learning style.

There are several learning styles programs that deserve your attention. *The 4 MAT System* by Bernice McCarthy is very thorough and Carbo's book, *Teaching Students to Read Through*

Their Individual Learning Styles, co-authored with Rita and Kenneth Dunn, is great.

Even without a formal learning styles program, teachers should lighten up and be tolerant of different preferences. Allow children to learn in whatever way is least painful to them. Then, both teachers and students will suffer fewer frustrations.

⌇

Students consistently behave better in classrooms where effective teachers rule, and it goes without saying that students deserve effective teachers. As Bloom has written, ". . . the schools can provide the best of education for virtually all of their students—if the schools choose to do so" (Bloom 1982).

We cannot humanely choose any alternative.

REFERENCES

Bloom, Benjamin S. *Human Characteristics and School Learning.* New York: McGraw-Hill, 1982.
Bloom, Benjamin S. "The New Direction in Educational Research: Alterable Variables." *Phi Delta Kappan,* February 1980.
Carbo, Marie; Dunn, Rita; and Dunn, Kenneth. *Teaching Students to Read Through Their Individual Learning Styles.* Englewood Cliffs, New Jersey: Prentice-Hall, 1986.
Carroll, J. B. "A Model of School Learning." *Teachers College Record,* May 1963.
Holly, William J. "Students' Self-Esteem and Academic Achievement." *Research Roundup* (NAESP), November 1987.
McKeachie, W. J. "The Decline and Fall of the Laws of Learning." *Educational Researcher,* March 1974.
Kerman, Sam; Kimball, Tom; and Martin, Mary. *Teacher Expectations and Student Achievement.* Bloomington, Ind.: Phi Delta Kappa, 1980.

Managing Behavior Problems:

Accentuate the Positive... Eliminate the Negative!

Jo Webber
Brenda Scheuermann

Jo Webber *(CEC Chapter #101) is an Assistant Professor of Special Education, and* **Brenda Scheuermann** *(CEC Chapter #241) is an Assistant Professor of Special Education, Southwest Texas State University, San Marcos.*

A former student called me yesterday.

"I need help. I'm teaching math to sixth, seventh, and eighth graders in a resource room, and my class is out of control. I've got Michael,

A student demonstrates an appropriate method for communicating anger.

Selina, Ryan, and Chris—all known for causing trouble—plus five others in this class. Everyone feels sorry for me. I thought teaching was supposed to be fun."

"What have you done with your applied behavioral analysis text-book?" I asked with amusement.

"I sold it," she said, sighing.

"OK" I said in my best professional voice. "Tell me what's going on."

"I've tried sending them to the office, calling their parents, giving them detention, and making them sit in the hall. Nothing seems to work. The principal and the parents just scold them and the kids are just as disruptive the next day. One of them called me a mean, mean teacher yesterday . . . and I feel like one."

As teachers try to maintain control in their classrooms, they often react initially by punishing undesired behavior (Morgan & Jenson, 1988). Teachers prefer punishment as a means to reduce undesirable behavior because they are reinforced by the immediate nature of its effects (Alberto & Troutman, 1986).

However, punishment often fails to create attentive, quiet, compliant students. By definition, it does not teach desirable behavior. Scolding, ridicule,

Reprinted from *Teaching Exceptional Children*, Vol. 24, No. 1, Fall 1991, pp. 13-19, by permission of The Council for Exceptional Children.

167

lowering of a grade, loss of privileges, temporary removal from class, suspension, or corporal punishment will not guarantee that a student will come to class on time, bring the necessary materials, or begin doing satisfactory schoolwork.

One reason for this failure might be that too often teachers *only* focus on reducing the inappropriate student behavior rather than actively teaching and reinforcing appropriate behavior (Winett & Winkler, 1972). They concentrate on what the student is *not* to do, as opposed to emphasizing which desired behaviors they want the student to exhibit instead.

To remedy this requires a shift in the traditional mindset: Rather than concentrating on the undesired behavior, the teacher should look for a positive alternative that will result in reinforcement for the student. This involves deciding what the student needs to do that he or she is not doing at the moment, then teaching it and reinforcing it. This positive approach to reducing misbehavior is an easy and effective strategy known as *differential reinforcement* or *positive reductive procedures* (Deitz & Repp, 1983). Differential reinforcement, in this context, means that positive behaviors receive reinforcement. The behavior targeted for reduction is not directly addressed. The result is an increase in more appropriate alternative behaviors and a decrease in the unde-

sired behavior. It is an instructionally sound technique and has been used successfully in clinics and classrooms to reduce a variety of behaviors such as aggressive behavior (Knapczyk, 1988; Poling & Ryan, 1982); out-of-seat behavior and talking (Ayllon & Roberts, 1974); in-class sleeping, talk-outs, and disruptions (Allen, Gottselig & Boylan, 1982; Deitz, Repp, & Deitz, 1976); inappropriate speech (Barton, 1970); and hyperactivity (Patterson, 1965; Twardosz & Sajwaj, 1972).

"I'm sorry you feel like a mean teacher. Punishment has a way of putting you in that role. Tell me about your reinforcement program."

"I let students work on the computer or have free time if they finish their work, and if everyone is cooperative all week, we have popcorn on Friday."

"Technically, you are using differential reinforcement, which is an effective technique, but you need to `fine tune' this system so it will work for you. Tell me more about Michael."

"He's a bully. He's big and loud and is always picking fights with the other kids. He was in four fights today!"

"Why don't you try a DRO technique with him?"

"DRO?"

Differential Reinforcement of Zero Rates of Behaviors (DRO)

DRO means that the student is reinforced for periods of time during which no inappropriate behavior is displayed. For example, if the goal is to reduce fighting, the student may be reinforced for every hour that he or she is not in a fight. Or, if the goal is to reduce cursing in the classroom, the teacher may reinforce the student for every 10 minutes of refraining from cursing. The frequency of the inappropriate behavior before the treatment intervention begins will determine the initial criterion for reinforcement. (During baseline, the teacher counts how much time elapses between instances of the target behavior; the average of all these times becomes the initial criterion.) The time intervals with "zero undesired behavior" will gradually be increased until the student's behavior approximates that of an average peer in a regular classroom setting.

For example, the teacher said Michael fights on an average of three times per 6-hour school day. Therefore, he might be reinforced for every 2 hours (6 divided by 3) that he does not fight. At the end of each 2-hour segment that he does not fight, Michael can give himself a point on his point card. His points can be turned in daily or weekly for classroom rewards.

When using differential reinforcement, it is usually recommended that any instances of the targeted inappropriate behavior be ignored. However, this is not always possible with severe behaviors such as fighting. Punishment for the inappropriate behavior may be necessary if the behavior is dangerous or if it is one that spreads quickly to other students (e.g., running in the school, horseplay, or calling out). However, the teacher should try a DRO procedure before considering punishment. DRO can work well with verbal aggression (e.g., name calling, threats), talking back, destruction of property, and tantrums.

"Well, I can see how DRO might work for Michael, but I don't see how it would work for Ryan. He refuses to do anything that I ask him to do. He doesn't work, doesn't pay attention, doesn't look at me, and doesn't answer my questions. He's

A student keeps track of his points each day. The teacher randomly tells the students to give themselves points for raising their hand, following directions, getting materials on time, etc.

already doing zero behavior—*good* behavior, that is."

"Why don't you try DRI with Ryan?"

"I feel like I'm taking one of your tests! What's DRI?"

Differential Reinforcement of Incompatible Behaviors (DRI)

With this strategy, the teacher reinforces a specific student behavior (e.g., following directions) that is impossible for the student to perform at the same time as the behavior targeted for reduction (e.g., noncompliance). For instance, if a teacher wishes to reduce name-calling behavior, then calling people by their appropriate names would be systematically reinforced. The student cannot both call people by their appropriate names and name call at the same time. Thus, as calling people by their correct names increases in frequency, name-calling behavior automatically becomes less frequent. As another example, if a teacher wishes to reduce talking, it would be wise to heavily reinforce in-

All students except this student will be eligible for "Bravo Bucks" for participating appropriately in class. These bucks can be used to purchase school tokens, the only currency accepted at the school store.

stances when the student's mouth is closed. The two behaviors (mouth closed and talking) are incompatible.

The behaviors chosen (the one targeted for reduction and the alternate behavior) should cover 90% to 100% of the possible alternative behaviors

(Donnellan, LaVigna, Negri-Shoultz, & Fassbender, 1988). This means that the child will have no other choices for behavior. For example, the child is either off task, quiet or talking, in seat or out of seat, on task. There are few other choices. It would not work well to reinforce "hands-to-self" behavior in order to decrease off-task behavior. The student can keep hands to self and sleep, which would be off task, and still be eligible for reinforcement. Likewise, it would not work well to reinforce task completion to decrease noncompliance. The student could finish the task but not follow the teacher's directions in doing so (noncompliance), the task could be handed in late or done in pencil instead of pen. The student would still be eligible for reinforcement even though the noncompliance was not reduced. If the student can be doing what is asked while still engaging in the undesirable behavior, another incompatible behavior should be chosen for reinforcement. Table 1 provides some examples of appropriate incompatible behaviors.

"Oh, I see . . . I can reinforce Ryan for following directions and probably reduce his refusal to do what I say. Maybe I can use a point system with Ryan, also, where he gets a point for every direction that he follows. I think I may need to prompt Ryan at first so he will know when I'm giving a direction. I think this might work!"

Table I

Positive Incompatible Alternatives for Common Classroom Behavior Problems

UNDESIRED BEHAVIOR	POSITIVE INCOMPATIBLE ALTERNATIVE
Talking back	Positive response such as "Yes Sir" or "OK" or "I understand"; or acceptable questions such as "May I ask you a question about that?" or "May I tell you my side?"
Cursing	Acceptable exclamations such as "Darn," "Shucks."
Being off task	Any on-task behavior: looking at book, writing, looking at teacher, etc.
Being out of seat	Sitting in seat (bottom on chair, with body in upright position).
Noncompliance	Following directions within _____ seconds (time limit will depend upon age of student); following directions by second time direction is given.
Talking out	Raising hand and waiting to be called on.
Turning in messy papers	No marks other than answers; no more than _____ erasures; no more than three folds or creases.
Hitting, pinching, kicking, pushing/shoving	Using verbal expression of anger; pounding fist into hand; sitting or standing next to other students without touching them.
Tardiness	Being in seat when bell rings (or by desired time).
Self-injurious or self-stimulatory behaviors	Sitting with hands on desk or in lap; hands not touching any part of body; head up and not touching anything (desk, shoulder, etc.).
Inappropriate use of materials	Holding/using materials appropriately (e.g., writing *only* on appropriate paper, etc.).

"Let's talk about what we can do about Selina," I said, encouraged.

"Selina wants to dominate the class and shouts out things when others are trying to talk. Her comments are often off task, and it really disrupts interactions."

"Well, you could use DRO or DRI, but it sounds like a habit and it might be easier for Selina to reduce the behavior gradually, rather than all at once."

"Let me guess—another differential reinforcement procedure?"

Differential Reinforcement of Lower Rates of Behavior (DRL)

For behaviors that do not need to be reduced quickly or reduced to zero occurrence (e.g., calling out for help), or for behaviors that are strong habits (e.g., talk-outs, burping, teeth grinding, self-stimulation), DRL may be the technique of choice. A teacher using this strategy would reinforce progressively lower rates of a behavior. For instance, if a teacher can tolerate some call-outs, then she can reinforce the student for progressively reducing the number of times that she calls out without permission. Or if a teacher wants to reduce teeth grinding, but does not need this to change immediately, he could reinforce the student for grinding his teeth no more than four times during a specific time period. When the student is successful at this level, reinforcement would next be contingent upon grinding teeth no more than three times. This criterion would gradually be lowered until the behavior is at an acceptable level.

The initial criterion for reinforcement is set by determining the average frequency or duration of the behavior before starting the procedure. If a student talks out on an average of four times per period, then setting the initial reinforcement criterion at four or less would be appropriate. The criterion for reinforcement is gradually lowered by reasonable intervals until an acceptable level of behavior is achieved. By allowing the student to change a habitual behavior gradually, rather than expecting immediate cessation, DRL helps ensure success as the student progresses toward the target level. Dangerous behaviors or contagious behaviors would not be appropriate for reduction with a DRL technique.

"Well, I can see that I could individualize my point system for each student. I could let Selina earn a point for every hour that she has fewer than eight call-outs. If she is successful this week, then next week it will have to be fewer than six call-outs until she has an average of only one call-out per hour. But what about Chris? He's a different one. He acts very immature, and anytime something does not go his way he cries and whines and stomps around the room. Even though the other kids make fun of him, he continues the behavior."

"You could use DRO, but it sounds like he needs to learn how to express his frustration. There is another technique that might work for him called *DRC.*"

Table 2

Problem Classroom Behaviors and Differential Reinforcement Strategies

PROBLEM BEHAVIOR	DIFFERENTIAL REINFORCEMENT TECHNIQUE
Talking back	Reinforce each 15-or 30-minute or 1-hour period with no talking back (DRO). Or reinforce each time that the student responds to the teacher without talking back (DRI).
Causing property damage	For each day that no property is damaged, reinforce the student and/or the class (DRO).
Cursing	Reinforce each 15- or 30-minute or 1-hour period with no cursing (DRO). Reinforce use of appropriate adjectives and exclamations (DRC).
Being off task	Reinforce each 5-, 10-, 15-, or 30-minute period of continuous on-task behavior (DRI).
Failing to complete tasks	Reinforce each task that is completed, half completed, or started (DRI).
Tardiness	Reinforce each day or period that the student is on time (DRI).
Being out of seat	Reinforce 5-, 10-, 15-, or 30-minute periods of continuous in-seat behavior (DRI).
Fighting	Reinforce the student after each hour or 1/2 hour that the student does not fight (DRO). Reinforce talking about feelings (DRC).
Picking on others, name calling, teasing	Reinforce the student each time he or she interacts appropriately with another student (DRI). Or reinforce the student each hour that he or she does not tease, pinch, etc. (DRO).
Noncompliance	Reinforce the student for each direction that he or she follows within 5 seconds (DRI). The schedule can be thinned to every 3 directions followed, 8, 10, etc.
Talking out	Reinforce the student each time that he or she raises a hand and waits to be called on (DRI). Thin the schedule to 3, 5, 10 times, etc. Or reinforce progressively less talking out (DRL).

Differential Reinforcement of Communicative Behaviors (DRC)

Recent literature (Sasso & Riemers, 1988) has proposed that some students may be acting inappropriately in order to communicate something. An analysis of aggressive and noncompliant behavior may reveal that the student is simply attempting to say, "Stop, I don't want to do it," or "I don't like you," or "I don't know the answer," or "I'm frustrated." Many students have not learned how to say these things directly. If this is the case, then teaching an appropriate alternative method for the student to communicate those thoughts and feelings will result in a reduction of the aggressive and noncompliant behavior.

The teacher's task is to analyze the student's inappropriate behavior and attempt to find communicative intent in it. If the teacher suspects communicative intent, then an appropriate communication strategy needs to be determined. For example, how should students communicate anger? Students with good language skills may learn to write about the anger or say "Being pushed makes me angry." Lower-functioning students may need to draw a picture of the emotion or use words or sign language. If the teacher demonstrates an alternative style of communication and heavily reinforces the student when appropriate communication is used, aggressive and noncompliant behaviors that have communicative intent should be reduced.

"So I could give Chris a point each time he says "I'm frustrated" with no crying, whining, or stomping. Maybe I could also give him points for each day that he has zero tantrums. That's DRO isn't it?"

"Yes, good! You can combine any of these techniques to make a more powerful intervention. By George, I think you've got it!"

Advantages of Differential Reinforcement

Differential reinforcement has many advantages. Among them are the following:

1. If the differential reinforcement system reduces the inappropriate behavior, the teacher can avoid punishment and its side effects. Most teachers are not effective punishers. They do not punish consistently, unemotionally, or contingently. Moreover, many students in special education have built up a resistance to commonly available punishers such as scolding, being sent to the office, or corporal punishment. They require a much stronger punisher that may not be available to school personnel. Use of differential reinforcement can also help the teacher forestall the rage, avoidance, and anger reactions that often accompany the delivery of punishment.
2. Differential reinforcement is a powerful intervention strategy that will

effectively reduce the majority of inappropriate behaviors without the concurrent use of punishment. Punishment should be used only after differential reinforcement techniques alone have been found to be inadequate. This may be true in the case of aggressive, dangerous, destructive, self-injurious, or extremely disruptive behaviors which, because of their severity, need to be extinguished immediately.
3. Use of differential reinforcement will help ensure that the teacher is teaching prosocial behavior because the teacher must specify a positive goal, assess the student's current skill level relevant to that goal, provide direct instruction in deficient skill areas, and give the student feedback (e.g., reinforcement) regarding progress toward the goal.
4. Differential reinforcement can be conducted in a variety of settings by a variety of people, thus adding to effective generalization.
5. Differential reinforcement allows the teacher to display and demonstrate

prosocial behavior (e.g., praising someone's efforts and giving rewards) as opposed to antisocial behavior (e.g., hurting someone).
6. Once a behavior is targeted for reinforcement, individualized education program (IEP) goals and objectives are easily written in positive terms.
7. Differential reinforcement tends to enhance the student-teacher relationship by setting up positive interactions between the target student and the teacher. It creates a situation in which the teacher delivers positive instead of (or in addition to) negative consequences.

Steps for Implementation

The following steps are recommended for classroom implementation.

Identify the behavior to be reduced or eliminated. This is generally the easiest step. However, a word of caution: Do not try to change every undesired behavior that a student exhibits. Start with

Student paying attention will earn a "ticket" for paying attention in class. The students write their names on the tickets and place them in a fishbowl for a Friday raffle. If their ticket is picked, they can "win" special privileges (i.e., eating a pizza lunch in the room with the teacher).

the behavior that is most intolerable in the school setting or the behavior that is causing the most problems for the student.

Identify positive alternatives to the undesired behavior. What would you like for the student to do instead? Provide the student with an alternative behavior that can be reinforced. For example, if the student is talking out without permission, reinforce only when he or she raises a hand to speak; if the student is frequently aggressive, reinforce during the times when he or she is not aggressive. If a student calls out frequently, provide reinforcement for calling out less often. If a student acts out feelings, model an appropriate way to communicate feelings.

Select a system of differential reinforcement. Use DRL for behaviors that can be reduced gradually; DRO for behaviors that need to be reduced to zero levels; DRI to teach a specific positive behavior as an alternative to the undesirable behavior; and DRC when the goal is to increase functional communication skills. Table 2 lists recommended differential reinforcement systems for common behavior problems.

Set up a reinforcement system. Pick reinforcers appropriate for the student's age and grade level. The reinforcers can be tangible reinforcers or privileges. Use school-related (natural) reinforcers whenever possible. Social reinforcers (smiles, praise, etc.) should always be used in conjunction with other reinforcers so that other reinforcers can be faded eventually. Survey the students, watch them, or ask other teachers and parents for appropriate reinforcer ideas. Make a list of at least 10 possible reinforcers.

Token reinforcement systems are a convenient way to reinforce systematically in the classroom. Checkmarks, stars, stamps, stickers, or initials can be exchanged for the reinforcers on the list. Tokens make it possible to give heavy reinforcement initially without disrupting lessons and without the danger of satiation. For more information on token systems see Alberto and Troutman (1986); Ayllon and Azrin (1968); Kazdin (1977); Polloway and Polloway (1979); and Stainback, Payne, Stainback, and Payne (1973).

Set a success criterion. Determine the *final* criterion for the desired behavior. For example, how long must the student stay seated? How many tasks must the

student complete each day? How long must the student display no teasing? The success criterion will vary according to the age and developmental level of the child, the setting in which the child must operate, and the behavior. One way to decide on a reasonable criterion is to determine how much or how long the same behavior is exhibited by an average student of the same age in a relevant setting. For example, if most students stay in their seats for an average of 40 minutes continuously, then do not stop the reinforcement strategy until this criterion is met by the student and the behavior is exhibited at this level over a substantial period of time. Be specific about setting a success criterion. It should not be decided haphazardly, but should be based on what the student needs to display to be successful in the mainstream setting. Begin by reinforcing small increments or short periods of time, and gradually lengthen these time periods or increase the amount of behavior required for reinforcement.

Evaluate results. Count both the inappropriate student behavior and the alternative behavior that had been reinforced. Simply saying that the stu-

dent is acting "better" does not provide the information necessary for further planning. If either behavior is not progressing in the desired direction, check the intervention for problems.

Potential Problems

The following are possible reasons why the differential reinforcement system is not working. Check these items before and during your intervention.

1. The target behavior has not been specified or assessed well. Pick one behavior at first and count it. Also, analyze it for communicative intent.
2. The reinforcers are not as rewarding to the student and/or are less powerful than the reinforcers the student is receiving for inappropriate behavior (e.g., teacher or peer attention, avoiding tasks, etc.).
3. The reinforcers are not delivered often enough for the student to recognize the value of exhibiting the desired behavior, or they are delivered so often that they cause satiation.
4. The reinforcers are not delivered consistently and contingently. Do not just give reinforcers when you

Students earn points toward their grade for staying in class and coming to class on time. This student must "punch out" or lose 10 points in order to leave class and go to the rest room.

feel like it, or stop the strategy because it "takes too much time." If the strategy is working, do not stop it until the success criterion is met.

5. The alternate behavior is not one that is achievable by the student. If the student does not know how to perform the behavior, then it should be taught using direct instruction and prompting.

6. The reinforcement schedule is thinned too quickly. Begin with frequent reinforcement of the alternative behavior and gradually reduce the amount and frequency of reinforcement.

7. The reinforcement schedule is thinned too slowly. Fade prompts and thin the reinforcement schedule as the student is successful at each stage. The goal is to eventually get to the point where an intermittent schedule of naturally occurring reinforcers will maintain unprompted behavior.

8. Generalization of the behavior to other settings has not been specifically addressed. Generalization should be taught before instruction is stopped. (See Alberto & Troutman, 1986, or Morgan & Jenson, 1988, for methods of generalization training.)

9. Instruction in new, appropriate behaviors is not continued. When the student has mastered one new appropriate behavior, teach another one. In this way, the student's access to reinforcers is increased. Furthermore, as the student masters more appropriate behaviors, fewer inappropriate behaviors will be displayed.

Summary

Differential reinforcement is a positive, relatively easy, and effective method of reducing inappropriate behavior by reinforcing positive alternatives to the undesired behavior. It requires a shift from concentration on what the student *needs to stop* to focusing on what the student *needs to do* instead. Differential reinforcement may be used alone, or, if necessary, in conjunction with punishment if the undesired behavior is extremely violent, dangerous, self-injurious, or destructive.

Differential reinforcement, like any other good behavior management system, places certain requirements on teachers if it is to work. The teacher must be consistent in delivering the reinforcers for the targeted desired behavior. It often is not easy to maintain this level of consistency, and it requires a high degree of commitment on the part of the teacher. However, the rewards resulting from this commitment are great. Time spent administering a system of differential reinforcement is probably less than that which is already being expended in dealing with inappropriate behavior, and the returns are far greater. It not only reduces inappropriate behavior, it teaches and reinforces appropriate behavior. Differential reinforcement is well worth the time and effort it involves.

References

Alberto, P. A., & Troutman, A. C. (1986). *Applied behavior analysis for teachers.* Columbus, OH: Charles E. Merrill.

Allen, L. D., Gottselig, M., & Boylan, S. (1982). A practical mechanism for using free time as a reinforcer in the classroom. *Education and Treatment of Children, 5,* 347–353.

Ayllon, T., & Azrin, N. (1968). *The token economy: A motivational system for therapy and rehabilitation.* New York: Appleton-Century-Crofts.

Ayllon, T., & Roberts, M. D. (1974). Eliminating discipline problems by strengthening academic performance. *Journal of Applied Behavior Analysis, 7,* 71–76.

Barton, E. S. (1970). Inappropriate speech in a severely retarded child: A case study in language conditioning and generalization. *Journal of Applied Behavior Analysis, 3,* 299–307.

Deitz, D. E. D., & Repp, A. C. (1983). Reducing behavior through reinforcement. *Exceptional Education Quarterly, 3,* 34–46.

Deitz, S. M., Repp, A. C., & Deitz, D. E. D. (1976). Reducing inappropriate classroom behavior of retarded students through three procedures of differential reinforcement. *Journal of Mental Deficiency Research, 20,* 155–170.

Donnellan, A. M., LaVigna, G. W., Negri-Shoultz, N., & Fassbender, L. L. (1988). *Progress without punishment: Effective approaches for learners with behavior problems.* New York: Teachers College Press.

Kazdin, A. E. (1977). *The token economy: A review and evaluation.* New York: Plenum.

Knapczyk, D. R. (1988). Reducing aggressive behaviors in special and regular class settings by training alternative social responses. *Behavioral Disorders, 14,* 27–39.

Morgan, D. P., & Jenson, W. R. (1988). *Teaching behaviorally disordered students.* Columbus, OH: Charles E. Merrill.

Patterson, G. R. (1965). An application of conditioning techniques to the control of a hyperactive child. In L. P. Ullmann & L. Krasner (Eds.), *Case studies in behavior modification* (pp. 370–375). New York: Holt, Rinehart and Winston.

Poling, A., & Ryan, C. (1982). Differential reinforcement of other behavior schedules: Therapeutic applications. *Behavior Modification, 6,* 3–21.

Polloway, E., & Polloway, C. (1979). Auctions: Vitalizing the token economy. *Journal for Special Educators, 15,* 121–123.

Sasso, G., & Riemers, C. (1988). Assessing the functional properties of behavior: Implications and applications for the classroom. *Focus on Autistic Behavior, 3*(4), 1–6.

Stainback, W., Payne, J. Stainback, S., & Payne, R. (1973). *Establishing a token economy in the classroom.* Columbus, OH: Charles E. Merrill.

Twardosz, S., & Sajwaj, T. (1972). Multiple effects of a procedure to increase sitting in a hyperactive retarded boy. *Journal of Applied Behavior Analysis, 5,* 73–78.

Winett, R. A., & Winkler, R. C. (1972). Current behavior modification in the classroom: Be still, be quiet, be docile. *Journal of Applied Behavior Analysis, 5,* 499–504.

ORDER in the CLASSROOM

Some teachers swear by Lee Canter's Assertive Discipline system. But if it's so good, why do critics call it "dehumanizing," "humiliating," even "dangerous"?

DAVID HILL

LINDA DARLING-HAMMOND HAD never heard of Assertive Discipline until her daughter, Elena, entered kindergarten two years ago. When she came home from school, Elena had plenty of stories to tell her mother, but they weren't the kind of stories Darling-Hammond expected to hear. Instead of being about new friends and new things to learn, Elena's accounts of her first days at Takoma Park (Md.) Elementary School focused on which kids in her class were being punished—and how. The teacher, Elena told her mother, wrote the names of the "bad" kids on the blackboard, which meant they could have certain privileges taken away from them. Elena wasn't among the "bad" kids; in fact, she brought home happy-face stickers because she had been "good." Yet she was frightened of what could happen if she played with the kids who had been punished.

"She was so terrified by the prospect of having her name placed on the board, being held in from recess, or being excluded from class activities that she stopped participating in class," says Darling-Hammond, an educational researcher for the RAND Corporation at the time and now a professor at Columbia University's Teachers College.

When Darling-Hammond went to observe her daughter's classroom, she learned that the teacher was using a system called Assertive Discipline, developed in the 1970's by Lee and Marlene Canter and now used in many schools across the country. The highly structured system, a mixture of common sense and behavior-modification techniques, stresses rewards and punishments as a way for teachers to "take charge" of their classrooms. Many teachers and administrators swear by it, but Darling-Hammond was appalled by what she witnessed:

"I saw a group of small children trying hard not to move or speak; a young, inexperienced, and unmentored teacher trying religiously to apply rewards and consequences. The list of names on the board grew whenever someone wiggled or spoke. The children appeared unhappy and confused. The stickers did not do much to offset their distress, since many of the children who got them felt bad about the children who didn't. Virtually all of the 'offenders' that day were boys; most of them were black. None of them had done anything that I could term 'misbehaving' during my visit. But they had broken rules forbidding talking and moving; i.e., normal 5-year-old behavior."

Takoma Park Elementary School no longer uses Assertive Discipline. And Lee Canter no longer advocates the discipline technique of writing down names on the blackboard. "People such as Linda Darling-Hammond interpret that as something that could be psychologically harmful to the kids," says Canter. "Personally, I don't think it is, but I have come out in all my latest materials saying that teachers should not use it. I think especially with kindergarten kids, I would not write their names on the board."

Darling-Hammond isn't the only critic of Assertive Discipline. In recent years, many educators and child psychologists have spoken out against the technique, calling it, among other things, "dehumanizing," "humiliating," and "dangerous." Yet it remains popular; Canter says that more than 750,000 teachers have been trained in Assertive Discipline during the last 15 years, and his company, Lee Canter & Associates, has grown from a mom-and-pop operation to a multimillion-dollar enterprise, with 75 full- and part-time employees. Proponents of Assertive Discipline speak of it as if it were the greatest thing since sliced bread. The bottom line, they say, is that it works. One middle school principal who recently began using Assertive Discipline at his school goes so far as to call it "a godsend."

I**N A MODEST, WINDOWLESS** office in Santa Monica, Calif., Lee Canter is explaining to a visitor the genesis of Assertive Discipline. If Canter were a student, he would no doubt get a happy-face sticker, his office is so tidy. On one wall, between two shelves of neatly arranged books, is a cartoon that depicts the kind of fantasy a teacher might have after an especially bad day. In it, a plump, innocent-looking teacher with glasses faces her wide-eyed students and says: "Good morning, children. My name is Miss Applegate. One false move and I'll kill you."

Despite waking up with a stomach virus, Canter, 43, is animated and energetic, constantly emphasizing his points with his hands. He often gives motivational speeches to teachers and principals, and his speaking experience shows, even in a one-on-one situation.

Canter received a master's degree in social work from the University of Southern California in 1970, and says he got most of the ideas for Assertive Discipline while working as a guidance counselor, helping parents and teachers deal with problem children. "I saw what was going on in the classroom," he says. "I saw teachers coming home every night so frustrated, kids not getting the opportunity they needed to learn, and I just sat down with my wife and said, 'We've got to do something about it.' And we came up with ideas that obviously worked.

"I think they probably worked because they're based upon nothing really new. I get a lot of credit for Assertive Discipline, and I get a lot of blame for it from people who don't like it. But there's nothing really brand new in this program. Throughout history, teachers have told kids what they wanted them to do, have had rules for the classroom, have established consequences if you break the rules, and have had positive consequences when you're good. All I really did was to put it together in a package.

"I watched a lot of effective teachers. I went into classrooms, and I sat down and watched teachers who did not have discipline problems. Number one, they were assertive. That meant they clearly and firmly told their kids what they wanted. They were positive with the kids, very straightforward. When the kids were good, the teachers would give them a lot of positive support. If the kids chose not to behave, the teachers would discipline them."

Canter and his wife, Marlene, a former special-education teacher, published *Assertive Discipline: A Take-Charge Approach For Today's Educator* in 1976. The book, now in its 26th printing, remains the basic text for the discipline technique, but Canter's company also publishes a number of other materials for teachers and parents, such as *Positive Reinforcement Activities*, *Homework Without Tears*, and *Assertive Discipline For Parents*. Canter's 25 instructors offer Assertive Discipline workshops all over the country, and there's something for everyone: teachers (K-12), administrators, parents, paraprofessionals, even bus drivers.

Canter says that, in the past, most of the training was done on a schoolwide or districtwide basis, usually in one-day, inservice seminars. (Teachers at Takoma Park Elementary, in fact, were required to be trained in the Assertive Discipline method.) But recently, he says, there has been increased interest in his five-day graduate-level course called "Beyond Assertive Discipline," for which teachers may earn college credit.

Canter promises results, too. Teachers who take the basic one-day training (at an average cost of $28 per person) are told that they will see "an 80 percent reduction in classroom disruptions," "fewer students in the principal's office," "a calm, positive classroom climate conducive to teaching and learning," and "more success in dealing with parents on behavior problems."

Here's how Assertive Discipline works: "Assertive" teachers should (in Canter's words) establish a "systematic discipline plan that explains exactly what will happen when students choose to misbehave." The key, says Canter, is consistency: "An effective discipline is applied fairly to all students."

Canter suggests that the plan include a maximum of five consequences for misbehavior. "For example, the first time a student breaks a rule, the student is warned. The second infraction brings a 10-minute time out [isolation]; the third infraction, a 15-minute time out. The fourth time a student breaks a rule, the teacher calls the parents; the fifth time, the student goes to the principal." Canter says he initially suggested that teachers write students' names on the board because he wanted to eliminate their need to stop the lesson and issue reprimands.

"Writing a student's name on the board would warn the student in a calm, nondegrading manner," Canter says. "It would also provide a record-keeping system for the teacher. Unfortunately, some parents have misinterpreted the use of names and checks on the board as a way of humiliating students. I now suggest that teachers instead write an offending student's name on a clipboard or in the roll book and say to the student, 'You talked out, you disrupted the class, you broke a rule. That's a warning. That's a check.'"

At the same time, Canter says that teachers should reward those students who obey the rules. He suggests, for example, that teachers drop marbles into a jar every time a student does something positive; when the jar is full, the entire class is rewarded by, say, 10 minutes of free time at the end of the day. Canter suggests that students be rewarded with material objects, such as cookies, ice cream, or even a hamburger from McDonald's.

"An effective behavior-management program must be built on choice," Canter has written. "Students must know beforehand what is expected of them in the classroom, what will happen if they choose to behave, and what will happen if they choose not to behave. Students learn self-discipline and responsible behavior by being given clear, consistent choices. They learn that their actions have an impact and that they themselves control the consequences."

Canter often makes the point that Assertive Discipline is not a cure-all. "This is not a perfect program," he says. "This is not the answer. And I keep saying that, because there are people out there who say, 'This is the answer.'"

Teachers and administrators who use Assertive Discipline *do* tend to gush about its benefits. Charles Warner, principal of Jackie Robinson Middle School in New Haven, Conn., has nothing but praise for the system. "It's fantastic," he says. "We're looking at it as a godsend for us."

Warner says that Jackie Robinson and two New Haven elementary schools (which "feed" students into Jackie Robinson) began using Assertive Discipline last

September. The middle school, he says, is located in a neighborhood with a lot of drug activity, an atmosphere that created "a fair amount of discipline problems" and "hostile children." Teachers at the school used to have their own individual discipline plans. "But we felt that we needed to do something different," says Warner.

Now, students at all three schools know exactly what is expected of them—and what will happen to them if they disobey the rules. "Assertive Discipline gave us consistency," Warner says. "That's one of its highlights." He says there has been "a drastic decrease" in discipline problems since the plan was implemented. "I'm sold on it. I had my reservations at first. I thought it was just another thing to spend money on. But once we had our first training session, I realized it was worth doing."

Henry Rhodes, who teaches 7th grade social studies at Jackie Robinson, agrees. "I couldn't wait to try it," he says. "It's easy to use. It's all spelled out for you."

Critics, however, contend that Assertive Discipline is harmful—to students *and* to teachers—precisely *because* of its apparent simplicity. "It totally dehumanizes the teacher by putting the control into a system," says educator Richard Curwin, co-author (along with Allen Mendler) of *Discipline with Dignity*. "Where's the teacher's judgment? For teachers who are insecure, it has a lot to offer."

Assertive Discipline's main objective, say Curwin and Mendler, is to teach kids to be obedient, not to be responsible for their actions. In their book, they write: "We define obedience as following rules without question, regardless of philosophical beliefs, ideas of right and wrong, instincts and experiences, or values. A student 'does it' because he is told to do it. In the short term, obedience offers teachers relief, a sense of power and control, and an oasis from the constant bombardment of defiance. In the long run, however, obedience leads to student immaturity, a lack of responsibility, an inability to think clearly and critically, and a feeling of helplessness that is manifested by withdrawal, aggressiveness, or power struggles. . . . Obedience models are far more interested in keeping students in line rather than maintaining their dignity."

(Curwin also says that the use of Assertive Discipline is "dying out," a charge that Canter disputes. "Every year, more and more teachers go through the program," Canter says. He estimates that his company will train 85,000 teachers this year; 50,000 of them will take the one-day seminar, while 35,000 of them will take the five-day graduate-level course.)

Linda Darling-Hammond believes that Assertive Discipline is especially harmful to children in the early grades, when they are still developing self-regulatory behavior and social skills. For one thing, she says, the rules Canter recommends are "inappropriate for young children" because "they suggest a curriculum in which conversing and moving about in the classroom are inappropriate and punishable activities." In addition, she says, "Designating children's behavior as 'bad' results for young children in them believing they themselves are bad. Under the age of 11, children cannot generally separate attributions about their behavior from attributions about themselves."

Darling-Hammond also cites research showing that the use of rewards actually *decreases* intrinsic motivation among students. Assertive Discipline, she concludes, "replaces the teaching of values and the development of intrinsic motivation for learning with a control-oriented system of rules and penalties stressing compliance, sanctions, and external motivation."

Canter is accustomed to such criticism. "The whole *point* of Assertive Discipline," he says, "is teaching children responsibility. The way you teach kids to be responsible is by telling them exactly what is expected of them and then giving them a choice. One thing that I've always talked about in my work is that children need to be given a choice." He pauses, assumes the role of an assertive teacher, and addresses me as a student. "Dave, you have a choice. If you choose to yell and stop me from teaching someone else, you choose to have this consequence. On the other hand, if you choose to behave, I will recognize that behavior."

He continues: "So Assertive Discipline is based upon choice. Curwin can say that he views it as an obedience model, but I think it's clearly spelling out to kids what's expected and then giving them a choice. Because how else do you learn responsibility but by making choices, and realizing there are choices in life, and that we have to be responsible for our actions?"

The concept of student choice in Assertive Discipline, contends Vincent Crockenberg, professor of education at the University of California-Davis, is "utterly muddled. It is fraudulent." In a 1982 article in the *California Journal of Teacher Education* titled "Assertive Discipline: A Dissent," Crockenberg pointed out that the notion of "choice" is distorted when children have only two options. "The Canters simply stack the deck in favor of the teachers. They give teachers a simple way out of their difficulties, but at the price of miseducating children by deeply misrepresenting to them what it means to choose to do something which affects others, what it means to act morally."

Crockenberg concluded: "Assertive Discipline is too simple. It 'works,' if it works at all, only by distorting moral language, by pandering to the defensiveness of teachers about their work, and by ignoring or even denying that children have any significant rights or needs that are independent of the needs of the adults who are their teachers. That is just too high a price to pay for order in the classroom."

"The thing that I've found," responds Canter, "is that kids need limits. It's not like you're doing something to harm a child when you give him some structure. We're not talking about hitting kids. We're not talking about verbally degrading kids. We're not talking about saying to kindergarten kids, 'You're

going to sit on the rug for an hour.' We're saying there should be some general rules so the kids know there's an adult there who really cares about them. That's what we're after."

Canter claims that Assertive Discipline is "based solidly on techniques that have been shown to work in the classroom," and he even distributes a publication titled *Abstracts of Research Validating Effectiveness of Assertive Discipline.* One study cited, for example, surveyed 129 teachers and 12 principals at three Indiana schools during the 1982-83 school year. Of the respondents, 86 percent said that they liked using Assertive Discipline, and 82 percent said that student behavior at the schools had improved. Yet critics contend that such evidence is scant and, further, that Canter has selectively reported it.

Gary Render, a professor of education at the University of Wyoming, along with Ph.D. candidates Je Nell Padilla and Mark Krank, conducted a study of the existing research on Assertive Discipline and found "a surprising lack of investigation of a program that is being so widely used. The literature supporting Assertive Discipline is not strong or generalizable. Much of it is based on perceptions of teachers, students, parents, and administrators." Their conclusion: "We can find no evidence that Assertive Discipline is an effective approach deserving schoolwide or districtwide adoption."

One of the most troubling aspects of Assertive Discipline is its abuse by some teachers and school districts. In 1983, parents of five children attending Germantown Elementary School in Annapolis, Md., sued the Anne Arundel County Board of Education for $17.3 million, claiming that their children's civil rights were violated when they were placed in solitary confinement for misconduct in 1980 and 1981. One student, 11-year-old Michyle Davis, testified that she was confined for five consecutive days during school hours in a "storage room" with a desk, after she was accused of laughing in class and throwing a chair. The suit also alleged that the children, aged 7 to 12, were discriminated against because they are black.

Ralph McCann Jr., the elementary school's principal at the time, testified that his policy of confining unruly children in isolation rooms was part of Canter's Assertive Discipline program, implemented in 1980 to stem runaway discipline problems at the school. Canter, however, said at the time that Assertive Discipline does not recommend isolating students without adult supervision. When an attorney for the children asked the principal, "Didn't you know that Lee Canter recommended no more than two consecutive hours of in-school suspension for elementary school students?" McCann replied, "No, sir." He also said that he had used Canter's basic concepts but had modified them to "suit our particular needs."

A $30,000 out-of-court settlement was reached in 1984. As part of the settlement, school officials agreed that students placed on in-school suspension would be supervised by an adult at all times.

Milton Shore, a Silver Spring, Md., child psychologist who testified on behalf of the five children, says that he asked Canter to testify in court that the Maryland school was using a "distortion" of his system, but Canter said his lawyer had told him he had "nothing to gain" by doing so. "His comment to me was, 'I wouldn't have approved it,' " Shore says. "Why he wouldn't say it in court is something I've never been able to understand."

Canter says that *both* sides wanted him to testify in the case, and that he was ready and willing to testify on behalf of the children. "Absolutely," he says. "What went on in that district was unconscionable." His lawyer, however, told him not to get involved. "He said, 'Don't get caught in the middle of this thing. You are being set up.' "

Canter admits that Assertive Discipline has taken on a life of its own. "It has become a generic term, like Xerox or Kleenex," he says. "A number of educators are now conducting training in what they call Assertive Discipline without teaching *all* the competencies essential to the program. For example, I have heard reports of teachers who were taught that they had only to stand in front of their students, tell them that there were rules and consequences, display a chart listing those rules and consequences, and write the names of misbehaving students on the board. That was it. Those teachers were never introduced to the concept that positive reinforcement is the key to dealing with students."

To Canter, the problem isn't with the system; rather, it's with the people who don't understand how to use it: "Negative interpretations have also come from burned-out, overwhelmed teachers who feel they do not get the support that they need from parents or administrators and who take out their frustrations on students. Assertive Discipline is not a negative program, but it can be misused by negative teachers. The answer is not to change the program, but to change the teachers. We need to train administrators, mentor teachers, and staff developers to coach negative teachers in the use of positive reinforcement. If these teachers cannot become more positive, they should not be teaching."

At the same time, Canter insists that the teachers who most effectively use Assertive Discipline are the ones who mold the system to their individual teaching styles. "That's fine," he says. "I don't want the legacy of Assertive Discipline to be—and I don't want teachers to believe they have to use—names and checks on the board or marbles in a jar. I want

teachers to learn that they have to take charge." Or, as he also has said: "The children must know that something will happen when they break a rule. The form it takes is not as important as the reality of a negative consequence."

In other words, don't take Canter's suggestions too literally. When Canter's son, Josh, was 13, his father sent him to his room after he had misbehaved. "An hour later," Canter says, "he comes out reading *Assertive Discipline for Parents*, and he says, 'Dad, how many times did you warn me about yelling and screaming?' And I said, 'Two.' And he said, 'But in your book, it says two warnings, maximum half-hour in the room. You sent me in for an hour! You can't even follow your own program!' " Canter laughs about the incident: "It's very hard to practice what you preach."

L INDA DARLING-HAMMOND wasn't the only parent upset over the use of Assertive Discipline at Takoma Park Elementary and other schools in the Montgomery County (Md.) school district. When a group of them began voicing their concerns about the system, they found an ally in school board member Blair Ewing, who had done some research of his own. "I thought [Canter's] materials were dreadful," he says. "Assertive Discipline doesn't examine the reasons *why* children are misbehaving. It values conformity above everything, and that's dangerous."

Ewing says he raised the issue "over and over" with School Superintendent Harry Pitt, who eventually issued a policy statement recommending that prepackaged discipline systems not be accepted wholesale by the district. "Assertive Discipline is not prohibited, but it's understood that it's not to be used," says Ewing. "I haven't seen it rear its ugly head again."

Darling-Hammond didn't wait around to see what would happen; she removed her daughter from the school. When she took her to look at another school, one that didn't use Assertive Discipline, Elena said, "Mom, I want to stay in this school, because they don't punish the kids."

Corporal Punishment: Used in a Discriminatory Manner?

JOHN R. SLATE, EMILIO PEREZ, PHILLIP B. WALDROP, and JOSEPH E. JUSTEN III

John R. Slate is an assistant professor in the Department of Counselor Education and Psychology and Emilio Perez is an associate professor in the Department of Special Education and Communicative Disorders, both at Arkansas State University. Phillip B. Waldrop is a professor and chair of the Department of Elementary and Special Education, Middle Tennessee State University. Joseph E. Justen III is a professor in the Department of Special Education and Communicative Disorders, Arkansas State.

Physical punishment is part of our pedagogical legacy (Clarke 1984). The rationale for physical punishment comes from Calvinistic theology, as illustrated by the old adage, "Spare the rod, spoil the child." Corporal punishment, despite research evidence to the contrary (e.g., Good and Brophy 1990; Henson 1986), is still believed to be an effective means of stopping student misbehavior, particularly by administrators and teachers in the South, the Southwest, and rural areas throughout the country (Hyman, Clarke, and Erdlen 1987). In fact, for many administrators and teachers, paddling and discipline are synonymous.

Within the last decade, data have been collected that indicate that sexual, racial, and age inequalities are present in the application of corporal punishment. Such punishment is not administered solely on the basis of a student's misbehavior. Rather, a student's misbehavior, race, sex, and age, as well as the sex of the punisher, all help to determine whether and to what degree corporal punishment is administered. This is true even though no research evidence that we are aware of indicates that corporal punishment is differentially effective with one sex, race, or age group over another, or differentially effective when administered by male or female principals.

Sexual and Racial Inequality

As most of us know from our own experiences in American public schools, it is primarily males rather than females who receive corporal punishment. According to a civil rights survey, boys are paddled more often than girls, at a rate of twenty-five to one (*Jonesboro Sun* 1988). Another study reported that males accounted for 80 percent of all paddling incidents (Jennings 1988). In a study by Rose (1984), 90 percent of respondents who used corporal punishment as a disciplinary procedure reported that they had paddled male students in the preceding 30 days, compared with 79 percent who had paddled female students in the same time period. Eighty-nine percent of the school principals and teachers in the study reported paddling five or fewer female students per month; only 45 percent reported paddling male students that infrequently. No principal in Rose's study who used paddling reported using corporal punishment with more than fifteen female students a month, but 14 percent indicated that they used corporal punishment that frequently with male students.

Another study (Wooldridge and Richman 1985), using fabricated situations and requesting teachers to recommend appropriate punishment, found a significantly greater number of teachers who recommended severe punishment for males than for females, even when the misbehavior was identical for the male and female students. In a similar survey study, Williams (1983) found that when students were described as black, teachers decided more frequently to send them to the office for disciplinary problems. In a finding of particular interest, teachers were much more likely to send black students than white students to the office for minor offenses.

Corporal punishment is not administered equitably to racial groups. Black students continue to be far more likely than whites to be the subjects of disciplinary action and are involved in more than twice as many incidents of corporal punishment. Data indicate that black students were involved in 31 percent of the 1.1 million instances of corporal punishment in American public schools in 1986. Yet they represent only 16.1 percent of enrollment. White students were involved in only 60 percent of instances of corporal punishment, even though they make up 73.3 percent of the student population (Jennings 1988). Nationally, 5.22 percent of black students were paddled in 1986, compared with 2.28 percent of white students and 2.06 percent of Hispanic students. In the state of Arkansas, for example, black students make up 24 percent of total school enrollment but were involved in 40 percent of recorded corporal punishment incidents. White students, who represented 75 percent of Arkansas's total school enrollment, accounted for 60 percent of the corporal punishment incidents. For states that recorded such data, Arkansas had the largest disparity in corporal punishment rates: 22.6 percent of black students were paddled, compared with 11.0 percent of whites and 5.6 percent of Hispanics (*Jonesboro Sun* 1988).

If a student who misbehaves is male or black, he is more likely to be paddled than a student who misbehaves and is female or white, even if they do the same thing. There is no evidence, however, that blacks break school rules more often than whites. McCarthy and Hoge (1987) concluded that racial differences in the administration of corporal punishment are not matched by racial differences in school misconduct. If black students do not engage in more misbehaviors than white students, why then are they paddled more often? Frahm (1983) speculated that academic frustrations, cultural differences in behavior, inconsistent rule enforcement, and teacher racism were the reasons. Frahm believed that the problem existed in the classroom setting, where teachers who are less tolerant of minority students usually overreact to their behavior. In agreement with Frahm, Burrell (1971) found that white counselors and disciplinarians often allowed bias or preconceived stereotypes to influence their judgment and, as a result, were unable to establish good rapport with black students. Another researcher (Ciminillo 1980) argued that those giving out punishment are subjective in their judgments and attitudes toward individuals: if the individual who misbehaves is perceived in a negative way, then the punishment is likely to be more severe than if the student is perceived in a more favorable light.

Age-Related Inequality

Although junior high school students engage in more documented misbehaviors than do students at other grade levels, the misbehaviors are most often nonviolent and not of a serious nature (Hyman, Clarke, and Erdlen 1987). Nonetheless, paddling occurs at a higher rate for junior high school students than for students at any other grade level. Hyman, Clarke, and Erdlen (1987) speculated that high school students may get a paddling less often than students at other grade levels because such action against older students (aged 14 to 20) may make the administrator or teacher more vulnerable to a hostile student reaction.

Use of Corporal Punishment by School Principals and Teachers

Not only are there sex, race, and age differences in who is paddled, differences also occur depending on who administers the paddling (Rose 1984). In a national survey, male principals reported that they paddled black students more often than did female principals. Interestingly, all the female principals in the study indicated that they used corporal punishment as a disciplinary technique, whereas only 70 percent of male principals did so.

Though more female than male principals reported having the use of corporal punishment at their disposal, male principals indicated that they paddled students much more frequently than the female principals. Seventeen percent of male principals administered corporal punishment to more than twenty students a month; no female principals paddled at this high rate. All female principals in the study indicted that they paddled less than fifteen students a month. Male teachers are three times more likely than female teachers to inflict severe corporal punishment on students (Hyman, Clarke, and Erdlen 1987; Hyman and Zelikoff 1988).

Rose's 1984 study reported that 59 percent of principals stated that they had paddled black students within the preceding thirty days. Every principal in the study who paddled more than ten black students a month was located in the South (Rose 1984). Given that the number of black students in each part of the country surveyed was not reported, one possible hypothesis for this differential application might be that more black students were enrolled in the schools surveyed in the South than in other areas.

Behaviors Resulting in Corporal Punishment

Typical behaviors that result in the administration of corporal punishment include fighting, being disruptive in class, showing disrespect for authority, and disobedience (Rose 1984). Fighting was the misbehavior identified by the majority of respondents as most likely to elicit the use of corporal punishment. One must question the logic of responding to one aggressive behavior (fighting) with another aggressive behavior (paddling).

Principals of smaller schools appear more likely to administer corporal punishment when the misbehavior is disobedience or fighting, whereas principals of larger schools appear more likely to do so when students show disrespect, are truant, or, to a lesser extent, engage in disruptive behaviors (Rose 1984). Thus, even the size of the school a student attends seems to influence whether or not he or she receives corporal punishment.

Determining the Use of Corporal Punishment

McCarthy and Hoge (1987) hypothesized that school authorities use criteria other than the seriousness of the misbehavior in meting out disciplinary sanctions. Variables they mention as possibilities include race, age, sex, socioeconomic status, a student's general school demeanor, and home situation. They found evidence that the strongest predictor of corporal punishment, other than the amount or severity of misconduct, is the amount of punishment received by the student in the last year or so. The next strongest influence is the teacher's perception of the misbehaving student's overall demeanor. The third contributor is the misbehaving student's grades. What is the logical relationship between a student's grades for performance on academic material and whether or not he or she is paddled for misbehavior? McCarthy and Hoge (1987) argued that, as a group, black students are perceived as exhibiting poorer overall demeanor, demonstrate poorer academic performance, and have been subjected to more past punishment than have white students.

Summary

Data strongly suggest that discriminatory elements exist in the use of corporal punishment in American public schools. In addition to problems of bias, considerable evidence exists that corporal punishment is ineffective in eliminating inappropriate behavior (Good and Brophy 1990). Though paddling may temporarily suppress unwanted behavior, it does not eliminate it, nor does it teach a student how he or she should behave. Rather, corporal punishment may have negative consequences, such as withdrawal, aggression, negative peer reactions, and negative self-statements.

We believe that the evidence that we have discussed forcefully argues for the banning of corporal punishment from American public schools. Too many other methods exist (e.g., Good and Brophy 1990) for us to view corporal punishment and discipline as synonymous. Eliminating paddling in favor of more positive methods is recommended. Hitting students for committing misbehaviors is not conduct that is conducive to a civilized society.

The banning of corporal punishment cannot be accomplished on the federal level but has to be done on a state-by-state basis because the Tenth Amendment to the Constitution reserves authority over education to the states. The process of banning corporal punishment from our schools will thus be a lengthy process, as each state legislature deals with this controversial issue. As a result, we are rather pessimistic that corporal punishment will be banned in the immediate future.

REFERENCES

Burrell, L. 1971. Black and white students' attitudes toward white counselors. *Journal of Negro Education* 40:25–29.

Ciminillo, L. 1980. Discipline: The school's dilemma. *Adolescence* 15:1–12.

Clarke, J. 1984. Analysis of recent corporal punishment cases reported in national newspapers. *Resources in Education*, ED253347.

Frahm, R. 1983. Minorities: Classroom crisis. Changes and challenges: City schools in American. Washington, D.C.: Institute for Educational Leadership. 7–23.

Good, T., and J. Brophy. 1990. *Educational psychology: A realistic approach.* 4th ed. New York: Longman.

Henson, K. 1986. Corporal punishment: Ten popular myths. *High School Journal*, 107–09.

Hyman, I., J. Clarke, and R. Erdlen. 1987. Analysis of physical abuse in American schools. *Aggressive Behavior* 13:1–7.

Hyman, I., and W. Zelikoff. 1988. Psychological abuse in the schools: An overview. *Resources in Education*, ED294328.

Jennings, L. 1988. Disparities in pupils' treatment persist, rights study finds. *Education Week* 14.

Jonesboro (Ark.) *Sun.* 1988. School discipline studied. 12 December.

McCarthy, J., and D. Hoge. 1987. The social construction of school punishment: Racial disadvantage out of universalistic process. *Social Forces* 65:1101–20.

Rose, T. 1984. Current uses of corporal punishment in American public schools. *Journal of Educational Psychology* 78:427–41.

Williams, J. 1983. Suspensions hit minority pupils. Changes and challenges: City schools in America. Washington, D.C.: Institute for Educational Leadership.

Wooldridge, P., and C. Richman. 1985. Teachers' choice of punishment as a function of a student's gender, age, race, and IQ level. *Journal of School Psychology* 23:19–29.

Exceptional Children

- **Educationally Disabled (Articles 33–35)**
- **Gifted and Talented (Articles 36–38)**
- **Culturally Different (Articles 39–40)**

The Equal Educational Opportunity Act for All Handicapped Children (Public Law 94-142) gives disabled children the right to an education in the least restrictive environment, due process, and an individualized educational program specifically designed to meet their needs. Professionals and parents of exceptional children are responsible for developing and implementing an appropriate educational program for each child. The application of these ideas to classrooms across the nation at first caused great concern among educators and parents. Classroom teachers whose training did not prepare them for working with the exceptional child expressed negative attitudes about mainstreaming. Special resource teachers also expressed concern that mainstreaming would mitigate the effectiveness of special programs for the disabled and would force cuts in services. Parents feared that their children would not receive the special services they required because of governmental red tape and delays in having their children properly diagnosed and placed.

It has now been more than a decade since the implementation of Public Law 94-142. Many of the above concerns have been studied by psychologists and educators, and their findings have often influenced policy. For example, research has indicated that mainstreaming is more effective when regular classroom teachers and special resource teachers work cooperatively with disabled children.

The articles concerning the educationally disabled confront many of these issues. Sally L. Smith discusses the characteristics of learning disabled students. Teachers who have worked with learning disabled children share their observations and teaching strategies. The article by Howard Margolis and Elliot Schwartz discusses the positive effects of cooperative learning in mainstreamed classes. Stanley C. Diamond's article provides examples of problem behaviors and what teachers can do to help emotionally disturbed adolescents.

Another dimension of exceptional children is the gifted and talented. These children are rapid learners who can absorb, organize, and apply concepts more effectively than the average child. They often have IQs of 140 or more and are convergent thinkers (i.e., they give the correct answer to teacher or test questions). Convergent thinkers are usually models of good behavior and academic performance, and they respond to instruction easily. Teachers generally value such children and often nominate them for gifted programs. There are other children, however, who do not score well on standardized tests of intelligence because their thinking is more divergent (i.e., they can imagine more than one answer to teacher or test questions). These gifted divergent thinkers may not respond to traditional instruction, may become bored, may respond to questions in unique and disturbing ways, and may appear uncooperative and disruptive. Many teachers do not understand these unconventional thinkers and fail to identify them as gifted. In fact, such children are sometimes labeled as emotionally disturbed or mentally retarded because of the negative impressions they make on their teachers. Because of the differences between these types, a great deal of controversy surrounds programs for the gifted. Such programs should enhance the self-esteem of all gifted and talented children, motivate and challenge them, and help them realize their creative potential. The three articles in this subsection on gifted and talented children discuss the nature of giftedness, and explain how to identify gifted students and provide them with an appropriate education.

The third subsection of this unit concerns the culturally different. Just as labeling may adversely affect the disabled child, it can also affect the child who comes from a minority ethnic background where the language and values are quite different from those of the mainstream culture. The term "disadvantaged" is often used to describe these children, but it is negative, stereotypical, and may result in a self-fulfilling prophecy whereby teachers perceive such children as incapable of learning. Teachers should provide culturally different children with experiences that they have missed in the restrictive environment of their homes and neighborhoods. The articles in this section address cultural and language differences and suggest strategies for teaching culturally different children.

Looking Ahead: Challenge Questions

Can mainstreaming have a positive effect on the intellectual and social development of disabled children?

What are the characteristics of children with learning

disabilities? What are some strategies that teachers can use to help students deal with their disabilities?

Who are the gifted and talented? How can knowledge of their learning needs help in providing them with an appropriate education?

What are some of the cultural differences that exist in our society? How can teacher expectations affect the culturally different child? Would multicultural education help teachers deal more effectively with these differences?

THE MASKS STUDENTS WEAR

Recognizing the behaviors learning disabled students use to hide their problems helps you to help them

Sally L. Smith

Sally L. Smith is the founder/director of The Lab School of Washington, a full professor and director of the graduate program in learning disabilities at The American University in Washington, D.C. and the author of the book, No Easy Answers: The Learning Disabled Child at Home and at School.

Learning disabled adults are telling educators what learning disabled children can't. What we learn from these adults can improve the teaching of children and the training of teachers.

There are many types of learning disabilities including auditory, vision and language disabilities. And students can have combinations of different learning disabilities.

One of the most important messages learning disabled adults are giving is that the greatest challenge learning disabled children face is the battle for self-esteem. These adults say they felt stupid and were treated in school as though they were. They felt defeated, worthless and "dumb." Over the years, these adults learned to mask their hurts.

"I learned to act a certain way so I couldn't be teased. I would appear bored, tired, eager to be of help, all-knowing or funny, depending upon what was going on. In other words, I would do anything but let them know I couldn't read the material," confesses one learning disabled adult.

"I faked my way all through school," says another. "I had the gift of gab and an excellent memory."

Unfortunately, many dyslexic and learning disabled adults started to develop masks in first or second grade when they could not read what others could. Few ever received special education. They were not identified as learning disabled or dyslexic. Instead, their teachers often

labeled them "lazy," "willful," "poorly disciplined" and "spoiled" when actually they were trying their hardest.

These students were called "retarded" if they had any speech and language problems and "disturbed" if they were hyperactive, impulsive or had any of the behavioral manifestations of a learning disabled child. Often these children were gifted, above average in intelligence, and unable to bear their inability to accomplish the simplest academic task.

Think of the energy many learning disabled students spend hiding their disabilities and masking the feeling of being stupid. The masks are an elaborate subterfuge that make students feel worse about themselves. The masks protect the students from being thought of as "stupid," but isolate them from others. Often the masks interfere with students' ability to learn.

Recognizing the masks learning disabled students sometimes wear to hide their inabilities will help you take action to have the problem treated. Masking behavior comes in many variations. The following types are among the most common masks students wear.

The mask of super competence

"Easy!" "Oh, sure! Everyone knows that!"

With a great deal of bravado, this student tries to make everything look simple. He knows he can talk his way

Reprinted from *Instructor,* April 1989, pp. 27-28, 31-32. Copyright © 1989 by Sally L. Smith. Reprinted by permission.

Characteristics of a learning disabled child

- Looks typical but doesn't learn typically.
- Is intelligent, often gifted.
- Has reading, spelling, writing and/or math achievements that are significantly below child's capability level.
- Has a short attention span.
- Is easily distracted.
- Has poor listening skills.
- Has trouble following directions.
- Doesn't seem to be trying, acts lazy or is defiant.
- Sometimes uses immature speech and language.
- Confuses left and right.
- Sometimes uses immature movements, is awkward, clumsy. Shows poor motor coordination (i.e., reaches one hand out and the other hand follows).
- Exhibits immature behavior.
- Displays general disorganization, poor organization of time and space.
- Often has difficulty with tasks employing paper and pencil.
- Produces many reversals (i.e., "b" instead of "d") and rotations (i.e., "b" instead of "q") in written work.
- Is inconsistent in behavior and work.
- Frequently displays exceptional ability in the arts, sports, science and verbalization.

Steps you can take if you suspect a student is learning disabled

1. List the child's personal and academic strengths and areas of weakness. Back up the list with anecdotal records after a week of careful observation and listening.
2. Check student's recent eye and hearing test records as well as general physical health records to rule out physical problems.
3. Confer with parents to discuss the list; ask them if they see similar strengths and weaknesses at home.
4. Recommend an evaluation by a school psychologist. In some schools, initial referral is to the pupil personnel worker; in others it is to the interdisciplinary team or principal.
5. Inform parents about Public Law 94–142, the *Education for All Handicapped Children Act.* Specify parents' rights to have their child evaluated, and if not satisfied with the evaluation results to seek a second evaluation.

If a child is diagnosed as being learning disabled, the child is entitled by law to appropriate services.

These range from support in the classroom to resource assistance to placement in self-contained classrooms. These services may or may not include speech and language therapy, occupational therapy and adaptive physical education.

Resources

Organizations

Association for Children with Learning Disabilities (ACLD)
This grassroots organization serves parents, teachers and other professionals. It provides needed support and information to help follow the latest educational and medical research and supports legislation for special education classes and teachers in the field. To find the organization nearest you, write the National ACLD, 4156 Library Road, Pittsburgh, PA 15234, or call (412) 341–1515.

Council for Exceptional Children (CEC)
This organization for professionals publishes books, media, journals, periodicals and research findings. Low-cost informational flyers are available. For a catalog or more information, write to CEC, 1920 Association Drive, Reston, VA 22091, or call (703) 620–3660.

Foundation for Children with Learning Disabilities (FCLD)
This organization for parents and professionals is a source of information for publications concerning the learning disabled child. It also provides grants. For more information, write to FCLD, 99 Park Ave., New York, NY 10016, or call (212) 687–7211.

The Orton Society
This organization for professionals is also open to parents. It studies preventive measures and treatment for children with specific language disabilities, sponsors research, and shares its findings. For more information, write to The Orton Society, 724 York Road, Baltimore, MD 21204, or call (301) 296–0232.

Books
Smith, Sally L. *No Easy Answers: The Learning Disabled Child at Home and at School*, Bantam Books, New York, 1981.
Stevens, Suzanne. *Classroom Success for the Learning Disabled*, John Blair Publisher, 1984.

through anything. His logic is impeccable. He's good with people, numbers, problem solving and trouble shooting.

Gen. George S. Patton, a dyslexic, assured his daughter that Napoleon couldn't spell, either, and quoted Jefferson Davis as saying, "A man must have a pretty poor mind not to be able to think of several ways to spell a word."

The mask of helplessness

"I don't know." "I don't understand." "I can't do anything."

Through pity, this person gets everyone around to help her do her work and assume responsibilities so she never fails. She refuses to risk failure, but feels even worse because she knows she didn't do any of the work.

The mask of invisibility

"I would hide in my shell, hold my neck in like a turtle, almost pleading with the teacher not to call upon me."

By looking frightened, whispering to teachers and acting terrified with peers, this person gets everyone else to do his work for him.

The student realizes he can get through school by not talking, just repeating when necessary, taking a low profile, and making no waves. With his head down and sitting quietly for a long time, nobody bothers him. He has the talent of melting into the crowd. Teachers and supervisors later realize they never got to know this student or acknowledge he was there.

The mask of the clown

"Isn't that a riot!" "Ha, ha, ha." "What a joke!"

Everything is funny when this student is around. Laughter, however, hides the real issue—a learning disability.

Cher, the Academy Award-winning actress/singer, admits she was the "class clown" to divert attention from her inability to read, write or do arithmetic in school. Despite her problems, she was exceedingly verbal and outstanding in the arts. A teacher proclaimed that she was not working hard enough. Feeling stupid, she dropped out of school at 16 and wasn't tested for learning disabilities until after she was 30.

The mask of the victim

"It's not fair." "Everyone picks on me." "There's no justice anywhere."

Injustice is a basic theme with this person. Often called a "jailhouse lawyer" because he has an argument for everything, this student feels victimized and takes on a "poor me" attitude. He assumes no responsibility for anything. He angers others around him.

The mask of not caring

"I don't care." "Nothing matters." With this mask, the student is never vulnerable, and risks no failure. If she tries to succeed and fails, she says she never tried and it doesn't matter. The mask is a way of keeping others at a distance, making her feel woefully inadequate. If nothing matters, it's very difficult to change or motivate this person.

The mask of boredom

"This is boring!" *Yawn*. "What time is it now?" *Yawn*.

With big yawns, loud sighs, tapping fingers and toes, this person lets the teacher know how bored he is. This behavior puts the teacher on the defensive. Usually this person is not bored, but frustrated, and can't do what he's been asked to do.

Thomas Edison was kicked out of schools for not following instructions. He probably did not understand the instructions due to his auditory problems. Severe learning disabilities prevented him from being able to write what he was told.

The mask of activity

"Gotta run." "Sorry, I'm in a hurry, I can't talk." "I'm busy now, I'll do whatever you want later."

This student is always on the move. Standing still may bring her close to others, and she precludes any intimacy. Constant activity wards away others and keeps her from having to perform.

The mask of outrageousness

"I'm way out." "I don't like being a conformist." "I believe in individualism to the extreme." Through wild clothing, hair style and color, wigs, extraordinary glasses, stockings, boots, and so on, this student projects eccentricity and hides his problems.

Robert Rauschenberg, a famous artist who had extreme difficulty with math and spelling, did outrageous, unheard of things in school and in his career. Many artists feel he expanded the definition of art for a generation of Americans by daring to innovate.

The mask of the Good Samaritan

"Let me help you." "What can I do for you?"

This student wants to please at any cost. Frequently, she is too nice and too accommodating. She will echo what you say, work longer hours than necessary and be overly helpful to get out of doing what she can't do.

The mask of contempt

"They don't know how to teach." "This whole place sucks."

Negativity encompasses this mask. This joyless student has a negative word for everything. If it's sunny out, it could be sunnier. He wears out the people around him because nothing is ever good enough. He takes no pleasure in small successes. He's angry at the world for making him feel stupid and believes the world owes him something. He puts everyone around him on the defensive.

The mask of the strong silent type

"I'm Joe Cool." "Nobody comes too close to me, but they follow me everywhere." "Get out of my face. Nobody moves on me." "Every sport is for me. I live for sports."

Personified by a sleek body and prowess in sports, this student is revered by many and endowed, in her own mind, with every fine feature.

Bruce Jenner, Olympic decathlon champion who is dyslexic, says sports gave him his self-esteem. Jenner says reading aloud in the classroom was much harder and more frightening for him than competing in the decathlon.

The mask of perfection
"If they don't recognize my talents, that's their problem." "Good artists don't have to read really well, anyhow."

Proclaiming loudly that there are machines to spell and write, secretaries to take dictation and lawyers to read for him, this student presents himself as perfection. He tolerates no mistakes in himself or others. He often carries an impressive book or magazine he can't read and saunters into a room looking completely pleased with life. He makes everyone around him miserable.

The mask of illness, frail health and vulnerability
"My head." "My stomach." "My side." "My bladder." "My migraine."

To receive extra attention and get out of the work she can't do, this student calls in sick, leaves sick, constantly pretends to be sick and talks about her frailties.

Given something to read, she uses her illnesses and frailties as an excuse or cries if necessary. Expecting special attention, special privileges, while avoiding what she can't do, this student confuses everyone around her and usually gets by with this behavior.

The mask of seduction
"Hey, woman, write this down for me. Men don't write." The "macho man" often gets a female to do for him what he can't do. He hides behind his macho mask, making himself appear sexy.

"Math is men's work, girls can't do it." The "helpless female" asks a "macho man" to do what she can't do and hides behind her female mask to make it appear sexy.

The mask of being bad
"Don't mess with me. You'll be sorry." "I threw the book at him, so what?" "I'd rather be thought of as bad than dumb."

Losers at school often become winners on the street.

This student feels stupid, powerless and useless at school and often directs his frustration and anger towards his teachers. His peers enjoy his bad behavior and encourage more of it.

Billionaire Dallas real estate manager Rick Strauss changed schools several times, always suffering the humiliation of not learning to read or write due to his severe dyslexia. He compounded his problems by cutting up. Doing so diverted his teachers' attention away from his poor work. It wasn't until he was a high school senior that he learned that his inability to read and write resulted from his learning disabilities.

The mask of fantasy
"I'm going to be a millionaire by the time I'm 30!" "The world will understand me soon." "I'll have a Ph.D. once I learn to read."

Characterized by a fertile imagination and a great deal of creativity, this student tends to live more in her hopes and fantasies than in reality, which is filled with daily frustrations.

Hans Christian Andersen didn't learn to read and write, even with the help of 10 royal tutors of the Danish Court. He dictated his wonderful fairy tales to a scribe. His mask of fantasy protected him from the pain of facing reality, even though glimpses of his suffering appear in some of his stories, such as "The Ugly Duckling."

Removing the masks
The masks can be removed when students reach a certain comfort level. This usually happens when a student realizes he is not stupid, but suffers from a learning disability. The student experiences enormous relief when he discovers why he has been having difficulties learning.

What learning disabled adults have to say about the masks they wore in school alerts educators to the need to reach children in their early years, identify those children who have trouble learning before they begin to wear the masks, and teach them in ways that will help them succeed.

What to Do When You Can't Do Anything

Working with Disturbed Adolescents

STANLEY C. DIAMOND

Stanley C. Diamond is director of the Mill Creek School, Philadelphia, Pennsylvania, and a consulting editor for The Clearing House.

"There is really no one around to help out."

"There is no place to send students to let them just calm down."

"There is no chance to see them afterward to explain things or to hear from them."

"There are just too many kids in the class (school)."

"I don't have training to work with these kids. We don't know much about them or their lives; we don't meet their parents."

"I can't be a counselor and a teacher; there is just no time for that kind of involvement."

These are some comments made by teachers in large city high schools during discussions about emotionally disturbed students. The teachers readily admit that there are plenty of such youngsters in their classes, or at least they assume that to be the case. They also know that these students will either drop out or self-destruct without proper attention to their needs. They know, too, that the capacity for evaluating and servicing such students in their schools is limited and that a referral to the counselor or special education team is likely to result in long delays at best or total neglect at worst. Most school systems are stressed to their very limits in this respect. Abstract and mysterious solutions such as providing the least restrictive environment or a "regular education initiative" seem to be imposed upon the schools and teachers by near-sighted and unrealistic educators miles from the everyday classroom experience.

However true the teachers' observations may be and however well grounded their expressions of frustration and confusion are, there are practical limits to the range of choices and interventions available in the classroom for students who exhibit disturbed behaviors. Teachers become concerned about the youngster who falls asleep in the middle of the day or expresses deep hostility in the absence of provocation, the child who displays bizarre behavior or dramatically withdraws, the one who changes a behavior pattern in a significant and obvious manner or talks or acts in a regressed fashion. There seems to be little that can be done. That is often the reality of the daily experience for teachers; those who care may have to make peace with the limitations of their power. To a great extent, they do face an unsatisfying level of helplessness. Many of the students who come to their attention will not be properly served; most will not be responded to at all.

Yet it is possible for a teacher to open opportunities for such students, to be helpful to them or, at the very least, less harmful. Some of the interventions that are possible are independent of the world outside of the classroom; nothing in the school system prevents such efforts from being made. Having limited power is not the same thing as helplessness. Here are some notions about what teachers can do when there seems to be little that can be done.

Relationship Enhancement

We always make a choice about how close or how available we are to our students. All too often the most disturbed of our pupils have few productive or caring relationships to draw upon. The presence of an adult who is perceived as interested in them is potentially valuable in itself. Should they feel self-destructive or especially needy in some way, they may recognize that there exists at least one alternative to total isolation. Merely noticing the students who are feeling bad or looking stressed or worried is a validation of their importance, something that may not happen to them in any other setting. A comment such as "How are you doing today? You look a little tired" may well be more than they receive from others during their daily activities. A question about how a student did in a particular situation you are aware of is a still stronger

From *The Clearing House*, March/April 1991, pp. 232-234. Reprinted with permission of the the Helen Dwight Reid Educational Foundation. Published by Heldref Publications, 1319 Eighteenth St., NW, Washington, DC 20036-1802. Copyright © 1991.

statement of caring and can make a difference in how that youngster feels about himself. It can "make his day" in a substantive and meaningful manner.

Sharing Yourself

The classroom is a more intimate and more comfortable place when a teacher is willing to be him- or herself. By simply sharing feelings or experiences or personal anecdotes, we bring our students closer and let them know that personal sharing is welcome. This opportunity may not be present in other aspects of their lives and can enable students to offer the kind of communication that will be helpful to them. People need to be known. The process of making oneself known is a step toward better mental health, a deeper sense of connectedness, and an enhancement of one's self-esteem. Setting an example for our students may involve more personal risk than we have been accustomed to taking, but the result can be a classroom where students are freer to be themselves and where we can enjoy one another more fully as people.

Changing Student Expectations

The youngster who drifts into class a bit after the bell has rung—or who has to tweak another student's ear in passing, or who slams a book on the desk—is behaving in a disruptive and unacceptable manner in a classroom. Understandably, our tendency is to respond with discipline, usually with a counterforce at least equal to the offense committed. All teachers know the variety of options available in their school for coping with such disruptive behavior.

But what happens if we don't give the anticipated response? What if we do not perpetuate the cycle? We do need to respond in some way to unacceptable behavior; yet our response does not have to be the one the student elicits repeatedly and predictably at home and in school. In fact, the usual responses have not solved the problem, or the behavior would not still be present. Thus dancing to that old tune holds little promise for change. Just trying new responses is a useful intervention in itself. It offers the possibility that an approach can be found that will help the student to learn new, more productive behaviors.

Suppose the late arrival were greeted with humor—"I see the matinee crowd has arrived"—rather than force—"This is your third tardy this month. Go to the office." Or how about making a statement to that student that you wish to talk with him or her after class and trying a problem-solving conversation in which you and the student come together to make arrival on time a project that you are both invested in. Or how about sharing how the late arrival makes you feel about your role with the class or about your ability to be the kind of teacher you want to be. Or can you make an encouraging statement designed to let the student know that you care about his or her achievement and performance?

In other words, try for a personal exchange that is not a struggle for power. The chances are the student is used

to the struggle and has difficulty finding a way out of it. We can occasionally help in that process and teach ways of resolving conflict without losing face.

Humor as a Classroom Tool

Students with emotional problems rarely come from homes where people play and have fun together. Life just is not very funny for them; nor are the people with whom they associate inclined to see and enjoy the lighter side of things. We can help to change that by allowing humor to become part of our classroom life. Not everyone is a comedian, but we all have the ability to respond to a comical setting. Many teachers fear that such relaxation threatens control in the classroom, and perhaps there is a limit beyond which each person will experience anxiety about classroom order. So be it. However, we can work within our individual limits.

A teacher I know threatens her unruly sixth-grade class of inner-city, below-average-ability students with her singing if they do not settle down. The thought of her singing to them is a source of comic distress. When she starts, they plead for silence and immediately become orderly. How refreshing for all concerned! Their fun has replaced power issues with a more salutary result than could otherwise be attained. How much easier it is for students to be part of that classroom. No wonder they love and respect that teacher!

How about a five-foot woman sidling up to a six-foot, husky, eighth-grade male student and whispering to him, "If I see that comic book on your desk again, I am going to take you outside, strangle you to death, call your mother to tell her to come pick up the body, and then I am going to collect the reward." This kind of overstatement is both private and preposterous. The book inevitably disappears, and the teacher's remedy is never tested. Two people have communicated with affection and with humor. No confiscation, no argument, no shame, and no repetition of the behavior. Those are the usual results. If humor doesn't work, some other intervention needs to be used. At any rate, it is fun to try.

Nonjudgmental Conversation

We can make another contribution by simply listening without judgment to a student's feelings, ideas, opinions, or struggles. Allowing a young person to talk with us, to select us for sharing something of him- or herself that is personal, perhaps even private, is a validation of that person. We too easily assume that what the student wants is "guidance." But that is not necessarily the case. If we are given the chance to listen, that may well be the service needed. Our interest may help the youngster to articulate whatever is bothersome in a way that causes productive reexamination. Or it may just be an answer to the need to be heard, to be respected, to be cared about. In any event, it is important not to rush to offer judgments about important things that are shared with us by our students. We may well serve them better by just being available to them.

Doing Just One Extra Thing

All the teachers with whom I have spoken know that they cannot do everything. In fact, they rarely feel they can do anything to make things better for their disturbed students. But the truth is that we can all do some little thing that has the potential to make a little difference. The warm greeting that we go out of our way to remember to give to the withdrawn student, the word of encouragement that we make sure the acting-out youngster receives after some small success, the welcome to the student who has been out sick, the phone call or note to a parent to commend a youngster's achievement, the few words after school on our "free" time, the offer of help that communicates sincerity and interest—these are all useful interventions, however minor they may seem. Each of them has the potential to make a student feel more accepted and to open up a relationship that need not be burdensome for the teacher at the same time that it is helpful to a student whose life is otherwise empty. One small action can be a start toward helping the troubled student, and each class setting offers the possibility of finding a way to fit such an effort into the daily events.

There are two levels at which caring teachers can work for the good of their neediest students. We can all be political and active within our school and our school systems. We can participate in committees, speak up at meetings where educational issues are discussed, and stand forcefully for what we believe in wherever our voice may count. In the meantime, however, we must never give in to helplessness no matter how great our odds for success may be.

Facilitating Mainstreaming Through Cooperative Learning

Howard Margolis

Queens College of the City University of New York

Elliot Schwartz

August Martin High School, Jamaica, New York

Regardless of their philosophical stance toward mainstreaming, teachers are often apprehensive at the prospect of having mildly handicapped students (for example, learning disabled, educable mentally retarded, and emotionally disturbed students) placed in their classes (Kavanagh, 1977; Knoff, 1985). Many already consider their classes extremely difficult to teach because of the wide range of competencies and diverse needs of their students. Teachers find it difficult to address the needs of mildly handicapped students in heterogeneous classrooms without inviting disorder or depriving their other students of needed attention (Knoff, 1985; Madden & Slavin, 1983). These concerns often prompt teachers' reluctance "to mainstream students for whom they must alter basic instruction" (Salvia & Munson, 1985, p. 126). Nonetheless, given current mainstreaming trends, many subject area teachers will be responsible for educating mildly handicapped students in their classes.

Fortunately, easy-to-understand instructional methodology, such as cooperative learning, can be highly effective as a way to assimilate mildly handicapped students into the mainstream. Cooperative learning can help teachers meet the individual needs of handicapped and nonhandicapped students without significantly altering the curriculum (Johnson & Johnson, 1986). Through the use of carefully structured group assignments, cooperative learning strategies help (a) individualize instruction in a time-efficient manner that avoids dependency on recurrent teacher-student dyads (which, paradoxically, reduce the amount of direct instruction per student); (b) guide planning; (c) teach essential cooperative skills and promote positive social interaction; and (d) increase understanding of disabilities and respect for differences. After reviewing the research on cooperative learning, Johnson and Johnson (1986) concluded that compared to competitive or individualistic learning:

> Cooperative learning experiences result in higher achievement and greater retention of learning. . . . Students in cooperative learning situations tended to use higher level thought processes, engaged in more higher level oral rehearsal, and discovered higher level strategies more frequently. . . . (Moreover, cooperative learning) promoted greater achievement motivation, more intrinsic motivation, more persistence in completing tasks, and greater continuing motivation to learn. . . . (It) also resulted in more positive attitudes toward the subject area and instructor (p. 556).

Cooperative learning activities are highly structured "so that students work together to achieve a shared academic goal (Schniedewind & Salend, 1987, p. 22)." Each student is viewed as having something important to offer other members of the group, which will contribute to the group's success. Students stimulate or complement each other. According to Cohen (1972), cooperative learning activities can be categorized as either (a) consensus-oriented tasks, in which the group reaches agreement on a common answer to some shared question; (b) a collegial model, in which group members share resources or teach each other to master a specific topic; or (c) divided labor, in which each group member has a specific, clearly delineated task(s) that helps satisfy a communal assignment when completed. To realize the benefits of cooperative learning, teachers must assign tasks that legitimately require cooperation and that tap the diverse skill and knowledge of the different group members. For example, writing and performing a play analyzing the causes of the Civil War from the perspectives of well-known historical figures—as opposed to adding columns of figures that students find simple, tedious and commonplace—would be an appropriate task. In addition, teachers need to monitor individual accountability, offer incentives based on group rather than individual performance, and foster student beliefs that cooperation will enhance accomplishment.

Success in most adult activities requires the cooperation of diverse individuals or groups. Cooperative learning attempts to prepare students for this challenge. At the core of cooperative learning is the premise that learning how to work effectively and efficiently with neighbors to achieve what cannot be accomplished alone is valuable in and of itself. For mildly handicapped and their nonhandicapped peers, cooperative learning also provides opportunities for individuals to contribute to the group's success and the achievement of its members regardless of their level of individual skills. It offers mildly handicapped students a chance to enhance their self-esteem by providing help, rather than only receiving it. For example, in English class, Doug, a highly intelligent, mildly handicapped adolescent with a severe reading problem, could be assigned a group task in which success depends on his strengths rather than on his poor reading ability. He may have the job of (a) collecting magazine pictures to illustrate the major themes of the group's report; (b) using a tape recorder to interview the school's principal to assess the principal's opinions about some controversial subject; (c) roleplaying a critical character in a group play; (d) sharing with the group his expertise on a relevant topic he learned about through personal experience (for example, what it's like working on a family fishing boat); (e) editing a videotape of relevant news events supporting the group's consensus position on some public issue; or (f) orally summarizing the group's conclusions to the class and enumerating potential implications. In a resource room, Lucy, a fourteen-year-old mildly handicapped student of average intellect, who reads at a third-grade level, may be assigned to teach match concepts she has mastered to Keith, a nonhandicapped student from another class who is having difficulty with a math concept that he missed due to an extended illness. Keith, in turn, has the responsibility of teaching Lucy ten basic sight words she needs to learn. When they have finished instructing each other and think that their partner is prepared for a test, the teacher assesses both on criterion-referenced measures which he discussed with them before initiating peer tutoring. Lucy is given a test on the sight words that Keith taught her, and Keith is given a test on the arithmetic concepts that Lucy taught him. Their grades are averaged and each receives the mean grade for the pair as the individual's grade. As the mildly handicapped student makes crucial contributions to the group, nonhandicapped peers have direct, structured, personal, and experiential opportunities to learn that although the mildly handicapped student has severe academic problems, the mildly handicapped student is not necessarily lower in intelligence, importance, personality, or human worth. In other words, given the right situation, we all are capable of making valuable contributions and learning from each other. Thus the teacher's challenge is how to structure cooperative learning situations to bring out the best in all students.

Schniedewind and Salend (1987) identified peer teaching, group projects, the "jigsaw" and the combination "jigsaw-counterpart" group as the basic formats for cooperatively-structured learning. In the example given above, Lucy and Keith performed peer teaching by instructing each other in their areas of competence. Group projects are often more ambiguously structured and the tasks less discrete. Students are asked to combine their knowledge and skill to develop a project or complete an assignment. This format makes maximum demands on student ability to analyze task requirements and assign responsibilities. If more structure is needed, Schniedewind and Salend recommend using the "jigsaw" format. This design assigns specific tasks to individual group members. All groups in class may work on the same project, with each having members assigned the same distinct task. For example, one member in each group is assigned task "A," another member task "B," and so on. The combination "jigsaw-counterpart" takes this one step further by having all students in class with the same assignment work with each other as well as with their original group. Counterparts work together to improve their skill, knowledge, or product. In some situations, they continue instructing and offering assistance to one another until a predetermined criterion is met. Counterpart participation usually improves contributions to the original group and helps instill confidence.

Expectancy theory (Hackman & Oldham, 1982) suggests that cooperative learning will yield success when students have the competence to perform whatever aspects of a group's work they are assigned, to believe in their ability to succeed at given tasks, to realize that they are in a productive interdependent relationship, and to value the outcomes or rewards associated with success. It is likely to work even better when students have a predilection for the topic and activities and are given adequate time and guidance. When group members realize that a mildly handicapped student has the prerequisite knowledge and skill to make positive contributions to the group, they may, for the first time, view the mildly handicapped student as a resource rather than a liability. Involvement in situations in which success depends on the mildly handicapped student's strengths, rather than his weaknesses, have the potential to increase achievement and peer acceptance, which, in turn, may enhance self-esteem.

Guidelines for Implementation: Conceptually, cooperative learning is relatively easy to understand. Individuals with a common goal form a group to achieve their goal, which can be accomplished only by working together. Tasks and responsibilities are identified and assigned by the teacher or by the students themselves.

Each student is dependent upon other group members for success. Individual grades are assigned on the basis of group achievement, product, and cooperative effort. Grades take into account the quality of team efforts at working together, as well as academic accomplishment.

Initially, implementing cooperative learning is often more complex than anticipated. With practice over time, and teacher analysis of what contributed to previous successful experiences, and an understanding of what still must be improved, cooperative learning becomes easier and easier for teachers to manage. The key is to start small with relatively easy tasks and gradually expand the program's scope as teacher and student facility with cooperative learning strategies increases. Adherence to the following guidelines should facilitate successful implementation.

1. Choose both academic and social learning objectives appropriate for the grade and skill levels of the group. Assignments and responsibilities for students of various achievement levels, experiential backgrounds, and predilections should be designed for success.

2. Explain assignment objectives and procedures clearly, explicitly, and completely. Ask group members to paraphrase what they are supposed to do and why. Use roleplaying and practice assignments to prevent misunderstandings.

3. Emphasize the importance of specific social-cooperative skills in attaining success. Explain to students which of these skills will be observed and the reasons for doing so. Discuss these before initiating academic activities. Make sure students can articulate the reasons for stressing these skills and working together.

4. Have students initially work on highly discrete tasks in groups of two or three. As they become more comfortable and skilled in group work, progressively less-distinct tasks may be assigned, giving students a greater role to play in defining tasks for themselves and in determining "who does what." Similarly, group size may gradually be increased, commensurate with student ability to handle larger groups. Groups of more than five should be avoided, since larger groups offer fewer opportunities for participation. When increasing the group size, do not simultaneously diminish the specificity of individual assignments or roles. Initially assign mildly handicapped students to groups with students most likely to be sensitive to the feelings of others.

5. Plan for group diversity. The greater the variety of skill, knowledge, and opinion, the greater the potential for interesting and creative groups. Discussion of how particular differences are strengths fosters an appreciation for differences. Providing positive feedback, on visible individual and group behavior that demonstrates how student differences helped produce success, promotes respect for individuality.

6. Make sure that each student ultimately has a well-defined role and clearly articulated responsibilities on which he can obtain feedback. Provide regular oral and written feedback to students on academic and group interaction efforts. This can be done by writing individual students, and the group as a whole, letters enumerating which of their actions positively influenced progress. Structure reinforcement (grades) so that group members realize that accomplishment depends on the cooperation of all group members. For example, if everyone in the group gets at least a 'B' on his assignment, then every group member could receive an 'A' for the project. Such linkage encourages members to help each other, if afforded ample opportunities to do so. Regular monitoring helps identify students who continue to experience difficulty. These students should be given individual or small group instruction. If necessary, modify assignments to more accurately reflect student abilities.

7. Monitor group collaborative processes as well as individual academic achievement. Make it clear that you are available to clarify instructions, review procedures, offer suggestions, conduct mini-lessons, and provide feedback on both academic and collaborative matters. If appropriate, review rating forms with students, forms that delineate distinct behaviors you will focus on during observations (for example, listening while others speak, asking clarification questions, soliciting suggestions, integrating different positions). This underscores the importance of these behaviors and encourages their use. Assigning students to particular roles often facilitates group productivity. Roles may include consensus seeker, academic coach, summarizer, and process observer. Before delegating students to roles, be sure they have the knowledge, sensitivity, and desire to handle the assignment. This may require coaching, roleplaying, and supervised practice. Reinforce students for new cooperative behaviors by giving verbal reinforcement that indicates which behaviors were beneficial and why.

8. Pay particular attention to the physical arrangement and sound level of the classroom. A circle usually works best for individual groups (Johnson & Johnson, 1986). Circles require members to face each other and establish eye contact. This promotes dialogue and cooperation. Provide members with safe places to keep their work. Although talk should be encouraged, extraneous noise should be kept to a minimum. It is often helpful to discuss this in advance and to assign one member of each group the task of monitoring the group's sound level.

9. Use materials and assignments that promote interdependence while respecting differences in student abilities. For example, if there are four students per group and four riddles to figure out to solve a mystery, "jigsaw" the assignment by giving each group member a different riddle. Students with lower reading

abilities could be given riddle sheet "A," written at a fourth grade readability level, and higher-functioning students could be assigned riddle sheets that make greater demands on their reading abilities. Thus, the teacher needs to prepare only four different riddle sheets for an entire class. Separate assignments, designed to help students achieve a shared goal, allow for differentiation according to ability levels while avoiding embarrassment. In another situation, two students per group may jointly write a script for the remaining three group members to perform.

10. Use reinforcement procedures that promote intergroup cooperation to prevent groups from becoming isolated, competitive entities. The teacher may say: "We'll begin videotaping the play after each group gets 80 points."

11. Before beginning the autonomous-group phase of a cooperative learning assignment, provide whatever critical information or instruction students need to be successful. Instruction on how to use a thesaurus, for example, may be necessary. Remember that a primary purpose of cooperative learning is to maximize individual student learning.

12. Periodically hold plenary class discussions in which students describe group or individual actions that fostered or hindered cooperation. Be careful to establish ground rules that preclude blaming. These might include: "Discuss specific behaviors, not personalities. . . . Before suggesting behaviors which possibly need improvement, first indicate what you liked about the student's cooperative efforts. . . . Before speaking, ask yourself if what you want to say is likely to improve the situation. . . . Avoid using names or identifying people who exhibited behaviors you thought needed improvement. . . . Speak in terms of improvement rather than 'blame' or 'fault.' " A common mistake is not allowing sufficient time for these mutual feedback sessions.

Conclusion: Mildly handicapped students need every opportunity possible to succeed in mainstreamed environments. Given the innumerable responsibilities of regular classroom teachers, the presence of mildly handicapped students often complicates their jobs and makes teaching difficult. Cooperative learning strategies offer one potentially productive and satisfying way to help individualize instruction, foster social responsibility, teach group skills, and promote interpersonal sensitivity within heterogeneous classes by using an organized framework that can enhance teacher effectiveness and student creativity. Careful planning and step-by-step implementation offer the promise of making cooperative learning strategies a valuable resource for both teachers and students.

REFERENCES

Cohen, E. G. (1972). *Designing Groupwork: Strategies for the Heterogeneous Classroom.* New York: Teachers College Press.

Hackman, J. R. and Oldman, G. R. (1982). "Motivation Through the Design of Work." In D. A. Nadler, M. L. Tushman, and N. G. Hatvany, (Eds.), *Managing Organizations: Reading and Cases* (pp. 158–172). Boston: Little Brown.

Johnson, D. W. and Johnson, R. T. (1986). "Mainstreaming and Cooperative Learning Strategies." *Exceptional Children, 52,* 553–561.

Kavanagh, E. (1977). "A Classroom Teacher Looks at Mainstreaming." *The Elementary School Journal, 77,* 318–322.

Knoff, H. M. (1985). "Attitudes Toward Mainstreaming: A Status Report and Comparison of Regular and Special Educators in New York and Massachusetts." *Psychology in the Schools, 22,* 410–418.

Madden, N. A. and Slavin, R. E. (1983). "Mainstreaming Students with Mild Handicaps: Academic and Social Outcomes." *Review of Educational Research, 53,* 519–569.

Salvia, J. and Munson, S. (1985). "Attitudes of Teachers in Regular Education Toward Mainstreaming Mildly Handicapped Students." In C. J. Meisel (Eds.), *Mainstreaming Handicapped Children: Outcomes, Controversies, and New Directions* (pp. 111–128). Hillsdale, NJ: Lawrence Erlbaum.

Schniedewind, N. and Salend, S. J. (1987). "Cooperative Learning Works." *Teaching Exceptional Children, 19*(2), 22–25.

Synthesis of Research on Gifted Youth

The research on identifying and educating gifted youth supports the use of multiple identification measures, accelerated instruction, and ability grouping.

JOHN F. FELDHUSEN

John F. Feldhusen is Director, Gifted Education Resource Institute, Purdue University, South Campus Courts–G, West Lafayette, IN 47907.

What is giftedness? What is talent? What should schools and parents do for gifted and talented youth? What are desirable short-term and long-range goals for their development? While definitive answers to these questions are not yet available to guide us, research and evaluation projects during the past 20 years have given us some insights about how to structure and conduct educational services for gifted and talented students.[1]

Conceptions of Giftedness

Educators often view giftedness as something calling for a label (Guskin et al. 1986). The most troubling report on conceptions of gifted and talented youth was presented by Richert, Alvino, and McDonnel in 1982. They conducted a national survey of school personnel and concluded that there is "a labyrinth of confusion" (p. 89) about what giftedness is.

Sternberg and Davidson (1986) made a major contribution to theory in their excellent compilation, *Conceptions of Giftedness*, which presents the views of 29 researchers. This work offers the clearest delineation of what is known and what remains unknown about giftedness and presents the conclusion that giftedness is often seen as cognitive processing capacity, following models of information processing.

Gagne (1985) presented one of the first major attempts to delineate talent as distinct from giftedness. He suggested that talent is an ability focus that emerges out of general ability. He proposed four domains of general ability or giftedness: intellectual, creative, socio-emotional, and sensori-motor. In individuals, these abilities develop differentially; they interact with environmental circumstances and personality factors in the child and emerge as talent in specific fields, such as leadership, art, natural science, dance, or photography. Schooling is essential in the development of specific talents from general giftedness.

Major determiners of school-based conceptions of giftedness are Renzulli (1986) and Stanley and Benbow (1986). Renzulli's three-ring concept of giftedness was first presented in 1978 and has been elaborated and updated in a chapter in *Conceptions of Giftedness* (Sternberg and Davidson 1986). This model proposes three interlocking sets of traits: above-average abilities, creative capacities, and task commitment. Renzulli stressed that it is more productive to focus on gifted behaviors than to attempt to determine whether or not children are gifted. He also emphasized the idea that giftedness is a set of traits that can grow with nurturance, not just a condition bestowed on some and denied to others. Major support for the three-ring model has been presented by Monks and colleagues (1985) from research conducted in Europe. Monks extended the three-ring concept to include the social context in which giftedness manifests itself (family, school, and peers).

Identification

Educators must, of course, identify gifted students before they can provide special enrichment and accelerated services. Many states make identification a prerequisite for receiving special funding for the gifted. Moreover, good identification procedures yield information about students that can guide program development.

Nevertheless, identification of signs of giftedness, of potential for high-quality creative achievement, remains a relatively inexact science. There is great variation in the procedures used to detect giftedness. Many practitioners search for the gifted *child*, not for *signs* of giftedness, of potential. They typically pay little attention to diagnosing children's particular strengths or talents. Most researchers and theorists agree that multiple measures should be used in identifying the gifted, but multiple data sources are rarely used to specify alternate types of giftedness or to specify appropriate program services. Often multiple scores are simply added up to identify the "all purpose" gifted child.

Interpreting the results of their national survey, Richert, Alvino, and McDonnel (1982) concluded that the "state of the art of identification of gifted and talented youth is in some disarray" (p. 39). They found that a wide variety of test instruments, many of them lacking any standardization, are used to identify gifted students, and are often used quite inappropriately.

Yarborough and Johnson (1983) surveyed the 50 state departments of education concerning identification of the gifted. They found that standardized achievement tests and tests of intelligence are widely used, in spite of prevailing pessimism that either form of testing really reflects giftedness.

More recently, Klausmeier, Mishra, and Maker (1987) surveyed school psychologists in the United States concerning their views and practices in identifying the gifted. Their first choices of tests were the Wechsler Scales and the Stanford-Binet. Very few used creativity tests or achievement tests. The school psychologists surveyed also viewed themselves as poorly trained for identification of the gifted.

The work of Stanley and colleagues on the identification and nurturance of mathematically and verbally talented youth has been presented in dozens of articles and a number of books. For example, in *Mathematical Talent, Discovery, Description, and Development* (1974), Stanley, Keating, and Fox presented a series of papers by themselves and others. In *The Gifted and Creative, A Fifty-Year Perspective*, Stanley, George, and Solano (1977) presented new research; and Stanley set forth the rationale for his Study of Mathematically Precocious Youth (SMPY) and its use of the Scholastic Aptitude Test (SAT) as a primary identification tool. Later research presented by Benbow and Stanley in *Academic Precocity, Aspects of Its Development* (1983) confirmed the value of the SAT as an identification tool and the efficacy of high-level, fast-paced instruction for the gifted. Van Tassel-Baska (1984) has presented a more specific rationale for use of the SAT and talent searches to identify gifted children.

Feldhusen, Baska, and Womble (1981) discussed problems in the way test scores are combined in identification systems, and Feldhusen, Asher, and Hoover (1984) reviewed the many technical problems that can arise in the identification process. Hoover and Feldhusen (1987) presented a comprehensive model for the identification of the gifted at the secondary level.

Despite this catalog of research, serious problems remain in identifying giftedness, especially in finding talent among children from poverty and minority backgrounds (Baldwin 1987, McKenzie 1986, Chambers et al. 1980), among very young children (Hollinger and Kosek 1985), and among those who are underachievers in school (Butler-Por 1987). Some promise has been shown in the SOI (Structure Of Intellect) tests and research by Meeker and colleagues (1985), which focus on the assessment of several factors of intelligence; but Clarizio and Mehrens (1985) have criticized the SOI tests as lacking adequate norms and having questionable reliability and validity. Heller and Haeny (1985) at the University of Munich are conducting a major research project on identification of the gifted, funded by the Federal Republic of Germany.

Acceleration

Acceleration means different things to its proponents and its opponents. To proponents it means providing instruction at a level and pace appropriate to the child's level of achievement or readiness. In a series of experiments,[2] my colleagues and I showed that if an effort is made to assess children's readiness level for learning a new task, and if a new task is then taught at that proper level, children will retain the new learning in both short- and long-term memory; and they will transfer the new learning to other related learning tasks. A host of other studies reviewed by Daurio (1979) confirmed the short- and long-term values of all forms of acceleration, ranging from early admission to school to early admission to college, and the absence of problems resulting from acceleration in the lives of accelerated youth.

From the point of view of proponents, *acceleration* is a misnomer; the process is really one of bringing gifted and talented youth up to a suitable level of instruction commensurate with their achievement levels and readiness so that they are properly challenged to learn the new material. Proponents of acceleration also argue that gifted children spend much time in school encountering new material at far too slow a pace or being instructed in things they already know. They argue that an excess of such experience demotivates the gifted and talented, and is at the heart of the widespread problem of underachievement among the gifted (Whitmore 1980).

Opponents of acceleration view it as rushing children through the curriculum without concern for their social and emotional development. Although Kulik and Kulik (1984) showed in their analysis of the research that acceleration does not cause social-emotional problems, critics—especially school personnel—fear that gifted and talented youth will suffer from social immaturity in an accelerated setting and hence experience emotional difficulty. However, a recent review of the social-emotional adjustment and maturity of gifted and talented youth by Janos and Robinson (1985b) concluded that:

• Gifted and talented youth are often precocious or advanced in their social adjustment; as a result, they often prefer older playmates.

• They are socially and emotionally well adjusted.

• Extremely gifted children have more social and emotional adjustment problems than those who are moderately gifted.

Major changes in educators' views of acceleration of the gifted and talented came from the work of Stanley at Johns Hopkins University in the Study of Mathematically Precocious Youth and the later Study of Verbally Precocious Youth.[3] This research clearly established the value of accelerated instruction for gifted youth, the validity of using the Scholastic Aptitude Test as an identification tool for gifted youth at the middle school level, and the effectiveness of a diagnostic/prescriptive teaching methodology to test gifted youth in the classroom and place them at appropriate levels of readiness. Brody and Benbow (1987) reviewed the research from the acceleration projects at Johns Hopkins University and concluded:

This study investigated the relationships between acceleration and academic achievement, extra-curricular activities, goals and aspirations, and social and emotional adjustment for highly able students who have selected accelerative options to varying degrees. This study did not reveal any harmful effects as a result of acceleration (p. 109).

On the contrary, they reported that accelerated students earned more state and national awards than non-accelerated students and more attended highly selective colleges. Brody and Benbow (1987) stress that accelerated students gain in being able to select challenging learning experiences in their special interests.

Several researchers have reviewed studies of early admission to school and grade advancement of precocious children.[4] They agree on the positive value of such acceleration for children of high achievement and ability and the relative absence of personal or social problems, if the advancement is made after careful examination of the individual circumstances. These researchers presented guidelines to help school personnel make decisions regarding candidates for early admission or grade advancement.

Several researchers have reported on studies in which middle school and high school students received advanced high school or college level courses while still enrolled as secondary students (Benbow and Stanley 1983), and additional research is reported on the effects of College Board Advanced Placement (AP) Courses on high school students (Willingham and Morris 1986). Compared to students of equal ability who did not take AP courses, students who did so in high school had better academic records in college, graduated from college with more honors, engaged in more leadership activities, and took more advanced courses in college. Benbow and Stanley (1983) reported on an eight-year follow-up of students who took accelerated classes in high school. They concluded:

Findings from the eight-year follow-up of the participants in SMPY's first fast-paced precalculus classes and equally able nonparticipants revealed that the most successful students in the mathematics classes achieved much more in high school and college than the equally able students who had not participated. The students were satisfied with their acceleration, which they felt did not detract from their social and emotional development. Furthermore, there appeared to be no evidence to justify the fear that accelerated rate of learning produces either gaps in knowledge or poor retention (p. 208).

Several researchers have also conducted studies of the progress and success of students who enter college early.[5] Compared to unaccelerated peers matched for ability, accelerated students earned higher GPAs, earned

more honors, associated with older and more intellectual students, were more satisfied with the academic climate, and were equal in psychosocial adjustment to unaccelerated peers. Clearly, students who are ready for the college experience thrive on the opportunity to enter college early.

Kulik and Kulik (1983, 1984) have done major syntheses of the research on acceleration of the gifted. They concluded that accelerated students perform as well academically as equally able students who are already in the advanced grade(s), and accelerated students show a year's advancement over nonaccelerants of the same age. Long-range performance indicators produced less clear findings but suggested that accelerants earned more advanced degrees, earned top salaries, and were viewed favorably by superiors. The Kuliks (1984) concluded that:

Together experimental and correlational studies provide strong evidence that acceleration leads to greater student achievement in school and in life for talented students (p. 89).

Given the evidence of superior achievement in school and in performance beyond school and an absence of evidence suggesting social-emotional problems due to acceleration, my colleagues and I conclude that, to provide for the gifted, we must upgrade the level and pace of instruction to fit their abilities, achievement levels, and interests. Further, for gifted youngsters, the only suitable enrichment—defined as extended learning beyond the regular curriculum—is instruction on special enriching topics at a high level and a fast pace.

Grouping

Providing special services for the gifted and talented almost inevitably requires some special grouping. Grouping the gifted for all or part of the school day accommodates achievement and readiness levels and can serve other purposes as well. Gifted and talented children complain a great deal about the boredom of their classroom experiences (Feldhusen and Kroll 1985); they are forced to spend a lot of time being taught things they already know, doing repetitive drill

sheets and activities, and receiving instruction on new material at too slow a pace. These experiences probably cause gifted youth to lose motivation to learn, to get by with minimum effort, or to reject school as a worthwhile experience.

Grouping gifted and talented youth for all or part of the school day or week also serves as a stimulus or motivator. Interaction with other students who are enthusiastic about astronomy, robotics, Shakespeare, or algebra motivates gifted and talented students. DeLisle reports (1984) that gifted children must often hide or suppress their special interests or their enthusiasms for academic topics or else face ridicule; peer pressure prohibits excitement about academics in many schools. In special classes for the gifted and talented, the reverse is true: mutual reinforcement of enthusiasm for academic interests and activities prevails.

For gifted and talented youth, grouping also confirms the legitimacy of their personal identity. Some of them worry about being viewed as outcasts because of their scholarly or bookish natures. Through interaction with other gifted or talented youth in special programs, however, they discover others who are like themselves and learn that it is legitimate to have strong intellectual interests and enthusiasm for reading and study. Thus, the sense of being abnormal is alleviated, and a new, positive self-image can emerge.

The Kuliks reported two meta-analytic evaluations of the research literature on ability grouping (1982, 1987). They found (1982) the average effect size for educational achievement to be small but significant, favoring grouped classes. However, when high-ability youth were grouped in special classes *and* given enriched or accelerated instruction, effect sizes were large. Grouped high-ability students also developed more favorable attitudes toward the subject matter than did high-ability students in ungrouped classes. And achievement of low- and average-ability students did not decline when high-ability students were removed to the special classes.

In a more recent meta-analytic study of the research on grouping, the Kuliks (1987) included a wider variety of studies. They concluded that the strongest and clearest effects of grouping came from programs designed especially for talented students. The talented students in these programs gained more academically than they would have in heterogeneous classes (p. 28). Special within-class grouping designed for talented students raised academic achievement substantially. The Kuliks (1987) concluded that "grouping can be a powerful tool in the education of gifted and talented students" (p. 29).

A frequent complaint from regular classroom teachers is that any special grouping of the gifted that removes them from the regular classroom will deprive children of low and average ability of role models to motivate them to higher achievement. Conversely, some teachers have reported positive effects when the gifted leave; they no longer dominate the classroom, and children of low and average ability get a chance to be leaders or top performers. Nevertheless, the idea that the gifted are needed to inspire other students is ubiquitous.

In a comprehensive review of the literature on peer role models in the classroom, Shunk (1987) concluded that the more alike observers and models are, the greater the probablity that the model affects observer behavior. In other words, watching someone of *similar ability* succeed at a task raises the observers' feelings of efficacy and motivates them to try the task: hence the superiority of "coping" role models over "mastery" role models. Coping models gradually improve their performance after some effort, and are thus effective models for peers who will also have to struggle to achieve academically. Mastery models (often the gifted), on the other hand, demonstrate perfect performance from the outset.

Overall, my colleagues and I conclude that grouping of gifted and talented students in special classes with a differentiated curriculum, or as a cluster group in a regular heterogeneous classroom (but again with differentiated curriculum and instruction), leads to higher academic achievement and better academic attitudes for the gifted and leads to no decline in achievement or attitudes for the children who remain in the regular heterogeneous classroom.

Meeting the Needs of the Gifted

Gifted and talented youth need accelerated, challenging instruction in core subject areas that parallel their special talents or aptitudes. They need opportunities to work with other gifted and talented youth. And they need highly competent teachers who both understand the nature and needs of gifted youth and are deeply knowledgeable in the content they teach.

If we fail to meet the needs of gifted students, we are harming not only those children but all of society, which benefits from their contributions. We must enable all students to realize their potential, including the gifted.

---

1. The research and evaluation evidence has been reported mainly in articles in the *Roeper Review*, the *Journal for the Education of the Gifted*, and the *Gifted Child Quarterly*, while evaluation and development projects have been reported in *Gifted Child Today*, *Gifted International*, and *Gifted Education International*. A number of books and technical reports have also documented the findings of researchers, developers, and evaluators.

2. Feldhusen and Klausmeier 1959; Klausmeier and Feldhusen 1959; Klausmeier, Check, and Feldhusen 1960; and Feldhusen, Check, and Klausmeier 1961.

3. Stanley 1978; Stanley 1980; Stanley, Keating, and Fox 1974; Stanley, George, and Solano 1977; Stanley and Benbow 1982; Benbow and Stanley 1983; Stanley and McGill 1986.

4. Feldhusen, Proctor, and Black 1986; Proctor, Black, and Feldhusen 1986; Proctor, Feldhusen, and Black 1988.

5. Janos and Robinson 1985a, Janos 1987, Janos et al. 1988.

References

Baldwin, A.Y. (1987). "I'm Black, but Look at Me, I Am Also Gifted." *Gifted Child Quarterly* 31, 4: 180-185.

Benbow, C.P., and J.C. Stanley. (1983). "An Eight-Year Evaluation of SMPY: What Was Learned?" In *Academic Precocity, Aspects of Its Development*, edited by C.P. Benbow and J.C. Stanley. Baltimore: Johns Hopkins University Press, 205-214.

Brody, L.E., and C.P. Benbow. (1987). "Accelerative Strategies: How Effective Are They for the Gifted?" *Gifted Child Quarterly* 31: 105-109.

Butler-Por, N. (1987). "*Underachievers in School*. New York: John Wiley and Sons.

Chambers, J.A., F. Barron, and J.W. Sprecher. (1980). "Identifying Gifted Mexican-American Students." *Gifted Child Quarterly* 24, 3: 123-128.

Clarizio, H.F., and W.A. Mehrens. (1985). "Psychometric Limitations of Guilford's Structure-of-Intellect Model for Identification and Programming of the Gifted." *Gifted Child Quarterly* 29, 3: 113-120.

Daurio, S.P. (1979). "Educational Enrichment Versus Acceleration: A Review of the Literature." In *Educating the Gifted, Acceleration and Enrichment*, edited by W.C. George, S.J. Cohn, and J.C. Stanley. Baltimore: Johns Hopkins University Press, 13-63.

DeLisle, J.R. (1984). *Gifted Children Speak Out*. New York: Walker Company.

Feldhusen, J.F., J.W. Asher, and S.M. Hoover. (1984). "Problems in the Identification of Giftedness, Talent, or Ability." *Gifted Child Quarterly* 28: 149-156.

Feldhusen, J.F., L.K. Baska, and S.R. Womble. (1981). "Using Standard Scores to Synthesize Data in Identifying the Gifted." *Journal for the Education of the Gifted* 4: 177-185.

Feldhusen, J.F., J. Check, and H.J. Klausmeier. (1961). "Achievement in Subtraction." *The Elementary School Journal* 61: 322-327.

Feldhusen, J.F., and H.J. Klausmeier. (1959). "Achievement in Counting and Addition." *The Elementary School Journal* 59: 388-393.

Feldhusen, J.F., and M.D. Kroll. (1985). "Parent Perceptions of Gifted Children's Educational Needs." *Roeper Review* 1: 240-252.

Feldhusen, J.F., T.B. Proctor, and K.N. Black. (1986). "Guidelines for Grade Advancement of Precocious Children." *Roeper Review* 9, 1: 25-27.

Gagne, F. (1985). "Giftedness and Talent." *Gifted Child Quarterly* 29: 103-112.

Guskin, S.L., C. Okolo, E. Zimmerman, and C.Y.J. Ping. (1986). "Being Labelled Gifted or Talented: Meanings and Effects Perceived by Students in Special Programs." *Gifted Child Quarterly* 30: 61-65.

Heller, K.A., and E.A. Haeny. (1985). "Identification, Development, and Analysis of Talented Children." In *Identifying and Nurturing the Gifted*, edited by K.A. Heller and J.F. Feldhusen. Toronto: Hans Huber, 67-82.

Hollinger, C.L., and S. Kosek. (1985). "Early Identification of the Gifted and Talented." *Gifted Child Quarterly* 29, 4: 168-171.

Hoover, S.M., and J.F. Feldhusen. (1987). "Integrating Identification, School Services, and Student Needs in Secondary Gifted Programs." *Arkansas Gifted Educators' Magazine* 1: 8-16.

Janos, P.M. (1987). "A Fifty-Year Follow-Up of Terman's Youngest College Students and IQ-Matched Agemates." *Gifted Child Quarterly* 31, 2: 55-58.

Janos, P.M., and N.M. Robinson. (1985a). "The Performance of Students in a Program of Radical Acceleration at the University Level." *Gifted Child Quarterly* 29, 4: 175-179.

Janos, P.M., and N.M. Robinson. (1985b). "Psychosocial Development in Intellectually Gifted Children." In *The Gifted and Talented, Developmental Perspectives*, edited by F.D. Horowitz and M. O'Brien. Washington, D.C.: American Psychological Association, 149-195.

Janos, P.M., N.M. Robinson, C. Carter, A. Chapel, R. Cufley, M. Curland, M. Daily, M. Guilland, M. Heinzig, H. Kehl, S. Lu, D. Sherry, S. Stotoff, and A. Wise. (1988). "A Cross-Sectional Developmental Study of the Social Relations of Students Who Enter College Early." *Gifted Child Quarterly* 32, 1: 210-215.

Klausmeier, H.J., J.F. Check, and J.F. Feldhusen. (1960). "Relationships Among Physical, Mental, Achievement, and Personality Measures in Children of Low, Average, and High Intelligence at 125 Months of Age." *American Journal of Mental Deficiency* 65: 69-78.

Klausmeier, H.J., and J.F. Feldhusen. (1959). "Retention in Arithmetic Among Children of Low, Average, and High Intelligence at 117 Months of Age." *Journal of Educational Psychology* 50, 88-92.

Klausmeier, K., S.P. Mishra, and C.J. Maker. (1987). "Identification of Gifted Learners: A National Survey of Assessment Practices and Training Needs of School Psychologists." *Gifted Child Quarterly* 31, 3: 135-137.

Kulik, C.C., and J.A. Kulik. (1982). "Effects of Ability Grouping on Secondary School Students: A Meta-Analysis of Evaluation Findings." *American Educational Research Journal* 19, 3: 415-428.

Kulik, J.A., and C.C. Kulik. (1983). "Effects of Accelerated Instruction on Students." *Review of Educational Research* 54: 409-425.

Kulik, J.A., and C.C. Kulik. (October 1984). "Synthesis of Research on Effects of Accelerated Instruction." *Educational Leadership* 42, 2: 84-89.

Kulik, J.A., and C.C. Kulik. (1987). "Effects of Ability Grouping on Student Achievement." *Equity and Excellence* 23, 1-2: 22-30.

McKenzie, J.A. (1986). "The Influence of Identification Practices, Race, and SES on the Identification of Gifted Students." *Gifted Child Quarterly* 30, 2: 93-95.

Meeker, M., R. Meeker, and G. Roid. (1985). *Structure-of-Intellect Learning Abilities Test (SOI-LA)*. Los Angeles: Western Psychological Services.

Monks, F.J., H.W. VanBoxtel, J.J.W. Roelofs, and M.P.M. Sanders. (1985). "The Identification of Gifted Children in Secondary Education." In *Identifying and Nurturing the Gifted*, edited by K.A. Heller and J.F. Feldhusen. Toronto: Hans Huber Publishers, 39-65.

Highlights of Research on Gifted Youth

The voluminous research on gifted and talented students provides educators with guidelines for serving this special population.

Identification. Schools are often ineffective in identifying gifted students, especially in finding talent among children from poverty and minority backgrounds, among very young children, and among underachievers. Identification is most often based on intelligence tests; use of creativity tests or achievement tests is rare. Multiple data sources should be used to identify alternate types of giftedness and to specify appropriate program services.

Acceleration. Acceleration motivates gifted students by providing them with instruction that challenges them to realize their potential. Accelerated students show superior achievement in school and beyond. Despite the fears of some educators, acceleration does not damage the social-emotional adjustment of gifted youth.

Grouping. Grouping gifted and talented youth for all or part of the school day or week serves as a motivator. In special classes or cluster groups for the gifted, mutual reinforcement of enthusiasm for academic interests prevails. Removing gifted students from regular classrooms does not deprive other students of role models; instead, it allows them to be leaders and top performers.

Overall, to provide for the gifted, we must upgrade the level and pace of instruction to fit their abilities, achievement levels, and interests. The only suitable enrichment is instruction on special enriching topics at a high level and a fast pace. We must also provide them with highly competent teachers and with opportunities to work with other gifted and talented youth.

Proctor, T.B., K.N. Black, and J.F. Feldhusen. (1986). "Early Admission of Selected Children to Elementary School: A Review of the Literature." *Journal of Educational Research* 80, 2: 70-76.

Proctor, T.B., J.F. Feldhusen, and K.N. Black. (1988). "Guidelines for Early Admission to Elementary School." *Psychology in the Schools* 25: 41-43.

Renzulli, J.S. (1986). "The Three-Ring Conception of Giftedness: A Developmental Model for Creative Productivity." In *Conceptions of Giftedness*, edited by R.J. Sternberg and J.E. Davidson. New York: Cambridge University Press, 53-92.

Richert, E.S., J.J. Alvino, and R.C. McDonnel. (1982). *National Report on Identification: Assessment and Recommendations for Comprehensive Identification of Gifted and Talented Youth*. Sewell, N.J.: Educational Improvement Center–South.

Shunk, D.H. (1987). "Peer Models and Children's Behavioral Change." *Review of Educational Research* 52, 2: 149-174.

Stanley, J.C. (1978). "SMPY's DT-PI Model: Diagnostic Testing Followed by Prescriptive Instruction." *ITYB* 4, 10: 7-8.

Stanley, J.C. (1980). "On Educating the Gifted." *Educational Research* 9, 3: 8-12.

Stanley, J.C., and C.P. Benbow (1982). "Educating Mathematically Precocious Youth: Twelve Policy Recommendations." *Educational Researcher* 11, 5: 4-9.

Stanley, J.C., and C.P. Benbow (1986). "Youths Who Reason Exceptionally Well Mathematically." In *Conceptions of Giftedness*, edited by R.J. Sternberg and J.E. Davidson. New York: Cambridge University Press, 361-387.

Stanley, J.C., W.C. George, and C.H. Solano. (1977). *The Gifted and Creative: A Fifty-Year Perspective*. Baltimore: Johns Hopkins University Press.

Stanley, J.C., D.P. Keating, and L.H. Fox. (1974). *Mathematical Talent: Discovery, Description, and Development*. Baltimore: Johns Hopkins University Press.

Stanley, J.C., and A.M. McGill. (1986). "More About Young Entrants to College, How Did They Fare?" *Gifted Child Quarterly* 30, 2: 70-73.

Sternberg, R., and J. Davidson, eds. (1986). *Conceptions of Giftedness*. New York: Cambridge University Press.

VanTassel-Baska, J. (1984). "The Talent Search as an Identification Model." *Gifted Child Quarterly* 28, 4: 172-176.

Whitmore, J.R. (1980). *Giftedness, Conflict, and Underachievement*. Boston: Allyn Bacon.

Willingham, W.W., and M. Morris. (1986). "Four Years Later: A Longitudinal Study of Advanced Placement Students in College." *College Board Reports No. 86-2*. New York: College Entrance Examination Board.

Yarborough, B.H., and R.A. Johnson. (1983). "Identifying the Gifted: A Theory-Practice Gap." *Gifted Child Quarterly* 27, 3: 135-138.

SUCCESS STRATEGIES

for Learners Who Are Learning Disabled as Well as Gifted

Christine Brown-Mizuno

Christine Brown-Mizuno *(CEC Chapter #188) is a Learning Handicapped Specialist, Sowers Middle School, Huntington Beach, and a Teacher, Coastline Community College, Fountain Valley, California.*

Robert W., a seventh-grader who is gifted, sits as if riveted to his desk. He never looks up at his classmates or even at the chalkboard to get the week's homework or lesson explanation. Instead, he ceaselessly sketches on any paper available—pictures of fallen angels with anatomical parts falling from their sides, pictures of war and destruction of people, aircrafts, angels. When told to pay attention and stop what he is doing, he does for a while, only to drift back and continue his compulsive distraction. Whatever **the etiology of his behavior, [he] is not attending to task and he is falling behind his classmates academically.**

Another student, William S., bursts into the learning handicapped/special day class classroom just as the class is pledging allegiance to the flag. He pulls out a mock machine gun and "shoots" the flag, making loud, shooting noises. His teacher tells him to sit down, asks for the toy gun, and then places a piece of paper on his desk. "Draw what you are feeling," she tells him. He draws a person shooting another person with a bow and arrow.

Their emotional overlay has prevented these students from achieving the po-tential indicated by their high IQs. They are gifted students with learning disabilities. Rather than performing above grade level, as many of their gifted peers do, they perform 3 to 4 years below grade level. In the broadest definition of the term *learning disability*, a significant discrepancy may exist in the development of their psychological behavior, perception, grasp of relationships, visual-motor integration, attention, or memory as related to their abilities (Kirk & Gallagher, 1979). A behavior disorder may or may not be caused by dysfunctional psychological development. However, as the disorder inhibits the gifted student's academic performance through its contribution to time off task, a lag between ability and achievement can develop.

Robert W., because of his early assessment as gifted, had been in a self-contained classroom for gifted and talented students since first grade. William S. had not been assessed as gifted earlier and had attempted to cope in a regular education setting from first until fourth grade, when he was placed in the learning handicapped/special day class because of his assessment as severely emotionally disturbed. By fourth grade, he was falling behind his other classmates academically and was not even identified as gifted. His self-esteem was suffering, and his emotional instability worsened. By sixth grade, when asked to choose two adjectives that described him, he labeled himself "crazy and bright."

Research has indicated that once a pattern of underachievement has been established it generally continues and becomes worse unless appropriate interventions are initiated. The eventual outcome too frequently is delinquency, dropping out of school, and emotional problems. Studies of fourth graders reveal the same factors as have been found with high school and college underachievers, suggesting that the pattern associated with underachievement is fairly well established by the fourth grade and apparently persists and increases over the years of schooling (Whitmore, 1980).

Common Difficulties

Although not all gifted students who have learning disabilities suffer from inhibited academic performance as well as emotional instability, the portraits of these

Reprinted from *Teaching Exceptional Children*, Vol. 23, No. 1, Fall 1990, pp. 10-12, by permission of The Council for Exceptional Children.

two students suggest underlying issues that need to be examined by educators who serve students who are gifted but lagging behind academically. Many underachievers of primary school age experience intense frustration created by either developmental immaturity or specific disabilities that prevent them from performing at a level comparable to that of average children in their classes. Often the difficulty stems from physical immaturity or perceptual-motor disabilities. Some gifted children are handicapped by a lag in their visual-perceptual development. They have difficulty in recognizing objects and their relationships to one another. Space can be distorted and unstable. When they arrive at school, their distortion and confusion of visual symbols make reading, writing, and arithmetic difficult or impossible in spite of their high intelligence. Their inability to cope with the academic learning situation can lead to emotional disturbance, with repercussions in the home and in their relationships with their peers and teachers (Whitmore, 1980).

Such children are often characterized not only by depressed academic skills but also by personality and behavior disturbances (Senf, 1983). The disruption of their personalities and social behavior does not seem to be a result of their academic learning problems; rather, it is an integral part of the total symptomatology.

As Piers and Harris concluded in their (1964) study of self-concept in children, underachievement and behavior problems of gifted children can be regarded as symptoms expressing conflict between internal needs for acceptance, success, and meaningful learning and the external conditions of the classroom environment. Therefore, underachievement can be viewed as a social product, not just as the problem of the child. This perspective acknowledges personal and social contributions to the problem but suggests that teachers focus on understanding the child's needs and modifying the school experience in order to reduce conflict and increase the achievement motivation of the child (Piers & Harris, 1964).

Issues for Educators

Proper techniques for assessing emotional maladjustment and specific learning disabilities, followed by proper placement in settings in which appropriate, effective strategies are used, and finally advocacy campaigns to maintain existing programs and provide more disability-specific programs are all necessary elements in meeting the needs of gifted learners with learning disabilities.

Assessment

Early assessment is essential. Specific disabilities might include attention deficit disorder with or without hyperactivity; emotional and behavioral disturbances; visual-motor integration difficulties, which affect reading, language, and mathematics performance; and dyscalculia, dysgraphia, or dyslexia, which affect mathematics, written language and reading skills. Testing of gifted students for these possible disabilities should be completed in the early grades by psychologists. Often, however, only IQ tests are administered to these students. Although they are not considered actual learning disabilities, low motivation and lack of a nurturing environment also should be detected early, before low performance manifests itself. By identifying and effectively programming for a low-achieving gifted student in the early grades, it is possible to reverse such a student's negative behavior and lack of accomplishment.

Despite high intelligence, gifted students are often insecure, with low self-confidence and perseverance compared to other students, according to Kirk and Gallagher (1979). Gifted students in general, as well as those with specific learning disabilities, are subject to a high probability of emotional stress and social conflict. High levels of adaptation are required to prevent the discomfort from reaching a degree of intensity that impairs mental health and general functioning (Whitmore, 1980). While some students are able to use their superior intelligence to cope effectively and adapt, a significant minority experience impeding maladjustment. Some of the specific problems unique to gifted learners are perfectionism, feelings of inadequacy, unrealistic goals, supersensitivity, demand for adult attention, and intolerance. Assessment in the early grades should include instruments designed to detect and predict behavior maladjustment based on a rating of these characteristics.

Early Intervention

Most psychologists and educators studying the phenomenon of under-achieving gifted students conclude their reports with recommendations for early identification and treatment (Whitmore, 1980). It is an accepted fact that early intervention to prevent the development of undesirable behavior patterns such as underachievement, social alienation, and emotional disturbance is the most cost-effective and successful approach to the problem (Whitmore, 1980). Prevention at an early age is much easier and more successful than remediation at a later age. In one study, an appreciable number of juvenile delinquents showed a marked disparity between high intellectual capacity and low achievement in British schools (Pringle, cited in Whitmore, 1980). Similarly, as many as one-third of the high school dropouts in the United States have been found to be gifted (Webb & Meckstroth, 1986).

Placement

Once a student is identified as gifted, appropriate placement is necessary if a learning disability or severe interference with learning caused by behavioral and emotional deficits is also present. Unfortunately, programming strategies are not always geared to meet a child's strengths and weaknesses. In California, for example, gifted students are assessed in the early grades and then are placed in classrooms with other gifted students of their age and grade level. In some classrooms a gifted student might be part of a homogeneous cluster of gifted students in a class of students who are not gifted. If a learning disability is present that affects overall performance in a subject area, the student remains with his or her gifted peers and falls farther behind in that academic area. Until the student can remediate learning disabilities or modify expectations in difficult subject areas, he or she will tend to quit altogether or develop a low self-image, which may inhibit learning further.

Instead of a placement in a classroom or cluster of gifted students, flexible programming with time spent in small groups or one-to-one with a teacher trained in special education techniques should be considered. Unfortunately, in California, for example, eligibility criteria discourage the placement of gifted students in special education classrooms. Because gifted students with learning disabilities can be "peak-and-valley" people, for whom the peaks of ability are high and the valleys of performance are low, the task of identifying their strengths and building on them can be easier if flexible, individualized programming is available.

Individualization should be the philosophy that permeates the entire program (Whitmore, 1980). Rather than prescribing the nature of instruction—individual, small group, or whole class—or a methodology and type of curriculum, this philosophy is the basis of an approach in which each child's needs are considered and alternatives are provided that allow the child to select learning activities that are appropriate in level of difficulty, relevance to interests, meaningfulness, and mode of instruction.

In the case of William S., to fulfill his need for enforced daily counseling and avoid further peer rejection, a placement in a private setting with only 4 to 5 students in the classroom and 20 to 25 in the larger playground area was chosen. After a few weeks in his new environment, his special day class teacher phoned him and asked him how he was doing and how his new school was different from the special day class. He replied, "the kids here are like me." Perhaps perceiving himself as not so different and isolated from the rest of the world, William had begun a big step toward self-acceptance and higher self-esteem. Rather than depending on his single parent to provide consistent counseling opportunities, he and his family received counseling within the private school setting.

Intervention Strategies

Strategies for teaching gifted students with learning disabilities should be geared toward the type of disability. Students with emotional and behavioral disorders and their families should receive individual and group counseling services as well as flexible programming or multi-grade-level instruction in a structured setting that modifies behavior through a positive reward system. In such a system, specific behaviors are evaluated frequently and students ultimately review their behavior and award points. Targeted behaviors include time on task, risk taking, following directions, completing assignments, relating to others, and cleaning up. Several studies have indicated that intervention during the elementary years, involving the entire family in group counseling, has had the largest and longest lasting impact (Clark, 1983).

Through this process of self-development, students' self-esteem may be enhanced as they gain a sense of internal control over what they will become. Behavior modification—establishing clear expectations and contingencies, ignoring inappropriate behavior, and rewarding approximations of the behavior desired—can effect some changes in behavior, particularly when students are motivated by the reward of attention. Teachers also must help such students become aware of the need to change, alternatives that are more rewarding, and assistance available to facilitate change (Whitmore, 1980). In addition, students need to identify their strengths in art, music, reading, sports, or other areas. Activities encouraging the development of these strengths are as important as remediating weaknesses, since self-recognition of strengths and its attendant increase in self-esteem can have a positive effect on academic performance.

If disabilities related to visual-motor integration such as dysgraphia or dyslexia are evident, such modifications as word processing or simply typing classwork can help in language arts. Systematic, sequential reading programs based on linguistics and phonics instruction such as the Herman Reading Method are successful in reading. Attention deficit disorder with hyperactivity can be treated successfully with medication as well as by a reward system that recognizes task completion. Biofeedback, visualization, and family management are also effective treatments.

Conclusion

Advocacy for gifted students with learning disabilities can occur only when it is recognized that these special students exist. No longer can their potential be wasted. From the district to the state level, their needs must be addressed continually in educational conferences and publications. Business and industry also need to be informed of what they can lose by not investing in the education of these learners through underwriting programs designed to meet their needs. An appropriate maxim is to find out what is right and encourage it; find out what is wrong and fix it; and find out what works and use it.

References

Clark, B. (1983). *Growing up gifted.* Columbus, OH: Merrill.

Kirk, S. A., & Gallagher, J. J. (1979). *Educating exceptional children.* Boston: Houghton Mifflin.

Piers, E. V., & Harris, D. B. (1964). Age and other correlates of self-concept in children. *Journal of Education Psychology, 55,* 91–95.

Senf, G. M. (1983). *Learning disabled gifted children: Identification and programming.* Austin, TX: Pro-Ed.

Webb, J. T., & Meckstroth, E. J. (1986). *Guiding the gifted child.* Columbus, OH: Psychology Publishing.

Whitmore, J. R. (1980). *Giftedness, conflict and underachievement.* Rockleigh, NJ: Allyn and Bacon.

Identifying and Serving the Gifted New Immigrant

PROBLEMS ◆ STRATEGIES

Carole Ruth Harris

Carole Ruth Harris *(CEC Chapter #695) is formerly Associate, Department of Human Development, Harvard Graduate School of Education, Cambridge, Massachusetts; is now Researcher, Hollingworth Longitudinal Study, Teachers College, Columbia University, New York City.*

The problems of accurately identifying and providing appropriate services are vastly compounded with children of new immigrant families. Linguistic and cultural complications, economic and health factors, attitudinal factors, socio-cultural peer group expectations, cross-cultural stress, and intergenerational conflict frequently deflect the efforts of educators to recognize giftedness and talent in these children and provide for them. The following analysis of the problem areas particular to immigrant populations is accompanied by practical suggestions that offer viable field-based solutions.

Problems

Linguistic

Many current immigrant groups have more difficulty with English than did the former immigrant groups from Europe. Native languages of new immigrants differ vastly from English in pronunciation, grammatical structure, and alphabet. These problems block the acquisition of reading skills and create an emotional barrier. Increased feelings of isolation can intensify frustration and confuse a child who is accustomed to learning with ease (Sheehy, 1986; Wei, 1983).

At home there is often limited or no use of English, and home-school interface is minimal thus limiting language skills further. Consequently, students with limited English proficiency are frequently perceived as not being ready for gifted education, and few are placed in such programs.

Cultural

Major conflict arises from customs that seem strange or are perceived as insulting, rude, or laughable. Sex-role conflicts are particularly apparent (Goffin, 1988; Sheehy, 1986), especially in the area of sports.

Cultural differences in listening behavior (Trueba, 1983) may be perceived negatively by the teacher. Response behavior patterns (Cohen, 1988; Harris, 1988) such as lowering of the eyes when being addressed or passive, seemingly unresponsive staring are frequently misinterpreted as inattentiveness. The gifted child, who already feels different because of giftedness, now has to contend with many other kinds of difference in a new milieu.

Economic and Health Factors

Many new immigrants are below the poverty line, with as many as 80% coming from Third World countries. Some support several households, both here and in the land of origin (National Coalition of Advocates for Students, 1988). In addition, the families may be large. Older students may work after school because of economic need.

One hidden factor is poor health caused by limited access to health care due to lack of knowledge or accessibility. Illegal status may result in neglect of basic prevention, including immunization procedures (Clark, 1988b). There may be some physical and psychological problems caused by torture. According to the report by the National Coalition of Advocates for Students (1988), authorities are aware of this problem, but no data are available.

Educational alternatives and opportunities are perceived as ephemeral by economically impoverished groups. Attempts at providing information on such opportunities for immigrant children with high potential are few, and follow-up is rare.

Attitudinal

The reasons for immigration play an important part in the attitudes of immigrants toward their adopted country.

Reprinted from *Teaching Exceptional Children*, Vol. 23, No. 4, Summer 1991, pp. 26-30, by permission of The Council for Exceptional Children.

The attitude of an immigrant who comes to the United States for economic betterment or as a result of an untenable political situation in the homeland is vastly different from that of a refugee who comes to escape danger.

All immigrants suffer social confusion in that they know neither what to expect from others nor what the expectations of others will be for them. This confusion deepens when fear either present or residual is resent (Sheehy, 1986). Emotional problems, including symptoms of "depression, impaired memory, panic, severe insomnia, periods of disorientation and confusion, reliving of war experiences, separation anxiety, family conflicts, isolation, and suicide" (National Coalition of Advocates for Students, 1988, p. 24), are heightened by guilt over survival when members of the family have been killed and by separation when family members remain in the endangered area. The heightened awareness of gifted children increases vulnerability to these problems.

Fear of authority may be present because a child or a near relative is an illegal immigrant (Gratz & Pulley, 1984; Portes, McCleod, & Parker, 1978; Vasquez, 1988). This mistrust of authority prevents the child from forming close relationships with teachers and results in a syndrome associated with exhaustion of coping behavior (Clark, 1988b), constantly aggravated by a feeling of not belonging.

Misinterpretation of actions or misinformation sometimes has tragic results, as in the case of the Vietnamese father who hung himself after being accused of child abuse when he treated his sick child with the traditional "cupping" technique practiced in the Vietnamese countryside (Wei, 1983). The technique uses suction to break a chest cold and often causes welts on the body. Authorities had no cultural knowledge of the technique or of the disgrace of such an accusation, and they proceeded with their charges without appropriate investigation.

Sociocultural and Peer Expectations

One growing problem in the area of sociocultural and peer expectation is racial conflict. Another is fear for personal safety, which is associated with the formation of youth gangs. New forms of self-hatred appear as a result of internalization of racial prejudice.

Trueba (1988) and Portes and colleagues (1978) have reported that economic, psychological, and political expectations differ among sociocultural groups. Differences in the aspirations of illegal immigrants, refugees, and other groups contribute to conflict.

Sociocultural and peer expectations differ markedly both among linguistic and cultural groups and within the groups. Residual expectations within geographically determined communities can aggravate tensions and conflict sharply with the gifted child's natural curiosity and innate love of challenge.

Cross-Cultural Stress

Problems related to sex roles are a major factor in producing cross-cultural stress (Vasquez, 1988). Confusing signals from two cultures can play havoc with ego development. The locus of control is weakened, and the way to realization of individual potential is essentially barred. Cross-cultural stress is a problem that will continue as long as there are new waves of immigrants. Continuation of the problem should not give rise to acceptance, however, it is time to seek ways of dealing with it.

Intergenerational Conflict

Intergenerational conflict extends from the placing of responsibility on young children who act as interpreters for their families to a shift in cultural values within generations. In the first case, the Americanized children and youth may resent the dependence of the elders, and in the latter, the younger generation is seen as disassociating itself from the old traditions. This double stress results in the development of coping strategies that have a negative effect on both self-concept and family relationships (Harris, 1988). A gifted child who attempts to surmount this problem may increase the conflict.

School System Conflict

One of the most severe problems associated with the identification of gifted students in the new immigrant misplacement in school. The accepted mode is placements are made according to chronological age rather than level of education. Students may have had little or sporadic schooling, possibly even no schooling, prior to coming to the United States. Wei (1983) reported the frequency of the wrong date of birth in school records. This is not always the fault of the school. Placement is difficult when there are no school records. Many children hide facts about years spent in former schools in an attempt to save face (OECDE, 1987; Vuong, 1988), bolster self-image, and gain peer approval. A parent may also hide these facts.

Overcrowded classrooms and schools, opposition of overworked staff to special programs, and the use of standardized tests often combine to preclude entrance to programs for gifted children. According to testimony by Steinberg and Halsted (National Coalition of Advocates for Students, 1988), immigrant children are commonly tracked into English as a Second Language courses and then steered toward vocational education.

Misplacement also occurs when gifted students, culturally different students, and immigrant children are classified only in terms of disabilities (Poplin & Wright, 1983), a problem not confined to immigrants. Some absurdities result from ethnocentric misplacement. In one case, a rigorously trained Japanese 14-year-old in need of calculus was placed with a Laotian 14-year-old who had but 2 years of schooling because they were both Asian (Vuong, 1988). On the other side of the coin, high barrier to proper placement may be erected by parents of immigrant children who mistrust any kind of special education, including classes for gifted and talented students (Wei, 1983).

Sugai and Maheady (1988) reported that a disproportionate number of immigrants are referred for psychological services. Research by Trueba (1988) revealed that teachers tend to identify behaviors in terms of adjustment and/or achievement problems. Field-dependent learning styles (i.e., working better in groups than individually) are open to misunderstanding along with problems arising in cultures that emphasize physical contact as a means of communication. For example, Haitian children who have field-dependent learning styles also use body language in lieu of verbal communication. The expressively gifted Haitian child may be viewed as manifesting behavioral difficulties or even perceived as incapable of concentrated effort.

Strategies

Provision for the new immigrant students who are gifted must include a variety of approaches to identification, service, and evaluation. A flexible framework encompasses a range of cultural differences and provides a combination of techniques that allow giftedness to surface. The strategies described here are practical actions that teachers can take in specific problem areas:

Linguistic

1. Give students with limited English proficiency who are perceived as "not ready" for gifted programs some form of enrichment to sustain them until their language skills show sufficient progress.
2. Institute independent or small-group research projects using reference books in the native language.
3. Cultivate an awareness of code switching (injecting or substituting phrases, sentences or expressions from another language, sometimes unconsciously) to increase linguistic sensitivity on the part of the staff (Trueba, 1983).
4. Explain the concept of gifted programs to immigrant parents in their own language, either verbally or via a simple publication such as a mimeographed booklet.

Cultural

1. Use an informal approach to allay the fears of parents and children about special programs for children who are gifted.
2. Conduct parent interviews in their native language, using culturally sensitive questioning that speaks to the giftedness valued by the culture. Examples include dance, weaving, storytelling, and calligraphy.

Economic

1. Take into account the aspirations of the immigrant group, giving attention to parental status variables such as occupation and education (Portes, McLeod, & Parker, 1978), especially when interviewing or planning curricular intervention.
2. Assume nothing about the economic status or economic perceptions of any ethnic group. Work from facts only.

Attitudinal

1. Work to increase home-school interface (Harris, 1988). This frequently results in lowered conflict and higher achievement.
2. Tap the sense of self-reliance by using a biographical approach, which concentrates on positive aspects of problem solving, task commitment, and decision making.
3. Encourage empowerment through

expression in publications or journals containing writings like those found in MOSAIC, from South Boston High School. Encourage students to keep journals and stories and poems.

Sociocultural and Peer Group Expectation

1. Use narratives, role playing, and bibliotherapy (Ramirez, 1988) to diffuse conflict in this sensitive areas.
2. Identify weaknesses in locus of control (Vasquez, 1988), ascertain the causes, and provide specific intervention.

Cross-Cultural Stress

1. Increase the motivation for self-identification as gifted, softening the cultural difficulty of self-proclamation by reference to the special program or class as an opportunity for students to work harder and learn more.
2. use care in selecting staff for identification, with specific attention to the sending cultures and ethnocentric attitudes.
3. Recommend the use of bicultural effectiveness training where appropriate. Szapocznik, Santisteban, Kurtines, Perez-Vidal, and Hervis (1983) have provided a good model.

Intergenerational Conflict

1. Use nonverbal expression such as music, dance, or drawing, which brings the parent or family into the product assessment.
2. Use peer referral both within and outside of the culture as an additional source of identification.
3. Involve outreach workers. This will be helpful to many parents who are illiterate and/or fearful of school authority.
4. Use media in the native language. These services are usually available through local agencies that serve specific cultural groups.

School System Conflict

1. Place or identify students according to educational background and potential, not simply according to chronological age.
2. Interpret bizarre behavior in the light of the child's experience (Ramirez,

1988). Symptoms of posttraumatic stress disorder should not influence identification of potential giftedness, but they should be taken into account in the learning environment.

3. Use extracurricular activities for input to identification procedures, and encourage incorporation of successful activities into the learning goals.

4. Ensure that the screening and selection committee has cultural knowledge of creative production and/or performance. Include representative community members in the committee.

5. Avoid the superimposition of past identification procedures.

6. Assess from the perspective of field-dependent and individual learning styles (e.g., Ramirez & Castenada, 1974).

7. Place the child in a minimal-stress, "culturally congruent" (Trueba, 1983, p. 412) environment and observe for a period of time. Attributes of giftedness will emerge if given an opportunity.

8. Assess teacher attitudes periodically. Hold informal sessions for teachers to air problems and exchange ideas.

9. Use the developmental (Reyes, 1988) rather than the crisis-oriented model.

Conclusion

When a new immigrant population is tapped for talent potential, both society and the individual benefit. However, problem areas must first be defined in the light of the specific culture and cultural conflict. Attention must then be directed to problem-specific techniques to ensure correct placement and opportunities for appropriately differentiated learning experiences.

If immigrants are to be included in the life of their new country, then they must also be included in a vision of education that speaks to the fulfillment of each child's capabilities. As Iaian Chrichton Smith (1976) so eloquently stated in his poem, "Two Girls Singing,"

> It neither was the words nor yet the
> tune,
> Any tune would have done and any
> words.
> Any listener or no listener at all.
> As nightingales in rocks or a child
> crooning
> in its own world of strange awaken-
> ing
> or larks for no reason but
> themselves.
> So on the bus through late
> November running
> by yellow lights tormented, dark-
> ness falling,
> the two girls sang for miles and
> miles together
> and it wasn't the words or tune. It
> was the singing.
> It was the human sweetness in that
> yellow,
> the unpredicted voices of our kind.

References

Clark, L. (1988a, June). *Early warning of refugee flows.* Washington, DC: Center for Policy Analysis and Research on Refugee Issues.

Clark, L. (1988b, October). Early warning of refugee flows. In *Research Seminar on International Migration.* Symposium conducted at Massachusetts Institute of Technology, Cambridge.

Cohen, M. (1988, April 21). Immigrant children need aid, study says. *The Boston Globe,* p. 25.

Goffin, S. G. (1988). Putting our advocacy efforts into a new context. *The Journal of the National Association for the Education of Young Children,* 43(3), 52–56.

Gratz, E., & Pulley, J. L. (1984). A gifted and talented program for migrant students. *Roeper Review* 6(3), 147–149.

Harris, C. R. (1988, April). *Cultural conflict and patterns of achievement in gifted Asian-Pacific children.* Paper presented at the meeting of the National Association for Asian and Pacific American Education.

National Coalition of Advocates for Students. (1988). *New voices: Immigrant voices in U.S. public school.* Research Rep. No 1988-1). Boston: Author.

Organization for Economic Cooperation and Development (OECD). (1987). *Immigrant children at school.* Paris: OECD, Center for Educational Research and Innovation.

Poplin, M. S., & Wright, P. (1983). The concept of cultural pluralism: Issues in special education. *Learning Disability Quarterly, 6,* 367–-372.

Portes, A., McLeod, S. A., Jr., Parker, R. N. (1978). Immigrant aspirations. *Sociology of Education, 51,* 241–260.

Ramirez, B. A. (1988). Culturally and linguistically diverse children. *TEACHING Exceptional Children, 20*(4), 45–51.

Ramirez, M. I., & Castenada, A. (1974). *Cultural democracy, bicognitive development, and education.* New York: Academic Press.

Reyes, L. (1988). The challenge. In *New Voices: Immigrant voices in U.S. public schools,* (pp.67-69). (Research Rep No. 1988-1). Boston: National Coalition of Advocates for Students.

Sheehy, G. (1986). *Spirit of survival.* New York: Bantam.

Smith, I. C. (1976). Two girls singing. In L. Lueders & P. St. John (Eds.), *Zero makes me hungry (p. 130).* Glenview, IL: Scott, Foresman.

Sugai, G., & Maheady, L. (1988). Cultural diversity and individual assessment for behavior disorders. *TEACHING Exceptional Children, 21,* 28–31.

Szapocznik, J., Santisteban, D., Kurtines, W., Perez-Vidal, A., & Hervis, O. (1983, November). *Bicultural effectiveness training: A treatment intervention for enhancing intercultural adjustment in Cuban American families.* Paper presented at the Ethnicity, Acculturation and Mental Health Among Hispanics Conference, Albuquerque, New Mexico.

Trueba, H. T. (1983). Adjustment problems of Mexican and Mexican-American students: An anthropological study. *Learning Disability Quarterly, 6,* 395–415.

Trueba, H. T. (1988). Culturally based explanations of minority students' academic achievement, *Anthropology & Education Quarterly 19,* 270–287.

Vasquez, J. A. (1988). Contexts of learning for minority students. *The Educational Forum, 6,* 243–253.

Vuong, V. (1988). Finding solutions. In *New voices: Immigrant voices in U.S. public schools.* (Research Rep. No. 1988-1). Boston: National Coalition of Advocates for Students.

Wei, T. (1983). The Vietnamese refugee child: Understanding cultural differences. In D. Omark & J. Erickson (Eds.), *The bilingual exceptional child,* (pp. 206–211). San Diego: College-Hill.

Educating Language-Minority Children: Challenges And Opportunities

Teachers facing the challenge of teaching children from different cultural communities find themselves hard pressed to decide what constitutes an appropriate curriculum. Ms. Bowman identifies a few developmental principles that can provide a conceptual framework.

BARBARA T. BOWMAN

BARBARA T. BOWMAN is director of graduate studies at the Erikson Institute, which is affiliated with Loyola University, Chicago, where she teaches courses in public policy administration and early childhood curriculum. She is a past president of the National Association for the Education of Young Children and currently serves on a committee on early education for the National Association of State Boards of Education and on a committee on day care for the National Research Council.

HY CAN'T all Americans just speak standard English? This plaintive question reflects the distress that many citizens feel about the linguistic diversity that has become a source of divisiveness in society and a source of failure in the schools. In many school districts, the number of languages and dialects spoken by children and their families is staggering, as the languages of Central and South America, Africa, and Asia mix with various American dialects to create classrooms in which communication is virtually impossible. Across America, language-minority children are not learning the essential lessons of school and are not fully taking part in the economic, social, and political life of the country.

And the problem will soon become even more serious. Over the next decade or two, language-minority children will become the *majority* in our public schools, seriously straining the capacity of those institutions to educate them.

In a nation that is increasingly composed of people who speak different languages and dialects, the old notion of melting them together through the use of a common language is once again attractive. Requiring all children to speak the same language at a high level of proficiency would make the task of educating them a good deal easier. Unfortunately, what seems quite simple in theory is often difficult to put into practice. One of the most powerful reasons in this instance is the interrelationship of culture, language, and the children's development.

CULTURE, LANGUAGE, AND DEVELOPMENT

Christian men show respect for their religion by removing their hats but keeping their shoes on in church, while Muslim men show similar respect by keeping their hats on and removing their shoes in a mosque. But differences in how groups think and act are more than a matter of using different words or performing different actions for the same purposes. Differences in culture are more substantial than whether members of a community eat white bread, corn pone, or tortillas. The behavior of people varies, and the beliefs, values, and assumptions that underlie that behavior differ as well. Culture influences both behavior and the psychological processes on which it rests; it affects the ways in which people perceive the world — their physical environment, the events that surround them, and other people. Culture forms a prism through which members of a group see the world and create "shared meanings."

Child development follows a pattern similar to culture. The major structural changes in children — changes that arise from the interaction of biology and experience, such as language learning — are remarkably similar in kind and sequence across cultural groups. However, the specific knowledge and skills — the cultural learning — that children acquire at different ages depend on the children's family and community.

Learning a primary language is a developmental milestone for young children and is, therefore, a "developmentally appropriate" educational objective. Moreover, the informal, social method by which children learn their primary language is also "developmentally appropriate." However, the specific uses to which that language is put are determined by the culture.

As the ideas from a child's social world are brought to bear through the guidance of the older members of the community, children come to know, to expect, and to share meanings with their elders. Children acquire *scripts* (sequences of actions and words) for various interactions with people and things, and the adults in their families and communities structure these scripts for children to help them learn. Gradually, children internalize the adult rules for "making meaning."

From *Phi Delta Kappan*, October 1989, pp. 118-120. Reprinted by permission of the author and *Phi Delta Kappan*.

207

Classroom discourse presents a challenge to children to learn new rules for communication. The use of formal language, teacher leadership and control of verbal exchanges, question-and-answer formats, and references to increasingly abstract ideas characterize the classroom environment, with which many children are unfamiliar. To the extent that these new rules overlap with those that children have already learned, classroom communication is made easier. But children whose past experience with language is not congruent with the new rules will have to learn ways of "making meaning" all over again before they can use language to learn in the classroom.

When teachers and students come from different cultures and use different languages and dialects, the teachers may be unaware of the variations between their own understanding of a context and that of their students, between their own expectations for behavior in particular contexts and the inclinations of the children they teach. When children and adults do not share common experiences and do not hold common beliefs about the meaning of experiences, the adults are less able to help children encode their thoughts in language.

Children are taught to act, believe, and feel in ways that are consistent with the mores of their communities. The goals and objectives presented, the relationships available, and the behavior and practices recommended by family and friends are gradually internalized and contribute to a child's definition of self. Language is an integral part of a group's common experience. Speaking the same language connects individuals through bonds of common meaning and also serves as a marker of group membership; it is the cement for group members' relationships with one another. The shared past and the current allegiances of the group are the bedrock for the "common meanings" taught to children through language.

TEACHING CULTURALLY DIFFERENT CHILDREN

The idea of a developmentally appropriate curriculum is inherently attractive. It evokes a vision of classrooms in which experiences are synchronized with each child's levels of maturity and experience, so that what is taught is consistent with the child's capacity to learn.

But teachers facing the challenge of teaching children from different cultural communities find themselves hard pressed to decide what constitutes an

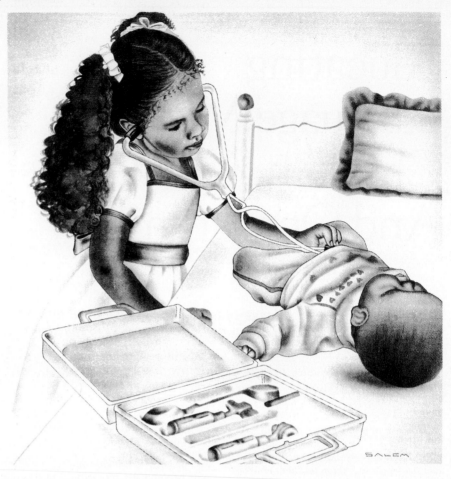

appropriate curriculum. If the children speak different languages and dialects, how should teachers communicate with them? If children from some groups are hesitant to speak up in school, how can teachers organize expressive language experiences? If children from some groups are dependent on nonverbal cues for meaning, how can teachers stress word meaning? If different groups have different ways of expressing themselves, how can teachers know what children mean to say or what children understand of what teachers and other children say? How can teachers test for mastery of the curriculum if children do not speak a standard language or use the same styles of communication? Cultural diversity makes it hard for teachers to assess each child's developmental status, to find common educational experiences to promote further growth, and to measure the achievement of educational objectives.

Given the complexity of the interaction between culture and development, is it possible to design a developmentally appropriate curriculum at all? If that question implies that the same curriculum can be used for all children, the answer must be no. Children who have been socialized in different worlds will not under-

stand material in the same ways. On the other hand, recognizing a few developmental principles can provide a conceptual framework for the culturally sensitive teacher. The following list of principles is not meant to be exhaustive; it merely provides a beginning for teachers who are trying to bridge the gap between children's cultural backgrounds and the school's objectives.

First, teachers need to learn to recognize developmentally equivalent patterns of behavior. Before they come to school, all children have learned many of the same things — a primary language, categorizing systems, interpersonal communication styles. Although these developmental accomplishments may look quite different, they can be said to be developmentally equivalent. There are a number of "equally good" ways to shape development. When a child does not respond to the social and cognitive expectations of the school, the teacher should look first for a developmentally equivalent task to which the child will respond. For instance, a child who does not talk in the classroom can be observed on the playground or at home. A child who does not separate buttons correctly can be asked to sort car logos or other personally rele-

amily values should reinforce school expectations; interpreting the school's agenda for parents is one of the teacher's most important tasks.

vant artifacts. A child who does not listen to stories about the seasons may be spellbound by a story about a basketball player.

Teachers who have doubts about the development of culturally different children should assume that the children are normal and look at them again, recognizing that their own vision may be clouded by cultural myopia. By assuming the developmental equivalence of a variety of tasks, adults can begin the search for the mismatch between their own and a given child's understanding of a situation or of a task to be performed.

Second, it is essential not to value some ways of achieving developmental milestones more highly than others, because young children are particularly sensitive to the ways in which adults view them. Asa Hilliard and Mona Vaughn-Scott point out that, because the behavior of African-American children is so different from that of their white peers, such children are often judged to be deficient in their development, rather than just different. The result is that normal, healthy children are sometimes diagnosed as sick or retarded.*

Speaking a common language is the cement that binds individuals to groups. Thus young children who speak languages other than English (or nonstandard dialects) are reluctant to give up this connection to the members of their own

group. When such children find that the way they talk and act is not understood or appreciated in school, they are apt to become confused or disengaged. And their rejection by the school presages their rejection of school.

Third, teachers need to begin instruction with interactive styles and with content that is familiar to the children. Whether this entails speaking in the child's primary language, using culturally appropriate styles of address, or relying on patterns of management that are familiar to and comfortable for children, the purpose is to establish a basis for communication. While fluency in a child's primary language may not be an achievable goal for many teachers, they can nonetheless become more adept at understanding, planning, and implementing a culturally sensitive curriculum. Such a curriculum must encompass more than tasting parties and colorful ethnic costumes; it must be more than shopworn introductions to the odd and amusing practices of people from different nations or different racial groups. In order to teach such a curriculum, teachers must have come to grips with their own ethnocentricity and must be able to deal with themselves and others fairly; teachers must know the difference between style and substance.

Fourth, school learning is most likely to occur when family values reinforce school expectations. This does not mean that parents must teach the same things at home as teachers do in school. However, it does mean that parents and other community members must view achievement in school as a desirable and attainable goal if the children are to build it

into their own sense of themselves. This means that interpreting the school's agenda for parents is one of the most important tasks for teachers.

Fifth, when differences exist between the cultural patterns of the home and community and those of the school, teachers must deal with these discrepancies directly. Teachers and children must create shared understandings and new contexts that give meaning to the knowledge and skills being taught. The challenge is to find personally interesting and culturally relevant ways of creating new contexts for children, contexts in which the mastery of school skills can be meaningful and rewarding. Learning mediated by teachers who are affectionate, interested, and responsive — teachers who are personally involved in the lives of young children — has greater "sticking power" than learning mediated by an adult who is perceived as impersonal and socially distant.

Sixth, the same contexts do not have the same meanings to children from different racial and ethnic groups. The meanings of words, of gestures, and of actions may be quite different. The assessment of learning outcomes presents a formidable problem when children misunderstand the meaning of the teacher's requests for information and for demonstrations of knowledge and skills. The same instructional materials and methods may take on meanings different from those that the teacher intended. Formal assessment should be delayed until teachers and children have jointly built a set of new meanings, so that the children understand the language and behavior called for in school.

A developmentally appropriate curriculum can never be standardized in a multicultural community. Thoughtful teachers, however, can use the principles of child development to make the new context of school meaningful, to attach new kinds of learning to what children have already achieved, and to safeguard the self-image and self-confidence of children as their knowledge and skills expand. It is not easy, but it is the only workable system.

*Asa Hilliard and Mona Vaughn-Scott, "The Quest for the Minority Child," in Shirley G. Moore and Catherine R. Cooper, eds., *The Young Child: Reviews of Research*, Vol. 3 (Washington, D.C.: National Association for the Education of Young Children, 1982).

Teaching to the Distinctive Traits of Minority Students

JAMES A. VASQUEZ

James A. Vasquez is an associate professor in the College of Education at the University of Washington, Seattle.

Researchers report that students at all levels find greater motivation and perform at higher levels academically when instructional methods complement student learning characteristics (Gentry and Ellison 1981). Yet it is not uncommon to find that many teachers, both minority and mainstream, are unable to identify distinctive traits among ethnic minority youths that require a unique set of instructional strategies if acceptable levels of learning are to be experienced by these youths. Equally disturbing is that, once such cultural traits have been identified, teachers have no idea how to adapt classroom instruction to these traits.

In this article I will identify several traits in each of three minority student groups and will show their notable distinctiveness when contrasted with traits commonly believed to characterize students from mainstream society. I will then suggest a procedure for adapting teaching to fit the distinctive traits of ethnic minority students.

Hispanic Students

An abundance of literature suggests that many Hispanic students are distinguished by a sense of loyalty to the family (Montalvo, Lasater, and Garza 1981; Vasquez 1979a; Ramirez and Castaneda 1974). Children from such homes are brought up with the notion that to bear the family name is a very important responsibility, that their behavior at all times reflects on the honor of the family, and that the family is to be their basic support group throughout their lives. Socialization of this type cannot help but produce in the individual a sense of motivation that is other-directed, one that seeks its impetus from a basically external source—the family. (Other minority groups seem also to imbue in their youth a sense of loyalty directed outwardly, although not necessarily toward the family.)

In contrast to this is the strong sense of individualism (Adams 1988; Brandt 1987) that is found in many typical mainstream families where young people are taught that life is in their hands, that they can go as far in life as they want, and that they will have only themselves to blame or to thank for what they have achieved at life's end. This concept is referred to as "rugged individualism" in textbooks. It is a deeply rooted value in American mainstream society, one that is said to have been of major importance in the move westward by Anglo-Americans when families lived in isolation and had to learn to depend largely on themselves.

Hispanic and mainstream students also differ significantly along the dimensions of cooperation and competition. The literature on Hispanic students abounds with reports on the preference of many of these youths, especially Chicanos, for activities in which they can achieve a goal with other students, not in isolation from them or in competition with them (Avellar and Kagan 1976; Kagan and Madsen 1971). The author remembers well his refusal to participate in a school activity in which he excelled simply because the teacher put him in a competitive position vis-à-vis his classmates. The experience is not uncommon among Hispanic students, as many will testify. In contrast, we find that mainstream youths are said to learn early on to be competitive (Elleson 1983; Nelson and Kagan 1972), that it is important to strive to be "numero uno," and that it is okay to achieve in school at someone else's expense. Because classes are essentially taught by mainstream, middle-class individuals, it is not surprising that such a high percentage of activities in the classroom require that students compete with one another.

A third trait of Hispanic youths in our schools (and one in which they are again in contrast with their mainstream peers) is their continual need for ethnic role models. Data from the U.S. Bureau of the Census (1980), for example, show that in a number of selected professions (computer specialist, engineer, math specialist, life scientist, physics scientist, psychologist, social scientist), Spanish-surnamed individuals are virtually nonexistent. This point must be well understood by teachers if they are to adequately serve students from

From *The Clearing House*, Vol. 63, No. 7, March 1990, pp. 299-304. Reprinted with permission of the Helen Dwight Reid Educational Foundation. Published by Heldref Publications, 1319 Eighteenth St., NW, Washington, DC 20036-1802.

this, and other, minority groups. Its importance is easily noted when we consider that the young persons' professional aspirations are so profoundly influenced by the presence or absence of role models in their awareness. Consider, for example, that mainstream children never have to ask themselves the question, "Can I really be a doctor (engineer, mayor, principal, etc.)? I've never seen one who looks like me." No, mainstream children are surrounded at all times by role models from their own ethnic backgrounds. That is the situation we would wish for all American children. Such is not the case, however, for many Hispanic children who have yet to see, or hear about, the first successful Hispanic in many of the professions in our society.

Black Students

Shade (1982) wrote that research has found black students, from an early age, to be significantly more person-centered than mainstream children who are characterized by an object-centered approach to learning. According to Young, the tendency of socialization techniques in the black community to orient the child toward persons tends "to frustrate the child's interest in the 'object world' " (in Shade 1982). Shade (1982) also reported that Yarrow, Rubenstein, Peterson, and Kowski found that preferences of black children for these two aspects of the environment (humans and inanimate objects) were "strikingly independent."

The roots of the person-centered preference may be found in historical settings that required that blacks, for survival purposes, be highly sensitive to the moment-by-moment moods of others, especially those who exercised total control over black people, and found in the enduring interpersonal relationships that existed between blacks and others in their social milieu. This distinction between black and white children takes on considerable importance when we become aware of the requirement in typical classrooms to focus on objects (mathematics, natural phenomena, letters of the alphabet, rules, etc.), not people, for extended periods of time in order to learn well.

Some research also suggests that many black children learn better when multiple stimuli are present. Following Young (1974), Shade (1982) noted that Afro-American children apparently "are taught to concentrate on many stimuli at one time rather than learning to concentrate on one." Shade also reported that Boykin (1979) concluded that although Euro-American children were apparently socialized to "tolerate monotony or unvaried presentation of material," black children "did markedly better if the formats had high variability" in problem-solving tasks.

Yet most classroom instruction apparently provides single or limited stimuli to students. If, as research suggests, single stimulus conditions are more conducive to learning among mainstream students than black students, we may be dealing, at this point, with an example

of typical classroom practice that favors one American ethnic group (the mainsteam) at the expense of another.

Finally, black children may be more receptive to learning that allows them to use their skills in the oral tradition (a trait Barwell [1981] also reports among native Americans), although mainstream children are thought to have a stronger orientation to the written word as a major source of gathering information. Britto (1983), for example, cites Smitherman: "The crucial difference in American culture lies in the contrasting modes in which black and white Americans have shaped their language . . . a written mode for whites, having come from a European, print-oriented culture; a spoken mode for blacks, having come from an African, orally oriented background." Britto urges teachers of black youth to pursue "this avenue of understanding and study" in their teaching.

Native American Students

Some native American students are said to be characterized by a deductive, or holistic, approach to learning (Barwell 1981), which is sometimes referred to as the field-dependent style (the terms *field sensitive* and *field attentive* are sometimes used). This approach to learning proceeds from the general to the particular. Students so characterized are thought to be more responsive to an overview or "big picture" presented at the beginning of a lesson. They presumably are in need of an early orientation to the entire field of information to be covered (thus the term *field dependent*), after which they can proceed to more specific details of the lesson. So important is this learning preference among some native American students that one researcher (Barwell 1981) has stated that, in teaching these students, "above all, the course should be taught holistically."

In contrast to this learning style is the field-independent learning style, believed by some researchers to describe many, if not most, mainstream students (Ramirez and Castaneda 1974; Witkin 1967; Witkin et al. 1962). This trait requires a more inductive approach to learning, meaning that the student learns better when details are presented first and the direction of learning is from the particulars of a lesson to the more general concepts. Although neither learning style is unduly difficult to conceptualize, the significant differences in teaching strategies each requires for maximal learning among students are obvious.

An important additional (but infrequently discussed) trait of some native American students is their preference for engaging in trial-and-error learning by means of private rather than public experiences such as those the classroom provides. Kleinfeld (1975), for example, notes the difficulty some native American students have in coping with the direct type of criticism that failure in classroom activities inevitably brings. Researchers reporting this trait suggest that in some native American communities, learning among youth often takes place as the learner practices the skill to be mastered privately, and only after an acceptable degree of mastery is attained in that context will he or she attempt to publicly demonstrate it.

Yet traditional practice in the public classroom assumes no difference in this area among students, and teachers regularly employ activities that make failure an inevitable experience in the classroom. Indeed, many teachers believe that failure is an important and necessary learning experience for students. It would seem that the competitive nature of so many mainstream students (Vasquez 1979a; Avellar and Kagan 1976) would better prepare them for trial-and-error learning in our classrooms. The emphasis on keeping one's errors within one's own private experience as much as possible, combined with a relative lack of competitive spirit among native American students (Barwell 1981; Kleinfeld 1975), seems to work to their disadvantage at this point, considering the present nature of many of our classrooms.

Bridging Traits and Instructional Strategy

I will not in this article fall prey to the temptation to compare the merits of values within different American groups, but I cannot help but point out the important implications that differing values have for teachers in our classrooms. Recall, for the moment, the sense of family loyalty that characterizes many Hispanic youth from traditional homes. Now consider a common phrase any teacher might say to a student: "Good work, Mary. You should be proud of yourself." In an effort to reinforce the student for high performance, the teacher will use this phrase on the assumption that Mary has within her value system the belief that she should be proud of herself for doing good academic work.

But what if this is Maria, and not Mary? What if the student in question comes, not from a traditional mainstream value system with its high sense of individualism, but from a traditional Hispanic value system where children are not taught so much to perform for the sake of pride in their own work as for the pride their family will have in them? In such a case the teacher's efforts to reinforce the student will be largely ineffective.

Our attempts to reinforce must be based on values the student holds (Gentry and Ellison 1981; Vasquez 1979b; Vasquez and Wainstein n.d.), and these often differ depending on the particular ethnic (and social class) background of the student. It is for this reason that teachers who boast that they "treat all students the same" are not showing their democratic disposition, but rather that they are not yet prepared to teach in the pluralistic classrooms of American schools where already more than one in every four students is an ethnic minority student (U.S. Bureau of the Census 1986).

Or, again, consider the ease with which instruction could be made culturally suitable for black children if the teacher would keep in mind a person-oriented approach to teaching. Even concepts dealing with naturalistic phenomena (math, science) can be couched in terminology that involves people interacting with people. Is that too much to ask of a teacher who has black children in the classroom?

And what about the notion that the black culture has a strong oral tradition? Is this not also a unique strength that teachers should be quick to capitalize on for the purpose of enhancing learning among these students? It is a fact that a strong oral tradition characterized the Jewish people for many centuries, and it served them well.

Native American students, too, will be better served in our schools as teachers learn to adapt instruction to their learning propensities. It is not difficult, after all, to teach in a manner that makes use first of the larger concepts, to "set the field" with broad strokes right from the beginning of the lesson, to proceed from the general to the specific in communicating a set of facts to students. Nor should it be difficult to reduce the number of classroom activities involving a public display (from the perspective of these students) of failure, for the sake of allowing native American students to fail privately so that they might succeed publicly.

Are there not some basic guiding concepts that will help teachers learn a practical procedure for adapting teaching to cultural traits for the purpose of enhancing learning among ethnic minority students? I believe there are. Rather than considering specific traits of each minority group in turn, it would be more helpful to discuss a few practical procedures that can assist us in bridging the gap between an observed student trait and an instructional strategy that is founded upon the trait.

Adapting Instruction to Cultural Traits

Earlier I stated that teachers do not generally know the cultures of ethnic minority students sufficiently to identify those traits that require an appropriate adaptation of instructional strategies to assure effective teaching. I suggested several such traits for students from three ethnic groups and indicated how they stand in clear contrast with common traits among many students of Anglo-American background. If teachers are willing to train themselves as close observers of student behavior (a trait recommended for teachers at all levels, including those in higher education) and to avail themselves of the sources of information on minority students (reading, workshops, academic courses, etc.), there is no reason why they cannot attain an adequate knowledge of their students in terms of cultural distinctives.

I also stated that once teachers do become aware of certain cultural traits in their students, they are often at a loss as to what to do with those traits. To resolve difficulties at this point, it would be helpful to keep in mind three elements of good teaching, each of which may become the means for moving from an observed student trait to an appropriate instructional strategy for that trait. The three teaching elements are content, context, and mode.

Content, of course, refers to the material that is taught. It is the information or data the teacher wishes to communicate to the students. *Context,* in this sense, refers to the physical and psychological environment of the classroom and may include such factors as the kind of teacher expectations projected by the teacher, the degree of feminization of the classroom, whether a spirit of cooperation or competition is dominant, whether students generally feel that their own efforts are effective in getting the reinforcements they desire in the classroom, and student perceptions regarding how much the teacher really cares about them. There are other contextual factors as well (Vasquez 1988). The *mode* refers to how the information is treated or presented. It can include the method, form, style, or manner of delivery used by the teacher. Aspects of the mode include the degree of globalism, complexity, and abstractness used, as well as the sequence and length of the presentation.

It would seem that teachers are somewhat more inclined to think in terms of the first element—the content—when a change in instructional strategy is needed and to avoid thinking in terms of the context in which teaching takes place or the mode of teaching. Although efforts that focus on adapting content to specific cultural traits of minority students are helpful, this approach greatly reduces the range of instructional adaptations needed for providing students with culturally appropriate instruction. Teachers must be aware of the ways in which both context and mode may also be changed for the sake of enhancing learning among non-mainstream students.

The approach to adapting instruction to student traits involves three steps. The first is to identify the particular student trait that may require some adaptation in the teacher's normal way of teaching. As stated earlier, this may come from direct observation on the part of the teacher. It may also be information that the teacher has learned from some other source. Although information characterizing groups should not be considered as infallible when applied to individuals, such information at least serves the teacher well as a starting point in adapting instruction to the cultural needs of minority students.

The second step, once a trait has been identified, is to pass the trait through the filter of several questions, each one relating to the content, context, or mode of instruction that might be required. For example, the teacher must ask whether any aspect of the student trait has implications for the content that should be taught. Similar questions are then asked with regard to the context in which teaching should take place, and with regard to the mode that should be used in teaching. The result of this activity may, of course, identify more than one aspect of teaching that could be appropriately changed for the purpose of assuring culturally appropriate teaching. A given trait—high motivation for the sake of pleasing the family, for example—may suggest to the teacher the need to both reinforce the student by making reference to the student's family (changing the psychological context for the student), and to teach more about the family's specific expectations for students in the classroom (changing the content of what is taught).

Although the practice of reexamining one's teaching in terms of the effect particular student traits should have on it (at the points of content, context, and mode) may seem new and even peculiar, this practice is at the heart of culturally appropriate instruction, and the dividends will be quickly evident for those who take it seriously.

Third, the teacher must define the new instructional strategy that will be used as a consequence of the first two steps. It would be helpful to actually write out the strategy. Assume, for example, that Carlos is the student in whom a high regard for pleasing his family has been observed. The procedure described above must end in some articulated strategy such as: "I'm going to tell Carlos that I will send his best work home to his parents." Although the actual final adaptation of instruction may take many forms, the importance of carrying the process through to this last step cannot be emphasized too strongly, for final success in teaching in culturally appropriate ways is dependent on reaching this practical point. Figure 1 illustrates the proposed steps in sequence, with several beginning points (student traits) developed to the point of an appropriate instructional strategy.

Conclusion

One might well ask why I do not suggest that culturally appropriate instruction could and should be provided by teachers who themselves are ethnic minorities. Two important facts argue convincingly against this solution. The first is that at present the enrollment in our teacher training institutions is proceeding in a direction quite opposed to that required by this strategy. Minority students simply are not choosing teaching as their preferred vocation. Those who enroll in college are quite aware that, at present, teaching as a profession is not one of the highly paid professions, nor does it enjoy particularly high regard in the public eye. These facts, combined with the phenomenon of a rapidly increasing minority student population in the public elementary and secondary schools, mean that a sufficient number of minority teachers is simply nowhere to be found in the foreseeable future.

A second argument against this solution is that some evidence suggests that ethnic minority teachers are not better teachers of minority youth than are mainstream (Anglo) teachers (U.S. Commission on Civil Rights

FIGURE 1
Three-Step Procedure for Adapting Instruction to Cultural Traits

Step 1	Step 2	Step 3
Teacher observes/ identifies student trait	Trait is passed through "filter" of three questions to identify which aspect of teaching (content, context, mode) should be affected.	Teacher verbalizes/writes out the new instructional strategy

Step 2 details:

Content
a. Does any aspect of the trait suggest the kind of material I should be teaching?

Context
b. Does any aspect of the trait suggest the physical or psychological setting I should create in the classroom?

Mode
c. Does any aspect of the trait suggest the manner in which I should be teaching?

Step 1	Step 3
1. Carlos is very concerned about pleasing his family.	1. I'll tell Carlos that I'll inform his parents when he does really good work. (Carlos should work with greater effort and expectation and thus for him the context is changed.)
2. Sammy and Joanna seem disinterested when given individual work and more "turned on" when interacting with others.	2. I'll provide more activities that allow Sammy and Joanna to work on projects with others in small groups. (Mode is changed since the means of instruction has shifted to include more student input.)
3. Ben seems intimidated and shy when I ask him questions to which he might not know the answer.	3. I'll focus on asking Ben questions in class that I'm fairly sure he can answer correctly, and work with him individually in areas in which he is less knowledgeable. (This strategy affects both the mode of instruction and the psychological context for Ben.)
4. Charlotte does better when the material I teach involves people interacting with one another; she is not strongly "object" oriented.	4. I will teach more math concepts in the context of people dealing with one another, as in buying, trading, borrowing. (The mode is basically changed to suit Charlotte's preferred style of learning.)

1973). It seems clear that, although minority teachers indeed serve in the capacity of role models for minority students, both groups—minority and mainstream teachers—are in need of special training if instruction in the classroom is to be appropriately adapted to the distinctive cultural traits of minority students.

The problem of insufficient knowledge on the part of teachers with regard to the distinctive learning characteristics of many minority students is one that is largely in the hands of teachers themselves to resolve. Teachers must become good observers of student behavior in the classroom. This practice in itself can be of significant help to teachers at this point. Then teachers can avail themselves of research and other educational literature to further their knowledge of value systems, reinforcement needs, cognitive styles, and other learning-related traits of these students.

The problem of not knowing what to do once minority student traits have been identified is a little more difficult to resolve, for, to my knowledge, proven models that will guide teachers through the practical steps needed in such a procedure has not yet been published. I have proposed here a basic three-step procedure that, it is hoped, will be of help to some who wish to move ahead in this pedagogical area.

This procedure is clearly student centered, for the teacher is required to begin with observed student traits, and the whole intention is to ultimately produce an instructional strategy that is uniquely fitted to those student traits. It is also a procedure that encourages continual professional growth for the teacher because revision of instructional strategies will be an ongoing practice given the changing nature of students in the classroom year by year.

Finally, it is a procedure that measures good teaching, not in terms of a set of traits we might observe in the teacher, but in terms of the teacher's response to student characteristics, for the basic point in seeking to implement culturally appropriate instructional strategies is to assure that the strengths students bring into the classroom are the factors that give shape to the content, context, and mode of instruction employed by the teacher.

REFERENCES

Adams, D. W. 1988. Fundamental considerations: The deep meaning of native American schooling, 1880–1900. *Harvard Educational Review* 58(1): 1–28.

Avellar, J., and S. Kagan. 1976. Development of competitive behaviors in Anglo-American and Mexican-American children. *Psychological Reports* 39: 191–98.

Barwell, J. 1981. Strategies for teaching composition to native Americans. Paper presented at the Annual Meeting of the Conference on College Composition and Communication, March, in Dallas, Texas. ERIC Document No. ED 199 761.

Brandt, R. 1987. Is cooperation un-American? *Educational Leadership* 45(3).

Boykin, A. W. 1979. Psychological/behavioral verve: Some theoretical explorations and empirical manifestations. In *Research directions of black psychologists,* edited by A. W. Boykin, A. J. Franklin, and J. F. Yates. New York: Russell Sage Foundation.

Britto, N. 1983. Teaching writing to minority students. Paper presented at the Annual Meeting of the Midwest Regional Conference on English in the Two-Year College, February, in Overland Park, Kansas. ERIC Document No. ED 233 343).

Elleson, V. J. 1983. Competition: A cultural imperative? *Personnel and Guidance Journal* (December): 195–98.

Gentry, R., and V. G. Ellison. 1981. Instructional strategies that challenge black college students in the area of exceptional child education. Paper presented at the Council for Exceptional Children Conference on the Exceptional Black Child, February, in New Orleans, Louisiana. ERIC Document No. ED 204 906.

Kagan, S., and M. Madsen. 1971. Cooperation and competition of Mexican, Mexican-American, and Anglo-American children of two ages under four instructional sets. *Developmental Psychology* 5(1).

Kleinfeld, J. S. 1975. Effective teachers of Eskimo and Indian students. *School Review* (February): 301–44.

———. 1973. Intellectual strengths in culturally different groups: An Eskimo illustration. *Review of Educational Research* 43(3), 341–59.

Montalvo, F. F., T. T. Lasater, and N. Garza. 1981. *Mexican American culture simulator for child welfare, trainer's manual.* San Antonio, Tex.: Our Lady of the Lake University.

Nelson, L., and S. Kagan. 1972. Competition: The star-spangled scramble. *Psychology Today* 6(4).

Ramirez, M., and A. Castaneda. 1974. *Cultural democracy, bicognitive development, and education.* New York: Academic Press.

Shade, B. J. 1982. Afro-American cognitive style: A variable in school success? *Review of Educational Research* 52(2): 219–44.

U.S. Bureau of the Census. 1980. *Population statistics in the U.S.* Washington, D.C.: The Bureau.

———. 1986. *Population statistics in the U.S.* Washington, D.C.: The Bureau.

U.S. Commission on Civil Rights. 1973. *Teachers and students.* Report V: Mexican American Education Study.

Vasquez, J. A. 1979a. Bilingual education's needed third dimension. *Educational Leadership* (November): 166–68.

Vasquez, J. A. 1979b. Motivation and Chicano students. *Bilingual Resources* 2(2), 2–5.

Vasquez, J. A. 1988. Contexts of learning for minority students. *Educational Forum* 52(3): 243–53.

Vasquez, J. A., and N. Wainstein. n.d. *The responsibilities of college faculty to minority students.* Unpublished manuscript, College of Education, University of Washington, Seattle.

Witkin, H. A. 1967. A cognitive style approach to cross-cultural research. *International Journal of Psychology* 2(4), 233–50.

Witkin, H., R. B. Dyk, H. F. Faterson, D. R. Goodenough, and S. A. Karp. 1962. *Psychological differentiation.* New York: John Wiley.

Young, V. H. 1974. A black American socialization pattern. *American Ethnologist* 1: 405–13.

Measurement and Evaluation

In which reading group does John belong? How do I construct multiple-choice tests? How do I know when my students have mastered the objectives? How can I explain test results to Mary's parents? Each of these questions, and many more questions that educators ask, are answered by applying principles of measurement. College students in education often groan when they come to the part of a course that deals with tests and measurements. They believe they will be forced to learn material that is unimportant and unrelated to teaching but is at the same time difficult. Yet the principles of measurement constitute a universal, generally agreed-upon set of concepts that are integral to the teaching-learning process. Indeed, it seems that with accountability and the stress on basic skills, testing has become more prevalent and more important than ever before.

Measurement provides a foundation for making sound evaluative judgments about students' learning and achievement. Teachers need to use fair and unbiased criteria in order to objectively and accurately assess student learning and make appropriate decisions about student placement. For example, in assigning John to a reading group, the teacher will use John's test scores as an indication of his ability and skill level. Are the tests valid for the school's reading program? Are his test scores consistent over several years? Are they consistent with his performance in class? How does John compare with other pupils in the class? These questions should be asked and then answered by the teacher before he or she can make intelligent decisions about John. On the other hand, will knowledge of the test scores affect the teacher's perception of classroom performance and create a self-fulfilling prophecy? Teachers also evaluate students in order to assign grades, and the question is how to balance test scores with subjective evaluation. Both kinds

of evaluative information are necessary, but both can be inaccurate and are frequently misused. What the field of measurement provides is a set of principles to improve all types of evaluation.

The first two articles in this section focus on grading. Teachers need to be aware of grading practices and procedures that are counterproductive for students, such as the indiscriminate use of zeros and averages, and the failure to understand the impact of measurement error in interpreting test scores. Teachers also need to differentiate between criterion-referenced grading for minimal objectives, and using norms to evaluate the achievement of higher-order objectives. The next two articles introduce and critique a new type of measurement, performance-based testing, which has great potential for more effectively integrating assessment of higher order skills with learning. The last article examines characteristics and limitations of standardized aptitude tests.

Looking Ahead: Challenge Questions

Many educators believe that schools should identify the brightest, most capable students. What are the implications of this philosophy for low-achieving students? Does the overall achievement of students matter?

What conditions need to be considered in deciding whether to use criterion-referenced or norm-referenced testing?

What principles of measurement should teachers adopt for their own classroom testing? Is it necessary or feasible to develop a table of specifications for each test?

How can teachers grade thinking skills such as analysis, application, and reasoning? How should objectives for student learning and grading be integrated? What are some practices to avoid in grading students? Why? What are appropriate teacher uses of standardized test scores?

216

Unit 6

It's a Good Score!
Just a Bad Grade

With 15 million children at risk of academic failure, the schools must shift their focus from sorting and selecting to teaching and learning, Mr. Canady and Ms. Hotchkiss maintain.

ROBERT LYNN CANADY AND

PHYLLIS RILEY HOTCHKISS

ROBERT LYNN CANADY is an associate professor in the Department of Educational Leadership and Policy Studies, Curry School of Education, University of Virginia, Charlottesville. PHYLLIS RILEY HOTCHKISS is an associate professor in the Division of Education, Midwestern State University, Wichita Falls, Tex. Both are members of the University of Virginia Chapter of Phi Delta Kappa.

ALGEBRA WAS quite a struggle for Amy. One afternoon she came home excited about her performance on an algebra test and announced, "I made a good score, an 80 — just a bad grade." For Amy an 80 was indeed a good score, the highest she had earned all semester. Translated into a letter grade, however, Amy had earned a D.

Amy's situation is but one example of the many common grading practices that make it difficult for many youngsters to feel successful in school.

One reason why the schools have not succeeded with students like Amy is that the schools have been reluctant to give up their traditional roles of sorting and selecting. Perhaps identifying and teaching the best students was once a valid function of the schools. After all, until fairly recently the American economy did not need large numbers of highly educated workers. However, when 15 million children are at risk of academic failure and of joining the ranks of the chronically unemployed, that time has clearly passed.[1] To help such children become productive citizens, schools must shift their focus from sorting and selecting to teaching and learning.

As a first step, we suggest that teachers reflect on grading policies and practices that might be counterproductive for students at all ability levels. For each grading procedure discussed below, we present a single illustration, which is a composite of many observations.

1. *Varying grading scales.* Martha, a high school freshman, and her brother David, a junior, moved from a highly rated private school in the South to a public high school in a mid-Atlantic state. Their mother and father held professional positions, and Martha and David shared similar ambitions for professional training at good universities. Martha and David liked their new school and were pleased to get grades in the 80s and 90s — as good as those they had received in private school. They were pleased, that is, until report cards were distributed. Then they discovered that their 80s and 90s no longer translated into A's and B's, but rather into B's and C's. Their performance had not changed, but the grading scale had.

In most schools it is common practice to establish grading scales with a passing range of 25 to 30 points. (Table 1 shows three examples.) Obviously, students in those schools that use a 10-point range for each letter grade have more opportunities to feel successful than do students in other schools. Depending on the grading scale employed, an 80 could be a B, a C, or a D.

Moreover, the ranges of failing grades on these three scales differ greatly: from 59 points to 74 points. We recommend strongly that, if teachers are going to play the "numerical averaging game," the

 From *Phi Delta Kappan*, September 1989, pp. 68-71. Reprinted by permission of *Phi Delta Kappan* and the authors.

TABLE 1.
Three Typical Grading Scales

Numerical Range			Letter Grade
95-100	93-100	90-100	A
88-94	85-92	80-89	B
81-87	77-84	70-79	C
75-80	69-76	60-69	D
0-74	0-68	0-59	F

range of passing grades be expanded and the grade of F have the same range as the other four letter grades.

2. *Worshipping averages.* Dale made A's in mathematics and scored at the 99th percentile on standardized tests. In seventh grade, he took the math section of the Scholastic Aptitude Test (SAT) as part of the Johns Hopkins Talent Search and scored 480. One day, while he was enrolled in Algebra I in the eighth grade, Dale had an argument with his best friend *and* a jammed lock on his locker. He arrived 15 minutes late for an algebra test. Consequently, he was unable to finish the test and scored 68, which translated into an F. This was his only score below 97 for the marking period, but it lowered his average to B. Although admitting that the grade did not reflect Dale's ability or knowledge, the teacher refused to consider his previous record and give him an opportunity for a retest.

Dale would have found it to his advantage to have faked illness and so postponed taking the test. At times, this strict devotion to averaging grades is practiced even when the "average" is inconsistent with what is known about a student's background, performance, and ability. No one works at peak efficiency at all times, and that includes students. A number of ways exist to make allowances for off days. For example, students can be permitted to drop their lowest grade or to repeat one test during a marking period. It seems to us that a teacher has an obligation to use professional judgment and occasionally decide to make an exception.

3. *Using zeros indiscriminately.* Bill's teacher had recently attended a workshop on direct instruction. After she presented each day's lesson, she asked a series of questions to "check for understanding." The students were to raise their hands if they could answer the questions. Bill liked the subject, studied hard, and knew the answers to most questions. However, after a week of having his raised hand ignored, he ceased to respond. What he did

not know was that his teacher had recorded zeros for him on the three occasions when he failed to raise his hand. At the end of the marking period these three zeros lowered Bill's grade from a B to a D. Had he merely been absent for three days, his grade would have stayed high.

One of the most punitive and damaging weapons in a teacher's grading arsenal is the use of zeros. We find this practice objectionable for at least two reasons. First, zeros are usually given for incomplete or missing homework. But far too many students go home to situations in which they have no place to work and no materials to use; other complications can also make completing assignments difficult. Second, homework should be assigned for independent practice to give students the opportunity to reinforce skills or concepts learned in class. If students are capable of performing well in class and on tests without completing homework, the students should not be penalized with zeros. Instead, teachers should examine their own teaching and assigning practices, which may not be challenging enough for the students.

Zeros have a devastating effect on students' grade-point averages. For example, assume that a student has the following numerical grades: 90, 92, 88, 90, 91, 89, and 91. The student's average grade is then 90.1. Add a single zero, and the average drops to 78.9. Add two zeros, and the student's average drops to 70.1 — a failing grade in many school districts. Clearly, a student who has learned 90% of the material on which he is tested has benefited from being in class. Can we justify giving that student a D or an F for the entire grading period?

We know of cases in which the zeros given to students were not related to academics. For instance, some teachers give zeros for late work — regardless of its quality. Behavior, class participation, respect for the teacher, and punctuality are among the nonacademic factors that influence grading in some classrooms. If teachers believe that students should be

judged in these areas, we recommend that separate grades from the academic grade be used.

4. *Following the pattern of assign, test, grade, and teach.* During the late spring, Mr. Slepp became concerned about covering all the remaining material in the textbook for his two honors classes in biology. Admonishing the students to move faster, he assigned a difficult chapter to read on Monday night. He promised the students a test on the following day on material that would have challenged college biology students. When the students arrived in class on Tuesday, they were given a true/false test. Mr. Slepp graded the test that evening and recorded the grades. On Wednesday he told the students that more than half of them had made C's, D's, or F's. He spent the entire period discussing the test and the material in the chapter, but it was too late for the students.

Far too often, students are told to read the next chapter and to be prepared for a test on the material. After they have been tested and their tests have been graded, the real teaching and discussion begin. In spite of all the emphasis that has been placed on effective instruction, we continue to an alarming extent to follow this pattern of assign, test, grade, and teach. Wouldn't it be far more logical to teach before testing and grading?

5. *Failing to match testing to teaching.* Bobby, who was interested in becoming a doctor, worked hard in his advanced chemistry class. Bobby felt comfortable with the material covered in class presentations and discussions. His teacher made straightforward presentations and then asked questions requiring mostly simple recall. Bobby read the assigned material in the text but concentrated on studying his class notes in preparation for the first test.

The test questions came as quite a shock to Bobby and his classmates. The items required application and synthesis and were based totally on the textbook. The students believed that they had received inadequate preparation for making the transition from recalling facts to synthesizing information. "He always does that," former students told Bobby. "You have to get used to it."

In this case, the quality of the test, the presentation, and the questioning strategies employed by the teacher are not in question. Rather, there was an obvious mismatch among the three. Students were given no instruction and no practice in answering the high-level questions that appeared on the test. If students are to have a fair chance to succeed, teachers need to monitor closely the match between teaching and testing.

6. *Ambushing students.* Ms. Romney frequently used pop quizzes "to keep the students on their toes." Confidential discussions with her students revealed that those who cared about grades were learning as much about how to cheat on the quizzes as about the material. Other students decided that they could not win at Ms. Romney's game and simply gave up. Her colleagues regarded Ms. Romney as a tough teacher who maintained high standards. No one asked the students.

No teaching and learning takes place when pop quizzes are given, nor can they be justified as "motivational." Pop quizzes are simply punitive measures that teachers employ when they suspect that their students have not learned the material. Rather than spend class time determining what the students have not learned and why, many teachers assume that students have not studied and decide to "get even." The validity of these quizzes, which are usually short and often composed on the spot, is questionable. Such tests will change the distribution of grades for the marking period. However, unless our primary focus is sorting and selecting rather than teaching and learning, we must question whether such practices represent the best use of teachers' and students' time.

7. *Suggesting that success is unlikely.* Ms. Brannet taught students in their first year of high school. At the beginning of the year she repeatedly told her students, "Remember that you are in high school now. Those middle school teachers gave more A's than we do. The fact that you got an A in middle school doesn't mean you'll get one in high school." After hearing this warning a few times, Judy, who had always been an A student, decided, "I'm going to let her keep her A's. She wants them more than I do." Judy got A's in all her other classes, but in Ms. Brannet's class Judy had decided that the deck was stacked against her. Think about the effect that Ms. Brannet's behavior could have on students who were less motivated to succeed than Judy.

Teachers employ other means of conveying to students the notion that success is unlikely. Consider the following statements, which we have heard in classrooms.

• "I can tell you right now, at the beginning of the second six weeks, that your grade is so low that you cannot possibly pass this course."

• "Your grade was so low last semester that you cannot pass the course for the year, regardless of your performance this

> **I**f the emphasis on sorting and selecting is to continue, we suggest that a formal appeals process for contested grades be set up.

semester. However, you keep coming to class, behaving, and trying. You're doing better!"

• "You almost earned an A. You needed a 95 average, and your average was 94.48. Maybe next time you'll make it!"

• "I had to change your B to an F. The three days you missed because you were suspended for shoving Mary while you were downtown last Saturday meant that you missed a vocabulary quiz, a homework assignment, and the test on *Beowulf.* Those three zeros really hurt you, but the school policy does not permit any makeup work for suspended students. My hands are tied."

8. *Practicing "gotcha" teaching.* Mr. Telly recently had a conference with his son's English teacher. Mr. Telly's son, John, had been an above-average, hardworking student prior to taking this English course. Even though he took copious notes in class and studied them diligently, John was making C's and D's on assignments and tests. Mr. Telly explained that John seemed to have difficulty discerning what was important in the lectures. The teacher explained that he always paused briefly before discussing the topics that would appear on the tests. "John must learn to read those pauses," said the teacher.

A nearly foolproof way to lower students' grade-point averages is to practice what we have come to call "gotcha" teaching. Teachers who have mastered this practice are skilled at keeping the objectives of their classes secret. Students are kept in the dark about what is important and what should be studied for tests. The students have to find out what it is that the teacher wants them to learn, and

the tests are ways of finding out how well students have read the teacher's mind. Wouldn't it be more reasonable to use pointed verbal markers and to share with the students those points that are worth stressing? What is wrong with letting students know what is expected of them?

9. *Grading first efforts.* Students in Tom's fifth-grade classroom were told to write an essay on the person they most admired. Tom wrote an eloquent essay on his older brother, Rob. He painted a vivid picture of his brother's free spirit. The paper was returned with a grade of F. Spelling and punctuation errors accounted for the points deducted. Yet mechanics had not been discussed as a factor to be graded. No comments appeared on Tom's paper regarding its excellent content. Tom is unlikely to bare his soul in writing again.

The standard practice, from kindergarten through college, seems to be to assign grades first and then to give feedback. (This happens frequently when teachers grade homework while students are still learning.) When are students given the opportunity to find out what we want them to learn? We have observed a few secondary English teachers and elementary language arts teachers who are providing feedback through a series of drafts of student writing. But we have not observed similar practices in other content areas.

10. *Penalizing students for taking risks.* Cynthia loved English. This was one subject in which she excelled. With the encouragement of her teachers, she decided to elect a "level 5" English course in her junior year. Her parents cautioned her that the course would be extremely difficult, because her previous experience had been in "level 4" classes. After four weeks of school and four difficult papers, Cynthia admitted that the class was "over her head." She asked to move to a lower-level class but was told that she could not do so. "What a fool I was to give this a try," Cynthia lamented to her friends. "There is no way out!"

Taking risks is not rewarded in most schools. From time to time, some students wish to take classes that may be too difficult for them. If they find that they are doing poorly, however, those students are given one of two options: take a low or failing grade with them to a lower-level class, or remain in the difficult class and continue to perform poorly. Many schools do not allow students to change classes once they have enrolled. Provisional placements without penalties might encourage students to risk trying more challenging work without jeopardizing their grade-point averages.

11. *Failing to recognize measurement error.* Ms. Corder proudly presented her grade book to Martha's mother, who had expressed concern about her daughter's grade. "Look, I have all the scores recorded," said Ms. Corder. "I carried them out to two decimal places when I averaged them, just to insure accuracy. Martha's average was 75.67, which gives her a D." This teacher's arithmetic may have been accurate, but she assigned equal weight to grades on homework, pop quizzes, papers, and tests. Is that likely to be appropriate?

12. *Establishing inconsistent criteria.* Judy and Stacey were reviewing their assignments on the way home from school. Judy was preparing to stay up all night to finish her social studies term paper. "Oh, don't bother," Stacey told her. "Mr. Kellogg will accept it a day late with no penalty." Judy thought that the grades for late papers would be lowered, but Stacey said, "No, that's what Ms. Trenton does. Mr. Kellogg takes papers late if you have a good excuse."

In some schools, each teacher establishes his or her own criteria for grading. Furthermore, these criteria may change from day to day or from grading period to grading period. We have seen a single school in which some teachers allowed students to drop one homework score per grading period, other teachers allowed students to drop one test score, and still other teachers insisted on counting all grades. Some teachers averaged all homework grades and counted this average as equal to one test grade; others averaged all grades as recorded. In other words, we could find no consensus among these teachers regarding grading practices.

If the emphasis on sorting and selecting is to continue, we suggest that, at the least, a formal appeals process for contested grades be established. The common practice of allowing the principal to arbitrate is unsatisfactory, because principals are placed in an untenable position: those who find for students are sure to be accused of not supporting teachers; those who find for teachers will certainly be accused of unfairness to students.

We propose that schools or school districts consider establishing appeals boards, each made up of a representative of the central office, a building-level administrator, a parent, and several teachers. Such boards would remove the burden of taking sides from principals and, more important, would focus the attention of teachers on the complexities of grading.

The student population served by the public schools continues to change. If demographic predictions for the next 20 years hold up, there will be a growing number of at-risk students. And these youngsters will remain in school *only* if there is more emphasis on teaching and learning and less emphasis on sorting and selecting. We are not advocating lowering standards. Rather, we wish to raise expectations for success by expanding students' chances to succeed. As long as schools insist on a narrow range of grading practices, educators will adopt curriculum materials and grouping practices that exclude many students from the best educational opportunities. Traditionally, the curriculum has been diluted — rather than the grading scale expanded — so that larger numbers of students will fit the narrow passing range.

The learning deficits that so trouble the recent crop of school critics[2] appear to support the need to enrich the existing curriculum in many schools. Changing grading practices to allow more students to succeed may help prevent students from dropping out even as opportunities for learning are enriched for all students. When educators cease to focus on sorting and selecting and begin to replace adversarial and inequitable grading policies with teaching and learning practices designed to increase students' chances of success, more students like Amy will come home announcing, "I got an 80 today. Not only is that a good score, but it's also a good grade."

1. Harold L. Hodgkinson, "The Changing Face of Tomorrow's Student," *Change*, May/June 1985, pp. 38-39.

2. The critics who have recently expressed concern about what students don't know include E. D. Hirsch, Jr., *Cultural Literacy: What Every American Needs to Know* (Boston: Houghton Mifflin, 1987); Chester E. Finn, Jr., Diane Ravitch, and Robert T. Fancher, eds., *Against Mediocrity: The Humanities in America's High Schools* (New York: Holmes & Meier, 1984); and Allan D. Bloom, *The Closing of the American Mind* (New York: Simon & Schuster, 1987).

Classroom Standard Setting and Grading Practices

James S. Terwilliger
University of Minnesota

James S. Terwilliger is Professor, University of Minnesota, Department of Educational Psychology, 319 Burton Hall, 178 Pillsbury Drive, SE, Minneapolis, MN 55455. He specializes in measurement and evaluation of educational achievement.

Assigning grades to students is undoubtedly one of the most distasteful aspects of teaching. If pushed, most teachers will state that the assignment of grades is, at best, a necessary evil that has little to do with the task of teaching. This point of view is also expressed in proposals for abolishing grading systems that appear in a cyclical fashion in professional journals aimed at teachers as well as in the popular press. Ebel (1974) summarizes the major arguments over grading and presents a strong case in favor of grades.

Interestingly, the process of grading has received relatively little attention in standard references on educational measurement. Textbooks on classroom measurement typically devote one chapter to issues related to grading, at least half of which deals with grading systems rather than the process of grade assignment.[1] Debates over

This is a revision of a paper presented as part of a symposium on classroom assessment research and training at the annual meetings of AERA and NCME, New Orleans, April, 1988.

grading systems have little to do with *grading as a judgmental process*. Therefore, this article presents an analysis of the grading process and recommends a specific approach to grading that can be employed regardless of the grading system in effect.

Assumptions Concerning Grading

I will start by stating six propositions concerning the grading process which I accept as self-evident truths.

1. Grading should be directly linked to an explicitly defined set of instructional goals that takes into account both the content of instruction and the cognitive complexity of outcomes. In principle, grades should reflect the *level* of the outcomes achieved by students with the highest grades being assigned to those who achieve the most advanced outcomes.

2. All data collected for purposes of judging student achievement should be expressed in *quantitative* form. This implies that (a) results on quizzes, tests, exams, and so forth, should be reported as scores or points earned based upon an explicit

scoring scheme; (b) homework, assigned projects, term papers, and so forth, should be scored using a clearly defined quantitative rating system; and (c) classroom performances, demonstrations, exhibitions, and so forth, should be evaluated using a well-defined system of numeric ratings or check lists.

3. The process of judging the quality of student performance (evaluation) should be distinguished from the process of collecting data about student performance (measurement). In particular, a valid judgment typically requires that (a) data be collected over a period of time, and (b) an explicit frame of reference be formulated as the basis for the judgment (evaluation).

4. From an educational viewpoint the assignment of a grade of failure, unsatisfactory, no credit, and so forth, has a special significance to students in terms of their future educational options. A failing grade should reflect a categorical judgment that the student does not possess a *minimal* level of competence independent of the student's performance relative to other students.

5. An evaluation plan should be

From *Educational Measurement: Issues and Practices*, Vol. 8, No. 2, Summer 1989, pp. 15-19. Copyright © 1989 by the National Council on Measurement in Education. Reprinted by permission of the publisher.

prepared for distribution to students. This plan should be explicit about (a) timing for data collection (e.g., dates for quizzes, exams, class presentations, etc.; due dates for assignments, projects, etc.), (b) conditions under which data collection takes place (e.g., format of items/questions in quizzes and exams, time limits for quizzes and exams, availability of reference materials, computational aids, etc., during quizzes and exams, penalties for late assignments, etc.), and (c) how the data are to be employed in making summative judgments about students (e.g., the relative weight to be given to each item of data in arriving at evaluations).

6. Teachers need time to establish an approach to grading that is both practical and consistent with the particular classroom setting in which they work. Realistic expectations concerning student performance can best be arrived at through trial and error.

A Recommended Grading Process

Over the past 15 years I have developed and employed an approach to grading which utilizes both criterion-referenced and norm-referenced concepts. I currently use some variation of the procedure in every class I teach. This approach has been adopted by several colleagues (both at my institution and elsewhere) and a significant number of public school teachers who have taken courses with me.

Two Classes of Objectives

A general overview of the procedure is shown in Figure 1. The first step is to distinguish what Gronlund (1973) has called *minimal objectives* from what he terms *developmental objectives*.

Minimal objectives represent essential course outcomes that all students are expected to achieve, whereas developmental objectives represent more complex goals of instruction toward which students strive but which few, if any, fully achieve. Gronlund (1973) argues that the mastery approach to learning and testing (Bloom, 1968) is clearly appropriate for minimal objectives but is of less value in reference to developmental objectives.

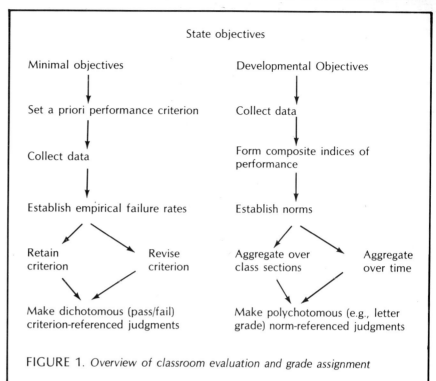

FIGURE 1. *Overview of classroom evaluation and grade assignment*

The distinction between objectives that are identified as minimal and those identified as developmental is somewhat arbitrary. Gronlund (1973) suggests a series of questions to help define minimal objectives that all students are expected to master. His questions include the following:

1. What minimum knowledge and skills are prerequisite to further learning in the same area (e.g., knowledge of terms, measurement skills)?
2. What basic skills are prerequisite to learning in other areas (e.g., reading skills, computational skills, language skills)? and
3. What minimum knowledge and skills are needed to function in everyday, out-of-school, situations (e.g., reading, writing, speaking)?

Obviously, the answers to questions such as these will vary from one teacher to the next. To identify objectives that are agreed upon by different instructors, it would be helpful if two or more teachers could share their judgments concerning what constitutes a set of minimal objectives in a given setting.

A rationale for the distinction between minimal and developmental objectives can also be based upon a cognitive analysis of instructional objectives. Minimal objectives typically correspond to lower level cognitive outcomes defined in terms of the acquisition of knowledge and basic skills. In contrast, developmental objectives are more clearly identified with higher level outcomes defined in terms of more complex cognitive processes.

For example, Presseisen (1986) has described *thinking skills* as falling into four categories:

Essential cognitive processes— the basic thinking skills that are the building blocks of thought development;
Higher-order cognitive processes —the more complex thinking skills, which may be harder to define but which are based on the essential cognitive processes;
Metacognitive processes—the learning to learn skills aimed at making thinking more conscious and the student more aware of the ways one can go about problem solving or decision making; and
Epistemic cognitive processes— the kinds of thinking related to particular bodies of knowledge or subject matters and the particular problems addressed by these knowledge areas as well as the in-

terdisciplinary relationships among content areas. (p. 9)

For present purposes, the first category could serve as a basis for minimal objectives whereas a mix of the other three would define developmental objectives. Presseisen's (1986) description of the differences between the first two categories is remarkably consistent with Gronlund's view. She states,

There is a decided difference between what is meant as a higher-order thinking and the exact, standardized, minimal competency objectives often included in basic skills instruction. Simplistic, rote information that fits limited instructional sequences is not sufficient as the material upon which to develop students' higher-order thinking. (p. 11)

Unfortunately, there is no universally accepted standard for differentiating minimal from developmental objectives based upon cognitive criteria. One concept that I employ is *novelty*. I believe that outcomes that are defined as minimal objectives are those that test students' ability to deal with familiar concepts and rehearsed skills. By definition, such outcomes have a low level of novelty. In contrast, developmental objectives test students' ability to apply learning to new material or situations. Others may argue for a broader definition of minimal outcomes. They prefer to include certain higher order outcomes (e.g., problem-solving skills) within the category of minimal objectives. This certainly is justified if sufficient numbers of students are able to achieve these objectives. The performance expectations for minimal objectives is the next issue to be addressed.

Minimal Objectives and Pass/Fail Decisions

Once the domain of minimal objectives has been defined, a series of special quizzes or exercises can be designed to measure student achievement with respect *to these objectives only*. For practical purposes, the minimal objectives quizzes and exercises function just like mastery tests. That is, a performance standard for passing is specified a priori with the expectation that at least 90% of the students will perform at or above the a priori standard. This raises the question of how to set the standard in order for the expected result to be realized.

Typically, some a priori performance standard is initially set, for example, 75% or 80% of the maximum possible score. Whether the a priori standard is "proper" depends upon how well the following assumptions are satisfied: (a) instruction has been effective, (b) students are motivated to achieve the minimal objectives, and (c) minimal objectives are achievable by most, if not all, students.

It is assumed that a teacher will do everything possible to meet the first two assumptions. But how can one know if an objective is within the reach of students? The only answer is an empirical one—test students and determine the success rate (difficulty level) for individual objectives and for the test as a whole. If the teacher has identified minimal objectives carefully, the success rate on each item will be high and the average performance on the total test will be well above the a priori standard. Few students will fail to reach the standard under these circumstances.

On the other hand, it may be that the success rate on certain items is extremely low. In such cases, the teacher needs to determine the cause of the problem. Perhaps the objective is one that is inherently difficult and should be removed from the domain of minimal objectives, or there may be a defect in the structure of the test question. In either event, items with low success rates obviously decrease the average score on the total test. Unless these items are omitted altogether, it may be necessary to alter the initial performance standard. After a couple of administrations of an instrument, a realistic and stable standard can be set.

This is one of the reasons I previously stated why a certain amount of trial and error is inevitable when designing a grading system. Performance standards must be calibrated to the difficulty level of the minimal objective measures in order to obtain results that are in line with expected (and acceptable) fail rates. Data from previous administrations of a measure are frequently essential to setting future standards.

Decisions to Fail Students

Decisions to fail students should be made strictly upon their performance on minimal objectives type measures (quizzes, exercises, etc.). The reason for this is simply that the Pass/Fail decision is a dichotomous one and criterion-referenced tests are well suited for that purpose.

Students should be given specific advance information concerning the minimal objectives. Therefore, the items and exercises should tap only familiar knowledge and well-rehearsed skills. Assuming that students are motivated to do well and are given proper instruction, it is quite reasonable to expect very small fail rates on such tests. Failure to reach the specified standard under such circumstances reflects a serious deficiency.

Developmental Objectives and Grade Assignment

Assessment of the more cognitively complex outcomes of instruction is undoubtedly the most difficult measurement job faced by a teacher. Analyses of teacher-made tests such as those reported by Fleming and Chambers (1983) reveal that the great preponderance of questions sample factual knowledge—knowledge of terms and rules. Such learning constitutes the lowest level outcomes and more properly belongs under the heading of minimal objectives. By asking teachers to differentiate minimal objectives from developmental objectives at the outset, I hope to create a greater curiosity among teachers concerning the entire range of possible learning outcomes. With luck, that may lead to more attention to complex outcomes than is currently the case.

Measuring Developmental Outcomes

Teachers who seek proficiency in designing measures of the more complex learning outcomes must (a) become generally familiar with cognitively based systems for classifying higher order outcomes, (b) study techniques for developing questions that tap such outcomes, and (c) practice constructing questions that are designed to measure complex thinking and reasoning skills. This is one area in which teachers can frequently help one another by working cooperatively on item construction and reacting to each other's efforts.

As previously noted, a basic criterion I employ in measuring higher order outcomes is the degree and type of novelty in the questions. One cannot claim to have engaged a student in any higher level cognitive process without presenting in the question a situation that is different in important respects from situations the student has previously encountered during learning. So-called *context dependent* items that make use of graphs, diagrams, tables, maps, and so forth, are excellent vehicles for tapping higher order outcomes. Teachers need to be encouraged to write questions that use such materials more frequently.

Score Distributions for Developmental Objectives Measures

By definition, higher order objectives are designed to "stretch" every student to their highest possible level of achievement. Gronlund (1973) notes that such objectives are open ended in the sense that each student can continue to progress toward greater expertise. Under these conditions it is impossible to set realistic a priori standards because of the great variation in student performances. Also, different types of data (written tests, classroom presentations, major projects, etc.) should be collected on each student to reflect the variety and complexity of higher level outcomes. These data are typically combined into a composite performance index[2] for each student as indicated in Figure 1. It is the composite score for developmental outcomes that becomes the basis for all grade assignments except for fail decisions previously made on the basis of minimal objectives scores.

Assuming that truly higher order outcomes have been tapped, the developmental composite score distribution will differ from score distributions yielded by the minimal objectives measures in three ways as summarized in Table 1. The dif-

---

TABLE 1

Expected Characteristics of Score Distributions Resulting From Minimal Objectives and Developmental Objectives Measures

Distribution characteristic	Minimal objectives	Developmental objectives
Shape	Definite negative skew	Approximately unimodal symmetric
Central tendency (difficulty level)	Mean score well above a priori standard (say .05 to .10) when divided by maximum possible score	Mean score divided by maximum possible score in interval between .50 and .70
Variability	Can be small or large; depends primarily upon degree of skew in distribution	Should be quite large

---

ferences in shape, central tendency, and variability are closely linked to the purposes that each serves. The unimodal symmetry (approximate), lower central tendency, and greater variability that characterizes the ideal composite distribution makes it much better suited to multiple category grading reflecting reliable differences in levels of achievement of higher order outcomes. It should be noted that the assumption of unimodality is not as important as the need for lower central tendency and greater variability.

In my experience, teachers have a built-in resistance to constructing instruments in which the difficulty level is in the .50 to .70 range. There are several reasons for this. As previously noted, one reason is that teachers simply are not in the habit of writing questions at levels beyond minimal objectives. Historically, difficulty levels on teacher-made tests are in the .80 to .90 range. A second reason is the prevailing belief that the average score is a direct reflection on the quality of the instruction. The lower the average score, the poorer the instructor. A third reason is that many teachers consider it to be unfair to ask questions that go beyond the specific material studied by students. For such teachers, the practice of asking students to respond to novel problem settings is strictly unthinkable. Obviously, these are beliefs that need to be dealt with before teachers will be receptive

to the grading system which I am advocating.

Grade Assignment

Assuming that the composite score distribution approximates the desired result, grades can be assigned on a norm-referenced basis within constraints, if any, imposed by school district guidelines concerning grade distributions. This is a trial and error process similar to that of standard setting in the case of minimal objectives outcomes. Initial grade assignments necessarily reflect the novice teacher's preconceptions concerning what quality performances are deserving of A's, B's, and so forth. With some experience, a set of implicit norms are formulated. With still more experience, the norms can become quite explicit.

It is important to note that I am *not* recommending grading on the curve. That would imply that a student's grade depends upon her/his performance in relation to others in the same class. Instead, I am suggesting that a more inclusive reference group be the basis for norms. This group might include (a) all students in various sections of the same general course for whom common performance data are available, or (b) all students who have taken a particular course under the same instructor over a specified period of time. If class sizes are reasonable (say 25 or more), fairly stable norms can be constructed in a relatively short amount of time.

One dilemma that arises in establishing norms by pooling data over time is the problem of *security* versus *comparability*. In order to make sure that the data base for grading remains constant over time, it is necessary to use the same (or psychometrically parallel) instruments year after year. Obviously, a teacher who decides to use the same assessment instruments year after year must take precautions to assure that the tests, quizzes, and so forth, are not in the public domain. Otherwise, there is likely to be a noticeable rise in the average performance level due to advance knowledge enjoyed by students in each successive year. A teacher who makes public the instruments employed as a basis for grading avoids the security problem only to sacrifice comparability in the data base employed.

I favor the practice of keeping assessment instruments as secure as possible. There are several reasons (besides comparability of data) for taking this position. First, the construction of measures of developmental outcomes is a time-consuming job. Teachers should be encouraged to think of this as an ongoing process in which instruments change incrementally based upon analysis of responses to specific assignments, questions, items, and so forth. It is a waste of valuable time and data to start from scratch every year. Second, by analyzing responses to classroom instruments and building an item bank from which instruments are constructed, it is possible to design high quality measures that assure substantial (if not strict) comparability of results. For example, quizzes or tests given in successive years can have 70% to 80% of their items in common with 20% to 30% new items added. If there is reason to suspect group differences, the performance on the common items can be employed as a check of the differences, if any, between students in the 2 years. Also, the general difficulty level of the common items can be compared with that of the new items added to a test. Third, it is not necessary to treat all assignments as secure. Major out-of-class term papers, projects, and so forth, can be designed and scored in a fashion such that it is of no great advantage for students to know in advance precisely what is expected of them. For such assignments there is no guarantee of strict comparability in the first place.

It should be noted that employing secure instruments does not deny students the benefit of valuable feedback from classroom assessments. I make it a practice of distributing and reviewing the results of quizzes, tests, and so forth, in class as soon as possible after each assessment. After students have reviewed their results, the instruments are returned to me and are available in my office for the balance of the term. At the end of the term all materials are destroyed.

Teachers have often asked me, "What is the ideal distribution of grades?" Of course, there is no generally acceptable answer. I do believe that it would be helpful if more school systems (and colleges) developed general guidelines suggesting reasonable grade distributions (10%–20% A's, 20%–30% B's, etc.). This could provide individual teachers with a framework within which to work. Teachers who wish to assign grades that are in conflict with the guidelines should be allowed to do so only if they can provide data to justify their action.

Some Concluding Remarks

The grading system outlined here can be adapted to a variety of settings. It is probably best suited to secondary school and undergraduate college classrooms where there is a need to use five or more grade categories. In settings where only a two-category Pass/Fail (or equivalent) system is used, the criterion-referenced approach using only minimal objectives would be sufficient. In classes where some students are enrolled on the Pass/Fail system and others are enrolled on a regular grading basis, the Pass/Fail students are required only to demonstrate achievement of the minimal objectives. Other students must complete both minimal and developmental objectives measures.

Of course, this flexibility is only possible if the two types of measures are constructed and administered as separate instruments. The minimal objectives measures should be treated as Bloom (1968) and others have described mastery tests, that is, each measure should be relatively brief, measures should be given fairly frequently, parallel forms should be designed to provide second trials for students who do not perform at the standard on the first administration, and so forth.

Finally, although I believe that measures of mastery and measures of minimal objectives are functionally equivalent, I think Gronlund's (1973) terminology has the advantage that it more honestly describes outcomes that the great majority of the students are expected to attain. As defined by standard dictionaries, the term *mastery* should be reserved for describing exceptional (i.e., high level) accomplishment or skill. Obviously, such level of achievement is much more consistent with developmental objectives than with minimal objectives.

Notes

[1] A notable exception is Hills (1981). This text contains several chapters dealing with a variety of issues associated with grades and grading.

[2] Technical issues associated with differences between the desired weights and effective weights for individual performances in composites will not be addressed here. These are discussed in Oosterhof (1987).

References

Bloom, B. S. (1968). Learning for mastery. *Evaluation Comment, 1*(2).

Ebel, R. L. (1974). Shall we get rid of grades? *Measurement in Education*, National Council on Measurement in Education, Fall.

Fleming, M., & Chambers, B. (1983). Teacher-made tests: Windows on the classroom. In M. E. Hathaway (Ed.), *Testing in the schools*. San Francisco: Jossey-Bass.

Gronlund, N. E. (1973). *Preparing criterion-referenced tests for classroom instruction*. New York: Macmillan.

Hills, J. R. (1981). Measurement and evaluation in the classroom (2nd ed.). Columbus, OH: Merrill.

Oosterhof, A. C. (1987). Obtaining intended weights when combining students' scores. *Educational Measurement: Issues and Practice, 6*(4), 29–37.

Presseisen, B. Z. (1986). *Thinking skills: Research and practice*. Washington, DC: National Education Association.

Teaching to the (Authentic) Test

Testing can once again serve teaching and learning if tests clarify and set intellectual standards.

GRANT WIGGINS

Grant Wiggins is a special consultant to the National Center on Education and the Economy in Rochester, New York, and the Coalition of Essential Schools on issues of assessment and curriculum. He may be reached through the National Center.

Practical alternatives and sound arguments now exist to make testing once again serve teaching and learning. Ironically, we *should* "teach to the test." The catch is to design and then teach to *standard-setting* tests so that practicing for and taking the tests actually enhances rather than impedes education, and so that a criterion-referenced diploma makes externally mandated tests unobtrusive—even unnecessary.

Setting Standards

If tests determine what teachers actually teach and what students will study for—and they do—then the road to reform is a straight but steep one: test those capacities and habits we think are essential, and test them in context. Make them replicate, within reason, the challenges at the heart of each academic discipline. Let them be—authentic.

What are the actual performances that we want students to be good at, that represent model challenges? Design them by department, by school, and by district—and worry about a

fair, efficient, and objective method of grading them as a *secondary* problem. Do we judge our students to be deficient in writing, speaking, listening, artistic creation, research, thoughtful analysis, problem posing, and problem solving? Let the tests ask them to write, speak, listen, create, do original research, analyze, pose and solve problems.

Rather than seeing tests as after-the-fact devices for checking up on what students have learned, we should see them as instructional: the central vehicle for clarifying and setting intellectual standards. The recital, debate, play, or game (and the criteria by which they are judged)—the "performance"—is not a checkup, it is the heart of the matter; all coaches *happily* teach to it. We should design academic tests to be similarly standard setting, not merely standardized.

Reform of testing depends, however, on teachers' recognizing that standardized testing evolved and proliferated because the school transcript became untrustworthy. An "A" in "English" means only that some adult thought the student's work was excellent. Compared to what or whom? As determined by what criteria? In reference to what specific subject matter? The high school diploma, by remaining tied to no standard other than credit accrual and seat time, provides

no useful information about what students have studied or what they can actually do with what was studied.

To regain control over both testing and instruction, schools need to rethink their diploma requirements and grades. They need a clear set of appropriate and objective criteria, enabling both students *and outsiders* to know what counts, what is essential—what a school's standards really are. Until we specify what students must directly demonstrate to earn a diploma, they will continue to pass by meeting the de facto "standard" of being dutiful and persistent—irrespective of the quality of their work. And standardized testmakers will continue to succeed in hawking simplistic norm-referenced tests to districts and states resigned to using them for lack of a better accountability scheme.

Exhibitions of Mastery

The diploma should be awarded upon a successful final demonstration of mastery for graduation—an "Exhibition" .... As the diploma is awarded when earned, the school's program proceeds with no strict age grading and with no system of "credits earned" by time spent in class. The emphasis is on the students' demonstration that they can do important things.

—From the Prospectus of the Coalition of Essential Schools

The "exhibition of mastery," proposed by Ted Sizer in *Horace's Compromise*

The Rite of Passage Experience (R.O.P.E.) at Walden III, Racine, Wisconsin

All seniors must complete a portfolio, a study project on U.S. history, and 15 oral and written presentations before a R.O.P.E committee composed of staff, students, and an outside adult. Nine of the presentations are based on the materials in the portfolio and the project; the remaining six are developed for presentation before the committee. All seniors must enroll in a yearlong course designed to help them meet these requirements.

The eight-part *portfolio*, developed in the first semester, is intended to be "a reflection and analysis of the senior's own life and times." The requirements include:
- a written autobiography,
- a reflection on work (including a resume),
- an essay on ethics,
- a written summary of coursework in science,
- an artistic product or a written report on art (including an essay on artistic standards used in judging artwork).

The *project* is a research paper on a topic of the student's choosing in American history. The student is orally questioned on the paper in the presentations before the committee during the second semester.

The *presentations* include oral tests on the previous work, as well as six additional presentations on the essential subject areas and "personal proficiency" (life skills, setting and realizing personal goals, etc.). The presentations before the committee usually last an hour, with most students averaging about 6 separate appearances to complete all 15.

A diploma is awarded to those students passing 12 of the 15 presentations and meeting district requirements in math, government, reading, and English.

Note: This summary is paraphrased from both the R.O.P.E. Student Handbook and an earlier draft of Archbald and Newmann's (1988) *Beyond Standardized Testing*.

Fig. 1. An Example of a Final Exhibition

(1984) and a cornerstone of the "Essential School," is one attempt to grapple with these issues. The intent of the exhibitions project is to help schools and districts design more authentic, engaging, revealing, and trustworthy "tests" of a student's intellectual ability.

The reference to engagement is not incidental. The exhibition of mastery was initially proposed as an antidote to student passivity and boredom, not merely as a more valid form of assessment. The idea is to capture the interest value of an authentic test of one's ability, such as is often provided in schools by literary magazines, portfolios, recitals, games, or debates. Thus, "any exhibition of mastery should be the students' opportunity to show off what they know and are able to do rather than a trial by question . . ."[1]

The exhibition of mastery, as the name implies, is meant to be more than a better test. Like the thesis and oral exam in graduate school, it indicates whether a student has *earned* a diploma, is ready to leave high school.[2] The school is designed "backwards" around these standard-setting

tests to ensure that teachers and students alike understand their obligations and how their own efforts fit in a larger context. Teachers "teach to the test" because the test is essential—and teacher designed.

But why institute a radically new form of assessment? Why not just improve conventional teaching and course-related tests? As the "Study of High Schools" documented, a major cause of the high school's inadequacies is the absence of direct teaching of the essential skills of inquiry and expression. Even in "demanding" schools, students often fail to learn how to learn. The culprit is discipline-based curriculums that lead to content-based teaching and testing: the essential (cross-disciplinary) habits and skills of reading, writing, questioning, speaking, and listening fall through the cracks of typical content-focused syllabi and course credits; as indicated, for example, when teachers say "I teach English, not reading."

A required final public exhibition of know-how ensures that those essentials are taught and learned. The final

exit-level exhibition reveals whether a would-be graduate can demonstrate control over the skills of inquiry and expression and control over an intellectual topic that approximates the expert's ability to use knowledge effectively and imaginatively. A final exhibition provides students with an occasion to make clear, if only perhaps symbolically, that they are ready to graduate.

An exhibition challenges students to show off not merely their knowledge but their initiative; not merely their problem solving but their problem posing; not just their learning on cue, but their ability to judge and learn how to learn on an open-ended problem, often of their own design. The experience thus typically focuses on the essential skills of "inquiry and expression"—a synthesis that requires questioning, problem posing, problem solving, independent research, the creation of a product or performance, and a *public* demonstration of mastery. Significantly, there is often a component calling for self-reflection and analysis of what one has undergone and learned.

Thus, a *final exhibition* is a misnomer in an important sense. Many Coalition schools provide a semester- or yearlong course, an adult adviser, and a committee to ensure that a student has adequate guidance, evaluation, and incentive (see fig. 1 for an example of a final exhibition from a Coalition school). The exhibition of mastery is as much a process as a final product, if not more so. The process of choosing topics, advisers, and committees and refining one's ideas and skills is a yearlong exercise in understanding and internalizing standards.

A similar approach to a diploma at the college level has been used successfully at Alverno College, Milwaukee, Wisconsin, for over a decade.[3] Assessment is a central experience, with coursework a means to a set of known ends: students must achieve mastery in the following eight general areas, with their progress in each area being charted on a multistaged scale:

1. effective communication ability,
2. analytic capability,
3. problem-solving ability,
4. valuing in a decision-making context,
5. effective social interaction,

6. taking responsibility for the global environment,
7. effective citizenship,
8. aesthetic responsiveness.

Performances: Better Classroom Tests

Course-specific tests also have glaring weaknesses, not only because they are often too low level and content heavy. They are rarely designed to be authentic tests of intellectual ability; as with standardized tests, teacher-designed finals are usually intended to be quickly read and scored.

It seems wise, then, to talk about a move toward more intellectual performances in course-bound testing as a way of stressing the need to make tests more central, authentic, and engaging—as in the arts and athletics. (The term *exhibitions* would be reserved for those culminating graduation-level exercises designed to assess ability in the essentials underlying all course-work required for graduation.)

Designing performances implies a very different approach to standard setting than is implied by typical criterion-referenced tests or outcome-based views of mastery, though the instincts behind the designs are similar. Performances would ideally *embody* and *evoke* desired outcomes in authentic contexts. Too often, specifying only outcomes leads to tests that atomize and decontextualize knowledge: the testmaker designs a set of isolated pat exercises designed to elicit each desired outcome. Genuine tests of ability rarely provide such blatant cues and simple recall; they require us to have a repertoire, the judgment and skill to "put it all together" in one central challenge, repeatedly tried. (Imagine the assessment of music ability in a series of little exercises tried once, rather than through practice and performance of a complete piece in recitals.)

In sum, the goals behind the exhibition of mastery and the performance are to design standard-setting tests that provide more direct evidence of a student's intellectual ability; design tests that are thus able to stand by themselves as objective results; design more authentic intellectual challenges at the heart of a discipline; and design tests that are more likely to engage students and motivate them to raise their own intellectual standards to do well on

---

An Oral History Project for 9th Graders

To the student:
  You must complete an oral history based on interviews and written sources and then present your findings orally in class. The choice of subject matter is up to you. Some examples of possible topics include: your family, running a small business, substance abuse, a labor union, teenage parents, and recent immigrants.
  Create three workable hypotheses based on your preliminary investigations and four questions you will ask to test out each hypothesis.

Criteria for Evaluation of Oral History Project

To the teacher:
  Did student investigate three hypotheses?
  Did student describe at least one change over time?
  Did student demonstrate that he or she had done background research?
  Were the four people selected for the interviews appropriate sources?
  Did student prepare at least four questions in advance, related to each hypothesis?
  Were those questions leading or biased?
  Were follow-up questions asked where possible, based on answers?
  Did student note important differences between "fact" and "opinion" in answers?
  Did student use evidence to prove the ultimate best hypothesis?
  Did student exhibit organization in writing and presentation to class?

Note: This example is courtesy of Albin Moser, Hope High School, Providence, Rhode Island. To obtain a thorough account of a performance-based history course, including the lessons used and pitfalls encountered, write to Dave Kobrin, Brown University, Education Department, Providence, RI 02912.

Fig. 2. An Example of a Test of Performance

---

them. (See fig. 2 for an example of a performance that illustrates and illuminates these design standards.)

Toward More Authentic Tests

Exhibitions and performances sound fine on a schoolwide basis, you say, but districtwide or statewide? Isn't that too costly and cumbersome? I contend that the supposed impracticality and/or expense of designing such tests on a wide scale is a habit of thinking, not a fact. The United States is the only major country that relies so heavily on norm-referenced, short-answer tests instead of performance- and/or classroom-based assessment on a national level. In addition, a national committee on assessment in Great Britain has called for an exemplary system requiring flexible, criterion-referenced, and performance-based tests.[4] Many of the tests would be created by classroom teachers, who would be part of the standardizing process through "moderating" meetings to compare and balance results on their own and national tests.

In the U.S., more authentic skill assessment can now be found in various districts and states due, in part, to the

work in writing assessment by the National Writing Project and its state offshoots (such as the California CAP writing test), and the American Council on the Teaching of Foreign Languages in the assessment of foreign language proficiency. Some states, such as Connecticut, have already designed and piloted performance-based assessment using ACTFL tests and criteria. In addition, they have piloted hands-on tests in graphics, small engines, and science. Vermont has proposed a statewide assessment system in writing and mathematics that would be portfolio based and teacher assessed.

We already have a national example in science: the 1987 NAEP pilot "Higher-Order Thinking Science Test," which includes some (though too few) hands-on experiments. One example:

Students are given a sample of three different materials and an open box. The samples differ in size, shape, and weight. The students are asked to determine whether the box would weigh the most (and least) if it were completely filled with material A, B, or C. There are a variety of possible approaches . . . NAEP administrators used detailed checklists to record each student's procedures and strategies.[5]

A. Structure and Logistics

1. Are more appropriately public; involve an audience, a panel, and so on.
2. Do not rely on unrealistic and arbitrary time constraints.
3. Offer known, not secret, questions or tasks.
4. Are more like portfolios or a *season* of games (not one-shot).
5. Require some collaboration with others.
6. Recur—and are *worth* practicing for, rehearsing, and retaking.
7. Make assessment and feedback to students so central that school schedules, structures, and policies are modified to support them.

B. Intellectual Design Features

1. Are "essential"—not needlessly intrusive, arbitrary, or contrived to "shake out" a grade.
2. Are "enabling"—constructed to point the student toward more sophisticated use of the skills or knowledge.
3. Are contextualized, complex intellectual challenges, not "atomized" tasks, corresponding to isolated "outcomes."
4. Involve the student's own research or use of knowledge, for which "content" is a means.
5. Assess student habits and repertoires, not mere recall or plug-in skills.
6. Are *representative* challenges—designed to emphasize *depth* more than breadth.
7. Are engaging and educational.
8. Involve somewhat ambiguous ("ill-structured") tasks or problems.

C. Grading and Scoring Standards

1. Involve criteria that assess essentials, not easily counted (but relatively unimportant) errors.
2. Are not graded on a "curve" but in reference to performance standards (criterion-referenced, not norm-referenced).
3. Involve demystified criteria of success that appear to *students* as inherent in successful activity.
4. Make self-assessment a part of the assessment.
5. Use a multifaceted scoring system instead of one aggregate grade.
6. Exhibit harmony with shared schoolwide aims—a *standard*.

D. Fairness and Equity

1. Ferret out and identify (perhaps hidden) strengths.
2. Strike a *constantly* examined balance between honoring achievement and native skill or fortunate prior training.
3. Minimize needless, unfair, and demoralizing comparisons.
4. Allow appropriate room for student learning styles, aptitudes, and interests.
5. Can be—should be—attempted by *all* students, with the test "scaffolded up," not "dumbed down," as necessary.
6. Reverse typical test-design procedures: they make "accountability" serve student learning (Attention is primarily paid to "face" and "ecological" validity of tests).[1]

1. Thanks to Ted Sizer, Art Powell, Fred Newmann, and Doug Archbald; and the work of Peter Elbow and Robert Glaser for some of these criteria. A more thorough account of them will appear in an upcoming issue of *Phi Delta Kappan* (in press).

Fig. 3. Characteristics of Authentic Tests

NAEP borrowed most of its experiments from the British Assessment of Performance Unit tasks, which have been used (and reliably scored) in Great Britain for a decade in reading, speaking, listening, math, and science.

Genuine tests *can* be widely implemented if we can overcome inertia and fatalism about current forms of standardized testing. Authentic, performance-based testing is a reality, not a romantic vision. There is also ample room for more intelligent design and use of conventional norm-referenced standardized tests.[6]

The state of Connecticut has developed a "Common Core of Learning," which lists objectives and criteria in all essential domains. Performance-based tests, built around criteria specified by experts in each field and involving tests administered by trained observers, are to be designed to honor those aims.

There are even standardized tests worth noting. ACT has developed a wide-ranging multimedia test of "general education knowledge and skills" called COMP, designed for colleges but easily adaptable to the high school level. The test uses art reproductions and audiotapes of news programs, for example, in testing writing and listening skills. On other items, students draft letters on different topics. There is even allowance for the student to respond orally on tape to a few test questions. The test takes six hours to administer, covers all the essential skills of inquiry and expression, and includes a 54-question self-assessment about one's patterns of activity related to each competency.

In sum, authentic tests have four basic characteristics in common. First, they are designed to be truly representative of performance in the field; only then are the problems of scoring reliability and logistics of testing considered. Second, far greater attention is paid to the teaching and learning of the *criteria* to be used in the assessment. Third, self-assessment plays a much greater role than in conventional testing.[7] And, fourth, the students are often expected to present their work and defend themselves publicly and orally to ensure that their apparent mastery is genuine. (See fig. 3 for a more thorough list of characteristics of authentic tests.)

Toward a Performance-Based Diploma

The diploma by exhibition implies radically different standards for graduation. Instead of seat time or the mere accrual of Carnegie units, the diploma is performance based and criterion referenced. We may not be ready for the demise of age grading and social promotion; but if the harm done by standardized testing is to be undone, we need to redesign schools "backwards" around graduation-level standards of performance.

The performances and exhibitions should be designed prior to instruction, thus setting the school's standards in functional, not merely abstract and idealized, terms. Seeing them as add-ons to the traditional curriculum is to miss the point. How must the school be redesigned to support exhibitions or any form of exit-level standards? This should be the question behind "restructuring" and the source of vigorous debate among faculties and school board members. Designing and institutionalizing exhibitions would better ensure, in other words, that the school had clear, coherent, and effective standards. Knowing the desired student abilities and work standards, as embodied in culminating performances and scoring criteria, would force key issues of policy: how will time, space, personnel, and other resources be best spent to ensure that diploma standards are met?

To talk with disdain of "teaching to the test" is to misunderstand how we learn. The test is the point of leverage—for learning and for reform. The issue is the integrity of the test: the genuineness, effectiveness, and aptness of the challenge. The finals (and the criteria by which they are graded) set the standards of acceptable work in a course and a school—irrespective of noble language in school district reports or teacher intentions as reflected in syllabi. Legitimate and effective assessment is as simple(!) as ensuring that tests, grades, diploma requirements, and the structures and policies of the schools practice what we preach as essential. If we so honor our professed aims, the problems associated with standardized testing will take care of themselves.

1. From *Horace's Compromise* (Sizer 1984), p. 68.

2. This (final) exhibition is patterned after the 18th century model of a public display of one's ability to engage in disputation: ". . . candidates for degrees expected to be academically tested at Commencement itself. Bachelor of Arts candidates prepared theses or topics on which they could be quizzed, and candidates for the Master of Arts submitted questions they were ready to defend. Titles of theses and questions were printed in advance and handed out at Commencement, and visitors often took the opportunity of challenging the candidates on their knowledge" (from the Harvard University Commencement program).

3. See the booklet *Assessment at Alverno College*, available from the college. For a history and an analysis of Alverno's program (as well as a general discussion of

competency-based higher education), see *On Competency* (Grant, Elbow et al. 1979).

4. *National Curriculum: Task Group on Assessment and Testing: A Report*. Available from the Department of Education and Science (1988). This is a landmark document, outlining in readable prose a plan for intelligent and humane assessment.

5. From *Learning By Doing* (Educational Testing Service 1987).

6. See the excellent article by Dan Koretz of the RAND Corporation in the Summer 1988 issue of *American Educator*, which sums up the current controversy about norm-referenced state testing (the "Lake Wobegon effect" of each state being above average) and provides a useful set of guidelines for assessing assessment.

7. At Alverno, self-assessment is often the first level of proficiency. Thus, in the speaking requirement, students must give a five-minute videotaped talk—with the first evaluations given on the student's self-assessment after watching the videotape.

References

Alverno College Faculty. (1979/1985). *Assessment at Alverno College*. Rev. ed. Milwaukee, Wis.: Alverno College.

Archbald, D., and F. Newmann. (1988). *Beyond Standardized Testing: Authentic Academic Achievement in the Secondary School*. Reston, Va.: NASSP Publications.

Department of Education and Science and the Welsh Office. (1988). *National Curriculum: Task Group on Assessment and Testing: A Report*. London: Her Majesty's Stationery Office, Department of Education and Science, England and Wales. A brief "Digest for Schools" is also available.

Educational Testing Service. (1987). *Learning By Doing: A Manual for Teaching and Assessing Higher-Order Thinking in Science and Mathematics*. A report on the NAEP pilot of performance-based assessment. A summary of the NAEP pilot of performance-based assessment. Princeton, N.J.: ETS. The full report: *A Pilot Study of Higher-Order Thinking Skills Assessment Techniques in Science and Mathematics*. ETS Report #17-HOS-80.

Grant, G., P. Elbow, et al. (1979). *On Competence: A Critical Analysis of Competence-Based Reforms in Higher Education*. San Francisco: Jossey-Bass.

Koretz, D. (Summer 1988). "Arriving in Lake Wobegon: Are Standardized Tests Exaggerating Achievement and Distorting Instruction?" *American Educator* 12, 2.

Sizer, T. (1984). *Horace's Compromise: The Dilemma of the American High School*. Updated ed. Boston: Houghton-Mifflin.

Wiggins, G. (In press). "A True Test: Toward Authentic and Equitable Forms of Assessment." *Phi Delta Kappan*.

Recommended Readings

Alverno College Faculty. (1984). *Analysis and Communication at Alverno: An Approach to Critical Thinking*. Milwaukee, Wis.: Alverno College.

Berk, R. A., ed. (1986). *Performance Assessment: Methods and Applications*. Baltimore, Md.: Johns Hopkins University Press.

Bloom, B., G. Madaus, and J. T. Hastings. (1981). *Evaluation to Improve Learning*. New York: McGraw-Hill.

Brooks, G. (1987). *Speaking and Listening: Assessment at Age 15*. Great Britain: The Assessment of Performance Unit (APU), Department of Education and Science. APU material exists on the results of performance-based assessment in language, history, math, science, and history in primary and secondary schools.

Elbow, P. (1986). "Trying to Teach While Thinking About the End" and "Evaluating Students More Accurately." In *Embracing Contraries: Explorations in Teaching and Learning*. New York: Oxford University Press. The former chapter originally published in Grant, Elbow, et al. (1979).

Higgs, T., ed. (1984). *Teaching for Proficiency, the Organizing Principle*. Lincolnwood, Ill.: National Textbook Company and ACTFL.

Sizer, T. (1986). "Changing Schools and Testing: An Uneasy Proposal." In *The Redesign of Testing for the 21st Century*. 1985 ETS Invitational Conference Proceedings. Princeton, N.J.: ETS.

Slavin, R., et al. (1986). *Using Student Team Learning*. 3rd ed. Baltimore: The Johns Hopkins Team Learning Project Press.

Snow, R. (1988). "Progress in Measurement, Cognitive Science, and Technology That Can Change the Relation Between Instruction and Assessment." In *Assessment in the Service of Learning*. 1987 ETS Invitational Conference Proceedings. Princeton, N.J.: ETS.

Spandel, V. (1981). *Classroom Applications of Writing Assessment: A Teacher's Handbook*. Portland, Oreg.: Northwest Regional Educational Laboratory.

Stiggins, R. (1987). "Design and Development of Performance Assessments." *Educational Measurement: Issues and Practices* 6, 3: 33-42. An Instructional Model (ITEMS), published by National Council on Measurement in Education (NCME). Comes with an Instructor's Guide.

Stiggins, R. (January 1988). "Revitalizing Classroom Assessment." *Phi Delta Kappan* 69: 5.

Wiggins, G. (Winter 1987). "Creating a Thought-Provoking Curriculum." *American Educator* 11, 4.

Wiggins, G. (Winter 1988). "Rational Numbers: Scoring and Grading That Helps Rather than Hurts Learning." *American Educator* 12, 4.

Innovation or Enervation?

Performance Assessment in Perspective

As sure as testing generally is not the answer to the multifaceted and complex problems facing contemporary American education, performance assessment is not the panacea either, Mr. Cizek contends.

BY GREGORY J. CIZEK

GREGORY J. CIZEK is a program associate in the Professional Assessment Services Division of American College Testing, Iowa City, Ia.

THE FIRST recorded performance assessment was literally a bloodbath. The interesting narrative of that event describes a truly "high stakes" examination, in which the Gilead guards "tested" fugitives from the tribe of Ephraim who tried to cross the Jordan River:

> "Are you a member of the tribe of Ephraim?" they asked. If the man replied that he was not, then they demanded, "Say Shibboleth." But if he couldn't pronounce the "H," and said "Sibboleth" instead of "Shibboleth," he was dragged away and killed. So forty-two thousand people of Ephraim died there at that time.[1]

Well, performance assessment is back. It is surely possible to overstate the parallels between the current calls for increased reliance on performance assessments and the Biblical example. Undoubt-

Illustration by Mario Noche

Its advocates
have yet to spell out
how the current ver-
sion of performance
assessment is different.

---

edly, the stakes involved in existing examination programs are not as momen-
tous as those in the story. But there are
similarities, not the least of which is the
almost religious zealotry of some proponents of performance assessment.

Before fully embracing the doctrine of
performance assessment, however, professional educators would do well to
scrutinize the movement's claims, costs,
and characteristics. Indeed, such scrutiny
is a professional responsibility. Addressing a related testing controversy over a
decade ago, Robert Glaser and Lloyd
Bond reminded us of that responsibility:

> In the heat of the current contro-
> versy, it is especially necessary to be
> our own sternest critics. It is not pos-
> sible to attend to every criticism, es-
> pecially those that are ill-founded and
> well beyond the state of the knowledge
> of human behavior. However, it is nec-
> essary to examine the point and coun-
> terpoint in public and professional de-
> bate in order to move forward with re-
> search and development in human as-
> sessment and with analysis of institu-
> tional policy and test use. The exami-
> nation should be conducted in a way
> that is open not only to the members
> of our own discipline but also the larg-
> er public that is affected by and must
> make decisions about tests.[2]

PERFORMANCE ASSESSMENT IN PERSPECTIVE

Performance assessment might be the
answer to many social and educational
problems, or so say its advocates. The
recent report of the National Commission
on Testing and Public Policy enthusiastically argues that this new kind of assess-

ment must be pursued in order to halt the
undermining of vital social policies and
to promote greater development of the
talents of all people.[3] Certainly these are
worthy goals. But is performance assessment the answer? The purposes of
this article are to define what is currently called *performance assessment*, to examine the goals of the advocates of performance assessment, and to offer practical and technical cautions to the makers and consumers of performance assessments.

WHAT IS PERFORMANCE ASSESSMENT?

Educational tests are, fundamentally,
attempts to gauge what students know or
can do. An *indirect* measure of, for example, a student's woodworking ability
might be obtained through a paper-and-
pencil test that asks the student to state
the uses of different lathe chisels, to
recognize grain patterns of different species of wood, or to identify the proper
way to feed stock into a planer. Another
way to gauge the student's woodworking ability would be to use a more *direct*
measure. Such a test might consist of
presenting the student with a block of
wood and the appropriate tools and requiring the student to turn a bowl. This
more direct way of assessing woodworking ability could be called a performance
assessment.

Of course, this kind of direct assessment has been going on for quite some
time and is not particularly new. Elementary students still solve problems in math
classes, middle-schoolers go to spelling
bees, high school students give speeches,
education majors do their student teaching, and dentists-in-training are evaluated on their ability to fill cavities. Indeed,
Walter Haney and George Madaus of the
Center for the Study of Testing, Evaluation, and Educational Policy at Boston
College have reminded us that performance assessment per se is not innovative:
"A point worth noting about evaluation
alternatives that have been suggested over
the last 20 years is that many of them
are not at all new. Evaluation tools such
as live performances, products, teacher
judgment, and school grades have a long
history in education."[4]

Elsewhere, Haney recounted three
trends in educational measurement that
were apparent *in the 1930s*:

> 1. A growing emphasis upon validi-
> ty and a consequent decreasing empha-

sis upon reliability as the criterion for
evaluating measuring instruments;

> 2. a decline of the faith in indirect
> measurement and an increasing empha-
> sis upon direct measurement as a means
> of attaining satisfactory validity; and

> 3. a growing respect for essay exami-
> nations as instruments for measuring
> certain outcomes of education.[5]

IF NOT NEW, THEN WHAT?

The three trends identified in the 1930s
must certainly sound familiar to policy
makers in the 1990s. They bear a remarkable resemblance to what the proponents
of performance assessment are currently urging. But if the idea itself is not new,
then what is original about the movement? Unfortunately, perhaps all we have
up to this point is a new *name* for these
activities — performance assessments.
And there may not even be consensus
on the name, with such aliases as genuine assessment, authentic evaluation, and
practical testing — to list just a few —
enjoying wide circulation. But performance assessment by any other name is the
same, and its advocates have yet to spell
out how the current version is substantially different from its relatives.

Whatever the name, one thing is certain: performance assessment is chic.
Many educational leaders, directors of
state-level assessment projects, and administrators of large-scale testing programs are seriously contemplating increased reliance on performance assessment. But the push for this type of assessment should be judged on more than
its current popularity. In a courageous
article on educational faddism, Robert
Slavin states that "education resembles
such fields as fashion and design, in
which change mirrors shifts in taste and
social climate and is not usually thought
of as true progress."[6] Slavin's article
was intended to document how educational innovations are often funded and
implemented before research on their effectiveness has taken place. The same insight should guide us in current policy
considerations involving performance assessment. It is my contention that we
have not yet been offered a well-con-
ceived rationale for action, when such a
rationale should be a sine qua non for
widespread change and the investment
of resources.[7] By my reckoning, performance assessment is flourishing somewhere between the "gee whiz" and the
"hot topic" stages in Slavin's schematiza-

tion of the 12 characteristic phases of the swinging education pendulum.

WHO ARE THESE PEOPLE AND WHAT DO THEY WANT?

The performance assessment bandwagon is evidently big enough to accommodate quite a crowd. Although proponents of performance assessment may not be totally sure of what they want, they know what they don't want: standardized, multiple-choice tests.

The National Education Association has encouraged the "elimination of group standardized intelligence, aptitude, and achievement tests."[8] David Owen, author of a critique of the Scholastic Aptitude Test (SAT), thinks that the answer might be to "abolish the Educational Testing Service."[9] Another article accuses standardized testing of being "harmful to educational health."[10] The final report of the California Education Summit goes even further, recommending that "all multiple-choice tests should be eliminated."[11] The recent report of the National Commission on Testing and Public Policy is more moderate, suggesting that "testing programs should be redirected from overreliance on multiple-choice tests."[12] Gerald Bracey, the director of research and evaluation for a Colorado school district, waxed philosophical about what needs to be done: "As a sociologist pointed out some years back, to make the world safe for democracy, it is not sufficient to destroy totalitarian regimes. You have to eliminate the *mentality* that produces totalitarianism. It will not be sufficient, similarly, to eliminate tests."[13]

But those touting performance assessment definitely want your money. It is highly surprising that a common complaint of testing prohibitionists is that testing is expensive. Bracey has assailed the SAT as "the $150 million redundancy."[14] The National Commission on Testing and Public Policy lodged a similar complaint, noting that "reported sales [of elementary and secondary tests and testing services] rose to over $100 million by 1986."[15] The proponents of performance assessment typically cite these figures and point out that the money could be better spent on programs for the disadvantaged, Head Start, or teachers' salaries. Certainly, education policy makers should be concerned about how limited resources are allocated. The irony is that, despite their advocates' apparent concern about cost, the vaguely defined

alternative assessments will surely be costlier. For example, the National Board for Professional Teaching Standards recently requested proposals for the development of a prototype credentialing program for "early adolescence/English language arts teachers" involving performance assessment. The estimated amount of the award for this *one* specialized program exceeds $1.4 million.[16] Another $1.4 million is expected to be awarded for the development of an "early adolescence/generalist" assessment.[17] These figures are for development only and *do not* include any printing, administrative, scoring, or reporting costs. If other performance assessments are as expensive – and surely large-scale assessments will be even more costly – the tab will be staggering.

The hidden price of increased reliance on performance assessments may be even more invidious than the actual monetary costs. For example, performance assessment advocate Ruth Mitchell of the Council for Basic Education noted in a recent interview that there is "no reliable way to compare the costs" of traditional tests and the proposed alternatives. Further, Mitchell asserts that "alternative assessment yields dividends for professional development and curriculum development. Such assessment efforts can, therefore, legitimately absorb other parts of a school district's budget."[18]

Whether such "absorption" is truly legitimate is – or should be – debatable. At minimum, Mitchell's observations should serve as a portent of future educational turf warfare if the high cost of the new assessments is balanced on the backs of other important budgetary considerations.

And what will be purchased in the rush to invest in this latest innovation? Proponents of performance assessments have offered only vague descriptions of what the new instruments will look like. For example, Mitchell has proffered that al-

ternative assessments "can take as many forms as the imagination will allow."[19] In essence, educators are being asked to purchase this amorphous product sight unseen.

Neither is it clear that the new instruments will actually measure something different from more traditional forms of testing. Bracey, a proponent of performance assessment, contends that the new assessments will measure abilities that "are hard, if not impossible, to measure with standardized, multiple-choice

> **A**lthough proponents of performance assessment may not be totally sure of what they want, they know what they don't want.

tests." He goes on to say that what *should* be measured is "higher-order thinking," which is "nonalgorithmic" and "complex," "yields multiple solutions," and involves "nuanced judgment," "uncertainty," and "imposing meaning."[20] Zowie! Such fantastic claims have led education policy analyst Chester Finn to note that performance assessment is "like 'Star Wars': the idea remains to be demonstrated as feasible."[21] Certainly, Bracey's descriptors *sound* good, but essential questions about what is actually to be measured and how these goals will be accomplished remain unanswered.

WILL PERFORMANCE ASSESSMENTS BE ANY GOOD?

I really don't mean to be a naysayer about innovation, but I do think that serious discussion about improving evaluation should not be muddied by the current euphoria surrounding performance assessment. Performance assessment advocates have built a straw person to knock down in the form of standardized, multiple-choice tests. This expenditure of energy could have been better invested elsewhere.

For example, no one claims that multiple-choice tests can solve all educational problems or that different types of measures shouldn't be matched with particular purposes. Even performance assessment zealots want whatever new meas-

Performance assessment advocates have built a straw person to knock down in the form of standardized tests.

ures are developed to be standardized in terms of administration and scoring. To fuss and fixate on format is to miss the point. Similarly, to intimate, as some proponents of performance assessment do, that testing may be the cause of "a palpable decrease in the quality of education" is to further obscure a troubling and enduring issue.[22]

Advocates of the new kinds of tests also frequently criticize current tests in general for being culturally biased or unfair. In bygone days it was newsworthy to discover a vocabulary test with the word *polo* or a reading selection using the word *quiche*. But real test-makers don't use quiche — anymore. Certainly, performance assessment enthusiasts would admit that impressive progress has been made toward the elimination of ethnic, gender, and socioeconomic bias. So it's difficult to comprehend why the proponents of performance assessment would now call for — I'm not kidding — more culturally biased tests. As one example,

Disciples of
the performance assessment movement generally tend to ignore the question of validity.

the National Commission on Testing and Public Policy reports favorably on efforts to "establish and maintain a program of research and development to provide accurate and *culturally specific* instruments" (emphasis added).[23] Educators would do well to consider seriously whether these culturally specific assessments represent a welcome advance or a misguided regression in fair testing policy.

WHAT MATTERS?

What really matters — ignoring cost for the time being — is whether performance assessment will actually be "fairer" or "better" by any reasonably rigorous and widely accepted standards. The early polls are in on this question, and the results are discouraging. It is my opinion that test-makers can develop performance assessments that rival multiple-choice tests in terms of reliability; many quite reliable performance assessments exist now. It is disconcerting, however, that standards for the new instruments are rarely discussed. One person who is concerned about the issue is Edward Haertel, who has recognized the obstacles to reliable, judgment-based measurement and who has suggested several factors to consider.[24] But such caution is not the rule. References to benchmarks such as the *Standards for Educational and Psychological Testing* or the *Code of Fair Testing Practices in Education*[25] are conspicuously absent from the discussion. What should especially trouble policy makers, educators, and testing professionals is that disciples of the performance assessment movement generally tend to ignore the question of validity.

In the first course I took on educational measurement, I recall discussing what was called "face validity." Anne Anastasi commented on the concept of face validity some time ago:

> Face validity . . . is not validity in the technical sense; it refers, not to what the test actually measures, but to what it appears superficially to measure. Face validity pertains to whether the test "looks valid" to the subjects who take it, the administrative personnel who decide upon its use, and other technically untrained observers. Fundamentally, the question of face validity concerns rapport and public relations.[26]

By the time I was in Robert Ebel's measurement class at Michigan State University, the professor had already penned his frequently cited sentences on validity: "Validity has long been one of the major deities in the pantheon of the psychometrician. It is universally praised,

but the good works done in its name are remarkably few." Indeed, Ebel was seriously concerned about test validity, reminding test-makers that it is "the quality we have said is more important than any other."[27]

So, whither validity? In the current press for more genuine assessment, the only talk about validity that one hears — if one even hears such talk — is about face validity. My fear is that we have begun a search for genuine-*looking*, authentic-*looking*, real-*looking* assessments and have eschewed more rigorous standards of validity. It would certainly be tragic if face validity were to become the reigning deity in the psychometrician's pantheon. Bracey has gone so far as to say, "Validity, to me, is a non-issue. . . . For the new assessments, if we agree that this is what children should know or be good at, *and* we agree that the assessment strategy used represents this well, then Q.E.D., the test is valid."[28] Similarly, Dale Carlson, director of the California Assessment Program, has labeled concerns about validity "a red herring."[29] One hopes that this kind of enthusiasm represents the far point of the pendulum's arc.

CONCLUSION

By the time the pendulum completes its downswing, the current calls for more performance assessment will surely have yielded benefits. A heightened awareness of the importance of examining the match between assessment and instruction has already developed. We are — however grudgingly — acknowledging the role that social policy and ideology play in putatively objective assessment practice. When appropriate, direct assessment of certain skills and abilities will receive renewed support and resources.

But the future of performance assessment is uncertain. As sure as testing generally is not the answer to the multifaceted and complex problems facing contemporary American education, performance assessment is not the panacea either. The euphoria of its proponents should give us pause. The lowered psychometric standards to which it is currently held should cause alarm. Its cost should cause us to hide the silver under the mattress.

Slavin comments that, "as each innovation swings up and down through the arc of the pendulum, we do learn something that may be of use now or in the future."[30] While we should possibly hesitate to put all our hopes in the promise of performance assessment, it would be useful now to embark on a careful analysis of its potential, so that this innovation does not fall by the educational wayside, another cast-off quick fix in the larger school reform effort.

1. Judg. 12:5-6, quoted in William A. Mehrens and Irvin J. Lehmann, *Measurement and Evaluation in Education and Psychology*, 3rd ed. (New York: Holt, Rinehart and Winston, 1984), p. 575.

2. Robert Glaser and Lloyd Bond, "Testing: Concepts, Policy, Practice, and Research," *American Psychologist*, October 1981, p. 997.

3. *From Gatekeeper to Gateway: Transforming Testing in America* (Chestnut Hill, Mass.: National Commission on Testing and Public Policy, 1990).

4. Walter Haney and George Madaus, "Searching for Alternatives to Standardized Tests: Whys, Whats, and Whithers," *Phi Delta Kappan*, May 1989, p. 685.

5. Walter Haney, "Validity, Vaudeville, and Values," *American Psychologist*, October 1981, p. 1023.

6. Robert E. Slavin, "PET and the Pendulum: Faddism in Education and How to Stop It," *Phi Delta Kappan*, June 1989, p. 752.

7. Gregory J. Cizek, "The 'Sloppy' Logic of Test Abolitionists," *Education Week*, 4 April 1990, p. 64.

8. Frances Quinta and Bernard McKenna, *Alternatives to Standardized Testing* (Washington, D.C.: National Education Association, 1977), p. 7.

9. David Owen, *None of the Above: Behind the Myth of Scholastic Aptitude* (Boston: Houghton Mifflin, 1985), p. 285.

10. D. Monty Neill and Noe J. Medina, "Standardized Testing: Harmful to Educational Health," *Phi Delta Kappan*, May 1989, pp. 688-97.

11. *California Education Summit Report: Meeting the Challenge* (Sacramento: California State Department of Education, 1989).

12. *From Gatekeeper to Gateway . . .* , p. 26.

13. Gerald W. Bracey, "Measurement-Integrated Instruction and Instruction-Integrated Measurement: Two of a Kind," paper presented at the Academy for the Colorado Association of School Executives, Denver, April 1990.

14. Gerald W. Bracey, "The $150 Million Redundancy," *Phi Delta Kappan*, May 1989, pp. 698-702.

15. *From Gatekeeper to Gateway . . .* , p. 16.

16. *Request for Proposals: Early Adolescence/English Language Arts* (Washington, D.C.: National Board for Professional Teaching Standards, 1990).

17. *Request for Proposals: Early Adolescence/Generalist* (Washington, D.C.: National Board for Professional Teaching Standards, 1990).

18. Scott Willis, "Transforming the Test: Experts Press for New Focus on Student Assessment," *ASCD Update*, September 1990, p. 5.

19. Ibid., p. 4.

20. Gerald W. Bracey, "Advocates of Basic Skills 'Know What Ain't So,' " *Education Week*, 5 April 1989, p. 36.

21. Chester E. Finn, Jr., quoted in Robert Rothman, "New Tests Based on Performances Raise Questions," *Education Week*, 12 September 1990, p. 1.

22. Grant Wiggins, "Reconsidering Standards and Assessment," *Education Week*, 24 January 1990, p. 36.

23. *From Gatekeeper to Gateway . . .* , p. 33.

24. Edward H. Haertel, "From Expert Opinions to Reliable Scores: Psychometrics for Judgment-Based Teacher Assessment," paper presented at the annual meeting of the American Educational Research Association, Boston, April 1990.

25. American Educational Research Association, American Psychological Association, and the National Council on Measurement in Education, *Standards for Educational and Psychological Testing* (Washington, D.C.: American Psychological Association, 1985); and *Code of Fair Testing Practices in Education* (Washington, D.C.: Joint Committee on Testing Practices, 1988).

26. Anne Anastasi, *Psychological Testing*, 2nd ed. (New York: Macmillan, 1961), p. 138.

27. Robert L. Ebel, "Must All Tests Be Valid?," *American Psychologist*, May 1961, pp. 640, 646.

28. Bracey, "Measurement-Integrated Instruction . . . ," p. 21.

29. Dale Carlson, quoted in Rothman, p. 12.

30. Slavin, p. 757.

Putting the Standardized Test Debate in Perspective

When used correctly, standardized tests *do* have value, but they provide only part of the picture and have limits—which we must understand and work to improve.

BLAINE R. WORTHEN AND VICKI SPANDEL

Blaine R. Worthen is Professor and Chair, Research and Evaluation Methodology Program, Utah State University, Psychology Department, Logan, UT 84322. **Vicki Spandel** is Senior Research Associate, Evaluation and Assessment Program, Northwest Regional Educational Laboratory, 101 S.W. Main St., Portland, OR 97204.

Are the criticisms of educational testing valid, or do most of the objections stem from the fact that such tests are often misused? By far the most common type of standardized test is the norm-referenced test—that in which a student's performance is systematically compared with the performance of other (presumably) similar students. Minimum competency and criterion-referenced tests—those that measure student performance against established criteria—can also be standardized. However, not coincidentally, most criticism has been leveled at standardized, norm-referenced tests.

Criticisms of Standardized Tests

Among the current criticisms, a few stand out as most pervasive and most bothersome to those who worry over whether to support or oppose standardized testing. In this article, we'll look at seven of the most common criticisms.

Criticism #1: Standardized achievement tests do not promote student learning. Critics charge that standardized achievement tests provide little direct support for the "real stuff" of education, namely, what goes on in the classroom. They do nothing, critics contend, to enhance the learning process, diagnose learning problems, or provide students rapid feedback.

True, standardized tests do paint student performance in broad brush strokes. They provide general performance information in content areas like math or reading—as the test developers have defined these areas. They do not, nor are they *meant* to, pick up the nuances of performance that characterize the full range of a student's skill, ability, and learning style. Of course, we hope that standardized test results are only a small portion of the assessment information a teacher relies on in making academic decisions about students or curriculum. Good classroom assessment begins with a teacher's own observations and measurement of what students are gaining from instruction every day. Standardized testing can never replace that teacher-centered assessment. But it *can* supplement it with additional information that may help clarify a larger picture of student performance.

Criticism #2: Standardized achievement and aptitude tests are poor predictors of individual students' performance. While some tests may accurately predict future performances of *groups*, critics of testing argue that they are often inaccurate predictors of *individual* performance. Remember Einstein flunked 6th grade math, the critics point out eagerly. Clearly, no test can tell everything. If standardized tests were thousands of items long and took days to administer, they'd probably be better predictors than they are now. But remember—there are predictions and predictions. When a person passes a driver's test, we can't say she'll never speed or run a red light. Similarly, when a child scores well on a standardized reading test, that doesn't mean we can kick back and say, "Well, he's a terrific reader, all right. That's how it will always be." Ridiculous. Maybe he felt extra confident. Maybe the test just happened to touch on those things he knew well. But if we look at *all* the students with high scores and *all* those with low scores, we can safely predict more reading difficulties among students with low scores.

What all this means is that in a standardized test we have the best of one world—a measure that is relatively accurate, pretty good at what it does, but necessarily limited in scope.

Because there are so many drivers to be tested and only a finite amount of time, we cannot test each driver in every conceivable driving situation; and, similarly, we cannot measure all we might like to measure about a child's reading skills without creating a standardized test so cumbersome and complex no one would want to use it. The world of testing is, to a large extent, a world of compromise.

Criticism #3: The content of standardized achievement tests is often mismatched with the content emphasized in a school's curriculum and classrooms. Because standardized tests are intended for broad use, they make no pretense of fitting precisely and equally well the specific content being taught to 3rd graders in Salt Lake City's public schools and their counterparts at the Tickapoo School downstate. Instead, they attempt to sample what is typically taught to *most* 3rd graders in *most* school districts. The result is a test that reflects most curriculums a little, but reflects none precisely. For most users, there are big gaps—whole lessons and units and months of instruction skimmed over or left out altogether. Or the emphasis may seem wrong—too much attention to phonics, not enough on reading for meaning, perhaps. Again, the problem is the size of the test. We simply cannot cover in 10 or 20 test items the richness and diversity that characterize many current curriculums.

Criticism #4: Standardized tests dictate or restrict what is taught. Claims that standardized tests dominate school curriculums and result in "teaching to the test" are familiar and can be leveled at any type of standardized testing that has serious consequences for the schools in which it is used. On the surface it may seem inconsistent to claim that standardized tests are mismatched with what is taught in the schools and at the same time to complain that the tests "drive the curriculum." But those two allegations are not necessarily at odds. The first is grounded in a fear that in trying to represent everyone somewhat, standardized tests will wind up representing no one really well; the second arises from the consequent fear that everyone will try to emulate the generic curriculum suggested by the test content. This doesn't have to happen, of course.

Further, to the extent it does happen, it seems absurd to blame the test. The question we really need to be asking is "How are decisions about curriculum content being made?" There's often considerable fuzziness on that issue. Here's one sobering note:

Achievement test batteries are designed around what is thought to be the content of the school curriculum as determined by surveys of textbooks, teachers, and other tests. Textbooks and curriculums are designed, on the other hand, in part around the content of tests. One cannot discern which side leads and which follows; each side influences the other, yet nothing assures us that both are tied to an intelligent conceptualization of what an educated person ought to be.[1]

Criticism #5: Standardized achievement and aptitude tests categorize and label students in ways that cause damage to individuals. One of the most serious allegations against published tests is that their use harms students who are relentlessly trailed by low test scores. Call it categorizing, classifying, labeling (or mislabeling), or whatever, the result is the same, critics argue: individual children are subjected to demeaning and insulting placement into categories. The issue is really twofold: (1) tests are not infallible (students can and do change and can also be misclassified); and (2) even when tests *are* accurate, categorization of students into groups that carry a negative connotation may cause more harm than any gain that could possibly come from such classification.

Published tests, critics claim, have far too significant an effect on the life choices of young people. Some believe that achievement and intelligence tests are merely convenient and expedient means of classifying children and, in some cases, excluding them from regular education. But here again, it's important to raise the question of appropriate use. Even if we agree that it's okay to classify some children in some cases for some purposes, we must still ask whether standardized tests provide sufficient information to allow for intelligent decisions. We must also ask whether such tests provide any really useful information not already available from other sources.

Here's something to keep in mind, too. Some test results rank students along a percentile range. For instance, a student with a percentile ranking of 75 on a reading test may be said to have performed better than 75 percent of the other students who took the same test. But a difference in performance on even *one test item* could significantly raise or lower that percentile ranking. Knowing this, should we classify students on the basis of standardized tests? That probably depends on the consequences, on whether the information is appropriate and sufficient for the decision at hand, and on whether there is any corroborating evidence. Suppose we identify talented and gifted students on the basis of standardized math and reading tests. We ought, then, to at least be able to show that high performance on those tests is correlated directly with high probability of success in the talented and gifted program.

Criticism #6: Standardized achievement and aptitude measures are racially, culturally, and socially biased. Perhaps the most serious indictment aimed at both norm-referenced and minimum competency tests is that they are biased against ethnic and cultural minority children. Most published tests, critics claim, favor economically and socially advantaged children over their counterparts from lower socioeconomic families. Minority group members note that many tests have disproportionately negative impact on their chances for equal opportunities in education and employment. We must acknowledge that even well-intentioned uses of tests can disadvantage those unfamiliar with the concepts and language of the majority culture producing the tests. The predictable result is cultural and social bias—failure of the test to reflect or take into account the full range of the student's cultural and social background.

A conviction that testing is biased against minorities has led some critics to call for a moratorium on testing and has also prompted most of the legal challenges issued against minimum competency tests or the use of norm-referenced standardized tests to classify students. It is tempting, in the face of abuses, to outlaw testing. But simplistic solutions rarely work well. A more conservative, and far more challenging, solution is to improve our tests, to build in the sensitivity to cultural differences that would make them fair for all—and to interpret results with an honest awareness of any bias not yet weeded out.

Making such an effort is crucial, if one stops to consider one sobering thought. Assume for the moment that there *is* a bit of cultural bias in college entrance tests. Do away with them, right? Not unless you want to see college admission decisions revert to the still more biased "Good Old Boy" who-knows-whom type of system that excluded minorities effectively for decades before admissions tests, though admittedly imperfect, provided a less biased alternative.

Criticism #7: Standardized achievement and aptitude tests measure only limited and superficial student knowledge and behaviors. While test critics and supporters agree that tests only sample whatever is being tested, critics go on to argue that even what is measured may be trivial or irrelevant. No test items really ask "Who was buried in Grant's Tomb?" but some are nearly that bad.

They don't have to be. The notion that multiple choice tests can tap only recall is a myth. In fact, the best multiple choice items can—and do—measure students' ability to analyze, synthesize information, make comparisons, draw inferences, and evaluate ideas, products, or performances. In many cases, tests are improving, thanks in large part to critics who never give up.

Better Than the Alternatives
No test is perfect, and taken as a whole, educational and psychological measurement is still (and may always be) an imperfect science. Proponents of standardized tests may point to psychometric theory, statistical evidence, the merits of standardization, the predictive validity of many specific tests, and objective scoring procedures as arguments that tests are the most fair and bias-free of any procedures for assessing learning and other mental abilities. But no well-grounded psychometrician will claim that tests are flawless, only that they are enormously useful.

What do they offer us that we couldn't get without them? Comparability, for one thing. Comparability in the context of the "big picture," that is. It isn't very useful, usually, for one

teacher to compare his or her students' performance with that of the students one room down and then to make decisions about instruction based on that comparison. It's too limited. We have to back away to get perspective. This is what standardized test results enable us to do—to back off a bit and get the big, overall view on how we can answer global questions: In *general*, are 3rd graders learning basic math? Can 6th graders read at the predefined level of competency?

Thus, such tests will be useful to us if we use them as they were intended and do not ask them to do things they were never meant to do, such as giving us a microscopic view of an individual student's range of skills.

Appropriate Use Is the Key
On their own, tests are incapable of harming students. It is the way in which their results can be misused that is potentially harmful. Critics of testing often overlook this important distinction, preferring to target the instruments themselves, as if they were the real culprits. That is rather like blaming the hemlock for Socrates' fate. It is palpable nonsense to blame all testing problems on tests, no matter how poorly constructed, while absolving users of all responsibility—not that bad tests should be condoned, of course. But even the best tests can create problems if they're misused. Here are some important pitfalls to avoid.

1. *Using the wrong tests.* Schools often devise new goals and curriculum plans only to find their success being judged by tests that are not relevant to those goals or plans yet are imposed by those at higher administrative levels. Even if district or state level administrators, for example, have sound reasons for using such tests at *their* level, that does not excuse any school for allowing such tests to be the *only* measures of their programs. Teachers and local administrators should exert all the influence they can to see that any measures used are appropriate to the task at hand. They can either (1) persuade higher administrators to select new standardized achievement or minimum competency measures that better match the local curriculum or (2) supplement those tests with measures selected or constructed specifically to measure what the school is attempting to accomplish.

Subtle but absurd mismatches of purpose and test abound in education. Consider, for instance, use of statewide minimum competency tests to make interschool comparisons, without regard for differences in student ability. Misuse of tests would be largely eliminated if every test were carefully linked with the decision at hand. And if no decision is in the offing, one should question why *any* testing is proposed.

2. *Assuming test scores are infallible.* Every test score contains possible error; a student's *observed* score is rarely identical to that student's *true* score (the score he or she would have obtained had there been no distractions during testing, no fatigue or illness, no "lucky guesses," and no other factors that either helped or hindered that score). Measurement experts can calculate the probability that an individual's *true* score will fall within a certain number of score points of the *obtained* score. Yet many educators ignore measurement error and use test scores as if they were highly precise measures.

3. *Using a single test score to make an important decision.* Given the possibility of error that exists for every test score, how wise is it to allow crucial decisions for individuals (or programs) to hinge on the single administration of a test? A single test score is too suspect—in the absence of supporting evidence of some type—to serve as the sole criterion for *any* crucial decision.

4. *Failing to supplement test scores with other information.* Doesn't the teacher's knowledge of the student's ability count for anything? It should. Though our individual perceptions as teachers and administrators may be subjective, they are not irrelevant. Private observations and practical awareness of students' abilities can and should supplement more objective test scores.

5. *Setting arbitrary minimums for performance on tests.* When minimum test scores are established as critical hurdles for selection and admissions, as dividing lines for placing students, or as the determining factor in awarding certificates, several issues become acute. Test validity, always important, becomes crucial; and the minimum standard itself must be carefully scrutinized. Is there any empirical evidence that the minimum standard is

set correctly, that those who score higher than the cutoff can be predicted to do better in subsequent academic or career pursuits? Or has the standard been set through some arbitrary or capricious process? Using arbitrary minimum scores to make critical decisions is potentially one of the most damaging misuses of educational tests.

6. *Assuming tests measure all the content, skills, or behaviors of interest.* Every test is limited in what it covers. Seldom is it feasible to test more than a sample of the relevant content, skills, or traits the test is designed to assess. Sometimes students do well on a test just because they happen to have read the *particular* chapters or studied the *particular* content sampled by that test. Given another test, with a different sampling of content from the same book, the students might fare less well.

7. *Accepting uncritically all claims made by test authors and publishers.* Most test authors or publishers are enthusiastic about their products, and excessive zeal can lead to risky and misleading promises. A so-called "creativity test" may really measure only verbal fluency. A math "achievement" test administered in English to a group of Inuit Eskimo children (for whom English is a second language) may test understanding of English much more than understanding of math.

8. *Interpreting test scores inappropriately.* The test score *per se* tells us nothing about *why* an individual obtained that score. We watched the SAT scores fall year after year, but there was nothing in the scores themselves to tell us *why* that trend was downward. There turned out, in fact, to be nearly as many interpretations of the trend as there were interpreters.

A student's test *score* is not a qualitative evaluation of performance, but rather, a mere numeric indicator that lacks meaning in the absence of some criteria defining what constitutes "good" or "bad" performance.

9. *Using test scores to draw inappropriate comparisons.* Unprofessional or careless comparisons of achievement test results can foster unhealthy competition among classmates, siblings, or even schools because of ready-made bases for comparisons, such as grade-level achievement. Such misuses of tests not only potentially harm both

the schools and the children involved, but also create an understandable backlash toward the tests, which should have been directed toward those who misused them in this way.

10. *Allowing tests to drive the curriculum.* Remember that *some* individual or group has selected those tests, for whatever reason. If a test unduly influences what goes on in a school's curriculum, then someone has allowed it to override priorities that educators, parents, and the school board have established.

11. *Using poor tests.* Why go to the effort of testing, then employ a poorly constructed or unreliable measure—especially if a better one is at hand? Tests can be flawed in a multitude of ways, from measuring the wrong content or skills (but doing it well) to measuring the correct content or skills (but doing it poorly). Every effort should be made to obtain or construct the best possible measures.

12. *Using tests unprofessionally.* When educational tests are used in misleading or harmful ways, inadequate training of educators is often at fault. When test scores are used to label children in harmful ways, the fault generally lies with those who affix the labels—not with the test. When scores are not kept confidential, that is the fault of the person who violated the confidence, not the test maker. In short, as educators, we have a serious ethical obligation to use tests *well*, if we use them at all.

In Search of a Balanced View

Not all criticisms of tests can be deflected by claiming that they merely reflect misuses of tests. There are also apparent weaknesses in many tests, partly because we have yet a good deal to learn about measurement. We know enough already, however, to state unequivocally that uncertainty and error will always be with us, and no test of learning or mental ability or other characteristics can ever be presumed absolutely precise in its measurements. The professional judgments of teachers and other educators will continue to be essential in sound educational decision making. But we also assert—as do test advocates—that tests are often a great deal better than the

alternatives. Thus, we find ourselves caught in the middle of the debate between testing critics and enthusiasts.

The stridency of that debate occasionally calls to mind the old rhyme, "When in danger or in doubt, run in circles, scream, and shout!" In more recent years, however, there has been some softening on both sides. Measurement experts spend less time defending tests and deriding their detractors and more time working to improve the science of measurement. At the same time, they have become more comfortable in acknowledging that test scores are approximations and less obsessed with claiming unflinching scientific support for every test they devise.

Meanwhile, critics seem less intent on diagnosing psychometric pimples as terminal acne. They seem more aware that many testing problems stem from misuse, and their calls for "testing reform" have quieted somewhat as they have recognized that even the best tests, if subjected to the same sorts of misuse, would prove no more helpful. Further, most critics are beginning to acknowledge that abolishing testing would leave us with many decisions still to make—and even less defensible bases on which to make them.

But even if there are no quick-fix answers to the testing dilemma, there are things we can do. We can: (1) scrupulously avoid any misuses of tests or test results; (2) educate ourselves and our colleagues about tests so that we understand their capabilities and limitations and do not ask them to tell us more than they can; (3) stretch to the limit our creative talents in test design, teaching ourselves to develop test items that not only resound with our own thoughtful understanding of critical content but that encourage students to think; and (4) recall, even when pressed for hasty or expedient decisions, that no matter how much any test may tell us, there is always so much more to be known.

---

[1]G. V. Glass, (1986), "Testing Old, Testing New: Schoolboy Psychology and the Allocation of Intellectual Resources," in *The Future of Testing*, Buros-Nebraska Symposium on Measurement and Testing, Vol. 2, p. 14, edited by B. S. Plake, J. C. Witt, and J. V. Mitchell, (Hillsdale, N.J.: Lawrence Erlbaum Associates).

Index

Credits/ Acknowledgments

Cover design by Charles Vitelli

1. Psychology Applied to Education and Teaching
Facing overview—United Nations photo by John Isaac.

2. Development
Facing overview—United Nations photo by Milton Grant.

3. Learning
Facing overview—United Nations photo. 113—Illustration by Marcus Hamilton.

4. Motivation and Classroom Management
Facing overview—Apple Computers. 167-169, 171-172—Photos by Mark A. Regan.

5. Exceptional Children
Facing overview—United Nations photo by O. Monsen. 204—Photo by Jim Higgins. 208—Illustration by Kay Salem.

6. Measurement and Evaluation
Facing overview—The Dushkin Publishing Group, Inc., photo.

PHOTOCOPY THIS PAGE!!!*

ANNUAL EDITIONS ARTICLE REVIEW FORM

■ NAME: _____ DATE: _____

■ TITLE AND NUMBER OF ARTICLE: _____

■ BRIEFLY STATE THE MAIN IDEA OF THIS ARTICLE: _____
_____
_____
_____
_____

■ LIST THREE IMPORTANT FACTS THAT THE AUTHOR USES TO SUPPORT THE MAIN IDEA:
_____
_____
_____
_____
_____

■ WHAT INFORMATION OR IDEAS DISCUSSED IN THIS ARTICLE ARE ALSO DISCUSSED IN YOUR TEXTBOOK OR OTHER READING YOU HAVE DONE? LIST THE TEXTBOOK CHAPTERS AND PAGE NUMBERS:
_____
_____
_____
_____
_____
_____

■ LIST ANY EXAMPLES OF BIAS OR FAULTY REASONING THAT YOU FOUND IN THE ARTICLE:
_____
_____
_____
_____

■ LIST ANY NEW TERMS/CONCEPTS THAT WERE DISCUSSED IN THE ARTICLE AND WRITE A SHORT DEFINITION:
_____
_____
_____
_____

*Your instructor may require you to use this Annual Editions Article Review Form in any number of ways: for articles that are assigned, for extra credit, as a tool to assist in developing assigned papers, or simply for your own reference. Even if it is not required, we encourage you to photocopy and use this page; you'll find that reflecting on the articles will greatly enhance the information from your text.

ANNUAL EDITIONS:
EDUCATIONAL PSYCHOLOGY 92/93
Article Rating Form

Here is an opportunity for you to have direct input into the next revision of this volume. We would like you to rate each of the 45 articles listed below, using the following scale:

1. **Excellent: should definitely be retained**
2. **Above average: should probably be retained**
3. **Below average: should probably be deleted**
4. **Poor: should definitely be deleted**

Your ratings will play a vital part in the next revision. So please mail this prepaid form to us just as soon as you complete it.
Thanks for your help!

Annual Editions revisions depend on two major opinion sources: one is our Advisory Board, listed in the front of this volume, which works with us in scanning the thousands of articles published in the public press each year; the other is you—the person actually using the book. Please help us and the users of the next edition by completing the prepaid article rating form on this page and returning it to us. Thank you.

Rating	Article	Rating	Article
	1. Improving Education for the Twenty-First Century		23. A Critique of the Research on Learning Styles
	2. Does the "Art of Teaching" Have a Future?		24. Fostering Creativity: The Innovative Classroom Environment
	3. Using Action Research to Navigate an Unfamiliar Teaching Assignment		25. Competition Doesn't Belong in Public Schools
	4. The Colors of Teaching: A Tale of Double Vision		26. Students Need Challenge, Not Easy Success
	5. How Well Do We Respect the Children in Our Care?		27. The Development of Intrinsic Motivation in Students With Learning Problems: Suggestions for More Effective Instructional Practice
	6. Developmentally Appropriate Education for 4-Year-Olds		28. Motivation for At-Risk Students
	7. The Great Experiment		29. Good Teachers Don't Worry About Discipline
	8. The Development of Self-Concept		30. Accentuate the Positive . . . Eliminate the Negative!
	9. Encouraging Prosocial Behavior in Young Children		31. Order in the Classroom
	10. Changing Conditions for Young Adolescents: Reminiscences and Realities		32. Corporal Punishment: Used in a Discriminatory Manner?
	11. Meeting the Needs of Young Adolescents: Advisory Groups, Interdisciplinary Teaching Teams, and School Transition Programs		33. The Masks Students Wear
			34. Working With Disturbed Adolescents
	12. Affective Dimensions of Effective Middle Schools		35. Facilitating Mainstreaming Through Cooperative Learning
	13. Putting Learning Strategies to Work		36. Synthesis of Research on Gifted Youth
	14. Linking Metacognition to Classroom Success		37. Success Strategies for Learners Who Are Learning Disabled as Well as Gifted
	15. Practicing Positive Reinforcement		38. Identifying and Serving the Gifted New Immigrant
	16. Guidelines for Implementing a Classroom Reward System		39. Educating Language-Minority Children: Challenge and Opportunities
	17. Two Decades of Research on Teacher Expectations: Findings and Future Directions		40. Teaching to the Distinctive Traits of Minority Students
			41. It's a Good Score! Just a Bad Grade
	18. Caring Kids: The Role of the Schools		42. Classroom Standard Setting and Grading Practices
	19. Cooperative Learning and the Cooperative School		43. Teaching to the (Authentic) Test
	20. Productive Teaching and Instruction: Assessing the Knowledge Base		44. Innovation or Enervation? Performance Assessment in Perspective
	21. Critical Thinking Through Structured Controversy		45. Putting the Standardized Test Debate in Perspective
	22. Survey of Research on Learning Styles		

(Continued on next page)

ABOUT YOU

Name_____ Date_____

Are you a teacher? ☐   Or student? ☐

Your School Name _____

Department _____

Address _____

City_____ State _____ Zip _____

School Telephone #_____

YOUR COMMENTS ARE IMPORTANT TO US!

Please fill in the following information:

For which course did you use this book? _____

Did you use a text with this Annual Edition? ☐ yes ☐ no

The title of the text? _____

What are your general reactions to the Annual Editions concept?

Have you read any particular articles recently that you think should be included in the next edition?

Are there any articles you feel should be replaced in the next edition? Why?

Are there other areas that you feel would utilize an Annual Edition?

May we contact you for editorial input?

May we quote you from above?

ANNUAL EDITIONS: EDUCATIONAL PSYCHOLOGY 92/93

BUSINESS REPLY MAIL

First Class   Permit No. 84   Guilford, CT

Postage will be paid by addressee

The Dushkin Publishing Group, Inc.
Sluice Dock
DPG **Guilford, Connecticut 06437**

No Postage
Necessary
if Mailed
in the
United States